9708

CURRENT = 16^{00}

8^{00}

D1604824

A Technological History of
Motion Pictures and Television

A Technological History of
Motion Pictures and Television

AN ANTHOLOGY FROM THE PAGES OF

THE JOURNAL OF THE SOCIETY

OF

MOTION PICTURE AND TELEVISION ENGINEERS

Edited, with an Introduction, by
RAYMOND FIELDING

UNIVERSITY OF CALIFORNIA PRESS

BERKELEY, LOS ANGELES, LONDON

Copyright © 1967 by The Regents of the University of California
First Paperback Printing 1983

All articles were copyright by the Society of Motion Picture
and Television Engineers upon original publication.
Reprinted by permission of the SMPTE

University of California Press
Berkeley and Los Angeles, California

University of California Press, Ltd.
London, England

Printed in the United States of America

ISBN 0-520-05064-9
Library of Congress Catalog Card Number: 67-10464

1 2 3 4 5 6 7 8 9

Contents

Introduction

Absurd as it must seem, we begin by conceding that we know more about the Greco-Roman civilizations of antiquity than we do about the first fifteen years of the motion picture.

Over 2000 years have passed since the cultures of Athens and Rome first rose, then flourished and finally decayed. Yet, for those who look to find it, the substance of those civilizations still survives today. It survives, of course, in the unconsciously inherited cultures of the western world. But it also survives in the artifacts which fill our museum cases and in the carefully preserved publications which line our library bookshelves.

The motion picture, by contrast, is scarcely 75 years old. Some of the people who made up its first audiences, and a few of those who pioneered its development, are still alive today. During this brief history, the motion picture has profoundly altered our way of life, exerting a cultural influence equivalent to that of the automobile, the telephone and wireless communication. For better or worse, it has helped to convert us from a print-oriented to a picture-oriented society—a change made all the more significant because of the film's immediate comprehension by both illiterate and literate peoples.

Sociologically, it has provided graphic and irresistible behavioral paradigms, as much for early twentieth-century adult immigrants as for today's native adolescents. Historically, whether in its fictional or documentary modes, it has mirrored the events of its days, providing vivid, if sometimes imperfect, reflections of contemporary culture. It has revolutionized the entertainment industry and has both popularized and compromised the fine arts. Above all, it is a unique art form in its own right.

Yet, for all of this, much of the film's history is still unrecorded. Its origins, although almost contemporary, are obscure. The factors which influenced its economy, technology, artistic form, and social impact are imperfectly understood.

Because of our fragmentary knowledge of the cinema's origins and development, it has not yet been possible for our best international scholars to produce a really reliable or "definitive" history of the medium, nor does it seem likely that they will be able to do so for some time to come. The scarcity of reliable data which prevails in this field follows from a variety of causes, some of which are no longer alterable, others of which are only recently being remedied.

In the first place, few of the people who founded the motion picture were inclined to record its development with care. Only a handful of the cinema's earliest pioneers had more than an inkling of their own work's significance. Even Thomas Edison, who, together with W. K. L. Dickson, is generally credited with the development of the first practical motion picture camera, regarded his own invention as a side-show novelty—a novelty whose income-producing ability was not expected by many people to survive the passing fancy of public attention.

In time, of course, the real economic potential of the film became apparent, and the young art passed into the hands of financial opportunists who left little behind them in the way of records and memorabilia. Even in later years, workers within the film industry were rarely inclined to record their own activities, unless it served some public relations function.

Because of the scarcity of contemporary records, the role of the film scholar is made excruciatingly difficult. Only the most meticulous detective work can produce a meaningful pattern from the bits and fragments which survive, and some of the jig-saw pieces seem permanently lost from the puzzle.

The failure of pioneers *within* the industry to record their own work precluded the accumulation of a body of reliable, basic information. The failure of the educated public *outside* the industry to take the motion picture seriously discouraged scholars from investigating and studying the medium.

For many of its early years, the cinema was regarded as the cheapest sort of entertainment, suitable only for the impoverished immigrant and the uneducated native. The better class of citizen refused to patronize its theaters. Artists from the legitimate stage derided its artistic potential. The organized clergy attacked its morality and the press represented it as a blight on the community.

Understandably, the technological crudity and puerile content of the early films did not encourage endorsement from the intellectual community. Still, the complete lack of vision of those who judged the medium did not accelerate its development either. Long after its technological and artistic crudities had been refined, the cinema remained a popular target for condescending criticism and censure.

In 1915, the year in which Griffith's *The Birth of a Nation* was released, the United States Supreme Court legally designated the motion picture a mere "spectacle" and ruled, in *Mutual Film Corporation vs. Industrial Commission of Ohio*, that the film was not entitled to constitutional protection under the first ammendment, thus shackling the motion picture within the constraints of arbitrary censorship for the next thirty-five years. If the intellectual and artistic communities were outraged by this decision, it was not apparent. Indeed, it was not until 1915, twenty years after the commercial introduction of the cinema, that the first serious study of this medium by a recognized American intellectual was published—Vachel Lindsay's *The Art of the Moving Picture*. Such works were rare, however, and in the decades which followed, the chronicling of motion picture history was left largely to gossip columnists, fan magazines, and a sensationalistic press.

The effect of such attitudes upon scholarly research was devastating. Scholars, being human, are reluctant to undertake research in areas which are considered trivial by other intellectuals. Confronting an art form which was abused by its owners and exploited by a penny-dreadful press, very few historians were encouraged to investigate the cinema during its first half century.

Happily, the prospects for future scholarship in this field appear much brighter than our failures in the past would indicate.

During the last twenty-five years, a generation of qualified film scholars has appeared throughout the world, enthusiastic in its love for the cinema and persevering in its efforts to bring order out of the chaos of a half-century's historical inaccuracies. Still another generation of film historians is now being trained within the world's universities and film schools. Increasingly, too, scholars from other disciplines within the humanities and social sciences are bringing their own specialized training to bear upon the cinema.

Outstanding film archives, museums, and libraries have been founded in New York, Rochester, London, Paris, Amsterdam, Copenhagen, Moscow, Prague, Sydney, Stockholm, and other international centers to which scholars and students may turn for those artifacts, documents, books, films, and memorabilia which have survived the ravages of time and an indifferent film industry. Under the aegis of the United States Library of Congress, a twelve-year-old program to restore several million feet of deteriorating early nitrate and paper-positive copyright prints is now drawing to a close. The collection, which was successfully salvaged by historian Kemp Niver, contains thousands of titles from both

American and European producers during the period 1894-1912. Hundreds of these prints are unique, known previously only by name. Scores more have been completely unknown until this time. Niver is now at work upon an annotated index of these materials which will allow, and undoubtedly require, a reappraisal of the first twenty years of world cinema.

For the first time, a fairly broad market for critical and historical books on the cinema exists among the general public. Inevitably, this expanded market encourages a certain amount of slipshod research and hastily compiled surveys. At the same time, however, it provides an economic base for the publication of serious scholarly studies.

Although the number of trained film historians is momentarily small, we can look forward to its amplification in the years ahead. This increase in the number of researchers will, of itself, help reduce the obstacles to good scholarship which prevail today. For reasons which are not clear, the field of motion picture history attracts a peculiarly polemic fringe of writers, into whose philosophy the more gentlemanly traditions of scholarship have not yet penetrated. The cacophony of their dissent, although marginally amusing, produces an environment ill-suited to mature scholarship. Additional obstacles to objective research are created by political pressures which operate within certain totalitarian governments and which distort the work of otherwise competent scholars. Finally, there is a pronounced, if understandable, inclination for historians in particular countries to exaggerate the contributions of their own people over those of foreigners. These perversions of the scholarly spirit will presumably diminish as increasing numbers of researchers from various countries begin work in the field.

Ideally, future research in film history will proceed along three different lines, and in the following order.

First, the consolidation and appraisal of studies which have already been conducted. This requires the preparation of up-to-date international bibliographies, the translation of foreign texts, and the republication, in convenient form, of information which is widely scattered in time and place.

Second, the execution of exhaustive, well-documented studies into particular aspects of film history. The need is for studies in depth rather than breadth.

Third, the production of broadly based international histories of the cinema which cut across geographical boundaries and different periods of time, and which embrace all of the differing artistic, economic, technological, and sociological factors which have shaped the medium.

The success of each of these lines of research depends upon that of the preceding. Broadly based studies will provide us with rich generalizations about the emerging history of the film and will allow for the development of tenable historiographic perspectives. But before such studies can be profitably attempted, many years of exhaustive investigation into particular aspects of the film must be conducted. Without such investigations, historians have no foundation upon which to build their more elaborate studies, but are doomed instead to redigest, perpetually, the hopelessly confused early histories of the motion picture. Finally, before any intelligently conceived program of research can be undertaken, the work that has been done before must be collected, appraised, indexed and made available to contemporary workers.

This anthology is an example of the most fundamental of these three lines of inquiry—a compilation of historical papers whose individual publications were widely scattered in time. About a third of the book's articles present the autobiographical reminiscences of prominent film pioneers. The rest of the anthology is devoted to historical studies which were prepared by engineers and scholars. All of the articles are concerned with the technology of the media; all were originally published in the *Journal of the Society of Motion Picture and Television Engineers.*

The SMPTE was founded in 1916 to advance the theory and practice of motion picture engineering, and to disseminate technical information through conferences and publications.* During its fifty-year history the Society's contributions to the motion picture and television sciences have established it as one of the world's most influential and prestigious engineering organizations.

Since the year of its founding, the Society has published reports of its members' research, first as the *Transactions,* then as the *Journal* of the SMPTE. Today, a complete collection of these journals provides the most complete and reliable record available of technical evolution in the film and television media. Fortunately for historians, the Society's Historical Committee has solicited and published historical papers regularly. Some of these papers have recorded basic historical information. Others have advanced conflicting technological claims from early film pioneers. Still others have offered broad, interpretive surveys of historical trends.

Unfortunately for historians, these studies are scattered throughout the more than 460 issues of the *Journal* that have been published since 1916. Few libraries own complete sets of the *Journal,* and so, few students enjoy access to its accumulated information. For the convenience of these individuals, as well as for the general reader who desires a technologically oriented survey of motion picture and television history, we have culled the most pertinent and useful of the *Journal's* historical articles and present them here, in collected form, for the first time.

This anthology is designed to fill a need for a historical survey whose perspective is distinctly technological. It is a survey which ignores the purposes to which film and television are put, but emphasizes, instead, the means whereby these ends are achieved.

There is a temptation for film historians in particular to interpret the development of the motion picture teleologically, as if each generation of workers had sketched out the future of the art far in advance of the technology required for its realization. In fact, however, the artistic evolution of the film has always been intimately associated with technological change, just as it has, in less noticeable fashion, in the older arts. Just as the painter's art has changed with the introduction of different media and processes, just as the forms of symphonic music have developed with the appearance of new kinds of instruments, so has the elaboration and refinement of film style followed from the introduction of more sophisticated machinery. The contribution of a Porter, Ince, or Griffith followed as much from the availability of portable cameras and improved emulsions as it did from their individual vision and talent. Similarly, the *Cinéma Vérite* movement of today could not possibly have appeared and prospered twenty years ago, prior to the miniaturization of camera and sound equipment, and without dramatic improvements in film stocks.

If the artistic and historical development of film and television are to be understood, then so must the peculiar marriage of art and technology which prevails in their operation. It is the involvement of twentieth-century technology which renders these media so unlike the other, older arts, for in no other media of artistic expression do so many technological impediments stand between the artist and his audience. No other media require so long an apprenticeship before even a minimal mastery is achieved, and before the simplest kind of communication can take place. It is this technology which renders film and television production so expensive. It is the expense, in turn, that determines which kinds of themes and treatments are economically feasible and which are not. Most significantly, it is this complexity of motion picture and television technique which renders every creative act a team effort rather than an individual one.

*Prior to 1950 the organization was known as the Society of Motion Picture Engineers.

What we have assembled here is by no means a complete and coherent history. Even the most superficial reading will reveal the many gaps in continuity and subject matter which interrupt the narrative, as well as the noticeable inconsistencies in style and viewpoint which distinguish one writer's work from another. Altogether, these thirty-three papers span a period of forty-three years, from 1920 to 1963; many of them need revision, updating, and a more contemporary perspective. Autobiographical accounts, in particular, require cautious appraisal. These are, at one and the same time, the most useful and the most misleading of historical documents, for many conflicting claims are presented here, together with personal reminiscences which are colored by time and personality.* Needless to say, the papers are reproduced as originally printed, except for the correction of a few typographical or spelling errors.

Taken together, whether autobiographical or scholarly, the papers collected here represent one of our most valuable resources for the investigation of film and television history, and it is hoped that this anthology will provide a convenient point of departure for students and scholars of the media. For those persistent workers who may wish to pursue this line of investigation still further, a list of additional historical papers from the JSMPTE is provided at the end of the book.

*Note, for example, the severe criticism of W. K. L. Dickson's autobiographical paper by Gordon Hendricks in his book, *The Edison Motion Picture Myth,* 1961.

Part I

Autobiographical Reminiscences

PUBLISHER'S NOTE

The papers in this volume have been reprinted, by permission, from *The Journal of the Society of Motion Picture and Television Engineers*. They are presented as originally published, except for the correction of obvious typographical and spelling errors.

History of the Motion Picture

By C. FRANCIS JENKINS

I have been asked by your Papers Committee to prepare a sketch of the conception, early history and development of the motion picture, but to compile an accurate account sufficiently complete without being too lengthy is not an easy task.

Where the motion picture idea originated I have not found out, though a hundred years before the Christian era, Lucretius strangely wrote his friend thus:[1]

"Do not thou moreover wonder that the images appear to move and appear in one order and time their arms and legs to use; for one image disappears and instead appears another arranged in another way, and thus seems each gesture to change; for you must understand that this takes place in the quickest time."

This is an exact description of the motion picture of today, and if this is really what he meant, then it took two thousand years to get a suitable picture ribbon and a proper machine to handle it. And it will be noticed that the subject naturally divides itself into these two main elements, i. e., the picture-carrying vehicle and the handling mechanism therefor. The mechanism is of two kinds, i. e., one of them continuous movement, the other intermittent movement of the picture carrier at the illuminated aperture. The process, as we know it today, is likewise divided into two steps; the first a photographic analysis of the animated subject, the second a synthesis of the elements into which the subject was divided by the analytical process.

The success of the attempt to simulate depends initially upon persistence of vision, that faculty of the human eye which enables the retina to hold onto a light sensation for an appreciable time after the light is cut off. And curiously enough this phenomena seems to have been first mentioned by a blind man.

The motion picture is not a sort of Minerva-birth of inventive genius, but like all notable achievements in mechanisms has had a long line of predecessors, for the difficult problem of recording and reproducing motion did not yield without much preliminary fumbling.

Obviously it would lengthen this paper beyond acceptable limits if description were made of the work of all who have contributed to the result in the form adopted and practiced at this time. I shall therefore endeavor to confine myself as far as this may be done to mention of the contributions of those who in turn first added a new step in the development of the idea.

By a process of knowledge additions and eliminations the motion picture of today reduces itself roughly to six historical periods; the first (1) a series of related picture elements; (2) the adoption of photography to secure them; (3) the use of a single camera; (4) of perforated film; (5) of intermit-

The Zoetrope

tent film movement; and (6) in making the period of illumination exceed the period of change or substitution of a new picture element, or frame, for the last in sequence throughout the series.

The first motion picture mechanism we have any record of is the zoetrope, or wheel of life, though its origin is buried in antiquity. It may be that this is the device Lucretius was writing about. It usually consists, as you all doubtless well know, of a paper cylinder having equi-spaced axial slits cut through its wall. Between the slits on the inside were arranged sketches of successive phases of an object in motion. By whirling the cylinder and viewing the sketches through the slits as they passed the eye one got the sensation of an object in motion.

The picture series were also put upon a slotted disc (this form may have antidated the drum type) and were viewed by looking through the slots at the reflection of the pictures in a mirror as the disc was whirled.

The first attempt at projection followed this line, that is, transparencies were mounted in disc form and illuminated from the back, a projection lens imaging these on a screen as the successive pictures of the series were momentarily exposed in the field of the lens.

Plateau, who seems first to have made up such a mechanism, mounted sixteen pictures on his disc, suitably illuminated them through a whirling opaque shutter having a single radial slot therein, the shutter disc rotating sixteen times as fast as the picture disc. Though blind, Plateau appears to have given diligent study to this persistence of vision phenomena, and at this early date, 1849, curiously enough, hit upon the same picture frequency now universally used. This picture disc, intermittently illuminated, was subsequently employed by several experimenters.

Another form was exactly the reverse of this plan, for instead of a single stationary lens and stationary light with a 16-picture transparent disc revolving between, consisted of a stationary disc with 16 pictures and 16 lenses, a single lens mounted in front of each picture, while the light whirled around to momentarily pass through each picture and adjacent lens. As all the lenses were adjacent to register at a single spot on the screen, the composite on the screen appeared, by persistence of vision, as a single uninterrupted picture.

The idea of simulating motion by intermittent illumination of a series of related elements seems to have been the preferred method for more than a hundred years, the last of the line being Edison's Kinetoscope of 1894 (to be described later).

The picture series were first made in a camera in 1860, to the best of my knowledge, by Coleman Sellers, an engineer, who, in one form, pasted the photo prints on an endless band for exhibition.[2] In 1894, I met Mr. Sellers who described his devices to me and gave me photographs of them and also strips of pictures used therein.

An acquaintance of Coleman Sellers, and likewise a Philadelphian, Henry R. Heyl, also made camera plates (of a dancing couple in action) making from the negatives wet-plate lantern slides which he mounted disc-wise, and revolved, step-by-step, in the light of a projection lantern. He gave a public demonstration at the Academy of Music, Philadelphia, Feb. 5, 1870.[3] I have paper prints off the negatives, which he gave me in 1895.

An examiner in the U. S. Patent Office, some ten years after allowing me a patent on a perforated picture strip in continuous and synchronous motion with a plurality of lenses passing a fixed opening in a camera, called my attention to an anticipating French publication, of March 1, 1864, in which Sr. Ducos illustrated and described much the same thing, i. e., a flexible picture band carried along by a sprock-

---

1 De Rerum Natura, Book IV, verse 766.
2 Sellers, U. S. Patent No. 31,357, issued Feb. 5, 1861.
3 Franklin Institute Transaction of this year (1870).

eted drum, synchronously with a plurality of lenses.[4]

The first use of the now almost universally employed geneva gear or star-and-cam in projectors appears to have been made by A. B. Brown, in 1869.[5] However, the use of this type of intermittent gear is practically the only interest his contribution has for the historian.

Marey, a French scientist, employed the zoetrope, the slotted cylinder described earlier herein, with solid figures

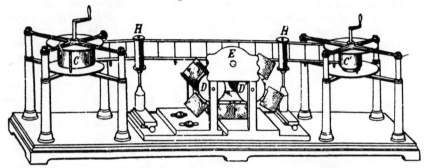

Projector with plurality of lenses.

instead of pictures, modeled in imitation of successive phases of an animal in action, which not only gave the action but the placity of solid bodies. One of his instruments of this type is still to be seen in the Museum of the Paris Physiological Station.

A variation of the picture-carrying drum, employed as a projector, had a series of vertical mirror-strips for reflecting the light beam which carried the picture to the screen. It depended for success upon the reflection phenomena that, to accomplish the desired result, the angular movement of the mirror must be one-half that of the

Reynaud's improved version
of the Zoetrope.

————
4 Unpublished French Patent, July 5, 1864.
5 U. S. Patent 93,594, 1869.
6 British Patent 2,295 of 1889.
7 British Patent No. 925 of 1868.
8 U. S. Patent No. 549,309, 1895.
9 U. S. Patent No. 779,364, 1905.

picture movement. Reynaud, in 1889, made such a device which was to be seen on the boulevards of Paris until the present type projector deprived it of public favor.[6]

Aside from the ribbon form of picture carrier, another which attained considerable popularity in its final and perfected form consisted in mounting the picture series as the leaves of a pad or book, which, bent back and exhibited by slipping from under one's thumb, brings the picture into sight in such rapid succession that a very good motion picture is produced.

The first mention I have been able to find of these thumb books, as they came to be called, was the invention of Linnett in 1868.[7] They appeared from time to time in one form or another, sometimes being mounted in a holder with a mechanical detent to press back the cards.

The most pretentious of these instruments was the Mutoscope of Herman Castler[8] in 1895. The picture cards stood out radically from a drum to which they were attached by their

The Phantascope

bottom ends, a thousand or more on a single drum, and these slipping from under a detent exhibited the pictures thereon with smoothness and precision. It was a coin operated machine and "picture parlors" equipped with Mutoscopes were established in the large cities, seaside and mountain resorts and pleasure parks, holding the public favor until the advent of the 5c-movie theatre.

The Messrs. Lumiere, of France, brought out a similar machine which they named the Kinora. The striking feature of this machine was the curved picture-carrying cards, curved to add resiliency.

My own contribution to this line was a Phantascope toy,[9] in which a

The Mutoscope

flexible band was employed, the cards being attached thereto by their lower ends and having a spaced relation of about five thousandths inch. This close spacing of the cards assured a firm adhesion to the band and to each other

But it is to the persistence of Eadweard Muybridge that we are indebted for the most scientific research in motion analysis, work which he began in 1879. His animal studies became classics with artists. Wet plates only were then available and he used above half a million of them in a plurality of cameras arranged in order along a track over which his subject was required to pass. He thus obtained consecutive impressions at regular intervals of time and distance during a complete stride.[10] His first work was financed by the Hon. Leland Stanford, of Califor-

The Phantascope

nia, a lover of fine horses.[11] Between 1883 and 1887, he was engaged in like work at the University of Pennsylvania, where his "Animal Locomotion" was published. On February 27, 1888, Mr. Muybridge interviewed T. A. Edison as to the possibility of combining his Zoopraxiscope projector with Edison's phonograph, but without result, though Mr. Edison did exploit such a combination some years later.

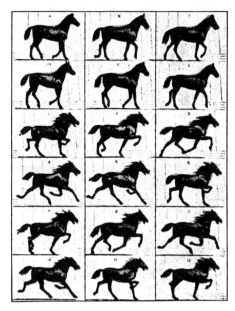

Some results of Muybridge's experiments

The next to come prominently into notice was Dr. Marey. Sometime after meeting Muybridge in Paris, in 1881, where Prof. Muybridge was exhibiting at the Electrical Exposition, Marey set about to determine by graphic methods

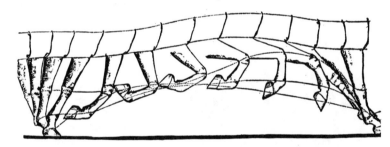

Dr. Marey's experiment with phases of animal locomotion.

the trajectories, velocities and accelerations of moving parts of the human body, acquatic locomotion, etc. At first, he used plates but later, 1888, used "a long roll of sensitive film" intermittently fed past the exposure aperture.[12] His work has a permanent value to science.

---

10 Franklin Institute Journal, April 1883.
11 The Century, July 1, 1887.
12 Academie des Sciences, Comptes Rendus 1888, CVII, page 677-678.
13 Philadelphia Photographer 1887, p. 328-688.
14 Serial No. 217,809; Patent No. 376,247.
15 Brooklyn Eagle, and Brooklyn Citizen, both of June 14, 1888.
16 Scientific American, June 20, 1891, also U. S. Patent 493,426.

In 1887, Anschutz published[13] a description of his tachyscope, a device which was later shown at the World's Fair, Chicago, 1893. The apparatus consisted of a glass wheel the pictures on which were lighted by the flash of a vacuum tube as they came into position; though the machine is the same as that described by Donisthorpe, of London, in *Nature,* issue of January 24, 1878.

To concentrate a considerable length of entertainment on a convenient area a disc picture carrier was attempted by several inventors. In one scheme a glass plate was employed upon which a series of pictures were spirally arranged, as in the Anthony device.

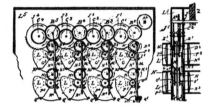

The LePrince Patent

A British patent of 1900 to Rosenberg discloses another plan, a film having two rows of pictures thereon, each row being half of the whole show. At the end of the first row the film was shifted and run in the opposite direction to show pictures of the second row. Edison in his home projector of 1911 followed the same scheme.

In 1886, Augustus Le Prince, of New York State, filed an application[14] for U. S. Patent which disclosed transparent picture ribbons having a row of perforations along each edge of each film. Four such strips were used in the machine, four pictures being made on each in succession behind sixteen lenses. A single lens modification is suggested, with perforated film driven by a sprocketed drum.

It is curious that those who came nearest anticipating future accepted methods and mechanisms should have failed to follow up their work. As another shining example I might cite Mr. Levison, who publicly exhibited at the Brooklyn Photo Club an apparatus much like present day devices; it had

flexible film, moved step by step, and behind a single lens.[15]

Plates, cards, paper strips, drums and glass discs had been used for animated pictures, but when in 1885 Rev. Goodwin invented the transparent celluloid flexible film the way was opened to rapid advance, for the necessary unlimited capacity in the picture carrier was then possible.

In 1889, Mr. Dickson began, at Thos. A. Edison's direction, the development of a picture machine.[16] News of what was being done appeared in print from time to time and the summer of 1894 saw the beginning of the public exhibition of his Kinetoscope, a box into which one looked to see picture in animation.

The picture ribbon was passed continuously between a small lamp and

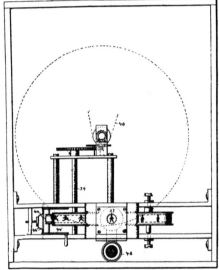

Appearance of first Kinetoscope.

the eye of the observer, the view being cut off by a rotating disc about a foot in diameter and having a one-eighth by one inch radial slit therein near the periphery. Through this flying slit the observer got a momentary sight of each picture frame as it came into position above the light. The frames passed at the rate of 46 per second, a high speed being required because of the instantaneous view and meagre illumination. The pictures were small, of course, but excellently done. The excellence of the Edison pictures without doubt proved a stimulus to the rapid development of the art, far more than any contribution in mechanical design or new methods, as was later demonstrated when the courts held that the Edison patents and re-issues were anticipated and invalid.

Among the early English workers were Friese-Greene and Mr. Evans who exhibited a camera before the Bath Photo Society, February 25, 1890, and in 1895 were working on a projector, work which was concurrent with the work of the Lumiere Brothers in France. The Lumiere camera was also used as a projector, however, and as such came to America in 1897.

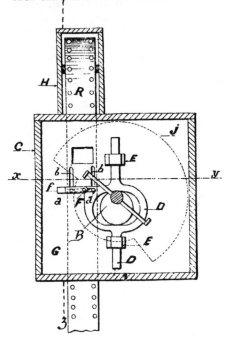

Lumiere Camera

The American Biograph, built by Herman Casler in 1896 was one of the very best of the projectors of these early development years. He worked on the theory that the larger the frame the sharper the definition on the screen because of the less enlargement required. This machine used 2¾″ width of film. The film, unperforated, was advanced through the projector by the gripping action of mutilated cylinders which contacted for only a fourth of a revolution. The resultant screen picture was excellent, but like all the other mechanisms employing film differing from the generally accepted standard, had its day, played its part and dropped from sight.

In 1890, I began work on mechanisms for recording and reproducing motion. Two systems were developed side by side; one employed intermittent motion at the picture aperture, the other continuous motion. Cameras were first made, in which film was used, split to width in the dark from Kodak film bought in local photographic shops. These pieces were spliced into strips, sometimes twenty-one feet long,

17 Richmond Telegram, Richmond, Indiana, June 6, 1894.
18 Baltimore Sun, Oct. 3, 1895; Atlanta Journal, Oct. 21, 1895; Albany, New York, Times-Union, Oct. 21, 1895.
19 Franklin Institute Bulletin, December 1895 and Franklin Institute Journal, January, 1896.

if I were lucky. Prints were made from negatives exposed in the cameras—usually in the continuous motion camera, for it made the steadiest pictures, though projection was mostly in the intermittent machine which had no interrupting shutter and therefore gave most illumination.

The continuous motion mechanism consisted of a rotating disc carrying a plurality of matched lenses arranged around its periphery and passing in single line sequence across an adjustable opening in exact synchronism with a film moving downward in the focus of the lenses. Different mechanisms were made, with an equipment of lenses ranging from five to forty-eight and in spaced relation depending on the height of the frame chosen.

In the intermittent mechanism the film was illuminated for about seven-eighths, and moved in about one-eighth of a period. A "beater type" was first employed and later followed by the geneva gear, a gear found in many makes of watches to prevent winding the spring too tight.

My work was my own, but viewing the art in historical retrospection from this late day, it is evident that the solution of the illumination problem was my only original contribution to the art as practiced from 1890 to the present time. I must confess that I

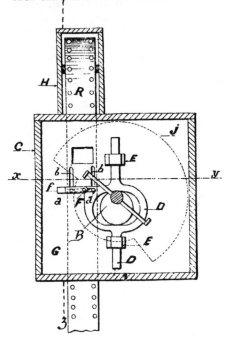

Continuous motion mechanism with plurality of lenses

don't quite understand why the thing wasn't hit upon by someone previously, it was so simple and so perfectly obvious when once done; like the half turn of the screw which made the constant contact transmitter, which, in its turn, made the telephone a commercial article.

All my old apparatus was acquired by the United States National Museum in 1895 and there it can still be seen (on exhibit in the Graphic Arts department).

My projectors were motor driven and by some accident of design were built left-handed, a type which has since been followed, consciously or unconsciously, in the design of machines the world over.

Exhibitions to friends were given from time to time in 1891, 1892 and 1893, though my first exhibition of which any account appeared in printed publications, was in June of 1894.[17]

In March following I secured the financial assistance of a local man and we built three copies of this early machine and exhibited them at the Cotton States Exposition, Atlanta, 1895.[18] These were the first of picture shows in a building built exclusively for the purpose.

In the winter following, I demonstrated the original instrument, the Phantoscope, before the Franklin Institute of Philadelphia[19] and at the close of the demonstration it was voted that the matter should go before the proper committee to determine whether it ought to receive scientific acknowledgement. The Committee in due course recommended the Elliott Cresson Gold Medal and published its findings in the Journal for three months. Thereupon the proposed award was vigorously opposed by two interested gentlemen, but after many months of taking testimony and considering evidence and data submitted, the originally recommended award was made. Eighteen years later a second award was made, the John Scott medal, for improvements, i. e., lateral projection, as demonstrated in a machine which I later christened the Graphoscope.

Efforts have been made from time to time to exploit synchronized pictures and sound, but without success. There is no difficulty in synchronizing. This has been accomplished in several ways by those engaged thereon, my own scheme being to put the sound record on the film as a sinuous edge so that accidental destruction of a part of the film would take out as much sound as picture, and when spliced again would still be in synchronism and without any adjustment of mechanism. The public, however, did not favorably receive any of the singing pictures and all such schemes disappeared when the novelty of a single exhibition had passed. The silent drama is attractive to a very large extent, I think, because it is the silent drama.

Stereoscopic motion pictures have been the subject of considerable thought and have been attained in several ways, as described in the October, 1919, transactions of this Society. but never yet have they been accomplished in a practical way. By practical,

I mean, for example, without some device to wear over the eyes of the observer. It is generally conceded that its acceptable accomplishment would enhance the beauty of the motion picture.

Motion pictures in natural color have been attained by several persons, one of the first to have wide public exploitation was that employed by Smith and Urban (Chas. Urban, one of our members). The film had color stencil frames alternating longitudinal-

consists, as you will remember, of a double coated film, the red-yellow frames being on one side and the blue-green frames on the other side of the film, each side tinted in its proper color throughout the length of the film. Such a natural color film can be run in the standard projector without change, and can, and often is, put into a split reel with monochrome film.

The suppression of flicker (and resultant headache) was the next problem to attract attention and the first

Projection has not been developed to the same high degree, perhaps because the accomplishment is far more difficult. The analytical end of the motion picture process has always been the least troublesome, principally because of the ample time latitude of film movement in the camera and printer. The projector still lacks the 100% quality for 100% of time of a completely developed machine, in addition to an efficiency of but 50% in light utilization.

And yet I think it one of the most remarkable mechanisms extant. Consider its intermittent sprocket for example; it handles a thousand feet of fragile and delicate film per minute, with a start-and-stop motion, at a speed of nearly 150 feet per second at the maximum point, stopping it with so nearly microscopical exactness that, magnified, say, four hundred diameters, and repeated sixteen times a second, the unsteadiness is almost nil.

The original Jenkins lateral projector.

ly of the film and which were projected respectively through red-yellow and green-blue tinters so that the film running through the machine at twice standard speed produced a composite screen picture in natural color and motion.

Gaumont in 1913 had a color scheme in which three rows of frames were arranged side by side on a wide film, each row being projected through its appropriate tint and, superimposed, produced a screen picture in natural color. With a synchronizing attachment sound was also added giving "talking motion pictures in natural color."

As each of these schemes required special apparatus difficulty was experienced in exploiting these processes and they fell by the wayside.

The process which will succeed is that which fits standard machines without change. Such, for example, as that patented[20] by Arturo Hernandez and skillfully developed by one of our members, Mr. Kelley. This was demonstrated at our Philadelphia meeting and described in the transactions of November, 1918, and April, 1919. It

mention I find is in 1900[21] and the description says that "the shutter rotates once in the interval between the movements of the film."[22] But as more commonly practiced flicker is subdued by adding one or more blades rather than by rotating the shutter oftener.

In France the Pathe Brothers have a notable establishment in which the requisites for the entire motion picture process are produced, i. e., raw stock, cameras, laboratory equipment, studio and projectors. In England, Chas. Urban, for several years maintained a similar plant and his accumulation of educational and scientific subjects are probably unequalled anywhere.

We have no similar establishment in America, the Yankee being more prone to specialize. And my sketch would be incomplete should I fail to mention the impetus initially given to quality picture production by Messrs. Bell and Howell, makers of fine cameras and printers. Another who has made himself paramount in his specialty, picture printing, is Mr. Rothacker. Both Bell and Rothacker are members of our Society. And just here let me note that quality production has been possible by the uniformly high standard of raw stock furnished by George Eastman, represented in our Society by Mr. Blair.

As for players our art now has such popularity that few actors and actresses of the speaking stage have been able to resist the lure of the silent drama, despite their prejudice, though none of them has made so great successes as those of less or no foot-light experience. Apparently stagecraft and cameracraft don't "gee." Certain it is that new names have attained stellar brilliance in the pictures, the new medium of expression having developed a new type of artist both in acting and in direction.

But we should not forget that while our art as an industry is the fifth largest in the world, and money has been spent with reckless disregard of values, it was the courageous spirit who established the first 5c movie house who made such expenditures and such returns possible. This was the real beginning of the expansion which made an industry of a scientific plaything, and a film exchange system which has endured to this day. For just as the central exchange made the telephone widely useful, so the movie theatre made the motion picture a profit paying entertainer.

So, as Sargent happily puts it, for fifteen years now we have had a device for dramatic representation which has given us every form of entertainment known to man since the beginning of time. We present the story teller in a pantomine far more effective than mere words alone; we show every form of spectacular reproduction in a splendor never dreamed of by a Caesar; we present every human emotion known to exist in a realism and costume true to nature; we multiply the magic lantern a thousand-fold in every reel; we bring every distant country, every

20 U. S. Patent 1,174,144.
21 British Patent No. 2283 of February 5, 1900.
22 From Digest in U. S. Patent Office Library.

strange people, every quaint custom, every new and wonderful invention, every scientific discovery; all this we bring to the stay-at-homes and an humble coin pays the fiddler. The child of today has seen more of the world than did the traveler of yesterday.

Many great enterprises have begun with the doing of some very simple thing. So in motion pictures when the opening in the shutter was enlarged scientific groping stopped and the development of an industry began, an industry grown already to great magnitude. But I firmly believe that because of its universal usefulness, the ability to convey information between all peoples of the earth (for you should remember that it is without language or literacy limitation), the motion picture is destined ultimately to be the greatest single industry known to mankind. I think, therefore, fellow engineers, we may justly be proud of our vocation.

Early Stages of Kinematography*

By C. H. BOTHAMLEY

Summary.—*The author, who presided over the meeting of the Photographic Convention of the United Kingdom at Chester, England, in 1890, describes some of the work of E. J. Marey, Muybridge, Friese-Greene, and Le Prince, pioneers in the art of producing and exhibiting motion pictures. The information given in this paper is particularly interesting in view of the personal acquaintance of the author with these pioneers during the time in which they were conducting their work.*

When an invention or development in pure or applied science rapidly receives recognition and wide application, especially if it be of a kind that achieves popularity, there is always a chance that the merits of the pioneers responsible for the invention or development will be underestimated, and even that the precise part that they played will be forgotten. For example, though the name of E. J. Marey, Professor in the College of France, is occasionally mentioned, it is doubtful whether the importance of his work is fully appreciated, notwithstanding the fact that his book, *Le Mouvement,* was translated into English by Dr. Eric Prichard, and published in 1895. It is not improbable that this is due to the fact that Marey restricted himself to his original line of work, the study of the movements of living things, from the scientific rather than from a popular point of view, and his book is a somewhat technical account of his results, with illustrations that are numerous, but on a small scale.

Marey himself states that the real originator of this line of work was the famous astronomer, Janssen, who, in December, 1874, took a series of successive photographs of the transit of the planet Venus across the face of the sun. A rotating circular plate was used, the interval between successive exposures being seventy seconds. Janssen, moreover, suggested that this method of making successive photographs at regular intervals might be applied to the study of the motion of animals, especially of locomotion.

After Janssen, came Eadweard Muybridge who, about the year 1880, or a little earlier, at the suggestion of a Mr. Stanford, a former Governor of California, applied the principle to the photographic study of the movements of the horse, and who subsequently extended his experiments to other animals and to human beings. As is well known, Muybridge's method was to use a long line of cameras, the lenses of which pointed across a defined track, along which the object moved, the successive exposures being made by permitting the moving body itself to operate a simple system of shutter releases. The method was cumbersome, being limited somewhat severely by the number of exposures possible, but the results were very striking and valuable. A selection of them can be seen in **Muybridge's book in the Library of the** Royal Photographic Society. Much new light was thrown on the mechanics of walking and other movements.

Muybridge was able to demonstrate his results by means of the projection lantern and, in 1889, gave lectures at Newcastle-on-Tyne and at other places in the north of England. Professor A. Smithells, F.R.S., then professor of chemistry in the Yorkshire College (now Leeds University), persuaded him to come to Leeds and give a demonstration of his results. I met Muybridge on that occasion, and was able to give him some help in setting up his lantern and other equipment. The plates carrying the successive images were fixed to a large glass disk, which rotated between the condenser and the lens, while an opaque disk with transparent slits in it rotated in the opposite direction. The results surprised as much as they delighted the large and somewhat critical audience before which they were shown. Perhaps the most striking of all the demonstrations was that of the wing motion of a large white bird (a cockatoo, I think). As the wing moved in the upstroke, brilliantly lighted by sunshine, we saw most distinctly every plume of the wing turn on its base, so as to present only its edge in the direction of motion, and thus offer as little resistance to the air as possible. As the wing came down, each plum turned back so as to present its flat surface to the air and thus gain the maximum impulse. I well remember the murmur of astonishment and pleasure that went through the whole audience, and the persistent demands for the repetition of what was as beautiful a picture as I have even seen on a screen.

Marey and Muybridge were early in communication, and in order to obtain simpler and more portable apparatus, Marey invented his "photographic" gun. This apparatus, it should be noted, required only one lens. It was built in the form of an ordinary sporting gun, but of course, with different relative dimensions of its parts, and was used on the shoulder and sighted in the same way as a gun. At first, plates were used, which were attached to a disk of glass contained in a drum fixed to the gun just as a revolver barrel would be. The disk could be rotated by clockwork actuated by the gun-trigger. The exposure was first made; then the shutter closed, and the disk moved around and brought another plate into position. With this apparatus, the number of exposures possible was 12 per second, and the plates were necessarily very small. Soon, "a continuous film very slightly coated with gelatin and bromide of silver" was substituted for plates, the film being wound on bobbins, at the end of which were flat plates having perforations that were engaged by a peg in a metal plate in order to rotate the bobbin. Black paper attached to the ends of the film made filling and changing possible in daylight. The images obtained with this apparatus were 9 centimeters wide. The improved apparatus and the increased sensitivity of the films obtainable made it possible to study the movements of a wide variety of living beings, the results of which study are set out in the book to which I have already referred.

In a delightful place in Beaune, bounded on one side by one of the great bastions of the fortifications, and on the other by a row of those dignified renaissance houses that give a distinct cachet to this quaint old town, there is a railed-in enclosure planted with graceful trees; in their midst is a life-sized statue of Marey, a sturdy thick-set seated figure with a face of marked character. Against the figure is a mass of stone, on the body of which are carved representations of his pictures of horses; while, as a frieze, there is a representation of his study of a flying bird. A long inscription sets out the achievements and honors of this distinguished Professor of the College of France, and the esteem in which he was held by his townsmen and countrymen.

Friese-Greene, on June 26, 1890, at a meeting of the Photographic Convention of the United Kingdom at Chester, over which I presided as president for the year, read a paper on *A Magazine Camera and Lantern.* He exhibited and described a long series of successive exposures on a sensitive film, which was moved by means of perforations in the film itself, instead of by perforations on a bobbin. He likewise

* Reprinted from the *Photographic Red Book,* London (1931), p. 78.

exhibited and described a lantern that he had devised for projecting the images so obtained. Unfortunately, on the journey from London, the projection apparatus had been damaged so that it could not be used, and the films that Greene had brought with him for exhibition could not be projected. This accident and the non-descriptive title which he gave to his paper were most unfortunate, and I am inclined to doubt whether any of the numerous experienced photographers at the meeting quite realized what a distinct advance Greene had really made.

It is a point of interest that the art now so widely applied for purposes of entertainment originated from a desire for making scientific investigations, of which most of the patrons of the cinema are probably ignorant; although to a very limited extent it is occasionally brought to their notice the methods used to produce the pictures that amuse them are still constantly employed in scientific studies of great importance from various points of view.

Le Prince, whose claims as one of the pioneers I have recently advanced, I knew well by sight; in fact, I met him once or twice at the house of Mr. and Mrs. Wilson, with whom he had gone abroad just before his mysterious disappearance. I have, however, no recollection of having heard anything about his work in kinematography up to the time when I left Leeds in August, 1891, although I was a fairly regular attendant at the meetings of the Leeds Photographic Society. Probably he did not desire publicity until he had made satisfactory arrangements for working his patent.

A Brief History of the Kinetograph, the Kinetoscope and the Kineto-phonograph*

By W. K. LAURIE DICKSON**

In the year 1879 at the age of 19 I had read much of a Mr. Edison in America and his scientific experiments, and so wrote to him to inquire whether he would take me on his staff of experimenters (Fig. 1). His reply was not encouraging. It read as follows:

Menlo Park, N. J.
March 4, 1879.
William Kennedy Laurie Dickson,
Care of Mrs. Aubin,
2 Tregunter Road. London W.
Dear Sir:
Your favor of the 17th ult. has just been rec'd.
I cannot increase my list of employees as I have concluded to close my works for at least 2 years, as soon as I have finished experiments with the electric light.
Very truly,
T. A. Edison.

However, in spite of this, I persuaded my mother and sisters to pull up stakes, and after a stormy crossing we landed in New York and continued down to Richmond, Virginia, by the Old Dominion S. S. Line. After residing there for two years, we youngsters made for New York City early in 1881. I took my book of credentials, *etc.*, to show Mr. Edison at his office at 65 Fifth Avenue, in case I should be lucky enough to gain an interview.

My reception was unique. "But I told you not to come, didn't I?" said Mr. Edison. I agreed, but told him I couldn't have done otherwise after reading about the work in which he was engaged. He watched my face while turning my testimonials over, until I had to remind him please to read them. He only replied, "I reckon they are all right; you had better take your coat off and get to work." I had won.

----

* Requested and recommended for publication by the Historical Committee. Presented at the Fall, 1933, Meeting at Chicago, Ill., at which meeting Mr. Dickson was elected an Honorary Member of the Society.
** Montpelier House, Twickenham, Middlesex, England.
EDITOR'S NOTE: Mr. Dickson was born of Scottish parentage at Chateau St. Buc, Minihic-sur-Ranse, in 1860.
†This letter was reproduced as a foreword to an article by the author and his sister, Antonia Dickson, which appeared in *Century Magazine,* 48 (1894), p. 206. Also published in "History of the Kinetograph, Kinetoscope, and Kinetophonograph" by the same authors; 1895, *Albert Bunn,* New York, N. Y.

He then gave me a note to Mr. Charles Clark, chief mathematician, and anoher to Mr. W. S. Andrews, superintendent of the Goerk St. testing and experimental department of the Edison Electric Works, under

FIG. 1. William Kennedy Laurie Dickson.

whose able and kindly tutelage I secured a good knowledge of what was wanted. The following year, with Mr. Edison's approval, Mr. W. S. Andrews gave me his place while he traveled through the United States planning and erecting electric light and power stations.

My tests and experiments under Mr. Edison's direct instructions were indescribably interesting. We attempted to arrive at a fixed standardization of all electrical apparatus for home and power stations, such as type of dynamo, motors, lamps, meters, *etc.* One test or series of experiments stands out very clearly in my mind. I had the good fortune to help Mr. Edison to determine the meaning of the "Edison effect," or first concept of the famous "valve" used now in radio apparatus.

In 1885 Edison took me away from the Electric Works at Goerk St. to assist him in his private laboratory at Newark, N. J., where I was given research problems to work on. In 1887 Mr. Edison, who knew that I was keen on photography, disclosed his favorite scheme of joining his phonograph to pictures taken photographically with a device like the *Zoetrope.*

He was then erecting his large laboratory at Orange, N. J., in which, as

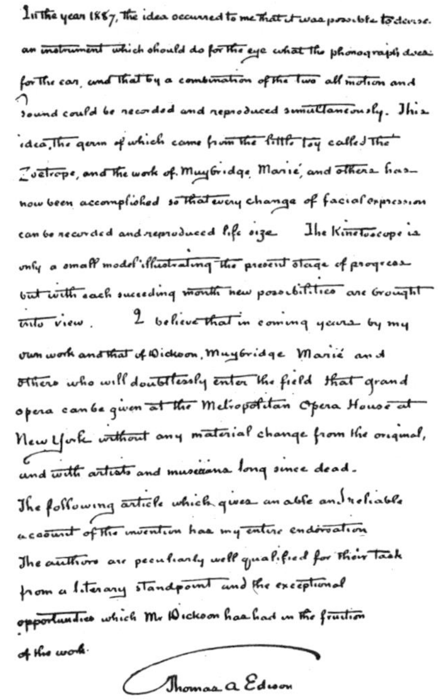

FIG. 2. Reproduction of original letter by T. A. Edison (courtesy *Century Magazine*).

soon as completed, I was allowed to select two large rooms: namely, No. 5 on the 1st floor for the kinetophonograph experiments, and No. 14 above for magnetic ore separation work, analysis, *etc.*

As to animated photography, Fig. 2 is a reproduction of a letter by Mr. Edison, in his own handwriting, regarding his conception of the work he wished me to carry out for him.† This proved entirely successful in the end by giving our kinetograph the double duty of taking the films and reproducing them on a screen in the simplest possible way. If the kinetograph could take good, steady pictures it followed that the same pictures could be projected — as they eventually were — by using a smaller sprocket wheel to allow for the slight shrinkage of the film after developing and fixing.

By his order, however, projection was put aside, and our experiments were concentrated on a "money earner," the kinetoscope, which as it proved left the field open for all.

EARLY EXPERIMENTS WITH CYLINDER RECORDS

Edison's idea, as disclosed to me in 1887 at the Newark Laboratory, was to combine the phonograph cylinder or record with a similar or larger drum on the same shaft, which drum was to be covered with pin-point microphotographs which of course must synchronize with the phonograph record (Fig. 3). I pointed out to him that in the first place I knew of no medium that was sensitive enough to take microphotographs at so rapid a rate while running continuously on the same shaft.

"Well, try it; it will lead to other things," was Edison's reply. I did as soon as I got to his new laboratory, then being erected at Orange, N. J.

Before making the drum, which was to fit over the phonograph shaft, I made a small micro camera, using various objectives or lenses taken from one of my microscopes to produce the pin-head photos. In this micro camera I tried Daguerre's process on highly polished bits of silver and developed in the usual way. The subject I used was a lantern slide of Landseer's stag for all these comparative single still pictures.

The time of exposure was about three-quarters of a minute. Of course, this method was soon abandoned. Next I tried silver nitrate on wet collodion, using an exposure of 10 seconds, which was finally shortened to 5 seconds. Then I had a light drum made and produced a few spirals of pictures on a dead slow shaft. These, even with ammonia acceleration, proved a failure. So I increased the size of the aluminum drum and of the pictures, and coated the drum with a bromide of silver gelatin emulsion; and would have obtained a fairly good result but for some chemical action which took place between the aluminum and the emulsion. That made me try a glass drum and a one-opening rapid shutter.

My second batch of emulsion was light struck, owing to the night-watchman's bursting in at 2 a.m., which so disgusted me that I just slotted the aluminum drum and wrapped a sheet of Carbutt's stiff sensitized celluloid over it. This proved quite satisfactory and did away with my home-made emulsion coatings. The pictures were sharp and good, and to save time in making prints or positives I turned the negative into a positive effect with bichloride of mercury. A reproduction of one of these sheets of ¼-inch pictures may be seen in the *History of the Kinetograph, etc.* (See footnote, p. 9, also Fig. 4.)

---

* EDITOR'S NOTE: This sketch and several others illustrating the article were prepared by Mr. Dickson at the request of the Historical Committee. Originals are on file at the Los Angeles Museum.

To view these small pictures was another matter. If run continuously the result, of course, would be a black streak, unless seen through a slotted disc. To obtain full illumination it occurred to me to rig up a small Geissler spiral tube without a shutter.

FIG. 3. Sketch of Edison's first method of synchronizing phonograph with picture records.*

These pictures, when viewed through a low-power microscope, were fairly good in spite of the curvature of the drum. A disk was tried next, to avoid the difficulty arising from the curved drum surface. However, for the sake of simplicity, we returned to the celluloid sheet and drum. The drum at one end had pins projecting exactly opposite each picture (Figs. 4 and 5).

Courtesy T. Ramsaye -

FIG. 4. Drum for inspecting microscopic pictures on film strip shown on right.

The pins came in contact with a stiff primary wire from an induction coil, whereas the secondary fed the Geissler tube placed directly over or a little to one side of these pictures. Owing to the extreme rapidity of the flash of light from the Geissler tube, when compared with the movement of the drum of pictures, the images appeared to stand still and were sharply defined.

I have not mentioned some of my earlier failures, such as the use of a vertical disk which, however, being flat, got rid of the distortion of the drum. Also, I need not go into a detailed description of my glass drum illumi-

nated intermittently from the inside by a back-and-forth straight shutter.

I was glad to get away from drums, disks, *etc.*, and a hopelessly limited number of pictures, looking forward some day to getting decent lengths of strips of film from Blair or Carbutt.

EXPERIMENTS WITH SHORT FILM STRIPS

My next attempt, after abandoning drums and the like (early 1888), was to proceed with narrow strips of Carbutt celluloid, 18 inches long, notched on the top, and impelled intermittently by a clock escapement movement (Fig. 6). A rotating shutter and a 1½-inch focus lens were used. The pictures were ¼-inch square. This tentative test or experiment seemed to be leading me in the right direction, as will be shown. On trying to join these strips, the usual trouble was that the joints stuck in the frame or open guide, which, however, we made as springy as possible.

While wandering through our museum of showcases containing many hundreds of models of Edison's inventions, I caught sight of his perforated paper automatic telegraph. By the end of a week my capable mechanic, William Heisse, had made me a perforator which made two round holes to a picture. The sprocket drive had a single row of sprockets to fit the newly punched Carbutt strips.

The escapement movement then in use was soon found to be much too slow to satisfy persistency of vision in the stopping and starting which we found imperatively necessary in the endeavor to get a quick change and a long rest. So we adopted the Maltese cross, and after some modifications found it to answer our purpose very well (Fig. 7). In less than a month we

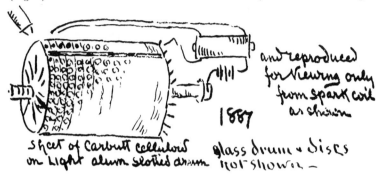

FIG. 5. Sketch of images on Carbutt film wound around drum and viewed with the aid of light from a Geissler tube.

had a good working camera. This occurred in the autumn of 1888.

The pictures were taken horizontally, but were only ½-inch in size—on Carbutt celluloid strips. Though the strips shot through the gate at a good rate, we didn't mind how often we threaded up to enjoy our success. The longest we could made was about 40 inches, or 3 joints of 14 inches each. This apparatus was finished, but neither Carbutt nor Blair could supply us with thinner or longer strips.

EASTMAN'S FILM AND ITS APPLICATION

Toward the close of the year 1888 it was rumored that the Eastman Company was experimenting on a new product for their cameras, and that it would be shown at the New York Camera Club by Mr. Geo. Eastman's representative. At the end of the meeting, which I attended, I approachd the demonstrator, explained what we wanted and asked for the 2 by 4 inch sample to show to Mr. Edison. The representative quickly grasped the situation and its great possibilities, and

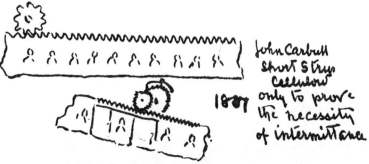

FIG. 6. Sketch of Carbutt film with notched edge.

invited me to come out to Rochester to see Mr. Eastman, which I did the next day. I knew then that we should reach our goal if the Eastman Company could supply this new product in good lengths. When I showed Mr. Edison my new find his smile was seraphic; "Good," he said, "we can now do the trick—just work like hell."

On reaching the Rochester Works, Mr. Geo. Eastman received me most courteously; and after a long talk he took my arm, guiding me through his long darkrooms while he touched on some of his ambitions. He showed considerable enthusiasm as to the new possibilities of the kinetograph requirements.

Clock Escapement stop motion to prove a principle only ie a stopping & starting action followed by

← The Geneva movement.

B Intermittent attached to sprocket shaft. (Sprocket & film) with slip pulley on Drive —

1890 Improved Edison Stop motion for Higher speeds —

Three of the Stop motions used between 1887 to 1890

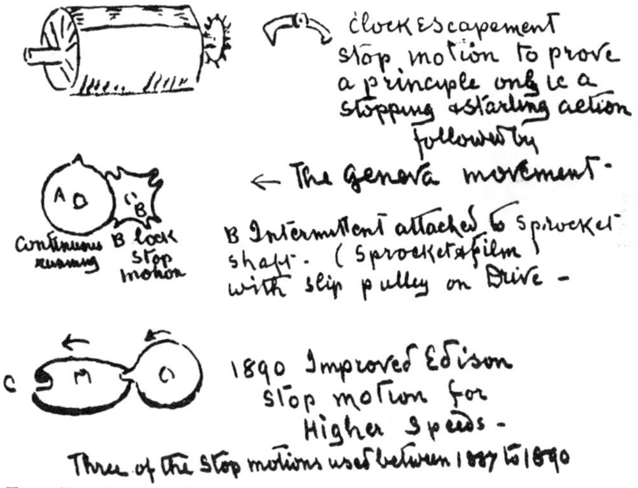

FIG. 7. Types of intermittent movements used 1887–1890.

The central table was covered with long sheets of plate glass, carefully fitted together in lengths. The atmosphere was pregnant with the fumes of

amyl acetate, and I was glad to get out of it. He then took me into another room and gave me many experimental samples wrapped in red and black paper for my tests; and invited me to come whenever I liked. That was the beginning of many years of friendship, strengthened by our mutual interest. Mr. Eastman was at all times ready to concede to my wishes, supporting me in my efforts to attain my great purpose for Mr. Edison.

On my return to Orange, my assistant and I were soon able to test some of these short samples of which we had a good supply, thanks to Mr. Eastman's generosity. However, we found that we should require greater sensitiveness and less coarseness. The silver grains were too apparent when magnified.

A few weeks elapsed before I saw Mr. Eastman again and explained our difficulties, which were remedied by reducing the coarseness of the silver bromide. This change proved most satisfactory. When perforating the film, however, the sprocket wheel often broke through and tore the film. I had to ask Mr. Eastman whether he could make his base tougher and less brittle, which he did.

Meanwhile we had to use this rapid negative for our positive prints; and although they lacked pluckiness, we partly overcame it by using potassium bromide in our developing bath to reduce its sensitiveness. This caused me to apply again to Mr. Eastman for a less sensitive product or emulsion similar to that used in lantern slide work, which we ultimately received.

We were, however, much troubled with "frilling," and often a gelatinous mass of pictures was left at the bottom of our developing or fixing troughs, while the base remained on the drum, a situation which we found very trying and necessitated further conferences on this matter. Mr. Eastman, however, managed to overcome this difficulty in part. An early film of a horse shoeing scene (May, 1889) shows partial frilling (Fig. 8).

About this time we received six rolls of improved negative film 50 feet long, and later slow positive film. All these samples and experiments were made exclusively for us by Mr. Eastman, who took an ever-increasing interest in what we were doing.

To return to the work in hand, we had to devise certain essentials, such as a circular film cutter or trimmer, a perforator, a clamp with steady pins to fit the punch holes, to use in joining the films with a thin paste of the base dissolved in amyl acetate, which, I suppose, is still commonly used. Room 5 at the Edison Laboratory was used principally for our photographic experiments and mechanical work. The precision workshop was located near our room.

Fig. 8. Print from one of first successful Edison negatives on Eastman film (Approximate date, May, 1889).*

To take these photographs or strips, our camera or kinetograph had to be carried down to a small improvised platform placed against our ore-milling outhouse. A bright sunny-natured Greek, Sacco Albanese by name, was one of my very earliest victims, figuring mostly in the ¼-inch, and later in the ½-inch, pictures Draped in white, he was made to go through some weird antics. (See Fig. 4.) Some time later, early in 1890, I persuaded Mr. Fred. Ott, Edison's chief mechanic, to give me an exhibition of sneezing.

The famous firms of Bausch & Lomb and Messrs. Gundlach, of Rochester, N. Y., produced some fine lenses for the work, and I have always felt that they should be brought into this early

---

history of the kinetograph for the perfection of their work and their patience with me and my demands. The lenses were at last standardized as 2½-inch mean focus. With such lenses we made our second kinetograph.

Our first outside subject was the dancing and wrestling bears, which we took early in 1889 in the open yard of the Edison Laboratory, long before any studio was erected. I found these performing bears on the main street of Orange, N. J., and persuaded their Italian owners to follow me to the laboratory to have their photos taken. After a few rehearsals my assistant was ready with a pieced sample of film and the picture was soon made.

My drawer full of samples and tests was destroyed after I left America, and there remain only a few scraps of originals and reproductions and my booklet *The History of the Kinetograph, etc.* I may add also that the studio and the "Black Maria" were razed to the ground as of no historical interest, as it was deemed by my successor. The "Horse Shoeing Scene" of May, 1889, was taken outside with an improvised background, as were other scenes taken prior to that date. (See Fig. 8.)

SYNCHRONIZATION OF THE EDISON PHONOGRAPH AND KINETOGRAPH

In the midst of this work Mr. Edison went abroad, leaving me his instructions. I accompanied him to the steamer. As the boat glided out I saw Mr. Edison leaning over the railing, his fists to his eyes to imitate the viewing of the pictures in our experimental kinetoscope. I understood the pantomine to mean that I was to have the kinetoscope completed before his return. A rough model of the instrument was constructed.

The gearing up of the kinetograph with the phonograph kept us busy day and night, experimenting until both were done in time. A smaller sprocket wheel had to be made for the row of perforations to fit the teeth better, owing to the shrinkage resulting from developing and fixing the negative film, which we had to use for all purposes.

On my return from the boat I persuaded my friend Mr. Charles Batchelor, who was in charge of the laboratory, to build an outside studio to my specifications, combining a sliding glass roof to let in the sunlight unobstructed, for photographing kinetograph subjects before a black or other suitable background.

Attached to this room, which was about 18 by 20 ft. in size, were two darkrooms — one for punching, trimming, joining the films, and printing the positives; the other for developing,

fixing, washing, and "glycerining"† the films. These operations were done by using large, black, enameled drums adjustably suspended at each end when immersed in long, shallow troughs.

The films were spirally wound around these drums and the ends clamped to hold the film in place. When deemed to be thoroughly developed, the drum was carried to a similar trough to revolve in water coming from a spray over the length of the film or drum. The used water was carried away by an overflow from the trough (Fig. 9). The film was then carried to the fixing trough and back to the washing arrangement, thence to the glycerine trough, and dried before a fan while revolving on the motor-driven drum.

Method of Making Prints. . . . As to our method of printing negatives, I had a large 8- or 10-inch sprocketed drum made, geared to run slowly, over which the films came in contact, the unexposed film being under the negative and the pins engaging both films. A small pea-lamp and reflector were placed above the negative. A square of ground glass was interposed between the light and the film, and the light was regulated by a small slide resistance to give the right exposure. Two spools on each side were used, geared to pick up the negative and positive films (Fig. 9).

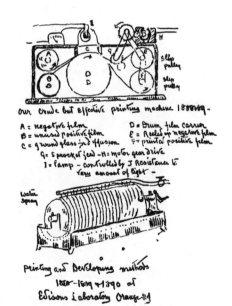

FIG. 9. Printing and developing equipment used at Edison laboratory.

Above these darkrooms I had another room for projecting tests with the kinetograph and phonograph (Fig. 10). Having succeeded in devising a very simple method of doing this, I hastened to get my assistant to take a short film, using me as the subject, in combination with the phonograph, to prove that Mr. Edison was right in supposing such a thing could be done as predicted in his preamble in the *History of the Kinetophone, etc.*

Mr. Edison's return to his laboratory took place Oct. 6, 1889.* Within the hour I had him by the arm and led him to the new studio and kinetophone exhibit, on which we had been working day and night. On seeing the studio, Mr. Edison asked, "What's that building?" I explained its necessity. "Well, you've got cheek; let's see what you've got." We went in. Gradually his face lit up, the clouds of disapproval were dissipated and finally dispelled. I had placed him in a chair in the upper projecting room to witness his first "talkie," or exhibit, of the kinetophone. For a wonder, the exhibition was good. No breakdown of the film occurred nor did the Zeiss arc lamp sputter. There was much rejoicing. Edison sat with the eartubes to the phonograph. My assistant started the arc lamp and removed the metal sheet interposed between the arc and the film. The phonograph motor controlled the projecting kinetograph.

I was seen to advance and address Mr. Edison from the small 4-foot

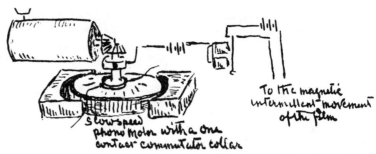

FIG. 11. Sketch of arrangement used to synchronize phonograph record and motion picture film.

screen; small, because of the restricted size of the room. I raised my hat, smiled, and said, "Good morning, Mr. Edison, glad to see you back. Hope you like the kinetophone. To show the synchronization I will lift my hand and count up to ten." I then raised and lowered my hands as I counted to ten. There was no hitch, and a pretty steady picture. If the pictures were steady in the taking, why not in the reproduction on the screen?

A rough description of the method adopted to synchronize the two instruments may be useful. The only modification made to the kinetograph, was to place a ratchet wheel at one end of the driving shaft. Thus one end of the shaft held the sprocket wheel

FIG. 10. Projection room (about 1894), showing phonograph attached to kinetoscope for synchronization of sound and picture. (*Century Magazine*, **18**, 207, 1894).

* It has been said that Mr. Edison sent me long, weekly cables and letters during his absence, to instruct me further as to what information he had gathered when in Paris from others working on these lines; which, of course, was absolutely incorrect. I wish to emphasize the fact that Mr. Edison never during his absence communicated with me either by cable or letter.

which engaged the perforated film, and the other end held a magnetic escapement device, which was controlled and timed through a relay and battery from an extra commutator collar on the phonograph motor shaft. The impulses electrically received through the ratchet wheel were spaced at ½-inch intervals for each phase or picture

(Fig. 11). This arrangement gave very good synchronization and was extremely simple though a little slower than when using the Geneva movement which, of course, was put temporarily out of gear for these kinetophone demonstrations.

A little later, about a year, I fancy, Mr. Edison devised an ingenious stopping and starting device, which took the place of the Maltese cross or Geneva movement for a time. A horizontal 1½-inch disk with one slot at its edge was centered on a shaft to run continuously. A disk of similar size with a nose or pin projecting and running vertically was driven forward on a slip collar. The nose rested and slid along the slotted horizontal disk; and as the vertical disk revolved, the nose or pin in the horizantal disk would fall rapidly through the slanting slot (Fig. 7). The film was therefore moved along, since it was engaged at the other end of the shaft by means of a sprocket wheel.

I waited for Mr. Edison's further approval of my model of the kinetoscope that day on his return, before going ahead with a standard model. He was quite enthusiastic, and the next day, Oct. 7, 1889, he brought in several visitors among them Samuel Insull, to see the "Wonderbox." A photograph of the studio interior taken a few weeks later shows both the No. 1 and 2 kinetoscope models (Fig. 12). Although this apparatus has often been described, I will venture to repeat a description.

THE FINISHED KINETOSCOPE

In the first place, the film or positive which was 47 feet long, ran continuously and not intermittently as in the kinetograph.

The kinetoscope mechanism was built up on a small platform, and consisted of an open gate through which the film ran, drawn by the sprocket wheel (Fig. 13). A 10-inch shutter revolved at high speed. The shutter was slotted in one place giving a 3/16-inch opening to admit the light from a small electric lamp after passing through the film. The light rays from the 8-volt lamp were converged by means of a reflector, causing the rays to cross through the 3/16-inch shutter opening to obtain a maximum of light.

The film, after leaving the gate and sprocket wheel, passed down and up over several velvet covered rollers or spools in an endless band. The last spool was weighted and controlled by a spring to take up any slack. The film used in the first model had one row of perforations. The pictures were ½-inch in width (Figs. 14 and 15), and the shutter opening was so set as to meet a picture centrally. To increase the magnification of the image, I further devised a two-eye plano-convex lens to increase the size of the image. As this whole device was approved by Edison, I forged ahead, and soon was using a larger film perforated along both edges. The mechanism was driven by a small 8-volt motor, using storage batteries. The manufacture of this device was started in 1893 and was soon carried out in quantities for exhibitors.* Meanwhile, the projecting kinetograph remained in *status quo,* to my great regret.

At the end of the year 1889, I increased the width of the picture from ½ inch to ¾ inch, then, to 1 inch by ¾ inch high (Fig. 15). The actual width of the film was 1⅜ inches to allow for the perforations now punched on both edges, 4 holes to the phase or picture, which perforations were a shade smaller than those now in use. This standardized film size of 1889 has remained, with only minor variations, unaltered to date (Fig. 16).

The demand for films for the kinetoscopes was somewhat of a problem as the machines were being manufactured. Just at this time I was switched off to carry out some further experiments on magnetic ore-milling machinery. However, I never failed to remind Mr. Edison of his risk in not patenting all these "movie" devices. I think it was Mr. Frank L. Dyer who at last persuaded him to move in the matter, after I had talked it over with him. This, however, was not done until a year or so later, while others anticipated us by a patent date though we could prove priority of invention and actual working models, *etc.*

---

* The first commercial showing of this device was at the Holland Brothers Peep Show Parlour, 1155 Broadway, New York, N. Y., April 14, 1894 (*"History of the Motion Picture,"* by T. Ramsaye, *Simon & Schuster,* N. Y., 1925).

* Completed on Feb., 1892, at a cost of $637.67.

THE MAKING OF COMMERCIAL KINETOSCOPE PRINTS

On my resuming movie work (which I did off and on), I had to do my best to secure attractive subjects for the kinetoscopes. It was only at certain times of the day that I could get such pictures in the studio with its glass roof slid back, so I decided in 1891 to build another studio revolving on wheels to meet the sun at all hours, which some wag later dubbed the "Black Maria."* This had a stage at one end, backed by a tunnel to give velvety black effects, and at the other end was a darkroom fitted to change the films.

The kinetograph camera was fixed on an adjustable table which we could wheel out on rails for focusing close-ups or whole stage effects. The roof was made to fold back to admit the sun after the building had been moved around (Fig. 17). Here we took most of the pictures, although some were made at the old studio and a few in the open.

The outside pictures were taken against a long or very wide grey painted wooden wall so that when the subject moved out of the picture we would still follow it by keeping it centrally framed against an even, gray background, as was necessary when photographing *Duncan C. Ross' Horsemanship* or *Mounted Sword Fencing.*

FIG. 12. Interior of first studio (1889), showing models 1 and 2 of the kinetoscope. (From *History of the Kinetoscope, etc.,* by W. K. L. Dickson and Antonia Dickson. *A. Bunn,* N. Y., 1895.)

FIG. 13. Interior view of the kinetoscope (Talbot, F. A.: "Moving Pictures," *Lippincott's,* Philadelphia, Pa., 1923).

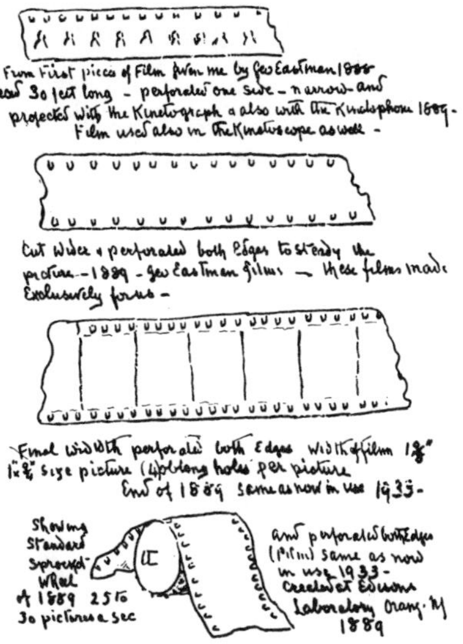

FIG. 14. Evolution of standard film width and picture size.

FIG. 15. Print from length of early narrow width film made with kinetograph (perforations cut off when first reproduced in book form).

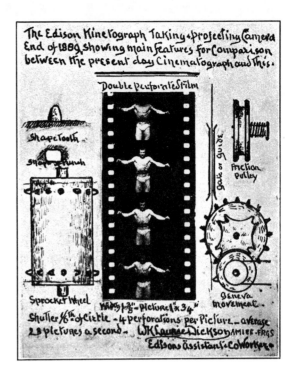

FIG. 16. Types of mechanisms and film used in the kinetograph.

The camera end of the "Black Maria" used to be swung around and such pictures taken through a small window inside the darkroom. The lighting and stage were so great an improvement, that I repeated several of the subjects I had taken earlier in the 1889 studio, such as the organ grinder and monkey, *Sandow,* and some others. I can give only an inadequate list of subjects, most of which were taken in the "Black Maria," built in 1891-92. A partial list of subjects taken at Edison's laboratory between 1889 and 1895 follows:

Trick Dog Teddy and other Dog and trick Cats.
Madame Bertoldi, contortionist.
The Gaiety Girls.
Colonel Cody's (Buffalo Bill) Shooting Skill.
Colonel Cody and his Sioux Indians.
Sioux Ghost Dance.
Sandow in Feats of Strength.
Texan Cowboy Throwing Lassos (in the open).
Alcide Capitaine.
Mexican Knife Thrower.
Madame Armand Ary.
Fencing Bout—Experts.
John Wilson, the Tramp.
Boxing Cats.
Sheik Hadji Tahar—Summersaults, *etc.*

———

* The Biograph Co., sometimes known as K.M.C.D. (after the initial letter of the founder's names) was formed in the summer of 1896. Their first commercial showing was on Oct. 13, 1896, at Hammerstein's Olympic Music Hall (in New York.

** The Biographic camera had an intermittent movement consisting of a double mutilated, rubber-covered roller. When portions of the roller having the thicker radii came together on revolving, the film was moved forward.

Walten and Slavin (long and short) comedians.
Japanese Dancers.
Chinese Opium Den Police Raid — a comic.
Milk White Flag (a play).

These subjects were taken on our full width film, having double perforations, four to a phase as used to this day, and standardized by me for Edison at the end of 1889.

In conclusion, when I left Mr. Edison's laboratory in 1895, having accomplished the problems assigned to me, I joined my friends Messrs. H. N. Marvin, E. B. Koopman, and Herman Casler* to carry out a new method of reproducing motion by means of a pack of cards, which I had devised shortly after I left Mr. Edison. This device we called the "Mustoscope." The cards were viewed both as a peep show and as booklets given out by manufacturers for publicity purposes. A syndicate was immediately formed, and our master mechanician, Mr. Herman Casler, worked out his famous "punch as you go" taking camera.** When it was ready, I managed to secure some very stirring pictures.

FIG. 17. "The Black Maria" motion picture studio; designed by Dickson in 1891, completed Feb., 1892.

———

BIBLIOGRAPHY

"The Life and Inventions of Edison," a series of 124 articles by A. and W. K. L. Dickson. *Cassier's Magazine,* 3 (Nov., 1892), p. 3; *et seq.*

"Edison's Invention of the Kineto-Phonograph," by A. and W. K. L. Dickson. *Century Magazine,* 48 (1894), p. 207. Also other articles for the *Century* and *Harper's* Magazines.

"History of the Kinetograph, Kinetoscope, and Kinteto-Phonograph," by A. and W. K. L. Dickson. *Albert Bunn,* New York, N. Y., 1895.

"The Biograph in Battle," by W. K. L. Dickson. *Unwin,* Paris and London, 1900.

Later, I secured pictures with this equipment in London, of Queen Victoria's Jubilee; in Rome, of Pope Leo XIII; and in Africa, of the Boer War. These films were exhibited in London and the United States. The pictures of the Boer War were shipped back periodically and exhibited first at the Palace Theater in London.

In conclusion, it is with considerable pleasure that I look back on these days and nights at Edison's laboratories; of strenuous work, defeat, and triumph.

My friendship and close association with Edison will always remain as a happy memory shadowed by his loss. I still watch with keen interest the development of this great industry—Edison's dream materialized.

My Part in the Development of the Motion Picture Projector[*]

By THOMAS ARMAT[**]

It is difficult to trace to its beginning and fix a date for the conception of an idea that leads to an invention. Of the interesting impressions of my childhood, the one made by the toy known as the Zoetrope was among the most outstanding. The idea that its principles might be applied to producing a series of consecutive instantaneous photographs of objects in motion, so as to reproduce the motion, was suggested by something I had read, and the fascinating thought persisted in my mind until the Anschutz tachyscope I saw at the Chicago World's Fair in 1893 brought a realization of its actual accomplishment.

A toy magic-lantern was also one of my much prized playthings, and from it I had learned, among other things, that microscopically small objects could be projected upon a screen and greatly enlarged. My first thought upon seeing the tachyscope was of the possibilities that would be presented if its pictures could be projected upon a screen. The tachyscope was a peep-hole apparatus, and the picture I saw was that of an elephant trotting along in a most realistic manner. It was an outdoor scene, a foreign setting. The idea of bringing scenes from far and interesting countries and projecting them upon a screen before comfortably seated spectators, was an exciting thought.

In the summer of 1894 I was at Washington the first exhibition there of the Edison kinetoscope. It interested me greatly. About that time Mr. H. A. Tabb, who had known me since my boyhood days, and who also was a friend of both members of the firm of Raff and Gammon, exclusive agents for the kinetoscope, dropped into my office in Washington and endeavored to interest me in a business way in the kinetoscope. He gave me glowing accounts of the public interest in kinetoscope exhibitions and as to the profits to be made out of them.

One of the places Mr. Tabb had in mind for the profitable exhibition of the kinetoscope was Atlanta, Georgia, anticipating the large crowds that would attend the Cotton States Exposition scheduled for the following year.

After investigating the matter I told Mr. Tabb that I could not see anything very promising in the kinetoscope as a commercial project, but that I could see a lot in a machine of the kinetoscope type if the pictures could be projected upon a screen, and that I believed that I could devise such a machine.

Mr. Tabb's answer to that was that he did not believe it was possible to project such pictures successfully, because he knew that Raff and Gammon had urged the Edison Company to produce such a machine and that they had failed to do so, and he, therefore, did not believe it could be done. From what I knew of stereopticons it did not seem to me that the problem presented insuperable difficulties, and I began a research to find out all I could as to the state of the art and what, if anything, had been accomplished in the way of projecting such pictures upon a screen, at the same time starting preparations for experimental work.

I had been inventing for a number of years and had received several patents, among them No. 361,664, filed January, 1887, covering an automatic car-coupler, which had been developed to the point of making a model and which received some very favorable consideration. A subsequent patent, No. 521,562, filed March, 1893, covering a conduit electric railway system, also received favorable criticism from various sources, among others from Professor Louis D. Bliss, founder and head of the Bliss School of Electricity of Washington, D. C., who wrote me a letter in which he said, "It is most decidedly a model of perfection when compared with the crude system of the General Electric Co., and the cumbersome, complicated, and unreliable mechanism of the Wheeless system."

In the fall of 1894 I enrolled as a student in the Bliss School, largely for the purpose of acquiring practical information as to handling an arc light that I proposed to use in my motion picture projection experiments. When I explained my purpose to Professor Bliss, he told me that there was another student in his school who was also interested in motion picture experiments. A few days later, at one of the classes, Professor Bliss introduced to me C. F. Jenkins, the student in question. Jenkins was a stenographer in the Life Saving Service, a branch of the U. S. Treasury Department.

It developed that Jenkins, with the cooperation and assistance of Professor Bliss and E. F. Murphy, the latter having charge of the Edison kinetoscope in the Columbia Phonograph parlors in Washington, had assembled a modification of the Edison kinetoscope, in which all Edison parts, films, sprockets, etc., were used. Jenkins called this peep-hole machine a "phantoscope," and applied for a patent on it November 24, 1894. The patent was issued as No. 536,539 on March 26, 1895. As the patent shows, the Jenkins modification differed from the kinetoscope only in respect to the shutter. Instead of using a rotating shutter with a slit in it for exposing the continuously running film over a stationery electric light bulb, Jenkins rotated the bulb itself. This modification accomplished no improvement in results. It amounted to a somewhat different way of doing the same thing in a somewhat less efficient manner. Its only virtue consisted in the possible avoidance of certain claims in the Edison kinetoscope patent, in which a specifically described shutter was included as an element. These claims were cited by the Patent Office against the Jenkins application.

Practically every night that we met at the Bliss School Jenkins urged me to join with him in experimental work to develop a motion picture projection machine. He was fully convinced that a successful projection machine could be built upon the principle of the continuously running film of the Edison kinetoscope type of exhibiting machine. I was not so certain about that, but I felt that an experimental start had to be made and the sooner the better, and finally agreed on March 25, 1895, to join with Jenkins under an agreement which he prepared. In April or May of 1895 we completed a projection machine built on the kinetoscope principle. The machine turned out to be a complete failure, for reasons now obvious to anyone familiar with motion picture projection problems.

After that I took complete charge of further experimentation, at my own expense, and finally we produced the first projection machine ever made that embodied an intermittent movement with a long period of rest and illumination of the pictures on the film. Application for patent on this machine was filed on August 28, 1895, and later

----

[*] Prepared at the request of the Historical and Museum Committee; received Jan. 7, 1935.

[**] Washington, D. C.

issued to Jenkins and Armat as patent No. 586,953 (Fig. 1). The patent drawings were made from the machine itself, completed a short time before the application was filed. As may be seen, we mounted an Edison kinetoscope sprocket upon the mutilated gear illustrated in the patent. This arrangement gave the desired long period of rest and illumination and quick shift of the pictures, and demonstrated the value of the method. The machine, however, was a mechanical failure.

The Edison films we used (the only kind available at that date) were all taken at the rate of approximately forty per second. The machine could not run the films at more than half that speed, and it thus gave a slow-motion effect to all the scenes. It made a terrific noise. The sprocket and mutilated gear weighed more than a pound, and after a few experimental exhibitions the recesses in the driven gear were battered out of shape and made useless. The machine was never exhibited outside my office at No. 1313 F St., Washington, D. C. I still have the original sprocket and mutilated gear in my possession.

Under date of August 30, 1895, Jenkins wrote his friend Murphy that the machine was a "grand success," but I regarded it as a complete failure so far as its having any commercial value was concerned, and addressed myself to the task of devising a practicable machine. This I accomplished a short time after the failure of the Jenkins and Armat machine, with a modification of the Demeny camera intermittent negative film movement, adapted to projection machine requirements. I hurriedly assembled a crude machine, tried it out and found it satisfactory. Immediately afterward I had a more substantial machine made, and with it gave a number of successful exhibitions in my office to friends and acquaintances. An account of this machine was published in the Baltimore *Sun* of October 3, 1895.

In the month of September, 1895, we took this machine to the Cotton States Exposition at Atlanta, Georgia. Subsequently I had two duplicate machines made and sent to us there for exploitation purposes. I obtained a concession from the Exposition author-

ities and built a theater in the grounds for giving exhibitions, with the thought that receipts from the theater would help to pay the exploitation expenses. The anticipated crowds did not materialize, the receipts were small, and a very considerable loss was incurred.

While at Atlanta, Jenkins borrowed one of the three machines, saying that he would like to take it to Richmond, Indiana, to give some exhibitions to his friends on the occasion of his brother's wedding, and that he would be back in a few days. Jenkins gave an exhibition with this machine in his brother's store in Richmond, as announced in the Richmond *Daily Telegram* of October 30, 1895.*

After Jenkins' departure from Atlanta I made some important improve-

ments in the machine, including a loop, or slack-forming means, that improved the exhibitions and greatly reduced the wearing of the films. Subsequently I remodeled the machine, to give it a more commercial form.

In the month of December, 1895, I got in touch with Messrs. Raff and Gammon of New York, who were the exclusive agents for the Edison kinetoscope and films. My idea was to arrange for a supply of films. In reply to a letter to them asking that they come to Washington to see my machine, I received an answer to the effect that they had no faith in motion picture projection machines, since they had endeavored to induce the Edison Company to produce one and they had failed to do so, and they did not believe motion pictures could be suc-

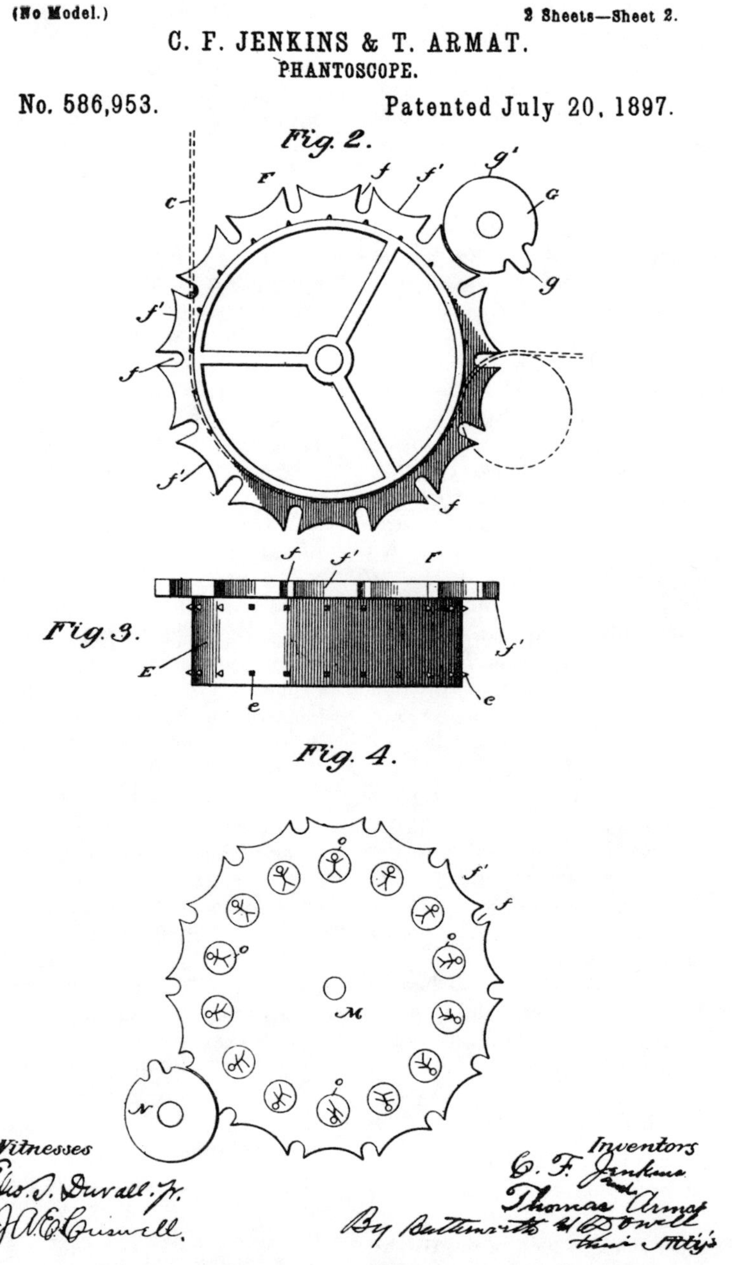

* EDITOR'S NOTE: It has been stated several times in the literature that C. F. Jenkins gave an exhibition with his projector at Richmond, Indiana, on June 6, 1894, but no proof of this earlier date has been obtained by the Historical Committee. A photographic copy of the Richmond *Daily Telegram* for Oct. 30, 1895, describing the showing on October 29, 1895, is in the files of the Committee.

(No Model.)   3 Sheets—Sheet 2.

C. F. JENKINS & T. ARMAT.
PHANTOSCOPE.

No. 586,953.   Patented July 20, 1897.

Fig. 2.

Fig. 3.

Fig. 4.

Witnesses   Inventors
Edw. S. Duvall. Jr.   C. F. Jenkins
J. C. Criswell.   Thomas Armat
                            By Batturworth & Dowell
                                              their Attys

FIG. 1.   Arrangement for providing a long period of rest and illumination, and quick shift of pictures.

cessfully projected. After a further exchange of letters Mr. Gammon agreed to come to Washington if I should pay his expenses, which I agreed to do. Mr. Gammon arrived with a sort of apologetic air of having being fooled into a wild-goose chase. When I took him into the basement of my office and threw a picture upon the screen, his attitude underwent a complete transformation. His excitement and interest were most apparent.

The result of the interview was a contract under the terms of which Raff and Gammon undertook to furnish films and to manufacture a certain number of machines, and licenses were to be granted upon a royalty basis to users of the machines and films, with territorial restrictions. No machines under any circumstances were to be sold. The Edison Company was to make the machines from a model I was to send them.

Mr. Edison wanted to see an exhibition of the machine before details as to the number of machines to be made by him, the supply of films, *etc.*, were to be decided. It was arranged that I should give Mr. Edison an exhibition. I sent a machine over to the Edison Works at Orange, N. J., and later Messrs. Raff and Gammon and I went over from New York to give the exhibition. The exhibition took place in a large room in the Edison plant and the sheet was a large one. Mr. Edison was obviously surprised at the excellence of the exhibition and so expressed himself. On the way back to New York Mr. Gammon told me that Mr. Edison had agreed to all our plans but expressed the opinion that we were planning to have more machines made than necessary. We planned to make eighty machines at first, but Mr. Gammon said that Mr. Edison believed that fifty machines would be sufficient to cover the country. This (oft quoted) statement might seem strange coming from a man of Mr. Edison's vision, but it should be borne in mind that up to that date (February, 1896) no pictures of outside scenes had been taken by the Edison Company. The scenes were all such as had been taken in the Edison "Black Maria," as they called it, a sort of open-air, black-lined stage adapted to be rotated so as to face the sun. The necessity for bright sunlight was largely due to the high speed of taking. The pictures were restricted to such as could be taken in the limited space of the small stage, and they were all of vaudeville subjects.

Arrangements were made by Raff and Gammon to introduce the machine, or rather its exhibitions, to the New York public, and I was asked to come to New York to supervise the installation and operation of the machine. This I did, and on the evening of April 23, 1896, I gave at Koster and Bial's Music Hall in New York, the first exhibition ever given in a theater of motion pictures as we know them today, embodying, as such exhibitions do, the feature of relatively long periods of rest and illumination of each picture on the film. I personally operated the machine the first night. All the scenes shown, with one exception, were what might be called vaudeville turns, or stage subjects. A crowded audience applauded each of the scenes with great enthusiasm. The one exception to the stage scenes was an outdoor scene that Raff and Gammon had succeeded in getting from Robert Paul, who by that date was experimenting with motion pictures in England. This scene was of storm-tossed waves breaking over a pier on the beach at Dover, England—a scene that was totally unlike anything an audience had ever before seen in a theater. When it was thrown upon the screen the house went wild; there were calls from all over the house for "Edison," "Edison," "speech," "speech."

A graphic account of the exhibition was published in the New York *Herald* and the New York *World* published long accounts of the exhibition that I had given at the Edison Works.

It should be here stated that, by mutual agreement, it was decided that Edison's name should be used in connection with the machine. This was done partly for the commercial advantage of the prestige of his name and partly because he was the producer of and had patents pending

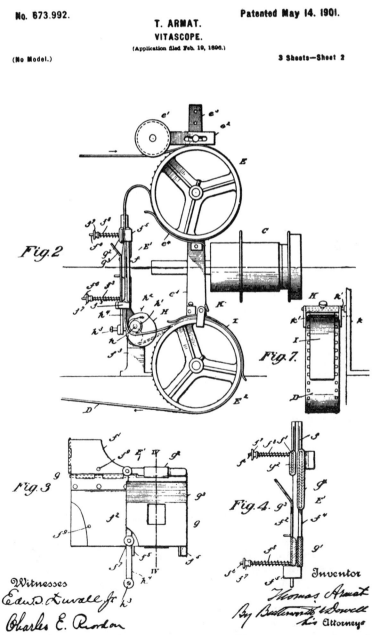

No. 673,992.   **T. ARMAT.**   **Patented May 14, 1901.**

VITASCOPE.

(Application filed Feb. 19, 1896.)

(No Model.)   3 Sheets—Sheet 2

FIG. 2. Mechanism of the *Vitascope.*

19

covering the films, an essential part of the machine, that he was to supply. Prior to this, when I had gotten the machine in all its details into what I considered practicable commercial shape, I applied for a patent on it on February 19, 1896 (Fig. 2), and selected *Vitascope* as a name for the machine. This name was applied to a projection machine for the first time in this patent application, and it would seem that I added a word to the English language as the word *Vitascope* now appears in most modern dictionaries. The Vitascope, Edison Vitascope, so-called, made an immediate hit and was in great demand all over the country.

Subsequently I invented and patented another projection machine with a greatly superior intermittent movement. This machine is shown in my patent No. 578,185 filed September 25, 1896, issued March 2, 1897 (Fig. 3). This intermittent movement is known as the "Star Wheel" or Geneva Cross movement, and it superseded all others by 1897 and is in use today in practically every motion picture theater the world over. It was not, however, a part of the Raff and Gammon arrangement, being a somewhat later development. The intermittent movement has been called, appropriately I think, the "heart" of the motion picture projection machine. In the early days this intermittent movement of my patent No. 578,185 was used in the Edison Projectorscope, the Powers Cameragraph, the Vitagraph, the Lubin machine, the Baird machine, the Simplex machine, and many other early machines.

The Raff and Gammon licensing arrangement started off auspiciously and the financial returns were satisfactory, but troubles developed shortly. None of my patents had been issued at that date, and the applications were still pending in the patent office, two of them involved in "interferences" which greatly delayed their issue. No patent protection could be given until patents were actually issued. Piratical machines began to appear, and, in the absence of patents, could not be stopped. Later on the Edison Company began to be slow in supplying films. Friction, for that reason among others, developed between the Edison Company and Raff and Gammon. Still later the Edison Company began to market a machine that infringed my pending patents. As soon as my patents were issued I organized a company, to which I transferred my patents. Warnings were sent out to infringers, and suits were filed. In many cases the suits were rendered fruitless by the simple expedient of fading away on the part of the sued infringer. The Edison Company was

making and selling large numbers of machines that they called *projectorscopes* which infringed no less than three of my patents. We notified users of the machines that they must promptly arrange to pay us royalties for their use or they would be sued for infringement and damages. The Edison Company notified users of projectorscopes they had sold that they would be protected against any suits that we might bring. That made it necessary for us to sue the Edison Company. In the meantime a suit we had brought against the Biograph Company reached its final stage and was decided in our favor, and the company was enjoined. On the strength of that decision an injunction was obtained against the Edison Company. The Edison Company had pending in the Patent Office an application

covering the only successful method of taking motion pictures and an application covering the perforated film.

So long as the Edison Company and my company were fighting each other, no exhibitor could give an exhibition without risk of being sued by one side or the other. I had pointed out a number of times to the Edison Company the obvious advantages of our getting together on some basis that would not involve the sale of projection machines, but without avail. After we obtained the injunction against the Edison Company they tried in various ways to obtain a license from my company under which they would be permitted to sell machines. To that I declined to agree. From the beginning I had refused to sell machines, or to license other to do so, for the reason that I felt that whatever monopoly we

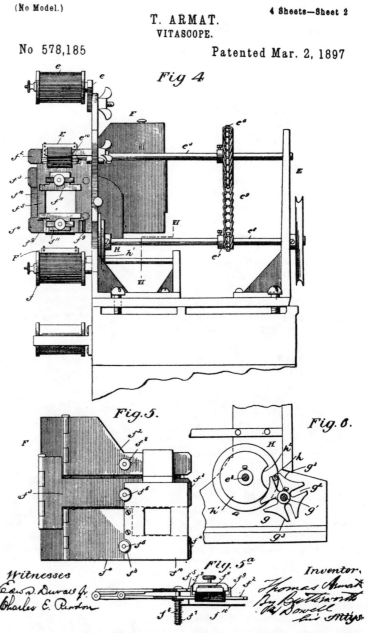

FIG. 3. Intermittent movement employing the star-wheel, or Geneva cross.

might be entitled to under our patents would be destroyed by any sale of machines; and I also felt that any profit we might make out of the sale of machines would not be remotely commensurate with the earning power of the machines themselves. I wanted a royalty from exhibitors, small enough not to be felt by them, but which in the aggregate would net a handsome income to my company.

The suit against the Biograph Company was for an injunction and damages of $150,000. Damages were also asked in the suit against the Edison Company. Both companies posted bonds and prepared appeals. While damages in patent suits are rarely collectible, a favorable decision in an injunction suit where damages are claimed creates a very uncomfortable feeling on the part of the defeated party and the holders of any of their securities.

The American Mutosope and Biograph Company had outstanding a bond issue of $200,000. Some of the bonds were held by the Empire Trust Company of New York, who took notice of the success of our suit for injunction and damages against Biograph Company.

Among the stockholders of the Empire Trust was J. J. Kennedy, a very distinguished counsulting engineer as well as a man of rare business ability, who was requested by the Empire Trust Company to study the motion picture patent and commercial situation and work out a plan that would help the Biograph Company and their bondholders out of their difficulties. Mr. Kennedy got in touch with Mr. H. N. Marvin, also an engineer of distinction and an inventor, who was the president and general manager of the Mutoscope and Biograph Company. Together Mr. Kennedy and Mr. Marvin, after holding consultations with all interested parties, formed a stock company to take over all the valuable patents in the art, the stock to be distributed to the patent owners. It was a closed corporation, the stock was placed in escrow, and none of it was sold.

This holding company was called the Motion Picture Patents Co., and the principal beneficiaries were the Edison Company, the Biograph Company, and the Armat Moving Pictures Company. I owned most of the stock in the latter. The Motion Pictures Patents Company was an immediate success. The royalties that it collected put no burden upon the industry but resulted in a large net revenue to the Patents Company. A royalty of half a cent a foot was paid by the producers, and a royalty of two dollars a week

was paid by the exhibitors to the Patents Company.

At the date of the organization of the Patents Company there were in this country between ten and twelve thousand small theaters, or *Nickleodeons,* as they were called. The royalty of two dollars a week was an entirely negligible sum to them, but, as it was collected without cost to the Patents Company by the simple expedient of having the distributors add two dollars a week to their weekly film rentals, it amounted to a practically net revenue of between $20,000 and 24,000 a week. The revenue of half a cent a foot as film royalties also amounted to a handsome total. Unfortunately for the stockholders of the Patents Company, as the Motion Picture Patents Company came to be known, its life was rather a short one.

Some of the producers, for reasons that I have never quite understood, were refused licenses by the Patents Company. These producers, calling themselves "Independents," formed an organization and put up an all-around fight. At that date anything that smacked of being a monopoly or trust was very unpopular with the public and the courts.

The Independents charged the Patents Company with being an unlawful monopoly under the Sherman Anti-Trust law, and instigated a suit by the Government against them on that ground. In a decision by Judge Dickinson it was held in substance, as I recall it, that while a patentee had a legitimate monopoly within his patent claims, he could not, under the Sherman act, lawfully combine his patent with other patents, and the Patents Company was ordered dissolved.

I have always felt that Judge Dickinson was influenced in his judgement by the fact that the Edison Company (under the domination of Gilmore) had sold thousands of projection machines without restrictions as to their use, in some instances guaranteeing the right to their use, and later, through the Patents Company, participated in royalties collected for their use.

Judge Dickinson said, "Every theater was required to pay royalties for the use of projection machines, even where the machine had been owned before the combination was formed." He appeared to overlook, or to ignore, the fact that the machines had been sold without license or other authority from the owners of the projection machine patents.

I have always felt that the Patents Company, instead of being an organization in restraint of trade, the thing that the Sherman law was designed to

prohibit, was in effect an organization to facilitate trade; for the reason that prior to the date of the Patents Company's acquiring the right to grant licenses, under the controlling patents, no producer or exhibitor could do a legitimate business—that is, a business that did not infringe one or more patents—and the fear of running counter to the patent laws could certainly have had a deterrent effect upon the business of all except those piratically inclined.

Many erroneous statements have been made and published as to when and by whom the first motion picture projection machine was made. To clarify the facts I have been asked several times to list the more or less basic inventions upon which the motion picture industry was initially established, as shown by U. S. Patent Office records. I have been regarded as qualified to do so because of my own pioneer inventions in the art and my connection with the beginning of the industry founded upon them. Subsequently to this early experience I was called upon to testify, as an expert in the art, in litigation under my patents, and later under the Edison and other patents owned by the Patents Company.

There have been a great variety of motion picture projectors, produced under different names, that vary as to their mechanical details but embody all the inventions that may be called basic—basic in the sense that they are necessary for successful projection and have been used since the beginning or near the beginning and are still being used. The following is my list of the eight most important inventions in the motion picture art:

(1) The Edison camera: Patent No. 589,168, dated Aug. 31, 1897. Filed Aug. 24, 1891. This was the first camera employing a perforated film which was given an intermittent motion so that a given number of perforations and a given number of pictures would be intermittently moved, rather than a given length of film. The result was a film having equally spaced, juxtaposed pictures throughout its length. The first practicable motion picture camera ever produced.

(2) The Edison motion picture film: Patent Reissue No. 12,038, Sept. 30, 1902. Filed Aug. 24, 1891. The first perforated motion picture film ever produced having equally spaced, juxtaposed pictures, necessary to successful motion picture projection and an essential part of every motion picture projector in use the world over today. This Edison film when first made some time prior to 1891 was 1⅜ inch wide over all, contained four perforations to each picture, the picture itself being 1 inch wide by ¾ inch high. The number of perforations per picture and the film dimensions have not been changed in standard size machines since they were first made by Edison some time prior to 1891.

(3) The Edison peep-hole kinetoscope: Patent 493,426, dated March 14, 1893. Filed Aug. 24, 1891. This was the first motion picture exhibiting machine employing a perforated film with equally spaced juxtaposed pictures. The first practicable motion picture exhibiting machine of *any* kind, but incapable of projecting pictures successfully because it gave the film a continuous motion instead of an intermittent motion.

(4) The Jenkins and Armat intermittent motion projection machine: Patent No. 586,953, dated July 20, 1897. Filed Aug. 28, 1895. The first motion picture projection machine giving the pictures an intermittent motion with a long period of rest and exposure. A mechanical failure, it nevertheless demonstrated the necessity and value of long exposure, essential to successful projection.

(5) The Vitascope: Invented and patented by Thomas Armat, Patent No. 673,992, dated May 14, 1901. Filed February 19, 1896. The first projection machine employing a loop-forming means and the first projection machine embodying a practicable intermittent movement giving the pictures the required long period of rest and exposure. A loop-forming means is essential in projection machines employing a long length of film.

(6) The star-wheel intermittent movement: Invented and patented by Thomas Armat. Patent No. 578,185, dated March 2, 1897. Filed September 25, 1896. By means of this intermittent movement a small sprocket carrying the film could be given a gradually accelerated intermittent movement without film wear and tear and without jar to the mechanism. This movement superseded all others by 1897, and has been continuously used up to date. The intermittent movement is called the "heart" of the projecting machine.

(7) The Albert E. Smith framing device: Patent 673,329, dated April 30, 1901. Filed March 15, 1900. This device frames the pictures while the machine is running, and is a practically essential device.

(8) The John A. Pross shutter: Patent 722,382, dated March 10, 1903. Filed January 19, 1903. An important improvement for reducing scintillation or flicker. Not so essential in the earlier days of 1895 and 1896 when Edison films were the only ones obtainable, since these films were taken at approximately forty per second, but quite essential with pictures taken at the later commercial lower rates.

The foregoing is a complete list of the pioneer inventions covering all the essentials of the motion picture camera, the motion picture film, and the motion picture projector, and they are all in universal use today in the most modern and up-to-date equipment. The addition of color and of sound accompaniment belong to a later period.

For the possible benefit of those who have not investigated the matter, I believe it might be well to point out some of the differences between a camera and a projection machine, from the patent and invention standpoint. These differences were pointed out by me in the Patent Office interference in which my Vitascope patent, No. 5 on the list, was involved. I am not an attorney, but my familiarity with the art and its requirements enabled me to conduct this case successfully myself, preparing the brief and arguing the case personally before the several tribunals of the Patent Office and the Court of Appeals of the District of Columbia, all of which tribunals accepted my views and decided in my favor. In taking a picture of an object in motion it is essential to make the exposure of the image on the sensitive film as short as possible, consistent with the sensitiveness of the film, for the reason that if this is not done there will be time for the image of the moving object to be displaced on the sensitive film, causing a blurred or indistinct picture. In an exhibiting apparatus the reverse is true. There is, in the exhibiting apparatus, a picture fixed beyond the possibility of any such image movement's causing blur, and the longer the picture is exposed to the eye, the better the results. In a camera we are dealing with a moving object and a sensitive film. In an exhibiting apparatus we are dealing with a fixed picture and the human eye. No question of flicker or scintillation enters into the problem of taking pictures. That question enters very ex-

tensively into the problem of exhibiting pictures.

In a camera, the sensitive film does not cooperate with the mechanism to produce a complete or final result. The film has to be taken out and developed and printed before the operation is complete. The film is run through the camera but once. The Patent Office and the courts held that the film is no more a part of a camera than the paper is of a printing press. In an exhibition machine the film with pictures on it is an essential part of the apparatus. It is a part of the mechanism which cooperates with the other parts to produce the complete and final results. In an exhibition machine the film is used over and over again in the apparatus and has to be so used whenever the apparatus is used. In passing upon this question the Patent Office had this to say:

"If Latham with his Exhibit Machine No. 12, and Casler with his Exhibit First Machine, both of which were taking cameras, could, without invention, have produced a machine of the construction called for by the issue, it is remarkable that they did not do so at any proven date before the filing of their application.

The evidence shows that neither Latham nor Casler was an ordinary mechanic but that they were inventors of considerable capacity, and yet neither of them produced a machine having the new and beneficial results which are claimed for the machine described in Armat's application."

The Patent Office said further:

"In our opinion, proof of the existence of a camera for taking pictures of an object in motion, said camera having in combination with a sensitive film, mechanism for giving an intermittent motion in which the periods of pause exceed the period of motion, said mechanism comprising in addition the other elements called for by the issue and a shutter, is not a reduction to practice of this issue; unless there is proof to show that when this camera was used for projecting the shutter was either omitted altogether, or was so adjusted as to provide for such relative periods of pause and illumination and periods of motion as are called for by the issue."

What Happened in the Beginning

By F.H. RICHARDSON[*]

When one seeks to delve into the history of the motion picture industry during the period we usually refer to as "formative"—the space of time during which the inventions upon which the future success of the industry would be based were in process of discovery—one is immediately confronted with many apparently conflicting claims.

When the writer undertook the preparation of this paper, he had nothing more in mind than the showing to you, by means of projected stereopticon slides, certain old pictures in his possession, together with some samples of old films and the relation of certain historic facts then in his possession.

When the time came for serious consideration of the matter, however, certain things came to the fore in mental vision which very greatly altered the plans. One by one the pioneers of the early days are slipping out into ghostland, and few indeed have left any consistent written record of their achievements in the industry. William T. Rock, Sigmund Lubin, Nicholas Power, Edward Earl, Frank Cannock, and others have passed into the Eternal Shades, and in every case, so far as I know, we must now depend upon bits of information picked up here and there for the very incomplete record we have of their doings in those early days around which so much interest centers.

We still have with us, however, some men who were pioneers on the very frontier of the industry, and it seemed to me to be of real importance to secure from them a personal, written statement of their activities in those days, for while we hope and trust they may be with us for many years, still, who may say when the Grim Reaper will speak the word which all humanity must obey at the last?

With this thought in mind I have approached Thomas A. Edison, George Eastman, Thomas Armat and C. Francis Jenkins, each of whom has been kind enough to drift back in memory into the past and set forth for the records of this Society their own personal recollections, supported in many instances by records, official or otherwise, as to their own individual activities during the period when the motion picture industry was in the process of changing from a peep-hole affair into the life size motion picture which we know today.

———
[*]*Motion Picture World,* New York City.

I have also been able to induce Mr. Albert E. Smith, President of the Vitagraph Company of America, to set down for us a record of his own activities in the early days, Mr. Smith and Mr. J. Stuart Blackton having been the original incorporators of the Vitagraph, which was, so far as I know, (though I do not make it as a statement of known fact), the first producing corporation outside of the Edison Company, and certainly the only producing company of them all, including the Edison Company, which started in the very early days, has endured through the years and is today still producing motion pictures. Also, it was the Vitagraph Company which created the very first "Star," who was Miss Florence Turner, long known as the "Vitagraph Girl."

The statements of all these various gentlemen are in the form of letters prepared and signed by them personally; hence, there can be no question as to their genuineness, or that they contain anything not personally written and approved by them. For reasons you can readily understand, I desire to retain the originals of these letters in my possession, when the records of the Society have been completed so far as they are concerned. I would therefore suggest, if I may, that these letters be incorporated into our proceedings in the form of cuts made from the originals.

I also take the liberty of most respectfully suggesting to this honorable body that a committee be appointed by its President to examine into and, so far as possible, reconcile any conflicting claims as between the various early inventors, most of which are, I believe, more apparent than real.

First, I will present the statement of Mr. Thomas A. Edison, who says:

Cable Address "Edison, New York"
From the Laboratory
of
THOMAS A. EDISON
Orange, N. J.
January 24, 1925

Mr. F. H. Richardson,
516 Fifth Avenue
New York, N. Y.

Dear Mr. Richardson:
In accordance with your request I will give you a brief account of my work in the development of the motion picture, with the hope that it will be filed in the proceeding of the Society, so as to constitute a permanent record.

One of my early notes on the subject made shortly after the kinetoscope was invented, not later than 1890, was the following:

"In the year 1887 the idea occurred to me that it was possible to devise an instrument which should do for the eye what the phonograph does for the ear, and that by a combination of the two all motion and sound could be recorded and reproduced simultaneously This idea, the germ of which came from a little toy called the zoetrope and the work of Muybridge, Marey, and others, has now been accomplished so that every change of facial expression can be recorded and reproduced life size. The kinetoscope is only a small model illustrating the present stage of the progress, but with each succeeding month new possibilities are brought into view. "I believe that in coming years, by my own work and that of Muybridge, Marey and others who will doubtless enter the field, grand opera can be given at the Metropolitan Opera House at New York without any change from the original and with artists and musicians long since dead."

I knew, of course, that both Muybridge and Marey had been able by photography to produce the *illusion of motion* by first securing instantaneous photographs of a *single cycle of movement* and indedefinitely repeating the same and that they had actually employed projectors by which the moving image would be shown on a screen. The work of these two pioneers was essentially scientific and in no sense utilitarian; they were interested only in *analyzing* movement and not in creating a source of entertainment. Their pictures were taken on plates and therefore were limited in number, so that a continued exhibition necessitated the constant repetition of a single cycle of movement. Furthermore, with both Muybridge and Marey, the photographic images were located *centrally* on the plates and for this reason when projected on the screen the image of the subject remained stationary with its arms or legs in motion. It was because of this limitation that, with the early pictures of Muybridge and Marey, it was impossible to utilize a distinctive background and therefore the pictures were taken before a screen of uniform color.

When I first turned my mind to the subject in 1887, it was with the thought of creating a new art. I was not interested in analyzing motion because that had been done with brilliant success by Muybridge and Marey before me. Just as with the phonograph which makes a permanent record of an indefinite number of successive sounds, I wanted to make a permanent record of an indefinite number of successive phases of movement, doing for the eye what the phonograph had done for the ear. This meant the photographing instantaneously of a scene *as viewed by the eye* and involved the following problems:

1. The pictures had to be taken from a single point of view and not from a changing point of view as with Muybridge

and Marey. In other words, the camera should not move with respect to the background but the moving object or objects should move with respect to the camera—exactly the reverse of what had been done before. And taking the pictures from a single point of view meant the use of a single lens.

2. The pictures had to be taken at a sufficiently rapid rate to give a smooth and uniform reproduction without jerking; that is to say, the displacement between the succeeding photographs had to be made very small. With my early pictures the rate at which they were taken varied from 40 to 50 per second. This gave a smooth and beautiful reproduction even though the movements photographed were quite rapid. With the modern art this rate has been reduced to about 16 per second, solely in order to prolong the exhibition. Therefore sudden and rapid movements were avoided.

3. The reproduction of the photographs either by direct view or by projection on a screen, had to be so effected that the interval between successive images would be less than one-seventh of a second. This was a purely physiological limitation made necessary to take advantage of the phenomenon of persistence of vision as had been done for many years with the zoetrope and toys of that character.

4. Since my conception involved the thought of permanently recording and reproducing a scene *of indefinite duration,* the use of disks or wheels on which to carry the pictures, as had been proposed by Muybridge and Marey, was impossible. A carrier of indefinite length was required and my conception included taking the photographs on and reproducing the positive prints from a *tape* of light, tough, flexible material, such as a narrow celluloid film. In this particular development I was very materially assisted by the intelligent and hearty cooperation of Mr. George Eastman of Rochester, New York. At the time the invention was being developed by me, it was the accepted belief that the size of the grains of a photographic emulsion bore a definite relation to its sensitiveness and that a very high speed film must necessarily be one with very large grains. If this belief had been true it would have been difficult to secure satisfactory results, especially if the photographs were enlarged on the screen. However, I did not believe it was true, and thanks to the skill of Mr. Eastman and his assistants, I was able to obtain from them for my experimental work and later for commercial use, an extremely sensitive film of very fine grain.

With the problems above stated before me, I took up my experimental work late in 1887 or early in 1888. As a preliminary and to test out the feasibility of my ideas, the first photographs were made on a cylinder (somewhat resembling a phonograph record) turning continuously, the pictures being of small or almost microscopic size and being arranged in a continuous spiral line on the cylinder. A positive print of the photographs was then made and placed upon the cylinder which, upon being again rotated, gave a reproduction of the original scene by illu-

minating each picture as it passed the eye by means of an electric spark. This was a purely tentative experiment and was eminently successful, a perfect reproduction of the object in motion background and all being secured.

I immediately perceived that my original conception of 1887 was entirely feasible and that it was possible to make a permanent record of a continuous scene just as it had been possible to make a permanent record of a continuous musical selection.

But the first experimental apparatus was obviously impracticable not only because the pictures were too small but also because the duration was limited by the length of the spiral path. The pictures were small because with the first experimental apparatus the sensitive surface moved continuously; to have made them larger would have meant inevitable blurring. I concluded, therefore, that in order to make larger pictures so as to secure sharp impressions it would be necessary to move the sensitive surface intermittently many times per second, thereby permitting the exposure to be made when the surface was stationary.

Turning then to my original thought of using a continuous film, I first employed a film width of one half inch but found that the pictures were still too small for satisfactory reproduction especially if enlarged by projection on a screen. I then experimented with photographs one inch wide by three-quarters of an inch high. These dimensions were adopted by me in 1889 and remain today the standard of the art.

The problem then arose as to the mechanical possibilities of feeding such a film intermittently past the field of a camera lens many times per second with the assurance that the film would be stationary at the instant of exposure and not shaking and vibrating to blur the image, and with the further assurance of such accuracy that the succeeding photographs would be exactly superimposed one upon the other in reproduction. Various methods and schemes were experimented with for thus feeding the film and I concluded to adopt the scheme of using sprocket holes or perforations outside the photographs in order to permit the film to be engaged accurately by the feeding devices and to be moved always precisely the same distance in making the successive photographs. In forming the sprocket holes in the film I first used only a single line at one side but finding this unsatisfactory, I utilized two lines of sprocket holes spaced so as to provide four holes for each picture which also has been and now is the present standard of the art.

Very many forms of start and stop mechanism were tried and by the summer of 1889 a satisfactory arrangement was adopted by me and was embodied in an actual full size camera by means of which the first motion pictures were taken on a celluloid film. These pictures were made in the summer of 1889; they were exactly like the present pictures except that they were taken at a considerably higher speed. In the latter respect they were actually superior to the present practice of the art, because the reproduction was smoother and less jerky.

Having by a long course of experiments thus made my first successful camera in the summer of 1889, I applied for a patent on it on August 24, 1891, and the patent thereon issued August 31, 1897, No. 589,168. This patent with its several reissues was recognized by the early manufacturers as the fundamental patent in the art and royalties under it were paid to me by the American manufacturers of films until its expiration in 1914.

My first camera constructed by me in 1889 and covered by this patent disclosed the following features which have always been utilized in the art:

1. A single lens.

2. A long celluloid film carrying a sensitive surface and having two rows of sprocket holes.

3. A reel from which the film is unwound and a second reel on which the film is wound after exposure.

4. Mechanism having a minimum inertia for moving the section of the film between the two reels intermittently past the lens many times per second, the film being stopped and brought to rest at each exposure.

5. A shutter coordinated with the feed mechanism to expose the film during the periods of rest.

The **following** quotation from my patent (written in the year 1891) may be of interest to you:

"The purpose I have in view is to produce pictures representing objects in motion throughout an extended period of time which may be utilized to exhibit a scene including such moving objects in a perfect and natural manner, by means of a suitable exhibiting apparatus.

"In carrying out my invention I employ an apparatus for effecting by photography a representation suitable for reproduction of a scene including a moving object or objects comprising a means, such as a single camera, for intermittently projecting at such rapid rate as to result in persistence of vision, images of successive positions of the object or objects in motion as observed from a fixed and single point of view, a sensitized tape like film, and a means for so moving the film as to cause the successive images to be received thereon separately and in single-line sequence."

The invention by me of this camera was in my opinion the egg of Columbus. By its means I had been able to secure as early as the summer of 1889 motion pictures on a long celluloid film representing exactly a scene as it would be observed by the eye with all of its details both as to background and as to objects moving with respect to the background. No such film had ever before been secured. No such camera for feeding a film intermittently and making exposures during the periods of rest had ever before been made or suggested.

After making my camera, the question then was, how shall the pictures be reproduced? It was obvious that they could be viewed directly through a suitable magnifying lens or that they could be projected on a screen as had been done by Muybridge and Marey in their classical work on the analysis of motion.

The most fruitful field immediately before me was the exhibition of the pictures by direct observation rather than by projection, because in the year 1890 and for some time afterwards a very popular form of entertainment in this country was the so called slot parlor where phongraphs were installed, arranged to be operated by coin-controlled mechanism. It therefore occurred to me to start out with a device by which the motion pictures could be made use of in the many hundreds of slot parlors which were then doing a flourishing business in the United States. This resulted in the development of the peep hole kinetoscope in which the film was moved continuously by a coin started electric motor passing a magnifying lens of about two diameters; the picture was illuminated by an electric light below it and was observed thrugh a slit in a shutter which exposed the picture when substantially in the optical axis of the lens. This gave an entirely satisfactory reproduction and anyone who remembers the old peep hole kinetoscope will I think agree with me that the results secured were remarkably clear and natural. Several thousands of these first kinetoscopes were made and distributed throughout the country in the years following 1890 and many of them were exhibited at the World's Fair in Chicago in 1893. Hundreds of films were made from 1890 and even earlier, for which purpose the first motion picture studio was erected, known as the "Black Maria."

I had always had in mind the projection of motion pictures on a screen even before the completion of my first successful camera in 1889. As a matter of fact, it was our practice from the very first to test the character and quality of films by projecting them on a screen by equipping the kinetoscope with a more powerful light and with a projecting lens.

Of course such a device would not have been suited for the public exhibition of pictures by projection owing to the insufficient light. For this purpose I saw that the successful projector should be based upon the principle of my camera wherein the periods of rest greatly exceeded the periods of motion of the film, thus giving the opportunity for much greater illumination, or in other words making it possible to very greatly prolong the shutter opening. But in the early days there was no demand for a projector; there were no motion picture theatres and even after projectors were made by me their introduction was slow. The competitive struggle between the motion picture theatre and the penny arcade lasted, as you will remember, for a good many years.

In the year 1895 I had reached the conclusion, largely as the result of urging on the part of my agents, Messrs. Raff and Gammon, to design and manufacture a projector based upon the principal of my camera, feeding the film intermittently so as to secure satisfactory illumination. This work was well under way when early in the year 1896, Mr. Thomas Armat of Washington, D. C. brought to my attention a projector which he had invented

and which he had exhibited in the previous Fall at the Cotton States Exposition at Atlanta. That exhibition, by the way, although technically successful, was a commercial failure. Any public interest in the possibility of motion picture projection was still dormant. Mr. Armat had worked out the details of the mechanism quite ingeniously and I concluded that the intermittent device which he had developed was more satisfactory than the one upon which I was working. I therefore arranged with him to use his type of projector, which was thereupon put on the market in 1896 as the Edison Vitascope and that machine (later known as the Edison Projecting Kinetoscpe) was with various modifications and refinements manufactured and marketed by me for many years thereafter.

The foregoing comprises the essential facts in connection with my invention and development of the motion picture art. Of course much of the success of the motion picture as we now know it has been due to many factors, such as the skill and artistic ability of the directors, the technical skill of the camera men, the exhibition value of the scenarios, the genius of the actors, and the business judgment and courage of the manufacturers, distributors and exhibitors.

But from a purely mechanical and technical standpoint the motion picture art was created when my camera was completed in the summer of 1889. That device made it possible for the first time to secure a permanent photographic record of a scene including movement — something never before accomplished—and that device also was the basis of and disclosed the principle used in the modern projector. In the latter respect it disclosed the two reels for storing and taking up the film after exposure, it disclosed intermittent mechanism for feeding the film step by step past the lens, it disclosed the feature of relatively long periods of rest with correspondingly short periods of motion, and it disclosed the shutter for exposing the film during the periods of rest. In a broad sense all that was necessary to convert the camera into a projector was to use a suitable source of illumination for the film and to enlarge the shutter opening to secure the maximum lighting effect.

Yours very truly,
(Signed) THOMAS A. EDISON

You will observe that Mr .Edison not only has covered the ground very thoroughly, but also he has cited certain official records in support of his statements. I am very sure there will be no shadow of a doubt in the minds of any of us but that Mr. Edison has set forth only that which he believes to be the even and exact truth with regard to things not directly supported by corroborative evidence.

I have myself examined many records not incorporated in this paper, all of which corroborate what Mr. Edison has said. More than this I do not feel it right and proper to say, since, as I have stated there are some

apparently conflicting claims, which I again respectfully suggest that this Society take steps to try to harmonize.

I next present for your consideration a statement by Mr. Thomas Armat, of Washington, District of Columbia. You will observe that the statements of Messrs. Edison and Armat agree throughout. There seems to be, so far as I am able to see, no conflict of claims with regard to the application of the old, well-known star and cam type of intermittent movement to the motion picture projector, in this country at least, but there was a bitter legal fight some years ago as to who invented what is known as the "Latham Loop," which is so very vital to intermittent projection.

The only serious controversy existing today, so far as my understanding goes, is with regard to who first projected life size motion pictures to a screen as we have them today, and it is this matter which I have suggested that this Society, through a commitee, attempt to settle. I have other correspondence from Mr. Edison, Mr. Jenkins and Mr. Armat, together with certain items of evidence, which I will be glad to turn over to such a committee.

Mr. Thomas Armat says:

THOS. ARMAT
1870 Wyoming Ave.
GRAYSTONE
KLINGLE ROAD
Washington, D. C.
April 4th, 1925.

Mr. F. H. Richardson.
516 Fifth Ave.
New York, N. Y.

Dear Mr. Richardson:
I have your letter of recent date and have delayed answering it in order to get copies of certain patents which I am now mailing you under separate cover.

These patents are Nos. 578,185 and 673,992 issued to me, and No. 586,953 issued to C. F. Jenkins and myself.

I am very glad indeed that you are taking the trouble to get at the facts in regard to the moving picture projecting machines covered by these patents, so many mis-statements concerning them having been published by uninformed, or misinformed, writers on moving picture history.

My patent No. 673,992, applied for on February 19th, 1896, covers the "Vitascope," and is no doubt the projector referred to by Edison, in his letter to you, as having been invented by me.

This patent although applied for in February 1896 did not issue until May 1901 for the reason that it was involved in a long Patent Office Interference proceeding. This is a proceeding for defining an invention and deciding who invented it. There were four claimants to this invention in this Interference to wit: Thomas Armat, Herman Casler, E. H. Amet and Woodville Latham. The applications were filed in the order named.

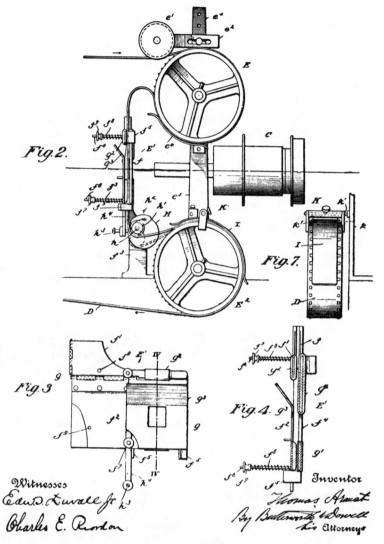

No. 673.992.   Patented May 14. 1901.

T. ARMAT.
VITASCOPE.
(Application filed Feb. 19, 1896.)

(No Model.)   3 Sheets—Sheet 2

Fig.2.

Fig.3

Fig.4.

Fig.7.

Witnesses
Edw D. Duvall Jr
Charles E. Riordon

Inventor
Thomas Armat
By Butterworth & Dowell
his Attorneys

FIG. 1.   Sheet No. 2 of U. S. Patent No. 673992.

The taking of testimony in such cases follows the rules laid down in courts of law and is very thorough. After taking volumes of testimony the case was decided in my favor by the Examiners-in-Chief, the Commissioner of Patents and finally, on appeal by Latham, by the Court of Appeals of the District of Columbia. The invention involved in this case was that of the "slack" or "loop" forming means in a projecting machine as set forth in claim 2 of my said patent 673,992.

Some fifteen years after my machines covered by this patent were made and extensively exhibited and long after this Interference had been decided in my favor, certain claims were set up to the effect that a projecting machine of this character and covered by this patent had been made prior to the dates claimed by any of the parties to this Interference. It is sufficient to say that all such claims are absurd and untrue and were based upon false or mistaken testimony.

Patent No. 586,953 was applied for C. F. Jenkins and myself on August 28th, 1895. The invention covered by this patent was the result of a series of experiments carried on under my direction after certain ideas of Mr. Jenkins had been tried out and proved to be valueless. These experiments extended over a period of about three months, from April to August, 1895. The first and only place the machine of this patent was ever exhibited was in my office in this city in the month of August 1895. This was also the first exhibition anywhere of a machine embodying the principle covered by the claims of this patent. The machine was a mechanical failure and commercially valueless for the reason that in it we attempted to give a rapid intermittent movement to a large and heavy kinetoscope sprocket. The claims of this patent however, if they could be sustained, had a certain strategic

value in connection with my later and successful projecting machines. The claims covered broadly the principle of giving, in a projecting machine, an intermittent movement to the motion picture film so that each picture on the film was given a relatively long period of exposure, as set forth in detail in the claims. This patent was also involved in a Patent Office Interference proceeding. I have recently had occasion to go quite fully into the facts of this Interference and will be glad to go over them with you, but will not take the time now to do so.

My patent No. 578,185 covers the co-called Geneva star type of intermittent movement as applied to moving picture machines. The claims are broad enough, as you will see, to cover this and all similar types of intermittent movements. The intermittent movement mechanism has been frequently referred to as the "heart" of the moving picture projector. This Geneva type of intermittent movement as you doubtless know, superseded all other forms soon after it was introduced in the fall of 1896, or thereabouts, and continues to be almost universally used up to the present time.

After I had produced a satisfactory projecting machine in the fall of 1895, it of course became necessary to secure an adequate supply of moving picture films for use thereon. All films I had used for experimental purposes in 1895 were Edison films secured from the Columbia Phonograph Company who had an Edison Kinetoscope parlor in Washington. They, in turn, secured them from Messrs. Raff and Gammon of New York, who were exclusive agents for Mr. Edison.

In December 1895 I started negotiations with Messrs. Raff and Gammon and shortly thereafter entered into a contract with them under the terms of which they were to supply Edison films for use on the "Vitascope" the name I had given the projector described in my patent No. 673,992, and the Edison Manufacturing Company were to obtain a certain number of these projectors from a model I gave them.

Raff and Gammon wanted to use the Edison name in connection with their exploitation of the Vitascope, for obvious commercial reasons and for the additional reason that they wanted to be assured of a continued supply of Edison films. Edison kinetoscope films were the only moving picture films obtainable anywhere in the world at that date. Mr. Edison had produced his kinetoscope and had pending patents covering his camera and the product of the camera, the moving picture film itself. The moving picture film has been held by the Patent Office and the Courts to be an essential element in the moving picture exhibiting machine. I have frequently stated that, in my opinion, when Mr. Edison produced his camera and film he did far and away more than anyone else ever did before or since, in the way of moving picture invention.

Recently certain misinformed writers on moving picture history have credited certain individuals, whose activities commenced years after Mr. Edison had produced his camera, his film and his kinto-

26

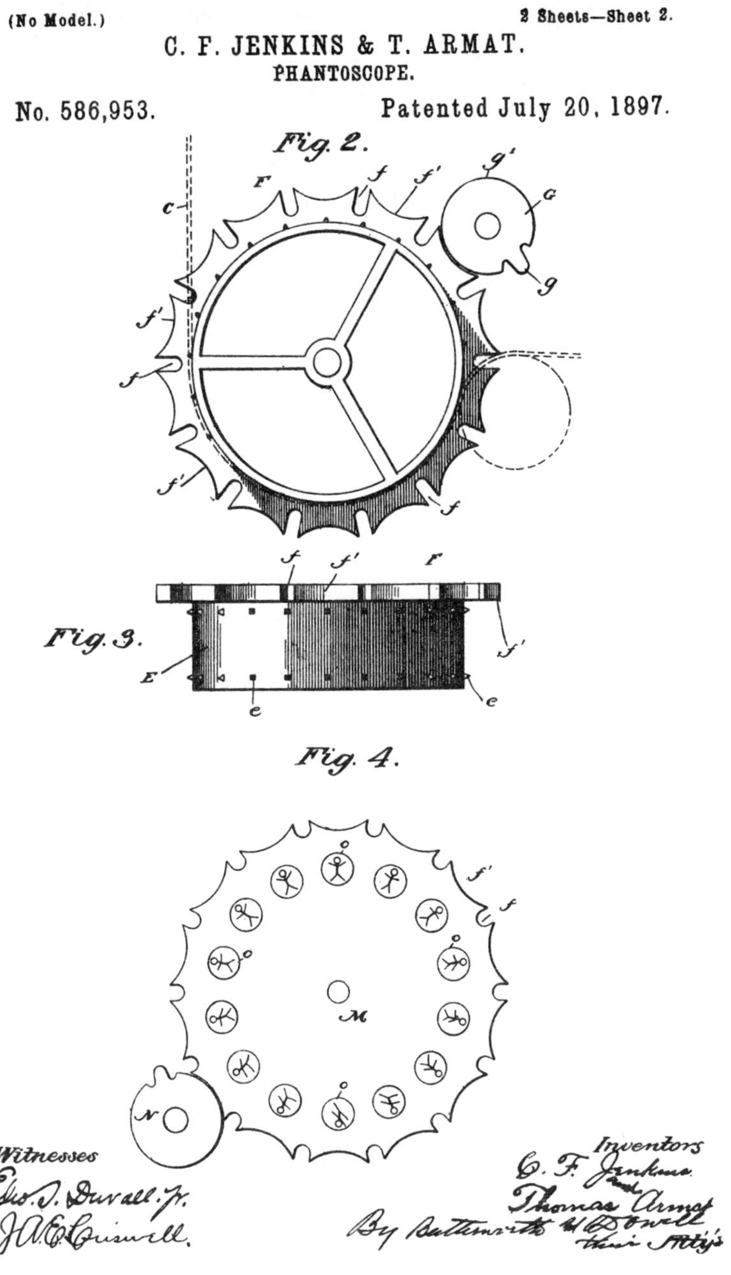

C. F. JENKINS & T. ARMAT.
PHANTOSCOPE.

No. 586,953.   Patented July 20, 1897.

Fig. 2.

Fig. 3.

Fig. 4.

Witnesses
Edw. J. Duvall. Jr.
J. A. C. Criswell.

Inventors
C. F. Jenkins
Thomas Armat
By Batturworth & McDowell
their Att'ys

FIG. 2. Sheet No. 2 of U. S. Patent No. 586953.

scope, with having "invented" or "discovered" moving pictures.

To set up such a claim from twenty-five to thirty years after the inventions covered by the patents I have referred to were made is of course absurd, as an intelligent search of the Patent Office records would disclose.

The moving picture art, like many others, has been a matter of evolution in which many people have had a part, some directly and some indirectly. Inventors and manufacturers in the art of instantaneous photography which had to be brought to a high state of perfection before moving pictures as we know them today became a possibility, as well as manufacturers of celluloid strips for carrying the highly sensitive emulsion for taking the pictures, all had an important part in the development of moving pictures, so that no one person can properly claim to have invented or discovered moving pictures.

I have never set up any special claims for myself one way or the other but I feel that I can justly claim to have done my full share of what Mr. Edison left to be done in the way of developing or inventing moving pictures, and, in the matter of projecting machines, I think perhaps that the patents I have referred to may entitle me to claim that I did more than anyone else in the way of inventing the first successful moving picture projecting machine.

Prior to the advent of such a machine the moving picture film was confined to the very narrow field of the peep-hole or direct view machine, where the pictures about the size of a postage stamp, were seen through a lens that magnified them but very slightly.

The patents whose numbers I have given were the first ones covering the essentials of the projecting machine, the machine that throws the pictures upon the screen.

The foregoing, I believe, answers all of your questions.

Yours very truly,
(Signed) THOMAS ARMAT

You will observe that the Jenkins and Armat patent was, as we all now know, not practicable. The "Vitascope," invented by Mr. Armat and patented by him March 2, 1897, has the regulation star and cam movement, which, somewhat to my surprise, is a one-pin movement. This was later changed by Mr. Edison to a two-pin. It was the change of the Edison two-pin movement into a one-pin which constituted Mr. Nicholas Power's first big improvement to the Edison projector.

The "Vitascope" as designed by Mr. Armat was intended to handle a continuous band of film over a "spool bank." This was the way Mr. Edison first used it. Apparently there is no means provided for cutting the light off the screen while the film is in motion over the aperture, which presumably was one of the improvements added by Mr. Edison. Also, I see no apparent method for effecting a framing of the film, though probably there was some method employed to accomplish this important and very necessary function.

In the year 1901 Mr. Armat patented an improved form of the "Vitascope," but what finally became of it I do not know.

I next present for your consideration the letter and two photographs sent by Mr. C. Jenkins, in response to my request for data.

C. Francis Jenkins
Frank H. Edmonds
Lewis M. Thayer

JENKINS LABORATORIES
1819 Connecticut Avenue
Washington, D. C.

January 8th, 1925

Mr. F. H. Richardson,
646 West 158th Street,
New York, N. Y.

Dear Mr. Richardson:

I am enclosing the two photographs you asked for, (1) an early portrait, and (2) a photograph of my *first projection machine,* the type now used in every theatre the world over.

This machine was built in 1893, and repeatedly exhibited in 1893 and 1894, and is the projector referred to in "The Photographic Times" for July 6, 1894 which I am quite sure you can find in any of the large public libraries in New York City, I know I found it recently in the National Library here.

In the Baltimore, (Maryland) "Sun," of October 2, 1895, appeared an account of the construction of three copies of this machine for the Atlanta Cotton States Exposition of that year.

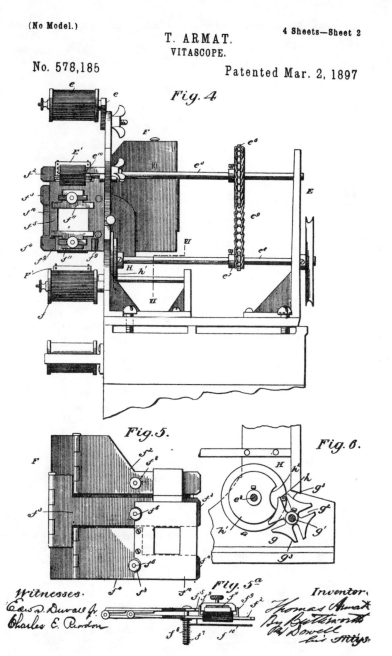

(No Model.)

T. ARMAT.
VITASCOPE.

No. 578,185.   Patented Mar. 2, 1897

4 Sheets—Sheet 2

Fig. 4

Fig. 5.   Fig. 6.

Witnesses.   Inventor.
Edwd Duvall Jr.   Thomas Armat
Charles E. Riordon   By Butterworth
                            Wm Dowell
                            his Attys.

Fig. 5a

FIG. 3. Sheet No. 2 of U. S. Patent No. 578185.

These machines were installed in a building, especially built therefor by my financier, Mr. Thomas Armat, the *first motion picture theatre* ever built exclusively for the purpose, the admission charged being 25c. Notices of this "marvelous exhibition" appeared in the Atlanta papers, and copied rather extensively elsewhere.

That winter the original machine of which the Atlanta machines were copies, was exhibited before the Franklin Institute (Philadelphia), and after the taking of much testimony for and against the claim that I was the inventor, the Elliott Cresson gold medal was awarded by the Institute to me.

It may interest you to know that within a few weeks, that is, before the next S.M.P.E. meeting, we expect to give public exhibitions of motion pictures, and performances from living subjects, transmitted by radio from our studio to private homes here in the city, a perfection of the present apparatus of daily demonstrations in our laboratory here.

Sincerely yours,
(Signed) JENKINS.
CFJ/sla

"You will observe that both projectors shown have the well known "beater" type of intermittent movement. You will also observe that the first mechanism (Fig. 4) apparently has no means for shutting the light off the screen while the film is in movement. There is no lamp house at all, and what seems to be a cell, which probably was filled with alum water to absorb a portion of the heat, is in front of the condenser. There is no upper sprocket, and a lower sprocket, driven by a worm gear, the upper sprocket being chain driven from the shaft of the lower one. These sprockets are apparently about three inches in diameter,

and of a width to take film of approximately, if not exactly, the present width and perforation. Mr. Jenkins' claim is that this projector was made and used by him to project life size motion pictures in 1893 and 1894. The means for driving the mechanism is not apparent.

The second picture (Fig. 5) is of the "Phantoscope," which is the projector Mr. Jenkins advises was made for use at the Atlanta Exposition. Apparently it is of the same general type, but an improvement on the one shown in the first illustration. There seems to be no upper sprocket shown. The cell in front of the condenser in the first projector is absent in this one. There is some attempt at inclosing the arc, though the lamp itself is stil outside.

The next statement is in the form of a letter from Mr. George Eastman to the author of this paper. I am very sure you will be deeply inerested in what it contains. Mr. Eastman has, at my request, personally prepared it with intent that it become a part of the records of this Society, and as such a permanent, official record of his activities in the matter of discovering flexible film and its application to motion pictures. Mr. Eastman says:

EASTMAN KODAK COMPANY
Rochester, N. Y.
March 18th, 1925

Mr. F. H. Richardson,
New York City,
Dear Mr. Richardson:

In reply to your letter of March 2nd, addressed to our Mr. Blair, asking for a statement in regard to my connection with motion picture film, to be made a part of the records of the Society of Motion Picture Engineers, I am writing this letter.

I have read Mr. Edison's statement of January 24th and am in full accord with the reference which he makes to me.

About the year 1883 or 1884, in connection with William H. Walker, I engaged in an effort to create a system of film photography. Mr. Walker was a skilled mechanic and had had some experience in manufacturing cameras. I was engaged in the manufacture of dry plates and had had experience in the making and handling of photographic emulsions, as well as some mechanical experience.

On looking over the ground we found that there were three things necessary to be accomplished:

1st. To find a suitable flexible support to take the place of glass.

2nd. To devise a method of applying emulsion to it, and

3rd. To create a practical mechanism for exposing the sensitive flexible support in the camera.

Walker and I worked together on the machanical problems, while I tried to work out the photographic and chemical side of the enterprise. The broad idea, of course, was not new. An exposing mechanism, called a "roll holder," for sensitized paper had been made as early as 1854, the

28

FIG. 4. The Phantoscope. Invented by Mr. Jenkins and used in 1893-94.

FIG. 5. The "Atlanta Exhibition" machine. One of three copies of the Phantoscope taken to the Atlanta Cotton States Exposition.

year that I was born. Warnerke, in about 1875, made a roll holder and a film, the latter consisting of paper coated with collodion emulsion. The image was stripped direct from the paper after exposure and development. This attempt to create a system of film photography was a failure and the field had been practically abandoned at the time Walker and I began. We soon worked out a practical roll holder. A machine for coating paper in bands 8 or 10 ft. in length, for the carbon process, was in existence. We devised a machine for coating continuously. I invented a film, known as "Eastman Stripping Film"; filed an application for patent on March 7, 1884, and the patent was issued October 14, 1884. This completed a practical system of film photography. A company, The Eastman Dry Plate and Film Company, was formed and the enterprise started in 1885. It was successful from the start but the use of the film was hampered by the necessity of sending it to the Company for development because the development and finishing of the negatives was too com-

plicated for the amateur, or even the dealer, to accomplish. The film consisted of a strip of paper first coated with soluble gelatine and afterwards with the sensitive emulsion. After the film had been exposed in the roll holder it was developed and then squeegeed down on to a glass plate which had previously been coated with a thin solution of rubber. This held it in a rigid position while the paper was dissolved off by hot water, leaving a very thin image on the glass plate. This had to be reenforced by a sheet of moistened gelatine. When dry the reenforced image could then be pulled off from the glass plate. This produced a negative which was very similar to the film of the present day. There were other objections to this process beside the complications. For instance: The time required to dry the gelatine sheet used for the backing; and the fact that the image sometimes was affected by the grain of the paper offsetting. It was quite obvious that what was needed to make a perfect substitute for the glass plate process was a substance which

had the properties of glass except its rigidity and fragility. Transparent celluloid had already been used as a substitute for glass in making single negatives but no way was known of producing it in sheets thin enough and long enough to use in a roll holder. After we got started with the stripping film I made many experiments to produce long sheets of transparent material, using cellulose nitrate "soluble cotton," which is the chief constituent of celluloid. I used the only solvents known in photography at that time, namely grain alcohol and ether. A mixture of these solvents would only dissolve about 10 per cent of its weight of the cellulose nitrate and this solution, when coated on glass, gave too thin a film to be of any use. I tried building up a thicker film by using successive coatings of this solution (known as "collodion") and rubber but I could not get a thick enough film to be practical. In the meantime, failing to succeed in producing this ideal support, I began to experiment in replacing the sheets of gelatine used for backing the stripping film with a varnish to overcome the objection of the slow drying. One day a young assistant whom I had assigned to this job came to me with a bottle of varnish and a glass plate bearing a stripping film negative which had been varnished and partially stripped from the plate. He said he had found just what we were looking for. I asked him what the varnish was composed of and he said: "Wood alcohol and soluble cotton." It was very thick, like separated honey. I saw at once that it was the solution which I had been looking for to make film base and immediately began to devise apparatus for producing film by drying the varnish on long strips of plate glass. We at once fitted up a small factory with tables 100 ft. long, having glass tops of the longest sheets of plate glass we could find, with the joints cemented together, and began to make the first practical transparent film in rolls that was ever put on the market. This was in August, 1889.

While we were engaged in fitting up this factory I received a call from a representative of Mr. Edison's who told me of Mr. Edison's experiments in motion pictures and how necessary it was for him to have some of this film. The idea of making pictures to depict objects in motion was entirely new to me but of course I was much interested in the project and did my best to furnish him film as near to his specifications regarding fineness of grain and thickness as possible. As far as I know the film we furnished him then, and from time to time later, was satisfactory. In the years during which the motion picture industry has been developing we made many improvements in the way of fineness of grain, photographic quality, and uniformity, but the film made today is substantially the same as the first film furnished Mr. Edison.

So far as I can recollect all the experimental film that was furnished Mr. Edison was negative film. Special film for printing positives was not made until about 1895.

The new film was a success for amateur purposes from the moment it was offered to the public. The use of film has super-seded glass plates for amateur use for many years past; and of late years has been replacing them for all professional uses as well.

The support, instead of being made on glass tables as at first, is now cast on the surface of great nickel plated wheels which run continuously night and day, week in and week out. One of these wheels, of which we have upwards of fifty, produces 25 times as much as the whole of our first factory. The base is turned over to the sensitizing department in rolls 41 inches wide and 2,000 feet long and is so accurately made that it does not vary over one-four thousandth of an inch in thickness. Of course only a part of this product is for motion pictures.

Yours very truly,
(Signed) GEORGE EASTMAN

It is understood that the above statement will be incorporated in the records of your Society as an unaltered whole.

The last personal statement I shall present is one by Mr. Albert E. Smith, President of the Vitagraph, and one of the two men who originally formed the company in March, 1897. Unfortunately, when I saw Mr. Smith he was about ready to leave for the west coast, and could only take time to dictate a very brief statement.

The information about the "Idoloscope" is interesting, also, you will note that Mr. Charles Webster, whose photograph I will show you later, and who was the projectionist the second night Thomas A. Edison saw motion pictures in their present form, was one of the firm known as the International Film Company.

I think but few of us knew that William T. Rock did not join the Vitagraph until two years after it was organized. I know I always had the idea myself that it was he who organized the company.

This thing called by Mr. Smith the "setting device," was what we now know as a "framer." Mr. Smith's explanation of its invention was that the film would "creep up" out of frame in the friction type of projector, and the framer was designed to overcome that fault, or to neutralize it, rather.

Mr. Smith says:

Albert E. Smith, *President*

THE VITAGRAPH COMPANY
OF AMERICA
Executive Offices
E. 15th Street and Locust Avenue
Brooklyn, New York
April 13th, 1925

Mr. F. H. Richardson,
646 West 158th Street,
New York, N. Y.

Dear Mr. Richardson:
The following statement covers dates of happenings of early items of interest in the history of the Vitagraph Company, which I trust will be of use to you:

The Idoloscope was brought out in 1896. It was a special machine, using a special film, in the camera of which the film ran continuously and in which the film was rendered optically stationary, by the aid of a slot in a 360° shutter.

The film was first projected with a machine in which the film ran continuously, but later was projected with the aid of a Pitman or Beater movement which Beater movement was later incorporated in the camera.

The film and apparatus of the old Idoloscope Corporation was purchased by Mr. J. Stuart Blackton and Mr. Albert E. Smith in the early part of 1897.

The International Film Co. was owned by Messrs. Webster and Kuhn. They operated from 1896 to 1898.

The Vitagraph was organized by Mr. J. Stuart Blackton and Mr. Albert E. Smith in March, 1897.

Mr. William T. Rock joined Vitagraph in the summer of 1899.

Vitagraph's first projector was built by Mr. Albert E. Smith in 1896. It had an intermittent movement, and the setting devise that was incorporated in all later Vitagraph machines and was copied on all Edison projectoscopes and was imitated by most other projectors, was the same setting devise that was devised on the original Vitagraph projector in 1896. The non-flicker shutter was devised by Mr. Albert E. Smith, and used on Vitagraph machines in 1898.

The first pictures by electric light were taken in 1899 by Mr. J. Stuart Blackton and Mr. Albert E. Smith, at the old Manhattan Theatre in New York, which was loaned for the occasion by William A. Brady. Upon demonstrating the success of photographing by electric light, Mr. Brady then contracted with Mr. Blackton and Mr. Smith, to photograph pictures of the Fitzsimmons-Jeffries Fight at the Coney Island Sporting Club, in 1899.

Unfortunately, the cylinder head of the engine of the special plant, which was installed at Coney Island to furnish the current for this operation, blew out at the start of the fight, and therefore, the entire fight was never photographed.

The enlargement over Mr. Rock's desk in the photograph showing the early Vitagraph Office, is an enlargement of one of the moving pictures taken of the Fitzsimmons-Jeffries Fight.

The first picture was made by Mr. J. Stuart Blackton and Mr. Albert E. Smith on the roof of the Morton Building, No. 140 Nassau Street, in the fall of 1897. It was a short comedy picture, about 45 feet in length, and was called "The Burglar on the Roof."

The average length of pictures at this period, ran from 40 to 75 feet.

The early pictures of the Vitagraph Company were either topical, that is, scenes of every-day occurrence, comedy, or magical pictures — the magical pictures being what were known as the "stop-motion" variety, that is to say, the action would be carried to a certain point, where the director would call "stop." Everyone then would hold the position that they happened to be in at the moment. Some change would then be made in the development of the action, that is to say, a character's coat might be taken off and laid on the floor, and when this action was carried out, the director would give the word "go." The camera would start to grind, the characters would start further business, until they again received the word "stop," when some other change would be made.

When the negative was finally cut and edited, the effect of this particular business would be that, during the course of the action, one of the character's coats would suddenly fly off onto the floor.

All the magical effects were instantaneous happenings, produced somewhat after this fashion and along these lines.

The first "stop-motion" picture of this nature produced by Vitagraph, which made a big hit throughout the country, was a "Visit to the Spiritualist," in which all kinds of mysterious things happened, the same being brought about by the above described method.

The foregoing relates to pictures taken prior to 1900.

The first animated cartoon was made by Mr. J. Stuart Blackton and Mr. Albert E. Smith, in the year 1903.

The first director engaged by Vitagraph was Mr. G. M. Anderson, who joined the Vitagraph forces in 1904. He later became the partner of Mr. George K. Spoor in the Essanay Film Producing Company, Chicago.

Florence Turner was the first Vitagraph star, and I believe the first film star. She joined Vitagraph in 1905, becoming popularly known as "The Vitagraph Girl."

Very truly yours,
A. E. SMITH, *President*

I shall now show you various pictures, some of which are my own property and some of which have been loaned to me. Many of them are very valuable, because of the fact that no known duplicates exist. Mr. William Reed, Motion Picture Projectionist at Atlantic City, New Jersey, is owner of some of the most rare and interesting ones.

Let me say that Mr. George Eastman and Mr. Thomas A. Edison are two of the great men on earth — men whose names and whose works will live so long as the history of our time shall last.

Both Mr. Edison and Mr. Eastman were pioneers in the very forefront of the motion picture industry. Both Mr. Eastman and Mr. Edison have told you the story of what they did in the early days. It would be presumptuous for me to dilate upon the tremendous influence these two gentlemen have had upon the perfection of the thing which has come to be the most widely patronized and the most keenly enjoyed form of public amusement the world has ever known.

Next I present (Fig. 6) to you a gentleman who needs no introduction to the Society of Motion Picture Engineers, because C. Francis Jenkins was chiefly instrumental in bringing about its formation and in literally nursing it through its first years of life.

Had C. Francis Jenkins done no other thing for or in the motion picture industry than to form this Society, surely that one act would be quite sufficient to write his name upon the Roll of Honor of the industry as a man who did really worthwhile things.

The next picture (Fig. 7) is that of William T. Rock, one of the pioneers in both the production and exhibition end of the motion picture industry. It was he, who, together with his partner, Mr. Wainwright and William Reed, projectionist, opened Vitascope Hall, corner of Canal Street and Exchange Place, New Orleans, Louisiana, in June, 1896, which was the first theatre

FIG. 6. Mr. C. Francis Jenkins.

used strictly and exclusively for the exhibition of motion pictures of which I have been able to discover tangible evidence — any evidence other than the personal statements of various individuals, which same I have invariably found to be more or less contradictory. I shall present to you a photograph of this theatre and of its programme before I have finished.

Mr. Rock, who was popularly known throughout the industry of that day as "Pop" Rock, joined the Vitagraph Company in its early days (1899) and, up to the time of his death a few years since, was its president. He was in many ways a picturesque character, an excellent business man, and very capable in the matter of forming correct judgment as to the amusement value of various things. He loved diamonds, his collection of them being famed

throughout the entire industry of that day. The picture selected is somewhat in the nature of a "freak," but it nevertheless is a most excellent likeness of Mr. Rock, as the writer remembers him. It was taken during the last years of his life.

The next picture (Fig. 8) is that of William Reed (left) and Charles Webster who acted as projectionist on the second evening that Thomas Edison witnessed the projection of life size pictures on a screen by means of Mr. Armat's "Vitascope" projector. On the first evening Mr. Armat himself projected the pictures. That was the first time Mr. Edison ever saw motion pictures projected to a screen at full life size, though at that time he was himself working on a projector designed to do that very thing.

FIG. 7. The late William T. Rock, President of the Vitagraph Company of America from the time it was organized until his death some years ago. Mr. Rock and his partner, Mr. Wainright, opened the Motion Picture theatre in New Orleans, in the year 1896, which was the first theatre, of which visible evidence still remains, devoted exclusively to motion pictures. Mr. Rock was, during his lifetime, one of the most widely known men in all the motion picture industry of that day.

William Reed was the man who left a position with Messrs. Raff and Gammon where he was "keeping tab" on Edison peep-hole Kinetoscopes in Boston and vicinity, and went with Messrs. Rock and Wainwright to New Orleans, Louisiana, in the spring of 1896, where he acted as motion picture projectionist, using an Armat "Vitascope," which same had then been taken over by Mr. Edison.

After having filled an engagement in a New Orleans park, Messrs. Rock and Wainwright opened "Vitagraph Hall," as will be hereinafter set forth.

Mr. Reed was the guest of this Society at its Atantic City dinner, in May, 1923. He had requested that I convey to you his felicitations and earnest good wishes. He has projected motion pictures continuously from the time he

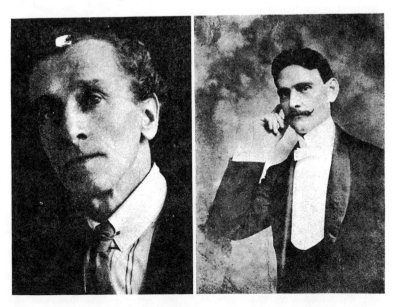

FIG. 8. Mr. William Reed (left) and Mr. Charles Webster (right).

started in New Orleans in 1896 up to the present time. He is today projectionist at the new Palace Theatre in Atlantic City, New Jersey.

While it cannot be said that Mr. Reed was the first man to project motion pictures, he was, nevertheless, the projectionist in the first strictly motion picture theatre of which we have printed, authentic record, and certainly his record entitles him to be hailed as the Dean of Motion Picture Projectionists.

Nicholas Power has passed to that bourne whence no traveler ever returns, into the shadows of which so many of the pioneers of the industry have already entered. Next to Mr. Edison himself Mr. Power was the first man to manufacture motion picture projectors on a commercial scale for use in the United States of America and Canadian America. In fact, so far as I have been able to find out, for some time after Mr. Power himself began manufacturing projectors the Edison Company was his only rival in that field. Certain it is, that the Edison Company and Mr. Power were the only ones who put out any considerable number of projectors in the very early days of the industry.

Just how Mr. Power, who I have been told, was a dabbler in real estate dealings before he took up projection, first came to take up projection I have not been able to ascertain. His family refused to give any information on the subject. Either in the fall of 1896 or the spring of 1897 he was acting as projectionist at the Koster and Bial Music Hall, on Twenty-Third Street, near Sixth Avenue, New York City. Afterwards he was projecting pictures at a vaudeville theatre in Brooklyn. The story is that one day when he took down the intermittent movement of his Edison projector, he was unable to get it back in time for the evening show, had a go-round with the theatre manager and quit—either voluntarily or "by request."

Shortly thereafter he leased a room on the third floor, 117 Nassau Street, where he startd a repair shop for Edison projectors. Soon he conceived the idea of making changes in the mechanism of the projectors. I am told that his first improvement was the changing of the two-pin Edison Geneva movement to a one-pin. He then added other changes and improvements of his own, and soon came out with what he called the Power's Peerless Projector, very few of which were actually made and sold. In the accompanying picture, (Fig. 10), notice the sack for catching the film after projection. This is a very genuine relic of the distant past of motion picturedom. I very much doubt if there is another picture of this projector in existence.

Shortly after the advent of the "Power's Peerless," which must have come out some time in either 1897 or 1898, Mr. Power brought out his "Power's No. 1" projector, which was followed by the No. 2, No. 3, No. 4 and No. 5 models, all of which appeared between 1897 or 1898 and 1907, in which latter year the No. 5 appeared, it being the first approach to a really high grade projector mechanism in general use up to that time, except that the Motiograph had appeared shortly before, and George K. Spoor, of the Essanay Producing Company had put out a limited number of "Kinedrome" projectors, which were distinctly high grade mechanisms, as also were the motiographs.

During the first ten years of the industry, or up to about 1907, the only projectors having anything like a general use were the Edison, the Power,

FIG. 9. Mr. Nicholas Power.

the Vitagraph, the Lubin, the Selig and (around Chicago, Illinois, only) the Motiograph, the Spoor Kinedrome and a claw-movement projector made by a man named Pink, called the "Viascope." I have been unable to ascertain the exact dates at which these various projectors appeared. Except for the Powers and the Motiograph (The Simplex did not come into the field until about 1911) they have all entirely disappeared, though being permitted to rummage through the "morgue" of the Nicholas Power Company, examples of several of their mechanisms were discovered, covered with the dust and grime of many years. Through the kindness of the Power's Company I secured photographs of these mechanisms, which will, I am sure, interest you. I

FIG. 10. The Power's Peerless Projector.

will show them to you a little later.

I show you (Fig. 16) the famous Edison "spoolbank projector," of which you doubtless all have heard, and many have wished to see. The photograph of this relic came into my possession as technical editor of the *Moving Picture World* some years ago. By looking closely you may be able to trace the path of the film, which was in the form of an endless band. The "spoolbank" was merely a device to permit of using a band of film having greater length than could be used without it. The two upper views are two views of the same projector, while the lower one shows it, minus the spoolbank and fitted to use an upper reel, which same you may see is merely a core, or hub, with four projecting spokes on either side, to hold the film roll in position. Notice the diminutive lamp house, and that the lamp mechanism was located entirely outside of it, only the long, flimsy carbon arms extending into its interior. Notice also how the lamp house sets up on a stand to bring the condenser in line with the projector aperture. The rheostat is, you will observe, well encased in a sheet metal cover.

In Fig. 17 you see the mechanism of the Edison spoolbank projector. It is the same general style, with its wooden frame, to which Mr. Edison clung, with slight variations, for many years—until about 1907.

In Fig. 18 you see Mr. Edison's final perfected projector. Very soon after it was finished, and before it was placed on the market, Mr. Edison decided to abandon the making of motion picture projectors, which he did, so that the "Super" never actually came on the market at all.

POWERS
NO 1

FIG. 11. The Power's No. 1.

FIG. 12. The Power's No. 2.

Lubin Projector

In Fig. 23 is shown the projector mechanism put out by Sigmund Lubin. It disappeared finally about 1912. It was crudely constructed and never very successful, though at one time rather widely used in the city of Philadelphia and territory immediately adjacent

FIG. 13. The Power's No. 3.

The only model of projectors Mr. Edison ever placed on the market was the Edison "Exhibition Model," of which many thousands were sold. It had, as you may see, a wooden frame. It had an "inside shutter," the interrupter blade of which was perforated.

The Model B came out about 1907 or 1908. It had a metal frame, but aside from that change and several improvements, it clung closely to the old Edison style of projector.

Motiograph Early Models

I present to you (Fig. 20) a picture of the Model No. 1A Motiograph, its predecessors the No. 1, No. 2 and No. 3 Optograph and the DeLuxe model Motiograph of today. Aside from the Spoor Kinedrome, the Motiograph was the first closely built projector mechanism given us. It was the invention of Mr. A. C. Roebuck, a member of the Society of Motion Picture Engineers, and a man we all know well. What you may not have known, however, is that he was the original Roebuck of Sears, Roebuck & Co., the famous mail order house.

Fig. 21 is of the old Selig projector mechanism. Observe the small crank and the chain upper sprocket drive. It had a claw movement, commonly termed, at that time, a "finger feed." It was great on ripping out the divisions between sprocket holes.

In Fig. 22 is shown another claw movement projector mechanism, which was very popular in and about Chicago, Illinois, about 1907 and 1908. It was roughly built, but gave results considered very good in that day.

FIG. 14. The Power's No. 4.

FIG. 15. The Power's No. 5.

thereto, also it was used somewhat in other eastern territory.

A Stranger

This picture (Fig. 24) is made from a photograph which has been in my possession for a long while. Evidently it is an early type, and I have suspected it was one of Mr. Power's first efforts toward changing and improving the Edison projector. Note the framing device which raises the gate bodily a short distance by means of a slow-acting screw.

Amet Magniscope

This picture (Fig. 25) is of the Amet Magniscope, a projector invented by a man namel Amet, who now is located in Mobile, Alabama. At the time he evolved this mechanism he lived near Chicago, Illinois. Its intermittent movement was of the clutch trip type, hence, enormously noisy and quite impractical. It projected nine pictures per turn of the crank. The picture is only of interest as showing one of the early efforts to evolve motion picture projectors.

Old Type Film

I show you in Fig. 26 some of the early types of film. It have lost the data connected with the one to the right. Note the wide spacing between the pictures and the round, queerly placed sprocket holes. The Veriscope film and projector were made especially to

"take" the Fitzsimmons-Jefferies prize fight. It was, so far as I know, never used for anything else.

Old Films

Some months since I published a picture of an Edison Model B mechanism, asking how many projectionists could identify it. One man sent the drawing shown in Fig. 27 in addition to the picture of the mechanism. It is distinctly interesting. I venture many of you had almost entirely forgotten some of these one-time popular films.

Vitascope Hall

I now present a photograph of "Vitascope Hall," opened by Messrs. Rock and Wainwright as a strictly motion picture theatre, in June, 1896. Its location was the corner of Canal Street and Exchange Place, New Orleans, Louisiana. They showed, among other things, the "May Irwin Kiss," "Waves of Dover," also a lot of short scenic stuff. Admission was ten cents. For ten cents additional patrons were permitted to peek into the "projection room" and for another ten cents they were presented with one frame of old film.

The projector used was the Armat Vitascope, then being produced by Thomas A. Edison, and, for business reasons, called the "Edison Vitascope." That last is on the authority of projectionist, Reed, who had it direct from Mr. Rock, who himself purchased the projector.

The theatre was a store room fitted with a screen, wooden chairs, an enclosure for the projector, a ticket booth and a name—Vitascope Hall. It seated about four hundred people. In the photograph you see its operators, Messrs. Rock and Wainwright, standing in front, together with its projectionist, William Reed. Mr. Rock is at the extreme right, with Mr. Wainwright next to him. Mr. Reed is at the extreme left. The names of the others are unknown. You will observe that "Li Hung Chang" was the bill on the day the photograph was taken.

Vitascope Hall Program

Here, gentlemen, is the printed program of that little theatre of far-off days. Doors open 10 to 3 and 6 to 10.

Letter of Raff and Gammon

Messrs. Raff and Gammon, whose office was in the Postal Telegraph Building, 253 Broadway, New York City, were agents for the Edison Phonograph, and sole agents for the Edison peep-hole kinetoscope. It was this firm who were responsible for Mr. Armat's invention being called to the attention of Mr. Edison. They heard of it, Mr. Gammon went to Washington and witnessed its performance, was so impressed with its apparent possibilities, even in its then very crude form, that he hastened to lay the matter before Mr. Edison, and plans were laid for a demonstration of the projector at the

34

FIG. 16. The Edison Spoolbank projector. In one, the film is in a roll. The reels were supplied with the outfit. In the other are two views of the Edison Spoolbank Projector. Note the diminutive size lamp house and how the film runs in a continuous band over the banks of spools.

FIG. 18. The Edison "Exhibition Model" projector.

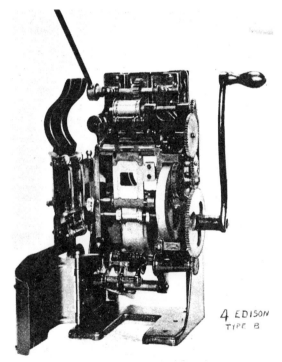

FIG. 19. The Edison "Model B" Projector.

Edison laboratories. Evidently the demonstration was satisfactory, for arrangements were entered into immediately between Mr. Armat and Mr. Edison to build the projectors at the Edison plant. Due to the commercial value of Mr. Edison's name, it was decided it would be best to use it in connection with the projector, which thus became the "Edison Vitascope."

Soon after this Messrs. Koster and Bial, who operated two music halls,

FIG. 17. The Edison Spoolbank Mechanism.

FIG. 20. Motiograph Early Models.

FIG. 21. Selig Projector Mechanism.

one on West Twenty-Third Street, New York City, and one at Broadway and Thirty-Fourth Street, where the Macy Department Store now stands, booked the "act" (life size motion pictures) for their Thirty-Fourth Street house, paying the sum of five hundred dollars per week therefor. I might add that as soon as Oscar Hammerstine saw the "act" he offered one thousand dollars a week for it, but his offer was refused because Messrs. Koster and Bial had it under contract. Keith also tried to secure it for his Fourteenth Street Theatre, but failed for the same reason, whereupon he at once proceeded to import Lumiere cinematographs, which arrived in July, 1896, together with men to act as projectionists. Mr. F. Keith had an Edison Vitascope in his Boston, Providence and Philadelphia theatres early in May, 1896.

The first show at Koster and Bial's consisted in "Anabella in the Butterfly Dance," "Shooting the Chutes at Coney Island," and the "Waves at Dover," the latter being a surf picture made by a man named Paul, in London, England. James H. White and P. L. Waters, were

projectionists on the night the "act" opened at Koster and Bials.

The Black Maria

In Fig. 31 is shown a photograph of what was the first strictly motion picture development plant in the entire world. It was a frame structure covered with black tar paper, and the Edison force quickly christened it the "Black Maria," which name clung to it and has been passed down to us as history. It was the building erected to develop motion picture films for use in the Edison peep-hole kinetoscope, but was used for a time to develop films for use with the Vitascope.

Mr. Edison still has the negative of this picture, from which he was kind enough to permit the making of a print for this paper. I feel that I cannot too strongly stress the advisability and desirability of this society, possibly acting in conjunction with others identified with the industry, devising some method by means of which such relics of early days may be collected and preserved in as nearly as may be a permanent way, for the benefit of posterity. I am sure that even so comparatively

short a while as one hundred years from now such things will have value beyond all computation.

Next I present (Fig. 32) two photographs, one of the office of the Vitagraph Company of America in its early days and one of the first development plant of the same company, the latter picture was taken in 1897.

In the first picture the late Mr. William T. Rock, then president of the Vitagraph Company, is seen at his desk at the left. Over his desk is an enlargement of one frame of the Fitzsimmons-Jefferies prize fight, taken by the company. At the right is J. Stuart Blackton, and in the center Alfred E. Smith, who became president of the Vitagraph Company after the demise of Mr. Rock. This office was at 116 Nassau Street, New York City.

It is most interesting to contrast the little plant shown in Fig. 33 with the motion picture development plants of today.

DISCUSSION

MR. JENKINS: I suggest that Mr. Richardson's alleged facts should be substantiated by citations where evidence

PINK'S "VIASCOPE" MUCH USED IN AND AROUND CHICAGO ABOUT 1907 TO 1909. IT IS CLAW MOVEMENT

FIG. 22. Pink's Viascope.

THE LUBIN "CINEOGRAPH" DISCONTINUED ABOUT 1910.

FIG. 23. The "Lubin Cineograph," discontinued about 1910.

FIG. 24. A Stranger.

one of the first projectors   one of the first projectors

FIG. 25. The Amet Magniscope.

may be found to support his allegations, i.e., public documents, records, publications, *ex-parte* statements, oaths, etc.

I believe no one denies that my name is associated in some way with the period of transition from peep-hole machines to life-size picture projection.

An analysis of motion picture apparatus discloses that the only new essential over old apparatus was the adoption of *means for getting long illumination of the film at the exposure aperture of the projecting machine.* That was my contribution, and that is why the shutters were left off my early

machines (Fig. 34), lantern slides of some of which were shown us by Mr. Richardson (see Figs. 4 and 5).

No projection of well-illuminated, life size motion pictures had been attained before the time I refer to, and no machine has been made since without this feature. This is conceded by the parties whose letters were read by Mr. Richardson. And as both Mr. Armat's and Mr. Edison's letters say that Edison got his projector from Mr. Armat and put his name to it in order to get more money out of the public, it would seem to be only a question of evidence of invention as between Mr. Armat and myself.

You doubtless noted yesterday that in Mr. Armat's letter he says he changed the name of his projector to the "Edison Projectoscope" or "Edison Kinetoscope" (from the original name Phantoscope).

Now, "Phantoscope" is the fanciful name I had given all my motion picture apparatus.

If you will look up the *Photographic Times* of July 6, 1894, which can be consulted in any of the larger public libraries, you will find that this name "Phantoscope" was applied to my machines, with descriptions and accounts of exhibitions of them, months before I ever met Mr. Armat.

Many friends saw these exhibitions, and their affidavits and testimony can be found in suit Equity No. 5/167, U. S. Circuit Court, Southern District of New York. There also can be found in affidavit and testimony of the workman who made several of these machines for me, including the construction of the "1893-94 Phantoscope," the construction of which was paid for by J. P. Freeman.

Mr. Armat, after investigating a machine of mine which projected motion pictures, believed he saw how he could make some money out of it as a promoter, as is explained in the preamble of our contract signed March 25, 1895, which reads as follows:

"This agreement, made and entered into this 25th day of March, 1895, in duplicate, by and between C. Francis Jenkins, of Washington, D. C., party of the first part; and Thomas Armat, of Washington, D. C., party of the second part, witnesseth, that—

FIG. 28.   Vitascope Hall.

Whereas, the party of the first part has filed application for letters patent of the U. S. for a certain invention of his known as the 'Phantoscope,' and also for letters patent on certain new methods of photography, it is agreed that—

First: For and in consideration of One Dollar and the immediate construction and subsequent public exhibition and proper promotion by the party of the second part * * * "

You notice he admits that the Phantoscope is my invention, and he proposes to make, exhibit and properly promote my "Phantoscope."

Under this contract, three copies of my 1894 machines were made and taken to Atlanta, Georgia, for exhibition at the Cotton States Exposition. Mr. Armat called in a reporter to write up the trip, and his account appeared in the *Baltimore Sun*, October 2, 1895. The article refers to the machine which would be used, as "the Phantoscope, the invention of a Washington stenographer."

MR. EDISON OUTDONE
————
PHANTOSCOPE MORE
WONDERFUL THAN HIS
KINETOSCOPE
————
LIFE-SIZE FIGURES SHOWN
————

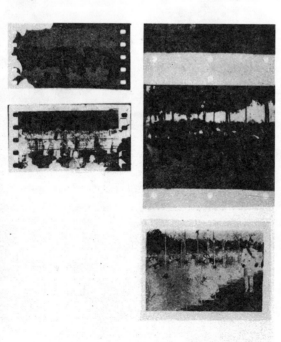

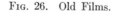

FIG. 26.   Old Films.

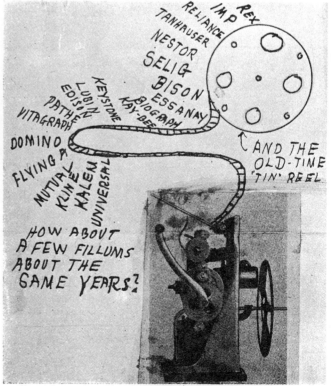

FIG. 27.   Old Type Films.

Here is a projector mechanism which was considered one of the best and most popular no longer ago than 1912. Thousands of them were then in use. How many of you can name it. I had the engraver remove the name plate in making the engraving.

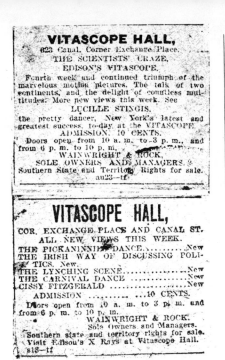

FIG. 29. Vitascope Hall Program. From the Bill of the Theater at 623 Canal Street, New Orleans, La., in the fall of 1896, of which you have been shown a photograph. Take note of the admission price. also the reference to "Edison's Vitascope" and "Edison's X-Rays."

THE REMARKABLE INVENTION OF A WASHINGTON STENOGRAPHER

It will be shown for the First Time at the Atlanta Exposition, Where it May Reproduce All the Details of a Mexican Bull-Fight Without Fear of Interference by Mr. Ballou—It May Also Figure Largely at the Corbett - Fitzsimmons Prize-Fight at Dallas.

(Special dispatch to the *Baltimore Sun*)
Washington, October 2, 1895.

Raff & Gammon
(ORGANIZERS OF THE KINETOSCOPE CO.)

EXCLUSIVE CONTROL OF THE
LATEST MARVEL
The Vitascope

SOLE AGENTS FOR THE
EDISON KINETOSCOPE
IN THE UNITED STATES AND CANADA
THE EDISON PHONOGRAPH

PHONOGRAPH AND KINETOSCOPE SUPPLIES,
ELECTRIC DESIGNS, ETC

Postal Telegraph Building, 253 Broadway
Removed to 43 W. 28th St.
New York,

Vitascope opened Keiths Theatre
May 4th — Boston, Mass.

N. C. R.
Harry Brooks, Esq.,
2995 Washington St.
Roxbury, Mass.
Dear Sir:-
Replying to your postal card of the 5th inst., we beg to say that the right to Massachusetts has been sold, and if you wish to exhibit in that state, you will have to address the purchaser, Mr. P. W. Kiefaber, 419 New Market St., Philadelphia, Pa.
Would be glad to sell you the right to any state remaining open, but they are nearly all taken, and you should act promptly if you wish to secure such a right.
Very truly yours,

FIG. 30. Letter from Raff and Gammon. This letter was written May 9, 1896, just about the time Mr. Edison had the Vitascope projectors ready for the market in considerabe numbers. The note in ink was presumably made by Mr. Brooks. This letter is especially interesting as showing the avidity with which state rights were taken up.

Mr. Armat was not, until much later, interested in claiming that he *invented* the machine, so he continued to give out news stories, even during my absence from Atlanta, about "The Phantoscope," for example, in the *Atlanta Journal* of October 15, 1895, and October 21, 1895, in which the exhibition of the machine continues to be referred to as the "Phantoscope."

Soon after Mr. Armat's return to Washington, he took one of the machines to New York, and there on the second floor of the Postal Telegraph Building, he exhibited it to Edison and his associates in December, 1895, as Mr. Armat explains in his testimony in the Armat-Latham-Castler [sic] suit.

About the same time I made another copy of the original 1894 Phantoscope machine and exhibited it before the Franklin Institute, Philadelphia. The invention was referred to the Committee on Science and the Arts for report. In due course, this committee recommended the award of the Elliott Cresson gold medal, their highest honor. This recommendation was published for three months in the *Journal* of the Institute, and Mr. Armat protested the proposed honor. His protest was dismissed. I quote from the report.

"Mr. Armat declined to submit testimony to substantiate his claims to inventorship, the protest is made up chiefly of aspersions upon the character of Mr. Jenkins, which matters are not relevant to the question. No allusion is made in said (Jenkins-Armat) agreement to any inventions made or contemplated by Mr. Armat. An interference was declared in the Patent Office to settle the question of inventorship. After Mr. Jenkins' testimony was given Mr. Armat declined to maintain his claim as inventor by giving testimony before the Patent Office, but he, at that stage of the case, bought for a cash consideration, all of Mr. Jenkins interests in the Phantoscope, and had Mr. Jenkins withdraw his application, which made the way clear for the allowance of the joint patent (Jenkins-Armat No. 586,953)." Fig. 2.

So the Elliott Cresson award was made; and thirteen years later a second, the John Scott Medal was given me, perhaps to confirm their earlier judgment. I quote from that award.

"Eighteen years ago the applicant exhibited a commercial motion picture projecting machine which he termed the 'Phantoscope.' This was recognized by the Institute and subsequently proved to be the first successful form of projecting machine for the production of life-size motion pictures from a narrow strip of film containing successive phases of motion."

After signing a contract with Edison, Armat asked the Court to stop me from making, using, selling, or exhibiting my machine, or publishing any description of it. But Judge Hagner dismissed the suit in my favor, from which decision I quote. (In Equity No. 17,416, D. C. Docket 40.)

"Its statements (Photographic Times filed by plaintiff Armat) would seem to be of value to defendant Jenkins, inasmuch as it showed his attention had been directed to this subject at a period in advance of any intercourse between Armat and himself, and long before the date complainants attach to the alleged inventions of Thomas Armat. The injunction is denied."

I might say that all the evidence referred to by me this morning and much more has been collected and bound, in three copies, one of which can be found on deposit in the Franklin Institute. This evidence was gotten together at the request of the National Museum, at considerable labor and cost, and delivered to Dr. Charles D. Walcott, Director, but later, on inquiry, I was told the evidence could not be examined as the museum could not consider controversial subjects. May I add that much of the old apparatus I made and used in developing motion pictures had been in the National Museum for twenty-eight years, unchallenged, and can still be found there on exhibit.

As to Edison's invention of anything original connected with motion pictures, the United States Supreme Court decided he had not invented anything which had not already been disclosed by others. The decision appears in U. S. Supreme Court Record Vol. 243, U. S. 502, 61 L Ed. 871; Vol. 235, Fed. 398; Vol. 232, Fed. 363; Vol. 231, Fed. 701; and many others.

Quoting from C. C. A. 2nd Ckt. March 10, 1902—Fed. 114, page 926, the court said:

"The photographic reproductions of moving objects, the production from the negatives of a series of pictures, representing the successive stages of motion, and the presentation of them by an exhibiting apparatus to the eye of the spectator in such rapid sequence as to blend them together and give the effect of a single picture in which the objects are moving, had been accomplished long before Mr. Edison entered the field.'

FIG. 31. The Black Maria.

FIG. 32. The Vitagraph Office.

FIG. 33. The Vitagraph Development Plant in 1897. Contrast it with those of today.

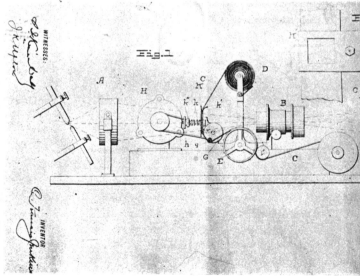

FIG. 34. The Jenkins Sole Application which was put in interference with Armat-Jenkins joint application.

40

Fig. 35.   A part of the exhibit of apparatus built and used by Mr. Jenkins in the development of motion pictures.

C. Francis Jenkins,
Washington, D.C.   March 13, 1923.

Dear Mr. Jenkins:
                Referring to the
attached photograph, I can say that
I recollect that when you were living at our house in 1892 you had a
camera of which I believe this to be
a photograph. I recognize the shape
and size of the wooden box, and also
the crank pin on the face of the rotating disc. Mrs. Bush says she remembers your giving two little darky
boys a nickle each to turn somersault
while you photographed them with this
camera.   *Philo L. Bush*

Fig. 36.   One of the first cameras built by Jenkins. It has a crank pin for giving the film an intermittent movement behind the lens, later called the "Beater Type."

Kinematographic Experiences[*]

By ROBERT W. PAUL[**]

Summary.—*The first commercial showing of motion pictures in England was probably made by two men with six Edison peep-show Kinetoscopes installed in a shop in Old Broad Street, London, in 1894. Six duplicates of these devices (which had not been patented in England) were built in that year by Paul, and sixty machines during 1895. A camera having a cam-driven intermittent movement was also built in 1895 from a design by Paul and Acres, the latter an English photographer. Printing and developing equipment were developed to process the films made with the camera. In 1895 a second camera was constructed in which intermittency was achieved by means of a modified Geneva stop. The public interest shown in the Kinetoscope and its adaptability for projection stimulated Paul late in 1895 to design a projector having an intermittent movement consisting of a seven-toothed starwheel.*

Many interesting experiences in making and exhibiting pictures during 1896 and subsequent years are described. The first motion picture studio in Great Britain was designed and built by Paul in 1899 at Muswell Hill, North London. Trick films and scientific pictures were made there as well as other subjects. The project was closed about 1910 because it was regarded as too speculative as a side-line to instrument making.

My first contact with animated photography occurred by chance in connection with my business, as a manufacturer of electrical and other scientific instruments, which I had started at Hatton Garden, London, in 1891. In 1894 I was introduced by my friend, H. W. Short, to two men, George Tragedes, who had installed in a shop in Old Broad Street, E. C., six Kintoscopes, bought from Edison's agents in New York. At a charge of twopence per person per picture, one looked through a lens at a continuously running film and saw an animated photograph lasting about half a minute. *Boxing Cats, A Barber's Shop*. and *A Shoeblack at Work* were among the subjects, and the public interest was such that additional machines were urgently needed. Finding that no steps had been taken to patent the machine, I was able to construct six before the end of that year. To supply the demand from travelling showmen and others, I made about sixty Kinetoscopes in 1895, and, in conjunction with business friends, installed fifteen of them at the exhibition at Earl's Court, London, showing some of the first of our British films, including one of the boat race and derby of 1895. The sight of queues of people, waiting their turn to view them, first caused me to consider the possibility of throwing the pictures upon a screen. Moreover, it had become evident that the weight of the Kinetoscope and the difficulty, at that time, of recharging its accumulators, militated against its extensive use.

Users of my Kinetoscopes shortly after that were refused supplies of films by the Edison agents, so I was forced to produce new subjects. Film stock, with a matte celluloid base, was procurable from Blair, of St. Mary Cray, Kent. For negatives, Kodak film having a clear base was preferred. In Birt Acres I found a photographer willing to take up the photography and processing, provided I could supply him with the necessary plant, which I did early in 1895. For perforating the film I made, for use in an ordinary fly-press, a set of punches, 32 in number, made to the Edison gauge and fitted with pilot pins. We had no information to guide us in designing a camera, but I worked out an idea due to Acres. The film was drawn by a continuously running sprocket from an upper spool, past the light opening, or gate, to another spool below, and was kept under slight tension. A marginal clamping plate, intermittently actuated by a cam, held the film stationary in the gate during each exposure. A shutter, whose opening synchronised with the cam, revolved between the lens and the gate. In our first trial we failed to get a picture on Blackfriars Bridge only because we forgot, in our excitement, to attach the lens.

Our printer (Fig. 1) was of the rotary type, consisting merely of a sprocket over which the positive and negative films passed together, behind a narrow slot illuminated by a gas jet. The sprocket was turned by hand at a speed judged by the operator, who inspected the negative as it travelled past a beam of red light. For development, a 40-ft. length of film was wound upon a birch frame with spacing pegs. Horizontal or vertical troughs held the solutions and washing water. At first drying was done in festoons, but a little later on light

* Requested and recommended for publication by the Historical Committee. Obtained with the cooperation of E. A. Robins, who was one of the early assistants of Mr. Paul.

** Cambridge Instrument Co., Ltd., London, England.

FIG. 1. Rotary printer.

wooden drums (Fig. 2). Our first successful Kinetoscope film was taken in February, 1895. We took a fair number of subjects, such as *Rough Seas at Dover,** An Engineer's Smithy,* and some comic scenes, in addition to the two typical films already mentioned. A number of such films, joined as endless bands of forty feet long, were exported, more especially to the United States and to Germany, but I do not believe that our total output for the year exceeded ten thousand feet.

A POSITIVE
INTERMITTENT MOTION

The intermittent motion in our first camera was, as I pointed out to Acres, not well suited to give accurate spacing, and the pictures compared unfavorably in that respect with the original Edison films. So soon as the camera was put into use I therefore proceeded to make a second with which many of our 1895 films were taken. In it I adopted a modification of the familiar Geneva stop, as used in watches, to give an intermittent motion to the sprocket. Because the 14-picture sprocket of the Kinetoscope had too great inertia, I made one of aluminum, one-half the diameter.

My first projector (Fig. 3) is described in *The English Mechanic* of February 21 and March 6, 1896. It was intended to be sold at a price of five

of an eccentric, and a hand-operated safety shutter was provided. Four light spring pads pressed upon the corners of the film, which was fed out into a basket. A fault, which I ought to have foreseen, was the unsteadiness caused by the inertia of the spool of films, and it became necessary to insert the films, 40 or 80 feet long, singly. So this model, by means of which I first saw a motion picture upon the screen, was promptly scrapped.

The next step (Fig. 4) consisted in duplicating the intermittent sprockets, the film near the gate being kept more or less taut between them.[2] At that time the likelihood of shrinkage of the film was not realized. The machine had a revolving shutter, in the form of a horizontal drum cut away on two opposite sides, and a rewind spool was provided, driven by a slipping belt. A large handwheel was belted to a small pulley upon the fingerwheel spindle, the latter being coupled to the shutter spindle by spur gears. After a few of these projectors had been put into operation the need for larger spools, to contain a series of films, became evident. So additional sprockets were arranged to give continuous feed above and below the intermittent sprockets.

The projector was furnished complete with lantern and illuminant, either arc or limelight. This model was

screen, this disadvantage was not regarded as serious.

EARLY DEMONSTRATIONS

I named the projector the *Theatrograph,* under which title it formed an item in an entertainment at Finsbury Technical College, London, on February 20, 1896. A week later the machine was shown at the Royal Institution. There the pictures were seen by Lady Harris, whose husband was a leading impresario, responsible for managing the Theater Royal, Drury Lane, and a big spectacle at Olympia. Next morning Sir Augustus Harris telegraphed me to meet him at breakfast, and proposed that a projector be installed at Olympia on sharing terms. He added that he had recently seen animated photographs at Paris, and prompt action was necessary as he was sure that the popular interest would die out in a few weeks. Though I knew nothing of the entertainment business I agreed to intall the machine in a small hall at Olympia in March, 1896, and was surprised to find my small selection of films received with great enthusiasm by the public, who paid sixpense to view them.

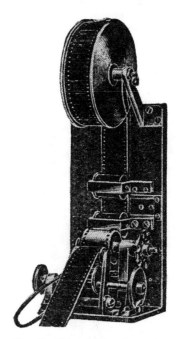

Fig. 3. Star-wheel intermittent projector (Feb., 1896).

Fig. 2. Developing racks and drying drums.

——
* This film was included in the program shown at Koster & Bial's Music Hall, New York, on April 23, 1896, when the Armat *Vitascope* was used to project the pictures.[1]

pounds, and to be capable of attachment to any existing lantern. The seven-toothed star-wheel was driven by a steel finger-wheel which acted also as a locking device during the period when the shutter was open. The latter was oscillated behind the gate by means

used in all my earlier public demonstrations and more than 100 of them were produced, many being exported to the continent and to the United States. One of these projectors, used at the Alhambra Theatre, is preserved in the Science Museum, London, together with a camera (Fig. 5) made in 1896, having a precisely similar driving mechanism. Both pieces of apparatus were decidedly noisy, but as the projector was then usually placed at the back of the stage, behind a translucent

The first public exhibition of the Lumière cinematograph in England took place, also on February 20th, at the Polytechnic in Regent Street, and the results were then superior in steadiness and clearness to my own. To compete with that machine, as shown at the Empire Theater in Leicester Square, the Manager of the Alhambra asked me to give a show, as a ten-minute item in the program, with my Theatrograph, which he renamed the *Animatographe.* This engagement was for two weeks, beginning March 25th, but actually

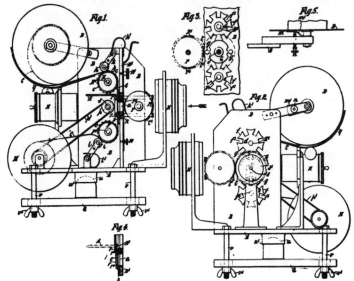

FIG. 4. Second model of intermittent projector (Brit. Pat. No. 4686, March 2, 1896).

THE
EMPIRE
Palace of Varieties, Limited. Charles Street, Newport.

Monday, Nov. 2nd, 1896, and during the week.

R. W PAUL'S
ANIMATED
PHOTOGRAPHS
R W PAUL is the Inventor of the Animatographe, now at The London Alhambra, and this Machine is a replica of that.

The Pictures will be selected from the following —

Papermakers	6. Blackfriars Bridge with Traffic	10. Children at Play
Fishwives	7. Comic Costume Race	11. The Gordon Highlanders
Chirgwin	8. Princess Maud's Wedding	12. The Soldier's Courtship
New Westminster	9. Steam Launch Child Overboard Rescue	13. Spanish Street Scene
Arrival of the Paris Express		14. Bathing at Lisbon
		15. The Derby of 1896.

FRANK BUCKLEY
Character Comedian.

The Celebrated Irishman! WALTER
MUNROE
Singer of Patriotic Songs and Impersonator of Humorous Characters.

Next Week - Horace Wheatley, Bros. Lloyd, Minnie Cunningham

LATE TRAINS.

MUSICAL DIRECTOR

Two Performances Nightly - Early one 7 o'clock to 9; Late one 9 o'clock to 11.

ALL ARTISTES ENGAGED APPEAR at EACH PERFORMANCE

PRICES OF ADMISSION.

Private Box	Stalls	Balcony	Pit	Gallery
7s. 6d.	1s.	6d.	4d.	2d.

Seats not guaranteed. No money returned. The right of refusing admission reserved.

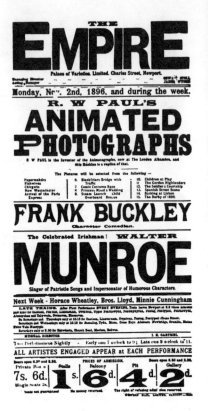

FIG. 6. Section of program at Empire Theater, Newport, England, beginning Nov. 2, 1896.

continued for about two years. The salary, or fee, was at the rate of eleven pounds for each performance, far more than I had expected. In April, the Alhambra manager, Mr. Moul, who wisely foresaw the need for adding interest to wonder, staged upon the roof a comic scene called *The Soldier's Courtship,* the 80-foot film of which caused great merriment. The climax came in June, with the presentation of the Prince's derby, won by Persimmon. The incidents connected with its taking were fully recounted in an illustrated article in *The Strand Magazine,* and His Royal Highness came to see the film. It is a little difficult today to visualize the mad enthusiasm of the closely packed audience, which demanded three repetitions of the film, and sang *God Bless the Prince of Wales,* while many stood upon their seats.

During the summer of 1896 we were busy getting new subjects, some of the leading entertainers being quite willing to participate in the scenes, often without payment. Further, I equipped my friend, Short, with a camera with which he took some interesting films in Portugal, Spain, and Egypt. Of these one of the most popular was taken from the interior of a cave near Lisbon, and showed enormous breakers which appeared to be about to overwhelm the spectators.

At this period the purchasers of many of my projectors worked them personally. Though we did our best to train lanternists and limelight operators to use the machine properly, their results were sometimes indifferent. Therefore, I attended in the evenings at many of the London music halls, the times of showing being carefully arranged in advance. This helped to maintain the reputation of the projector. I drove, with an assistant, from one hall to another in a one-horse brougham, rewinding the films during the drive. Figs. 6 and 7 are reproductions of sections of original programs of showings given at the Empire Theater, Newport, on Nov. 2, 1896, and at the Cheltenham Cricket Club on Dec. 4, 1896.*

SELLING PROJECTORS IN 1896

As a result of these demonstrations an extraordinary demand arose, first from conjurors and then from proprietors of halls, fair-ground showmen, and speculators who wanted exclusive rights for a territory. The first purchaser was David Devant, then with Maskelyne. The latter refused to join in the venture, but engaged Devant to perform with the machine twice daily at a salary, the projector being eventually used thus for two years. Devant also gave evening shows at private houses for a fee of 25 guineas. Through him I sold several projectors to Meliss, the Parisian conjuror, who converted one of them into a camera with which he took his first trick films. Another "mystery merchant," Carl Hertz, took a machine to South Africa in April, projecting the first animated photographs ever seen at sea, on board the S.S. *Norman.* Customers came from nearly every country, and beset the office with their interpreters, while each insisted upon waiting until a projector could be finished. Additional premises and assistants became necessary in order to provide instruction, which was sometimes rather difficult. Four Turks, speaking little English, came daily for weeks, put on their slippers, and practiced. Finally they found that the attractiveness of night life in London had led to the complete exhaustion of their financial resources. A gentleman from Spain,

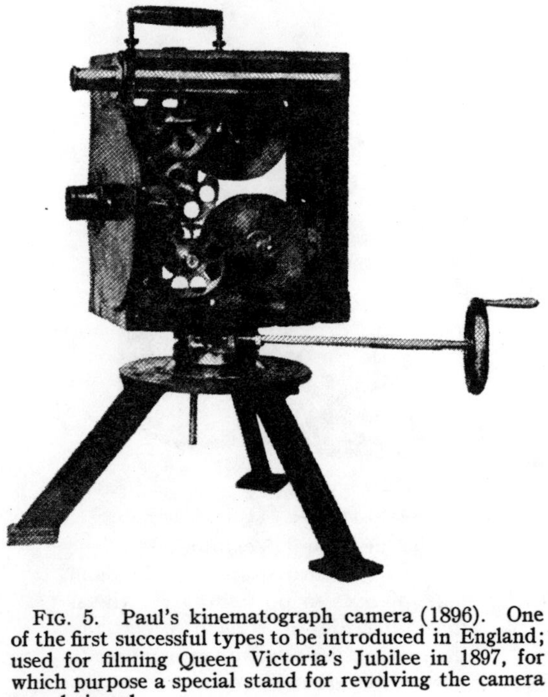

FIG. 5. Paul's kinematograph camera (1896). One of the first successful types to be introduced in England; used for filming Queen Victoria's Jubilee in 1897, for which purpose a special stand for revolving the camera was designed.

---

* The original programs were supplied to the Historical Committee by E. A. Robins, one of Mr. Paul's assistants at the time. Mr. Robins is now an official of Kodak, Ltd., Wealdstone, Middlesex, England.

anxious to return quickly, proved too impatient to learn how to center the arc light, and left with his projector, unboxed, in a cab. Arriving at Barcelona his first attempt at projection failed, whereupon the disappointed audience threw knives at the screen and wrecked the theater. He himself retired to serve a term in a Spanish prison. The court painter to the King of Denmark, sent over by his royal master to fetch a projector, also had trouble with the arc lamp and had to return for further instruction. Fortunately, such mishaps were rare. A little later the King of Sweden and Norway sent his artist for a projector, with instructions that the maker was to accompany the projector and see it properly installed in the palace at Stockholm. This I did, I hope, to his satisfaction, and I was granted special facilities for getting Swedish pictures.

Here I must point out that these reminiscences are personal in character, and in no way an account of the industry or of the work of my competitors. From 1896 onward was a period of great activity, as may be judged from the number of patents for animated picture devices taken out in England, France, and Germany. In the 5 years, 1896 to 1900, these totalled 566, as against 63 for the five previous years.

EVENTS IN 1897

An outstanding event of 1897 was the Diamond Jubilee of Queen Victoria,

FIG. 8. Enlargement from single frame, showing construction of miniature railway set.

was related of one that when the Queen's carriage passed he was under his seat changing film; and of another, that hanging on the railway bridge at Ludgate Hill, he turned his camera until he almost fainted, only to find, upon reaching a darkroom that the film had failed to start. An event of 1897 of a different character, which had serious repercussions, was the disaster at a Charity Bazaar at Paris, when 73 lives were lost in a fire at a kinematograph booth. The operator, using limelight with an ether saturator, attempted to recharge the latter, which exploded and set fire to the films which were

upon a stiff tripod. In this year, after the Jubilee, the public interest in animated pictures seemed to be waning, in spite of the prompt presentation of topical films supplemented by a considerable output of amusing subjects. So soon as a topical film had been taken, all likely purchasers were informed by telegram or post, and the darkroom staff, under J. H. Martin, worked hard to turn out prints, often continuously throughout the night. The work was not then specialized, any operator being ready to take or project pictures as occasion arose. The possibility of presenting upon the screen long films giving complete stories had yet to be exploited, and its realization formed a new phase in the development of the art.

WORK ON THE OPEN-AIR STAGE

To obtain space for taking subjects upon a more ambitious scale than was possible in London, I purchased a four-acre field at Muswell Hill in North London. Pending the erection of a studio, to be described presently, work proceeded upon an open-air stage in an adjacent garden, where temporary buildings accommodated the processing operations. The stage was merely a platform having uprights for supporting a back-cloth, but it proved useful for many simple comic and dramatic pictures. Sometimes a picture combined scenes in natural surroundings with others upon the stage. For example, two divers were filmed, descending and ascending, close to Nelson's flagship *H.M.S. Victory*. Between these views was inserted one on the stage, set with a back-cloth representing a wreck on which the divers worked, sending up treasure. We placed a large narrow tank containing live fishes between the stage and the camera. Strange as it may now seem, the result appeared suffi-

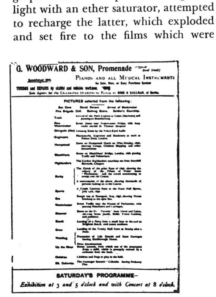

FIG. 7. Section of program at Cheltenham Cricket Club, Dec. 4, 1896, of showing with the *Theatrograph*.

with its magnificent pageantry of royalty and troops from all parts of the world, and the touching ceremony at the steps of St. Paul's Cathedral. Large sums were paid for suitable camera positions, several of which were obtained for my operators. I myself operated a camera perched upon a narrow ledge in the churchyard. Several continental kinematographers came over, and it

loose in a basket. This sad event caused a widespread fear of similar disasters. I then produced a fireproof projector in which the film spools were enclosed in casings, the film passing through narrow slots to and from the mechanism. This machine had a four-picture sprocket actuated by a four-star Maltese cross; it was far more portable than my earlier projectors and was set ciently natural to cause the Prince of Wales and Lord Rothschild, after seeing it upon the Alhambra screen, to ask me how it had been possible to photograph under water.

As an example of "model" work I recall a film (Fig. 8) representing a railway collision, of which the effect upon the screen was regarded very thrilling: A railway track runs alongside an embankment, below which is a lake bearing a yacht. A slow train comes along toward a tunnel and overruns the signal. While the driver backs the train an express dashes out from the tunnel, and a collision occurs in which the trains are thrown down the embankment. This film had a large sale, and I was told that a great number of pirated copies appeared in America.

In 1899 I sent out two cameras to the Boer War. One of them was lent to Colonel Beevor of the Scots Guards, one of the first regiments to leave, who was able to get about a dozen good films, including one of the surrender of Cronje to Lord Roberts. Nobody made pictures of actual fighting, though several operators obtained interesting scenes on the lines of communication. To meet the demand for something more exciting, representations of such scenes as the bombardment of Mafeking and the work of nurses on the Battlefield were enacted on neighboring golf links, under the supervision of Sir Robert Ashe, an ex-officer of Rhodes' force. These were issued for what they actually were, although I can not vouch for the descriptions applied to them by the showmen.

TRICK FILMS IN THE STUDIO

In 1899 we commenced work in a studio (Fig. 9) erected in a corner of the field. I believe it was the first in Great Britain to be designed for kinematograph work. It comprised a miniature stage, about 28 by 14 feet, raised above the ground level and protected by an iron building with wide sliding doors and a glass roof facing north. At the rear of the stage was a hanking frame to which back-cloths painted in monochrome could be fixed: the frame could be lowered through a slot to facilitate the work of the scene painter. Traps in the stage and a hanging bridge above the stage provided means for working certain effects to which I shall refer later. Eventually a scene-painting room was added behind the studio. A trolley mounted upon rails carried the camera, which could thus be set at any required distance from the stage, to suit the subject. Sometimes the trolley was run to or from the stage while the picture was being taken, thus affording a gradual enlargement or reduction of the image upon the film.

FIG. 9.   Photograph of Paul's motion picture studio (1899).

Adjacent to the studio, a laboratory (Fig. 10) was erected, having a capacity for processing up to 8000 feet of film per day. With the valuable aid of Walter Booth and others, hundreds of humorous, dramatic, and trick films were produced in the studio.

A specimen trick film may be briefly described (Fig. 11): Upon the moon-lit battlements of a castle a knight meets his lady-love. The twain are startled by the appearance of a ghost, which, at the approach of the knight, fades away. Meanwhile a witch, complete with broomstick, appears in the sky and attempts to carry off the lady, but being driven off by the knight, she flies away over the moon. Then a grim ogre, several times the size of the knight appears over the battlements and picks up the lady, who hands him a flaming sword. The scene dissolves to the cave of the witch, where many exciting and fantastic events occur, culminating in the rescue of the lovers and a banquet at the castle. I have summarized this fairy story, which lasted three minutes upon the screen, as an example of what was done at the beginning of this century to pack the maximum of movement into 180 feet of film. It is also an example of the position of the art as regards trick photography. The black magic effects were produced by photographing the ghost against a black velvet cloth, then superimposing the negative upon that of the main scene, in which is a suitable blank space, and printing the two together.

When dissolving from one scene to the next, the exposure was gradually reduced at the end of the first negative and gradually increased at the beginning of the next. Either a mask, having a wedge-shaped aperture, was moved across the lens by means of a screw feed, or the iris diaphragm was slowly contracted or enlarged during the exposure of an appropriate number of pictures or frames. In the case of a fig-

FIG. 10.   Paul's film processing laboratory.

FIG. 11.   Scenes from an early trick film (about 1900).

ure taken against a background, the image could be traversed in any direction either by the aid of a mechanically actuated rising front, or by a panoramic movement of the camera itself. By feeding the film upward instead of downward in the camera, the motions could appear as reversed, and a building made to disappear brick by brick.

By repeating in the print a single frame of the negative, a diver could be made to pause in mid-air as long as he desired. By rotating the camera about the axis of the lens, a person could be made to appear to perform the movements of a butterfly, floating about and turning over.

By speeding up the camera, slow-motion pictures were taken, and in this way we were able, under the guidance of Professor Vernon Boys and Professor Worthington, to obtain pictures of sound-wave "shadows" and falling drops, respectively. A little later Professor Silvanus P. Thompson prepared several series, each consisting of hundreds of diagrams, illustrating lines of force in changing magnetic fields; these we converted into animated pictures by the one-turn-one-picture camera. I had the pleasure of personally presenting copies of these films to Thomas Edison at Orange, N. J., in 1911.

In projectors having the Maltese cross type of intermittent movement, the shutter covering the motion of the film subtended an angle of about 90 degrees, thus involving a noticeable amount of flicker. To reduce the flicker, and at the same time maintain the illumination, I designed a projector (Fig. 12) in which the Maltese cross, or four-star wheel, was replaced by one having only three slots.[3] Thus the shutter had to cover only about 90 degrees; in other words, the ratio of light to darkness was 11 to 1 instead of 3 to 1. The outfit included a sliding lantern, so that lantern slides as well as films could be shown (Fig. 13). A camera with a similar movement, now in the Science Museum, is shown in Fig. 14; it had detachable dark boxes, full-sized finder, interchangeable lenses with turret mounting, and other features common in present-day practice. This three-slot mechanism did not eventually supersede the four-slot Maltese cross so generally used in modern projectors.

SELLING FILMS

Turning for a moment to the business side of the kinematograph work, showroom premises were taken in High Holborn, and Jack Smith joined the firm as sales manager in 1900. Our maximum output of new film subjects was reached in the period 1900 to 1905. As the staff at Muswell Hill was fully occupied there, taking topical films became the care of Jack Smith and his assistants. Smith also travelled abroad and photographed many popular subjects. In 1900 I produced, through the good offices of the adjutant-general, a whole series depicting life in every branch of the British army.

It soon became the practice of firms, owing to competition, to send out batches of films on approval to many of the exhibitors, in order that the latter might see the latest productions. Many of the less conscientious showmen repeatedly used the samples for a week or more before sending thm back as unsuitable. This abuse grew to such an extent as to cause much loss to the makers, and it was eventually abolished by their mutual action. In 1907 there existed in England about ten firms producing pictures, while several exhibitors had cameras and produced occa-

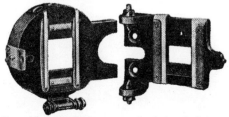

FIG. 12.   Three-slot star-wheel intermittent, and gate of projector (1899).

FIG. 13.   Complete projector using three-slot star-wheel intermittent (1899).

sional topical and dramatic films. Some of them started renting their films, and played off the foreign against the British producer in order to cut prices. To regularize trade conditions Will Barker called the producers together and the Kinematograph Manufacturers' Association was formed. In 1909 this Association, in cooperation with George Eastman, called together at Paris all the producers of films in Europe, and a Convention of conditions of supply was signed by thirty-five firms. Of these, few, if any, exist today. Other activities of the K.M.A. included standardizing film dimensions, training operators and certifying them, and arbitrating in commercial disputes. By 1910 the expense and elaboration necessary for the production of any salable film had become so great that I found the kinematograph side of the business too speculative to be run as a side-line to instrument making. I then closed it down, and destroyed my stock of negatives, numbering many hundreds, thereby becoming free to devote my whole attention to my original business, now a part of that of the Cambridge Instrument Company.

Fig. 14. Camera using three-slot star-wheel intermittent.

REFERENCES

[1]Armat, T.: "My Part in the Development of the Motion Picture Projector," *J. Soc. Mot. Pict. Eng.*, XXIV (March. 1935), No. 3. p. 241.

[2]Paul, R. W.: Brit. Pat. No. 4686, March 2, 1896; covering segment shutter, marginal pressure pads, and spring compensation for sprocket variations.

[3]Paul, R. W.: Brit. Pat. No. 487, 1899.

The Lumière Cinematograph[*]

By LOUIS LUMIÈRE[**]

Summary.—*A historical account of the development of the cinematograph camera and projector. Work on the apparatus was begun in 1894, and a private demonstration given in March, 1895, at Paris. The first public showing at which admission was charged took place in the Grand Cafe on the Boulevard des Capucines, Paris on December 28, 1895. Motion pictures were also projected upon a screen approximately 80 x 100 feet in the Galerie des Machines at the Paris Exposition grounds in 1898, using a projection distance of more than 600 feet. The paper contains an illustrated description of the apparatus.*

When the Edison Kinetoscope appeared in Paris in 1894 in a shop on the boulevards, there were many who thought, after having peered into the eyepiece of this ingenious device, that the projection of the moving images, which were produced then for only one spectator at a time, would be of considerable interest. However, the continuous motion of the film in the Kinetoscope permitted the eye to perceive each of the elementary images during only a very short time (1/6000 second), and this feeble illumination, which necessitated examining the images in direct light, without interposing any diffusing surface, could not pass sufficient light for good projection. Moreover, the sharpness suffered considerably because of the motion of the elementary images, even during the very short time they were illuminated.

My brother and I decided to investigate the problem, and I soon succeeded in making a device in which the film was kept stationary, for a time corresponding to two-thirds of the total time, each time an elementary image appeared exactly on the lens axis. The device allowed the frequency of 16 images per second which I had previously established, and an illumination time of 1/25 second per image, which is more than is needed for projection. This device consisted of a sliding block (Fig. 1) driven with a reciprocating vertical motion by means of a triangular eccentric, which stopped the motion of the block completely at the top and at the bottom of its travel during one-sixth of the total time. When the block was sationary, the tines or claws (Fig 2) of a kind of fork located at the side sank into the perforations of the film, under the control of a helical cam (Figs. 3 and 4). These pins described a rectangular path and carried the film along during their downward motion and left it motionless during their withdrawal, their upward course, and their sinking in. A pressure member, acting upon the film as a light brake, was sufficient to hold the film in perfect

alignment with the gate behind which the image appeared, thus absorbing any play in the apparatus. The principle of the movement is shown in Fig. 5.

As I contemplated producing only short scenes, the length of the film was only 17 or 18 meters. I had not deemed it necessary to complicate the instrument by having a continuously running sprocket, the effects of the inertia of the small roll of film containing the images being deadened by a spring-lever (Fig. 6).

I shall not undertake to write the history of the motion picture industry; and without going back to Zoetropes, Phenakistoscopes, *etc.*, I shall cite only the work of the astronomer Janssen, of Muybridge, and especially of Marey of the Institute, of Demeny, and of Reynaud, who at times carried out remarkable analyses of motion; although none of the instruments of these men was

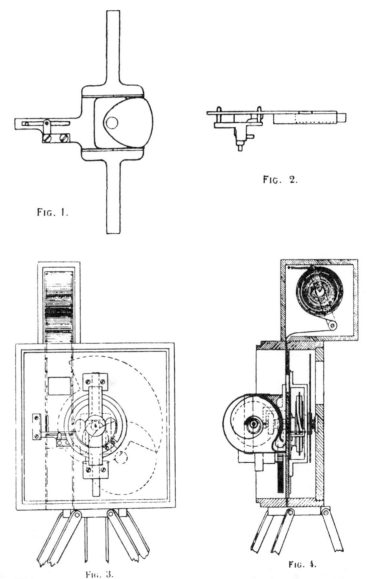

FIG. 1.

FIG. 2.

FIG. 3.

FIG. 4.

FIG. 1. Sliding block and triangular eccentric of pull-down device.
FIG. 2. Section through sliding block, showing mounting of pull-down pins.
FIG. 3. Front elevation of camera mechanism, showing arrangement of sliding block and pull-down pins.
FIG. 4. Side elevation of camera mechanism, showing helical cam controlling movement of pull-down pins.

———
[*]Requested and recommended for publication by the Historical Committee.
[**]Neuilly, Paris, France.

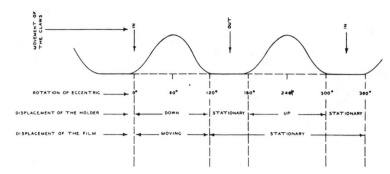

FIG. 5. Movements of film and various parts of pull-down mechanism during one exposure and pull-down cycle.

able to achieve the animation of more than about 30 images, the projection of which involved much difficulty.

The first outfit I developed was made in 1894 in our factory at Lyons, according to my drawings and under my supervision, by our chief mechanic, Mr. Moisson. The first images I succeeded in obtaining were printed upon the photographic paper we were manufacturing at the time. Later, we obtained base film from the New York Celluloid Co. which we coated with sensitive emulsion in our machines, and made into perforated rolls.

The film described above had only two circular holes per image and assured unusual steadiness in projection. I demonstrated the outfit, patented in February, 1895, during the course of a lecture at the Societe d'Encouragement pour l'Industrie Nationale, in Paris, in March, 1895. At the time, I had only one film, which showed the employees leaving the Lumiere factory—an easy subject, since I had simply to set up my camera in front of the factory gate at closing time.

This first demonstration was a great success. I met there Mr. Jules Carpentier, an engineer, member of the Scientific Academy, and a well known manufacturer of precision instruments, who immediately proposed to undertake to manufacture a series of Lumiere cinematographs. I accepted the offer at once, and the Carpentier factory forthwith manufactured much of the appara-

tus, which could be used as cameras, projectors, and printers, since by providing a double-film magazine, both the raw film and the negative could be run in together and printed. Figs. 7, 8, and 9 are illustrations of the equipment.

The results obtained were submitted to the Congress of the Photographic Society of France at Lyons, on July, 1895, and greeted with a tremendous acclaim. We decided to give public demonstrations with the equipment, and on December 28, 1895, opened a place in the basement of the Grand Cafe, on the Boulevard des Capucines, Paris, where, for a small admission fee people could witness the projection of the following short films: *Men and Women Employees Leaving the Lumiere Factory, Arrival of a Train at the Station of La Ciotat, The Baby's Lunch, The Sprinkler Sprinkled (!)*, and *Boat Leaving the Harbor, etc.* The success of the showing when the existence of our place became known, was considerable, although no publicity was sought. Thus, on that date, December 28, 1895, was really born the expression: "I have been to a movie."

In 1897, I announced a device (Fig. 10) utilizing as a condenser, a simple glass flask, as nearly spherical as possible, filled with water, and carrying in the upper part a small piece of pumice stone suspended by a thread in order to regulate the boiling of the water which occurred after prolonged use. The device thus formed a block system,

since the concentration of the light-beam upon the film would cease in case the flask were broken. All our machines were furnished with these devices.

When the Paris Exhibition of 1900 was decided upon, in 1898, I was called to Paris by Mr. Picard, the general secretary, to whom I proposed the experiment of projecting greatly enlarged motion pictures at the Exhibition. With the small apparatus described above, I succeeded in projecting ordinary cinematograph images covering a screen 24 meters high and 30 meters wide, set up in the middle of the Galerie des Machines, a huge building, 400 meters long by 114 meters wide, which had been constructed for the Exposition of 1889. Fig. 11 gives an idea of the size of the screen, set 200 meters from the projector. As a fabric for the screen I had selected a material that reflected, when wet, as much light as it transmitted, so that one could see the projected images from any position in the big hall. To moisten the screen on the day of the experiment required the assistance of the Paris Fire Brigade, since the screen was the height of a six-story building. The results were so remarkable that the screen was retained for the Exposition of 1900. Unfortunately, the Galerie des Machines was cut in the middle to make a circular hall more than 100 meters in diameter, and having a capacity of 25,000 seats. This forced me to reduce the dimensions of the screen to 16 meters high by 21 meters wide, and place it along a diameter of the hall. To avoid the difficulty of moistening the screen at the time of projection, the screen was kept immersed in a large rectangular tank of water, and each evening was raised out of the tank by a hand-winch under the cupola after removing the trap door that closed the tank during the day. I had to be satisfied with an arc of only 100 amperes, which, however, was sufficient because of the optical instruments used. The demonstrations occurred each evening, without trouble, throughout the Exposition.

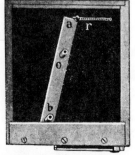

FIG. 6. Spring-lever in supply magazine to reduce effects of inertia of the film roll.

FIG. 7. Front view of camera with shutter removed.

FIG. 8.　Rear view of camera, showing method of threading film.

FIG. 9.　Take-up magazine, unassembled.

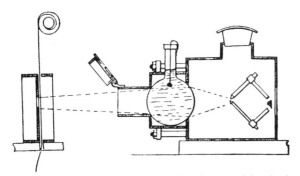

FIG. 10.　Illuminating system of projector, with spherical flask acting as combination condenser and heat absorber.

FIG. 11.　Large screen 24 by 30 meters (79 × 98 feet) used for projection of motion pictures at Paris Exposition of 1900.　Note figures of men at base of screen.

To obtain better definition in the images projected upon so large a screen, I had a camera built, with the collaboration of Mr. Carpentier, capable of producing images, 4.5 by 6 cm., having perfect definition, as shown in Fig. 12, which was taken on the opening day of the Exposition of 1900. Unfortunately,

FIG. 12.　Print from film taken on opening day of Paris Exposition of 1900 in Lumière camera using wide film (4.5 × 6 cm. frame).

the camera was not finished in time to be used for the more ambitious programs we had planned, so we kept to the original small films. Since at Lyons we were unfavorably situated to undertake the production of longer films, and since we were more interested in our laboratory investigations, we abandoned the project in 1905.

Every one knows how tremendously the motion picture projector has been developed, especially through the impetus and improvements that are due to a great extent to the efforts of American engineers and industry.

REFERENCES

COISSAC, G. M.: "Histoire *du Cinematographe*," *Gauthier-Villars* (Paris), 1925. According to this authority, the first public showing of the Lumiere Cinematograph in New York occurred in May, 1896.

RAMSAYE, T.; "A Million and One Nights—the History of the Motion Picture," *Simon & Schuster* (New York), 1926; 2 vols.

"Geschichte der Photographie" (Vol. I of "Ausfuhrliches Handbuch der Photographie"), J. M. Eder, ed., *W. Knapp*, Halle, 1932.

"Agenda Lumière-Jougla," *Gauthier-Villars* (Paris). Issued annually; contains accounts of early motion picture research and a complete bibliography of scientific articles published by Louis Lumière and his associates.

Adventures in Cinemaland[*]

By H. T. KALMUS[**]

Summary.—An account of some of the highlights in the history of the development of the business of Technicolor Motion Picture Corporation primarily from the point of view of its contact with motion picture producers, distributors, and exhibitors; incidental to which is an account of the development and growth of the various Technicolor processes from a semi-technical point of view but with a special reference to practical application in the motion picture industry.

Webster defines adventure as *chance of danger or loss; the encountering of risks; a bold undertaking, a daring feat; a remarkable occurrence or experience, a stirring incident; a mercantile or speculative enterprise of hazard; a venture.* The excursions of Technicolor into the domain of the producers, distributors, and exhibitors of motion pictures have been all of these.

Technicolor has manufactured and shipped prints of many hundreds of productions (during 1937 alone of over 350 subjects for some fifty different customers including more than twenty features) and since some phase of adventure usually develops during the photography or printing of any production, it is clear that this account does not pretend to be complete.

Nor are the events described in detail necessarily those of greatest importance. The writer having played a continuing part will no doubt unduly emphasize some which he found particularly interesting, whereas with the passage of time others only lightly touched upon or omitted may be found to be of greater significance. However, it is hoped that this paper may be a fitting preliminary to a more ambitious one which I have been asked to prepare, reviewing the progress of color cinematography over the past quarter of a century, with special reference to the contributions of Technicolor.

Early in the development of any color process, two decisions of policy must be made: first, how far will it permit departure from standard equipment and materials, and, second, how will it attempt to divide the additional requisites of recording and reproducing color between the emulsion maker, the photographic and laboratory procedure, and the exhibitor's projection machine. Technicolor assumed at the outset that special cameras and special projectors were permissible, provided raw film of standard dimensions were employed.

The earliest Technicolor laboratory was built within a railway car. This car was completely equipped with a photo-chemical laboratory, darkrooms, fireproof safes, power plant, offices, and all the machinery and apparatus necessary for continuously carrying on the following processes on a small commercial scale; sensitizing, testing, perforating, developing, washing, fixing and drying negative; printing, developing, washing, fixing and drying positive; washing and conditioning air; filtering and cooling wash water; examining and splicing film; and making control measurements and tests. In 1917 the car was rolled over the railway tracks from Boston, Massachusetts, where it was equipped, to Jacksonville, Florida, where the first Technicolor adventure in feature motion picture production was to take place. The camera was the single-lens, beam-splitter, two-component type, without the refinements which came later. The picture was *The Gulf Between*, with Grace Darmond and Niles Welch playing the leads. Technicolor was the producer. Dr. D. F. Comstock, Mr. W. B. Wescott, Professor E. J. Wall, Mr. C. A. (Doc) Willat, Mr. J. A. Ball, Mrs. Kalmus, and I were all on the job. The process was two-color, additive, standard size frame, and hence demanded a minimum of the laboratory procedure.

During the progress of this production, February, 1917, I was invited by the American Institute of Mining Engineers to deliver a lecture at Aeolian Hall, New York, to expound the marvels of the new Technocolor process which was soon to be launched upon the public and which it was alleged by many could hardly do less than revolutionize their favorite form of entertainment.

The Gulf Between had been preceded by *The Glorious Adventure*, a feature picture made in England by the Kinemacolor Process. Since Kinemacolor photographed the color components by successive exposure, it was nothing for a horse to have two tails, one red and one green, and color fringes were visible whenever there was rapid motion. The Technicolor slogan was two simultaneous exposures from the same point of view, hence geometrically identical components and no fringes. At that time hundreds of thousands were being spent by others trying in impossible ways to beat the fringing of successive exposures and the parallax of multiple lenses.

I thought the Technicolor inventors and engineers had a practical solution, commercial at least temporarily, so I marched bravely to the platform at Aeolian Hall. It was a great lesson. We were, of course, introducing the color by projecting through two apertures, each with a color filter, bringing the two components into register on the screen by means of a thin adjusting glass element. Incidentally, Technicolor had to invent and develop a horizontal magnetically controlled arc which gave one-third more light for the same current than the then-standard vertical arcs and which could be relied upon for constancy of position of the source. This latter was vitally important with a double aperture. During my lecture something happened to the adjusting element and, in spite of frantic efforts of the projectionists, it refused to adjust. And so I displayed fringes wider than anybody had ever before seen. Both the audience and the press were very kind but it didn't help my immediate dilemma or afford an explanation to our financial angels.

Arrangements were made with Messrs. Klaw and Erlanger to exhibit *The Gulf Between* by routing the photoplay one week each in a group of large American cities. During one terrible night in Buffalo I decided that such special attachments on the projector required an operator who was a cross between a college professor and an acrobat, a phrase which I have since heard repeated many times. Technicolor then and there abandoned additive processes and special attachments on the projector.

As early as 1918 Technicolor had in mind two principal methods of attacking the color problem. Dr. Leonard T. Troland, who, at the time of his death, was Director of Research of Technicolor Motion Picture Corporation, had done some important pioneer work on the Monopack process. Some of his inventions were embodied in numerous patent claims which have been issued and which were intended broadly to cover the multi-layer method both for taking and printing. The other Technicolor attack was by the imbibition method. Both Monopack and imbibition were obviously capable of ultimate development into multi-component processes, but since imbibition seemed to load more of the problems

---

*Presented at the Fall, 1938, Meeting at Detroit, Mich., received October 28, 1938.
**Technicolor Motion Picture Corp., New York, N.Y.

on the laboratory and relatively less on the emulsion maker, we pursued it with the greater vigor.

A first approximation to the Technicolor imbibition method consisted of two gelatin reliefs produced upon thin celluloid which were glued or welded together back to back and dyed in complementary colors. Combined with the Technicolor two-component cameras, this method provided an immediately available system (1919-21) capable of yielding two-component subtractive prints. A small laboratory or pilot plant was built in the basement of the building occupied by the Technicolor engineers, Kalmus, Comstock & Wescott, Inc., on Brookline Avenue, Boston, Mass.

In 1920 Judge William Travers Jerome first became interested in Technicolor; he brought as associates the late Marcus Loew, Nicholas M. Schenck, now President of Loew's, Inc., and Joseph M. Schenck, now Chairman of the Board of Twentieth Century Fox, Inc.

Both Joseph and Nicholas Schenck have on many occasions been most helpful to Technicolor by giving practical advice to Judge Jerome and to me, but at no time more so than when it was decided to produce the photoplay which was later called *The Toll of the Sea.* This was the first Technicolor production by the subtractive method. It was photographed in Hollywood under the general supervision of Mr. Joseph M. Schenck, Chester Franklin, Director, Anna May Wong, lead, and J. A. Ball, Technicolor cameraman.

Mr. Nicholas Schenck arranged for the release of *The Toll of the Sea* by Metro-Goldwyn-Mayer. The first showing was given at the Rialto Theater in New York, the week of November 26, 1922. Letters of praise were received from Maxfield Parrish, Charles Dana Gibson, and other artists. But because of insufficient laboratory capacity we were not able to supply prints fast enough to follow this up immediately and not until 1923 was the picture generally released in the United States. It grossed more than $250,000, of which Technicolor received approximately $160,000.

The prints of *The Toll of the Sea* were manufactured in the original pilot plant on Brookline Avenue, at a manufacturing cost of about 27 cents per foot.

Every step of the Technicolor work in *The Toll of the Sea* was carefully watched by the executives of the industry. Rex Ingram, who was in the midst of producing *Prisoner of Zenda,* wired Mr. Loew for permission to scrap everything he had done in black and white on that picture and start over again in

color. D. W. Griffith wanted to produce *Faust* and Douglas Fairbanks telephoned about producing a feature.

Our first adventure in Hollywood seemed successful! We were told that with prints as good as we were manufacturing if offered at 8 cents per foot the industry would rush to color.

But, thus far we had only inserts and one feature production, *The Toll of the Sea,* of which Technicolor was itself the producer. We had no adequate means of giving rush print service in Hollywood, and we were charging 20 cents a foot for release prints. It was another matter to convince a producer to employ the Technicolor company to photograph and make prints of a production at his expense and risk and under the conditions which prevailed in the motion picture industry.

Meanwhile Technicolor Plant No. 2 was being built in Boston in a building adjoining the one containing the Pilot Plant. It had a capacity of about one million feet of prints per month and cost approximately $300,000. And in April, 1923, the late C. A. Willat, in charge, J. A. Ball, Technical Director, G. A. Cave, Assistant Technical Director, were sent from Boston to establish a small Technicolor laboratory and a photographic unit in Hollywood. This was established in a building in Hollywood rented for the purpose.

In November, 1923, Mr. Jesse L. Lasky and I finally agreed upon the terms of a contract between Technicolor Motion Picture Corporation and Famous Players Lasky Corporation for the production of *The Wanderer of the Wasteland.* We were told by Mr. Lasky that they had appropriated not more for this picture than they would have for the same picture in black and white. Also that the time schedule allowed for photographing was identical with what it would have been in black and white. The photography was to be done by our cameras in the hands of our technical staff, but following a budget and a time schedule laid out for them by Famous Players. Rush prints and the quality of negative were to be checked by them each day. During the six weeks of photography our entire staff worked from early morning to late at night, including Sundays and holidays. At one time we were accumulating negative which we did not dare to develop because of inadequate facilities in our rented laboratory. A few of us in Technicolor carried the terrorizing thought that there was no positive assurance that we would finally obtain commercial negative, and that the entire Famous Players investment might be lost. However, Mr. Lasky was not permitted to share that doubt. His confidence and help during the darkest hours were

really marvelous and finally the cut negative emerged satisfactorily. We delivered approximately 175 prints which were shown in several thousand theaters over the country. These prints were billed at 15 cents a foot, for which Technicolor received approximately $135,000. Some of these prints were made in the pilot plant, but more of them were made in Plant No. 2 which was now being run by operators we had trained.

Nevertheless there were reasons why we could not obtain a volume of business. Every producer in Hollywood knew that the first important production by the Technicolor process under actual motion picture conditions and not controlled by the Technicolor company, had just been completed by Famous Players Lasky Corporation. A considerable group of producers expressed themselves as interested, but were waiting to see the outcome. Another group believed the process to be practical and might have paid our then price of 15 cents a foot, but considered it impracticable to send the daily work to Boston for rush prints.

A small plant, primarily for the purpose of developing negative, making rush prints, and providing a California headquarters was installed at 1006 North Cole Avenue, Hollywood, in a building erected for our purpose. A large part of the equipment was built by our engineers in Boston and shipped to California. The installation was ready for operation about the middle of the year 1924.

Neither *The Toll of the Sea* nor *The Wanderer of the Wasteland,* nor any of the inserts made until the middle of 1924 had given us experience photographing with artificial light. We were therefore very glad to obtain an order for an insert in a production directed by Mr. George Fitzmaurice, called *Cytherea,* photographed in the United Studios lot in Hollywood, giving us our first experience in photographing an interior set on a dark stage. Mr. Fitzmaurice was delighted with the results.

In the Fall of 1924 we had six men and four cameras working in Rome on the Metro-Goldwyn-Mayer production, *Ben Hur.*

One of the great adventures of Technicolor in Cinemaland and a milestone in its progress was in the photography, print manufacture, and exhibition of Douglas Fairbanks' *The Black Pirate.* Mr. Fairbanks had the idea that the screen had never caught and reflected the real spirit of piracy as one finds it in the books of Robert Louis Stevenson, or the paintings of Howard Pyle, and that he could catch it by the use of color. He said, "This ingredient has been tried and rejected countless times.

It has always met overwhelming objections. Not only has the process of color motion picture photography never been perfected, but there has been a grave doubt whether, even if properly developed, it could be applied, without detracting more than it added to motion picture technic. The argument has been that it would tire and distract the eye, take attention from acting, and facial expression, blur and confuse the action. In short it has been felt that it would militate against the simplicity and directness which motion pictures derive from the unobstrusive black and white. These conventional doubts have been entertained, I think, because no one has taken the trouble to dissipate them. A similar objection was raised, no doubt, when the innovation of scenery was introduced on the English stage—that it would distract attention

But Mr. Fairbanks' attorneys pointed out that this production would cost a million dollars, and asked what assurance there was that Technicolor would be able to deliver prints, much less satisfactory prints. This difficulty was finally resolved by making a tripartite agreement in which the engineering firm of Kalmus, Comstock & Wescott, Inc., which still had the pilot plant in the basement of its building, agreed under certain conditions that it would deliver the prints in case Technicolor company failed. There was great discussion as to the color key in which this picture would be pitched. We made test prints for Mr. Fairbanks at six different color levels, from a level with slightly more color than black and white, to the most garish rendering of which the Technicolor process was then capable. Mr. Fairbanks set to work on the shore of Catalina Island and off that shore on his pirate ship, with four of the seven Technicolor cameras then in existence, to capture moods after the manner of impressionistic painting. The picture was released through United Artists in 1925. So far as audience reaction, press reviews, and box-office receipts were concerned, it was a triumph from the start, but for the Technicolor company it was a terrible headache.

Technicolor was still making the double-coated cemented together relief prints, so that the red and green images were not quite in the same plane, and the pictures didn't project too sharply on the screen. This double-coated film is considerably thicker than ordinary black-and-white film, with emulsion on both sides which tends to make it cup more readily and scratch more noticeably than black-and-white film. And the cupping could occur in either direction, more or less at random. Judg-

ing from the complaints, at each such change in the direction of cupping, the picture would jump out of focus. We sent field men to the exchanges. We provided these men with a supply of new prints to replace the cupped ones in the theaters, in order that the latter might be shipped back to our laboratory in Boston for decupping. The newly decupped prints were temporarily satisfactory; the picture was a great success, but our troubles never ended.

It had been clear that this double-coated process was at best but a temporary method, and the work of developing a true imbibition process was being pressed in our research department.

But unfortunately the imbibition process was not ready for *The Black Pirate,* or for *The Wanderer of the Wasteland.*

Early in 1925 Mr. Sydney R. Kent, then head of distribution of Famous Players Lasky Corporation, said: "We have concluded not to do more Technicolor pictures for the present, for two reasons: first, because we have had a great deal of trouble in our exchanges due to the fact that the film is double-coated and consequently scratches much more readily than black and white, with the necessity of having to order more replacements, and it is an added bother to our operators; and, second, because the cost is out of all proportion to its added value to us. We paid $146,-000 additional for *Wanderer* prints. We understand that you need volume to get your costs down. At an 8-cent price we would be interested to talk volume."

Evidently Technicolor needed the single-coated imbibition prints and volume to lower the price to meet his conditions.

Meanwhile Mr. Nicholas Schenck, then President of Loew's, Inc., was advising us to produce a picture ourselves, to prove both quality and costs.

And so in 1926-27 I once more found myself explaining to the directors of Technicolor that I always had believed and still believed very thoroughly in the ultimate success of the Technicolor project, always provided, however, that it was recognized by all the Directors to be a tremendously difficult undertaking technically and one which requires business sagacity and financial endurance. These directors, including the late Wm. Travers Jerome, the late Wm. Hamlin Childs, the late A. W. Erickson, the late Wm. H. Coolidge, the late Thomas W. Slocum, James C. Colgate, Eversley Childs, and Alfred Fritzsche, had many earlier reminders of the necessity of financial endurance. Prior to 1926 over two and one-half million

dollars had been spent, but this time I was not calling for money for cameras and printers, for imbibition machines and research salaries; it was to go into production. When they asked me what I knew about production, I frankly told them nothing, but at least I could start from scratch without some of the fixed ideas and prejudices concerning color that some of the Hollywood producers seemed to have accumulated. I wanted to make short subjects, not primarily to make money as a producer, but to prove to the industry that there was nothing mysterious about the operation

what the emulsion recorded was susceptible of reasonable control through understanding, that black and white cameramen could easily be trained to light for Technicolor cameras, that talented art directors could readily begin to think in terms of color, that rush prints could be delivered promptly, and generally that the job could be done efficiently and economically, utilizing but not minutely imitating black-and-white experience.

The first short we produced was a story of the creation of the American flag, an episode involving George Washington and Betsy Ross. George M. Cohan probably never produced anything more certain of applause than when George Washington unfurled the first American flag in glowing color. Another subject was the divorce episode of Napoleon and Josephine, photographed in November, 1927, which was booked all over the world as a companion short to Charlie Chaplin's then tremendously successful production, *The Circus.* We made twelve of these two-reelers, an experience which established the fundamntals of our studio service both in the camera and color control departments, and altogether disclosed the answers to a multitude of practical questions which have served us no end since that time.

They were produced economically and yet we were continually praised about them by Metro who distributed them. In my opinion Technicolor would not have survived without the experience of this series of short subjects.

Our friends and customers both in Hollywood and New York praised and applauded these short subjects, *but* they were only shorts. Mr. Nicholas Schenck advised us to produce a feature production which Metro would distribute.

I had been much impressed with a production called *The Covered Wagon,* a touching love story with the epic quality of slowly and laboriously conquering a continent. Why not have a love story of the vikings with the epic quality of fighting mutiny and storms to conquer an ocean. Jack Cunningham, recently a writer and associate producer at Paramount, wrote *The Covered Wagon,* so we engaged him to write *The Viking.* We spent $325,000 on this production and got our full money's worth of experience in all departments. But also we got our money back. The late Irving Thalberg, who was always our friend and a believer in Technicolor, thought we had a lot of production for that amount of money, and bought it for Metro by reimbursing our cost to us.

There seemed to be two principal troubles with *The Viking,* both of which I suspected but without certainty. First, it came out among the very last silent pictures in 1929 and, second, whiskers. Lief Erickson, the viking hero, true to character, had a long, curling mustache, whereas American audiences prefer their lovers smooth-shaven. At times the whole screen seemed filled with viking whiskers. But the picture was a good color job and the first to be synchronized with music and sound effect.

But thus far we had only isolated feature productions. The building of color cameras on the scale they exist today, the building of laboratories of sufficient capacity that prints could be made cheaply enough to make color generally available could not be carried on in terms of an occasional picture.

We brought out two-color imbibition prints with silver sound track in 1928. The advantages in respect to focus, cupping, scratching, size of reel, and cost of manufacture were immediate. The gelatin on the Technicolor imbibition film is harder than on ordinary black and white, and through the years there is substantial evidence that the life of Technocolor imbibition prints is greater than that of ordinary black and white.

By early 1929 all the important studios in Hollywood had become thoroughly sound conscious. This was a great help to us in introducing color. Prior to that, studio executives were loathe to permit any change whatsoever in their established method of photography and production. But with the adoption of sound, many radical changes became necessary. Technicolor was always confronted with objections that photographing in color required more light, different costumes, a knowledge of color composition, additional time, and one or the other of these points, plus the added forceful argument that it cost more money, made it difficult for us to get started. In my opinion the turning point came when we ourselves produced the series of

short subjects. By entering the field as a producer, by keeping very careful records of our time and money schedules, and by openly discussing with studio executives everything that we were doing as we went along, we dissipated most of the prevailing misinformation. Meanwhile our quality was improving; our costs were decreasing. Warner Bros. and Metro-Goldwyn-Mayer were regularly coming out with satisfactory short subjects in Technicolor, and two inserts were highly successful, namely, *Broadway Melody* and *Desert Song.* Paramount had produced a successful feature length picture in Technicolor, *Redskin.* The studios were beginning to be *color* conscious.

But it remained for Warner Bros. and its affiliated company, First National, to take the first step on a *large* scale. Mr. J. L. Warner, with foresight and courage, signed up with us for a series of more than twenty features. These included *On with the Show,* the first all-talking all Technicolor feature picture, and *Gold Diggers of Broadway,* which has grossed over $3,500,000 and which still ranks high among the all-time outstanding box-office attractions. The Technicolor mechanical service of providing and maintaining cameras in good working order and of delivering rush prints on time was well established. Two more subtle departments of service, namely, helping producers' cameramen to learn how to light and operate to advantage in Technicolor, and consulting and advising in matters of color control, were being demanded. Cooperation under the head of color control was ranging all the way from deciding the details of the color composition of sets, choice of materials and costumes, to the broad planning and preparation of a picture by writing a color score after the manner in which the musical score is written.

As evidence of the increased color-mindedness throughout the industry, Technicolor had contracts for the ten months beginning March, 1929, covering the photography and delivery of prints of the footage equivalent of approximately seventeen feature length productions. This required a doubling of the Hollywood capacity which was accomplished in August, 1929. For the year 1930 Technicolor had closed contracts for thirty-six feature-length productions which would call for some 12,000,000 linear feet of negative to be sensitized, photographed and developed during that year in the Hollywood plant, and a print capacity of approximately 60,000,000 feet.

During this boom period of 1929 and 1930, more work was undertaken than could be handled satisfactorily. The producers pressed us to the degree that

cameras operated day and night. Laboratory crews worked three eight-hour shirts. Hundreds of new men were hastily trained to do work which properly required years of training. Many pictures were made which I counselled against, and all in the face of the fact that to book a picture in our crowded schedules called for a deposit of $25,000. At one time we had $1,600,000 of such cash payments.

Among the features photographed and released during this period were: *Bride of the Regiment,* Vivienne Segal (First National) ; *Bright Lights,* Dorothy Mackail (First National) ; *Doctor X,* Lionel Atwill and Fay Wray (Warner Bros.) ; *Fanny Foley Herself,* Edna May Oliver (RKO) ; *Fifty Million Frenchmen,* all-star cast (Warner Bros.) ; *Follow Thru,* Charles "Buddy" Rogers and Nancy Carroll (Paramount) ; *Gold Diggers of Broadway,* all-star cast (Warner Bros.) ; *Golden Dawn* (Warner Bros.) ; *Hold Everything,* Winnie Lightner, Georges Carpentier, and Joe E. Brown (Warner Bros.) ; *King of Jazz,* Paul Whiteman (Universal) ; *Kiss Me Again* (First National) ; *Life of the Party* (Warner Bros.) ; *Mamba* (Tiffany Productions) ; *Manhattan Parade* (Warner Bros.) ; *On with the Show,* all-star cast (Warner Bros.) ; *Runaround* (RKO) ; *Show of Shows* (Warner Bros.) ; *Song of the West,* John Boles and Vivienne Segal (Warner Bros.) ; *Song of the Flame,* Bernice Clair and Alexander Gray (First National) ; *Sweet Kitty Bellairs,* Claudia Dell and Perry Askam (Warner Bros.) ; *The Rogue Song,* Lawrence Tibbett and Catherine Dale Owen (Metro-Goldwyn-Mayer) ; *Sally,* Marilyn Miller (First National) ; *The Toast of the Legion,* Bernice Clair, Walter Pidgeon, and Edward Everett Horton (First National) ; *The Vagabond King,* Dennis King, Jeanette MacDonald (Paramount) ; *Under a Texas Moon,* Frank Fay, Noah Beery, Myrna Loy, and Armida (Warner Bros.) ; *Viennese Nights,* all-star cast (Warner Bros.) ; *Wax Museum,* Lionel Atwill (Warner Bros.) ; *Woman Hungry,* Sydney Blackmer and Lila Lee (First National) ; *Whoopee,* Eddie Cantor (Samuel Goldwyn and Florenz Ziegfeld) .

In Warner's *Wax Museum* and Goldwyn's *Whoopee* the Technicolor two-component process may have reached the ultimate that is possible with two components.

By reason of the fact in Technicolor of complete separation of the sound-track technic from the picture technic, the necessity (as in black-and-white procedure) of compromise between the sound and picture quality is avoided and relatively better sound-track should result. The first to take advantage of this was Ted Reed who was in charge of Mr. Goldwyn's sound department during the production of *Whoopee*. When that picture was shown in Hollywood the sound quality elicited much favorable comment and discussion among producers and technicians.

My greatest anxiety at the time was that there might be thrust upon the public productions which would be very crude in color composition and unfaithful in color reproduction. Our own color control department was doing everything possible to consult with and advise directors, authors, art directors, wardrobe heads, paint departments, and others in the studio, and this department was being expanded as fast as practicable. But there was more involved than questions of composition and design. There were the limitations of the process. As early as May 29, 1929, I reported to our directors: "The fact that we have signed this large volume of business on the basis of our present two-color process has not altered, in my opinion, the fact that the quality of this two-color output is not sufficiently good to meet with universal approval, and hence cannot be regarded as ultimate. I feel confident that the short-comings of our two-color process will be aided by the fact that they are combined with voice, and particularly by the fact that the work includes so many girl and music type productions like *Sally* with Marilyn Miller, and *Paris* with Irene Bordoni. Also this combination will offer a very considerable novelty angle for a time which is always important in the amusement world. Gradually, however, I believe the public will come to realize that these two-color pictures do not represent an ultimate natural color process. Consequently I feel urgently that our drive to put our process on a three-color basis as soon as possible should not in the least be abated because of our success in getting business on the two-color basis. This three-color work is moving ahead and involves a very considerable research department in Hollywood under the direction of Mr. J. A. Ball."

This premature rush to color was doomed to failure if for no other reason because the Technicolor process was then a two-color process. In the last analysis we are creating and selling entertainment. The play is the thing. You cannot make a poor story good by sound, by color, or by any other device or embellishment. But you can make a good story better. Broadway has a terrible struggle each season to find good stories or plays for a dozen successes. Hollywood is trying to find over five hundred. They don't exist. The industry needs all the help it can get, all the

showmanship it can summon—it needed sound; it needs color.

But color must be good enough and cheap enough. The old two-component Technicolor was neither—hence it failed, but it was a necessary step to present-day Technicolor.

During the rush to color, Technicolor had not only its own shortcomings to contend with, but also a surfeit of poor stories that were to be saved by color, and a monotony of musicals more or less on the same formula. An injustice was no doubt done Technicolor by causing it thus to be identified so largely with musical and period productions. I counselled at the time that producers were no doubt losing an opportunity in not taking advantage of the fact that color can be used to intensify dramatic effect and bring out the best points of personalities, advantages which have been later used with striking effectiveness.

During the years 1929 and 1930 Technicolor appropriated over $3,000,000 for plants, equipment, and research work, which increased its plant capacity from one million to six million feet of two-component prints a month. At the same time that it had been building those plants and training personnel to operate them, it had been filling its orders. Such conditions were not conducive to the highest quality product, even if the orders had been normal. The fact that this rush was largely forced upon Technicolor by the producers wouldn't help in the slightest degree with the exhibitor or the audience, even if they knew of it. And executives who were glad to try to work it out with us gradually over a period of time, were suddenly confronted with the necessity for drastic curtailment of their own budgets because of a sharp drop in motion picture theater attendance. At the peak of the rush Technicolor had twelve hundred men employed with a payroll of approximately $250,000 per month, whereas by the middle of 1931 these had dropped to two hundred thirty men and approximately $70,000. In the middle of 1931 picture production in Hollywood was at an extremely low ebb and the last week in July is said to have been the worst for theater receipts in fifteen years.

During 1931 the base price of Technicolor prints was reduced from 8¾ to 7 cents per foot.

But Technicolor had persisted in its research and development work so that by May, 1932, it had completed the building of its first three-component camera and had one unit of its plant equipped to handle a moderate amount of three-color printing. The difference between this three-component process

and the previous two-component process was truly extraordinary. Not only was the accuracy of tone and color reproduction greatly improved, but definition was markedly better.

However, we could not offer the three-component product to one customer without offering it to all, which required many more cameras, and the conversion of much of our plant. To allow time for this and to prove the process beyond any doubt, we sought first to try it out in the cartoon field. But no cartoonist would have it. We were told cartoons were good enough in black and white, and that of all departments of production, cartoons could least afford the added expense. Finally Walt Disney tried it as an experiment on one of his "Silly Symphonies." This first attempt was the delightful *Flowers and Trees,* following which Disney contracted for a series. For Christmas 1932 came *Santa's Work Shop,* the following Easter, *Funny Bunnies;* in May, 1933, came *Three Little Pigs,* which made screen history, and in March, 1934, *Big Bad Wolf.* I needn't relate the story of Disney's extraordinary success with Technicolor. The "Silly Symphonies" in Technicolor surpassed the "Mickey Mouses" in black and white, and then both Mickies and Sillies adopted Technicolor.

Both the Disney Company and Technicolor were rather undersized at birth and in recent years both have grown rapidly in importance. A frequent conversation has been as to which helped the other most. Much like the conversation between two Irishmen after a considerable session at the bar: "Yer know, Clancy, when I was born I weighed only five pounds." "Yer did, and did yer live?" "Did I live? Yer ought to see me now."

What Technicolor needed was someone to prove for regular productions, whether short subjects or features, what Disney had proved for cartoons. But the producers asked: "How much more will it cost to produce a feature in three-component Technicolor than in black and white?" This question is always with us and it seems to me the answer must be divided into two parts; the added cost of prints, negative raw stock, rushes, and lighting can be numerically calculated and requires little discussion. But then there are the less tangible elements about which there is much discussion. I have said to producers and directors on many occasions: "You have all seen Disney's *Funny Bunnies;* you remember the huge rainbow circling across the screen to the ground and you remember the Funny Bunnies drawing the color of the rainbow into their paint pails and splashing the Easter eggs. You all admit that it was marvelous entertainment. Now I will ask you how much more did it cost Mr. Disney to produce that entertainment in color than it would have in black and white?" The answer is, of course, that it could not be done at any cost in black and white, and I think that points to the general answer. A similar analogy can be drawn with respect to some part of almost any recent Technicolor feature.

If a script has been conceived, planned, and written for black and white, it should not be done at all in color. The story should be chosen and the scenario written with color in mind from the start, so that by its use effects are obtained, moods created, beauty and personalities emphasized, and the drama enhanced. Color should flow from sequence to sequence, supporting and giving impulse to the drama, becoming an integral part of it, and not something super-added. The production cost question should be, what is the additional cost for color per unit of entertainment and not per foot of negative. The answer is that it needn't necessarily cost any more.

In 1932 we marked our base print price down from 7 cents to 5½ cents a foot.

Early in 1933 Mr. Merian C. Cooper and Mr. John Hay Whitney began to show a practical interest in Technicolor. After thorough investigation of the Technicolor situation by Mr. Whitney and his associates, and as a result of many conferences, a contract was signed between Technicolor and Pioneer Pictures, Inc., on May 18, 1933, which provided for the production of eight pictures, superfeature in character and especially featuring color. There were some conditional clauses, among others a provision for extensive preliminary tests. Certain doubts remained in the minds of Whitney and his associates as to the performance of our three-component process under certain conditions. Would the process reproduce the various shades of green in woodland and jungle? For one story they were considering a lead with very dark coloring and black hair. Would she photograph satisfactorily against light backgrounds? For another story they thought of placing a decided blonde in the leading part; how would she photograph against various backgrounds? What about make-up? What about the visibility of extremely small figures in the distance. An exhaustive sets of tests were made with results satisfactory to Mr. Whitney and Mr. Cooper.

Then began the hunt for the first story to be produced. At one time Whitney told me they had given consideration to no less than two hundred stories.

While Mr. Whitney was searching, Pioneer Pictures made a very practical and complete test of the process by producing the picture La Cucaracha. This short subject met with tremendous success.

La Cucaracha, together with "Silly Symphonies," caused a tremendous interest in three-component Technicolor. The industry was now waiting to see what the first Whitney feature production would be like. Meantime Technicolor business was improving. Positive film shipments for the first six months of 1933 were double what they were for the first six months of 1932. Appropriation was made to increase the number of cameras under construction from three to seven.

The first test of the three-component process on a very large set was for Twentieth Century Fox on the closing sequence of The House of Rothschild.

Since Whoopee in 1930 Mr. Goldwin and I had talked regularly each year about another picture in Technicolor, so that on one occasion Eddie Cantor asked me if I were coming for my annual ritual. This time it was the closing sequence in his Cantor picture, Kid Millions, which was another important early three-component insert.

No amount of Technicolor adventures in the realm of producers would be complete without affectionate mention of Mr. Andrew J. Callaghan. He was a Vice-President of the company, active in sales and studio contracts through our most troublous times. He was Hollywood's most popular man—loved by all—and has been tremendously missed by everybody in Technicolor since his death in 1934.

Mr. Whitney and his Pioneer Pictures associates finally settled on Becky Sharp as their first production of the series of eight. Becky was a champion for hard luck. The original director, Lowell Sherman, was taken ill and died during the period of photographing. He was succeeded by Reuben Mamoulian. Unusual difficulty was encountered in the sound recording so that Mr. Whitney found himself in the ironically anomalous position of having produced the first three-component Technicolor feature, of having surmounted all the hazards of color, yet being in difficulty with an spect of the work which he had naturally taken for granted.

During the 1935-36 season we were manufacturing in the neighborhood of 2¾ million feet of prints a month, which included a larger volume of Warner Bros. short subjects than ever before and about forty per cent of all Metro-Goldwyn-Mayer short subjects.

A very interesting and important adventure in the history of Technicolor development was the organization of a British affiliate, Technicolor, Ltd., which I organized as a subsidiary of Technicolor Motion Picture Corp. and later developed in association with Sir Adrian Baillie, Mr. Alexander Korda, and The Prudential Assurance Company, Ltd.

The first Technicolor feature picture photographed in England was Wings of the Morning, a race-track story which has had very successful distribution throughout the world. This production was produced before the London laboratory was built, and was serviced from Hollywood. In 1936 the British laboratory was built at West Drayton, just outside of London where it is now regularly operating to service British made productions and prints of American made productions for distribution in the United Kingdom. Mr. Alexander Korda has been outspoken in his enthusiasm for color, as evidenced by a series of pictures which he has produced, including the current release Drums. He is now planning and all-Technicolor series of pictures, of which the first is The Four Feathers, at present being photographed in the Sudan.

Since Becky Sharp there have been produced at Hollywood and in London a large number of important feature productions in Technicolor, including: Adventures of Robinhood, Errol Flynn, Olivia de Havilland (Warner Bros.); A Star Is Born, Janet Gaynor and Fredric March (Selznick International Pictures); Drums, Valerie Hobson, Sabu, Raymond Massey (London Films Productions); Ebb Tide, Ray Milland, Frances Farmer (Paramount); Garden of Allah, Marlene Dietrich, Charles Boyer, Basil Rathbone, Joseph Schildkraut (Pioneer Pictures); God's Country and the Woman, George Brent, Beverly Roberts (Warner Bros.); Gold Is Where You Find It, George Brent, Olivia de Havilland (Warner Bros.); Goldwyn's Follies, all-star cast (Samuel Goldwyn Pictures, Inc.); Her Jungle Love, Dorothy Lamour, Ray Milland (Paramount); Men with Wings, Ray Milland, Louise Campbell, Fred MacMurray (Paramount); Nothing Sacred, Carole Lombard, Fredric March (Selznick International Pictures); Ramona, Loretta Young, Don Ameche (Twentieth Century Fox Productions); Sixty Glorious Years, Anna Neagle, Anton Walbrook (Herbert Wilcox); Snow White and the Seven Dwarfs, Walt Disney (RKO Pictures, Inc.); Trail of the Lonesome Pine, Sylvia Sidney, Fred MacMurray, Henry Fonda (Walter Wanger Productions); Tom Sawyer, Tommy Kelly, Anne Gillis (Selznick International Pictures); Valley of the Giants, Claire Trevor, Wayne Morris

(Warner Bros.) ; *Vogues of 1938,* Joan Bennett, Warner Baxter (Walter Wanger Productions) .

Generally speaking, these pictures have been extraordinarily well received, some of them having broken attendance records in many parts of the world. Thus Technicolor has met the second great rush into color with steadily improving quality of its product and a broadening range of service. It is the purpose of Technicolor, during the time that prints of any picture are being manufactured in its plant, to hold the laboratory open for and at the disposal of the customer as if it were his own. His representative may inspect each of his prints and any changes suggested will be undertaken if practicable. To do this he simply moves into the inspection room where each print before shipment is compared by simultaneous projection with a standard print approved by the customer for the purpose.

William Wellman who has directed more three-component Technicolor pictures than any other individual, all of them successes, namely, *A Star Is Born, Nothing Sacred,* and *Men with Wings,* has said repeatedly of Technicolor photography that he takes it in his stride, at substantially the same number of setups per day as black and white. It is noteworthy that most of the camera work is now done by cameramen in the direct employ of the studios.

Broadly considered, this recent array of feature pictures is of such a late date that it is too early to render a verdict based upon any sort of generalization with respect to them.

Looking ahead, Technicolor has contracts for about forty feature-length productions spread among most of the outstanding producers, constituting a very substantial volume of business. Among these there are now either being photographed or in preparation the following: *Dodge City,* Errol Flynn, Olivia de Havilland (Warner Bros.) ; *Gone with the Wind,* Clark Gable (Selznick International Pictures) ; *Heart of the North,* Dick Foran, Gloria Dickson (Warner Bros.) ; *Jesse James,* Tyrone Power, Henry Fonda, Nancy Kelly (Twentieth Century Fox) ; *Kentucky,* Loretta Young, Richard Greene, Walter Brennan (Twentieth Century Fox) ; *Little Princess,* Shirley Temple, Richard Greene, Anita Louise (Twentieth Century Fox) ; *Northwest Passage,* Robert Taylor, Spencer Tracy (Loew's, Inc.) ; *Sweethearts,* Jeannette MacDonald, Nelson Eddy, Frank Morgan, Ray Bolger (Loew's, Inc.) ; *The Light That Failed,* Ray Milland (Paramount) ; *The Mikado,* all-star (G. & S. Productions, Ltd.) ; *The Thief of Bagdad* (London Films Productions) ; *The*

Wizard of Oz, Judy Garland, Jack Haley, Bert Lahr, Ray Bolger (Loew's, Inc.) ; and a second feature-length production is being prepared by Walt Disney Enterprises, Inc.

To meet this growing volume of business Technicolor many months ago appropriated some $1,500,000 to increase the number of its cameras and to double its plant capacity. This expansion program is now well on its way to completion.

I have thus passed over rapidly the matter of eighteen pictures to be produced in Technicolor during the last part of this year and the first six months of next year, although they will probably represent an investment of some fifteen million dollars.

The foreign situation is becoming increasingly difficult. Sales to Germany, Spain, Japan, and China have practically ceased, and in many other foreign countries they are below normal. The Italian Government controls the entire distribution of films in Italy, which probably means that everything possible will be done to distribute Italian-made pictures at the expense of English and American-made pictures. To cope with the various regulations of censorship, the various languages requiring either superimposed titles or dubbing with new sound-track, has for years been difficult enough, but with the more recent quota laws, import duties, exchange difficulties, and especially in the face of the impossibility of getting money out of several foreign countries, to continue in the motion picture business there means adventures in other businesses, possibly including banking and politics. The establishment of Technicolor laboratories at various points over the world is a practical necessity and despite all these difficulties definite progress is being made.

About a year ago Technicolor established a department to contact exhibitors directly. Its representatives travel over the country to call upon exchange manager, theater managers, and projectionists. The purpose has been to study projection and screen conditions at the theater; to advise how to get the best results with Technicolor prints, to listen to complaints and establish good will, and particularly to obtain projectionist, manager, and audience reactions to productions in Technicolor. The results have been most gratifying; we have found that the public reaction to Technicolor pictures is extremely favorable and that exhibitors throughout the country are realizing more and more that Technicolor has great box-office value.

In the letter from Dr. Goldsmith, suggesting for himself and Mr. Crab-

tree, that I write this paper, he said, "I believe it would be of particular interest to the engineers and the industry if you cared to indicate how you happened to cling so tenaciously to these developments through the 'dark ages' when color motion pictures were not so well appreciated." All I have said points to the answer; it was marvelously interesting; it was great fun; we couldn't let anybody down, neither customers, employees, stockholders, nor directors. But there was something else too; there was always something just ahead, a plan for tomorrow, something exciting to be finished—yes, and something more to be finished after that; and I am willing to predict that it won't be finished for many years yet. The type of film which will be standard for natural color pictures ten years hence may not yet have emerged. I predict that within two years Technicolor will have done away with special cameras and be regularly employing single strips of negative through any standard motion picture camera and that within two months for special purposes and within six month for more general purposes it will be offering to its customers a negative for use in its present cameras with from three to four times the speed of its present negative. That's why we cling so tenaciously; there's always something ahead; there always will be; our pride is enlisted; it's our job.

DISCUSSION

Mr. Crabtree: I have been greatly impressed by the way in which color develops the loveliness of the ladies, especially the blondes and the redheads. Are the producers sold on the fact, and do they make screen tests of potential stars in both color and black and white?

Dr. Kalmus: The program of testing is always with us. There has been no end of tests, both in black and white and in color, for comparative purposes. Relatively few are being made now; many producers think they are not necessary.

Mr. Crabtree: I have been wondering whether the usual methods of inserting backgrounds are being used with Technicolor. Were there very many background shots in *Men with Wings?*

Dr. Kalmus: We do projection background work regularly.

Mr. Crabtree: Is it as flexible as with black and white?

Dr. Kalmus: Not quite, but sufficiently flexible to be very practicable.

Mr. Wolf: I understand Technicolor will be available in a single film for use in standard cameras. Will the processing be difficult or will it be as simple as with black and white?

Dr. Kalmus: That is getting into a realm I am avoiding for the present. However, I think it will be some time before the processing will be as simple as black-and-white, if ever. The program as we have it outlined will be simple and practicable as compared with the programs we have been through before.

MR. KELLOGG: When you have a two-color system, do you leave some silver in the film in order to get some black in addition to what you get from the dyes?

DR. KALMUS: The two-component system was strictly two-component. The present system is really four-component—the three components ordinarily thought of as the color components, and black.

MR. THOMAS: Have you obtained any data of value, from the projection standpoint, from the questionnaires sent out with the prints of *Goldwyn Follies?*

MR. RACKETT: We have received valuable information from the projectionists' comments on the cards sent to theaters in advance of the showing of Technicolor pictures.

The comments may be divided into two classes: first, those referring to the physical condition of the film, which have occavisibility of instruction titles and changeover cue marks; the second, relating to the density and color values of prints, which are a little more difficult to classify as they have to be interpreted in connection with data from our field division relating to projection equipment.

Most theaters are epuipped with high-intensity arcs which produce a screen image that is slightly bluish. Technicolor prints are balanced to yield a neutral image on such a screen.

Small projection units equipped with Mazda light produce a screen image that is slightly orange. When a print balanced for a high-intensity arc is projected by a Mazda light the screen result will be slightly orange.

When we are establishing the density and color balance of a feature picture, we make a series of prints and usually arrange to view these with the producer of the picsioned our making minor changes in the ture in a number of first-run theaters, as far as time permits. We then compare a number of prints in a room where we can project simultaneously on matched screens as many as six prints of the same reel. We get a comparison of such fineness that we have not been able to find quantitative methods of measuring the differences.

All the data, including the important and welcome comments of the projectionists on the print comment cards attached to the print suggestion booklets, are very helpful in establishing the final results.

MR. GRIFFIN: How quickly is the rush print available in the three-component process after the negatives leave the camera?

DR. KALMUS: Regular twenty-four hour service.

My First Fifty Years in Motion Pictures*

By OSCAR B. DEPUE**

Summary.—*This is an intimate, chronological account of the author's experiences as a partner of the world's leading travelog exponent, Burton Holmes. Their first meeting is described in 1893 as well as their world-wide wanderings through the years up to 1917, and the problems encountered in devising camera, developing, projection, and film-printing equipment in those early days. The period from 1917 to date is concerned with the establishment of the Burton Holmes Films Laboratory, the theatrical release of a weekly travelog for six years, and the author's invention and manufacture of 35-mm and 16-mm printers and automatic light-control boards.*

In 1887 I was employed by the McIntosh Battery and Optical Company in Chicago, a firm operated by Dr. McIntosh, inventor and designer of many electrical and optical devices for the medical profession. The doctor gave many lectures before medical students and medical conventions. Work with him gave me the opportunity to learn the art of slide projection, microscopic work, and the handling of battery appliances and static machines for doctors' offices.

Ultimately, in addition to assisting Dr. McIntosh, I became a projectionist for other doctors and for various public lectures. I was frequently sent out of the city and my ingenuity was taxed in overcoming the difficulties of installing projectors and screens in a wide variety of halls, churches, and theaters which, at that time, had little equipment of their own. The illumination for stereopticon projectors was the calcium light. In fact, this was the only illumination even up to the time of motion pictures, and we used it for them during the years of 1897, 1898, and 1899.

It was while working with Dr. McIntosh that I first met Burton Holmes, who was searching for someone to project some lantern slides that he had made in Japan in 1892. He had brought back enough snapshots of the country to give an evening's entertainment or lecture on his travels. For his initial tryout on the Chicago public, he rented the recital hall on the seventh floor of the Auditorium building, counting quite heavily on his family's acquaintanceship with many of Chicago's society leaders.

This tryout in November, 1893, The World's Fair year, was a complete success—even with only the four performances planned. The hall seated about three hundred and fifty persons, and before the series was completed, the audience was sitting on camp stools in the aisles. That was the beginning of my association with Burton Holmes which eventually led to motion pictures and my work today.

---

*Presented Apr. 21, 1947, at the SMPE Convention in Chicago.
**Oscar B. Depue and Burton Holmes Films, Inc., Chicago, Ill.

In 1895 I traveled in Europe taking still pictures with Mr. Holmes. The trip was a bicycle tour through England, France, Corsica, Italy, and Switzerland. The pictures were made into hand-colored stereopticon slides which we showed in the winter at lectures in an ever-widening circle of cities.

In 1896 we realized that we had a growing rival—the motion picture. As a result, in 1897, at the end of the 1896 season, Mr. Holmes sailed for Sicily and Italy and I sailed for London, the Mecca for motion pictures at that time. My intention was to search out and buy a motion picture camera. I found little from which to choose, and the prices were exhorbitant. I was forced to go to Paris to see what I could find there. The situation was almost as bad—with one exception. Mr. Leon Gaumont had a Demeny camera for 60-mm film—the only machine that I could find in all of Paris. It was not what you would call a facile piece of apparatus; it was cumbersome and its tripod was a piece of two-inch plank fitted with solid iron legs (not adjustable). I was somewhat fearful of what I could do with this equipment, but nevertheless I purchased it and took the first train to Rome to join Mr. Holmes.

It was there that I made my first motion picture exposure. I chose St. Peter's Cathedral and the great Piazzo with its obelisk and fountains as a subject—a subject, I admit, that lacked animation until a herder with his flock of goats passed in front of the fountain to give it movement.

It may seem ridiculous now to consider that then I thought I must always have some famous background for my motion pictures. I had not quite broken away from still photography enough to realize that movement was the chief function of motion pictures.

That photographic expedition led me to Naples, Venice, and Milan and then up to Paris again where I took just one motion picture. This was of the Place de la Concorde—a scene that had *real* animation. I secured the picture by planting a cab at the busiest place in the Concorde. With the driver's seat for my tripod, I was able to photograph the teeming traffic at close

range. The police remonstrated with me vigorously for blocking traffic, but I "failed to comprehend" what they were after until I had finished what I was after—fifty feet of picture.

This negative and those made previously in Italy were taken to the Gaumont studio for development. I left the negatives with them in exchange for one print from each. Some fifteen years later, Mr. Gaumont graciously sent us these negatives, which are now in the Burton Holmes Films' storage vaults.

My next step was to return home and start to get equipment together for developing, printing, and projecting these motion pictures and others that I was soon to make of New York, Yellowstone Park, and other points of interest.

En route, I stopped in Rochester to visit the Eastman Kodak Company and had an interview with Mr. George Eastman. He agreed to cut film, both negative and positive, in a 60-mm width for me. He also gave me some ideas of how he thought I might build a printer.

I did build the printer, following his ideas and some of my own. It was a very amusing gadget when I look back at it today. The printer was mounted on a wall in a darkroom, with a hole through the wall to admit the exposure light from a lamp in the next room. The lamp was mounted on a rod so that I could slide it nearer or farther away from the film to suit the density of the negative which was observed as it passed in front of a slit. The lamp, mind you, was a Welsbach gas lamp—no such luxury as the electric light which came two years later.

The major problem of providing power to operate the printer was solved with a small water-wheel motor that I attached to the water faucet in my basement. This power, little as it was, was sufficient to drive the printing machine and a film perforator which I built as well. All this equipment had to be completed in time to have the films ready to be shown in the fall of 1897.

In addition, I had to convert the Gaumont camera into a projector. It proved to be quite satisfactory. The motion pictures were shown after Mr. Holmes' lecture proper, as a fifteen- or twenty-minute added attraction. With the spontaneous outburst of applause that followed the first roll, we had the great satisfaction of feeling that it was a real success, which, indeed, it proved to be during the rest of the season. As far as I know, these programs in the fall of 1897 marked the first time that motion pictures were used by any public lecturer in this country.

By the end of the 1898 season, I had constructed a larger camera which would accommodate 200-foot rolls of negative. I also made some improvement on a portable tripod. This equipment was taken to the Grand Canyon of the Colorado for the *first motion pictures* made of that great sight.

We then went on to Honolulu for a tour of the Hawaiian Islands. The American troops were passing through Honolulu on their way to Manila, for the Philippines had come into our possession through Dewey's victory at Manila Bay.

Returning from Hawaii, we stopped again at the Grand Canyon to make more footage and also visited the Hopi Indians' snake dance at Oraibi to make the very first motion pictures of such a ceremony. One year later I returned to photograph a snake dance at Walpi, the largest of the region's villages.

This second visit afforded an opportunity to show the Indians the pictures taken the year before so, on my way back to Canyon Diablo to take the train for home, I spent a few days at an Indian trading post called "The Lakes" run by Mr. Volz. My projecting equipment, a calcium-light outfit, and tanks of oxygen and hydrogen had been sent out in advance. Through Mr. Volz's co-operation, we gathered an audience which I believe was the most interesting I've ever seen. We set the projector in the back end of a lumber wagon and attached the screen to the side of the trading post. Several hundred Indians squatted around in circles on the ground waiting for something to happen.

In addition to the snake-dance pictures, I had photographed some Indian sports at the same location. One of these was called a "Gallo Contest." A rooster was buried up to its neck in sand, then the riders swooped past, leaned down, and attempted to pluck it from the ground without falling from their horses. You can hardly call this a humane sport, but it was the Indians' idea of fun—not mine. And you can imagine the reaction of my audience, who had never seen movies before, when they saw their own actions reproduced on the screen.

Another "sport" which I had photographed was the pursuit of a white girl on a fleet pony by a band of one hundred mounted Indian braves. The Indians entered into the chase with such zeal that I feared for the girl's safety and that of my camera as they raced by at full tilt. This part of the film made a hit too—but the high spot of the evening came with a mad scramble away from the screen when I showed pictures I had made of the Empire State Express dashing toward the camera, and of the Omaha Fire Department in action. Seats "front and center" went begging after that, but finally the Indians' fears were allayed and the show went on.

One of the pictures taken the year before showed a storekeeper of the post who had since died. There was a shout from the Indians when they saw him and his dog on the screen. The "magic" of the movies made fans of them very quickly and the next time I wanted to film their games, I had no trouble in obtaining the assistance of the whole tribe. When the show was over, the audience was curious to know where the pictures came from; they touched the screen and looked behind it, but strangely enough paid no attention to the projector in the wagon.

In 1899 I built a new camera with a capacity of 400 feet of negative. It had some modern conveniences such as a footage counter, a punch for marking scenes, and a film magazine which allowed loading and threading of the camera in daylight. However, in unloading, the film had to be removed from the camera in a changing bag, or in the darkroom. I had also built an improved projector which was patented on April 4, 1899.

In 1900 I spent my time building a portable developing outfit for a trip around the world. This trip, in 1901, took us first to Berlin, Warsaw, St. Petersburg, and then to Moscow where the trans-Siberian railway journey started. Before leaving Moscow, however, I hired some carpenters to make the wooden tanks to go with the developing racks which I had made at home—but the difficulty I experienced in getting the work done and the poor workmanship convinced me that I should wait until we reached Japan before building the drying racks which I also needed. There I found clever carpenters who constructed them quickly. Each rack held 200 feet of 60-mm film, and weighed twelve pounds. They folded down to fit into a box about four feet long and ten inches square.

The journey across Siberia was a memorable one. The trans-Siberian railroad only extended as far as Stratensk, a town three days' travel beyond Lake Baikal. After waiting there for several days, we secured passage on a river steamer for the first leg of a long journey down the Shilka and Amur rivers to Khabarovsk. The steamer stuck on the first sand bar, so we were transferred to one of shallower draft. We were on many boats before the trip was finished; in most of them we had to sleep on the upper deck—if there was one. Many of these craft were open barges. They got stuck the same as the steamer so on several occasions we were obliged to change to other barges with less draft. Each transfer lightened the load of the one that was stuck, so that it could be floated again.

We were twenty-eight days on this river trip, but finally we landed at Khabarovsk and proceeded by rail to Vladivostock. As soon as passage could be secured, we took a steamer to Nagasaki and from thence to Korea where we visited Fusan and Seoul, the capital.

From Seoul we went to Peking where the Boxer Rebellion had just been subdued. We saw troops of all the allies that took part in the siege—they were still there and in other parts of China. It was an opportune time for our visit because we were allowed, through the aid of our own troops, to see and film things that might not have been available to us otherwise. For instance, a company of American troops from Indiana guarded the north half of the Emperor's Palace in the Forbidden City. Japanese troops were stationed at the south half—our allies at that time—if not forty years later.

We sailed from Chefoo, China, returning to Nagasaki again where we took the train to Tokyo. We made a number of pictures in Japan, and in September I set about developing them and all the rest taken since leaving Moscow. I was permitted to use the old clubhouse of the Yokohama club near the Grand Hotel. The developing caused little difficulty, but the question of drying the film in that very damp and heatless building was a critical one. I had film looped all over the place. It refused to dry thoroughly and finally I was forced to coil it up the best I could in order to sail on the *Coptic* for America. I finished the drying job in my stateroom aboard ship. This experience and previous ones convinced us that 60-mm films were more difficult to handle than the smaller 35-mm that had become standard. In addition, by being off-standard, we could not always obtain film when we needed it, nor could we sell our wide film to the trade. In short, the 60-mm was passe.

The next year, 1902, I purchased a 35-mm Bioscope camera from the Warwick Trading Company in London and put it to work on our tour of Norway, Denmark, and Sweden. It was in Norway that I conceived the idea of making single-frame exposures at intervals to speed up the action seen from the bow of our steamer as it sailed through the turning, twisting fjords of that beautiful country.

In Bergen, I found a watchmaker who made me a small crank which was attached to the camera's pull-down mechanism in such a way that a single turn of the crank exposed one picture. By closing the shutter to a mere ⅛ inch wide, the exposure was about right although it depended on the speed at which the crank was turned.

Thus equipped, I planted my camera in the very bow of a steamer and by carefully observing the steamer's movements as it went straight ahead or turned for the bends in the fjords, I could increase or decrease the number of exposures to fit the apparent movement of the foreground. This first experiment, made on a short trip from Vick to Ulvick, proved quite satisfactory, but before ending our Norway trip to Christiania (Oslo) I had a chance to make a "fast" motion picture that turned out to be very successful. It showed a series of seven locks, with our steamer going into the top one and down through all the rest, then sailing away. By making single exposures at proper intervals, the action was condensed to a very short time on the screen. I really had to scramble to get the picture and then board the steamer again.

That picture was probably the first example of that type of cinematography —which we called "crazy pictures." It so impressed the Bioscope people that one of the principles, Mr. Charles Urban, asked us to leave the negative with him so that he could sell prints on a royalty basis. It was not a bad deal for us because many prints were sold. The short fjord picture was used also.

Several years later (in 1907) I made another trip to Norway and took "crazy pictures" the whole distance of a fjord journey of 120 miles. It was shown in about three minutes on the screen and gave a very good impression of such a journey. By this time I had constructed a shutter and crank that equalized the exposures. They no longer depended on how fast the crank was turned; the shutter, similar to a focal plane shutter, was activated by a spring which always gave the same exposure.

In 1903 we toured Alaska, taking the railroad over the White Horse Pass to White Horse, and then a stern-wheel steamer down the Yukon to Dawson. There we filmed the gold miners and their sluicing and hydraulic operations. During the remainder of our journey down the Yukon and on to Nome, we traveled and slept on a barge lashed to a river steamer. Returning from Nome to Seattle on the *Ohio* we passed through the Aleutian Islands with never a thought that they would one day be the scene of fierce encounters between Japs and Americans.

In 1905 we visited Germany and Austria again. We also visited Ireland, touring leisurely by jaunting car. This acquainted us with the country much more intimately than the usual trip by rail.

In 1906 we made an extended trip through Egypt, going up the Nile on a private yacht to the town of Wadi Halfa near the second cataract. On the way we visited the Valley of the Tombs of the Kings, the Temples of Luxor, and the Pyramids. We climbed Cheops, the largest Pyramids, and photographed other American tourists as they struggled up those great three-foot steps. All the films taken in Egypt were developed in Shepherd's Hotel in Cairo—a wonderful place at a wonderful time of the year—the last part of March.

Next we sailed for Italy, arriving in the Bay of Naples on April 8, just as the famous eruption of Vesuvius took place. This was the largest eruption in 300 years and it blew off the whole top of the mountain. We went ashore as soon as possible, secured hotel accommodations, then drove some fourteen miles to the base of Vesuvius. There we saw the great flow of lava which came down from its sides. The lava was engulfing and burning the homes of farmers and villagers. Part of the lava had cooled sufficiently to allow us to scale it and just as darkness came on, the lightning played around the top of the mountain, creating a wonderful display. Simultaneously we became aware of a veritable snowstorm of ashes falling on us, so we turned toward Naples in a hurry. The drive back through the blinding ash storm was a terrifying, wearying experience.

When we finally got back to our hotel, we found that only three guests remained out of about eighty that had been staying there that morning. The rest had left to get as far away as possible. That night two inches of ash fell on Naples and tremendous quantities fell on the slopes of Vesuvius.

We set sail from Brindisi for Greece and went by rail from Patras to Athens where the Olympic Games were being held. A memorable thing about the rail journey was that passengers getting on at a way station had Greek newspapers telling of another great tragedy caused by nature — the San Francisco earthquake and fire.

Filming the Olympic Games was a pleasant task. One of my best pictures was of the high-diving contest at Phalaron. Among the contestants was Annette Kellerman making her European debut and besides putting on a marvelous exhibition, she created a stir by introducing the one-piece bathing suit. Even though the suit was perhaps two or three times larger in area than those we see at the beaches today, it was considred very daring in that day and age.

We returned to Naples where I searched for a suitable darkroom in which to develop the Olympic Games pictures. I found a small photographic studio operated by a young Austrian who rented it to me for a few days so that I could set up my portable developing machine. The ashes from Vesuvius were still falling and I had considerable trouble in keeping the films clean.

This young Austrian offered to assist Mr. Holmes in photographing around Naples when it became necessary for me to return to Chicago. He became intensely interested in motion picture work and asked Mr. Holmes how he might go about getting into it on a permanent basis. Mr. Holmes gave him a letter of introduction to Mr. Charles Urban in London. The young man spent several weeks studying English to prepare for the interview, only to find that Mr. Urban spoke German as well as he did.

The young man was hired and in four weeks time absorbed all that the Bioscope Laboratory could teach. Then Mr. Urban sent him to South Africa to make motion pictures of the diamond mines at Kimberley and the great Victoria Falls of the Zambesi River. The films that he sent back were excellent in quality; no detail had been overlooked in the taking and packing. Urban was so pleased that he sent the young man to India at the time of the Durbar to photograph the processions and ceremonies of the Coronation in Kinema-color—probably the first great event ever photographed in color. I saw these films at the Alhambra in London where they ran for over a year.

You may wonder who this young man is. I think that most of you know him—Joseph De Frenes—who today has a motion picture production business in Philadelphia.

I have mentioned previously the second trip to Norway in 1907 to make another film of the fjord trips. It was on this trip that I purchased a Poulson wire recorder in Copenhagen. It was driven by a direct-current 110-volt motor, and so I was able to operate it in my steamer cabin while en route home. I had a lot of fun talking into it and playing back, and soon had a procession of passengers eager to record and hear their own voices. Several theatrical notables were present, including the famous Jimmie Powers who had just finished a London season. He was full of hit songs and stories, so we recorded a few. When he finished, I spoke into the recorder saying that Powers' record was made on the twenty-eighth day of August, 1907, in mid-ocean aboard the S.S.

Augusta Victoria.

Thirty years later, aided by Walter Hotz, Burton Holmes Films' sound engineer, I re-recorded Powers' voice on film. The wire had retained the record as clearly as when it was first made. When amplified, it appeared to have lost none of its original quality, although it may have lost some volume.

This re-recording was presented to the Society of Motion Picture Engineers at a time when wire recording was again in the limelight. Today there is a strong possibility of its having widespread use in the film industry.

In 1908 we made our second world tour, going first to Hawaii, Japan, and China. From Hong Kong we took a Dutch freighter to Java, a voyage of eight days. The ship was manned by seven or eight Hollanders and a Malay and Chinese crew. The other passengers, besides the two of us, were two Japanese and two hundred and fifty coolies on their way to work in the tin mines on the Isle of Banka just off Sumatra.

One day some petty incident caused a near riot which had us fearing for our lives until the Hollanders put the whole lot down the hatchway and fastened down the cover. It sounds easy when you tell it, but it took a lot of "doing." It was very interesting to watch a handful of men handle a mob of two hundred and fifty coolies without bloodshed. They used a number of sticks which landed where they did the most good and thus achieved order again—much to our relief.

From Banka we took a little coastal steamer for a two-day run to Batavia, Java. The craft was so crowded with Javanese, Chinese, and Japanese that it was difficult to find a place to sleep on the deck.

Sometimes things were not only different, they were difficult. This was especially true in regard to our photographic equipment. For instance, Mr. Holmes had a Gaumont 9- $\times$ 12-centimeter hand camera with a delicate shutter which failed as soon as we started photographing in Batavia. One of the leaves of the shutter had broken. It took a gunsmith three days to make a new one which, after half a day's photographing, broke too. I decided that this time I would do the fixing. A tin can provided material for a new leaf. In my developing kit was a small Godell Pratt drill which I clamped to a table so that it served as a turning lathe. I turned out a couple of rivets from brass pins, and attached the leaf to the shutter and then blackened it. Strange as it may seem this improvised shutter served very well for the rest of the tour and the resulting pictures were

as good as those made before the mishap. From that time on I carried an ample tool kit which proved its worth many times.

Developing film in Java was another problem. While in Batavia, we stayed in a "hotel" hungalow which had a square concrete bathtub which I used for developing, but I had to wait until two o'clock in the morning for sufficient coolness. Even then the water was never cooler than 86 degrees for it came from a tank in the patio exposed to the hot sun during the day. The tank was filled by coolies who carried the water from a well some distance away.

I solved the problem by using ice, which was a scarce item, to cool the developer. I could never get enough for the hypo and wash too, so I fixed the film hurriedly, and gave it a short rinse, thus avoiding loosening of the emulsion. When we returned to the United States I refixed and rewashed all the film and lost none as a result of it all.

The discomfort and inconvenience of the heat in Java in midsummer were compensated for by the interest that the country provided. Our round-trip railroad journey took us from one end of Soerabaja at the other. We passed many beautiful terraced rice fields on the mountainsides and many quaint villages and visited mountain resorts and historical monuments such as Boro Bodor, Soerakarta, and Djokjakarta. Each night was spent at a station hotel becuse there were not enough night travelers to make train operation pay and besides it was rather dangerous.

When our train returned to Batavia, I discovered that my film case was missing. I thought that it had been stolen, but the hotel manager said not to worry and he telegraphed an alarm over the entire rail system. In an hour he had an answer. When I had gone into the diner, the train stopped at Padalarang, a junction. The porter removed my film case by mistake and put it on a train bound for Buitenzorg at the end of the other line. The wire further stated that the case would be back on th next train to Batavia—and it was. The hotel man said that pilferage and robbery were rare things in Java because escaping the law was too difficult on such an island.

After leaving Java, we spent a few days in Singapore and then went on to Ceylon to visit the tea plantations. Colombo, the seaport, was uncomfortably hot, but in Kandy, 2500 feet above sea level, we found the temperature at 75 degrees—an ideal climate. I had no trouble developing films there, and set to work immediately, for I had found out years before that film should be developed as soon as possible after ex-

posure — especially old film. I had tested exposed film which had not been developed for two years and found it had lost the image entirely. However, if such film were re-exposed and developed immediately, it gave a beautiful negative with no sign of the first exposure.

Rio de Janeiro in April, 1911, was delightful, but we could not tarry. The day after our arrival we were bound for Argentina and Chile. We found Buenos Aires a magnificently laid-out city, an exciting new experience. It was booming, with new streets and buildings being built everywhere. Our hotel, the Plaza, was brand new, having just opened before our arrival.

By train we crossed the great plain called La Pampa to Mendoza at the foothills of the Andes and up those rugged mountains to a resting place called the Bridge of the Incas. So thrilled were we with the awesome scenery en route that, through the cooperation of the railroad company, we did our filming from the engine's cowcatcher. This gave us an unobstructed front view, but, at the same time, the natives had an unobstructed view of us as we perched there an a sofa-like seat secured to the cowcatcher. A ludicrous sight no doubt—but we did not mind so long as we got our pictures. It was rough riding at times—in fact, the jiggling finally put my camera out of commission. But the knowledge gained in similar experiences in Java, and a good day's work with my tool kit put the camera in working order again.

We left the train at an elevation of 10,000 feet and proceeded on horseback to the great statue of the Christus, over 13,000 feet up in the bleak, snow-covered pass.

We found Valparaiso partially in ruins from an earthquake similar to the one that devastated San Francisco five years before. Santiago offered a number of good camera subjects and a hotel which proved excellent as a place to develop the films taken so far. I kept at it so late one night that I had to miss dinner. But a handy fruit stand supplied me with the most delicious pears I have ever eaten. Some of them were cactus pears. The climate in that region is very much like Southern California, but California never gave me pears so tasty.

Our return over the trans-Andine railroad occurred in a midwinter snow. That line was abandoned a few years later because of the difficulty in keeping it open and the costly repairs resulting from the rough going through the passes. Today, people cross by plane several hundred miles to the south over a beautiful lake region, not snow-clad mountains.

In Buenos Aires we heard of the great Iguassu Falls, an eleven days' journey north up the Rio de la Plata and the Alto Parana. The river steamer took us to within thirteen miles of the falls; the rest of the way was traveled by wagon over a road cut through the jungle. Because of the rapid growth of plants and trees, the road had to be cleared every two weeks to keep it open.

The difficulty of reaching the falls was forgottn when we beheld them—the most beautiful series of cataracts in the world. And to have the opportunity of being the first to photograph them successfully made the trip even more worth while. We carefully filmed each group of falls — the colorful, inspiring Brazilian group, the Argentine, the Three Muskateers, and the Union, which drops 220 feet in one great plunge. We remained there nearly a week and slept on crude bunks in a barn with only the rats to keep up company. But we had the constant roar of the falls to lull us to sleep—an even better sleep-producer than lapping waves or rippling brooks.

When we returned to Rio de Janeiro, we chose the hotel Corcovado, up 2300 feet where the temperature was ideal for developing. Well do I remember standing on the site where now the great statue of Christ is located. I photographer a sunset and far below, the lights of the city and of the great seaside boulevards as they twinkled on at dusk. While I was turning a slow series and not making any noise, suddenly a wild fox leaped out on the sheer slanting rock not over twenty feet in front of me. As soon as he saw me, he turned carefully and fled. I say carefully because one misstep would have meant a fall of one hundred feet or more.

Time will not permit me to tell of other foreign journeys to the Orient and European lands and in our own United States. The tour of the Philippines in 1913 was one of the high spots in our careers.

I must touch briefly, however, on our association with the Paramount Company for whom we had contracted to produce weekly releases of our tours from 1908 to 1922. This resulted in six years of unbroken weekly travelog releases in Paramount Theaters.

And so I come to the end of my first fifty years of motion picture work, stretching back through the years to 1893 when Burton Holmes and I first met. But the final chapter is still in the making — for we both are still going strong. He is carrying on his lectures and packing the houses all over the country, and I am busy every day, turning out Depue printers. Surely we two have been fortunate in having the opportunity to "grow up" with the motion picture industry and to choose phases of it in which we were intensely interested. Certainly we "got what we wanted."

Gaumont Chronochrome Process Described by the Inventor

By LEON GAUMONT

Editorial Note: *A paper found among the effects of Leon Gaumont after his death in 1946 describes his early attempts to sychronize sound and image and discusses apparatus which he invented, such as the Chronophonograph and the Elgephone. As a tribute to this inventor, whose name is on the Honor Roll of the Society, and for the interest it may hold for contemporary scientists and inventors, the Historical and Museum Committee has contributed the following translation. Special assistance was given by L. J. J. Didiee of Paris in connection with the obtaining and preparing of this paper.*

My FIRST METHOD of synchronizing sound and image was presented at a meeting of the Photographic Society in Paris on November 9, 1902. Although the idea of synchronization was not new, the first patents on this subject had just appeared at that time. Serious attempts had been made previously, especially by the French inventor, Baron, the principles of whose method have been partly incorporated in my method.

The phonograph was the most delicate of the two kinds of apparatus used in this sound motion-picture projection presentation. It had to assume the functions of an orchestra leader, that is to say, an instrument controlling the motion-picture projector. Since the projector and the phonograph cannot be

A contribution received on October 2, 1958, from John B. McCullough, Motion Picture Assn. of America, 28 W. 44 St., New York 36, Chairman of the Historical and Museum Committee.

placed side by side, one would think of connecting these two units by a flexible cable. However, in this instance, cables were impractical, in view of the distance of several meters between the two apparatus and the impracticality of using cables for the synchronization of sound and image.

For this reason an electrical transmission was designed. A dynamo with a split circuit was connected to the phonograph and its speed adjusted to the normal speed of the latter. The dynamo was connected with the projector drive motor through a rheostat mounted on the projector base. If both units were started at the same time, they ran in perfect synchronism (Fig. 1).

The Chronophonograph

The first Chronophonograph was also presented to the Photographic Society on the same day, which gave the audience a glimpse of what they probably could expect in future meetings of the Society.

Since that time we have constantly improved distant sound recording by amplifying the emission from the phonograph, and on July 17, 1902, we presented the following films marking our introduction of sound motion pictures:

1. Introduction by Mr. Wallon
2. Lecture by Mr. D'Arsonval at the Academy of Sciences
3. *Double Tax* by Mr. R. Champigny (two persons)
4. *The Dentist* monologue by Mr. M. Zamacois
5. *Crowing Rooster*
6. *Telephone Communication* by Mr. Galipaux
7. *Banjo Player*
8. *At the Dentist's* by Mr. H. Francois (three persons)
9. *Voices of the Night* by Mr. Versse

The equipment used in this demonstration represented the results of all our previous experimentation.

The fact that the loudspeaker was placed near the projection screen, while the projector was at a great distance from it, created the necessity of additional electrical design.

Since the phonograph had to be operated at the same speed as the original recording to maintain proper

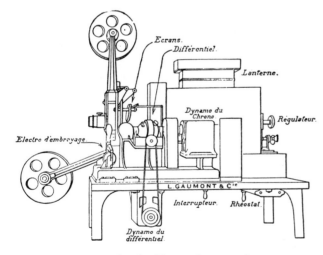

Fig. 1. Arrangement for the Chronophonograph.

Electro d'embrayage	electric clutch
Ecrans	fire shutter
Différentiel	differential
Lanterne	lamphouse
Régulateur	carbon feed
Interrupteur	switch
Dynamo du chrono	projector dynomotor
Dynamo du différentiel	differential motor

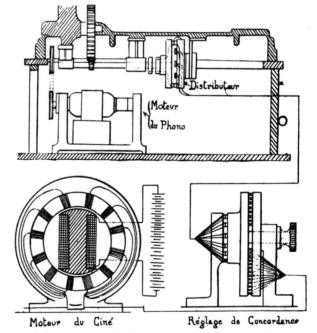

Fig. 2. The Synchronization Regulator.

Réglage de concordance	synchronization regulator
Moteur du ciné	projection motor
Moteur du phono	phonograph motor

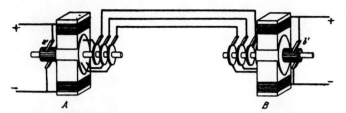

Fig. 3. Armatures of motors connected to turn at same angular displacement.

sound quality, and with the projector speed depending upon the phonograph, slight corrections, which became necessary due to the differences of one movement with respect to another, were made by means of a synchronization regulator (Fig. 2).

Several methods of connecting the apparatus were patented by our organization. One uses two small shunt d-c motors of almost the same power and supplied by the same current source.

The armatures of these motors contained the same number of sections, and each section of one armature was connected with a corresponding section of the other armature and in the same order. Consequently, the first armature turned at the same angular displacement as the second (Fig. 3).

The first armature controlled the phonograph and the second the projector. Synchronization was obtained by adjusting the speed of unwinding of the motion-picture film to the speed of the disk recording.

Some time after this presentation it was learned that the same synchronization method had been patented by E. Thompson for the operation of looms. The General Electric Co., owner of this patent, kindly granted the Gaumont Company the right to use this patent for the special purpose of obtaining synchronization of the phonograph and projector. It is, of course, understood that photography and sound recording were made simultaneously by synchronizing the sound recorder with the camera.

Synchronization of sound and image was perfect, provided the simple precaution was taken of placing the first image in the projector picture gate and at the same time the needle at the extreme start of the disk.

In later models the projector was started electrically by placing a contact on the phonograph disk. A rheostat in the motor circuit controlled the speed of both and kept the projector in accurate step with the phonograph. The speed of the latter, in turn, corresponded to the speed of the original sound recording, so that normal tone was reproduced after the speed adjustments were made.

By this method, the slightest difference between the emission of the sound and the lip movement of the actor could

be easily corrected by means of the following device:

A special motor acting on a differential gear mounted on the shaft connecting the projector with the control motor could be operated in either direction by a reversing commutator. Depending on the direction of rotation of the small motor, the projector speed could be accelerated or retarded to correspond with the speed of the phonograph, until the two units were again in perfect synchronization (Fig. 1). In addition to this, a panel within reach of the operator and near the phonograph connected all controls under one button, so that the projector could be instantly started at a chosen sound produced by the phonograph. A voltmeter served as speed indicator and a multiple commutator as speed regulator (Fig. 4). Finally, a reversing commutator was used on the small motor of the differential gear.

The phonograph contained two disks which were alternately and automatically operated to assure operation for an indefinite time.

Different phonograph models were constructed in our factories for the use of disks with lateral impressions. This method gave, in fact, greater clarity and volume and permitted the needle to follow the groove more easily than the sapphire which is used in vertical position.

The Elgephone

In one of our inventions, the Elge phone, sound amplification was obtained by releasing compressed air through a double distributor. The Elgephone distributor insured a constant flow of compressed air without acting on the distributing disk, since this would be a source of distortion.

The compressed air is forced through a small tube A (Fig. 5) into a metallic chamber C. The disk P carrying the needle a vibrated between two rectangular openings 0 and $0'$ following the sinuosities of the grooves on the disk by letting varying amounts of air escape through the apertures N and N'.

This method of amplification was more satisfactory than any other method known at that time. The volume was so great that the phonograph recordings could be heard in halls seating several thousand persons.

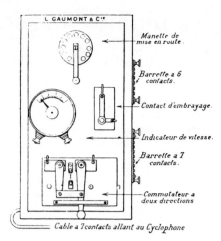

Fig. 4. Arrangement of voltmeter and multiple commutator.

Manette de mise en route	correction control
Barrette à 6–7 contacts	contact bar
Contact d'embrayage	electric clutch switch
Indicateur de vitesse	speed indicator
Commutateur à deux directions . .	reversing switch
Cable à 7 contacts allant au cyclophone	7-contact cable to cyclophone

Figure 6 shows the two units connected by the necessary cables, as well as the electric air compressor feeding the Elgephone.

We knew that this solution of the problem was not final at that time, because the use of the disks limited recording and reproducing possibilities. However, we were very sure that the application of sound by optical methods on film would no doubt eliminate this problem. Our tests were made on film different in dimension to the standard motion-picture film. The current modulated by the sound vibrations striking several very sensitive microphones flowed into a multistage amplifier and then into a two-wire mirror galvanometer. A very fine light beam oscillating on the film between the picture and the perforations (our film was 25mm) recorded these modulations. The speed of move-

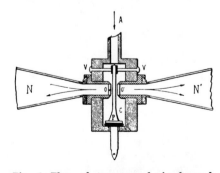

Fig. 5. Flow of compressed air through double distributor in Elgephone.

ment of this film was 500 mm/sec. This device represented the result of investigations with the Danish engineers; Petersen and Poulsen.

We experimented also with recording on two separate films, one for the image and the other for the sound. The eventual solution was the recording of sound and image on the same film strip.

Research in Color

The problem of sound recording was not the only one we studied. Our research on color motion-picture photography is recorded in history. We preferred the well-known three-color additive method used throughout all our experiments. The principle of this method was explained by Gros and Ducos de Hauron in 1869.

Each image appearing on the screen in natural colors was formed by superimposition of three images, violet, green and orange. The combined radiation of these three colors results in the reproduction of natural colors. The image was photographed on the film by three objectives placed one above the other, each provided with a glass color filter. These three images were projected in superimposition through carefully aligned objectives and filters. In this process the single image of ordinary motion pictures is replaced by three images simultaneously projected and superimposed.

If these three images had the same dimensions as used in ordinary motion pictures, 18 by 24 mm, each scene would require three times the length of film ordinarily used, and would necessitate very rapid movement of the film. Therefore, it was decided to reduce the height of the film by one quarter. By this method, the film length was approximately two and one-half times that of ordinary films.

As a further means to solve this difficulty, an intermittent movement capable of very long pulldown had to be made which was capable of transporting the film without undue strain, while guaranteeing absolutely perfect registration of the three images. The composi-

Fig. 6. The two units, with electric air compressor for Elgephone.

tion of the separation filters had to be carefully studied to obtain the best possible natural color rendition, especially of pure whites, by superimposition of three monochrome images. The film had to be sufficiently hypersensitized to all colors to obtain panchromatization.

The following color films were projected at the general meeting of the Photographic Society on November 15, 1912:

Projections of flowers taken in the Vilmorin-Andrieux Gardens were shown, the vase containing the flowers was slowly turned giving a marvelous stereoscopic effect; projections of butterflies with brilliant colors magnificently reproduced their iridescent luster; and finally, outdoor views were shown, especially a view of the Deauville beach at the height of the social season. Other pictures showed harvesters and other very pleasant country scenes creating the impression of a sunlit countryside with the most perfect reality.

A demonstration of these three-color chronochrome motion pictures and of talking pictures was given by the U.S. branch of the Gaumont Company, at the 39th Street Theatre, New York, in June 1913. The following program was presented:

Gaumont
Chronochrome   Talking Pictures
1. (a) Flower Studies
   (b) Farmyard Scenes
2. Views of the Riviera
3. *Mandolinette* — study by artificial light
4. The Nice Carnival Fetes, 1913
5. Rustic Scenes in France
6. *The Cock That Crowed in the Morn* (nature study)
7. *The Broken Window* (sketch)
8. *Justice* (illustrated fable)
9. *The Bad Son* (illustrated fable)
10. *Caught* (sketch)
11. (a) Funeral of King George of Greece, at Athens
    (b) Paris Fashions
    (c) Studies of Nature
12. *Venice* (a) town and canals
    (b) glass works. (Salviati & Co.)
13. National Flags — *The Tricolor The Stars and Stripes*
14. *In the Lion's Den*
15. Bert Earle, in humorous sketch
16. A French comedy entitled *Le commissaire est bon enfant* by Courteline & Levy.

Part II

Historical Papers -- Motion Pictures

Pioneer Experiments of Eugene Lauste in Recording Sound*

By MERRITT CRAWFORD**

Summary.—Among the pioneers who were engaged in developing the motion picture art, the name of Eugene Augustin Lauste prominently appears. In the January, 1931, issue of the Journal a brief outline of Mr. Lauste's career was presented by the Historical Committee of the Society. This paper deals more intimately with the various stages of Mr. Lauste's career, particularly with regard to his long-continued experimentation with various methods of recording and reproducing sound on film. A replica of one of Mr. Lauste's original sound picture recording and reproducing machines was exhibited at the Spring, 1931, Meeting of the Society at Hollywood.

Too often the contrivances and machines built by early workers in an art, after a brief though strenuous existence, find their way to the junk heap long before their value as historical documents becomes apparent. Once in a while fragments survive, and occasionally whole machines find a safe resting place and later come to life, although somewhat battered by the vicissitudes through which it passed.

Some time ago when investigating the history of the development of the sound picture art, investigators of the Bell Telephone Laboratories were impressed with early work along this line as disclosed in patents and other publications of a Frenchman, Eugene A. Lauste. It was learned that Mr. Lauste was in this country and had preserved a number of parts of his original apparatus. It was considered desirable by the Bell Laboratories to preserve the Lauste apparatus and to have replicas made of it, both because of its general historical interest and because, in connection with pending patent litigation, it was desirable to present Lauste's work in concrete physical form to the Court. Accordingly, Mr. Lauste was employed to collect his apparatus and to reproduce a complete sound picture recording and reproducing machine. Two of these machines were built in the shops of the Laboratories under Mr. Lauste's direction, and one of them is on exhibition at this meeting of the Society of Motion Picture Engineers. This piece of apparatus has served its purpose as an exhibit, and it is planned eventually to place it in a suitable museum where it may be inspected by those who are interested in the historical records of the sound picture art. An outline of Mr. Lauste's early experi-

————
*Presented at the Spring, 1931, Meeting at Hollywood, Calif. A contribution of the Historical Committee. Additional details of the career of E. A. Lauste were given by the author in a previous paper published in *J. Soc. Mot. Pict. Eng.*, XVI (Jan., 1931), No. 1, p. 105.
**New York, N. Y.

FIG. 1. Eugene Augustin Lauste. Born in Paris, France, Jan. 17, 1857.

ments forming a historical setting for the apparatus on exhibition follows.

Efforts to record sound photographically are usually dated from Cermak's experiments in 1862, when the Viennese scientist photographed the vocal cords in action, although he made no attempt to record the actual sound vibrations.

Prof. Alexander Blake, of Brown University, in 1878 photographed the vibrations of a microphone diaphragm by means of a small mirror which reflected a beam of light on a sensitized plate kept in motion by a clock-work mechanism.

Several years later, Prof. Hermann at the International Congress of Physiology at Liege, Belgium, used a microphone in connection with a phonograph, the sound vibrations being recorded on a strip of sensitized paper. The microphone used by Hermann was furnished with a tiny mirror which vibrated or oscillated in accordance with the sound produced by the phonograph record, the beam of light varying accordingly.

For more than a decade thereafter, numerous other experimenters, using various methods and various materials—glass, paper, celluloid, *etc.* — with suitable sensitized surfaces, sought to record sound vibrations photographically. None of them, however, was able to reproduce the graphic curves of sound which their devices had photographically recorded.

Among the experimenters of this period whose names may be mentioned are Dr. Marage, the famous Sorbonne otologist, who photographed the elementary sounds of the human voice as early as 1898, using an acetylene flame; and an American, Edmond Kuhn, a pioneer inventor and constructor of camera and projection apparatus, who, in 1900 experimented with a mirror diaphragm, a lens, and an incandescent lamp, using motion picture film. Kuhn used an ordinary telephone receiver and a phonograph.

R. W. Wood described his experiments (1899) in photographing sound waves using a chronophotographic camera (*Phil. Mag.*, Aug., 1899, and *La Nature*, Aug. 9, 1900). He also described the work of Toepler along similar lines.

But, as already state, prior to the year 1900 no experimenter had succeeded in reproducing the photographed sound vibrations recorded by the various ingenious methods employed.

FIG. 2. The improved string recorder which Mr. Lauste used in 1912–13, a double string light valve, with which his best records were made. The records, as were all those made with the string recorder, were variable width records.

In that year Ernst Ruhmer of Berlin announced his "Photographophone," the first device successfully to reproduce sound photographed on film. Ruhmer's method is described in an article under his own signature in the *Scientific American* of July 29, 1901. He used a "speaking arc light" in conjunction with a microphone and transformer in recording, and an arc light in reproducing, the interruption of the light waves by the developed film being registered by an "exceedingly sensitive selenium cell connected with two telephone receivers in the circuit of a small dry battery." To direct the light beams he used a cylindrical lens and an optical slit.

In his announcemen in the *Scientific American* Ruhmer stated that it was his intention to employ the Photographophone in connection with the cinematograph to ascertain, as he said, whether it was "possible to record the movements of bodies and sounds (such as music) upon the same film." But he never attempted to carry his experiments further than the recording and reproduction of sound by photographic means and, as we know now, his "speaking arc" method could never have been successfully adapted for the talking picture.

It remained for Eugene Augustin Lauste, a Frenchman, who had received his early training in the laboratory of Edison, to be the first to record and reproduce sound and scene simultaneously and synchronously upon the same strip of sensitized celluloid and to disclose fundamental processes that are still embodied in present-day talking picture equipment.

Lauste first conceived his idea of photographically recording sound pictures in the year 1888, when he read an account, published some years before in the *Scientific American Supplement* (May 21, 1881), of the invention by Dr. Alexander Graham Bell and Sumner Tainter of the Photophone. Lauste reasoned that if sound could be transmitted through space by means of radiant energy these electrical sound waves could also be recorded photographically and reproduced, using the selenium cell in the same manner as Dr. Bell had used it.

At first it was Lauste's idea to record the sound vibrations photographically on a ribbon or band of bromide paper and he hoped to find means to reproduce them, using a mirror and the reflection of light. About a year later, however, he first saw a specimen of Eastman's new film at the Edison laboratory, and realized that this phase of the problem did not require further consideration. The sensitized celluloid ribbon of Eastman furnished the ideal base for photographing sound as well as motion.

It was to be many years, however, before he could undertake his experiments in a practical way. He was first to become the inventor and designer of the Eidoloscope camera and projector, and the inventor of the so-called "Latham loop" and indispensable second sprocket, which are still essential elements in most modern projection machines, and which for years were a much-mooted factor in the patent litigation that marked the early history of the film industry.

Following his invention of the Eidoloscope camera he was associated with the American Biograph and Mutoscope Companies for several years, and it was not until the year 1900 that he was enabled to make his first grate light valve, parts of which are still in existence. But in the interval, he made many experimental drawings and designs which have for the most part, unfortunately, been lost.

In 1904 Lauste devised a crude apparatus to prove that sound could actually be photographed. He was then associated with William Kennedy Laurie Dickson, who had been his superior during the early days in the Edison laboratory, and he wanted to convince Dickson that his idea was practicable.

Lauste has stated that the device was little more than a toy—a box with a narrow slit behind which the film passed, a crank to wind the film, and an adjustment of a mirror fitted on a diaphragm which reflected light on the slit in response to the sound vibrations. In a way, the device was not greatly different from that used by Dr. Blake in 1878 in his experiments in photographing sound, except that Lauste used film instead of a sensitized glass plate.

It was sufficient, however, to prove to Dickson that Lauste's idea had possibilities and he directed Lauste to proceed with his experimental work. During the remainder of that year Lauste made several grate light valves and parts of a recording apparatus to run the film continuously, and also experimented with acetylene and incandescent lighting means.

FIG. 3. Mr. Lauste's combined camera for sound and scene, employing the double string light valve; used by Mr. Lauste in 1912–13.

In 1905 he built a complete experimental apparatus for recording and reproducing pictures and sound simultaneously on the same film at one operation. The sound waves were recorded as variations in density and the results, it need not be added, were not highly successful. Nevertheless, crude as the device was, it reassured Lauste that if he was enabled to record vibrations accurately he could also reproduce them.

In 1906, in association with an Australian experimenter named Haines, and John St. Vincent Pletts, a British engineer, he filed an application at the British Patent Office (No. 18,057) for *"A New and Improved Method of and Means for Simultaneously Recording and Reproducing Movements and Sounds."*

Haines, Pletts, and Lauste, in the order named, were recorded as the inventors, but the inclusion of their names in the patent was unknown to Lauste until its issuance, and as thereafter in all the testimonies and published accounts of the invention their names do not appear, there seems to be no evidence that either of the co-patentees contributed anything to the invention that Lauste had not previously disclosed to others.

According to Lauste, himself, their association with him was simply for the purpose of securing for him the necessary capital to conduct his experiments, and when they failed to do so, neither had any further interest in the development of the invention.

In 1908 Lauste was enabled to secure the needed financial backing from Mr. George W. Jones, who was then the General Manager of the London Cinematograph Company, and in that year he visited Ernst Ruhmer in Berlin, with whom he had been corresponding for some time. He wished to study at close range the characteristics of Ruhmer's Photographophone and to ascertain whether the great German technician had made any further discoveries in the art of recording and reproducing sound. He soon satisfied himself that Ruhmer's method of recording and reproducing sound, using the so-called "singing arc" would never be suitable for talking pictures.

The difficulty of maintaining an "arc" of constant area limited this method so definitely as to make it quite impractical for talking picture purposes. Only when the flame was continuously elongated was the reproduction even moderately adequate.

In addition to this, the reproduction at best was very weak and uncertain, and it was only with difficulty that music or the voice could be heard in the earphones. Lauste purchased a Photographophone from Ruhmer and also a

new selenium cell, the cell which he had been using previously made by Bidwell in England, having proved unsatisfactory.

Lauste was using a mechanical slit at this time in all his apparatus, with a convex lens to concentrate the light rays. After his visit to Ruhmer he experimented with a cylindrical lens, but later used a larger convex lens for this purpose in all his experiments.

It is worthy to note that Ruhmer was very skeptical at this time as to the possibility of Lauste's successful reproduction of the sound recorded by his method for the reason that the natural inertia of his mechanical grate light valve was too great. The vibrations were too slow to record sound accurately and many sound cycles were missing. Thus, the photographed sound waves when reproduced were inevitably greatly distorted and constantly interrupted.

The record of Lauste's work between 1908 and 1910 shows the logical development of his idea. Each partially unsuccessful experiment led naturally to the next. Nevertheless, at one point in his progress, it is related, he despaired so of success in ever obtaining adequate results that for nearly three months he practically discontinued his experiments. Then almost by accident he hit upon the idea which at last assured him that his work had not been in vain, in his adaptation of the diamagnetic wire acting between the poles of two strong magnets, which was to prove the solution of his problem.

In 1910 he had reached an *impasse* which he believed marked the end of all his painstaking efforts to record and reproduce sound on film successfully. In addition to Ruhmer, such distinguished scientific men as Marage of Paris, Blandel, and others of equal note, assured him that his efforts to reproduce sound by these methods would inevitably fail.

The London Cinematograph Company, which had supplied his scant capital, had got into financial difficulties and could no longer provide him with the means to continue his experiments. For days and weeks he racked his brains to find a method which would overcome the mechanical inertia that seemed to be an inescapable characteristic of his grates and light valves, but to little purpose.

Lauste, himself, has related how the idea which was to prove the answer to his problem, based on the principle of the string galvanometer, came to him in the early hours of the morning as he lay in bed. He arose forthwith, and at 2 A.M. was at work in his laboratory. In his first experimental recorder he used a silicon bronze wire because of its non-magnetic qualities, and his first attempt at reproduction of the record made

with this instrument demonstrated that at least he was on the right track.

To record the progress of Lauste's experiments in their exact sequence is, of course, impossible, but in a general way the apparatus that he made tells its own story. In 1909 he constructed several types of grate light valves for mechanically recording sound waves. One was constructed on the principle of an electrical motor field in conjunction with an armature; another was a solenoid magnet—a plunger working within a hollow magnet; a third was a magnet and a diaphragm operating on the same principle as the telephone receiver.

This period constituted what might be called the first stage of his real progress and in 1910 he began experiments with a vibrating mirror, with which he obtained better, but still inadequate, results. During the early part of this year he also experimented with another principle of the light valve, using a solution of hydroxide of iron, based on the discovery of Majoranna in 1902.

Lauste's knowledge of chemistry, however, was too limited and he was unable to make the magnetic solution properly. He constructed the instruments but could not blend the hydroxide solution in its proper solutions to get the results desired, so he discontinued his experiments along this line.

FIG. 4. Mr. Lauste's projector for sound and scene as completed and perfected by him in 1913. The picture is projected by means of the upper lantern, the lower lantern effecting the reproduction of sound. The light from the lower lantern passes through the film to the selenium cell on the front of the machine.

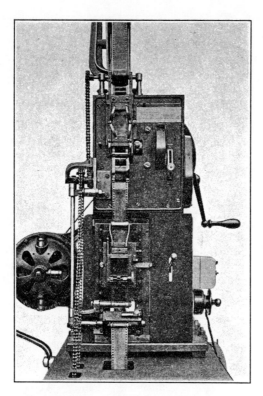

FIG. 5. A close-up of the projector mechanism, the upper part being the standard Pathé projector of the time, and the lower part the special Lauste sound reproducing equipment.

With his vibrating mirror he obtained better results than he had secured previously, but became convinced that this method would never be practical outside the studio or, at least, commercial, owing to the fact that the mirror recorded the vibrations of the camera as well as the sound waves which impinged on the microphone diaphragm. Lauste's experiments with his mirror recorder differ from those of previous experimenters, who, using similar means, had secured only a graphic curve of sound. He used, however, a *beam* instead of a point of light, and his negatives, of the variable area type, were half white and half black. It is similar to the method used by RCA Photophone today. His experiments with the electrodiamagnetic recorder, as already described, were almost completely successful from the outset.

Lauste has related how, upon the day when he had completed his first mechanism of the string galvanometer type and had recorded a few words from a French gramaphone record on the film, he was still very dubious of success. Nevertheless, when he attempted to reproduce it and heard through the earphones a few words spoken distinctly, his amazement and delight knew no bounds.

By a curious coincidence the words which he heard, as reproduced from the French gramophone record, were *"J' entends tres bien maint"*—"I hear very

well now." When he heard it, Lauste hardly believed his own ears. He called his wife and son to listen and then his assistants, one of whom, Mr. E. Sotain, who now resides at 39 Lonsdale Square, London, N. 1, has since told of this occasion. Sotain still recalls it vividly.

From this point on, Lauste's progress was very much more rapid. He devised several types of recording and reproducing apparatus using one and two non-magnetic wires in a magnetic field, several of which are still in existence and illustrate the ingenuity as well as the fine mechanical ability of the inventor. In 1910 Lauste also obtained a selenium cell from Bronk of Berlin, which gave him results far superior to those that he had previously obtained. This cell was in use by Lauste up to the time of the War.

Concerning Mr. Lauste's experiments in 1910, perhaps the testimony of Mr. L. G. Egrot, a member of the Society of Motion Picture Engineers, who personally observed his experiments, is of interest. His report was made at the request of Mr. Simon Rowson, as Chairman of the then British Section of the Society early in 1930. An extract from his report follows:

"I met Mr. Lauste in June, 1910, for the first time. He was introduced by Mr. Letuelle, French representative of the *Kinematograph Weekly* (the London film paper) . I was then working on a colour patent which had been granted to me, and was very much interested in sound and

synchronization of both sound and picture. When Mr. Lauste heard that I was going to London shortly, he asked me to make my trip coincide with his return, and we traveled together; as he was pleased to be with someone who knew something about the subject, he asked me to stop at his house instead of going to a boarding house, and there I stayed, with all his machines and experiments under my eyes.

"The old man had a workshop where he made his pieces of apparatus with his own hands, working on the patterns and fitting himself the most delicate pieces of apparatus. Above his workshop, he had installed a small laboratory where his son Henry used to develop the tests of the films recorded. This recording business was taking place continuously and records of the variable density system were obtained of a consistent quality and capable of reproduction on a listening apparatus made by Mr. Lauste, where the light variations caused by the passing of the film at a constant speed acted on a selenium cell modulating the electrical flow in a telephone.

"The recording apparatus was at the time (June, 1910) working with a microphone, transformers, and a solenoid acting on a set of very light grids exquisitely balanced; these were placed in a beam of light, controlling the amount passing through a cylindrical lens which focused it onto the film which was ordinary cinematograph standard film, perforated, and moving at an even speed; and if I remember well, the taking speed was in the neighborhood of the speed adopted in our days.

"The results thus obtained were very promising. Listening to the music, *via* microphone, beam of light modulated by the grids, selenium cell, and telephone, was as good as listening through microphone and telephone only. But Mr. Lauste was not satisfied and, with a cabinet already packed with different recording machines, he was turning his attention to galvanometer oscillographs and, I must say, he even approached the possibility of using the light of Geissler tubes and the bending of cold light by electrical means.

"He had already started building his camera to take pictures and sound together, the front part of the camera allowing to test the different systems he was experimenting with for sound recording; he had already records on both principles, variable density and variable area.

"Naturally, I was very much struck with all this, and when I heard, after returning to Paris, that Mr. Lauste was in financial difficulties, I arranged with a friend of mine, Mr. Weiss, to supply him with further capital. And later we introduced another gentleman, Mr. Salomon, a Belgian broker, who entered into an agreement with him to improve his machines.

"Mr. Lauste was doing everything himself—designs, patterns for casting, all the delicate engineering and precision work, all electrical fitments, coils, transformers, *etc.*; experiments, testing, and work were of necessity very slow, although he used to be the first one up in the house and at work at six o'clock every morning, unless he happened to suffer from his leg, in which case he would take things easy and do lighter work. Very often on a Sunday, a bandmaster friend of his, Mr. Norris, would come along with his band and play in the garden of the house where, in 1911, Mr. Lauste had had a wooden building erected as an experimenting studio. The machine was taken out, with all leads, some picture would be made and some sound recorded.

"Things were thus proceeding, improvement after improvement being adopted after tests, when the war started. You know all the rest, even better than I do."

Lauste continued to develop his string light valve up to the outbreak of the War. Between 1910 and 1913 he photographed many thousand feet of film, some with sound records only, and some with both sound and picture. In 1911 he came to America on a brief visit, chiefly in search of capital, with a combination camera and projector of a portable type which he had constructed to record and reproduce sound and scene.

He was able to make only a single experimental picture with this apparatus before being recalled to England, but this may be properly considered as the date when the first true sound picture was photographed in the United States. A short length specimen of this 1911 sound film is now in the museum of the Bell Telephone Laboratories.

Altogether Lauste designed and constructed at least six different types of his electrodiamagnetic recorder, on the principle of the string galvanometer. In some he used a single non-magnetic vibrating wire, in others two.

In the first string recorder he made, the single wire was held by spring tension. Later types employed bridges, and others an oil damper to absorb the secondary vibrations of the wire. His most satisfactory recorder, perfected in 1913, employed a double vibrating wire.

Lauste paid a second visit to Ruhmer in Berlin in 1912 to demonstrate his new method of recording sound waves photographically, and the German scientist, already stricken with the illness which caused his death the following year, was amazed at the clarity and distinctness of the record of a piano selection which Lauste made for him. For a time they considered continuing their experiments jointly, but Ruhmer's failing health would have made it impossible, even if it had not been impracticable for other reasons.

Lauste had brought his recording system to a point where but little further experimentation was needed, when the War came. He had then been experimenting for several years with various methods of amplification, using compressed air as its motive principle, as he felt then that all that was needed to make his sound·pictures commercially available for public presentation was an adequate loud-speaking system.

England's entrance into the struggle between France and Germany definitely ended his experiments, and when he came to the United States in 1916 hoping to find capital for the commercialization of his invention, it was only to encounter a similar situation.

The experiments he carried on prior to 1913 in photographing sound and scene, however, furnish some of the fundamental processes of the art which we know today, and there seems little doubt but that future authorities will assign to Lauste a distinctive place in the long and disinguished list of pioneer inventors and experimenters whose work has helped to make possible the modern sound motion picture.

Career of L. A. A. Le Prince*

By E. KILBURN SCOTT**

Summary.—*In November, 1886, Le Prince, an inventor and scientist living in New York, N. Y., applied for a U. S. patent covering a photographic camera which would expose successively a number of images of the same object or objects in motion and reproduce the same in the order of taking. Although the patent granted him on January 10, 1888 (U. S. Pat. 376,247), described a camera having sixteen lenses, it is shown that the original application specified "one or more lenses." His British patent No. 423, accepted Nov. 16, 1888, provided for both a camera and projector with one lens as well as multiple lenses. Most of Le Prince's important work was done in England and France from 1887 to 1890 with a single-lens camera, at least two of which were built and used. Descriptions are included of these cameras as well as a multiple lens camera. Evidence is introduced concerning the design of the cameras, such as the use of the Maltese cross intermittent movement, and of the building of and demonstrations with a projector.*

Louis Aimé Augustin Le Prince was born 89 years ago (Fig. 1). His father was a major of artillery in the French Army, an officer of the Legion of Honor, and was an intimate friend of Daguerre, the famous pioneer of photography, who gave his son some early lessons in the art.

Le Prince was educated in colleges at Bourges and Paris and did postgraduate work in chemistry at Leipsic University, which was very useful for his future career. He was a born artist, and, after some training in Paris, took up oil painting and pastel portraits; he also specialized in the painting and firing of art pottery.

In 1866, he met a friend, John R. Whitley, who afterward became famous as the builder and organizer of the first exhibitions at Earl's Court, and also as the builder of Le Touquet in France. He invited him to Leeds. and Le Prince decided to remain and join the firm of Whitley Partners, brass founders, of Hunslet, as designer, afterward taking charge of the valve department.

In 1869 he married Miss Whitley, who had been trained as an artist under Carrier Belleuse, the director of the Government pottery of Sèvres. His father-in-law, Joseph Whitley, was a remarkably clever inventor, who introduced, among other things, the method of spinning large cylinders and pipes from molten metal.

During the Franco-Prussian War, as an officer of volunteers, Le Prince went through the siege of Paris After returning to Leeds, he and Mrs. Le Prince started a school of applied art in Park Square, the first of its kinds in Leeds.

Le Prince carried out color photography on metal and pottery and fixed the colors in a special kiln. He executed commissions for Royalty, and his portraits of Queen Victoria and W. E. Gladstone were placed in the foundation stone of Cleopatra's Needle, along with other records of the time.

In 1875 the series of photographs taken by Eadweard Muybridge at Palo Alto, Calif., were published, and Le Prince was attracted to the idea of producing a series of photographs, in other words, "motion pictures" with one camera. Muybridge employed about two dozen separate cameras, and his mode of taking the photographs in sequence was limited and not suitable for reproducing the illusion of motion.

Le Prince had been working at this for some time, when, in 1881, his brother-in-law, who had become interested in the Lincrusta-Walton process, invited him to go to New York to assist in introducing that process. He went, and, on the patent rights being sold to an American company, had to find something else to do.

Mrs. Le Prince and the family had joined him meanwhile and deciding to stay on, he became manager of a group of French artists who produced large circular panoramas. One in New York showed the battle between the *Monitor* and the *Merrimac*. Others were in Washington and Chicago.

Jean Le Roy, of New York, who was employed by Joseph T. Thwaites, the English photographer, from 1872 to 1879 and from 1882 to 1888, has written as follows:

"I met and became acquainted with Le Prince about the spring of 1884, when he came to my employer's studio and photograph gallery at No. 1 Chambers Street, New York City. I recollect an order was for a number of lantern slides of military scenes, that he explained were to be made to scale so that he would be able to project them without any varying sizes or proportions. It was to help him to make outline drawings on convas to be used in a panorama of war. This was built at 59th St. and Lexington Ave., in later years converted into the 71st Regt. Armory, and now the site of the Plaza Theater. The last time I saw Le Prince was in 1887."

At this time, Mrs. Le Prince was teaching art at the Institute for the

Fig. 1. Louis Aimé Augustin Le Prince.

Deaf on Washington Heights, New York, N. Y. Her husband became friendly with the principal, Isaac Lewis Peet, and was permitted to use the tools and facilities of the institution's well-equipped workshop. Joseph Banks, the mechanic, who is still living in New York, assisted Le Prince in the constructional work and recalls the early attempts to make motion picture machines.

When a child of 14, Miss M. Le Prince went one evening to the institute. Seeing a light shining under the door, she entered and saw her father and Joseph Banks operating a machine which threw dim outlines of figures on the whitewashed wall Thus the first projected motion pictures of Le Prince —the earliest in America—were screened in the Institute for the Deaf.

In 1886 Le Prince drew up a specification giving full details and working drawings, and applied for an American patent in November of that year. Three clauses of the application read as follows:

(1) The successive production by means of a photographic camera of a number of images of the same object or objects in motion and reproducing the same in the order of taking by means of a "projector" or "deliverer," thereby producing on the eye of the spectator a similar impression to that which would have been produced by the original object or objects in motion.

(2) In an apparatus for producing "animated" pictures the continuous alternate operation of the film and its corresponding shutter or series of shutters.

(4) As a means of producing "animated" pictures on a photographic receiver pro-

*Reprinted with permission from the *Photographic Journal*, May, 1931. Recomended for publication by the Historical Committee.

**Consulting Engineer, London, England.

vided with one or more lenses and one or more shutters, in combination with one or more intermittently operated film drums.

Being a good mechanical draughtsman, he made his own drawings for the specification and showed the most difficult proposition, namely, a machine with 16 lenses. It is important, however, to note that his specification, as first filed, covered any number of lenses from one upward.

On January 10, 1888, the U. S. Patent Office in Washington granted his patent, No. 376,247, entitled "Method of, and Apparatus for, Producing Animated Pictures." They, however, cut out claims for machines with one lens and with two lenses, giving as the reason that Dumont's British patent No. 1457 of 1861 was an interference.

Le Prince was in England at the time and did not know that this had been done until it was too late for effectual protest. His patent attorneys, Munn and Co, very foolishly permitted the patent to be issued without challenge, and so it stands in the American records.

Many consider the attitude of the Patent Office to have been wrong because the Dumont patent was in no sense a motion picture device. It was for photographs on glass plates, arranged to form the facets of a prismatic drum, the object being to enable one to choose the best single photograph out of several successive ones. Dumont's object was not to show continuous movement by projecting pictures on a screen, which was the purpose of Le Prince.

In a statement of his father's claims, made in 1898, Adolphe Le Prince wrote quite fairly that:

"He was the first investigator to grasp the value and necessity of an unlimited amount of pliable film, moving from a *supply* drum, on which it was *wound* as many times as desired; not just a circumference length as Dumont had in mind. In the Le Prince apparatus the part of the film acted on was, at that instant, *between* the upper and lower drums, and therefore *flat*, being additionally aided by a clamping pad and tension device; this enables the Le Prince apparatus to take large pictures, and yet have perfect focus; both these points are *primary necessities* for good projection of 'Animated Pictures' on a screen.

"Marey, in 1885-1886, working independently on somewhat the same lines as my father, added greatly to the understanding of 'Animal Locomotion' and its more specific allies, but he had not used an endless pliable film, nor a means for definitely cutting off one phase from the next. His work has been given the credit it deserves."

Miss M. Le Prince, who saw pictures which her father took between 1885 and 1887, and which he projected on a wall of the Institute for the Deaf, has stated that some were taken with a single-lens camera-projector, and others with a four-lens camera. The pictures were about 1½ inches in diameter.

It is important to note that his British patent No. 423, applied for on the date of the issuance of his American patent, January 10, 1888, and accepted November 16, 1888, provided for a "receiver" (camera) and "deliverer" (projector) with one lens as well as multiple lenses. Otherwise it differs in no other essential particular from his United States patent.

Later, similar patents were issued by France, Italy, Austria, and Belgium, without the Dumont patent or any other being cited against them.

Obviously, if a machine could be designed and made to work with 16 lenses, it was easier to make it with 8 or 4, and easiest of all with only one We do know that practically all Le Prince's most important work was done with one-lens machines. The camera which Le Prince made in Leeds in 1887-1888 had only one lens, as Mr. Frederic Mason (who helped to make it) and myself have repeatedly stated. (See appendix.) This is fully demonstrated by the actual machine now in the Science Museum, London.

Le Prince returned to England in May, 1887, and then stayed with his mother in Paris. While there he gave attention to the taking out of his French and other continental patents. To facilitate this and demonstrate "proof of working," as it is called, he made a camera-projector with 16 lenses (Fig. 2).

The particular model brought from New York by Miss Le Prince is now in the Science Museum. It is constructed to take two bands of film of sensitized gelatine, mounted side by side on rollers in a chamber attached to the back of the camera. Of the sixteen lenses, eight facing one film were released in rapid succession, after which the remaining eight lenses were discharged while the first film was being moved on ready for another set of pictures Each film was clamped during exposure by a frame operated by a cam.

The lenses were operated by an ingenious system of double shutters worked by a series of electromagnets connected to a battery and a circular electric switch. On rotating the handle of the switch, the shutters operated in regular and rapid succession. Two additional lenses were provided as view finders, one for each film, in conjunction with a bellows at the back of the apparatus; focusing could be done while the machine was working.

Several sets of motion pictures were taken, including one of the mechanic who assisted Le Prince to make the machine. They were projected on a screen in the Paris Opera House on March 30, 1890. The Secretary of the National Opera made a statement, of which the following is a translation:

"I, the undersigned, Ferdinand Mobisson, Secretary of the National Opera, Paris, residing at 38 Rue de Mauberge, certify by this present to have been charged with the study (or examination) by means of the apparatus brought before me, of the system of projection of animated pictures, for which Mons. Le Prince, Louis Aimé Augustin, of New York, United States, has taken out in France patent rights dated the 11th of January, 1888, having the number 188,089, for 'Method and Apparatus for the projection of Animated Pictures, in view of the adaptation to Operatic Scenes,' and to have made a complete study of this system.

"In faith of which, I have delivered the present certificate to serve whom it may concern.

"Paris, March 30th, 1890.
        " (Signed) F. Mobisson."

Before going to Paris he had been to see William Mason and Son, woodworkers, of 150 Woodhouse Lane, Leeds, and secured the services of

Front view.   Rear view.
FIG. 2. Le Prince 16-lens camera.
(Reproduced by courtesy of the Science Museum, London.)

Frederic Mason to make parts of cameras, *etc.* On returning to Leeds, he rented a workshop at 160 Woodhouse Lane, and employed as assistant a clever mechanic, James W. Longley, who had done work for him at Rhodes Bros., Engineers, of Leeds. Some of the metal work was also carried out at Whitley Partners, his father-in-law being much interested in the invention. J. W. Longley was also an inventor, and made his first machines to deliver tickets automatically with coin-freeing mechanism. They were used at the Leamington athletic ground, Leeds.

By the summer of 1888, he had completed two cameras, each with a single lens, and (with the one also shown to The Royal Photographic Society and now in Science Museum) had photographed a series of pictures at the rate of 12 per second in the garden of his father-in-law at Roundhay. The following is a description of the camera (Fig. 3 and Fig. 4).

through the "gate" behind the lens in a series of jerks. At each exposure, it is held fast by a flat brass plate also operated by a cam. The plate moves back slightly when the film is being pulled through, to prevent scratching Many years later, this last device was claimed by firms as being original with them.

Light is cut off from the film during movement by a circular slotted brass shutter which revolves behind the lens in the same way as in modern machines. The shutter is a robust affair, and the opening in it is adjustable. Focusing is accomplished by means of a rack and pinion movement operated by a lever at the side, the front, bearing the lenses, and shutter being moved backward and forward. There is, of course, a finder lens attached above.

To assist in promoting smooth, even motion the spindle of the lower spool carries a heavy brass flywheel. The intermittent drive on the top spool was

and start the delivering machine with the same end of band of pictures. They would travel at the same rate in both the machines."

A series of pictures (Fig. 5) was taken by Le Prince in 1888 in the garden of his father-in-law, Joseph Whitley, at the residence now called Oakwood Grange, Roundhay, and occupied by Sir Edwin Airey, and the window shown in the photographs can still be seen. His son, Adolphe Le Prince, wrote the following on a print of these pictures:

"Portion of a series taken early in October, 1888, by the second one-lens camera. Le Prince's mother-in-law in this picture died October 24, 1888. Le Prince's eldest son is also in the picture, as is his father-in-law. Taken from 10 to 12 a second. There was no trial of speed contemplated here."

The following statement was also made by him on prints of the series of pictures taken from a window of the premises of Hick Brothers, at the south-

FIG. 3. Le Prince single-lens camera; 1888 (front). (Reproduced by courtesy of the Science Museum, London, England.)

FIG. 4. Le Prince single-lens camera; 1888 (interior). (Reproduced by courtesy of the Science Museum, London, England.)

The film, 2⅜ inches wide, is wound from one to the other of a pair of ebonite spools about six inches in diameter, one above the other. The top one is *revolved intermittently* by a cam bearing a number of teeth which engages with projections on the hub of the spool. The film is thus drawn up

unvaried, whatever the amount of film the latter carried. Le Prince's assistant, James Longley, wrote:

"As the drum gets larger, it takes more material to go round. All we had to do was simply *rewind the band of pictures off the drums of the camera machine on to the drums of the delivering machine*

east corner of Leeds Bridge, which firm supplied Le Prince with tools and materials:

"Portion of a series taken by Le Prince with his second one-lens camera in October, 1888. A view of the moving traffic on Leeds Bridge, England, taken at 20 pictures a second in poor light. His eldest son was with him when he took the picture."

James W. Longley wrote about them in the following characteristic way:

"Leeds Bridge—where the tram horses were seeen moving over it and all the other traffic as if you was on the bridge yourself. I could even see the smoke coming out of a man's pipe, who was lounging on the bridge. Mr. Augustin Le Prince was ready for exhibiting the above mentioned machine in public. We had got the machine perfect for delivering the pictures on the screen."

For taking these pictures, Le Prince used sensitized paper film, and one of the exhibits at the Science Museum is a reel of this material. It is on record that Le Prince used gelatin stripping film when Eastman introduced it In any case he had no trouble in getting good photographs at 12 to 20 per second. The pictures of Leeds Bridge were on film 2⅛ inches square.

To project the pictures was more difficult, for the reason that the film had to pass close to a lamp, and the heat made the material cockle or blister, and put the pictures out of focus.

FIG. 5. Two Frames of a series taken by Le Prince, October, 1888.*

His great problem was to obtain a suitable supporting base for his emulsion and, as mentioned in the specification, he tried horn, mica, hard gelatin sheets, and collodion sheets; also, at one time he used glass positives, at-

*This series was taken with a lone-lens camera at rate of 10 to 12 images per second, in the garden of his father-in-law, Mr. Joseph Whitley, Roundhay, Hunslet, Leeds, England. Le Prince's son, Adolphe, and Mr. and Mrs. Whitley are shown in the picture, with a younger lady. The date is definitely determined because of the death a few days after of Mrs. Whitley. Le Prince cranked the camera and probably used gelatin or glass plates on the carrier in his camera, not having yet obtained celluloid film.

FIG. 6. Spools for developing film; Le Prince, 1888. (Reproduced by courtesy of the Science Museum, London, England.)

tached to bands moved by sprocket wheels.

His patent specification refers to material carrying the film transparencies, reading:

"Punched with holes fitting on the pins of the guide rollers; also sensitive film for the negatives may be an endless sheet of insoluble gelatin, coated with bromide emulsion or any convenient, ready made, quick-acting paper."

His eldest son, Adolphe, who left a record of the experiments, stated that his father went to all the photographic supply houses in England, France, and the United States to obtain suitable material.

He obtained a supply of sensitized celluloid in sheets about a foot square, which he cut into positives and printed from the roll negative films. These he mounted on flexible, robust carrying bands.

Finally, the coming of long sensitized celluloid strip or film did away with the bands.

Evidence of his skill in making apparatus is well shown by the two large reels of celluloid, one of which is in the Museum (Fig. 6). They are of strips of celluloid 3 inches wide and about 12 inches long, cut from sheets and joined by pieces of silver. Two strips of silver along the edges are bent to form regular projections to keep the layers apart.

These particular reels were used for developing his exposed films, which were rolled up in the spool of celluloid, the whole being then immersed in the developer. The silver projections allowed space between each coil for the solution to reach the film. The celluloid is pierced with holes to allow the developer free access to the film. The strip has a matte surface on one side. This idea was patented years later by another inventor, but if the authorities had known of Le Prince's arrangement they would not have allowed the patent.

Examination of the clever mechanism of the camera and the construction of the spools gives the impression that

Le Prince had the ability to cope with all the problems necessary to make motion pictures a commercial success. Had he lived, he would have been a master figure in the industry.

He had the usual characteristics of the true inventor, and was always making improvements. His projectors or "deliverers" went through many stages with the object of simplifying the mechanism.

In the winters of 1888-1889 he built a "deliverer," or projector, having three lenses and three belts, which is thus described by his son:

"In this machine the belts, at slight tension, were moved by teeth pulling in the eyelets of the three belts, and rapidly stopping and starting at equal intervals (depending on speed of rotation of main shaft) by means of three 'pintooth' wheels timed to correspond with the opening and closing of the three lenses. The opening and closing were governed by a slotted circular shutter, rapidly rotating on a shaft. A gear wheel on the end of this shaft connected with the feed gear, and completed the harmonious action of the feed shutter and stopping and starting device. This deliverer gave continuous illumination on the screen.

"He also constructed in 1889 a one-lens deliverer, the picture belt being arranged in an endless spiral, the pictures appearing before the lens in rapid succession, and storing automatically as soon as projected and released."

A sketch made by his assistant, Longley, with descriptive letters, shows that the three-lens "deliverer" used the Maltese cross to give intermittent picture shift (Fig. 7). He says:

"g is the star wheel arrangement for allowing the band to work at the proper time. The wheel with the pins is for gearing into the band of pictures and should have two rows of pins, one on each side—and we had brass eyelets fixed in the band similar to the eyelets of boots."

Being an artist, Le Prince appreciated the importance of color, and the patent specification he wrote in 1886 says:

"Once developed and toned the transparencies may pass through the hands of artists who will tint them in transparent

79

colours, dyes, or lacquers as the subject may require."

In 1889, Le Prince constructed a projector to work with one lens, and decided to use an electric arc light instead of oxy-hydrogen previously employed. For this purpose, he came to his friend, Wilson Hartnell, an electrical engineer, of Leeds, by whom I was employed. I went to see about it and entering the workshop at 160 Woodhouse Lane, saw his assistant, Longley, whom I had known for some years. Noticing a large sheet at the end of the room, I asked if it was for a magic lantern, and his reply was, "Much better than that; the pictures actually move and represent life."

In due course, the plant was installed, direct current being generated by a Crompton dynamo driven by a semi-portable Robey boiler and engine in Mason's yard. That was at No. 150, and permission was obtained to carry the cables over intervening buildings to No. 160.

A difficulty in recording the history of events is that those who were eye-witnesses die. However, I state positively that the projector and the camera worked with single lenses, and William Mason and Wilson Hartnell have told me about seeing Le Prince's pictures on the screen.

The unveiling of a tablet on Le Prince's workshop (Dec. 12, 1930) has brought forward letters from people who would not otherwise have been traced. One from Walter Gee, chief engineer to the British Barnsley Co-operative Society, says:

"I am very pleased to give my testimony about the pioneer work of the late Louis A. A. LePrince and confirm what I know of particulars given in your pamphlet about the electric installation.

"During the late eighties I was an electrician with Wilson Hartnell, M.I.Mech.E., Consulting Engineer, of Basinghall Street, Leeds, and worked on the installation for the supply of electricity to an arc lamp in Le Prince's workshop at 160 Woodhouse Lane, Leeds.

"Mr. Le Prince worked his projector machine and showed moving pictures on a white sheet hung at the other end of the room.

"At the time of the first switching on, there was one other person present beside Mr. Le Prince and myself, namely, James W. Longley, who was his assistant.

"I know nothing of details of construction of the projector machine, but I was very pleased to see it work so well. I noticed how Mr. Le Prince opened his mind as he was working it, for he had been very quiet up to then. . . .

"Regarding the time of the electrical installation, my recollection is that it was about the middle of 1889. In 1890, I came to Barnsley, to put in plants for the Barnsley British Co-operative Society, where I have been ever since and am chief engineer.

" (Signed) Walter Gee."

J. T. Baron, chief electrical engineer of the Metropolitan Borough of St. Pancras, 57 Pratt Street, London, N.W.1, writes:

"I well remember the occasion of Mr. Le Prince's experiments about 1889 in Woodhouse Lane, when, along with others of Mr. Wilson Hartnell's staff, I was sent to see about fixing up the equipment, consisting of a dynamo and electric arc projector, for what was known to us then as moving pictures.

"I trust you will get further support for the interest you have taken in the recognition of Le Prince.

" (Signed) J. T. Baron."

Arthur Wood, engineer and machinist, of 331 Pietermaritz Street, Pietermaritzburg, Natal, wrote on the 25th of November, 1930:

"In 1888, two years prior to my leaving Leeds for South Africa, I was with the firm of Whitley Partners, Railway Works, Leeds. The head of the firm in those days was Mr. Joseph Whitley, a very capable man, one who would spend thousands of pounds in experiments for his business, and greatly interested in anything unusual.

"I can very well remember Le Prince's invention, as, while I was with Mr. Joseph Whitley, I personally made mechanical parts of the projector, such as the pedestal, gears, chains, etc. I was shown the film for which it was made, and if my memory holds good this film was of a horse galloping, although I did not see it actually projected.

" (Signed) Arthur Wood."

Certain people have said that Le Prince was not the pioneer he is claimed to be because he only made machines with multiple lenses. This mistaken idea has been helped by the description given in Hopwood's book, *Living Pictures,* and on seeing what he had written, I told the author he was wrong. Unfortunately after Hopwood died, Mr. Bruce Foster, also of the Patent Office, repeated the error in a second edition. He has, however, written me the following letter:

"I have been away for a few days and have been looking through the various documents you have sent me, more par-

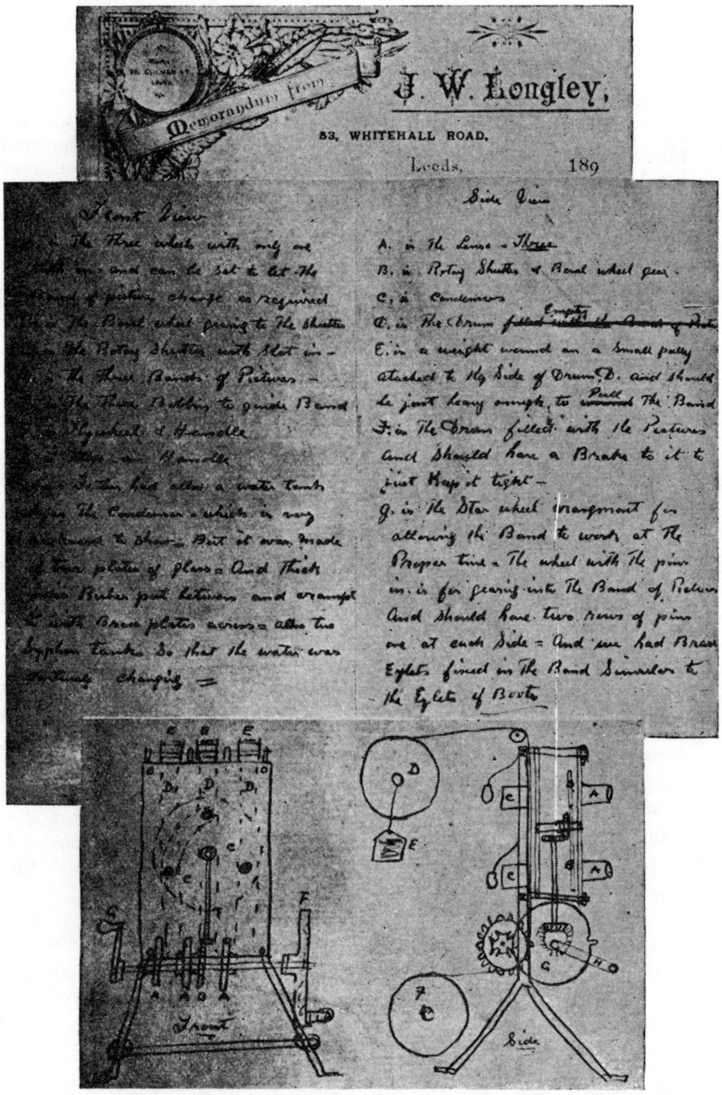

FIG. 7. Photostat of memorandum and sketch prepared by Longley, who assisted Le Prince in constructing his cameras.

ticularly in respect of the bearing of the information thereon in the relevant matter of Hopwood's *Living Pictures*—for the second edition of which I must plead guilty.

"There can be no question of fact that Le Prince's specification of 423/1888 includes the proposition of a 'one-lens' camera and projector. The specification includes the following passages in addition to the claims cited on p. 7 of the pamphlet:

"'When the receiver is provided with one lens only as it sometimes may be, it is so constructed that the sensitive film is intermittently operated at the rear of the said lens which is provided with a properly timed intermittently operated shutter, and correspondingly in the deliverer, when only one lens is provided, the band or ribbon of transparencies is automatically cooperated so as to bring the pictures intermittently and in the proper order of succession opposite the said lens.'

"It is a matter for regret that this aspect of Le Prince's specification was not brought out clearly in the second edition of Hopwood's book. The reason probably was that the specification described in greater detail the multiple-lens construction. This fact cannot, however, be relied on to exclude a 'one-lens' construction according to the specification.

"If, as it would appear from the information you have, the film referred to on p. 6 of the pamphlet shows Mr. Whitley walking in the garden, and can be identified as taken with a 'one-lens' camera, then, as Mrs. Whitley died on the 24th October, 1888, these facts alone would appear to date the 'one-lens' camera as made before that date.

"I am sorry the storm of controversy should be so tied up with the detailed paragraphs in Hopwood's *Living Pictures*, and apart from my regret that the existing text does not give due weight to the 'one-lens' proposition in the specification of 423/1888—if the story has to be rewritten—it will have to be modified also in other particulars, in the light of new facts which were not put in my possession when the second edition was published.

" (Signed) E. Bruce Foster."

Le Prince worked with collodion and gelatin for several years and, when living in New York, must have heard that Hyatt Bros., of Newark, were engaged on the problem. They made sheets of transparent celluloid by veneering it from a large block. Afterward it was made by spraying on glass.

John Carbutt sold sensitized celluloid sheets late in 1888, and showed this material and photographs made on it at the Franklin Institute, Philadelphia, in November of that year.

Rev. Hannibal Goodwin, of Newark, N. J., was evidently in touch with Hyatt Bros., for in 1887 he knew

REFERENCES

[1]Scott, E. Kilburn, "The Pioneer Work of Le Prince in Kinematography," *Phot. J.*, 63 (Aug., 1923), pp. 373-8.

[2]Crawford, Merritt: "Louis A. A. Le Prince," *Cinema*, 1 (Dec., 1930), pp. 28-31.

enough about the possibilities of celluloid film to apply for an American patent in that year. Dr. Marey, of Paris, is said to have used sensitized film in the late eighties.

There is very little doubt that long sensitized celluloid strip became available in 1889, and Le Prince had some reels of it in that year. Frederic Mason was employed to cut each reel into two to suit Le Prince's machines, as declared before a Commissioner. (See appendix.)

The 1889 patent of W. Friese-Greene and Mortimer Evans makes mention of "sensitive photographic film"; however, there is no special merit in mentioning a material which anyone could buy. If celluloid film had been on the market when Le Prince applied for his first patent 2½ years before, *i.e.*, in 1886, he would most certainly have mentioned it along with the other materials.

Le Prince had trouble with his film cockling and getting on fire with the heat of the lamp, and the water screen he made is thus described by Longley:

"It was made of two plates of glass and thick India-rubber put between and clamped with brass plates across, also two syphon tanks so that the water was continually changing."

They fully recognized that in the use of sensitized celluloid film the last hurdle had been cleared. It was the production of satisfactory transparent, pliable, and robust films that finally brought motion pictures into commercial use in the middle nineties. In that work many inventors, engineers, and commercial men helped.

In the spring of 1890, Le Prince decided to return to his family in New York, and ordered special boxes to be made to carry his apparatus. These boxes recently came back to Leeds as containers of the original apparatus, which was shown at the unveiling of the memorial.

In preparation for showing her husband's apparatus and pictures, Mrs. Le Prince rented the Jumel Mansion in New York and had it redecorated. The home life of the family was ideal and she was a splendid helpmate.

"Proof of working" of his first French patent was granted in June, 1890, and there is no doubt but that he then had business in that country. In August he went to France with his friends, Mr. and Mrs. Richard Wilson, and left them at Bourges to visit his brother, an architect and surveyor of Dijon. He was last seen entering the train for Paris with his luggage. Intensive searches were made by French and English detectives, but not a single clue was ever discovered.

Some time after his disappearance, Mr. Richard Wilson collected such

things as he thought worthy of preservation. As a banker he did not know their technical and historical value, and thus films, *etc.*, were lost that would now be considered valuable. Charles Pickard, commercial photographer of Leeds, has the tripod of the camera and Frederic Mason picked up a few photographs.

It will be remembered that much the same thing happened in the case of Friese-Greene, practically all his apparatus being sold for "junk," only a few pieces of film being saved. In the case of Friese-Greene, no machines remain, but in the case of Le Prince there are two, fortunately, to testify to his ingenuity.

When it became certain that her husband was lost, Mrs. Le Prince consulted Mr. Choate, sometime American Ambassador to Great Britain, but all he could tell her was that she would have to wait until the death could be legally "presumed," which took seven years. In 1898, the eldest son visited England and France and took back to New York the camera and other things, some of which are now deposited in the Science Museum at South Kensington.

APPENDIX
DECLARATION OF FREDERIC MASON*

In 1887 I was near the end of my apprenticeship with my father's and brother's firm, Wm. Mason & Son, joiners and contractors, of 150 Woodhouse Lane, Leeds, and one day there came to the works a Mr. Louis Augustin Aimé Le Prince who previously had been with Whitley Partners of Hunslet, and also had a Technical School of Art in Park Square, Leeds.

He said that he required some woodwork which must be very accurately made, and it was given to me to carry out. During the next 2½ years I was engaged almost continuously for Mr. Le Prince. I made all the woodwork and the patterns for metal castings.

I discovered that he was constructing apparatus for the purpose of taking photographs in rapid succession and projecting them on a screen, so as to give the illusion of motion; in other words—moving pictures.

Mr. Le Prince equipped a workshop at 160 Woodhouse Lane, now occupied by the Auto Express Company, on which a bronze memorial tablet was unveiled by the Lord Mayor of Leeds on December 12, 1930.

At this unveiling the camera which Miss M. Le Prince brought from New York was shown, and this I at once identified as the one I assisted to make and which was completed about the summer of 1888. It was constructed to scale drawings made by Mr.

____

*Builder, 11 Quarry Mount, Hyde Park, Leeds, England.

Le Prince; he was a very clever draughts-man. The metal parts were cast at Whitley Partners and machined and fitted by Mr. J. W. Longley, who was the mechanic of Mr. Le Prince.

The camera has two lenses, one being for taking the photograph and the other for the view finder. The gate mechanism behind the lens is constructed to hold the film firmly in position during exposure, and then to momentarily release it while being drawn upward without it being scratched. The intermittent movement consists of a toothed cam which engages with a projection on the side of the top reel, the latter pulling the film through the gate and also winding it up.

The handle projecting from the side of the camera operates the mechanism through gear wheels. A brass shutter revolves in front of the lens which has in it an adjustable diaphragm. Turning the

materials. Their premises are at the south-east corner of Leeds Bridge, and the pictures showed very clearly the moving of traffic across the bridge.

Mr. Le Prince found the construction of the projecting machine much more difficult than the camera; it evolved through several stages, and when making changes existing parts were re-used as much as possible. One projector had three lenses, and was like a sketch of Mr. J. W. Longley's which he sent to Mr. Adolphe Le Prince in 1898, a photostat copy of which is in my possession (Fig. 7).

As indicated in his patent specification, Mr. Le Prince first dealt with the positive pictures by mounting them on bands, one material that he used being thin red fiber. Small holes were punched along the edges of the bands to engage with pins in the sprocket wheels.

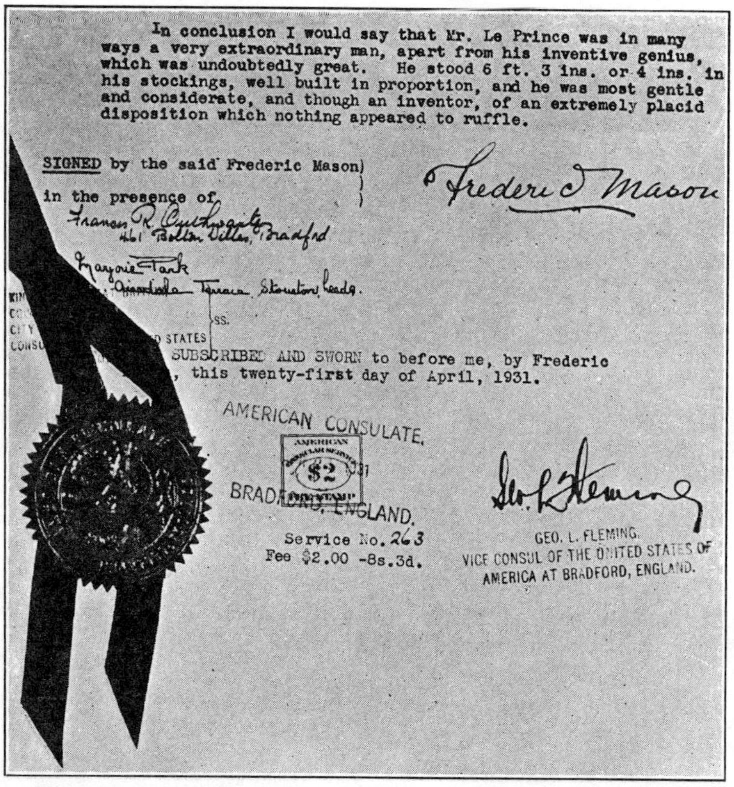

In his earlier experiments Mr. Le Prince

a higher voltage, and I took the risk of placing extra weights on the safety valve in order to get more speed on the dynamo.

When the arc lamp was first switched on there were present, besides Mr. Le Prince, Messrs. J. W. Longley and Walter Gee, the last-named being an electrician for Mr. Hartnell. He is now chief engineer to the Barnsley Co-operative Society. They were the first people to see moving pictures projected with the arc lamp illumination, but afterward a few others had an opportunity, including Mr. Hartnell and my brother William; the latter said the pictures showed well except for some flickering.

It is important to note that details of the camera and projector with which Mr. Le Prince did his best work in Leeds departed considerably from those shown in his British patent No. 423 of 1888 and his United States patent serial 217,809 of 1886. It was his intention to take out further patents, and naturally he was therefore reluctant to show his machines.

Miss Le Prince brought back with the camera, *etc.*, two long reels which her father had built up of strips, each about 3 inches wide and a foot long, fastened together and having silver along the edges to keep the layers apart. These he used for developing films.

At a later date, long reels of somewhat similar material, sensitized and nearly transparent, became available. It would be in the early autumn of 1889 that Mr. Le Prince came to me in high spirits to say he had obtained some rolls of sensitized film called celluloid. As these were too wide I cut them in halves on a lathe, working with a red lamp at night. The incident is clear in my mind because I had to wait until it was dark, about 9 p.m.

The coming of celluloid film solved the last difficulty, and in the spring of 1890 Mr. Le Prince decided to go to New York, where his wife and family were, to show moving pictures there. He ordered from Mr. Trinder, a maker of port-manteaux in Woodhouse Lane, special cases to hold the apparatus. The cases which Miss Le Prince brought back were the originals with the maker's name still on them.

Before sailing he went to France to see about patent business, also to bid adieu to his brother, an architect and engineer of Dijon, who saw him off at the station en route for Paris on 16th September, 1890. Unfortunately, from that moment he disappeared completely and, although exhaustive enquiries were made by detectives and members and friends of the family, no clue was ever found.

After waiting about a month, Mr. Longley and myself entered the workshop and found everything quite normal, the machines intact, and tools, drawings, photographs, as well as a quantity of discarded material, lying about. Mr. Richard Wilson, a friend of the family and manager of Lloyds Bank, Leeds, took charge of all the effects and proceeded to dispose of such parts as could readily be sold.

A large tripod I made for the camera passed into the possession of Mr. Charles Pickard, photographer, of Leeds, who showed it at the unveiling ceremony. I picked up a few relics, and am sorry now that I did not secure some exposed films

FIG. 8. Signatures and witnesses to declaration by Frederic Mason.

handle at the proper rate enabled pictures to be taken at the desired speed.

For his cameras Mr. Le Prince used sensitized paper film and gelatin stripping film. Miss Le Prince brought along with the other apparatus a reel of the paper film which was found in the camera.

In the early autumn of 1888 the camera was used for photographing a series of pictures, at about 12 per second, in the garden of Mr. Joseph Whitley, father-in-law to Mr. Le Prince. In them Mrs. Joseph Whitley is shown, and as she died on 24th October, 1888, this conclusively shows that the series was taken before that date.

Another series, taken about the same time, but at a higher speed, was from a window of Hick Brothers, Ironmongers, from whom he had purchased tools and

used oxy-hydrogen lime-light, but when finally he was able to get quick enough movement of pictures to employ only one lens, then he decided to have an arc lamp. This envolved installing an electric generating plant, and he called in the assistance of his friend, Mr. Wilson Hartnell, electrical engineer, who lived close by in Blenheim Terrace.

He supplied a dynamo and arc lamp, and his men installed them and ran cables over the roofs of intervening buildings from our yard at 150 to the workshop at 160 Woodhouse Lane.

The dynamo was driven by belt from our semi-portable Robey engine and boiler, which I operated at night. I have reason to remember the first time because Mr. Le Prince sent round that he wanted and the drawings, as unfortunately nothing was done to preserve them. That they might have historical importance was not appreciated.

Mr. Wilson retained the camera, parts of the projector, including a lens, the above-mentioned reels, and a machine with multiple lenses that Mr. Le Prince made in Paris in 1887 for the purpose of 'proving his patent." They eventually went to Mrs. Le Prince in New York City, and were kept there until October, 1930, when they were brought back to Leeds by Miss Le Prince. They are now housed in the Science Museum, South Kensington, London.

In conclusion, I would say that Mr. Le Prince was in many ways a very extraordinary man, apart from his inventive genius, which was undoubtedly great. He stood 6 ft. 3 in. or 4 in. in his stockings, well built in proportion, and he was most gentle and considerate and, though an inventor, of an extremely placid disposition which nothing appeared to ruffle. (See Fig. 8.)

(Signed) Frederic Mason
Signed by the said Frederic Mason in the presence of
    Frances R. Outhwaite
    461 Bolton Villas, Bradford

Subscribed and sworn to before me, by Frederic Mason, this twenty-first day of April, 1931.
(Signed) Geo. L. Fleming
    Geo. L. Fleming
[Seal]   Vice-Consul of the United States of America at Bradford, England

The History of the Animated Cartoon*

By EARL THEISEN**

Summary.—The history of the animated cartoon is traced from the earliest devices used to depict motion, before the introduction of photographic processes, to the realistic and artistic colored cartoons of the present day. The various innovations developed for reducing the labor and cost of producing the thousands of different photographs in seriatim for motion picture cartoons, is described briefly in relation to their chronology and application.

This history of the animated cartoon goes back farther than that of the motion picture; in fact, motion pictures had their beginning as hand drawn pictures. Long before photography had become practicable, many devices were introduced that portrayed motion by a series of cartoon pictures. These early devices were nothing more than toys, and were impracticable for depicting a story; however, they were popular and did much to crystallize the demand for motion pictures.

Five years after the discovery of the "persistence of vision" by Peter Mark Roget, in 1826, the first attempts were made to show motion pictorially by a series of drawings. With a device, called the *Phenakistoscope,* invented by Joseph Antoine Plateau, motion was depicted by a sequence of drawings, fourteen in number, each drawing blending with the next in the series to show some simple bit of action. The device was composed of two disks mounted on a shaft, the front disk having a series of slits around its outer edge, while the rear disk carried the drawings. The drawings were aligned with the slits, and on peering through the slits as the two disks revolved, the illusion of motion was created.

This was followed by the *Daedaleum,* or *Wheel of the Devil* (Fig. 1), invented by William George Horner, in England, in 1834, which consisted of a shallow cylinder, mounted on a stand, having slits around the top. The drawings, made on strips of paper about 2½ feet long, were inserted on the inside of the cylinder. In these drawings, the chief character was the devil, waving his trident. The *Daedaleum* was later re-invented in France as the *Zoetrope* by Desvignes, in 1860. It came to be known as the *Wheel of Life* because it showed action, and portrayed little every-day happenings, such as a child jumping rope, or a man pumping water, or a cast of actors, including an erring husband, his wife, and her rolling pin. The rolling pin here used may be said to be one of

the forerunners of the assorted "props" that are now so valuable to the motion picture. Many other events were faithfully recorded by hand drawings for the Zoetrope, which were motion pictures 2½ feet in length.

The *Wheel of Life* was first introduced in the United States by William Lincoln, in 1867, and was patented on April 23, 1867, which can be said to be the date of introduction of the animated cartoon into this country.

The most notable of the pre-photographic inventions was the *Praxinoscope,* devised by Emile Reynaud, in 1877, in France. To Reynaud goes the credit of drawing short bits of dramatic action in the forms of plays, which he projected on a screen in the Reynaud Optical Theater (Fig. 2). His most notable picture was *Pauvre Pierrot,* drawn on a thirty-foot length of a transparent medium which he termed "crystaloid." It should be noted that this was twelve years before either

FIG. 1. The *Wheel of Life,* one of the early devices for showing animated pictures.

the first Eastman raw stock with celluloid base, or the Edison motion picture apparatus was demonstrated.

Space will permit mention only of the first few pioneers who struggled to make pictures move before photography was available to them. There were a great number of others, some of whom spent a lifetime at the work. One man continued grimly to peer into his devices until he sacrificed his eyesight. Another lost his sight, yet continued his work with the assistance of his wife. To such men as these our gratitude must be extended. The revaluation that followed the perfection of the screen cartoon should not be al-

lowed to discredit those early movie devices; in perspective they may seem crude. But they were received in their day with all the acclaim accorded to Mickey Mouse today.

It was not until 1906 that the first cartoon was made on motion picture film. It was a picture made by J. Stuart Blackton, for Vitagraph, and was entitled *Humorous Phases of Funny Faces* (Figs. 3-6). A recent screening of this picture, with its 1906 copyright, and Vitagraph trademark, showed it to consist of such cartoon bits as a man rolling his eyes and blowing smoke at his sweetheart, a large-nosed Semite, a dog jumping over a hoop, and ended by showing Blackton doing a chalk-like type of drawing, in which apparently the cartoon starts as one thing and ends as another. This first cartoon picture required about three thousand drawings and its running for an early-day audience, which was largely composed of the more solid citizenry, was a signal for great mirth. The man blowing the smoke at his sweetheart was the highlight of the picture. Since cartoon technic at that time permitted the girl to show her displeasure only by suitable eye movements, the picture had its elements of humor.

The next man to make animated pictures was Winsor McCay. The first was completed early in January, 1911, and was known as *Little Nemo.* It was photographed in one-reel length by Walter Arthur, directed by J. Stuart Blackton and released by Vitagraph as *Winsor McCay Makes His Cartoons Move.* It contained over 4000 drawings, each complete with a background and was considered a mammoth undertaking at that time, despite the fact that the present cartoon requires as many as 12,000 drawings, which are run for a screen time of only six minutes. McCay's second picture, *How a Mosquito Operates,* was made in December, 1911, in 600 feet and was sold to Carl Laemmle. The third, *Gertie, a Trained Dinosaur,* was sold to William Fox. These pictures were used also as a vaudeville act by McCay, who toured with them and explained their making and technic.

To McCay goes the credit of making the first serious attempt at a dramatic cartoon. *The Sinking of the Lusitania,* released on August 15, 1918, by the Jewel Productions, was a cartoon of feature length. According to the *Motion Picture News,* of August 18, 1918 [it was], "made from 25,000 drawings

*Presented at the Spring, 1933, Meeting at New York, N. Y.

**Honorary Curator, Motion Picture Division, Los Angeles Museum.

FIG. 2. Reynaud's Optical Theater, showing an audience viewing the play *Pauvre Pierrot*.

on gelatin by the famous artist, Winsor McCay, requiring 22 months of work." The picture attracted attention at this time by virtue of its length and because it was a propaganda picture for the war. To date it has been the longest cartoon ever made.

John R. Bray, during the period 1914-16, was granted patents on making animated cartoons. The first, filed January 9, 1914, and granted the same year as No. 811,165, describes a method of registration so as to hold each picture in correct relation to every other for photographing. The most important claim in this patent, however, relates to the use of a translucent background over the character drawing. It will be noted that this is a departure from the tedious process of drawing each cartoon complete with a background and character, as was heretofore done. With this patent, Bray introduced the idea of making one background serve for all the action occurring in that scene (Fig. 7). He printed his background from a zinc plate on thin translucent sheets of paper, which he laid over the character drawing for photographing. This system did not permit good quality and was used only for the first few pictures, after which he adopted a system similar to the Earl Hurd method. Bray further eliminated unnecessary drawing by introducing the "stationary" drawing, which comprises the use of separate sheets of celluloid when a part of the character is motionless while other parts are moving. One drawing is made for the motionless part, while the action of only the moving part of the character is drawn out.

Cartoon history may be said to date from the announcement, on June 12, 1913, of the first Bray cartoon, *The Artist's Dream* (Fig. 8). This, while not the first of the animated cartoons, was the forerunner of the cartoon vogue. Previously to that, cartoons were largely considered a novelty, or photographic trick. They had been used at the end of newsreels, or vaudeville acts, and were shown more or less apologetically. Now, audiences seeing *The Artist's Dream* were left in a mood bordering on the hysterical, from laughter, and demanded more cartoons. The central character of this cartoon was a dachshund, with the long "wheel base" and the short legs. This dog, which resembles so much an animated sausage, experienced difficulties with a flea, which interrupted the dog in obtaining his sausages for dinner.

Another Bray cartoon, *Col. Heeza Liar*, which was the "Mickey Mouse" of that day, was by far the most popular of the early cartoons. The first of the series, *Col. Heeza Liar in Africa*, was released by Pathé in December, 1913. They were discontinued about five years, and again resumed in 1922 as an *Out of the Inkwell* combination. Walt Lantz, who draws the Universal *Oswald*, drew the later series, which consisted of a combination of the conventional motion picture into which was introduced *Col. Heeza Liar*.

Bray has the distinction of having made a hand-colored cartoon in 1917; it attracted much attention, but was impracticable because of the high cost of coloring each frame.

Earl Hurd introduced the modern technic of making cartoons. On December 19, 1914, he filed an application for a patent which, on June 15, 1915, was granted as No. 878,091. In this patent, he claimed the use of a transparent medium bearing the moving parts of the cartoon over an opaque background. Hurd was the first to use celluloid for his action drawings, which

he laid over a background, as is done today. It will be remembered that Bray, in his efforts, drew his backgrounds on a translucent medium, which he laid over his characters for photographing, and wherever the background interfered or covered the character, that part of the background was removed. Earl Hurd's first cartoons were the *Bobby Bump* series. Bray and Hurd combined their patents and formed the Bray-Hurd Company early in 1917.

Another early worker was Sidney Smith, who made *Old Doc Yak* for the Selig Polyscope Company. The first of this series was released on July 8, 1913. Wallace Carlson, who made *Dreamy Dubb*, and later the *Caminated News*, which was an *Out of the Inkwell* combination, was prominent at that time. Paul Terry drew *Farmer Al Falfa*. Leslie Fenton drew the *Hodge Podge* series which were released at the end of the Pathé newsreels.

Max Fleischer was the first to make the *Out of the Inkwell* type of drawing. This is a photographed picture to which is added a cartoon character by photographing a series of opaque cartoons drawn on celluloid placed over previously photographed conventional motion pictures. Fleischer's first series was *Koko, the Clown*, released by Paramount in 1917.

During this period Leon Searle made what was known as "cut-outs." They were jointed characters cut out of paper and animated across a background. Their animation was rather jerky, as were the marionettes made about the same time by Tony Sarg. The Sarg marionettes were figures illuminated from the rear, thus producing a silhouette effect.

Raoul Barre, who began making the Edison cartoons, introduced the "slash" system, whereby the motionless parts of the characters were drawn once, and the animated parts of the characters torn away. These moving parts were then drawn on another sheet so as to coincide with the stationary parts. The two were then photographed simultaneously, one over the other, thus saving unnecessary drawing. Barré also originated the use of registering pegs and punch holes in the drawings for holding them in place during the photographing.

Bill Nolan, working with Barré, was the first to use a panorama background. The panorama, with the characters moving past the background, was an innovation and made a decided improvement in the action. That was in 1916.

Most of the cartoons shown on the screen in 1917 were greatly inferior to those of today. They were crude and

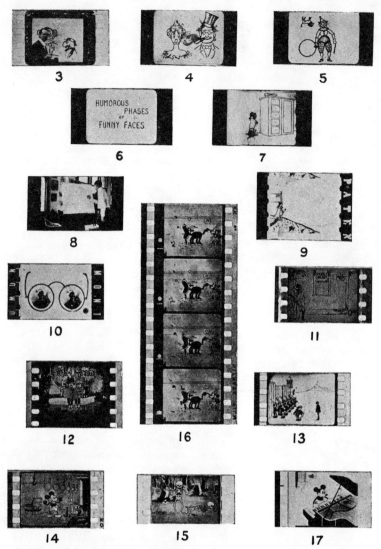

FIGS. 3 TO 6. Copies from specimens of cartoon films made by Blackton in 1906 (FIG. 3, picture of Blackton doing a chalk talk in his 1906 cartoon). FIGS. 7 and 8, the first Bray cartoon, *The Artist's Dream*, by J. R. Bray. FIG. 9, Pathé newsreel cartoon of about 1912 (note the Patents Company stencil on the edge of the film). FIG. 10, Gaumont cartoon of about 1912. FIG. 11, Packer cartoon of 1916. FIG. 12, the first Disney series made in St. Louis, 1921. FIG. 13, one of the *Alice Cartoons* made by Disney, 1923; a combination of real-life characters and cartoon. FIG. 14, first Mickey Mouse, *Steamboat Willie*. FIG. 15, first Silly Symphony, *Skeleton Dance*. FIG. 16, first method of synchronizing sound and picture; originated by Disney. The bouncing ball kept time for the musicians when scoring. FIG. 17, a recent Mickey Mouse, showing the sound track.

the characters imperfectly synchronized. They would walk either too fast or not fast enough; the leg movements seemed to create the illusion that the feet were being dragged somewhat in the manner of a skater's sliding over the ice. Another characteristic was the "bubble" type of title. This title was similar to the present press cartoon title, in which the wording appears in a balloon with a line leading down to the character. When the title appeared on the screen, the character would come to a pause, face the audience, and "yap" or rapidly open and close its mouth to represent talking. This, of course, greatly interfered with the continuity of the story.

Into this period entered the International Feature Syndicate formed by William R. Hearst. He placed Gregory La Cava in charge, who immediately set about improving the cartoons. He increased the number of drawings from the 2000 of the average cartoon of the time to 3500, resulting in smoother animation. Further, he changed the animation of the characters from the stiff, angular movements of the legs and arms to a smooth "rubbery" animation, such as is used at present. La Cava also discontinued the "bubble" title for the conventional title of the silent days.

Beginning in 1917, the International Syndicate released such cartoons in series as *Jerry on the Job* (Fig. 18), drawn by Walt Lantz, *Katzenjammer Kids*, by John Foster, *Tad's Indoor Sports*, drawn by Bill Nolan and re-

leased at the end of the International Newsreel. *Happy Hooligan*, drawn by Jack King, *Bringing Up Father*, by Bert Green, *Krazy Kat* (Fig. 19), drawn also by Bill Nolan and Leon Serle, and the best of the Internationals, *Silk Hat Harry*, were the principal cartoons released at this time by that company. This last-named was drawn by Walt Lantz and La Cava, and was first released in 1918.

The first International cartoons were made somewhat after the principle of the first Bray cartoons, in which the background was drawn on a translucent medium and the characters on an opaque sheet. The background was then laid on top of the character drawings. Where any part of the background interfered with the character animation, that part of the background was drawn on the same sheet with the character. This system was discontinued after the first few cartoons in favor of the now conventional "celluloid over the background" method.

Other famous cartoons during the 1917-20 period were the *Mutt and Jeff* series, made by Budd Fisher. The Kay Company released the *Terry Cartoon Burlesque*, and Sterling Pictures the *Zippy* series.

Skipping over the years to the sound era, we come to Walt Disney and his *Mickey Mouse* series, which were the first cartoons with sound. *Steamboat Willie* (Fig. 14), was the first of this series and had its premiere on September 19, 1928, at the Colony Theater in New York. An earlier Mickey Mouse had been made but it was released later as *Plane Crazy*. Mickey Mouse is probably the most popular of any screen character, whether in real life or cartoon. He is certainly the acme of all that the screen has to offer as entertainment.

Disney started cartoon making in St. Louis, in 1921, when he made the Laugh-O-Gram (Fig. 12) series. In October, 1923, he and his brother, Roy, went to Hollywood and produced the *Alice Cartoons* (Fig. 13), which were a combination of real life characters and cartoons.

Disney's first Silly Symphony, *The Skeleton Dance* (Fig. 15), was released at the Carthay Circle, in Los Angeles, in July, 1929. It was later shown at the Roxy in New York. It was the first cartoon picture to be rebooked for a second showing at the Roxy.

The method of synchronizing the first Mickey Mouse was by the "bouncing ball" method (Fig. 16), in which a ball was made to bounce in time with the music as a guide for the musicians, who watched the picture and the ball as they appeared together on the screen. This ball was photographed along the edge of the film, which space was later occupied by the sound track in the release print. Disney next used a wavy line, and finally adopted an aural method. The last method, employing head-phones, is still in use. Disney controls many of the sound cartoon synchronization patents.

The first Silly Symphony in color was *Flowers and Trees,* first shown at Grauman's Chinese Theater, Hollywood, on July 15, 1932. This was the first cartoon to employ the Technicolor Cartoon Process, a three-color imbibition process. Judging from today's standards it seems that it will be impossible to improve upon the beauty of these Disney cartoons colored by this process.

Many will remember the cartoon sequence that served as an introduction to the Universal picture, *King of Jazz,* released on March 30, 1930. It was colored by the Technicolor two-color process and was the first cartoon on record to be mechanically colored.

Another cartoon to follow this was Ted Eshbaugh's *Goofy Goat,* made by Multicolor and released at the Loew's State Theater, Los Angeles, on March 2, 1932. It had been previewed earlier at the Warner's Alhambra Theater, on July 6, 1931. Many will credit this cartoon with being the first in color, since it was the first complete cartoon story done in color, whereas the earlier Lantz cartoon was only an introduction for a real-life picture.

The current cartoon characters besides those named are *Oswald* and *Pootch-the-Pup,* drawn by Walt Lantz and Bill Nolan for Universal; *Krazy Kat* and *Scrappy* made by the Mintz Studio; *Looney Tunes* and *Merrie Melodies* made by Leon Schlesinger; *Flip-the-Frog,* by U. B. Iwerks for M. G. M. release; *Aesop's Fables* and *Tom and Jerry* by the Van Buren Corporation; *Betty Boop* by Max Fleischer; *Bosko* by Harman and Ising, released by Warners as a "Looney Tune;" *Magazine of the Screen* by Bray; and *Terry Tunes* by Paul Terry. *The Wizard of Oz* will shortly be released as a series, in Technicolor.

Such is the history of cartoons. It is interesting to observe their popularity today and then to recall their reception back in 1911-14, when they were always coupled with real-life characters in order to give a reason for their existence. *The Artist's Dream* had as an introduction an artist who drew a picture, and fell asleep; then the drawing came to life. The McCay cartoon had, as an introduction, a bet that he could not draw motion. He was pictured making the bet, and then the cartoon followed. Pathe, more or less hesitantly, ran a few short, terse bits of action in cartoons on the ends of their news-reels during 1911.

Today cartoons are a source of wonder. Those making animated cartoons lift out and re-shape human experiences in their more lovable form. They instill into the screen a gaiety and glow that depicts human traits in their more desirable form. They re-create again lost childhood. It is a form of entertainment that the screen must never lose.

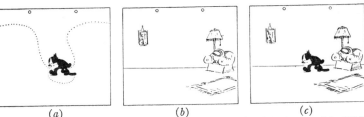

FIG. 19. *Felix the Cat,* animated by Wm. Nolan for International in 1917, showing the "slash" system used by Raoul Barré in the early Edison cartoons; the drawing of the cat (*a*) is cut as indicated by the dots and is superimposed on the background drawing (*b*). The photograph of the combination is shown at (*c*).

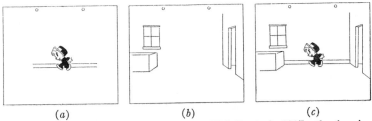

FIG. 18. *Jerry on the Job,* animated by Walt Lantz in 1917; the drawing (*a*) is placed beneath the drawing made on celluloid (*b*), and the two photographed together, producing the effect (*c*).

Another Armat Intermittent Movement

By ALEXANDER J. WEDDERBURN

A fourth mechanism by Thomas Armat for intermittently moving film through a motion-picture projector has recently been discovered in his old workshop. The movement was designed for a 17.5mm projector intended for home use.

THE NAME of Thomas Armat is a familiar one in the history of motion pictures. His pioneer work in motion-picture projection methods provided one of the basic patents in the field which became the basis for modern screening techniques.* Armat's use of the "star-wheel" or Geneva cross to move film intermittently through the projector was the first practical answer to the deadly screen flicker that retarded progress of the motion-picture industry.

What is not generally known is that

A contribution submitted on May 16, 1955, by Alexander J. Wedderburn, Div. of Graphic Arts, Smithsonian Institution, Washington 25, D. C.
* U.S. Pat. No. 578,185, March 2, 1897; see also Thomas Armat, "My part in the development of the motion picture projector," *Jour. SMPE* 24: 241–256, Mar. 1935.

Armat, far from resting on his laurels, continued his experiments with intermittent movement long after his Geneva cross had been accepted as one of the basic patents of the motion-picture industry. Only last summer was it discovered that Armat had perfected a fourth mechanism for advancing the film through the projector with a stop-start motion.

Mrs. Thomas Armat widow of the Washington inventor, while going through material stored in a small building that had formerly been Armat's workshop, came across a small projector that had been forgotten with the passage of the years. Sight of the machine brought back a flood of memories. Mrs. Armat recalls the details of a little-known episode in the life of the inventor. This is the story.

After the Edison interests had acquired rights to manufacture his Vitascope projector in 1896 Armat became interested in the potential market of amateur cinematography. Foreseeing that eventually the motion-picture camera and projector would attain equal prominence in the home with still apparatus, Armat began work on a machine he believed would appeal to the amateur.

He recognized the obvious fact that 35mm machines were too cumbersome, complex and expensive for any but the professional cameraman. With this in mind he set out to produce a camera and projector, small, simple to operate and inexpensive—in short a motion-picture prototype of the Eastman Number I Kodak camera that had brought photography into millions of homes.

Armat commenced this undertaking in 1911 and by 1916–17 had worked out a rough model of a projector which met the specifications he himself had set for it. To cut size and cost of operation simultaneously Armat decided to reduce the film size and accomplished this by simply

Fig. 1. Recently discovered 17.5mm motion-picture projector made by Thomas Armat about 1916–17. Rectangular metal housing contains the intermittent mechanism. The machine was intended for amateur use. (*Photographs from the Smithsonian Institution.*)

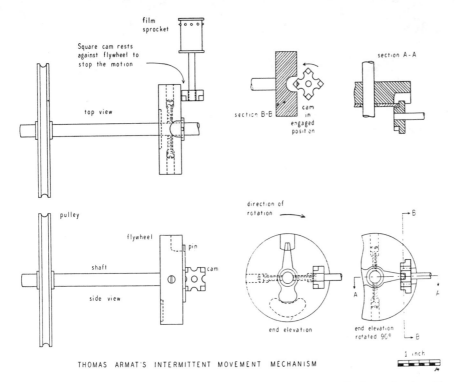

film sprocket

Square cam rests against flywheel to stop the motion

top view

section A-A

section B-B

cam in engaged position

pulley

flywheel

shaft

pin

cam

side view

direction of rotation →

B

A A

A A

B

end elevation

end elevation rotated 90°

1 inch

THOMAS ARMAT'S INTERMITTENT MOVEMENT MECHANISM

Fig. 2. The projector contains a type of mechanism not identified previously with Thomas Armat. A pin on the flywheel strikes a square cam rotating it one-quarter turn and advancing the film a frame at each revolution of the flywheel. Between times the cam is locked at rest against the face of the flywheel. (*Photograph from the Smithsonian Institution.*)

cutting a roll of 35mm standard-size film down the middle. This gave him a length of film 17.5 mm wide with an effective image size near to that of the present-day 16mm film. Of course the sprocket holes ran only on one side of the film and both camera and projector were adapted mechanically to meet this condition.

The projector, which is of primary interest, was powered with a small electric motor. A motor speed control allowed the operator to change the film speed at will.

In the accompanying illustrations (Fig. 1) Armat's amateur projector is shown mounted on a circular pedestal whose diameter is only 11 in. The overall height of the machine is 15 in.

and its longest measurement is 14 in.

But the most significant aspect of this machine was disclosed for the first time since it was reluctantly laid away in 1926 by its inventor when the author removed the top plate that hid the intermittent movement. We were expecting to uncover the familiar Geneva cross which Armat had incorporated in his 1896 projector. Instead we found a mechanism considerably different from any of the three previously attributed to Armat and/or his onetime partner C. Francis Jenkins.

It will be remembered that Armat and Jenkins together designed the first device that eliminated the screen flicker. This was the so-called mutilated gear which proved to be too noisy and heavy

to be practical. This was in 1895. Later that year after dissolution of the partnership with Jenkins, Armat adapted an eccentric cam or beater movement to his Vitascope projector. This too proved not to be the full answer because the constant striking of the beater tended to break the film.

It was in 1896 that the now famous Geneva cross movement was introduced in Armat's second Vitascope. This so far as was known until last year, was the last of Armat's improvements in the field of intermittent mechanism. Now we know that Thomas Armat was one of those inventors who never assumed that his most recent effort could not be improved upon. Apparently he decided to use still another stop-start device for his amateur projector.

As may be noted in the accompanying drawing (Fig. 2) the film sprocket is on a drive shaft which advances the film one frame at a time with a stop-start motion. The intermittent movement is imparted when a pin on the flywheel of the main drive shaft engages a square cam on the sprocket shaft, rotating it one-quarter turn and advancing the film a frame at each revolution of the flywheel. Between times the cam is locked at rest against the face of the flywheel providing a period of rest for each frame of the film.

This machine, together with its companion piece, a 17.5mm motion-picture camera, was to have been offered to the public for amateur use under the name "Fireside Movies," according to Mrs. Armat. But Armat and Henry N. Marvin, of the American Mutoscope and Biograph Co. who was to have been a partner and promoter of the new Company, lost interest in the project when they learned of apparently successful attempts by Edison and others to produce sound motion pictures. Unaccountably, they came to the conclusion that with the advent of sound a silent machine would have little appeal to the public.

It was for this reason that the fourth intermittent movement by the noted inventor was laid aside and forgotten until its recent discovery by the author.

Thomas Alva Edison's
Early Motion-Picture Experiments

By HAROLD G. BOWEN

In the year 1887, Thomas Alva Edison conceived the idea of devising an instrument by means of which, used in combination with his phonograph, "all motion and sound would be recorded and reproduced simultaneously." Historical objects, documents, photographs and prints from early movies have recently been discovered in the archives of the Thomas Alva Edison Foundation and Museum in West Orange, N.J. This paper will reveal for the first time some aspects of the development of motion pictures from an idea in Edison's mind to his contributions to the technological and artistic aspects of the infant industry.

THERE IS a familiar statement of Thomas Alva Edison's which was published in the *Century Magazine*, June 1894,[1] in which Edison said:

"In the year 1887, the idea occurred to me that it was possible to devise an instrument which would do for the eye what the phonograph does for the ear, and that by a combination of the two all motion and sound could be recorded and reproduced simultaneously. This idea, the germ of which came from the little toy called the Zoetrope, and the work of Muybridge, Marié and others has now been accomplished so that every change of facial expression can be recorded and reproduced life size. The Kinetoscope is only a small model illustrating the present stage of progress but with each succeeding month new possibilities are brought into view. I believe that in coming years, by my own work and that of Dickson, Muybridge, Marié and others who will doubtlessly enter the field, that grand opera can be given at the Metropolitan Opera House at New York without any material change from the original, and with artists and musicians long since dead."

In 1894, at the time Edison recorded these reflections, he had already accomplished a great deal. A practical strip film kinetograph and projector had been covered by patent applications. The 35mm film had been introduced which became the standard for the industry. The first motion-picture studio — the Black Maria (Fig. 1) — was built in West Orange, N.J. This kinetographic theater, which has been reconstructed (Fig. 2) as a part of the Thomas Alva Edison Foundation Museum in West Orange, N.J., revolved 360° on a pivot with its roof gaping at the elusive sun in order to floodlight the stage (Fig. 3) on which actors were performing kaleidoscopic glimpses of vaudeville acts.

During the middle and latter part of 1894, a great cast of performers were to troup across the boards of the Black Maria stage. A few of the films made in 1894 in the Black Maria might be of interest:

(1) First motion picture of a knock-out in a prize fight — six rounds of a ten-round fight between Leonard and Cushing.

(2) First motion picture of a staged prize fight — six rounds of Corbett and Courtney — a kinetograph exclusive.

(3) Short subjects galore — cock fights, boxing cats, Sandow in feats of strength, dog tricks, acrobats, fencers, knife duels, Spanish, English, Japanese and French dancers, scientific pictures of insects taken through a microscope, "westerns" with Buffalo Bill Cody and Indians.

(4) Comedy and slapstick described as a barber shop skit, a burlesque boxing bout with two comedians named Long and Short and a tramp clown.

(5) Twenty-four actors gave us the first stage show motion-picture spectacle.

(6) Trick photography had not been overlooked as W. K. L. Dickson appeared in company with himself in a film as a ghostly conscience in one sequence; and, beheaded, carried his head on a platter in another.

(7) Sound pictures had been successful since Dickson played a violin as two men danced. This film incidentally has been preserved and is available for viewing. An organ grinder had been recorded for eye and ear and a still photograph in the archives of the Edison Foundation shows an audience of one seeing and listening to a peep-hole kinetoscope equipped with ear tubes.

As techniques were sharpened, Edison made so bold as to twist the tail of the unknown by pointing the camera out of the window of the Black Maria for outdoor scenes of Professor Batty's Trained Bears, a picnic alongside the Black Maria fence, an acrobat doing somersaults on the greensward and an outdoor picture of charging horsemen.

Where would this lead? Even a motion picture of Thomas Alva Edison at work in his chemical laboratory on June 5,

1897, would be filed for posterity. Shortly, commercial movies, newsreels and shorts were to be made by the hundred and screened by Edison in the library of what is now the Edison Museum in West Orange, N.J. All sorts of subjects were to be filed in the film library "without any material change from the original and with artists and musicians long since dead." In the late 1890's and early 1900's, motion-picture films were to be taken by Edison with thousands and millions of frames showing matters of interest such as world's fairs and other expositions, disasters, Presidents, wars, travel and science, documentaries, advertising, education, human interest, sports, fantasy, comedy, glamour, and finally, in 1903, the first stories: *The Life of An American Fireman* in January 1903, and *The Great Train Robbery* in December 1903.

Films with a plot had arrived, and instead of a series of unrelated travelogues, newsreels and gimmicks, aimed at catching the curious public's attention as they marvelled at Thomas Alva Edison's latest technological wonder, films now had a beginning and an end heralding the advent of the motion-picture industry as entertainment.

But let us go back to the beginning. How did Edison bring to fruition in a practical way what the human race had been trying since the time the first cave man scratched on a cave wall—to permanently record motion?

In searching through the files of the Thomas Alva Edison archives, a person must be careful not to get bogged down in the wealth of material pertaining to the varied interests of Edison. The temptation to follow interesting trails that open up to an author must be sternly resisted. We have therefore endeavored to skim the cream off the top of the dish which contains successful experimentation on the motion-picture camera and report documentary material which sheds new light on Edison's pioneering accomplishments. Much work still must be done in the archives before the full story can be told. We have learned many new interesting things in the last year and we have made many exciting discoveries of Edisonia—the most important of which were first exhibited at the Library of Congress, Washington, D.C., and are now to be seen at the Edison Museum. We expect there will be more.

We might logically raise the question of what prompted Edison to send W. K. L. Dickson, a "young laboratory assistant keen on photography" to New York

Presented on May 3, 1954, at the Society's Convention at Washington, D.C., by Paul Busse for the author, Vice-Admiral Harold G. Bowen, USN (Ret.), then Executive Director, Thomas Alva Edison Foundation, West Orange, N.J. (This paper was received on March 21, 1955.)

Fig. 1. The "Black Maria," the first motion-picture studio in the world, erected on the grounds of Edison's West Orange Laboratory. It was completed on February 1, 1893. This was three and one-half years after his invention of the first practical and commercially successful strip-film motion-picture camera.

Fig. 2. This replica of the first motion-picture studio in the world, which was nicknamed the "Black Maria," has been built on the grounds of the Thomas Alva Edison Foundation Museum, West Orange, N.J., a short distance from the site of the original. The structure moves around on a pivot and the roof can be raised in order to use the sun's rays as for early movie making. Films are shown in the "Black Maria" daily, except Mondays and Tuesdays, at 11:30 A.M. and 4:00 P.M.

City during early December of 1887 to purchase photographic material from the Scovill Manufacturing Company. Aside from Dickson's own account[2] of preliminary project planning by Edison while at his Newark Laboratory, a letter from Scovill to Edison dated December 17, 1887, is the first direct evidence that systematic experiments were to be started in Room No. 5 of the new West Orange Laboratory "to do for the eye what the phonograph had done for the ear." The new Laboratory was opened in late November 1887, and there were big plans for the new project.

Dickson himself had said that one large room in the Laboratory was to be set aside for kinetographic experiments. In making a cursory examination of the extensive documentation in the archives, we are able to conclude that through Edison's avid reading of the *Scientific American* and other scientific and technical publications, he was undoubtedly aware of articles being published as early as October 19, 1878, on the advances being made throughout the world in the techniques of photography and particularly experiments by Muybridge on animal locomotion. Edison himself stated that the biggest spur to his interest in living photography came from his work in the development of one of history's most classical inventions, the recording and reproducing of sound by his device to be popularized as the phonograph.

After the successful invention of a commercially practical incandescent lamp and a system for the generation and distribution of electrical energy, commemorated in 1954 as Light's Diamond Jubilee, Edison turned, in 1887, to the further development of the phonograph which he had set aside in 1878. He also was free to begin his experiments on the problem of accelerated photography as well as the development

of a mechanism for both taking and viewing pictures in rapid succession.

Characteristically, Edison approached his photographic problem in a most practical manner. Unlike previous investigators, Edison realized that he needed to devise a mechanism that would start and stop many times per second with little or no inertia as it recorded tiny pictures. In his earliest experiments, microscopic photographs were made on the surface of a revolving cylinder similar to that of Edison's wax cylinder phonograph; and, in fact, using an adaptation of his phonograph mechanism. The pictures were "photographed in a continuous spiral line on a cylinder or plate in the same way that sound is recorded on the phonograph."

But perhaps Edison's own accomplishments and thoughts written in his own hand on October 8, 1888, and filed as caveat No. 110 on October 17, 1888,[3] will provide the best summary of his cylinder experiments.

This caveat, the handwritten draft

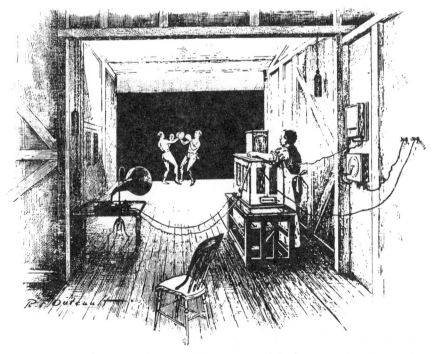

Fig. 3. This drawing of the inside of the "Black Maria," the world's first motion-picture studio, first appeared in the "Electrical World," June 16, 1894. The camera is seen at the right while the phonograph apparatus indicates that the picture being filmed was an early "talkie."

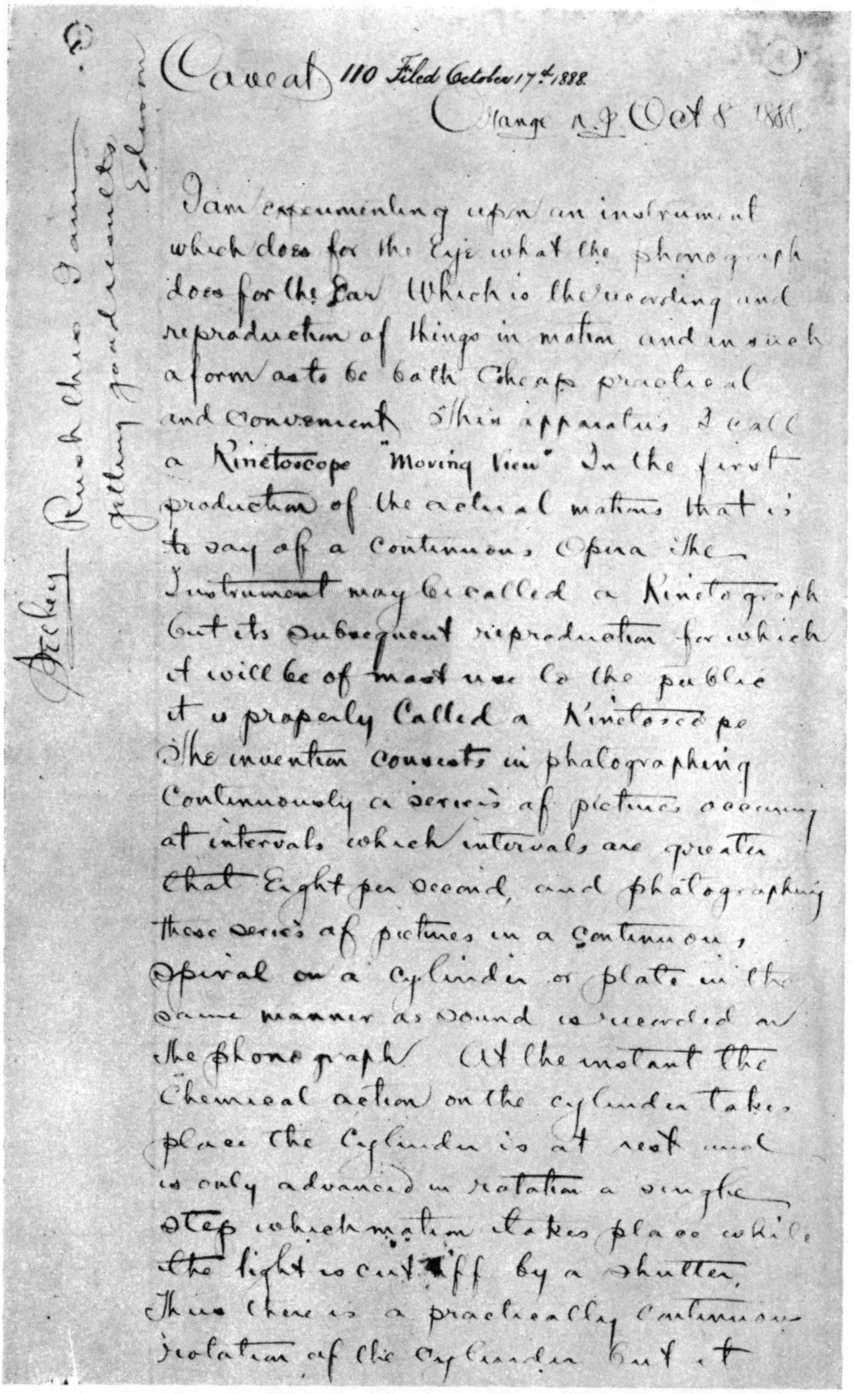

Fig. 4. First page of Edison's handwritten caveat of October 8, 1888, announcing preliminary experiments on motion-picture apparatus.

never before published, shows Edison's personal annotation to his lawyer: "Seeley, rush this I am getting good results;" signed/Edison.

The text is as follows (Fig. 4):

"I am experimenting upon an instrument which does for the eye what the phonograph does for the ear, which is the recording and reproduction of things in motion, and in such a form as to be both cheap, practical and convenient. This apparatus I call a Kinetoscope 'moving view.' In the first production of the actual motions that is to say of a continuous opera the instrument may be called a Kinetograph but its subsequent reproduction for which it will be of most use to the public it is properly called a Kinetoscope. The invention consists in photographing continuously a series of pictures occurring at intervals which intervals are greater than eight per second, and photographing these series of pictures in a continuous spiral on a cylinder or plate in the same manner as sound is recorded on the phonograph. At the instant the chemical action on the cylinder takes place the cylinder is at rest and is only advanced in rotation a single step which motion takes place while the light is cut off by a shutter. Thus there is a practically continuous rotation of the cylinder but it takes place step by step and at such times as no photographic effect takes place. For illustration say the cylinders may be about the same size as the phonograph, the number of threads to the inch on the feed screw is about 32. This will give a photograph image about $\frac{1}{32}$ of an inch wide, giving about 180 photographs per revolution or 42000 for the whole cylinder. It is probable that 25 per second will be sufficient to give the illusion as if looking at the actual scene with all its life and motion this will therefore record and reproduce all the motions or scenes occurring during a period of 28 minutes.

"By gearing or connecting the Kinetograph by a positive mechanical movement, a continuous record of all motion is taken down on the Kinetograph and a continuous record of all sounds are taken down by the phonograph and by substituting the photograph recording devices on the Kinetograph for a microscope stand and objective it becomes a Kinetoscope and by insertion of the listening tubes of the phonograph into the ear the illusion is complete and we may see and hear a whole opera as perfectly as if actually present although the actual performance may have taken place years before.

"I prefer to use the cylinder form instead of a plate with volute spiral. A continuous strip could be used but there are many mechanical difficulties in the way while the cylinder with the microphotographs taken on its surface in continuous spiral permits of the use of very simple mechanism. The cylinders which are hollow shells slip onto a taper cylinder permanently connected to the instrument just as in the phonograph. The shells may be of any substance which will preserve its shape such as plaster paris and other mouldable bodies. The collodion or other photographic film may be flowed over it just as if it was an ordinary flat photo plate, a positive being taken; but if it is desired to produce a negative series of photographs a glass cylinder is used—surface of the cylinder or shell is flowed and the records taken. The cylinder or shell being exceedingly thin say of mica is slipped over the regular cylinder to be used in practice whose surface is sensitized and printed from the negative by light in straight lines without reflection from side surfaces. A positive may be taken and with proper lenses reproduced on another cylinder just as one photograph may be taken from another.

"The permanent cylinder may even be covered with a shell and a thin flat film or transparent tissue sensitized be wrapped around it which after being filled with images may be detached from the shell and used as a negative to print many positives on sheets which are permanently pasted on shells for actual use, perfect alignment and no eccentricity of

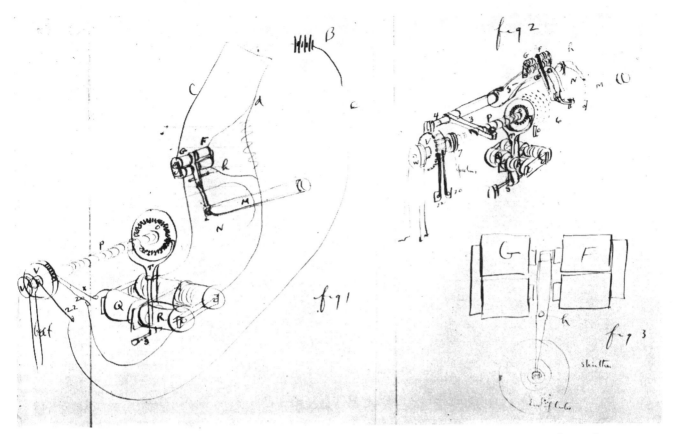

Fig. 5. Figure 1, Edison's first motion-picture caveat — cylinder Kinetograph with electromagnet intermittent motion control.

Fig. 6. Figures 2 and 3, Edison's first caveat on cylinder Kinetograph.

the surface must be had as the focus of the observing objective will be changed, although a presser foot might move the objective and thus keep it in focus even if the surface of the cylinder did not run true.

"In figures 1 [Fig. 5], 2 [Fig. 6], 3 [Fig. 6], I illustrate diagrammatically the principal feature of the apparatus. W, figure 2, is the drive pulley preferably run by a belt from an electromotor. V, the breakwheel. P is the feed screw as in the phonograph. 7 a friction connecting the drive pulley and break wheel with the screw P and attached apparatus 3 the traveller arm for carrying the micro-photographic apparatus while recording and the observing microscope when re-producing. 5 is the arm carrying the above. A shutter with two openings see figure 3 is vibrated by double magnets G and F between the surface of the cylinder and the recording or reproducing apparatus M. The lever of the vibrator is pivoted at h. When the lever is to the right or to the left the aperture is opposite the objective but when in the act of mov-ing the line of vision between the cylinder and objective is cut off by the space be-tween the two holes in the shutter. When the shutter is at either the left or right limit and still the cylinder is also in a state of rest and no movement of the cylinder takes place while an aperture is opposite the objective, hence in recording and reproducing the photographic sur-faces are in a state of rest, the intermittent

rotation of the cylinder takes place by means of an escapement O and fork T reciprocated by the double magnets Q and R. The reciprocation of the shutter as well as the escapement being con-trolled by magnets and the break wheel V and springs 20 and 22, one spring being in contact with the metallic part of the wheel (see figure 1) while the other is on the space between. On a further rotation of the break wheel the opposite effect occurs and the spring which was previously on insulation now comes in electrical contact with the wheel and the other set of magnets are energized thus advancing the cylinder $\frac{1}{32}$ of inch only at the time the shutter has closed the

vision between objective and cylinder. As the speed of W should be much greater than P, the break wheel V need have but few breaks. This insures greater rapidity of advancement of the cylinder during the interval when the shutter closes the light beam off.

"The motor should be governed so as to produce even results. Of course in practice the mechanism will be con-siderably changed from that shown as the figures are merely diagrammatical so as to simplify the explanation of the in-vention.

"A tuning fork with break might con-trol the magnets, the fork being kept in continuous vibration by a magnet and

Fig. 7. Motion-picture camera, or strip Kinetograph, made and used by Thomas A. Edison at his West Orange Laboratory in 1889.

Fig. 8. Hand perforator used for punching film strips for Edison's 1889 strip Kinetograph.

automatic make-and-break contact. The levers T and the shutter lever may be reeds or tuning forks themselves, their magnets being in one circuit and controlled by a master fork or reed electrically operated or by a self make-and-break attached to one of them. The break wheel V might be run by a governed motor or mechanism independent of the motor driving the main devices. The levers T and shutter may be operated mechanically by means of an undulating surfaced rotating wheel which reciprocates a lever which not only serves to release the escapement O but works the shutter, a strip parallel to the cylinder and between the objective and surface of cylinder may be reciprocated up and down two continuous apertures are in the strip. The whole of the shutter is then detached from the travelling arm rendering the images free from blurring due to any movement or vibration of the arm. A plate machine in the feeding mechanism, say a volute spiral or worm, or multiplying gearing may be used and flat records taken instead of using cylinders but I do not think this form is so practical. By using very large transparent shells the pictures may be even projected on the screen as in microphotographic projection or enlargement, the cylinder

being revolved and the source of light inside of the cylinder, negative records being only recorded." s/Thos. A. Edison

A few parts of this early cylinder apparatus have survived thanks to their having been used as exhibits in patent litigation. One piece is a slotted cylinder of phonograph size, another is a larger cylinder still showing patches of photographic emulsion on its surface, a third is a large cylinder with one edge studded with pins for making electrical contacts. These pins are $\frac{1}{4}$ in. apart, and may have served as circuit-closers for illuminating, by electric spark, the $\frac{1}{4}$-in. pictures. This cylinder, which was on exhibit with the others at the Library of Congress in 1954, is slotted and would hold a sensitized sheet 3 in. wide by 14 in. long, on which about 700 $\frac{1}{4}$-in. pictures could be taken in a spiral line. Prints of portions of three different sheets of these $\frac{1}{4}$-in. pictures have survived the ravages of time. They show Fred Ott, one of Edison's workmen, wrapped in a white sheet tied in the middle, waving his arms and "making a monkey of himself."

These and similar pictures were being made, on steadily improved cylinder mechanisms, up to the early part of 1889, as disclosed in two more recently dis-

covered Edison caveats dated February 2 and May 20 respectively. Mechanisms that had "done for the ear" were persisting in their influence on the development of mechanisms that were to "do for the eye." Better photographic materials facilitated progress, especially sheets of Carbutt celluloid 18 in. long which were wrapped around the cylinders to take the $\frac{1}{4}$-in. pictures described above. These $\frac{1}{4}$-in. pictures appear to be the last attempts to use the phonograph-cylinder conception for recording motion pictures.

By this time Edison and Dickson had recognized that to achieve their goal a radical departure from the cylinder approach would be necessary. New apparatus had been constructed and tried out for taking pictures in a straight line, using narrow strips cut from the 18-in. sheets of celluloid. As the experiments progressed, pictures were made larger, and strips of film were cemented end to end to obtain greater length. They were getting closer to success.

Before referring to Edison's handwritten original draft of his fourth caveat on motion pictures, dated November 2, 1889, in which he described the successful strip kinetograph, one important technological event must be described in which George Eastman plays the leading role. In the biography of George Eastman by Carl W. Ackerman,[4] there are quoted two letters which document the Edison-Eastman connection:

"Opening the mail at the office one morning Eastman found the following inquiry from Edison:

Orange, N.J., May 30, 1889
The Eastman Dry Plate Co.,
Rochester, New York

Gentlemen:
Please quote us discount upon your Kodak camera, your list price, $25.00. Also discount upon reloading camera, list price $10.00.
Yours truly,
EDISON PHONOGRAPH WORKS,
T.A.E.

On September 2, Eastman received another letter from the Edison Laboratories:

Dear Sirs:
Enclosed please find sum of $2.50 P.O.O. due you for one roll Kodak film for which please accept thanks — I shall try same today and report — it looks splendid — I never succeeded in getting this substance in such straight and long pieces —
Sincerely yours,

W. K. L. Dickson

Can you coat me some rolls of your highest sensitometer — please answer."

Dickson's own account of Eastman's film and its application was described in the December 1933 issue of this *Journal*[2] from which I quote:

"...it was rumored that the Eastman Company was experimenting on a new

94

product for their cameras, and that it would be shown at the New York Camera Club by Mr. George Eastman's representative. At the end of the meeting, which I attended, I approached the demonstrator, explained what we wanted and asked for the 2 by 4 inch sample to show to Mr. Edison. The representative quickly grasped the situation and its great possibilities, and invited me to come out to Rochester to see Mr. Eastman, which I did the next day. I knew then that we should reach our goal if the Eastman Company could supply this new product in good lengths. When I showed Mr. Edison my new find his smile was seraphic; 'Good,' he said, 'we can now do the trick — just work like hell...'

"A few weeks elapsed before I saw Mr. Eastman again and explained our difficulties, which were remedied principally by reducing the coarseness of the silver bromide. This change proved most satisfactory. When perforating the film, however, the sprocket wheel often broke through and tore the film. I had to ask Mr. Eastman whether he could make his base tougher and less brittle, which he did.

"Meanwhile we had to use this rapid negative for our positive prints; and although they lacked pluckiness, we partly overcame it by using potassium bromide in our developing bath to reduce its sensitiveness. This caused me to apply again to Mr. Eastman for a less sensitive product or emulsion similar to that used in lantern slide work which we ultimately received.

"We were, however, much troubled with 'frilling,' and often a gelatinous mass of pictures was left at the bottom of our developing or fixing troughs, while the base remained on the drum, a situation which we found very trying and necessitated further conferences on this matter. Mr. Eastman, however, managed to overcome this difficulty in part.

"About this time we received six rolls of improved negative film 50 feet long, and later some slow positive film. All these samples and experiments were made exclusively for us by Mr. Eastman, who took an ever-increasing interest in what we were doing."

With this valuable contribution of George Eastman, the continuous strip film Kinetograph was now practical. The 1889 strip Kinetograph took pictures $\frac{1}{2}$ in. in diameter on a strip of film $\frac{3}{4}$ in. wide which ran horizontally through the camera. Along its lower edge the strip had perforations which fitted the teeth of a sprocket wheel; and the sprocket, by means of a Geneva movement or the equivalent, moved the film intermittently, one step for each exposure, past a revolving shutter. Like the earlier cylinder apparatus, this machine was also used for viewing the pictures. By changing to a smaller sprocket wheel to allow

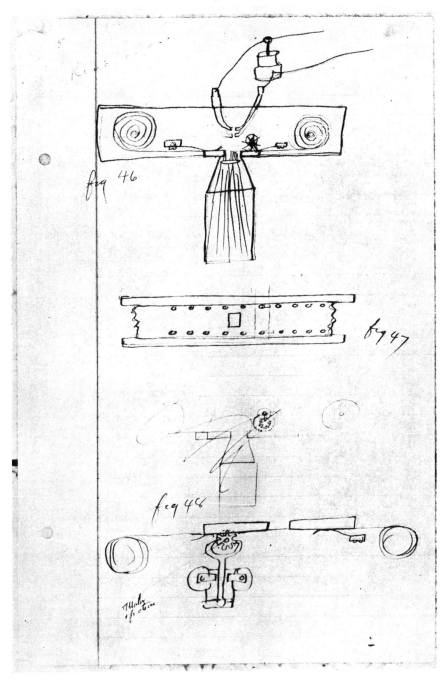

Fig. 9. Sketches from Edison's motion-picture caveat, November 2, 1889, showing the double perforated film — the prototype of modern standard film.

for shrinkage of the film when developed, the finished picture could be run through the camera, where it could be viewed directly, or, with a change of lens and addition of a light source, the picture could be projected on a screen. This camera (Fig. 7) has survived, almost complete, as a legal exhibit labelled "Edison's 1889 Strip Kinetograph." It was on display at the Library of Congress and is now on permanent exhibit in the Edison Museum, West Orange, N.J. With it is a little hand-operated device for punching the holes along one edge of the $\frac{3}{4}$-in. strips (Fig. 8).

The Edison 1889 Strip Kinetograph embodied the solution of the basic problems of the motion-picture art, both for making the pictures and for exhibiting them. The Strip Kinetograph (1889) is the first practical and commercially successful motion-picture machine to use a continuous film strip. On August 24, 1891, a patent was applied for and issued on August 31, 1897, as No. 589,168. This machine made practical the strip-film motion-picture camera. All later cameras and projectors, including Edison's own, are merely refinements of this primitive apparatus — the prototype for all.

Having solved the basic problems, Edison proceeded to build a better and larger camera. The pictures were eventually enlarged to 1 in. × $\frac{3}{4}$ in. The film strip, now available on special order from Eastman in 50-ft lengths, was used

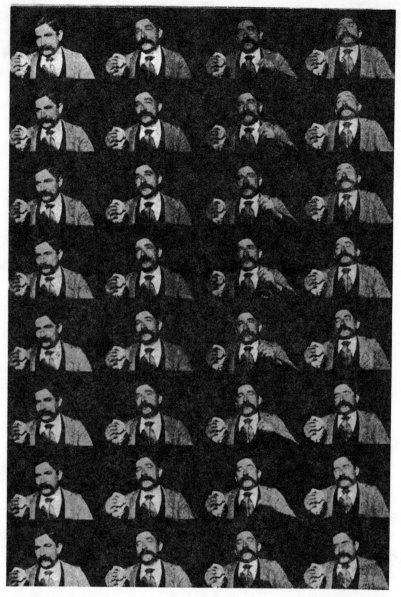

Fig. 10. "The Record of a Sneeze," one of the earliest motion-picture films made by Thomas A. Edison at West Orange, N. J. The first copyrighted motion picture — 1894.

in 1⅜ in. (35mm) width, and perforations were made along both edges — four to a frame. This film size is still standard. Cameras incorporating these improvements took motion pictures circa 1890 to 1894, including the early Black Maria films. One of these cameras, perhaps the first one, is now on display in the Henry Ford Museum in Dearborn, Mich.

Thus, by the close of 1889, Edison had solved the major problems in doing for the eye what the phonograph had done for the ear and a crude kinetographic camera as described in his handwritten caveat No. 4 dated November 2, 1889,[5] had been constructed and tested:

"Figure 46 [Fig. 9] is a kinetoscope. The sensitive film is in the form of a long band passing from one reel to another in front of a square slit as in Figure 47 [Fig. 9]; on each side of the band are rows of holes exactly opposite each other and into which double toothed wheels pass on (as) in the wheatstone automatic telegraph instrument. This ensures a positive motion of the band. The film being transparent, the Leyden jar spark illuminates back and by means of a lens the image is projected on a screen. Instead of the Leyden spark a continuous light with revolving shutter may be used. The operation of photographing is as follows — in front of the apparatus where the film is exposed the microphotographic apparatus is placed. A motor, preferably an electric motor, drives a shaft at great velocity; on this shaft is a sleeve carrying double toothed wheels engaging in the holes of the band of photo film. The connection between this sleeve and shaft is a friction one; on the sleeve is a release escapement with fork connected to the tongue of a polarized relay. This po-

larized relay is reciprocated by means of a break wheel alternating currents through it or by an alternating small dynamo. The time is so arranged with these currents that the band is advanced one step for a photograph 10 times in one second, the escapement working of course 10 times in a second, but of this $\frac{1}{10}$ of a second, $\frac{9}{10}$ths of the $\frac{1}{10}$ the band is still, with (while) $\frac{1}{10}$ of the $\frac{1}{10}$ of a second the band is moving. In other words: if there were but one photograph to be taken in ten seconds the band would be shifted in one second and stand still nine seconds, and this proportion holds good up to any number of photographs per second until the mechanism fails to act, by thus causing the band to be in a state of rest $\frac{9}{10}$ of the time, yet taking 10 photographic images per second, most perfect results are obtained and the great necessity of a shutter is modified. The break wheel which controls the polarized relay may be connected to the screw shaft of the phonograph, hence there will be a positive connection and all the movements of a person photographed will be exactly coincident with any sounds made by him.

"Figure 48 [Fig. 9] gives rough idea of positive feed mechanism; of course this principle can be applied to cylinder covered with the photo material as well as in bands. When a Leyden spark is used the break wheel is arranged that it takes place while band is in state of rest, or if shutter used reciprocating or revolving it is to be released by the same devices that release and move the band and the shutter so devised that light only passes to the image while projecting it on the screen when in a state of rest."

Edison's goal of 1887 described in the 1894 issue of *Century Magazine* quoted in the opening paragraph of this paper, had at last been attained.

The idea had been reduced to practice. A patent application had been filed. An instrument had been devised that could do for the eye what the phonograph had done for the ear. The very change of facial expression could be recorded on standardized 35mm film and reproduced life size without any material change from the original with artists long since dead— and copyrighted too! (Fig. 10).

References

1. A. and W. K. L. Dickson, "Edison's invention of the Kineto-Phonograph," *Century Magazine*, 48: 206–214, June 1894.
2. W. K. L. Dickson, "A brief history of the Kinetograph, the Kinetoscope and the Kineto-Phonograph," *Jour. SMPE*, 21: 435–455, Dec. 1933.
3. Edison Caveat No. 110, Handwritten Draft in Archives of Thomas Alva Edison Foundation, West Orange, N.J.
4. Carl W. Ackerman, *George Eastman*, Houghton Mifflin Co., Boston and New York, 1930.
5. Edison Caveat No. 117, Handwritten Draft in Archives of Thomas Alva Edison Foundation, West Orange, N.J.

Early Projector Mechanisms

By DON G. MALKAMES

Foreword

By BERNARD D. PLAKUN

Don Malkames' personal collection of old projectors, gathered over the past 25 years, includes more than a hundred machines and numerous accessories, dating back to the middle 1800's.

To see and handle the material on the shelves (Fig. 1), and to hear Malkames glowingly describe the place that each piece occupied in the history of motion pictures, is a memorable experience. On picking up a small brass film can, just large enough to fit snugly into a shirt pocket, you may learn that it had once been used to carry all the film needed for an entire evening's show — which might run only 40 ft. The background hangings in the museum breathe of a past era. Billboard posters advertising the triumph of motion photography or a scene from President McKinley's inauguration (both from the year 1897) create a feeling of excitement, as though one had just been newly introduced to the miracle of pictures that move.

It is difficult to convey adequately this excitement in the pages of a book; or to show, in still pictures, the action of an intricate rotary mechanism. Willy Borberg tried to do this in a paper which he

A contribution submitted in final form on April 24, 1957, by Don G. Malkames, 7 Plymouth Ave., Yonkers, N.Y.

presented at the 75th Convention of this Society in April 1954. He used the machines at the museum as a valuable source of research material for his paper. During the course of this early collaboration, Malkames became interested in the possibilities of a film record, and started work on a 35mm motion picture describing the projectors in his collection. The first two reels of this film were completed in time for showing at the Society's 79th Convention in New York City on May 2, 1956. A third reel was later added, and the completed film was shown at the Society's 80th Convention.

Malkames' production was well received, and he was soon beset by numerous requests for repeat booking. Unable to meet this huge task, but unwilling to refuse, he transferred the original to National Theatre Supply, through whose courtesy the film is now being made available for showing to groups.*

Although the production was a one-man operation, without financial support, it was so well done that the narration recorded in the soundtrack could be set down here almost word for word as a finished story. All photography in the film and in the article is original, from material in the museum. The author has

*Requests for loan of 16mm or 35mm prints with optical sound may be made to: Herbert Barnett, National Theatre Supply, 92 Gold St., New York 38. The name of the group and the purpose of the showing should be stated.

tried to create valuable new illustrations by avoiding widely recognized material, such as the original Edison Kinetoscope, for which numerous adequate photographs already exist.

One obvious, important omission is a discussion of Thomas Armat's work on basic projector design. The Society on two occasions has recognized the significance of Armat's work: first, when he was made an Honorary Member in 1935; and again in 1946 when he was honored with a scroll on the occasion of the 50th anniversary of his motion-picture projection demonstration in a theater on Broadway in April 1896, the first of its kind in the United States. A complete description of Mr. Armat's work was published in the *Journal* in March 1935.

Malkames regards his collection as incomplete, and is still searching for additional machines. He may, at some time in the future, prepare a story on the evolution of lighting devices leading to today's carbon arc. The museum already holds much of interest for such a story. We hope it is not long in coming.

Dates and other factual data given in the paper are supported by references in various forms. Letters from early inventors, out-of-print catalogues (i.e., J. B. Colt Catalogue, of 1894, Sears Roebuck Catalogue of 1898) and advertisements from early trade magazines were used as source material.

Fig. 1. One wall of the projector collection in Don Malkames' Movie Museum.

DURING THE latter part of the nineteenth century, the traveling exhibitor with his magic lantern supplied popular entertainment all over the country. Lectures on Temperance, Religion and World Travel, illustrated by lantern slides, were given in churches, rented schoolhouses, and town halls. The lecturer was also the operator. As he adjusted the light and changed the slides, he dramatically described the scenes to his audience.

Early exhibitors tried many ingenious contraptions to create movement on their screens. With hand-manipulated slide overlays, they could show what might happen to a man who imbibes too much brew (paunch expands alarmingly) or one who tries to rob a bird's nest (man and bird battle over nest). Howls of laughter resulted from such scenes as these. And for a more dramatic interlude, imagine a lonely graveyard on a sunny afternoon. As the sun sinks into the hills, the ghosts of our dear departed rise from the ground. The skeletons dance to the strains of the church organ wafting over the evening breeze. But all too soon, the night is over, and the grey dawn chases the dead back to their quiet repose.

Such scenes thrilled thousands just before the Gay Nineties. But by 1890, photography was being wedded to the rapid exposure of a series of pictures, to create the illusion of motion on a projector screen. Before the turn of the century, a complete performance usually consisted of several short films, each about 40 ft in length. These were single scenes, such as, *Empire State Express Going Sixty Miles per Hour*, or a scene of *President McKinley's Inauguration*.

An early camera built by Demeny in France made a series of rapid exposures on a revolving glass plate. After the plate

Fig. 2. The Lumière Projector.

Fig. 3. Demeny Projector with beater movement.

was developed and printed onto another similar one, the camera became a projector by the simple addition of a light source at its rear.

The first motion-picture film exhibition charging admission to the general public opened in Paris, December 1895, using the Lumière *Cinematograph*. This was a combination camera, printer and projector. The intermittent movement was of the claw type and the film was perforated with only one sprocket hole on each side, per frame of film. When used as a camera, 40 ft of film was fed from a small wooden magazine on top. After exposure, it was wound into a little metal magazine, inside. When used as a projector, a small spoolholder was mounted on the top to feed the film. After projection, the film fell into a wooden box under the mechanism. No sprocket wheels were necessary for such short lengths of film. Later, the Lumière

camera and projector were made as separate units. A Lumière projector was the original machine used in the Eden Musee when it opened in 1896. Figure 2 shows the projector mechanism.

An early Demeny film projector of about 1898 used the popular beater movement shown in Fig. 3. This simple mechanism gave very satisfactory results and was widely used for some years thereafter. In fact, it was used as late as 1913 in this country, in the *Kinemacolor* Projector to be described later.

The first model of the Edison projector was sold outright to the exhibitor in 1897. It became known as the *spool-bank* model, inasmuch as the film, instead of being fed from a reel, was in a continuous loop. In Fig. 4, you will note that there were no upper or lower sprockets and no means for framing. Edison used a 2-pin cam in his Geneva movement. It must be remembered that Edison's early films

Fig. 4. Edison (Spool-Bank) Projector.

Fig. 5. The Colt Criterioscope.

Fig. 6. Movement of the Colt Criterioscope.

Fig. 7. German Vitascope Projector.

Fig. 8. The Lubin Projector.

were photographed at 40 frames/sec and the 2-pin cam allowed projection at this speed without undue wear on film or mechanism.

The Colt *Criterioscope* of this same period, built in New York City, using a rear shutter and a 40-tooth intermittent sprocket, is shown in Fig. 5. This first American rear-shutter machine might have continued in successful production but for a fire which destroyed the factory in 1900, after which production stopped. The sturdy movement in this projector

(Fig. 6) reminds us of some of those used in some recent 16mm "sprocket intermittent" projectors.

Another type of movement, used about this time, periodically gripped the film between two rubber rollers to bring the picture down one frame. Several makers used this principle. A German *Vitascope*, made in Berlin by Deutsche Bioscope Gesellschaft, is shown in Fig. 7. The gate tension is relieved during the period the film is moving in the gate. The upper sprocket acts as a stop, after the film has

been pulled down one frame. Framing is accomplished while running, by turning the knob on the upper sprocket, thus moving the sprocket ahead or behind in relation to the rest of the mechanism.

The Edison projecting *Kinetoscope* of 1899 ran the film into a bag or basket underneath the mechanism. Up to this time, film magazines were not used on projectors. Instead, the reel, usually holding only a few hundred feet of film, was mounted on a so-called "reel hanger" above the mechanism. This also held a

Fig. 9. Powers No. 3 Cameragraph.

Fig. 10. The Selig Polyscope.

Fig. 11. Pink's Viascope.

Fig. 12. The Optigraph, made by Enterprise Optical Co., used a lantern slide projector as a light source.

Fig. 13. Edison's Universal Projecting Kinetoscope.

Fig. 14. Cannock's Cinematograph.

Fig. 15. Powers Cameragraph No. 4.

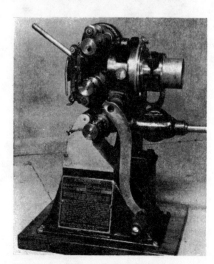

Fig. 16. Bell & Howell Kinodrome.

Fig. 17. The Optigraph No. 4.

Fig. 18. Cannock's Edengraph.

Fig. 19. Lubin's Cineograph.

Fig. 20. French Pathé Frères Projector.

Fig. 21. American Standard Projector of 1910·

geared crank which enabled rewinding of the film between showings. The mechanism was mounted on a wooden front board and could be slid up and down for framing, only the lens and aperture plate remaining stationary.

The Lubin Projector of 1899, complete with limelight, is shown in Fig. 8. The light source will be described later. This projector was similar to that of the Edison. One of the few changes is in the framing device. Here the aperture plate and lens move up and down together. Lubin used a single-pin cam in the Geneva.

Another projector of this same period and design was the Powers *No. 3 Cameragraph*. This machine (Fig. 9) was to be greatly improved and widely used for many years to come. Powers also used a single-pin cam. Framing was accomplished as in the Edison, by shifting the entire mechanism on the wooden front board.

The Selig *Polyscope* (Fig. 10) was built by Andrew Schustek in Chicago, for Col. William N. Selig. Copied in much detail from the Improved Lumière Cinematograph, this projector used a claw movement. Note the crudely constructed screw for framing. Although these machines gave a very steady picture on the screen, they wore out very rapidly as film lengths were increased from 40 to 400 ft or more. The claw movement had six pulldown pins.

Another claw-movement projector, also manufactured in Chicago, was the *Viascope* built by John J. Pink (Fig. 11).

In 1898, A. C. Roebuck (of Sears, Roebuck fame) marketed a projection head to be used with a dissolving stereopticon which had been sold by this firm for several years. The machine shown in Fig. 12 was made under the name of Enterprise Optical Co. The projector mechanism was called the *Optigraph*. This ingenious little mechanism, not

much larger than your fist, gave very acceptable projection and probably more of them were sold than all other makes combined. The mechanism was mounted on sliding rails in front of the lower lantern and could be slid out of the way when projecting slides, or dissolves could be made to a slide in the upper lantern. The Optigraph was actually the first model of the well-known Motiograph, which is still considered one of the finest projectors manufactured today. Just above the Geneva movement, between the aperture and lens, was a barrel-type shutter. Framing was accomplished by simply moving the aperture up and down. Because of its light weight, this machine became very popular with the traveling exhibitors in rural communities.

Because of the lack of electricity in most of these one-night stands, the limelight was the most popular type of light source. An intensely hot flame was directed against a stick of unslaked lime. The flame was produced by burning oxygen and hydrogen gases in proper combination. One tank, known as the saturator, supplied the hydrogen gas by vaporizing sulfuric ether. Oxygen was generated in a larger tank, where water dripped onto an oxygen-generating compound.

Inspired perhaps by the popularity of the small-sized Optigraph, Edison brought out the Edison *Universal* Projecting Kinetoscope designed by A. White in 1903. This, the first all-metal machine to come from Edison, was also designed so that it could be slid to one side to project lantern slides (see Fig. 13). Most entertainments of this period still consisted of a lecture, illustrated by slides, and interspersed with short scenes on motion-picture film. Incidentally, the sprockets, gears and bearing of most of these early machines were made of brass. Edison still retained the two-pin cam in the intermittent movement.

About 1903, Frank Cannock, who was employed as a projectionist in the Eden Musee in New York City, built the projector shown in Fig. 14 and named it the *Cinematograph*. Cannock had been a mechanic trained in the Singer Sewing Machine factory in Scotland. His mechanism probably showed the greatest mechanical precision used in a projector up to this time. This model was the forerunner of an improved machine which was later marketed as the *Edengraph* and which, still later, developed into the first model of the *Simplex*. This was, I believe, the first mechanism in which the Geneva movement was enclosed in an oil bath.

Nicholas Powers brought out his first all-metal projector, the Powers *Cameragraph No. 4*, in 1905. It immediately became very popular and thousands were sold during the next five years (see Fig. 15). The Powers *Cameragraph No. 5* had the first automatic fire shutter built in America, or, at least, so claimed the Nicholas Powers Company.

In 1907, Bell & Howell built the *Kinodrome* projector (Fig. 16) for Major George K. Spoor. This was the first machine in which framing was accomplished by revolving the intermittent, as is done in most modern projectors. Another innovation in this finely built mechanism was the double front shutter, with the disks revolving in opposite directions by using a shaft within a shaft, similar to the Century projectors of today.

The 1907 *Optigraph No. 4* (Fig. 17) used a relay condenser mounted on the gate. This model also had an arrangement for revolving the intermittent sprocket for framing. This was accomplished by a sort of sliding-screw arrangement. The Sears Roebuck catalog listed, as one of the features of this model, its ability to be operated either forward or backward. Thus, short films could be made to run more than twice their orig-

Fig. 22. Early Simplex Projector.   **Fig. 23. Baird's Projector of 1913.**

inal running time. Imagine the amusement of the audience at seeing horses going backward at full gallop; or divers springing out of the water, feet first, and alighting on the springboard! Thousands of other humorous actions were possible with the new Optigraph.

In 1908 the name of Optigraph was dropped when a new model was introduced under the name of *Motiograph No. 1*. This was the first machine having all gears enclosed. By simply pressing a button on the crank handle, the film could be rewound back onto the upper reel, ready for the next show. It must be remembered that an entire performance, in those days, consisted in most cases of only one reel of 1000 ft in length.

A double-cone shutter, mounted back of the lens and close to the aperture, gave an improvement in shutter efficiency. The completely enclosed Geneva movement slid up and down to frame, and was driven by a ball-and-socket shaft. This was the first movement that could be removed easily or replaced as a unit — a common practice today. A motor attachment could also be supplied, if desired.

In 1908, Frank Cannock introduced the *Edengraph* shown in Fig. 18. The successful years of operation of his earlier model at the Eden Musee had encouraged him to place this improved projector on the market. Although a finely designed and well constructed machine, its success was short lived. The industry was not ready to pay for the precision demanded by Cannock. Three years later, in 1908, his dream was realized when he and Edwin S. Porter designed the first Simplex.

S. Lubin's *Cineograph* (Fig. 19) was introduced as its first all-metal mecha-

nism. It had but few improvements over earlier models.

The French *Pathé Frères* projector (Fig. 20) also enjoyed some successs in this country during this period. It was considered a well-built and sturdy machine.

The Powers *No. 6 Cameragraph* reached the market during 1909. This very ruggedly built projector was destined to become one of the most successful for many years to come. It was the first to revive the front revolving shutter which was used almost exclusively thereafter, until about 1930, on all projectors. It introduced adjustable tension springs in the gate. However, the intermittent movement was the greatest innovation in this newest Powers Projector.

A five-to-one pin cross movement of entirely new design was used. It gave longer exposure without imposing strain on the film or the mechanism. Many old timers, today, still wonder why this movement hasn't been revived in some modern projector. Instead of a pivoted idler roller on the top sprocket, there were two small rollers at a fixed distance from the sprocket, similar to the design of many 16mm projectors today. A shoe was used on the lower sprocket, instead of a roller. The pin cross movement was mounted inside the flywheel.

A short time after the first of these machines was used in theaters, and after many complaints from users, the Powers Company announced that, due to the fact that the industry was changing over to the complete use of noninflammable film, several elements in the design were found to be impractical and would be changed at no cost to the purchaser. The changes consisted of replacing the upper and lower idlers with the type formerly

used, as well as enclosing the intermittent in an oil-tight casing. But it was to be more than 40 years before the industry would finally adopt noninflammable film.

In 1910, the *American Standard* projector (Fig. 21) reached the market and was quite popular for several years. In fact, it is claimed that for a short time there were more American Standards in use in Broadway houses than any other make.

In 1911, a new trend in projector design took place. The first *Simplex* had arrived. This mechanism (Fig. 22) is so well known to the industry today that it is unnecessary to describe its many advantages over other machines of that period. It was the first completely enclosed mechanism with center frame bearings. It had means for adjusting the revolving shutter during operation, a new style of sliding gate instead of the former hinged types, a new type of fire shutter and governor, and a precision-focusing and lens-mount adjustment.

The Edison *Model D* was a modernization of its old design made by adding a front shutter and semi-enclosure of the gears. This model used flanged sprockets and is believed to be the first mechanism to use side guides for the film passing through the gate.

In 1913, Motiograph brought out its *1A* model which had a front shutter, double flywheels and other improvements.

The *Baird* projector, manufactured in New York, was also announced in 1913. This machine (Fig. 23) was closer to the general appearance of a modern projector than any others of that time, and was still offered for sale as late as 1922. It had the first lamphouse of proportions

Fig. 24. The German Ernemann Projector.

Fig. 25. The English Kamm Projector.

such as we presently use, a heavy iron pedestal, 3000-ft magazines of heavy construction, and a mechanism designed for simplicity of gearing and construction. The particular Baird projector illustrated saw service from 1915 to 1923 in the Hersker Theater in West Hazelton, Pa. When it was demonstrated in the theater lobby, prior to installation, as an example of the latest and best in projection equipment, it made a certain schoolboy play truant to examine it in awestruck wonder. That schoolboy is now the author of this paper.

Figure 24 shows the 1912 model of the German *Ernemann*. Here some attempt was made at a centralized oiling point.

As in all foreign projectors, the film side of the mechanism was in the open, and 32-tooth feed and take-up sprockets were used. When using short-focus lenses, they could easily be moved out of the way to open the gate.

The English *Kamm* projector (Fig. 25), with its front barrel shutter, was also of an unusual design as compared with American projectors of that day.

The *Kinemacolor* projector of 1913 reverted to the, by then, seldom used Demeny beater movement (see Fig. 26). The color wheel behind the aperture projected alternate frames through red and green filters at about 32 frames/sec. The results on the screen were really the

first semisuccessful presentation of actual color motion-picture photography. These projectors were, of course, used with road shows rather than permanently installed, although they would project standard black-and-white prints by removing the revolving color filters.

In 1921, Motiograph brought out the *Model F*. By this time all American projectors had enclosed mechanisms, center frame bearings and front revolving shutters.

Even the Nicholas Powers Company designed its *Cameragraph No. 7* with completely enclosed mechanism featuring automatic upper and lower loop setters. Before this machine (Fig. 27) was

Fig. 26. The Kinemacolor Projector.

Fig. 27. Nicholas Powers Cameragraph No. 7.

placed on the market, the original company merged with International Projector Corporation. Then, with the coming of talking pictures, the esteemed Powers mechanism quietly disappeared from the field.

Perhaps the greatest single improvement in projector design during the 1920's came from Germany. In 1925, the German AEG projector introduced the conical rear shutter. This shutter made possible the greatest light efficiency, coupled with the utmost heat elimination. It was the forerunner of the shutters found in the most modern projectors of today.

In 1928, Motiograph equipped its machines with rear cylindrical shutters. With the introduction of sound-on-film, the reduced picture aperture size, plus the perforated sound screens, made an increase in arc amperage necessary. Rear shutters became very desirable. One designed by Bassen and Stern reduced the heat on the film, as well as supplied a stream of cool air around the aperture.

The *Super Simplex* of 1930 was designed with a rear disk shutter. This model could also be supplied with a turret to hold three lenses. By changing lenses during projection, the screen could be enlarged suddenly for spectacular sequences of the picture.

We have seen many of the early projector mechanisms developed during the first 35 years of our industry. But there were 25 more years of development and expert engineering before we had the excellent projectors of today, with their efficient optical systems, foolproof automatically lubricated mechanism, film take-ups which provide uniform tension of 7 to 8 oz, whether using a 2-in. hub, or taking up 5000 ft of film, conical rear shutters, operating less than 1 in. from the film aperture, water-cooled aperture plates and, of great importance, the recently introduced curve gate which gives the utmost in picture sharpness on the screen. This gate greatly reduced buckling and damage to the film image, which has proven so troublesome since the introduction of the various wide-screen techniques.

Yes, we've come a *long* way from the Edison spool-bank Kinetoscope of 1897.

The Historical Motion-Picture Collections at George Eastman House

By JAMES CARD

Opened in 1949 as a museum of photography and cinematography, George Eastman House contains a priceless collection of motion-picture apparatus and a library of more than seven million feet of film which is stored in specially constructed vaults. Some of its rare and historically significant cameras and projectors are described.

THE EXTENSIVE historical collections of photographic apparatus, photographs, motion-picture equipment and motion-picture films of the George Eastman House of Photography in Rochester, N.Y., are preserved in the stately mansion which George Eastman built for his own home in 1905.

Opened in 1949 as a public educational institute, the George Eastman House now serves as a living and lasting memorial to the man who brought photography to all.

The main building is used for the presentation of the historic collection of photography. The large garage and stable building has been converted for the display of contemporary photography and the manufacturing of photographic materials. Between these buildings, and joining them, a 550-seat theater has been erected with a special exhibition gallery on its second floor. Motion pictures from the collection are shown to audiences every week end and three nights during the week.

The George Eastman House came into being as an educational institution through the generosity of the University of Rochester. The University donated the building, which it had inherited from George Eastman, and the Eastman Kodak Co. supplied funds for the transformation of the building into a public museum and for its maintenance. The House is independently administered by a Board of Trustees and is chartered by the University of the State of New York as an educational institution.

The motion-picture study collection was begun in 1950 and is designed to enable students to:

(1) examine each film which constitutes a major development in technique or style of film-making;

(2) observe the manner in which changing social problems affected the motion picture and how they were in turn affected by the public's reaction to popular films;

Presented on April 21, 1958, at the Society's Convention at Los Angeles by George Pratt on behalf of the author, James Card, Curator of Motion Pictures, George Eastman House, 900 East Ave., Rochester 7, N.Y.
(This paper was received on November 3, 1958.)

(3) trace the growth or decline in the work of leading motion-picture artists;

(4) learn the major steps in the development and use of motion pictures, specialized in their purposes;

(5) refer to newsreels and documentaries as source material in the study of specific events, or to obtain authentic details of dress and architecture; and

(6) compare the several versions of identical stories many of which have been repeated at intervals spanning most of the history of motion pictures.

These objectives have been pursued through the operation of various programs.

Films in the study collection are shown on request and without charge to anyone having a specific and serious interest in any phase of motion-picture history.

A group of the films selected by area educators is shown on the premises

Fig. 1. Projecting Praxinoscope invented by Emile Reynaud, 1880.

throughout the school year to groups from the area universities, secondary and elementary schools.

Such films in the collection as are not specifically restricted against public showing, are shown free to the public on Saturday and Sunday matinees at Eastman House. These free matinee programs

continue throughout the year. Each screening is preceded by a lecture from one of the staff members.

The Dryden Theatre Film Society, with membership currently at 3000, meets at Eastman House for twenty programs each season. At these meetings, film programs are shown, also preceded by lectures concerning the history of motion pictures,

The Film Society is supplemented by two special study groups: the foreign-language group concentrates on a special series of German, French or Italian films and enables school groups working with these languages to attend the programs. The Cinema Seminar is a discussion group, composed of the most keenly interested members of the Film Society, which meets once a month to view films of highly limited interest or esoteric nature.

In 1955 the George Eastman House sponsored the First Festival of Film Artists to give motion-picture actors, directors and cameramen a unique opportunity to honor their own colleagues for past achievements. The first festival honored film artists of the 1915 to 1925 period. In 1957 a second retrospective award ceremony honored the outstanding players, directors and cameramen of the 1926 to 1930 period. On both occasions award winners received the Eastman House Medal of Honor, the so-called George award, in Rochester ceremonies.

Supplementing the collection of historical motion pictures, Eastman House maintains the world's largest collection of motion-picture cameras, projectors and associated equipment.

Many of the early cameras and projectors are on display and mechanized so that by pressing a button, visitors can examine the operation of the various types of intermittent movements characterizing these devices.

Among the extremely rare pieces, some of which exist in no other collection or institution, are the following:

Reynaud's Projecting Praxinoscope, 1880

In 1877, Emile Reynaud, the French inventor, developed his ingenious and very practical device (Fig. 1), which differed from existing zooetropes by having a strip of hand-painted pictures, mounted inside a revolving drum and reflected by similarly revolving mirrors. In the same year he patented his apparatus for projecting the pictures in apparent movement by combining his device with a magic lantern. The projecting Praxinoscope was completed in 1880. By 1892, Reynaud had expanded and enlarged the system to his Theatre Optique where his pictures were shown from perforated strips on a large theater screen, with the strips cued for sound effects.

Bouly's Cinematographe, 1892

It is curious that French historians give priority to the Lumières for their Cinematographe which did not appear until 1894, at the earliest. Bouly's system, patented in France in 1892, and bearing the same name — Cinematographe — was thought for many years to exist only as a patent application. The device itself, in the Eastman House Collection (Fig. 2) is an extremely interesting combination

Fig. 2. Bouly's Cinematographe, a rare device, patented in 1892.

camera-projector. It was designed to use film between 38mm and 48mm, although no positive film-size has ever been established. The film transport mechanism was a pair of friction rollers. The intermittent action was provided by broken rollers functioning with an intermittent grip. The shutter was a cylindrical drum with two openings. There is no available record of the practical use of this apparatus. Its ability to function adequately is improbable as the film transport system does not seem adequate to space images regularly on unperforated film.

Mutograph, 1895

The Mutograph produced the first motion-picture negatives for the American Mutoscope and Biograph Company and was probably the first motor-driven motion-picture camera in the United States. The Mutoscope, a peep-show viewing machine, is still in service in many penny arcades, but the ponderous Mutograph, the camera, is exceedingly rare (Fig. 3). It was invented by Herman Casler in 1895. It used unperforated film, 70mm in size. Average film length was 160 ft. Transport mechanism for the film

was friction rollers and the intermittent was of the intermittent-grip type. Normal operating speed of the battery-powered, motor-driven camera was 40 frames/sec with a possibility of increasing the speed up to 100 frames/sec. Perforations were made in the film as it passed through the camera. The perforations were used to bring the images into proper register in printing. The perforator also functioned like registering pins to hold the film steady in the aperture at the instant of exposure.

Armat Vitascope: Inventor's Model, 1895

This prototype of the refined Armat Vitascope was made in October 1895. It used 35mm film with the standard Edison perforations. The intermittent was an eccentric cam, also known as a beater movement or dog movement and similar to the intermittent first devised by Demeny in France with his 1893 Chronophotographe. The Armat Vitascope (Fig. 4) was shown to Edison in December of 1895. When Edison was finally and belatedly persuaded by Raff and Gammon to authorize the screen projection of his Kinetoscope films, he decided to adapt the Armat Vitascope for this purpose rather than to attempt building a projector of his own. Thus it was only after widespread projections of the Kinetoscope films by unauthorized showmen using a variety of projectors, that Edison reluctantly permitted Raff and Gammon to install the "Edison" Vitascope, Armat type, in Koster & Bial's Music Hall for the undeservedly famous showing of Edison films in New York City on April 23, 1896. Although a plaque on the R.H. Macy store which occupies this site commemorates the event, the showing definitely was not the first theater projection of motion pictures. It was simply the first showing of Edison Kinetoscope films on a screen to a paying audience, which was authorized by Edison himself.

Fig. 4. Armat Vitascope (made about October 1895). This model was used to demonstrate motion-picture projection to Thomas A. Edison on December 8, 1895. This projector was said by its inventor Thomas Armat to be the first projecting machine using an essential loop-forming means for the film and embodying a practical intermittent movement giving the pictures the required long period of rest and exposure.

Fig. 3. The Mutograph, an early motion-picture camera.

Chronophotographe (also known as the Biographe), 1893

The Demeny Chronophotographe is a motion-picture camera using 60mm, unperforated film. It was patented in France, October 10, 1893. The film transport mechanism was confined to the action of the take-up spool. The intermittent was the Demeny eccentric cam, beater, or dog movement.

Lumière Cinematographe, 1894

The Lumière Cinematographe (Fig. 5), the first eminently practical motion-picture camera-projector-printer, was patented in France, February 13, 1895. Lumière claimed that he exposed his first negative in the device, "Workers Leaving the Lumière Plant," at the end of 1894.

Fig. 5. Lumière Cinematographe.

Film size was 35mm with round perforations, two to each frame. Film length was 17 m. The intermittent movement was provided by a triangular eccentric shaft; film was transported by a pulldown claw. The shutter was circular and single-bladed.

Kinetographe, 1896

Rider De Bedts' camera-printer-projector (Fig. 6) was patented in France, January 14, 1896. It used 35mm film with Edison perforations in 30-m lengths. Film was transported by sprocket wheels. The intermittent was a wheel with three equally spaced teeth which at every revolution activates two other wheels sufficiently to replace one image with another. The apparatus could also be used for direct viewing like the Kinetoscope.

Phototachygraphe Sanson, 1896

This 35mm camera-projector was patented in France, March 5, 1896. It used film with Edison perforations transported with sprocket wheels. The intermittent was a notched sector oscillating from side to side which intermittently engaged the projecting teeth of a revolving wheel, then allowed the teeth to escape when the notch swung into position (Fig. 7). This device was used continuously and successfully at the Rouen Exposition in May 1896. It provided the greatest commercial competition in France to the Lumière Cinematographe.

Its inventor, Raoul Grimoin-Sanson also invented Cineorama, which was first presented to the public at the Paris World Fair of 1900, modified fifty years later as the Waller Cinerama and returned to Europe at the World's Fair in Brussels in the guise of Circarama, under the auspices of Walt Disney.

Gaumont Sound and Color System, 35mm

The Gaumont color system (Fig. 8) was a three-color additive process. Three lenses are used in the camera and three pictures (frames) are taken simultaneously through the primary color filters on a single strip of 35mm film, the frames of which are only three normal sprocket holes in height; one frame is exposed for each primary color so that the whole set of three color pictures corresponds to nine sprocket holes. Thus after each exposure the film must be advanced nine sprocket holes at a time. This is accomplished at a rate of 16 triple frames per second. The projector is fitted with a corresponding pulldown and gate and with three condensers and three sets of objectives with special registering devices.

Fig. 6. De Bedts Kinetographe.

Sound, which often consisted of lip-synchronized dialogue, was provided by high-quality disks amplified with compressed air. Synchronization was attempted through a system of rotating brushes and collector rings. By means of an electrically operated clutch, either one of two turntables could be rotated. A control panel was provided to be placed at the screen to synchronize sound and picture manually should the collector ring system fail to operate.

Other Items of the Collection

In addition to the devices just described, fifty pieces of motion-picture apparatus are on display at Eastman House, many of them mechanized. Over a hundred more are stored in the vaults as a study collection. Some three thousand motion-picture films are now available for screening at Eastman House and over six million feet of nitrate film is being held for eventual preservation on acetate stock.

There are still enormous gaps in the collection which the motion-picture department at Eastman House is constantly striving to fill in. But the prospects are encouraging and it is now possible for scholars and historians working with the collections at Eastman House to obtain useful clues to the real pattern of the history of motion pictures.

Fig. 7. Phototachygraphe Sanson, patented 1896.

Fig. 8. Gaumont sound-color projector circa 1912.

Oskar Messter and His Work

By ALBERT NARATH

This is a survey of the life of Oskar Messter, founder of the German Motion-Picture and Film Industry, and of his achievements in the development of cinematography.

OSKAR MESSTER, founder of the German Motion-Picture and Film Industry, was born in Berlin on Nov. 21, 1866. His father, Eduard Colmar Messter, had founded the firm of Eduard Messter in 1859. The senior Messter was only nineteen years of age and possessed very little capital when he founded the firm, a machine shop, which chiefly produced optical and medical instruments.

Today it might appear strange that a firm producing instruments for science and research, such as ophthalmoscopes, laryngoscopes and microscopes, would also produce equipment for stage and variety artists. The explanation is that optical equipment was of unit manufacture and could be built only by specialty firms. When Eduard Messter built equipment for the well-known magicians Bellachini and Basch, he occasionally presented his son with copies of these implements. Oskar Messter mentions in his autobiography that a musical box, the construction details of which he carefully inspected, had a ratchet-type lock for the spring winding, which was similar to a maltese cross.

The occupation with these varied instruments was not only stimulating but it also showed him how problems brought to his father were solved. It is no surprise that he, following his preference for mathematics and physics, decided on a technical career. He was only 26 when he took charge of his father's enterprise, and he sold his first motion-picture projector on June 15, 1896 (Fig. 1). This date can be considered as the birth date of the German motion-picture industry.

The Era of the Silent Film

The Beginnings of Cinematography and the Motion-Picture Projector

Like nearly all inventions, cinematography had its predecessors. One should avoid making sharp distinctions in a technical development, where there is actually a constant flow of transition. Many inventions in cinematography were

A contribution by Albert Narath, Professor at the Institute for Applied Photochemistry and Film Technique of the Technical University, Berlin, West Germany. This manuscript in German was translated into English by Dr. Eric I. Guttman, Manufacturing Experiments Dept., Kodak Park, Eastman Kodak Co., Rochester 4, N. Y.

made and patented about the same time by different people in different countries. Frequently, due to lack of communication, one individual was not informed about work done by others in an identical field. The same situation exists today, and just as frequently as in the past because the growing volume of papers can hardly be mastered.

At the time Oskar Messter took posses-

sion of his father's business, Anschütz had already introduced his "Rapid Viewer." Edison's Kinetoscope was on display at Castan's Panopticum in Berlin (summer of 1895) and Anschütz demonstrated his projector on Nov. 25, 1894, in the Post Office Building on Artillerie Street. He held performances and charged admission in the Parliament Building on Leipziger Street from February 22 until the end of March, 1895. Ultimately, the Skladanowsky brothers had the first performance of their Bioskop on Nov. 1, 1895, at the Winter Garden. This can be considered as the earliest date in Europe for paid motion-picture public performances.

By 1897 Oskar Messter had become so involved with the new art that he had published a 115-page illustrated catalog in which he offered his film projectors: the Kinetograph and the Thaumatograph with all their attachments, cameras for professionals and amateurs, also perforators and processing and printing equipment.

Oskar Messter delivered his first projector on June 15, 1896, to the showman Rogulino in Moscow. This instrument had a five-slotted maltese cross with a ratio of about 2.6:1 and a one-pin disc without a fly-wheel (Fig. 2). Drive and film path were mounted on a brass plate which was transverse to the optical axis. The hand crank was attached to a crankshaft which drove the pin disc through straight-toothed wheels. It was on the left side of the projector and had to be turned counter-clockwise. The single-blade, rotating shutter which was driven by beveled gears was between the aperture and the objective. The film path and gate did not have slide rails, but were velvet-covered. The transport sprocket below the aperture had a brass pressure roller. The film was unwound from a round box of about 60-ft capacity. It was open on the service side but had a small safety catch. The film ran free in a basket. The lamphouse had doors on both sides and on the back, was lined with asbestos and contained an arc lamp which could be observed through a small ruby glass window. The condenser had a diameter of 105 mm. In addition there was a sliding shutter which could be operated from the left. The instrument was delivered with six Edison films, each about 55 feet long. An illustration of this first projector is not in existence.

Seemingly, the projector satisfied the customer, because he reordered films by the end of July and October of 1896. During 1896 Messter obtained orders for 64 projectors, of which 22 were from abroad (Europe). One projector was installed in a theater owned by Messter in Berlin at 21 Unter den Linden. Furthermore, Messter projectors were used in the Apollo Theater starting the first of November and in the Hansa Theater in Hamburg on Dec. 1, 1896.

It was a lucky decision that Messter used a maltese cross in his projector from the start. In the beginning he used a 5-slotted cross, just like the one used by Max Gliewe from the Optical Works Gliewe and Kügler, Berlin.* Because of the smoother transport Messter replaced this in 1896 by a 4-slotted maltese cross (Fig. 3). One like it with a tangential entry is pictured in D. R. P. 127913,†

---

* He worked closely with Mr. Betz, an engineer of the firm Bauer & Betz. Both obtained registered designs (Gebrauchsmuster) and trademarks which are contained in the first catalog of Messter on page 3.

† All patents mentioned (except one) are Deutsches Reichspatents (German State Patents) and therefore the letters "D.R.P." will not be repeated.

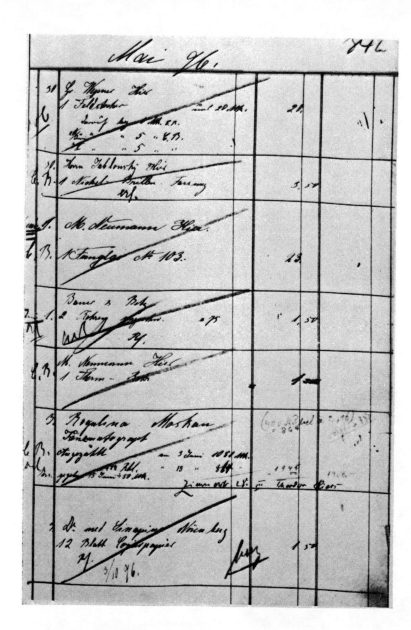

Fig. 1. Sale of the first projector by Oskar Messter to showman Rogulino in Moscow: Recorded on page from ledger from May 1896, with the entry June 3: 1,081 Marks down-payment; and June 15: on balance of 400 Rubels = 864 Marks were received.

Fig. 2. 5-slotted maltese cross with a ratio of 2.6:1.

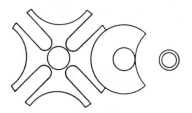

Fig. 3. 4-slotted maltese cross, ratio of 2.5:1.

June 26, 1900. This is reproduced in Fig. 4. It is the 4-slotted maltese cross with tangential entry which is missing from U.S. patent 578,185, issued to Armat in 1896, and which was the necessary prerequisite for a smooth movement.

Immediately after building the first projector, Messter introduced improvements on the new model. It turned out that the velvet in the aperture scratched the film. He changed to edge guiding by means of spring-loaded rails. The pressure roller, which pressed the film against the drive sprocket, contacted the film only on the edges, and not in the picture area. Later Messter chose pressure pads. To obtain a well-positioned, steady image, he took pains to see that all fast rotating parts were balanced. The single-blade shutter received a counterweight and to the shaft of the one-pin disc he then added a flywheel. Feed and take-up sprockets were installed, also a wind-up and fire-resisting magazine.

Important also was the installation

of the three-blade shutter (invented by Theodor Pätzold, Berlin) which eliminated the flicker (1902) and the picture framing mechanism (invented by Max Gliewe in 1900). In 1913 Messter boxed the entire movement and equipped it with automatic oiling. Between 1896 and 1913 he brought out 17 types, a proof that he constantly tried to add improvements. Figure 5 shows the projecting mechanism of the Kinetograph, System "Apollo," Model 1896. Figure 6 shows the Kine Messter Projector, Model 1908 with changeable base. Figure 7 shows the mechanism of Messter's "Armored Movie," Model 1914. Figure 8 shows the same projector open.

Besides many registered designs,‡ he obtained patents in the field of projector construction. Some of his patents were as follows: 126353, Sept. 20, 1900, and 212763, Apr. 5, 1908, for fire-protective installations; 222863, Mar. 17, 1908, for a supplementary speeding of the ad-

‡ "Registered design" or "petty patent" or *Gebrauchsmuster* (DRGM).

vance mechanism; 216236, June 14, 1908, for image positioning; 280618, Dec. 21, 1913, for a magnetically actuated windup; and finally noted is 330508, June 12, 1919, for a windup with tapered elements around the shaft. Interesting also is 278228, Feb. 12, 1913: With incandescent bulbs in the projector it was difficult to obtain uniform illumination without a point light source; the patent 278228 protected a method where the light source rotates around an axis which is perpendicular to the optical axis, whereby it behaves like a uniformly illuminated disc.

By 1900 Messter was interested in the problem of an optically compensated projector. First he used a ring made up of concave lenses. Later he changed to a many-sided rotating prism. In 1909 he began work with Dr. Thorner, an opthalmologist and professor of physics. Patents were recorded under either's name. For an optically compensated projector with two tilt mirrors and rotating mirror segments Messter obtained the German patents 230022,

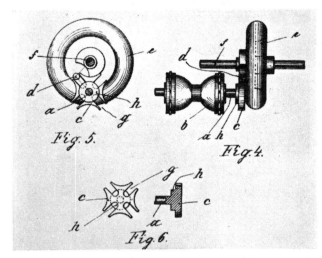

Fig. 4. 4-slotted maltese cross with tangential entry. Figures 4, 5, and 6 are from the Messter patent 127913 (6-29-1900).

Fig. 5. Kinetograph-Messter, System "Apollo" from Fig. 10 of Messter's first price list. (printed Oct. 1897, published 1898).

Fig. 6. Kine-Messter-Projector, Model 1908, with changeable base.

Fig. 7. Messter's Panzer-Kino, Model 1914; drive viewed from service side.

Nov. 25, 1908; 331550, Mar. 21, 1918; 332273, Aug. 12, 1919; and 336649, Aug. 12, 1920. These experiments, stretched over many years, were expensive; on the other hand they proved that Messter did not leave anything untried and caught every opportunity to solve a problem by himself. From the many who during the years occupied themselves with this problem, only Mechau achieved a design which was practical and is still used for special effects.

The Film Material

With his first projectors (1896) Oskar Messter furnished Edison Films, which he purchased in London from Maguire and Baucus. However, when he decided

to take his own pictures he had to find a dealer of raw films. The choice was between Blair and Kodak (Eastman Photographic Materials Co., Ltd.) in London, and Lumiere in Lyon (France). Blair and Kodak furnished longer strips free of splices. Since Kodak's films were the best, Messter intended to contract a large amount. The deal did not come through because Kodak shipped only for cash, which condition at that time Messter could not meet. In 1897 he saw Mr. Eastman in Berlin and obtained sufficient credit in spite of the policies of the company. One can conclude from this that Eastman was greatly impressed by Messter's work. Since Kodak delivered the films unper-

Fig. 8. Same model as Fig. 7, from back; view looking into the housing.

111

Fig. 9. Motor-driven perforator (Fig. 17a in Messter's first catalog).

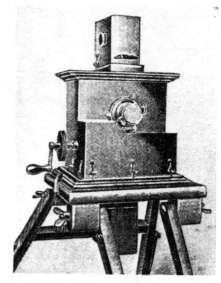

Fig. 10. Messter's first professional camera. Thaumatograph used as camera (Fig. 9 in Messter's first catalog).

forated, Messter built his own perforator, choosing a perforation which was in between the Edison and the later Pathé. A few years later he changed to the Pathé perforation. Figure 9 shows a perforator from 1897, which used a maltese cross drive, advanced the film always four pitches at a time and punched four pairs of holes. Later (1905-1910) Messter changed to single-hole perforating with a claw movement because he wanted to be able to change the pitch of the film to compensate for shrinkage in order to obtain perfect prints.

The Recording Camera

Before Oskar Messter attempted to build his own camera, he made an interesting preliminary experiment, which could be done cheaply. He used his projector mechanism as film transport and the rotating shutter as an instantaneous shutter. He converted his living room at 29 Georgen Strasse in Berlin into a camera obscura by pasting brown wrapping paper over the windows. In one window pane he installed a wooden board with two holes, inserting into one the objective lens and a red glass disc into the other. He observed through the red disc when a railroad train came by near his apartment and then put his mechanism in motion. The camera was loaded with 30 inches of regular roll film (used normally to take $3\frac{1}{2}$ by $4\frac{3}{4}$-in. pictures) slit to 35mm width. After processing the film in a wash basin, it showed that the experiment was successful and yielded sharp single exposures. Messter then built the first camera from an existing projector mechanism, effecting slight changes on the shutter and the aperture.

Near the end of October, 1896, he sold his first camera, while the camera by Lumiere was still kept secret. Messter's first cinema catalog lists two types,

a professional (Fig. 10) and an amateur camera (Fig. 11). Both contained a maltese cross drive. The amateur camera, with the addition of a film holder, could also be used as a projector, as shown on the illustration (Fig. 12). These two cameras had to be loaded in the dark; only later did Messter use magazines, similar to the Messter-Camera 1900, in which the magazines for the negatives were located below the camera drive, a logical design in regard to the location of the center of gravity. Another handy camera (Fig. 13) had interchangeable metal magazines for 90 feet of film. These magazines were side by side and he obtained patent 127543, Nov. 11, 1900, for this novel arrangement.

The handy Kine-Messter-Camera 1900 was used by many explorers, such as the Africa explorer Prof. Schillings, Prince Adolph Fredrick of Mecklenburg and many others. About 1910 Messter introduced the claw transport for his camera, also for the Studio Camera Model XIV (Catalog 1913/14). In this camera the open sector of the rotating shutter could be changed during exposure with the aid of the movable shutter blade. The exposure time could be changed thereby, down to complete dimming. This arrangement was especially important for fading one scene into the other and for trick shots (patent 324194, April 1, 1914).

The Processing and Printing of Films

After the first makeshift equipment Messter used drums for processing, on which 60 feet of film could be wound. For drying he used drums of several meters in diameter. In 1898 he used developing racks with pins and trays which he had seen in England. Later he changed to troughs 5 feet tall and used racks holding about 200 feet of film. His patent 304738, July 14, 1914, in

which he used very long pipes for the processing of film, going through many floors of the building, did not prove important. (Patents 352083, 352084 and 352085, all dated April 27, 1920, were assigned to the Bavarian Polytechnical Research Society at Tegernsee, a foundation established by Messter.)

The first printing experiments involving films were made with a homemade box having a slot 3mm wide and a transport roller with 20 teeth. After these experiments, he built a printer with maltese cross gear. He brought the two films into contact only in the printer gate and transported them below it by two separate sprockets. It is remarkable that Messter obtained a patent as early as 1907 for a printer design (144136, Dec. 20, 1907) where the positive and negative films are held together in the gate by compressed air. The equipment was built originally for paper prints; the patent, however, protects all kinds of contact prints.

The difficulties involved in film printing are shown by patent 338773, June 12, 1920. Due to lack of standards, films taken with different cameras could have the frame-line in different locations. The patent describes a printer with an attachment between the stock roll and the take-up roll for the positive which permits the calibration of the differing frame-lines into a common position.

A method of optical printing was also patented by Messter (121591, Feb. 18, 1900). It was orginally intended for his "Westpocket living photographs" and for his "Kosmoskop," which required enlarged paper prints made from motion-picture film negatives. This patent protects also any kind of optical prints, the patent claim being: "common drive providing the advance of both strips in a definite relationship to each other."

Even after his film companies were taken over by UFA in 1917, Messter's firm processed its own films until 1921.

The Motion-Picture Studio

Messter opened his first studio in November, 1896, on the fifth floor of 94a Friedrich Strasse. The illumination consisted of four Körting & Matthiessen 50-amp arc lamps. They were on portable mounts, so that Messter was able to take motion pictures for the first time of the ball held by the Berlin Press Club at the beginning of the year 1897. In 1902 he purchased in Cologne 24 Regina-Arc lamps and experimented later with arc lamps of Weinert-Berlin, which were enclosed in glass covers. He found help through Carl Froelich, who later became a famous movie director. Froelich left the electrical industry and became his apprentice without pay. Messter then moved to a studio at 156 Friedrich Strasse, which became his

first glass studio with southern exposure. The previous studios all had northern exposure, since they were built for portrait photography. In spite of his arc lamps, Messter still could not do without the sun. He considered building a floating studio on Lake Rummelsburg, to be able to rotate his studio and become independent of the sun. Some studio shots had to be retaken occasionally because his "sun watcher" erred in predicting the exposure time. Due to the variability of daylight Messter returned to the somewhat more dependable arc light. Most of the time he used mixed lighting.

Since the size of the business increased steadily, the present quarters became insufficient, and in July, 1911, he moved to the 5th and 6th floors of buildings at 31 and 32 Blücher Strasse. The glass studio there measured 46 by $78\frac{3}{4}$ feet with $24\frac{1}{2}$ feet height. Besides regular

production many sound films were also made there. To satisfy the increasing demand he installed a motor-driven suspension bridge under the glass roof, which permitted movement of either the camera or the subject.

By the end of 1917 he acquired the Literaria Studio at Berlin-Tempelhof. It was built in 1913 by Alfred Duskes for Pathé Frères to produce their German films. Messter started using it early in 1919. At the same time he moved his printing facilities there from 32 Blücher Strasse.

In 1914 he erected the first large film studio, for the Sascha-Messter-Film Company in Vienna in the Sievering District. It began operation in 1915 and is still operating today.

Color Film

Messter made some of his early sound films and his "Alabastra Films" (see below) hand-colored. He had become interested in color film around the turn of the century. For the additive system he built cameras with three objectives, whereby he divided the picture area into separate fields according to diverse methods. One of these cameras and many other instruments of importance to the development of cinematography are at the German Museum in Munich.

The "Three-Dimensional" Film

A process to achieve a three-dimensional screen image interested Messter from the beginning. A patent application for a sterco rapid viewer dated July 23, 1896, is one of the proofs. (The patent was not granted.)

In 1909 Messter learned about the existence of Engelmann's process which was based on Pepper's ghost images, whereby the audience viewed the projected cinematographic image showing persons apparently standing on the floor

of a dimly illuminated stage. The height of the persons who appeared to be moving freely about the stage was about 30 inches. Due to dimensional differences on the film, viewers "saw" the persons move both back and forth, so that an illusion of depth was sensed. Messter developed a projection system which he named "Alabastra." He showed the hand-tinted films with music and song accompaniment and received excellent press reviews. In spite of this his specially equipped Alabastra Theater was short-lived. Nevertheless, at the Court Theater in Darmstadt, the Czar of Russia, his son and Prince Heinrich of Prussia attended similar performances.

Special-Effect Photography

To eliminate defects in background projection, Professor Thorner perfected a method whereby the background was projected with a special projector over a partially transparent mirror onto a large

Fig. 11. Messter's Amateur-Kinetograph (Amateur camera, Fig. 6 in Messter's first catalog).

Fig. 12. Same as Fig. 11 — Left: instrument with mechanism ready for projecting. Right: Double magazine for picture taking (Fig. 5 in Messter's first motion-picture catalog).

Fig. 13. Messter's portable camera from 1900, with exchangeable metal magazines and 30-meter film capacity.

113

concave mirror in front of which the actors moved. The concave mirror and the objective combined the image of the actor with the background on the film (patent 598712, May 19, 1932). Messter carried out practical experiments with this system. It could not gain acceptance, because the manufacture of similar mirrors was expensive and dimensionally limited.

The Amateur, Instructional and Commercial Film

In his first price list Messter had the previously mentioned amateur camera (Fig. 12). Later he added a projector with a maltese cross drive which was mainly intended for school use.

To save on expensive film, he constructed in 1908 the "Salon-Kinemesster" with four rows of pictures on a 35mm strip (patents 235550, 224610 and 222393, all dated Feb. 24, 1909; and 225878, Sept. 30, 1909). The single frame of the 35mm film was subdivided into 16 pictures. The adjoining strips were projected alternately from top to bottom and from bottom to top after appropriate displacement of the objective and the light source. The 2-meter long film equalled in number of frames and projection time that of 32 meters (105 ft). A Nernst lamp was used as a light source. By using a metalized screen, he obtained a picture size of $3\frac{1}{2}$ by $6\frac{1}{2}$ feet. Grain size of films of the day did not permit greater magnification.

An even smaller piece of equipment was the "Fun Movie Projector," a miniature device which projected small pictures on a white surface such as the shirt front of a person (patent 193026, Nov. 14, 1906).

After 1897 Messter also engaged in the production of small booklets whose pages had to be flipped quickly. For the booklets, and for his "Kosmoskop" which worked like the Mutoscope and permitted the viewing of phase-pictures printed on a paper strip, he developed appropriate processing equipment (patents 108715, July 10, 1898; 107607, Nov. 8, 1898; 106784, May 13, 1899; 108810, July 7, 1899; 161163, Dec. 12, 1902; 154513, Dec. 20, 1902).

For commercial or advertising work Messter constructed a projector mounted in a box. By means of a mirror the pictures were projected on the opened box lid (patent 263818, Sept. 21, 1912).

Applications of Cinematography

Messter occupied himself extensively with developing motion-picture equipment for use in technical and scientific fields. In 1897 and 1898 he developed a high-speed camera for film 60mm wide. The frame size was 30 by 55mm and its speed 100 frames per second. Among other things he photographed the fall of a cat together with a stop watch made by

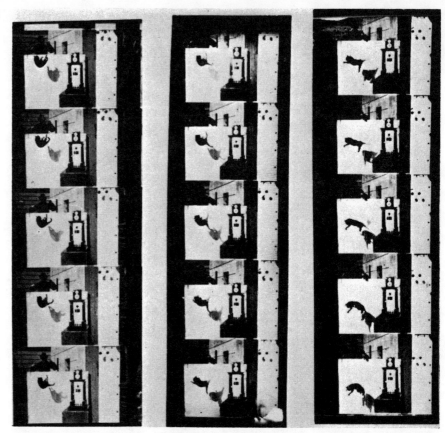

Fig. 14. Slow-motion pictures of falling cat (66 frames per second) beside millisecond watch by Hipp. Right: the shadowgraphs of two falling balls (iron and cork). (Camera developed by Messter 1897–1898.)

Hipp (Fig. 14). He worked on important problems during World War I for the German Army, Navy and Air Force. For the Navy he developed a camera which registered hits fired from warships at floating targets. The 35mm film moved from right to left and reproduced the target and its surroundings on a picture size 20 cm (7.874 in.) wide by 2.5 cm (0.984 in.) high. Simultaneously a clock and a glass scale were photographed. The zero point on the scale had to be adjusted onto the target. Each film advance amounted to 22.5 cm (8.858 in.).

The aerial cameras developed by Messter were of special importance. When he received the order during the first world war, he immediately decided on using film. Until then glass plates were customary. The first construction, which was called in soldiers' slang "Strandhaubitze" (beach howitzer), used unperforated film 120-mm wide (4.724 in.). The pictures were 10 by 10 cm (4 by 4 in.), 250 frames on a roll 25 m (82-feet) long. A 300mm focal length Zeiss-Tessar was used as the objective.

The success of this camera resulted in an order from the German Army High Command for the manufacture of an automatic camera. It was used for the first time on May 26, 1915. It was called Reihenbildner (multiple picture camera), used unperforated 35mm film and the negative size was 3.5 by 24 cm

(1.378 by 9.449 in.). The drive moved the film frame by frame in a horizontal direction. The camera was driven by a small air propeller. The objective was Zeiss-Tessar, focal length 250mm. The narrow strips, mounted properly, gave an uninterrupted image of the covered terrain. The ultimate camera used unperforated film, and the frames were 6 by 24 cm (2.362 by 9.449 in.). From 1915 to 1918 a total of 933,000 meters (3,061,017 ft) of film were exposed. For his process of taking small aerial pictures, photographed transverse to the direction of the flight and covering an area many times larger than the field of view in the direction of flight, and for his process of mounting the pictures, Messter received patents 298086, June 6, 1915; 300688, Aug. 25, 1915; and 301382, Jan. 28, 1916. The previously mentioned patents (331550, Mar. 21, 1918; 332273, Aug. 12, 1919; and 336649, Aug. 12, 1920) concern a continuously running film with alternately working optical compensation.

Another piece of equipment which Messter constructed during the first world war was designed to improve the marksmanship of machine-gunners. This camera was shaped like a machine-gun with identical sighting and identical hand controls. Instead of the bullet strip it was loaded with a film strip on which the target was recorded. In its center was a cross-hair and a clock face. Each picture showed the location of the shot and the time. This instrument was built extensively and Messter received patents 309108, July 18, 1916; 309109, Oct. 6, 1916; and 317487, Apr. 13, 1917.

The Age of the Sound Film

Strictly speaking, the silent film was never silent, since the very first pictures were shown with accompanying music. Furthermore, many tried from the start to have synchronized sound and picture, using the phonograph method even though it gave mediocre quality and insufficient sound intensity. Only short films could be recorded with synchronized sound because in those days the running time of turntables and records was limited. When pictures increased in length, this first epoch of the short sound films ended and accompanying music gained more and more importance.

The first sound film epoch in Germany lasted from 1903 until 1913. A total of around 1500 sound negatives were made, with an average length of about 220 feet.

Oskar Messter deserves recognition in both sound recording and sound reproduction. Many patents and contemporary registered designs prove the manifold solutions of the problems. The main problem was the synchronization of picture and sound. Messter solved this first with electrical attachments. According to patent 154372, Apr. 9, 1903, the current went from a separately driven commutator to the motors of the phonograph and projector. Here he used one battery for both motors. In a supplementary patent, 155978, July 16, 1903, he employed one battery for each motor.

All these contrivances were tested by Messter in practice. It was found that, while the two motors ran completely synchronously, the slightest overload threw them out of phase and finally stopped them entirely. Consequently he finally used two direct-current series motors, with three collector rings, which were connected to corresponding armature windings. The three-phase alternating current generated in this manner served to maintain synchronous speeds since the armature windings of the two motors were connected through the collector brushes.

While this provided for synchronous operation of the two motors, line voltage variations or poorly spliced film passing through the projector mechanism caused speed variations, which in turn led to variations in pitch of the sound. Lacking better equipment Messter first accepted these disadvantages and demonstrated his "Kosmograph" on August 30, 1903 at the Apollo Theater in Berlin. It is possible that he used a synchronizing system described in patent 145780, Feb. 19, 1903, to couple the projector to a (master) drive-motor, while at the same time using an identical clutching device to couple the phonograph with its drive motor.

His sound pictures were well received by the public and the press and brought him contract engagements from variety houses at home and abroad. At the World Exposition in St. Louis in 1904 he also gave performances. Special films were taken in English such as *The Whistling Bowery Boy*. For 25 cents 5 to 6 films could be seen. The Biophon Theater there contained about 250 seats and on the average 500 tickets were sold daily. These sound films ran 20 frames per second.

While synchronization between picture and sound was faultless, the above-mentioned speed variations produced undesirable effects. Messter tried further approaches, in which synchronization could be controlled by optical or acoustical signal transmittance.

The film advance was first operated by means of a handcrank and later governed by a periodic bell or light signal, according to patent 177685, Sept. 8, 1903. This patent gained importance especially in the fight against competitors, who intended to reproduce this equipment, because it was simple and inexpensive. An improved version, with the addition of a Wheatstone bridge hookup and galvanometer, is the subject of patent 175905, Oct. 21, 1904, and the application of a differential drive with an auxiliary motor drive is part of patent 200469, Apr. 29, 1906. This synchronizing equipment, which was mechanically coupled to the projector, while the auxiliary motor of the gramophone was electrically controlled, became the most used instrument of the following years. By 1913 five hundred theaters installed Messter's synchronized sound projector equipment. He named it the Biophon and sold it on a license basis to Biophon Theaters.

The difficulties which one had to contend with in the phonograph industry, when one did not intend to use a certain playback method, are described in patent 237961, Dec. 8, 1910. To make a recording on a cylinder or disc, it was necessary to use a long funnel (horn) to obtain the greatest influence on the stylus. The unsightly horn had to be kept out of the picture. Patent 237961, Dec. 8, 1910 describes a large cabin with slanted glass plate to direct sound toward the horn, fastened to the roof of the cabin, which remains outside the field of the camera lens. This recording technique was especially necessary when big scenes were taken and when sound was recorded simultaneously. This method prevented the recording of camera noise on the phonograph disc. It is interesting that this approach is just the opposite of the present method, in which the noise of the camera is kept from the studio stage by enclosing the camera itself.

After the development of amplifying systems had made large gramophone records possible, Messter occupied himself again with the problem of synchronization. He obtained the following patents: 592478, Feb. 1, 1928; 561660, Feb. 23, 1929; 561661, Mar. 28, 1929; and 541791, June 8, 1929. They deal with an indicating and regulating device, mounted outside the projection room, a start marking device, the application of colored edge marking (to enable one, in case of film tear, to re-establish synchronization quickly in semi-dark rooms) and finally an automatic spring prewinding device to permit quick starting of gramophone tables.

When the picture *Submarine* by the Messtrofilm Exchange (a Messter subsidiary) was acquired in May, 1929, the sound was reproduced on his Messterphon, a disc instrument, connected mechanically to the projector and equipped for handling the normal 78 rpm and also the large 40-cm (15.748 in.) $33\frac{1}{3}$-rpm discs.

The era of the disc-films, which were the forerunners of the modern sound films, was short. The different carriers of picture and sound and consequently the differences in the necessary reproducing equipment, the limited life of the gramophone discs and the difficulty in case of film tear to re-establish synchronization, were the reasons why "needle sound film" gave way to the optical sound film. When this happened — about 1930 — Oskar Messter was 64 years old. Only two patents came out of this period: 545807, Oct. 24, 1929, which protects an optical printing method for sound recordings by the variable-area method; 702940, Nov. 25, 1930, granted to him jointly with Kurt Breusing, for a process where the picture is taken at a lesser speed than the sound and then through multiple printing steps the two recordings obtain equal length. Neither of these patents proved important.

Messter also occupied himself with the problem of post-synchronization. Patent 593277, Oct. 16, 1929, deals with a system whereby a text is projected in correspondence with the picture, which should aid the speaker or singer at post-synchronization. The patent specified that, in order to facilitate the synchronization with instantaneously projected pictures or reproduced sound, the corresponding word parts, such as letters, syllables, etc., were made especially apparent by changes in size, in boldness, density and other means.

The Musical Accompaniment

From the beginning motion pictures were shown with music accompaniment. The phonograph was replaced by a live piano player. His duty was to adapt the music to the action.

When orchestras appeared and these, or a singer, were supposed to accompany the action, the picture had to be watched constantly by the conductor or the singer. To relieve them of this burden, Messter developed the Messtronom consisting of a line of music, running synchronously with the picture. In this manner only the music notes had to be watched (patent 293634, Aug. 13, 1913). Since the tape of the music moved at a constant speed, the writing had to differ from the normal type; according to the tempo the writing had to be more, or less, set apart. Of course, this process could be applied at the time of recording. This approach was tried by Messter in cooperation with the conductor and composer, Dr. Becce.

Later Messter decided to use pneumatically driven musical instruments, like the "Pianola," or "Phonola" (which became known about 1900), to insure agreement between subject matter on the screen and the accompanying music. Here the speed of the music tape changed together with the loudness of the music, when the pedals were pushed harder or gentler. To keep in tempo an additional hand lever had to be operated. To eliminate these disadvantages of the pneumatic drive, Messter added an auxiliary drive for the tape, obtained from an electric motor (patents 334585, Nov. 14, 1918; 334586, Jan. 21, 1920; 334587, Feb. 18, 1920; and 334588, March 11, 1920).

A little later Messter obtained patent 388509, June 18, 1922, which dealt with an improvement on the Messtronom. It was found that it was still burdensome for the conductor, and restrictive to his artistic talent, to watch the rolling music tape while he was also conducting. Messter's basic idea was that the conductor should not be governed by the projector, but that the projection should follow the conductor. The patent provides that a type of steering arrangement, connected to the projector, should be hand-operated by one of the musicians, who follows the conductor. Different possibilities were listed in the patent.

To enable one speaker to be heard during the showing of a film simultaneously in different theaters, which also may be in different cities, good synchronization was needed. Messter developed for this purpose the "Chronomesster," a clock with a second hand, making two revolutions per minute. On the outside of the clock two additional hands were located. These hands were coupled to the projector by means of a flexible shaft. The projector was adjusted in such a way that the position of one hand always corresponded with the second hand of the timer. Text or music could then be transmitted by radio. On Oct. 29, 1929, Messter showed in Berlin at the meeting of

the Deutsche Kinotechnische Gesellschaft that the two systems (Chronomesster and Messtronom) worked.

Finally, Messter's Conductor-Films should be mentioned. The goal was that of having the orchestra conducted by projecting the motion picture of the conductor. He aimed to obtain the same effect a living conductor achieves and with this invention he planned to preserve the art of famous conductors for posterity. Patent 293573, Nov. 4, 1913, provides for a specialized piece of pro-

Fig. 15. Oskar Messter medal, established by the Deutsche Kinotechnische Gesellschaft, Nov. 23, 1926; first bestowed on Oskar Messter, Dec. 1, 1927.

jection equipment, showing the conductor to the orchestra members from the front and to the audience from the back. The two views can either be taken with two cameras, or according to patent 324057, June 12, 1919, with a single camera and mirrors on a single strip of film. Messter himself operated with the latter scheme as early as 1913. Projection was done on a split screen. On the lower, opaque half, the orchestra sees the conductor from the front; on the upper half of the screen (which is transparent) the audience sees the conductor from the back. One of the pictures has to be taken with a mirror so that the image does not appear reversed left and right. This rearrangement is protected by patent 327228, Aug. 12, 1919. Messter photographed a number of leading conductors by this process.

While this type of conductor film did not achieve general acceptance, it was a lasting contribution by Oskar Messter toward preserving the appearance and art of famous conductors. These films are preserved as priceless music historical documents at the German Museum in Munich.

The Importance of Oskar Messter in Connection With the Motion-Picture Industry

So far we have discussed only Messter's merits in the technological field. His biography would be left incomplete by failure to mention his importance in the

German film economy. He was founder of the German motion-picture equipment industry since he manufactured all the necessary equipment for picture taking, processing and printing; however, he occupied himself also as producer and theater manager and was the founder of the German film trade.

His first movie catalog printed in October, 1897, and published in 1898, listed no less than 84 self-produced films. These were studio and location shots, scientific and technical films, also news shots, which have since obtained great historical value as documentary films. In 1898 he equipped, with his own funds, a film expedition, and as his own camera man took pictures in Turkey, Palestine and Egypt. When in 1896 Messter started to make entertainment films, he was author, director, operator, processor, printer and projectionist, all in one. In 1897 he made his first close-ups. The title of the picture was *From Seriousness to Laughter* (No. 4 in the Messter listing). His first trick film was *Rapid Painter Clown Jigg* (No. 5 in Messter's catalog). He took the scene at a slower speed and projected it at normal speed to increase the impression of the speed at which the painter worked. He produced the first German time-lapse picture. His film taken in 1897 with a lapse factor of 1500 frames per 24 hours, showing the blooming and wilting of a flower, can be considered the first German documentary. When in 1910 the longer entertainment pictures appeared, he employed artists for scripting, directing and acting, but he reserved for himself the planning, casting and the production of the film.

In 1901 he founded the Projektion GmbH when he changed in 1902 to "Messter's Projection GmbH." This firm, which was not dissolved until 1930, produced all his pictures prior to 1913. He founded — also in 1901 — the Kosmograph Compagnie GmbH which specialized in the manufacture, professional demonstration and display of equipment.

The Kosmograph concern was converted into Messter Film GmbH in 1913 and assumed the production of the Messter films. All these restricted liability companies (GmbH), to which (in 1913) he added the Author-Film Co., operated with independent capital structures. The *Messter Week*, a weekly newsreel which became famous through its truthful news reporting, was started Oct. 1, 1914. The old trademark of the Messter films, the globe rotated by a strip of film, became a familiar sight abroad. On Jan. 1, 1920, the *Messter Week* was taken over by the *Deulig-Week*. Messter also owned theaters. His first was at 21 Unter den Linden, and the last (in 1913) was the Mozart Hall. This was absorbed in 1917, together with the Messter Film GmbH, the Author-Film and other companies by the newly founded Universum Film Co., Ltd. (UFA).

Messter was also one of the founders of the Tonbild-Syndikat A. G. (Tobis) in 1928, a merger of his company, Triergon, Küchenmeister and Deutsche Tonfilm A. G.

Oskar Messter was mostly interested in films of literary or historical background but he did produce some comedies, thrillers and serials. Well-known technicians, cameramen and directors were his pupils and are indebted to him for the thorough education which was responsible for their later successes. Nearly all great actors and actresses worked with Messter and many of those who were discovered by him reached stardom. Henny Porten should be mentioned especially. At a very young age she became a world-famous star, the first one in Germany. Authors and musicians were among Messter's friends, because they felt that he tried to reproduce their work to the utmost perfection.

The Deutsche Kinotechnische Gesellschaft honored him on Nov. 23, 1926, by establishing the Oskar Messter medal, which is given to outstanding promoters of cinematography. He was made the recipient of the first medal on his sixtieth birthday (Fig. 15). On Nov. 26, 1936, the Technical University, Berlin, granted him the title of honorary senator, in recognition of his services to university education. The German Museum in Munich appointed him a life member of its committee and bestowed on him the golden museum ring.

He died on Dec. 6, 1943, on his estate at Leitenbauernhof on Tegern Lake. His last patent, granted when he was 72 (717925, Feb. 27, 1940) was for a film stopwatch. It probably is the smallest item he ever built. It is not a normal stopwatch, which has a meter scale added to the face, but a watch on which film has priority over time. One complete revolution of the hand does not equal 60 seconds but 10 or 100 meters. Beyond all, this watch stands as a symbol of Oskar Messter. In Messter's life, as on this watch, time and film are inseparably connected.

Acknowledgments

The present work is based chiefly on Messter's autobiography: *Mein Weg mit dem Film*, (*My Way With the Film*), Berlin, 1936, and on his patents and registered designs (*Gebrauchsmuster*).

The author is grateful to Oskar Messter's widow, Mrs. Antonie Messter, for the material from the Oskar Messter Archives; to Director L. Henning and Inspector R. Reitberger for furnishing items about the exhibit and in the storage of the German Museum in Munich; for several investigations of patent rights to Dipl. Ing. A. Essel, patent attorney and chief of the patent department of Siemens and Halske A. G., Munich, and to Dr. H. Atorf, senior government councillor at the Berlin branch of the German Patent Administration, for several legal patent investigations and helpful suggestions.

Much additional information was furnished by Gerhard Lamprecht, member of the "Comité Directeur du Bureau International de la Recherche Historique Cinematographique."

The History of Nitrocellulose as a Film Base

By EARL THEISEN*

Summary.—*The following chronology deals with the evolution of motion pictures as produced photographically on a nitrocellulose support carrying a light-sensitive emulsion of one kind or another. Even though the later dates of the preceding chronology overlap the earlier dates of the one that follows, the two chronologies have been kept distinct in order to present the history of the nitrocellulose film base as a unit in itself.*

1845-6—The discovery of the cellulose nitrates about this time is credited to Schoenbein, who became associated with Böttger sometime subsequently to August, 1846.[1,2]

1847—The solubility of the cellulose nitrates, especially in alcohol and ether, was accurately investigated by Gladstone; these experiments no doubt led to the subsequent discovery of collodion.[1]

1848—Iodized collodion was used by Frederick Archer Scott in his *calotype* wet-plate process.[3]

1855—Alexander Parkes was granted an English patent on *parkesine,* a substance similar to collodion, made by mixing anhydrous wood alcohol with guncotton.[4]

1868—Daniel Spill invented *xylonite,* a combination of pyroxylind, alcohol, and ether; he was associated with Parkes in some of his work.[5]

1869—John W. Hyatt, of Newark, N. J., invented celluloid by combining collodion with camphor, for which he was granted a U. S. patent[6,7] on June 15, 1869; in the patent specifications the name *pyroxylin* was used. Numerous patents were granted to the Hyatt brothers covering various uses of this material as artificial ivory. The name *celluloid* first appeared in the U. S. Patent Gazette on July 2, 1872, in the name of the Celluloid Manufacturing Company, of Albany, N. Y., assignee of the various Hyatt patents.[8,9,10]

1876—On November 9 of this year, an English patent[11] was issued to Wordsworth Donisthorpe on the *Kinesograph,* a device to be used for taking photographs on glass plates arranged as a pack, each plate dropping out of the way of the succeeding plate after being exposed. Pictures were taken at the rate of eight a second. The patent specified that the pictures were to be finished on paper and spaced equidistantly thereon. Another patent was granted to Donisthorpe on August 15, 1889, specifying the use of an electric spark for providing intermittent illumination in a viewing device. In *La Nature*[12] appears the following description of

Donisthorpe's work: "If the apparatus be arranged to take the successive pictures at sufficiently short intervals of time they may be printed at equal distances upon a continuous strip of paper; this paper, with the whole series of pictures upon it, may be used in the instrument known as the *Zoötrope* or *Phenakistoscope* . . . this strip may be wound on a cylinder, to be unwound from it at a uniform speed to another cylinder, and so carried on past the eye of the observer, any ordinary means being used for insuring that the pictures shall be exposed only momentarily to the observed. By this means the movements made by a person or group of persons, or any other object during the time they were being photographed, may be reproduced to the eye of the observer."[13]

1884—W. H. Walker and George Eastman, on June 27, 1884, assigned to the Eastman Dry Plate & Film Company a patent application on the process of coating paper with an emulsion having a soluble under-coating so that it might be applied to a stripping process; granted in 1890.[14]

1887—Hannibal Goodwin, in May of this year, applied for a U. S. patent on a method of preparing a celluloid support for photographic emulsions, the title being "Photographic Pellicle and Method for Producing Same." The patent[15] was granted on September 13, 1898; it is said that Goodwin did not reduce it to practice. This patent was later the subject of lengthy litigation, which was ultimately decided in favor of Goodwin's successors.[16,17]

1888—John Carbutt, in Philadelphia, began the commercial manufacture of films coated on sheet celluloid, obtained from a company in Newark, N. J. He apparently experimented with this product for two or three years before he could make it commercially.[18,19]

1888—Wallace Gould Levinson on June 26 applied for a U. S. patent,[20] which was subsequently granted, describing further developments along these lines.

1889—On April 9, Harry M. Reichenbach applied for a U. S. patent, which was granted on December 10, on a method of making transparent sheets of celluloid; a mixture of methyl al-

cohol, camphor, nitrocellulose, amyl acetate, and fusel oil was dried on a polished support, after which it was stripped off and coated with the photographic emulsion. This patent was assigned to the Eastman Dry Plate Company. The apparatus for coating the film base was patented by Eastman on March 22, 1892.[21] According to present records, the first supply of this stock to be used for producing successful motion pictures was sent to W. K. L. Dickson at the Edison Laboratories in July or August, 1889.[18,22]

1891—Eastman daylight-loading roll introduced.

1895 — In August, Eastman introduced the first positive motion picture stock; prior to this time motion pictures were made on negative film, which could be bought in 100-foot lengths. Many experimenters in Europe at this time bought the Eastman uncoated nitro-cellulose film bare and coated it themselves, notably the Lumiere brothers in France.

1903—Eastman introduced film having a gelatine coating on the rear surface in order to counteract curling of the film; the process had been patented by him in 1890.

1904—W. C. Parkin, in France, was granted a patent[23] on a method of making celluloid non-inflammable by adding a soluble metallic salt to ordinary celluloid. Subsequently, many others, chiefly in France, were granted patents on various ways of rendering celluloid non-inflammable or slow-burning, by means of adding various metallic salts.[24]

1913—In September, Eastman introduced panchromatic negative motion picture film.

1919—Eastman, introduced for the first time film that had latent image footage numbers printed on its edge; the markings included also the date, which was later omitted, and the markings evolved into the form as used today. The system was patented by Joseph Aller in 1922, the application being made in 1917.

1921 — On March 1, Eastman introduced colored base positive raw stock in nine colors: orange, amber, light amber, yellow, pink, red, green, blue, lavender to clear (black and white). Prior to this time, colored stock had been made in the various finishing laboratories by dyeing the emulsion after the processing of the picture.

1923 — In January Eastman introduced the 16-mm. reversal film and apparatus for amateur use.

---

*Honorary Curator, Motion Picture Collections, Los Angeles Museum, Los Angeles, Calif.

REFERENCES

[1]Worden, E. C.: "Nitrocellulose Industry," *D. Van Nostrand Co.*, New York, 1911, Vol. I, pp. 22-24.

[2]*International Encyclopedia*, 2nd ed., Vol. IV, *Dodd, Meade & Co., New York*, 1920, p. 753; *Encyclopedia Britannica*, 14th ed., Vol. 5, 1929, p. 97; *Encyclopedia Americana*, 1932 ed., Vol. 6, p. 175.

[3]*The Chemist*, 1851.

[4]Worden, E. C.: "Nitrocellulose Industry," *D. Van Nostrand Co.*, New York, 1911, Vol. II, p. 568.

[5]*Ibid.*, p. 571.

[6]U. S. Pat. 88,634.

[7] U. S. Pat. 91,341. Method of Making Solid Collodion.

[8]U. S. Pat. 91,233. Process and Apparatus for Manufacturing Pyroxyline.

[9]U. S. Pat. 133,229, Nov. 19, 1872.

[10]Worden, E. C.: "Nitrocellulose Industry," *D. Van Nostrand Co.*, New York, 1911, Vol. II, pp. 576-582.

[11]Brit. Pat. 4344, Nov. 9, 1876.

[12]*La Nature*, Jan. 24, 1878.

[13]Jenkins, C. F.: "Animated Pictures," *H. L. McQueen*, Washington, D. C., 1898, pp. 26-44.

[14]U. S. Pat. 420,130.

[15]U. S. Pat. 610,861.

[16]Ackerman, C. W.: "George Eastman," *Houghton Mifflin Co.*, New York, 1930.

[17]Worden, E. C.: "Nitrocellulose Industry," *D. Van Nostrand Co.*, New York, 1911, Vol. II, p. 846.

[18]*British Journal Photographic Almanac*, 1926, p. 480.

[19]*Philadelphia Photographer*, 25 (Nov. 3, 1888) , p. 672.

[20]U. S. Pat. 578,249.

[21]U. S. Pat. 471,469.

[22]Ramsaye, Terry: "A Million and One Nights," 2 vols., *Simon & Schuster*, New York, 1926.

[23]French Pat. 344,501.

[24]Bockmann, Friedrich: "Celluloid, Its Raw Materials, Manufacture, Properties, and Uses," translated from the 3rd German ed., by H. B. Stocks; *Scott & Co.*, London, 1921.

BIBLIOGRAPHY OF GENERAL REFERENCES

Sanford, P. G.: "Celluloid," 2nd ed., *Crosby, Lockwood & Son*, London, 1906.

Cross, C. F.: "Cellulose," *Longmans Green & Co.*, London, 1901.

Neblette, C. B.: "Photography, Its Principles and Practice," *D. Van Nostrand Co.*, New York, 1927.

Worden, E. C.: "Nitrocellulose Industry," 2 vols., *D. Van Nostrand Co.*, New York, 1911.

History of Motion-Picture Studio Lighting

By CHARLES W. HANDLEY

Historically, the use of artificial light in the motion-picture industry has followed a number of recurring cycles. The use of various types of lighting equipment has not always been a matter of evolution. On several occasions there has been a revolution in which carbon arcs were moved down from the top place by incandescent tungsten lamps and vice versa. The influences behind these cyclic changes were the advent of panchromatic film, the arrival of sound, the application of three-color photography, and finally an economic factor which resulted in a major change in the spectral sensitivity of all color films. During these various cycles, illuminants such as mercury tubes, fluorescent tubes and even mercury combined with other gases were experimented with, or used to some extent, but the main artificial light sources were carbon-arc lamps and incandescent tungsten lamps, used separately or in combination, and with one source or the other usually in a dominant position.[1,5,6,7,20,28]

THE ENERGY with which some people have attempted to reduce motion-picture set lighting to a strictly mechanical function indicates that the importance of light in motion-picture photography was probably not fully appreciated even by some of the people who depended upon the control of light for their livelihood. Basically, the visual part of the illusion we call the motion picture is nothing but the accurate control of light.

In modern motion-picture photography, light from the sun, light from the carbon arc or light from incandescent tungsten is directed to the object to be photographed. By reflection, this light is redirected to the film where it provides a photochemical reaction. The film, so modified, acts as a filter to control the intensity and quality of light from a projector. The modified projected light that is left after it has passed through the film is reflected from the screen to the eyes of the audience where it again makes an impression which should coincide dramatically with the original action. It would all be a simple matter of floodlighting if the word "dramatically" did not carry such strong implication. In order to enhance dramatic action the cinematographer must have as perfect control of the quality and quantity of light as possible.

A natural desire on the part of production units to simplify lighting to the extent of a pushbutton formula and to arrive at a Utopian position where pictures are made on a production-line basis has influenced historical trends in motion-picture set lighting. Some of these shifts have been responsible for major improvements in picture quality, while others, which were based on supposed economic

gains alone, have often forced compromises with dramatic effect to the serious detriment of the finished product.[2,30,31,34]

A close duplication of production items in a manufacturing process may result from strict adherence to engineering principles. And it is not to be denied that when it becomes necessary to deviate from engineering formulas, the one who does so with a complete understanding of what he is doing has an advantage over the empirical worker. Nevertheless, the one who works largely on a trial-and-error basis often produces a more successful motion picture if he keeps his thoughts on the emotional end result. This often requires a departure from strictly engineering efficiency in order that the production may be the same as the previous like group, but will provide a seemingly fresh presentation. An engineer who defends a position of strict adherence to basic engineering principles, regardless of the boxoffice value of the finished product, on the basis that he is an engineer and not an artist, is doing a bit of rationalization.

The film technician may desire a negative showing some detail in all shadow and highlight areas with most of the density range on the straight-line portion of the gamma curve. It is this desire for his own limited goal that has often encouraged him to extol the merits of flat light. The art director may desire sufficient overall density to insure an appreciation of the beauty of his set. But the director and cinematographer may be striving for a dramatic effect that fails to meet the desired requirements of either film technician or art director, yet does achieve the end result in that particular shot of affecting the senses of the theater patron in a manner which will forward the total desired effect of the story.[9,10,15,16,19,21,22,23,29]

In the beginning, little thought was given to anything except a sufficient

amount of light to provide exposure. Novelty effect took the place of dramatic effect. The motion picture was a magic lantern with movement, "just a passing fancy."

It is true that as early as the turn of the century, Thomas Edison built an experimental motion-picture stage which was mounted on a turntable so it could be rotated to follow the changing relative location of the sun. The infant industry, however, was in no position to try any costly experiments. As a matter of fact, where the cameraman helped to write the script, build the sets and even double in brass for all types of production work, there was little time for artistic expression.

Fortunately, as the motion-picture industry began to expand, there was a considerable number of people who saw the possibilities of the medium as a means for dramatic effect and the cameraman was one of the major leaders toward creating dramatic results that would entertain people by affecting them emotionally.

At that time in motion-picture production, sunlight was the only available light source and sets were photographed on open stages with muslin diffusers mounted on wires so they could be adjusted to control the light. Various types of reflectors were also used to redirect the rays from the sun and avoid heavy shadows on the faces of the characters and throughout the set. A wide assortment of translucent and opaque objects are still in general use to diffuse and control light (Fig. 1).

Because pictures were made in black-and-white, the question of color quality was not so important as it is today. However, the cameraman was handicapped by wide variations in intensity and position of his sunlight source throughout the day, and during inclement weather he was unable to work at all.

As a natural outgrowth of this situation, glass stages similar to large greenhouses were constructed and diffusers were installed as on the open stages. The reason for the glass stage was to permit the picture companies to operate during inclement weather; however, the advent of artificial lighting at about the same period made them obsolete and they were seldom used in the manner for which they were originally designed. The advantages of working under artificial light were so great that most of the sets built inside of the glass stages were covered over with canvas, or other means were employed to exclude the natural light. Later, the glass panels were painted black so the natural light could not interfere with the

Presented on May 4, 1954, at the Society's Convention at Washington, D.C., by Charles W. Handley, National Carbon Div., Union Carbide and Carbon Corp., 2770 Leonis Blvd., Los Angeles 58.
(This paper was received on May 24, 1954.)

Fig. 1. A Paramount picture photographed in 1939. Sunlight is the light source. Note the use of reflectors and circular scrim protecting some of the principals from overly strong shadow effects. Street set is rigged with canvas roof that may be pulled over to make closed set if artificial light is used.

controllable artificial illumination being used.[26]

In the earlier serious attempts at set lighting the cameraman worked with old-type, street-lighting carbon arcs and banks of Cooper-Hewitt mercury tubes placed directly overhead and at angles in an attempt to obtain a flat, diffused light all over the set. Cooper-Hewitt mercury lamps were installed in the Biograph Studios, New York, as early as 1905. Overall exposure requirements, lack of adequate equipment and economics made anything but flat lighting difficult, if not impossible, to attain.

It was known by the cameramen that added interest, improved perspective, increased illusion of depth and much greater dramatic effect would be obtained if they could skillfully utilize powerful light sources that would give them the effect of a one-source lighting such as could be obtained from the sun under ideal conditions, but the industry had not yet attained the position where such specialized equipment could be properly designed and made.

The time finally arrived when the public had accepted the silent pictures and fortunes were being made in production. This brought competition, which in turn opened the door for the cameraman to take some chances, to try anything he could get his hands on, to use his creative ability without fear of sudden replacement by a penny-wise management. In 1912, white flame carbon arcs replaced the low-intensity enclosed arcs at Biograph.

One of the cameraman's first demands

was for a controllable light source that would give him twice the power and twice the penetration capacity of anything he had. His only source of equipment was to follow precedent and adapt from other fields as had been done with the street-lighting carbon arcs and the Cooper-Hewitt mercury banks.

Carbon-arc floodlamps, better adapted to floor lighting than the other equipment, were obtained from the graphic-arts and still-photographic fields (Fig. 2). Carbon-arc spotlamps were purchased from the theater-projection and stage-lighting fields. Such lighting equipment companies as M. J. Wohl & Co. and Kliegl Bros., of New York, turned their attention to motion-picture studio lighting equipment. It was from the name Kliegl that the "Klieg-light" originated. Even the military searchlight was adapted for use where a greater amount of light was needed (Fig. 3).

Later, various adaptations of these units were built, or assembled by newly formed lighting companies in Hollywood. Among these concerns were Winfield-Kerner, a manufacturer of lamps for the graphic-arts trade, Creco Co. and Cinema Studio Supply Co., started by people from within the motion-picture industry.

The status of the cameraman improved with his increased ability, from both the equipment and economic angle, to show what could be done with light and his title was changed to Cinematographer, or Director of Photography.

To obtain dramatic effect, the cinematographer has always been forced to

compromise with engineering efficiency. The only time he would ever, or will ever, compromise with dramatic effect is under economic pressure that he cannot control. The equipment he searched for was something that provided a wide latitude of utilization even at the sacrifice of overall efficiency from the light-output, or power-consumption, viewpoints.[32]

Because they could be placed where the carbon arc could not, and because they provided a soft, more or less nondirectional source of light, the cinematographer often tried to use incandescent tungsten bulbs for certain effects. His efforts in this direction were largely frustrated at the time because of the low speed and limited color sensitivity of the film then used. The preponderance of light from the tungsten bulb is in the red end of the spectrum and his film was blind to red.[13]

Color motion pictures were not a major factor in those days, but color rendition in shades of gray of the same saturation as seen by the eye when looking at the original was something the cinematographers needed badly. Even a reasonably light-red object would photograph black. The advent of panchromatic film gave the cinematographer a better control of his gray scale and also made it possible for him to start experimenting with incandescent tungsten bulbs.

In spite of equipment that was ill-

Fig. 2. An early type of solenoid feed carbon-arc floodlamp.

Fig. 3. Sunlight arc lamps — 24-in. and 36-in. — popular during the 1920's and early 1930's. This equipment was adapted from the military searchlight.

Fig. 4. Grouping of incandescent tungsten lamp equipment of the types more popular in the late 1920's and early 1930's with some still in use.

adapted and inefficient, the cinematographer was beginning to achieve an art form when the advent of sound in 1927 imprisoned his cameras in static, awkward, soundproofed booths. The importance of the new sound medium transcended all demands for photographic quality and the cinematographer was forced to reduce his art to a mechanical function in order that an acceptable, audible result might be obtained.

Restricted to small sets and with his camera static, the cinematographer began to experiment with fresh approaches to his goal of photographic dramatic effect. Soon a number of cameras were running on the same set in order to achieve the effect of movement, and the cinematographer began casting about for light sources that would not be restricted, as were his cameras, by the noise they created.[3-9]

He had been experimenting with panchromatic film which was not blind to the red light, and in the incandescent tungsten bulb he saw a lighting medium with which he could obtain soft effects and which he could use for base lighting.

It was in 1927 that the Mole-Richardson Co., of Hollywood, was formed to manufacture, sell and rent all types of specialized studio-lighting equipment. This firm now operates all over the world wherever motion pictures are made and has provided many versatile lighting tools exclusively for motion-picture set lighting. Another firm established at a somewhat later date was the Bardwell & McAlister Co., of Hollywood.

Some people in studio management saw in the incandescent bulb a means of economic gain whereby set lighting would be accomplished by a push of a button. They put all of their publicity efforts behind an incandescent-bulb campaign and for a time the carbon arc was virtually discarded, with orders in some places

that it could be used only by special permission from the management.

Fortunately the novelty and value of added sound helped to overcome the photographic deficiencies of the period which followed. Camera lenses were not corrected for the red end of the spectrum and focus problems were legion. Sufficient incandescent-bulb equipment was not immediately available and certain motion pictures took on a dark, soft-focus appearance that was highly touted as the "new look" of the day. The pressure against the use of the supplementary carbon-arc lamps for sunlight, streaklight and other of the depth- and drama-producing effects was not only unfair to the efforts of the cinematographer, but to the value of the incandescent bulb itself. Partly as a result of this, many pictures were made where scope was limited to the techniques of the legitimate stage.

The sudden demand for housings to utilize incandescent tungsten bulbs resulted in adapting equipment from other fields and in the manufacturers imitating some of the carbon-arc lamp housings that had proven useful.

But as sound was absorbed into the industry, the cinematographer was again recognized as a creative artist. His immediate demands were for a lamp with twice the light and twice the penetrating power of anything available from the existing incandescent tungsten bulbs.

A rifled glass reflector, which had been used for incandescent tungsten flood-lighting at a distance from the source, was used as a basis for this demand for twice the light and twice the penetrating power.[25] From a light collecting and distribution standpoint it was particularly well engineered; from a utilization standpoint it was not flexible (Fig. 4). What the cinematographer wanted was a light with twice the intensity, twice the penetrating power and one that could

be used at varying distances with control of beam spread and light distribution.

Of course the demand was fantastic! In order to give the cinematographer what he wanted, it would be necessary to sacrifice engineering efficiency all the way along the line. It would mean more powerful incandescent bulbs, bulkier equipment and higher operating costs. What had to be learned was that the efficiency of utilization was the all-important factor and that strictly engineering or tight-drawn economic factors must be made to compromise.

Compromises were made. Ten-kw bulbs were produced and even a 50-kw bulb was tried. The equipment became more flexible. Compromises were also made by the sound departments. Carbon-arc lamps, now filtered with electrolytic capacitors to reduce generator ripple, again appeared on sets where the effects of sunlight, streaklight and back-

Fig. 5. Stepped-prism, Fresnel-type lens introduced in 1934. Controllable beam spread of from 8° to 48°. Introduced to the motion-picture industry by Mole-Richardson Co., Hollywood.

light would allow the cinematographer to express his individuality and to produce the illusion for which he was striving.[11,24]

It was this era that marked the first of the major changes made by manufacturers of studio-lighting equipment to provide units with maximum power and maximum utilization. Specialized incandescent bulbs were produced to replace those which had been adapted from other fields. In 1934, lamps with large-diameter, mirror-type optical systems were replaced with stepped-prism condensers made along the lines of the well-known Fresnel lens system (Figs. 5, 6 and 7). It appeared as though the industry was settling down to a lighting technique in which the incandescent bulb and the carbon arc were lighting tools available to the cinematographer depending upon his own interpretation of his artistic needs.

The one exception was the clarion cry, "I want a lamp with twice the light and twice the penetrating power!" But in the entertainment field, standardization of techniques often result in formula without novelty or apparent difference. It is quite true that people want formula, that they will not accept anything which does not carry a familiar connotation. They will pay money to see the same thing they saw last week or last year. They want it to be the same, but they want it to be *differently the same*.[27]

The first major revolution was in the advent of sound. Now color stepped in for a go at it!

Technicolor, who had been struggling with a two-color process, announced that they were ready to launch motion pictures in the full color scale and that the white light of the carbon-arc lamp would be needed for the process.[17]

The announcement by Technicolor did not produce chaos in the industry as had the arrival of sound, because the studio people believed that color was something they could take or leave alone.

Many believed that color would never replace black-and-white and others reasoned, correctly, that if it did eventually replace black-and-white it would be by evolution and not by revolution.

The advent of *Becky Sharp*, Technicolor's first major three-color release in 1935, did cause a revolution in the studio-lighting field. The carbon-arc lamp was again to be the predominant studio-light source and the unbalanced spectrum and comparatively low light output from a single unit of the incandescent bulb made its future appear quite bleak to many observers.[10-15]

Some work had been done on the design of a new type of carbon-arc spotlamp and these were hurried into production. For floodlighting, an adaptation of the older carbon-arc floodlamps was made and later a completely new design was manufactured and replaced the earlier units.[18] It was the heyday for the carbon arc. It would be necessary to throw away more than half of the energy from the incandescent lamp to make it match white light, so to all intents and purposes it was through insofar as use on color sets was concerned.[12]

But the cinematographer missed the soft diffusion, the small overall equipment size and the fill-light quality he obtained from the incandescent lamp almost as much as he had missed the small source size and great power from one unit of the carbon arc in the early days of sound; so color filters were made and incandescent lamps found their proper niche in Technicolor photography even though the film sensitivity did not indicate their use as an economic value.

Until the introduction of three-color photography, the photographic exposure meter was not used to any extent in the motion-picture studios. The cinematographer lighted his sets by visual judgment and depended upon photographic exposure tests when in doubt. Some worked almost entirely from their interpretation of a dramatic effect and refused

to compromise with certain basic engineering demands, with the result that there was a constant feud with the developing laboratories over who did what with which.[19,21]

The more restricted latitude, and even the handling of color itself, made it necessary to apply greater engineering efficiency to motion-picture photography in order to obtain added dramatic effect which color itself could provide. For the successful introduction of three-color, motion-picture photography, Technicolor found it necessary to demand certain engineering requirements so that the finished product would provide this dramatic effect.

In order to accomplish this result they supplied their own technicians to operate the three-strip cameras and contracted with a number of successful cinematographers to supervise the set lighting. As soon as possible, all cinematographers were made familiar with color requirements, one of which was the accurate control of light.[14-16,22] The cinematographer still does much of his light balancing by visual means, but he also reads the incident light in various areas and when he goes beyond the latitude of the system in order to obtain a certain dramatic effect he has been forewarned.

One of the major advances made by Technicolor was the announcement that they had doubled the photographic speed of the system. When the cinematographer was asked if this would bring about the use of smaller units, the response was that much of it would be used for increased depth of focus and greater latitude of operation. What was wanted was a light source with twice the penetrating power of existing lamps. A new super high-intensity, carbon-arc lamp was designed to fill this demand.

It should be noted that the first change from a preponderance of carbon arcs to a preponderance of incandescent bulbs was made possible through a change in film sensitivity. The next revolution in

Fig. 6. Modern carbon-arc lamp equipment.

Fig. 7. Modern incandescent tungsten lamp equipment.

123

lighting was the result of the film sensitivity of the new Technicolor process. In each case one type of light source was almost superseded by the other, until management pressure was relaxed giving the cinematographer a chance to fit the units in where they could be used for the greatest dramatic effect.

The next revolution came during 1950 when, due to loss of revenue, the carbon arc, because of manpower requirements, was singled out as the heavy in the melodrama of economics versus production values.

Technicolor changed the basic sensitivity of its system to match the color temperature of the incandescent bulb so it could be used unfiltered with incandescent lamps, or filtered with sunlight or carbon arcs. Eastman and Ansco soon did likewise with their color films. If mixed lighting was to be used the incandescent tungsten lamps would have to be filtered to the temperature of the carbon arcs, or vice versa.[33] The changed film was faster to incandescent tungsten than to white light and it appeared as though a revolution had taken place which would give the cinematographer much greater latitude of operation.

On a small set, or where a preponderance of incandescent lamps was indicated, he could use them and filter whatever arcs he wished to use. On a large set, he would go on a white-light basis and filter what incandescent units he had, thus providing a possibility for more latitude of operation first, and added economy second. The man with the pocketbook did not agree with this logic. The system had been changed to match incandescent lamps and incandescent lamps it would be. One studio even announced the sale of carbon-arc equipment.

Higher-powered incandescent lamps were demanded, a lamp that would produce twice the light and twice the penetrating power. The result was a revival of 10-kw lamps adapted to optics improved beyond ones that had been tried before, plus the wide usage of the highest-powered, carbon-arc lamps filtered to the spectrum of the incandescent lamp.

An occasional cinematographer ventured color production on a white-light basis, but on the whole he remained with the tungsten balance because of so-called economics. He now wanted a lamp with the penetrating power and light output of twice that of the highest-powered, carbon-arc lamp, but with the color temperature of the incandescent lamp so he could use it on his sets freely mixed with incandescents and without the necessity of a lamp filter.

What he actually needs is more freedom of choice for the improvement of production values rather than for small economic squeezing which robs him of the initiative it takes to make something *differently the same*.

Now comes the revolution of 3-D and wide screen with requirements of smaller lens apertures, much larger sets and the extreme in production values. As always, more light, the maximum of latitude of operation, and the extreme in creative ability will be needed. If history repeats itself, as the pendulum swings toward fewer and better pictures, the choice of set-lighting equipment will again revert to the man who directs the use of it and he will be casting about for a controllable light source with twice the light output and twice the penetrating power of any existing equipment, whether it be incandescent tungsten, carbon arcs, or some other form of radiant energy.

References

1. W. Roy Mott, "White light for motion picture photography," *Trans. SMPE, No. 8:* 7–41, Apr. 1919.
2. Loyd A. Jones, "Incandescent tungsten lamp installation for illuminating color motion picture studio," *Trans. SMPE, No. 22:* 25–45, publ. Sept. 1925.
3. E. W. Beggs, "Lighting by tungsten filament incandescent lamps for motion picture photography," *Trans. SMPE, No. 26:* 94–106, publ. Nov. 1926.
4. Peter Mole, "The tungsten lamp situation in the studio," *Trans. SMPE, No. 31:* 582–590, publ. Sept. 1927.
5. L. J. Buttolph, "Cooper-Hewitt neon lamps," *Trans. SMPE, No. 34:* 557, Apr. 1928.
6. R. E. Farnham, "The effective application of incandescent lamps for motion picture photography," *Trans. SMPE, No. 34:* 464–483, Apr. 1928.
7. D. B. Joy and A. C. Downes, "Characteristics of flame arcs for studio lighting," *Trans. SMPE, No. 34:* 502–520, Apr. 1928.
8. Peter Mole, "The use of incandescent equipment in motion picture photography," *Trans. SMPE, No. 34:* 521–536, Apr. 1928.
9. Karl Struss, "Dramatic cinematography," *Trans. SMPE, No. 34:* 317–319, Apr. 1928.
10. R. E. Farnham, "The use of Mazda lamps for color photography," *Jour. SMPE, 21:* 166–171, Aug. 1933.
11. C. W. Handley, "Lighting for Technicolor motion pictures," *Jour. SMPE, 25:* 423–431, Nov. 1935.
12. R. E. Farnham, "Recent developments in the use of Mazda lamps for color motion picture photography," *Jour. SMPE, 24:* 487–492, June 1935.
13. R. E. Farnham and R. E. Worstell, "Color quality of light of incandescent lamps," *Jour. SMPE, 27:* 260–266, Sept. 1936.
14. E. C. Richardson, "Recent developments in motion picture lighting," *Jour. SMPE, 29:* 178–183, Aug. 1937.
15. C. W. Handley, "The advanced technic of Technicolor lighting, *Jour. SMPE, 29:* 169–177, Aug. 1937.
16. G. Gaudio, "A new viewpoint on the lighting of motion pictures," *Jour. SMPE, 29:* 157–168, Aug. 1937.
17. F. T. Bowditch and A. C. Downes, "Spectral distributions and color temperatures of the radiant energy from carbon arcs used in the motion picture industry," *Jour. SMPE, 30:* 400–409, Apr. 1938.
18. Peter Mole, "The evolution of arc broadside lighting equipment," *Jour. SMPE, 32:* 398–411, Apr. 1939.
19. C. W. Handley, Chairman, Report of the Studio Lighting Committee, *Jour. SMPE, 33:* 97–100, July 1939.
20. G. E. Inman and W. H. Robinson, "The fluorescent lamp and its application to motion picture studio lighting," *Jour. SMPE, 33:* 326–335, Sept. 1939.
21. C. W. Handley, Chairman, Report of the Studio Lighting Committee, *Jour. SMPE, 34:* 94–97, Jan. 1940.
22. Winton Hoch, "Technicolor cinematography," *Jour. SMPE, 39:* 96–108, Aug. 1942.
23. John W. Boyle, "Black and white cinematography," *Jour. SMPE, 39:* 83–96, Aug. 1942.
24. B. F. Miller, "A motion picture arc-lighting generator filter," *Jour. SMPE, 41:* 367–373, Nov. 1943.
25. R. G. Linderman, C. W. Handley and A. Rodgers, "Illumination in motion picture production," *Jour. SMPE, 40:* 333, June 1943.
26. Peter Mole, "If it isn't on the film," *Intl. Projectionist, 21:* 36–38, 81, July 1946, Section 2.
27. Charles Handley, "Differently the same," *The Author and Journalist,* Nov. 1946.
28. F. E. Carlson, "New developments in mercury lamps for studio lighting," *Jour. SMPE, 50:* 122–138, Feb. 1948.
29. John Alton, *Painting with Light,* Macmillan Company, New York, 1949.
30. Wayne Blackburn, "Study of sealed beam lamps for motion picture set lighting," *Jour. SMPTE, 55:* 101–112, July 1950.
31. G. R. Stevens, "Independent frame — an attempt at rationalization of motion picture production," *Jour. SMPTE, 57:* 434–442, Nov. 1951.
32. Peter Mole, "Will there always be a need for carbon arcs?" *Am. Cinemat.,* Feb. 1951.
33. Charles W. Handley, Chairman, Progress Committee Report, *Jour. SMPTE, 56:* 568–583, May 1951.
34. Charles W. Handley, Chairman, Progress Committee Report, *Jour. SMPTE, 58:* 397–409, May 1952.

History of Professional Black-and-White Motion-Picture Film

By C. E. KENNETH MEES

Beginning with the regular roll film emulsion-coated on a length of clear support, which was sent to Mr. Edison for his first experiments, there have been many changes and improvements in the negative motion-picture films and the addition of positive films, sound-recording films and other special films which have themselves been improved from time to time, resulting in improved techniques and better motion pictures.

THE PRODUCTION of motion pictures involves a combination of the theatrical art and photographic technique, and its history has depended upon the development both of the theater and of photography. I have been asked to give you an account of the development of the films used in making motion pictures, and in doing so I must call attention to the close relation between the methods used in the production of pictures and the nature of the films which have been available.

This account deals only with the films manufactured by the Eastman Kodak Co., a record of which was available to me. A number of other manufacturers have played an active part in the development of the industry and have made a variety of films. The Lumière Co., of Lyons, France, made film at a very early date in connection with the development of motion pictures by Auguste and Louis Lumière and later sold a considerable quantity of motion-picture film to American users.

In 1918 the Du Pont Co. commenced the manufacture of motion-picture positive film and have since made a range of films for motion-picture purposes. The Agfa-Ansco Co. manufactured motion-picture positive film, and their successors, the Ansco Division of the General Aniline and Film Co., have been active in the supply of film to the industry.

This account of the development of motion-picture films deals only with the films which produce monochrome images.

The beginning of motion-picture production in the United States was associated with the first production of transparent film, made for use in Kodak cameras. In 1887, W. K. L. Dickson was working in Edison's laboratory in West Orange on an instrument to be used with the Edison phonograph to reproduce motion as well as sound. In this instrument, very small images were photographed in a continuous spiral on a

Presented on May 3, 1954, at the Society's Convention at Washington, D.C., by C. E. Kenneth Mees, Eastman Kodak Co., Kodak Park Works, Rochester 4, N.Y.
(This paper was received on May 17, 1954.)

cylinder, as sound is recorded on the phonograph cylinder. In September 1889, however, Dickson sent an order and $2.50 to George Eastman for a roll of film 35 mm in width. This film was used in a new type of kinetoscope for taking motion pictures on a continuous strip of film which was standardized at a width of $1\frac{3}{8}$ in. with four perforations to a frame along both edges, the film which, in essence, is that used today.

The emulsion was that used in the Kodak cameras and at first this film was used for making both negatives and prints, but in a very short time a special film was made for positive prints. It gave more contrasty and brighter prints, and, being of lower speed than the camera film, it was easier to handle in printing.

In 1916, when the Society of Motion Picture Engineers was formed, only two motion-picture films were available—a negative film for use in the camera and a positive film for making prints. The negative film was sensitive to blue, violet and ultraviolet light, and it was necessary to expose it outdoors by daylight or in studios by the use of arc lamps. Thus motion-picture studios found California, with its abundant sunshine, a convenient location, and a number of excellent lighting units using arc lamps were developed, at first to supplement and later to replace sunlight.

In January 1917, a change was made in the basic emulsion of the negative film which was known simply as "motion-picture negative film" until, owing to the introduction of other films in August 1925, its name became Motion-Picture Negative Film Par Speed. As new films were introduced, it became necessary to use some identification for the type of film other than rather indefinite names, and the Eastman Kodak Co. adopted the practice of assigning type numbers to the films, using new numbers not only for new kinds of films but for new varieties of the same kind, the old type being continued on the market for the convenience of customers until it was effectively replaced by the new introduction. The type numbers constituted to some extent a code. Thus 1 indicated a film on nitrate base; 2 in the second place

indicated a negative film. Par Speed negative film was therefore assigned Type 1201, and its emulsion continued essentially unchanged until it was discontinued in July 1942.

Panchromatic Negative Materials

As early as 1913, experiments were being made at Rochester on the production of a panchromatic negative film. The first panchromatic film was made for use in the Gaumont process, an additive process of color cinematography in which negatives were made simultaneously through three lenses equipped with suitable filters, and the pictures were projected in register by a three-lens system. This process was introduced by Léon Gaumont in France, and Mr. Eastman decided to consider its introduction upon the American market. Gaumont made his panchromatic film by bathing negative film in dye solutions, but this process is very prone to give spots and other defects, and experience with the Wratten panchromatic plates had shown that there was no great difficulty in sensitizing an emulsion to make it panchromatic. The real difficulties lay in the conditions necessary for coating the emulsion. Much credit is due to the workmen and supervision who succeeded in coating the panchromatic film in those early days. The operatives were accustomed to red light in the coating rooms, and it was not easy to work in almost total darkness.

Panchromatic film was originally supplied in small quantities as experimental material. Some of this was used as early as 1919 by Charles Rosher. In 1923 it became a regular product of the Eastman Kodak Co. One of the first, if not the first, regular productions made on panchromatic negative film was *The Headless Horseman*. The cameraman was Ned Van Buren. It was photographed in 1922, and the negative is now in the vaults of Eastman House in Rochester, N.Y.

The panchromatic film was at first higher priced than the blue-sensitive film, but in 1926 the price of the panchromatic film was lowered to that of the Par Speed Negative Film, and its sale began to increase rapidly. In 1928 the film was assigned Type 1203, and the name Motion-Picture Negative Panchromatic Type I was given to it.

In 1926 L. A. Jones and J. I. Crabtree published, in the Transactions of the Society of Motion Picture Engineers, a paper on "Panchromatic Negative Film for Motion Pictures," in which they summarized the properties of panchromatic film, its use with various light sources, the reproduction of colored objects obtained by its use and its handling in the darkroom. The use of infrared-sensitive film was also discussed and illustrated. The first infrared negative film was introduced under the name Panchromatic K in 1928 as Type 1210. Infrared film renders blue skies as black, and green foliage as white, and is used chiefly for the simulation of night effects in pictures taken by sunlight. Very great improvements have been made from time to time in the sensitizing of infrared film.

The use of panchromatic film became general in the studios by 1927, and tungsten light was being used to an increasing extent instead of arc lamps, especially for supplementary lighting. In 1928 the Du Pont Company put panchromatic film on the market, and the Kodak Company introduced Cine Negative Panchromatic Type II, Type 1218, which continued on the market until 1935. The year 1928 was, as we shall see later, one of great activity in the production of new types of motion-picture films.

Sensitizing Dyes

At this point, it is necessary to say something of the development of sensitizing dyes. Up to 1928, the dyes used for photographic film were those which had been developed by E. Koenig and his colleagues and which had been introduced by the German dye company, Farbwerke Hoechst. All these dyes were derived from quinoline. The green sensitizers were isocyanines; the red sensitizer generally used was pinacyanol, a dye made by the same reaction as the isocyanines, with the addition of formaldehyde. This reaction had been discovered by B. Homolka. Curiously enough, the chemical structure of pinacyanol was unknown or, if its originators knew its structure, they didn't publish it. During the First World War, sensitizers having the same structure and properties as the German dyes were made both in England and in the United States, and a study of the chemical structure of the dyes, and especially of pinacyanol, was carried out by W. H. Mills and W. J. Pope at Cambridge University. As a result of this work and of its extension by Mills and his pupils, it became evident to dye chemists that cyanine dyes similar in general structure to the German dyes could be made from a great number of organic compounds other than quinoline, and that a vast number of these dyes must exist. Starting in 1928, therefore, the laboratories of the photographic manufacturers in England, Germany and the United States began to produce new

sensitizing dyes at a very rapid rate. A summary of the work in the Kodak laboratories alone can be given by saying that since the beginning of 1930 the sensitizer laboratory has on the average produced one new sensitizing dye a day. The use of these new dyes, and especially their use in combinations, made possible a great increase in the color sensitivity of photographic materials.

In 1931 Super-sensitive Cine Negative Panchromatic Film was introduced as Type 1217 and rapidly displaced the 1218 panchromatic film which had been the standard Eastman material for negative making in Hollywood. A faster film known as Type 1227 was made in 1935. This was named Super-X Panchromatic Negative Film. It had a new basic emulsion with ortho-panchromatic sensitizing. It had a comparatively short life, however, because in 1938 a group of new films was introduced characterized by appreciably higher speed and lower graininess. They were made possible by basic developments in emulsion making which affected practically all high-speed films. The new motion-picture negative films were Type 1230, Background X Panchromatic; 1231, Plus-X Panchromatic; 1232, Super-XX Panchromatic. Of these, Type 1231 quickly became the most popular motion-picture camera film made by the Eastman Kodak Co. It is currently in production and is still our largest-volume camera film. Type 1232 was similar to 1231 except that its emulsion was appreciably faster and coarser in grain. It was the fastest Kodak film made at that date and is still a current product, though the recently introduced Tri-X Negative Film Type 5233 will probably take its place.

Special reference should be made to 1230, the Background X Cine Negative Panchromatic. This film was a successor to films introduced in 1932 for making background shots. Type 1212, a panchromatic emulsion of medium speed and finer grain than the 1217 negative panchromatic film of that date, was replaced a year or two later by Type 1213, and in 1938 Type 1230 largely replaced 1213.

Release-Print Positive

Now let us turn from the negative-making material to the release-print positive, of which such very large amounts have always been used in the motion-picture industry. The positive film has two characteristics in which it differs from the negative material. It must be of sufficiently fine grain to increase to the smallest possible degree the graininess inherent in the negative. It must also have a contrast which, when combined with that of the negative material, will give a satisfactory contrast

in the projection print. Using as a measure of contrast the slope of the straight-line portion of the characteristic curve, Hurter and Driffield's γ, experience has shown that the projection print should have an overall γ of approximately 1.3. The exact reproduction of the tone scale of the original would, of course, require a γ of 1.0, but loss of contrast owing to light scattering, and so forth, requires a somewhat higher γ than 1.0 for the best tone rendering. To obtain the required overall γ with a minimum of graininess, it has been found advisable to develop the negative material to a γ of 0.65, so that the positive material must have a γ of approximately 2.0. Thus the positive material should have the finest possible grain, should give a γ of 2.0 at convenient times of development and, at the same time, must have sufficient speed for printing in the standard motion-picture printers. The positive emulsion supplied as Eastman Cine Positive Film in 1916 met these requirements satisfactorily and remained unchanged for many years. When type numbers were introduced, it was assigned Type 1301.

Many attempts were made to produce a positive film having a lower graininess, but all failed because the film was too slow for use on the standard printers and also tended to give a warm-toned image, which was not generally satisfactory for projection. It was not until 1940 that Fine-Grain Release Positive Type 1302 was made having sufficient speed, provided that the printers were modified to increase the light available, and having definitely lower graininess than Type 1301 with an image of pleasing tone. Types 1301 and 1302, therefore, cover the whole history of motion-picture positive film up to date.

Colored Bases for Tints

About 1920 a demand arose for positive films on colored base, which enabled a tinted film to be obtained by simply printing upon film having the right color in the base. In 1921 positive films were available on lavender, red, green, blue, pink, light amber, yellow, orange and dark amber bases. When by 1929 sound films had displaced the silent films, difficulty arose with the tinted bases because the dye absorbed the light used for exciting the photoelectric cells by which the sound record was reproduced. A new range of tinted positive supports were therefore introduced under the name of Sonochrome. They were designed to provide satisfactory monochromatic scenes and, at the same time, enable the sound record to be utilized without difficulty in projection. They were described by L. A. Jones in a paper in the Transactions of the Society. After the fine-grain cine positive was introduced in 1940, three of the Sono-chrome tints were used for this new emulsion.

In 1926, J. G. Capstaff and M. W. Seymour published an important paper in the Transactions of the Society on the duplication of motion-picture negatives. At that time, prints made from duplicate negatives were notably inferior to direct prints. Duplicate negatives were usually made on Par Speed Negative material from projection positives and showed graininess, distorted tone scale and edge effects. A new duplicating film was made by the use of a fine-grained emulsion, the contrast of which was controlled by the addition of a water-soluble yellow dye. It gave little increase of graininess, good tone rendering and a minimum of edge effects, because development could be prolonged to eliminate the effects without producing too much contrast. At first, the same film, Type 1503, was used for both negative and positive.

In 1929 a duplicating positive, Type 1355, was introduced. Its speed was somewhat higher and its contrast somewhat lower than the standard release-print material of that date. In 1930 a fast, yellow-dyed negative material was coated as Type 1510. In 1933 a duplicating positive Type 1362 was introduced; in 1936 two new duplicating films were made having a finer grain than the regular positive of that date. These were 1203, Fine Grain Duplicating Negative Panchromatic, and 1365, Fine Grain Duplicating Positive.

Films for Sound

When the motion-picture trade adopted the reproduction of sound, interest arose in the use of special films for sound recording. There were two different methods of recording sound upon film: (1) that in which the density of the track was modulated, the variable-density method; and (2) that in which the width of the track was modified, the variable-width method. In 1930 L. A. Jones and O. Sandvik published a discussion of the "Photographic Characteristics of Sound Recording Film" in the *Journal* of the Society. The variable-width recording method did not present a serious problem since release positive film gave very good results, but in 1928 a yellow-dyed, negative-type emulsion was introduced as Type 1507 for use in variable-density sound recording. Not until 1932, however, was a sound-recording film, Type 1359, supplied which gave results in variable-density sound recording sufficiently better than those obtained on motion-picture positive film for it to be generally adopted by the trade. In 1936 Type 1357 was introduced for variable-area recording. Types 1357 and 1359 were very similar, and new films, Type 1372 for variable-area and Type 1373 for variable-density recording,

were introduced at approximately the same time in 1944 and are still in use.

Films specially made for color photography are dealt with in another paper, but it should be mentioned that since 1916 many films have been made for use in current processes of color photography. The Technicolor Corp., for instance, has used special red-sensitive, green-sensitive and blue-sensitive negative films in its three-strip cameras. It has also used specially made matrix films and positive films on which the final image was built up by transfer printing. Many of these films have been made to the specifications of the Technicolor Corp., and their development is a part of the history of the Technicolor process.

Bipack film for taking negatives by means of red and green light, Type 1208, was made first in 1930. It was a fast emulsion, green-sensitized with one of the first of the modern sensitizers and overcoated with an orange-red dye. It was exposed through the back in contact with a panchromatic film, so that the green negative was made upon Type 1208 and the red record was made on panchromatic film. A blue-sensitive film overcoated with a red filter dye was introduced as Type 1239 in 1938. This could be used in contact with a red-sensitive film to give the blue record in a three-strip system. For printing two-color negatives, yellow-dyed positive film single- and double-coated had been introduced in 1923, the single-coated material being used for the then current Technicolor process, and the double-coated film, for the Prizma process of color photography. Although the Prizma process had a short life, the duplitized, yellow-dyed, cine positive Type 1509 is still in production. It has been used in many color processes employing two-color systems.

Safety Base Films

Ever since 1909, efforts have been made to replace the highly inflammable cellulose nitrate base of motion-picture films by a cellulose acetate base. The earlier acetate films were unsatisfactory as regards their physical properties. They retained more solvent than nitrate film and as this solvent evaporated they shrank, until finally they might not fit the sprockets. The shrinkage also manifested itself as cockle and curl. Nevertheless, safety positive film was made in appreciable quantities before 1916 and has been made ever since. It was absolutely necessary for projectors used without a booth. Safety film, as will be seen later, also played a great part in the development of the 16mm program. Improvements in the acetate base were continuous until 1950, when a marked change was made by the adoption of triacetate base. Cellulose triacetate

gives much improved physical qualities to the base, compared with the earlier material which contains slightly less acetyl in the structure of the molecules. As a result, the triacetate base proved to be as suitable as the earlier nitrate base. In 1950 nitrate base was discontinued, and from the beginning of 1951 all film has been made on the safety triacetate base. Since 1928, safety film has been distinguished by the substitution of Type 5 for 1 as the initial number. Thus Plus-X Panchromatic Negative is now known as Type 5231 and Fine Grain Release Positive as Type 5302.

The first 16mm film was introduced in 1923 as part of a program of home cinematography. An orthochromatic film, Type 5204, was first manufactured in May 1923 under the name of Kodak Safety Film for the Cine-Kodak and other cameras using 16mm film. This film, after exposure in the camera, was from the beginning developed by a reversal process to a positive and used as a final print for projection. It was this system which was responsible for the success of the 16mm program which has had such wide application in the whole development of motion pictures.

Panchromatic Cine-Kodak Film, Type 5255, was placed on the market in 1928. The camera film was first supplied for daylight loading with a paper leader. Many experiments were made on the use of an opaque backing to avoid the troubles involved in the use of the paper leader. Finally, in 1931, a jet-black backing was made which gave the necessary protection to the film and which was removed in the processing machines. Supersensitive Cine-Kodak Panchromatic Type 5256 was introduced early in 1931, and this was replaced in 1939 by Super-X Cine-Kodak Panchromatic Film having the same type number, 5256, which is a current product. In 1938 Super-XX Cine-Kodak Panchromatic Film, Type 5261, supplied the need for an ultraspeed reversal film.

Undoubtedly, new black-and-white films for use in motion-picture photography will be introduced from time to time and will embody improvements made possible by the advance of the emulsion-maker's art. The future of motion-picture photography, however, involves the use of color, and the principal advances in motion-picture films will depend upon the improvement of the materials and processes used for color photography.

Acknowledgment

My thanks are due to Mr. F. H. Reed, of the Film Emulsion Division, Kodak Park Works, who extracted from the records of the Emulsion Making and Film Coating departments much of the information included in this paper.

BIBLIOGRAPHY

Film Supports

A. F. Victor, "The portable projector: its present status and needs," *Trans. SMPE, No. 6:* 29–32, Apr. 1918. A discussion of inflammable film as used in portable projectors, ending with an appeal to standardize a non-inflammable film for portable projectors.

W. B. Cook, "Advantages in the use of the new standard, narrow width, slow-burning film for portable projectors," *Trans. SMPE, No. 7:* 86–90, Nov. 1918. A discussion of the history of 28-mm film and mention of the economy and durability of this film in use.

C. R. Fordyce, "Improved safety motion-picture film support," *Jour. SMPE, 51:* 331–350, Oct. 1948.

E. Theisen, "The history of nitrocellulose as a film base," *Jour. SMPE, 20:* 259–262, Mar. 1933.

Panchromatic Negative Materials

L. A. Jones and J. I. Crabtree, "Panchromatic negative film for motion pictures," *Trans. SMPE, No. 27:* 131–178, Oct. 1926.

D. R. White, "Characteristics of Du Pont Panchromatic Negative Film," *Jour. SMPE, 17:* 223–229, Aug. 1931.

E. Huse and G. A. Chambers, "Eastman Supersensitive Motion-Picture Negative Film," *Jour. SMPE, 17:* 560–567, Oct. 1931.

D. R. White, "Photographic effects obtained with Infra D Negative," *Jour. SMPE, 20:* 54–59, Jan. 1933.

P. H. Arnold, "A motion-picture negative of wider usefulness," *Jour. SMPE, 23:* 160–166, Sept. 1934. Describes properties of Agfa-Ansco Super Pan Negative Film.

W. Leahy, "New emulsion for special fields in motion-picture photography," *Jour. SMPE, 25:* 248–253, Sept. 1935. Describes Agfa-Ansco Finopan, Superpan Reversible and Infrared Films.

P. H. Arnold, "Sensitivity tests with an ultra-speed negative film," *Jour. SMPE, 30:* 541–558, May 1938. Agfa-Ansco product.

P. H. Arnold, "Problems in the use of ultra-speed negative film," *Jour. SMPE, 31:* 307–314, Sept. 1938. Agfa-Ansco product.

A. W. Cook, "Characteristics of Supreme Panchromatic Negative," *Jour. SMPE, 32:* 436–441, Apr. 1939. Properties of Agfa-Ansco Film.

J. A. Ball, "Infra-red photography in motion picture work," *Trans. SMPE, No. 22:* 21–24, May 1925.

Printing Materials

C. R. Daily, "Improvement in sound and picture release through the use of fine-grain film," *Jour. SMPE, 34:* 12–25, Jan. 1940; "Report on the adaptation of fine-grain films to variable-density sound techniques," *ibid., 34:* 3–11, Jan. 1940.

C. R. Daily and I. M. Chambers, "Production and release applications of fine-grain films for variable-density sound-recording," *Jour. SMPE, 38:* 45–55, Jan. 1942.

J. R. Wilkinson and F. L. Eich, "Laboratory modification and procedure in connection with fine-grain release printing," *Jour. SMPE, 38:* 56–65, Jan. 1942.

V. C. Schaner, "Note on the processing of Eastman 1302 Fine-Grain Release Positive in Hollywood," *Jour. SMPE, 38:* 66–73, Jan. 1942.

H. W. Moyse, "Du Pont Fine-Grain Sound Films — Types 232 and 236," *Jour. SMPE, 45:* 285–293, Oct. 1945.

R. M. Corbin, N. L. Simmons and D. E. Hyndman, "Two new Eastman fine-grain sound recording films," *Jour. SMPE, 45:* 265–284, Oct. 1945.

Additive Color Processes

L. Gaumont, "Vues cinématographiques en couleurs naturelles," *Bull. Société française Photographie, 3ème Serie, Vol. III:* 370–371, 1912.

C. E. K. Mees, "Color photography," *Photo-Miniature, 16:* 97–131, July 1921.

G. E. Mathews, "Processes of photography in natural colors," *Jour. SMPE, 16:* 188–219, Feb. 1931. Contains discussion and bibliography of various color films.

Duplication Materials

J. G. Capstaff and M. W. Seymour, "The duplication of motion-picture negatives," *Trans. SMPE, No. 28:* 223–229, Oct. 1926.

Eastman Duplicating Film — Its Properties and Uses, Eastman Kodak Co., Rochester, N.Y., 1927.

C. E. Ives and E. Huse, "Notes on making duplicate negatives," *Trans. SMPE, No. 34:* 382–389, Apr. 1928.

C. E. Ives and J. I. Crabtree, "Two new films for duplicating work," *Jour. SMPE, 29:* 317–325, Sept. 1937.

Sound Recording Films

E. I. Sponable, "Some technical aspects of the Movietone," *Trans. SMPE, No. 31:* 458–474, Sept. 1927. Describes dimensions and location of variable-density sound record on 35mm film.

A. C. Hardy, "The rendering of tone values in the photographic recording of sound," *Trans. SMPE, No. 31:* 475–491, Sept. 1927.

H. B. Marvin, "A system of motion-pictures with sound," *Trans. SMPE, No. 33:* 86–102, Apr. 1928.

O. Sandvik, "A study of ground noise in the reproduction of sound by photographic records," *Trans. SMPE, No. 35:* 790–798, Sept. 1928. This issue of the Transactions contains several papers on sound recording.

L. A. Jones and O. Sandvik, "Photographic characteristics of sound recording film," *Jour. SMPE, 14:* 180–203, Feb. 1930.

Tinted Film Supports

Tinting and Toning of Eastman Positive Motion-Picture Film, Eastman Kodak Co., Rochester, N.Y., 1918; 4th ed., 1927. Originally published in *Motion Picture News,* p. 3255, Nov. 30, 1918.

G. A. Blair, "Tinting of motion-picture film," *Trans. SMPE, No. 10:* 45–53, May 1920. Methods of tinting and choice of dyes are discussed. Properties of acid dyes and formulas for use are given.

L. A. Jones, "Tinted films for sound positives," *Trans. SMPE, No. 37:* 199–226, May 1929.

Amateur Cine Materials

C. E. K. Mees, "A new substandard film for amateur cinematography," *Trans. SMPE, No. 16:* 252–258, May 1923.

Physical Properties

A. C. Hardy and L. A. Jones, "Graininess in motion-picture negatives and positives," *Trans. SMPE, No. 14:* 107–124, May 1922.

M. Briefer, "Physical properties of motion-picture film," *Trans. SMPE, No. 18:* 177–205, May 1924.

J. I. Crabtree, "Graininess of motion-picture film," *Trans. SMPE, No. 29:* 77–92, Apr. 1927.

C. G. Weber and J. R. Hill, "Stability of motion-picture films as determined by accelerated aging," *Jour. SMPE, 27:* 677–690, Dec. 1936.

E. K. Carver, R. H. Talbot and H. A. Loomis, "Film distortions and their effect upon projection quality," *Jour. SMPE, 41:* 88–93, July 1943.

J. M. Calhoun, "The physical properties and dimensional behavior of motion-picture film," *Jour. SMPE, 43:* 227–266, Oct. 1944.

R. H. Talbot, "Some relationships between the physical properties and the behavior of motion-picture film," *Jour. SMPE, 45:* 209–217, Sept. 1945.

Manufacture and Testing of Film

G. A. Blair, "Motion-picture film in the making," *Trans. SMPE, No. 7:* 16–19, Nov. 1918. Describes process of film manufacture, care taken in keeping film uniform, and the inspection made during manufacture to check the finished film for uniformity.

A. B. Hitchins, "Testing and maintaining photographic quality of cinematographic emulsions," *Trans. SMPE, No. 13:* 136–151, Nov. 1921.

E. K. Carver, "Manufacture of motion-picture film," *Jour. SMPE, 28:* 594–603, June 1937.

Care and Preservation

G. A. Blair, "The care and preservation of motion-picture negatives," *Trans. SMPE, No. 14:* 22–27, May 1922.

A. H. Nuckolls and A. F. Matson, "Some hazardous properties of motion-picture film," *Jour. SMPE, 27:* 657–661, Dec. 1936.

J. G. Bradley, "Changing aspects of the film-storage problems," *Jour. SMPE, 30:* 303–317, Mar. 1938.

Illumination

E. W. Beggs, "Lighting by tungsten filament incandescent electric lamps for motion picture photography," *Trans. SMPE, No. 26:* 94–106, May 1926.

P. Mole, "The tungsten lamp situation in the studio," *Trans. SMPE, No. 31:* 582–590, Sept. 1927.

General Early History

F. H. Richardson, "What happened in the beginning," *Trans. SMPE, No. 22:* 63–114, Sept. 1925.

W. K. L. Dickson, "A brief history of the Kinetograph, the Kinetoscope, and the Kineto-Phonograph," *Jour. SMPE, 21:* 435–455, Dec. 1933.

Robert W. Paul, "Kinematographic experiences," *Jour. SMPE, 27:* 495–512, Nov. 1936. In 1895 Paul used Kodak film for his negative — probably printed on same film.

L. Lumière, "The Lumière Cinematograph," *Jour. SMPE, 27:* 640–647, Dec., 1936. Lumière obtained from N.Y. Celluloid Co., film base coated with emulsion at the Lumière factory at Lyons, France, and perforated with two circular holes per frame. He demonstrated the outfit in Paris in March 1895. Film shows employee leaving the Lumière factory (only film available); copy at Eastman House.

Early History of
Amateur Motion-Picture Film

By GLENN E. MATTHEWS
and RAIFE G. TARKINGTON

A review is given of the status of motion-picture films for amateur use prior to 1923. Up to that date, lack of standardization of film size, the use of the negative-positive method, and cost of apparatus and printing held back extensive use of film for amateur motion pictures. Research in the manufacture of safety acetate film support was started by Eastman Kodak Co. in 1906–1907, and limited quantities of film were manufactured and sold between 1912 and 1923. Film on safety acetate base, a fundamental requirement for home movies, was introduced in 1912 for a portable projector made by Thomas A. Edison, Inc., and also for equipment made by Pathé Frères, a French firm. A safety film 9.5mm wide, introduced by Pathé Cinéma in 1923, was developed either to a negative, or directly to a positive by the conventional reversal method.

Research on film for amateur motion pictures was started in 1914 by Eastman Kodak Co. and led to the introduction of the Ciné-Kodak process on January 8, 1923. A safety film 16mm wide was used which was developed directly to a positive by an improved reversal process using controlled second exposure. The factors are analyzed that made this process successful and encouraged the standardization of 16mm film throughout the world. Included is a short account of the processing of 16mm films, of improvements in 16mm film emulsions, the printing of duplicates, the use of sound on 16mm film, the history of 8mm reversal film, and the introduction of amateur motion pictures in color.

I‌n 1888 George Eastman coined a slogan, "You press the button — we do the rest," expressing the simplicity of the new era in still photography introduced by the first "Kodak" camera and roll film. Thirty-five years later, the simplicity of still photography was extended to motion pictures with the announcement on January 8, 1923, of the Ciné-Kodak process using a new film 16mm in width and developed by a reversal process. The announcement was made at a joint meeting of several technical societies in East High School, Rochester, N.Y. (Fig. 1). On that occasion motion pictures were made on the new 16mm safety film of several members of the audience, processed to a positive by reversal and projected at the end of the lecture. The new film and the method of processing were described to the Society of Motion Picture Engineers[1] at their semi-annual meeting in Atlantic City, N.J., in May 1923. This development raised the curtain on a new era in the field of motion pictures for the amateur with portable equipment. During the 30 years that have followed the introduction of the reversal process for amateur motion pictures, the use of 16mm film has

expanded very extensively both for amateur and professional applications.

In the quarter century before 1923 many attempts had been made by numerous inventors and firms to introduce equipment and film that would provide motion pictures for home use (Table I). Several of these systems have been described by Crawford, Stull and others.[2] Most of these systems used the negative-positive process which was costly and probably accounts in large measure for their limited commercial success.

Motion-picture film as first supplied by Eastman and used by Edison in 1889 was on nitrate support, 35mm wide, which is the same width that is still used in the theater today although the picture dimensions have been changed from time to time. One of the first attempts to make apparatus using a narrower-width film was that of Acres (London) who in 1898 slit the 35mm negative lengthwise to make two filmstrips, each 17.5mm wide, perforated along one side. His camera was called the "Birtac" and the picture made with it was about half the standard 35mm frame. Subsequently, many others adopted a film 17.5mm wide with various types of perforations for use with their equipment. Other film widths that were used included 22mm, 21mm, 15mm and 11mm, some of which are shown in Figure 2. Many of these early films were exposed, printed and shown on the same piece of equipment. Most of these earlier films were coated on highly inflammable nitrate supports.

The Significance of Safety Acetate Film Base for Amateur Motion-Picture Use

In 1912 Thomas A. Edison, Inc., Orange, N.J., announced the Edison Home Kinetoscope (Fig. 3) which used cellulose acetate safety film 22mm wide (Table I and Fig. 2), developed to a negative, and printed. This safety film was supplied by the Eastman Kodak Co. who were convinced that only safety film

Presented on October 22, 1954, by Norwood L. Simmons for the authors, Glenn E. Matthews and Raife G. Tarkington, Research Laboratories, Eastman Kodak Co., Rochester 4, N.Y. (This paper was received on August 2, 1954.)

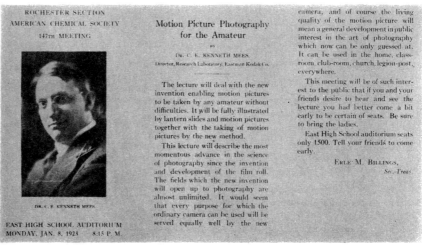

Fig. 1. Program announcing lecture about 16mm Ciné-Kodak process on January 8, 1923.

should be used for amateur motion pictures. This conviction was emphasized as shown by the following quotation from Mr. Eastman's letter to the Edison Company, dated June 4, 1912: "Concerning the cellulose acetate film which we are furnishing you for your Home Kinetoscope, we beg to say that we believe the article to be a perfectly safe one for use in such an apparatus or we would not consent to supply it. In our opinion, the furnishing of cellulose nitrate for such a purpose would be wholly indefensible and reprehensible."

Also in 1912, the French firm of Pathé Frères introduced portable motion-picture equipment using 28mm film with a cellulose acetate support.[3] The acetate-type base and the 28mm width of film were recommended by A. F. Victor[4] in 1918 as a standard for portable projectors. In his plea for the adoption of the new standard, Victor pointed out the grave importance of using only safety film in portable projectors for use in the home, the school, and other locations where safety from fire hazards is paramount. A standard was adopted in April 1918, by the Society of Motion Picture Engineers[5] for a safety standard film 1.102 in. (28mm) wide for portable projectors. It differed slightly from Pathé 28mm film but Pathé projectors could take the new 28mm standard film (Fig. 4).[6]

Research in the manufacture of a non-inflammable motion-picture film support by the Eastman Kodak Co. began in 1906–1907 and the results seemed so successful that by 1909 the Kodak Company was prepared to give up manufacture of nitrate and go entirely to acetate film.[7] Limited quantities of 35mm film on acetate support and some 22mm and 28mm film were supplied to the trade between 1912 and 1920. Experimental work was continued, especially after World War I, and after a great deal of research and many trials, a better product was made available for use in the 16mm Ciné-Kodak process and equipment as well as equipment made by other manufacturers. The research continued and improved safety films were introduced from time to time until today safety film support is made and used almost exclusively throughout the world.[8]

Early Research on Amateur Motion Pictures by Eastman Kodak Company

In 1914 F. W. Barnes, then manager of the Hawk-Eye Works of the Kodak Company, demonstrated at the Research Laboratory an experimental camera that had been built several years earlier for exposing two rows of pictures along short lengths of 35mm film, one row being exposed on the first run through the camera, much as 8mm film is exposed today (Fig. 5a). The film was developed to a negative and then printed in the

Table I. Chronology of Motion-Picture Film for the Amateur (1898–1923.)*

Year	Name	Film width, perforation location	Support type	Inventor or manufacturer
1898	Birtac	17.5mm perf. along one side	nitrate	B. Acres (London)
1900?	Biokam	17.5mm perf. in center	nitrate	Wrench & Son (London)
1900	Mirographe	21mm notched on each edge	nitrate	Reulos, Goudeau & Co. (Paris)
1900?	La Petite	17.5mm, 1 square perf. in center	nitrate	Hughes (London)
1900	Pocket-Chrono	15mm center perf.	nitrate	L. Gaumont & Co. (Paris)
1902	Vitak	17.5mm center perf.	nitrate	W. Wardell (a mail-order project)
1903	Kino	17.5mm center perf.	nitrate	Ernemann (Dresden)
1905?	Ikonograph (first projector that could reverse the movement of the film)	17.5mm	nitrate	E. J. Rector (N.Y.) (Ikonograph Commercial Co. of Manhattan, N.Y.)
1910	Empire Cinematograph	35mm	nitrate	W. Butcher & Son, Ltd. (London)
1910	Picturescope	35mm with 2 rows of pictures	nitrate	Chas. E. Dressler (N.Y.)
1911	Animatograph	Spiral film disk	nitrate	A. F. Victor (Davenport, Iowa)
1912	Duoscope	17.5mm with two center perf.	nitrate	
1912	Pathé K-O-K in France	28mm, 3 perf. on 1 edge; 1 perf. on other edge	safety	Pathé Frères (Paris)
1913	Pathescope in U. S.	Same as Pathé K-O-K	safety	Pathescope Co. (N.Y.)
1912	Home Kinetoscope	22mm, 3 rows of pictures, perf. between rows	safety	Thomas A. Edison, Inc. (Orange, N.J.)
1914	Atlas	35mm	nitrate	Atlas Educational Film Co. (Chicago, Ill.)
1914	Animatograph	35mm	nitrate	Victor Animatograph Co. (Davenport, Iowa)
1915	Animatograph (Model 2)	35mm	nitrate	Victor Animatograph Co. (Davenport, Iowa)
1917	Victor Projector	35mm	nitrate	Victor Animatograph Co. (Davenport, Iowa)
1914	Ensign Cinematograph Camera	35mm	nitrate	Houghton's Ltd. (London)
1913	Spirograph	Images on circular film disk in spiral order	nitrate	Charles Urban Trading Co., Ltd. (London)
1915	Sinemat	17.5mm	safety	Sinemat Motion Picture Machine Co.

conventional way. To project the film the camera was converted to a projector by replacing the back with a lamphouse.

J. G. Capstaff, of the Research Laboratory staff, saw the demonstration and asked if he might borrow the camera for experimental use on an idea for amateur motion pictures. From 1914 to 1916 he worked with this equipment from time to time and began almost immediately to develop the exposed films directly to a positive using a variation of the procedure that was recommended for *reversal* development of Lumière Auto-

chrome Screen Plates* (Fig. 5b). He became convinced that reversal processing and high-quality pictures would succeed commercially where other methods had failed.[10] He felt that the reversal process, which eliminates the need for additional film for the positive print and the printing operation, would reduce greatly the excessive cost of motion pictures for the amateur. Then, by making easy-to-use, low-cost equipment a method would be available to do for the potential motion-

* The reversal process of photographic development was described originally in 1899 by R. Namias.[9]

Year	Name	Film width, perforation location	Support type	Inventor or manufacturer
1916–1917	DeVry	35mm	nitrate	H. DeVry Co. (Chicago, Ill.)
1915–1916?	Autograph	17.5mm	nitrate?	
1915–1916?	Duplex	11mm, 2 round perf. on each edge	nitrate?	G. J. Bradley
1917	Safety Cinema	28mm, 3 perf. on each edge	safety	A. F. Victor, Victor Animatograph Co. (Davenport, Iowa)
1917	Movette	17.5mm, 2 circular perf. on each edge	nitrate neg. safety pos.	Movette Camera Co. (Rochester, N.Y.)
1917	Simplex	35mm	nitrate	Simplex Corp. (Long Island, N.Y.)
1917	Cub	35mm	nitrate	American Cinematograph Corp. (Chicago, Ill.)
1918	Actograph	17.5mm	nitrate	Wilart Instrument Co. (New Rochelle, N.Y.)
1920	Home Cinema	28mm-Pathescope	safety	Victor Animatograph Co. (Davenport, Iowa)
1920	Clou	17.5mm, 2 perf. per frame	nitrate	Firm name unknown (Austria)
1920	Sept.	17 ft of 35mm motion pictures or 250 still pictures	nitrate	A. Debrie (France)
1921	Coco	17.5mm	nitrate	Linhof (Munich)
1921	Defranne	35mm	nitrate	Bass Camera Co., (Chicago, Ill.)
1921	Kinamo	35mm	nitrate	Ica, A.G. (Dresden)
1922–1923	Pathé-Baby or Pathex	9.5mm, 1 center perf. between frames	safety, dev. to a positive by reversal	Pathé Cinéma (Paris)
1923	Baby Standard	35mm	nitrate	Vicam Photo Appliance Corp., (Philadelphia, Pa.)
1923	Ciné-Kodak	16mm	safety, dev. by controlled reversal	Eastman Kodak Co. (Rochester, N.Y.)
1923	Victor	16mm	safety	Victor Animatograph Co. (Davenport, Iowa)
1923–1924	Filmo	16mm	safety	Bell & Howell Co. (Chicago, Ill.) first spring-motor-driven camera

* Based on survey of the literature; but list may not be complete.

picture amateur what roll film and the snapshot camera had done for the amateur still photographer.

In 1916, the preliminary results were shown to Mr. Eastman. At first he was reluctant to enter a field of manufacture in which so many other firms had been unsuccessful. However, Mr. Capstaff's demonstration of the quality of small picture images obtainable by using the reversal process and the assurance that an appreciable lowering of cost would result from the adoption of this method encouraged Mr. Eastman to regard the proposal more favorably and he gave his approval that a development program should be started. At this time Mr. Eastman restated his conviction that only safety film should be used for amateur motion pictures and only this type of film has been manufactured by the Eastman Kodak Co. for this purpose.

Early in the experimentation (before 1916) it appeared that images made by reversal were of finer grain than those that were developed to a negative. This encouraged trials to be made of smaller picture areas than the standard 35mm size. Various apertures such as $\frac{1}{4}$, $\frac{1}{6}$ and $\frac{1}{8}$ that of the 35mm size frame in use at that time (1-in. by $\frac{3}{4}$-in.) were tried in the Barnes experimental camera. With the film emulsions then available, it was decided that a picture $\frac{1}{6}$ of the area of the standard frame was the smallest that could be used and still give good picture quality. Upon calculation this gave a picture area 10mm by 7.5mm and, allowing 3mm on each edge for perforation, resulted in a film 16mm wide and carrying 40 pictures to the foot. This smaller size reduced still further the cost of this method, and also it was advantageous in that chances of using nitrate (by splitting 35mm, for example) were very much lessened.

The reversal process of development, as generally used, consists essentially of the following steps: (1) a first development to form a negative image, (2) bleaching of the image with acid-bichromate or acid-permanganate to change the negative image to a soluble salt of silver that can be dissolved out, (3) a full exposure to light and (4) finally developing *all* of the remaining silver halide completely to form a positive image.[11]

The first experiments by Capstaff with the reversal process used these well-established procedures. However, this process as applied to film available at that time had two disadvantages.[1] It gave satisfactory results only through a limited range of original exposures and variations in the evenness of coating of the film emulsion resulted in inferior quality in the final, positive image. During the early research (before 1917) Capstaff[12] worked out a method that used a *controlled* second exposure or re-exposure which overcame these major disadvantages.

If a heavy or full exposure is given in the camera, much of the silver will be developed at the beginning, and when this is removed, there will only be a small amount of silver halide left for the production of the positive. A very heavy second exposure to light is then desirable, otherwise the positive image will not have enough density. On the other hand, if the camera exposure is light or on the short side, there will be a great deal of undeveloped silver halide available to form the final image, and a short second exposure is desirable, as otherwise too dense an image will be produced. Therefore, by the proper control of the second exposure during processing, the effective latitude of the reversal film was increased.

When complete re-exposure is used, variations in thickness of the emulsion will show up as a density difference, resulting in mottle, streakiness and other defects in the final image. With controlled re-exposure all the residual silver halide is not, in most instances, exposed completely; and the defects, while not eliminated entirely, are greatly reduced, in effect. This variable or controlled

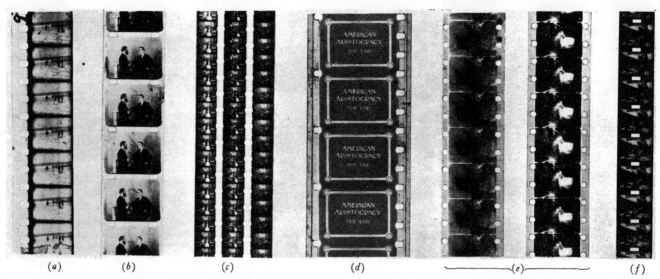

Fig. 2. Several varieties of film widths available before 1923: (a) Birtac—17.5 mm (1898); (b) Duoscope—17.5 mm, center perforation (1912); (c) Edison Home Kinetoscope—22 mm (1912); (d) Pathescope—28 mm (1912); (e) Movette negative and positive—17.5 mm (1920); (f) Pathex—9.5 mm (1923). (See Table I)

second exposure has been considered an important phase of reversal processing of Ciné-Kodak black-and-white films for many years.

The "timing," as it is called, of this second exposure was done in this experimental stage by exposing separate frames of a short length of the scene to different intensities of light. When developed, the correct exposure to be given the rest of the film could then be judged by examination of this test strip.

Another modification in the conventional reversal process invented by Capstaff[12] was the addition to the first developer of a silver halide solvent and a hardening agent. The former gave clearer highlights in the resulting image and the latter prevented reticulation of the gelatin during subsequent chemical treatment.

Work on the process was disccntinued during World War I but was resumed early in 1919. Many experiments were conducted to determine the emulsion, the formulas and the processing conditions that gave the best results. The design of a camera, perforator, and projector built to precision requirements was carried out by the Hawk-Eye Works. The prototype of the Model A Ciné-Kodak was completed early in May 1920 (Fig. 6), and the projector some months later (Fig. 7), and both were turned over to Capstaff for testing. He worked in close collaboration with the film manufacturing departments at Kodak Park and tried out many coatings of film. An orthochromatic emulsion on acetate base was finally chosen. Black paper leader and trailer on each 50- and 100-ft roll permitted daylight-loading. The film had two perforations (rounded-end type) per frame located one at each side on the frame line. The first perforator for 16mm safety film was built in the spring of 1920 and put into use by the film department early in May 1920 (Fig. 8). The rectangular perforation with rounded corners was adopted in January 1923, and is still in use. Although the first films did not have anti-halation backings, these were found necessary to control halation and considerable research was conducted on the best type of backing for suppressing such effects. Examples of early reversal test pictures on 16mm film are shown in Fig. 9.

Edison Home Kinetoscope

Motion Pictures for the Home, Schools, YMCA Clubs, etc.

EDISON HOME KINETOSCOPE

APPROVED BY FIRE AUTHORITIES

Fig. 3. Edison Home Kinetoscope booklet (cover and frontispiece), April 12, 1912. (Courtesy Thomas Alva Edison Foundation, Inc.)

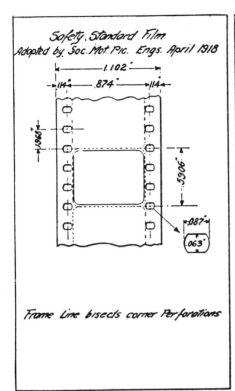
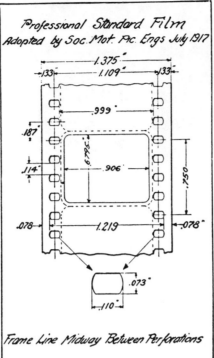
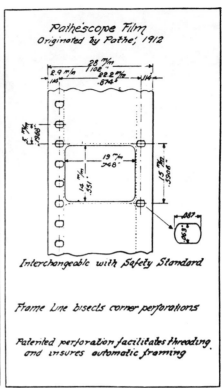

Fig. 4. Comparative sizes of Pathescope film (1912), 28-mm Safety Standard (SMPE—April 1918) and Professional Standard (SMPE—July 1917). (Reproduced from *Motion Picture Photography for the Amateur* by H. C. McKay, Falk Publishing Co., New York, 1924.)

Introduction of the Ciné-Kodak Process

By the latter part of 1922 development work had progressed sufficiently that it was decided by the Kodak management to place the Ciné-Kodak process on the market the following year. In talks and demonstrations given before several technical societies during 1923, it was pointed out[1] that the new system of amateur motion-picture photography was founded on "the use of film smaller than that used in the standard camera and on a new process for finishing it, the object being to reduce the cost of the finished picture to as low a point as possible" (Fig. 10). Actually, it was estimated that the new process cut the cost of motion pictures to $\frac{1}{6}$ that of the nega-tive-positive method — a very significant saving. An advertisement for the Ciné-Kodak appeared in the New York Times and the New York Tribune on July 5, 1923 (Fig. 11).

In discussing the advantages of the new reversal process, it was indicated that images developed with it were "astonishingly free from graininess" partly as a result of the special film but largely as a result of the reversal process itself, the largest grains and clumps of grains formed during first development being removed by the bleach, leaving the smallest grains to be developed as the final positive image.[1]

Because of the special equipment and skill required to develop the film, the Kodak Company decided in 1923 to establish a policy that they would undertake, for a time at least, the work of processing all the film that was exposed with the cameras in use.

The reversal process with controlled second exposure was an instant success. There is little doubt that it was this development that determined the success of the 16mm program of amateur motion pictures. Other factors were good equipment design for processing the film

Fig. 5a. Barnes experimental camera (closed and open) for exposing two rows of images linearly on short lengths of 35mm film.

Fig. 5b. Negative and reversal-positive test films exposed by J. G. Capstaff with Barnes experimental camera.

Fig. 6. Altered original 16mm camera used by J. G. Capstaff for experimental research with 16mm reversal film (1920–1922). Original camera about 2/3 as long as camera shown; section added about 1924 permitted use of longer focal length lenses.

Processing Apparatus for 16mm Ciné-Kodak Films

At first all 16mm reversal test films were processed with a hand-cranked reel and a tank of 50-ft capacity. Subsequently the processing was done on a so-called twin-reel machine consisting of two developing reels arranged end to end, each of 100-ft capacity, and above them, one 200-ft capacity drying reel. Each reel had two parallel, circular, hard rubber end-plates connected by glass rods. The film was wound spirally on one reel and became immersed in the processing solution as the reel was rotated manually. Motorized units of these machines were installed in Rochester in 1923, in Chicago in March 1924, and in San Francisco by

and a world-wide distribution and service facilities.

In his first lectures about the new process when comparing the cost of a single scene by motion pictures or as a snapshot, C. E. K. Mees[1] said, "On the whole, it appears as if amateur cinematography . . . will not be more expensive to the user than is still photography."

In commenting on this development A. F. Victor[13] in 1923 stated: "The reversal process has lowered the cost of picture-making to a point never before considered possible. At such a low cost it is almost certain that motion picture cameras and projectors may become as universal as still hand cameras." Victor also suggested that 16mm safety film

should be standardized for home use. A standard for 16mm safety film was proposed by the SMPE in May 1924 (Fig. 12), and approved by the American Engineering Standards Committee in April 1928.

Within the year of 1923 the Victor Animatograph Co. (Davenport, Iowa) and the Bell & Howell Co. (Chicago, Ill.) introduced equipment using the new 16mm film, recognizing the probability that it would become a standard for home use.

Interest in amateur motion pictures was encouraged and fostered in this country by the Amateur Cinema League which was founded in 1926. The first issue of the League's official publication

Fig. 7. Experimental 16mm projector (1920–1923).

1925. A hand-controlled light was used for the "timing" of the re-exposure, the amount of light being determined by the judgment of experienced operators.

The twin-reel machine did not have enough capacity for quantity processing and work began in 1926 on the design of a continuous processor known as the "tube machine." It consisted of a long series of vertical glass tubes, each 6-ft long, through which the film moved in a sinuous path driven by sprockets between consecutive tubes. Manual control of a density step tablet was used for the second exposure and the operator set it by judgment for each scene change. With a machine of this type it was possible to process hundreds of feet of film continuously.

Because of mechanical difficulties, glass

Fig. 8. First perforator for 16mm film (1920–1923).

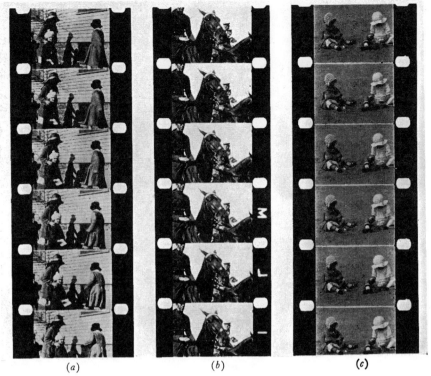

Fig. 10. Comparison of relative sizes of 35mm (standard) images and 16mm reversal image.

(a)　　　　　(b)　　　　　(c)

Fig. 9. Examples of early reversal pictures on 16mm film (about twice actual width): (a) May 1920—first tests—W. Vaeth; (b) Sept. 1920—Rochester Horse Show—H. B. Tuttle; (c) July 1922—children at play—J. G. Capstaff.

breakage and problems of control related to replenishment, agitation and temperature encountered with the tube machine, a tank-type machine was designed in which the film was wound on a series of rolls in spiral form passing several times from the top to the bottom of each of several tanks. The tank machine was more compact than the tube machine and also permitted continuous

processing of long lengths of film (Fig. 13). Improved methods of agitation, temperature control, replenishment and drying were devised. Early in 1925 the first tank machine was installed in Rochester at Kodak Park. Later these machines were installed in processing stations in several cities in this country as well as in stations throughout the world. Subsequently, a small tank ma-

chine was designed and a group of machines was built for use in the processing stations having a lower volume of work. Several of these smaller machines were installed on cruise ships that went around the world and permitted the amateur 16mm camera-users to see their pictures while en route. These installations were removed within a year or so as soon as processing stations were set up in different countries throughout the world.

The Automatic Printer for Controlled Re-Exposure

With the increase of production on the continuous machines it became apparent that manual control of re-exposure was difficult to perform consistently and offered many supervisional problems. The

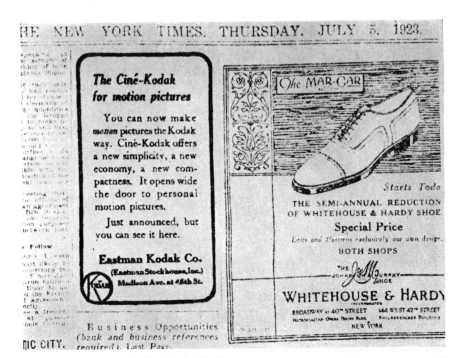

Fig. 11. Early advertisement of Ciné-Kodak process, New York Times, July 5, 1923.

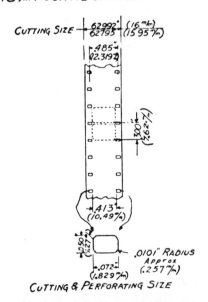

Fig. 12. Proposed SMPE Standard for 16mm film (1924). (Reproduced from *Trans. SMPE*, No. 18, 238, May 1924.)

Research Laboratories were assigned the problem of design of an automatic printer. Results of experiments were sufficiently good that an order was placed in February 1927, to build a number of them for distribution to existing processing stations.

The system of re-exposure used a source of non-actinic light and a thermopile to control the intensity of the printing light. The current from the thermopile, produced by the heating effect of the non-actinic light passing through the film, controlled the movement of a galvanometer vane that was interposed in the optical system and this, in turn,

Pathé 9.5mm Reversal Film

Just before Christmas of 1922, the French firm of Pathé Cinéma (formerly Pathé Frères) introduced in France under the name of "Pathé Baby"[15] a small projector for projecting films 9.5mm wide. At the same time films 9.5mm wide by 8.5 meters long, with a single perforation in the center between frames, and wound on a special spool were made available for use with the projector. The subject matter of these films was obtained by reduction printing from 35-mm professional motion pictures which had already been shown in theaters

the market. Since it was planned that the film could be reversal-processed by the customer, a developing outfit, consisting of two tanks and a combined frame on which three loops of film could be placed, was made available at the same time.

The negative film was processed, whether by the customer or by a laboratory, by reversal development, thus, like the 16mm Ciné-Kodak process, eliminating the cost of printing and print film stock. The second (positive) development was either by the use of an uncontrolled full exposure to light followed by development, or directly by the

Fig. 13. Early tank-type processing machine for 16mm reversal film (1925).

varied the amount of actinic light that was projected on the film. Thus the printer exposure was dependent upon the current in the thermopile and, therefore, upon the transmission of the red light by the residual silver halide (positive) image in the film.[14]

Many control problems arose and required solution during the attempt to improve the quality of processing, such as measurement of developer activity, methods of replenishment, control of the stability of bleach solution, recovery of silver, and so on. Expert supervision of quality control at processing stations throughout the world has insured the maintenance of a high level of picture quality throughout the years.

belonging to the Pathé Company, and a library of these films, known as Pathé Library Films, was established (Fig. 14).

Encouraged by the initial acceptance of this small film and projector system for home entertainment and realizing that only half the amateur motion-picture enthusiast's desire had been satisfied, Pathé Cinéma designed a 9.5mm motion-picture camera for amateur use. Experiments with reversal processing of 9.5mm film were conducted in December 1922 by L. Didiée of Pathé Cinéma.* In December 1923, this camera and an orthochromatic negative film, 9.5mm wide by 10 meters long and with center perforations, were placed on

_____
* Private communication, March 31, 1954.

use of a solution containing hydrosulfite which converted the remaining silver halide to a black silver image.[16] Customer processing apparently gave generally inferior results and the amateurs soon started sending their films to the Pathé Cinéma factory where precise control of processing conditions gave assurance of a more satisfactory product. Controlled second exposure during processing was not employed by the Pathé factory until 1936 when its use was begun for the same reasons that this method has been used in the 16mm Ciné-Kodak process. The 9.5mm Pathé Baby process of complete home motion pictures became very popular in France and has continued to be used quite widely there to the present day.

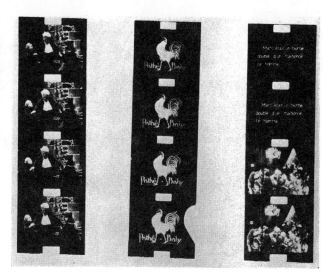

Fig. 14. (Above) Pathex (Pathe Baby) film carton and reel; (right) examples of Pathex films. (Twice original size.)

Other Reversal Films

Subsequent to the introduction of Ciné-Kodak Safety 16mm Film and Pathé 9.5mm film, other manufacturers introduced reversal films including those made by Agfa,[17] Gevaert, Mimosa, Ilford, Ansco and Du Pont.

Duplication of 16mm Reversal Films

The need for occasional duplicate prints was recognized from the beginning when 16mm reversal film was first introduced. In his early paper on the film,[1] Mees indicated that the making of extra prints was "provided for by use of a special printer in which a positive can be duplicated, the duplicate being reversed into a positive in the same way as the original picture," and at the same cost as the original picture. After the duplicating service was established in 1924 for making duplicates of films taken by the amateur, it made possible the use of this service for certain professional motion-picture purposes and probably encouraged wider use of 16mm film. Subsequently a variety of subjects became available for educational, industrial and other uses. This type of material was frequently made by reduction printing from 35mm film negatives. Libraries of educational and entertainment films were made available for the amateur and served to increase his general interest in amateur motion pictures.

Research and Development of Improved Ciné-Kodak Films

As noted previously, the first Ciné-Kodak Film was an orthochromatic emulsion coated on safety acetate support. From the beginning a research program has been in progress constantly to find ways of improving the quality of both the support and the emulsion. Problems of stripping, halation, resolution and many other difficulties have been studied and thousands of experiments made to overcome them. Reversal processing imposes stringent requirements upon the uniformity of coating thickness. In recent years improvements in the manufacture of reversal films have been made so that thickness variations are not now as serious a limitation on the picture quality as when the film was first introduced.

In 1928 Ciné-Kodak Panchromatic Film was introduced. This step insured better tone reproduction, particularly when photographing subjects having orange or red colors. It gave improved quality of tones in close-ups of people. In 1931 improved methods of sensitizing and new sensitizing compounds[18] resulted in the introduction of Super Sensitive Ciné-Kodak Panchromatic Film and in 1938 Super-XX Ciné-Kodak Panchromatic Film was introduced.

Sound on 16mm Reversal Film

Not long after the rapid growth of sound on 35mm film started in 1927–1928, interest began to grow in the problem of recording sound records on 16mm reversal film. The first sound records used were on disks synchronized with the picture film. Although the first projector[19] for 16mm sound films did not appear on the market until 1930 (Model PG-30 manufactured by the Radio Corp. of America), research in the problem of sound recording and reproduction on 16mm film began in the Kodak Research Laboratories in 1927. Considerable research was done because it was difficult to process both pictures and sound track simultaneously, since each type of record had different density, speed and gamma requirements. A steady light source, for example, is required for the second exposure of the sound track in contrast to a variable-intensity light for the re-exposure of the picture. Special 16mm film emulsions were developed by Kodak and others for separate recording without pictures for professional use.

In 1929 the Eastman Kodak Co. suggested the use of 16mm film having one row of perforations along one side, leaving the other edge of the film available for the sound track. A standard for this type of 16mm sound motion-picture negative and positive was proposed by the Society of Motion Picture Engineers in 1932[19] (Fig. 15), and adopted by the American Standards Association in 1935. Considerable research has been conducted in the problem of optical printing of 16mm sound tracks by reduction from 35mm records.[20]

History of the 8mm Reversal Film

Steady progress in emulsion manufacture toward finer grain and more speed between 1923 and 1928 made it possible to consider even smaller-sized motion pictures than 16mm film. Serious attention was given in 1928 at the Kodak Research Laboratories to the idea of a

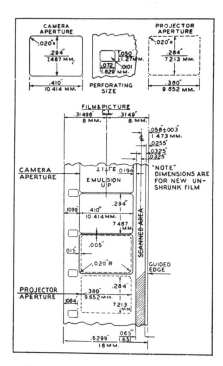

Fig. 15. Proposed Standard for 16mm Sound-On-Film (1932). (Reproduced from *Jour. SMPE,* 19: 478, Nov. 1932.)

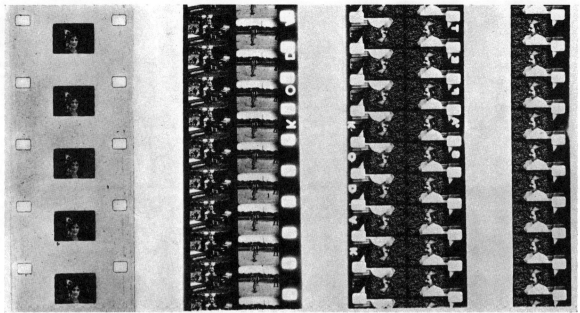

Fig. 16. Early experiments on 8mm film images and examples of unslit and slit "double-eight" film: (left) 5-mm image reduction-printed; (left center) 8mm experiment on single perforated 16mm film; (right center) standard 8mm pictures before slitting; (right) standard 8mm picture after slitting. (All films twice actual width.)

film one-half the size of 16mm although experiments had also been done by Capstaff on even narrower-width films (Fig. 16). While a smaller-sized film offered the possibility of further economies in amateur motion pictures, reducing the size from 16mm to 8mm does not reduce the cost in the same proportion. The operations of manufacturing, packaging, handling and processing remain essentially unchanged whether the film size is 16mm or 8mm. In order, therefore, to realize the reduction in cost commensurate with the reduction in film size to 8mm it was considered necessary to use existing 16mm equipment as far as possible.

Based in part on the Barnes experimental camera used in the very early work in the 16mm reversal process and on other inventions, a camera was built in 1930–1931 that would expose two rows of pictures linearly on 16mm film by exposing one row and rethreading the film and then exposing a second row (Fig. 16). The film spool and the two camera spindles were so designed that the user could only thread the film in the correct way.

After development in a 16mm process-

ing machine, the film is slit down the center and spliced end to end. Two hundred feet of this film are equivalent in projection time to 400 ft of 16mm or 1000 ft of 35mm film. Each picture on 8mm film is about one-fourth the size of a 16mm frame. Cameras and projectors for 8mm film were marketed by Kodak in August 1932,[21] and subsequently by several other manufacturers.

The extremely small size of the 8mm film image required the development of emulsions and processing solutions which would give a reversal image of very high resolving power and definition. New perforators had to be built for this film, slitters had to be supplied to the processing stations and a new automatic printer designed to give the controlled re-exposure to two rows of pictures differing in subject matter. With continuing im-

provement in photographic equipment and materials, the use of 8mm film for strictly amateur home movies is increasing rapidly, while the 16mm size is being used more and more extensively for non-theatrical-type purposes, such as in schools, churches, industry and science.

Introduction of Amateur Motion Pictures in Color

For more than a hundred years it has been the dream of nearly every experimenter in photography to produce pictures in natural colors. In this field the Kodak Company and several other firms have been experimenting since the early years of this century. Prior to 1925, however, no process of color motion-picture photography was considered by the Kodak Company to fulfill the requirements that would permit its

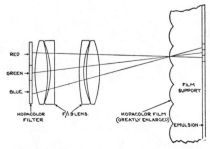

Fig. 17a. Diagram of Kodacolor lenticular film (1928).

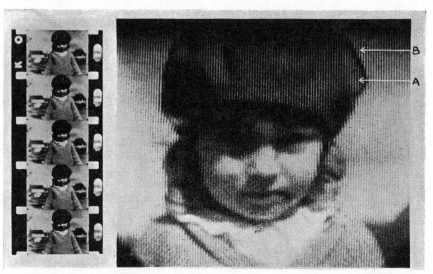

Fig. 17b. Picture on Kodacolor film of child with red hat (A) against blue sky (B), showing displacement of lines in these two areas.

adaptation to a simple process for color motion pictures for the amateur.

In 1925, rights were acquired by the Eastman Kodak Co. from Société du Film en Colours Keller-Dorian to adapt the additive color process of R. Berthon, a French inventor, to amateur cinematography. Berthon's lenticular screen process was originally patented in 1908. As finally worked out by Kodak and introduced under the name *Kodacolor*[22] in July 1928, it consisted of a panchromatic 16mm film having embossed on its film support hundreds of tiny cylindrical lenses (about 560 in an inch) extending lengthwise of the film (Fig. 17). For exposure in a standard 16mm camera, a banded three-color filter was placed over the camera lens. When the film is threaded into the camera with the base side toward the lens, the embossed lenses guide the rays from each of the three filters during exposure and impress these filtered images on the emulsion. After processing by reversal, a monochrome positive image is produced which becomes a color picture when projected with a projector having a banded three-color filter over its lens.

To make a successful process, a great deal of study was involved such as standardization of the embossing operation, making a suitable panchromatic emulsion and working out the best reversal processing conditions. The utmost care had to be taken to avoid dirt, surface irregularities and other possible causes of trouble with the lenticulated support during manufacture and processing of the film, otherwise color distortions would be produced when the film was projected. The major disadvantages of the Kodacolor process were the large loss of light in both the taking and projecting steps resulting from the use of filters, and the necessity of maintaining the optics, particularly those of the projector, to very close alignment.

The Kodacolor process was used successfully for several years. However, it lost favor quite rapidly with the amateur soon after the introduction of the Kodachrome process, which used a subtractive-type film that gave a brighter projected image and was considered easier for customers to use.

The German firm, Agfa, introduced a lenticular 16mm film called Agfacolor[23] in 1932, but this film also lost favor with the amateur after the introduction of a subtractive-type multilayer film.

Dufaycolor, another additive process, was introduced in 1934 for use in 16mm amateur motion pictures.[24] A regular mosaic screen or réseau was produced on the film support and then a fast panchromatic emulsion was coated over the mosaic screen. Exposure was made through the film base. The mosaic screen consisted of a geometrical pattern of blue and green squares separated by

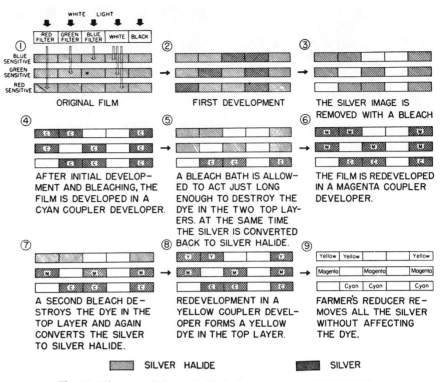

Fig. 18. Diagram of the early Kodachrome process (1935–1938).

red lines, producing roughly one million color filter elements per square inch. The film was developed by reversal and gave a color image on projection.

Multilayer Color Films Involving Reversal Development

The use of multiple-coated films having three emulsion layers, each sensitive to one of the three primary colors, has been suggested by various inventors from time to time. In 1912, R. Fischer, a German experimenter, proposed that chemical substances (later called couplers) be incorporated in each of the three emulsion layers of a multilayer color film. During development these substances would combine with oxidized developing agents to form dyes such as cyan, magenta and yellow.[25] This process required couplers and sensitizers that would remain within a layer and not wander into the next layer, and cause color degradation. In the existing state of knowledge at that time and for some years later this ingenious process was not converted to commercial practice.

In the Kodachrome process, developed by L. Mannes and L. Godowsky, Jr., in collaboration with the Eastman Kodak Co. and as originally marketed as 16mm film in 1935, the multilayer film contained only the sensitizing dyes, the couplers being in the developer solution.[26] After exposure, the film was developed to a negative and the negative image in each of these layers was removed by bleaching with permanganate. The film was then given a fixed exposure to light to make the silver bromide images developable and the whole film was developed to produce a cyan dye in all

three layers. After drying, the film was treated with a bleach of low penetration which removed the dye from the top and middle layers and regenerated the silver bromide which was then developed to form magenta images. The film was dried again and treated with a very low penetration bleach which removed the magenta dye from the top layers and converted the silver to silver bromide, so that it could be used to form a yellow dye image. The remaining silver was then changed to silver halide and removed by fixing, leaving the three dye images which formed the positive color image (Fig. 18). Although slow and clumsy, this process was operated successfully by skilled technicians for a few years.

With this type of reversal process, controlled second exposure is not practical. Nevertheless, the process uses a modified form of reversal development and much research has been done to work out special bleaches and other processing details. In 1936, Kodachrome 8mm film was announced, thus making color motion pictures available to the many users of 8mm equipment. In a new method of Kodachrome processing introduced in 1938 a simpler form of reversal process was used.[27]

Color motion pictures by the Kodachrome process can be made by anyone as easily as making ordinary black-and-white motion pictures because the complex phase of producing the color pictures, the color development of the film, is done at processing stations or laboratories under precise technical control.

In 1936, in Germany the new Agfacolor 16mm film was announced which is a commercial realization of Fischer's process. In this process, as marketed at that time, a coupler which will not wander was incorporated in each of the three emulsion layers and the dye images were formed during development.[28] Subsequently, other multilayer reversal 16-mm color films have been introduced including Ansco Color, Ilford Color and Gevacolor. Duplicating reversal color films have been made available as color print films for 16mm use.

Summary

This short historical survey has shown how motion pictures for the amateur came into wide commercial use within a few years after the introduction of the Ciné-Kodak process which was announced in January 1923. This process used a new safety film 16mm wide that was developed by the film manufacturer by an improved reversal process incorporating the unique feature of controlled second exposure. This process lowered the cost of amateur motion pictures in several ways: (1) it used a small-sized film having $2\frac{1}{2}$ times as many pictures per foot as 35mm film; (2) it used reversal development that avoided the conventional negative-positive method requiring additional film material and costly printing stages; (3) it used mass processing techniques; and (4) the film size and apparatus encouraged international standardization with the useful feature of interchangeability. As a direct result of the wide acceptance of standard reversal films in both black-and-white and color for amateur motion pictures, a new industry has grown up employing many thousands of persons and home movies have been enjoyed by millions throughout the world.

Acknowledgments

The authors wish to acknowledge valuable suggestions for this historical paper received from James Card, G. A. Gillette, Jr., N. B. Green, H. A. Hartt, W. T. Hanson, Jr., V. J. Moyes, D. W. Rupert, R. S. Scott, W. C. Vaeth and A. K. Wittmer. We are especially grateful for the many constructive comments made by J. G. Capstaff, C. E. K. Mees and H. B. Tuttle.

Significant useful data were obtained from Charles Bass (Bass Camera Co.), Paul Busse (Thomas A. Edison Foundation, Inc.), L. Didiée (Kodak-Pathé), S. G. Rose (Victor Animatograph Corp.) and M. G. Townsley (Bell and Howell Co.).

Demonstration Reel of 16mm Pictures

Following the presentation of the paper a short 16mm motion picture (about 250 ft) was projected which included examples of amateur motion pictures that were taken shortly before and after the introduction of the Ciné-Kodak Process on January 8, 1923. The titles of these examples were as follows:

(1) *Early May 1920:* First reversal processed test film taken with first model of 16mm camera (duplicate print);

(2) *Several Test Films:* Taken with experimental 16mm camera during year 1920 (duplicate prints);

(3) *June 1921:* First amateur motion-picture story with planned and directed continuity taken with experimental 16-mm camera (duplicate print); and

(4) *1922-23 Family Scenes:* Taken with first production Model A Ciné-Kodak (original film).

References

1. C. E. K. Mees, "A new substandard film for amateur cinematography," *Trans. SMPE,* No. 16, 252-258, 1923; also "Motion picture photography for the amateur," *J. Franklin Inst.* 196: 227-245, Aug. 1923.
2. M. Crawford, "The first thirty years," *Movie Makers,* 5: 755-757, 783-785, Dec. 1930; see also W. Stull, "Forty-eight years of home movies," *Am. Cinemat.,* 24: 58-60, 73-74, Feb. 1943; G. Cushman and C. Randall, "Biography of an idea," *Home Movies,* 11: 406-408, 430, Oct. 1944; Vorläufer und Wege zu den modernen Schmalfilmformaten," *Film Kino-Technik,* 8: 263-265, Sept. 1954.
3. W. B. Cook, "Description to accompany demonstration of Pathescope," *Trans. SMPE,* No. 16, 266, 1923; see also "The Pathescope Home Cinematograph," *Brit. J. Phot.,* 60: 216-217, Mar. 14, 1913.
4. A. F. Victor, "The portable projector, its present status and needs," *Trans. SMPE,* No. 6, 29-32, 1918.
5. W. B. Cook, "Advantages of the use of the new standard narrow width, slow burning film for portable projectors," *Trans. SMPE,* No. 7, 86-90, 1923; also Report of the Standards Committee, *Trans. SMPE,* No. 10, 6, 1920.
6. H. C. McKay, "Kinematography for the amateur," *Photo Era,* 51: 296, 1923; also *Motion Picture Photography for the Amateur,* by H. C. McKay, Falk Publishing Co., New York, 1924, Chapter II, p. 21.
7. *The Evening Times* (Rochester, N.Y.), June 15, 1909, p. 6.
8. C. R. Fordyce, "Improved safety motion picture film support," *Jour. SMPE,* 51: 331-350, Oct. 1948; also J. M. Calhoun, "The physical properties and dimensional behavior of motion picture film," *ibid.,* 43: 227-266, Oct. 1944.
9. R. Namias, "Uebermangansaures Kali zur Abschwächung zu harter Negative und die Herstellung direkter Positive in der Camera," *Phot. Mitteilungen,* 36: 366-367, 1899; also *Brit. J. Phot.,* 47: 679, Oct. 26, 1900.
10. C. E. K. Mees, "John George Capstaff," *Jour. SMPE, 44:* 10-17, Jan. 1945; also H. B. Tuttle and G. E. Matthews, "The Father of Home Movies," *PSA Journal, 18:* 418-420, July 1952.
11. V. H. Reckmeyer and H. S. Baldwin, "Reversal process," *The Complete Photographer,* Nat. Educational Alliance, Chicago, 1943, pp. 3145-3149.
12. U.S. Patent 1,460,703 (July 3, 1923); also *Brit. J. Phot.,* 70: 409, July 6, 1923; and Brit. Pat. 167,357.
13. A. F. Victor, "The motion picture, a practical feature of the home," *Trans. SMPE,* No. 16, 264-265, 1923.
14. U.S. Patent 1,908,610 (May 9, 1933); also C. Tuttle, "Devices for the photoelectric control of exposure in photographic printing," *J. Franklin Inst.,* 224: 615-631, Nov. 1937.
15. L. P. Clerc, Paris Notes, *Brit. J. Phot.,* 70: 49, Jan. 26, 1923; also L. Lobel, "Le projecteur de salon 'Pathé-Baby'," *Sci. Tech. et Ind. Phot.,* 3A, No. 4, 38-40, Apr. 1923; and "Le Pathé-Baby," *ibid.,* 3A, No. 12, 126-128, Dec. 1923.
16. "Le Film Vierge Pathé"—Etablissements Pathé Cinéma, Paris, 1926, Chapter VII, Le Film Inversible Pathé, p. 83.
17. C. Emmermann and K. Brandt, "Agfa-Umkehrfilm," *Filmtechnik,* 4: 463-466, Nov. 24, 1928; also "Agfa Film Available," *Movie Makers,* 4: 408, June 1929.
18. C. E. K. Mees, "The history of professional black-and-white motion-picture film," *Jour. SMPTE,* 63: 134-138, Oct. 1954.
19. R. P. May, "16mm sound-on-film dimensions," *Jour. SMPE, 18:* 488-502, Apr. 1932; also *ibid., 19:* 228-236, Sept. 1932, and 477-480, Nov. 1932.
20. O. Sandvik and J. G. Streiffert, "A continuous optical reduction sound printer," *Jour. SMPE, 25:* 117-126, Aug. 1935.
21. R. C. Holslag, "Enter the eight," *Movie Makers,* 7: 335, 356, Aug. 1932; also H. B. Tuttle, "Beginning with the eight," *ibid.,* 8: 190, 207-208, May 1933.
22. J. G. Capstaff and M. W. Seymour, "The Kodacolor Process for amateur color cinematography," *Trans. SMPE,* No. 36, 940-947, 1928; also C. E. K. Mees, "Amateur cinematography and the Kodacolor Process," *J. Franklin Inst.,* 207: 1-17, Jan. 1929.
23. G. Heymer, "Das Agfacolor-Farbenverfahren für 16mm Film," *Phot. Industrie,* 30: 1199-1202, Nov. 30, 1932.
24. *Brit. J. Phot.,* 81: 449, July 27, 1934.
25. Brit. Pat. 15,055 (1912); also *Brit. J. Phot.,* 60: 595, Aug. 1, 1913.
26. C. E. K. Mees, "Presenting Kodachrome," *Movie Makers,* 10: 197, 220-221, May 1935; L. Mannes and L. Godowsky, Jr., "Kodachrome Process for amateur cinematography in natural colors," *Jour. SMPE,* 25: 65-68, July 1935; also E. R. Davies, "The Kodachrome Process of 16mm Colour Kinematography," *Phot. J.,* 76: 248-253, April 1936.
27. C. E. K. Mees, "Direct processes for making prints in color," *J. Franklin Inst.,* 233: 41-50, 1942; also C. E. K. Mees, "Modern colour photography," *Endeavour,* 7: 131-140, Oct. 1948.
28. P. Hatschek, "Der neue deutsche Agfa-Farbenfilm," *Die Kinotechnik,* 21: 345-346, Nov. 5, 1936; also *Brit. J. Phot.,* 83: 709, Nov. 6, 1936 and W. Schneider and G. Wilmanns, "Agfa-color-Neu," *Veröffent. Wiss. Zentral-Lab. Agfa,* 5: 29-36, 1937.

Norman O. Dawn: Pioneer Worker in Special-Effects Cinematography

By RAYMOND E. FIELDING

Norman Dawn's early career as cameraman, director and producer is outlined. The special-effects techniques which he developed, including glass and matte shots, are described.

ALTHOUGH DRAMATIC CHANGES occur regularly in most areas of motion-picture technology, much of the technique of special-effects cinematography has remained substantially the same for the last fifty years. Because of this, it seems historically appropriate to establish the identities of those early pioneers who contributed so much to the development of this specialized art. One such pioneer, active in the film industry from 1907, was Norman O. Dawn: artist, inventor, special-effects cinematographer, director, and producer.

Because of the difficulties involved in determining technological precedence, Dawn has never claimed to have been the first to employ the processes which he developed independently for his own work. The dates on which he first employed them are sufficiently early, however, to establish him as one of the first and most active workers in this field. Fortunately for historical purposes, Dawn was a methodical film-maker and, from the time of his earliest efforts, kept copious notes and numerous examples of his work. Over 800 of his notebooks survive today, covering a period of over 50 years, their yellowing pages filled with exposure data, production dates, records of technical failure and success, and illuminating references to the personalities and productions with which he was associated.

In this article, Dawn's early career as a cameraman, director and producer is briefly traced; then there is given a description of the special-effects techniques which he developed during those years.

Production Background

Norman O. Dawn was born on May 25, 1886, in a railroad camp tent in Humahuaca Canyon, Bolivia, not far from the border separating that country from Argentina. His father was an American engineer who helped design and build Bolivia's early railway system.

Shortly after birth, Norman was taken to Salta, Argentina, where his birth

A contribution submitted on November 16, 1962, by Raymond E. Fielding, Motion Picture Div., Department of Theater Arts, University of California, Los Angeles 24.

and American citizenship were recorded. From there, at the age of three months, he was taken to Monterey, Calif., where he spent much of his early childhood. When Norman was ten years old, his father was killed in South America and from that time until the age of twenty, the boy lived with his aunt, a well-to-do property owner, in Pasadena and Alhambra.

Norman's early interest in photography was stimulated by his father's activities as an amateur "wet-plate" photographer, and later by his membership

Fig. 1. Norman Dawn, in 1906 at the age of 20, at work in his Alhambra, Calif. studio.

in a teen-age "pinhole camera" club. At the age of fourteen, he purchased an Eastman view camera which took 8 by 10-in. plates, set up his own darkroom, and began his photographic studies in earnest; by the time he had finished high school, he had long since decided to make his career in photography.

In 1905, at the age of 19, he went to work as a still photographer for the Thorpe Engraving Co. of Los Angeles. One of his co-workers and close friends there was Max (Matt) Handschiegl, later to achieve prominence in motion-picture circles as an inventor and technical innovator.

During this period, Dawn also developed his quite considerable talent as an artist. Largely self-taught, he had achieved sufficient skill as a commercial artist by his twentieth year to hope for the kind of career in which both his

photographic and sketching talents could be combined. In 1906 he traveled to Paris to pursue his art studies through formal instruction at the French schools. It was during this visit to France that he first met Georges Méliès, the brilliant French film-maker in whose fantasy and trick films many of the basic cinematic effects which survive in practice today had already been introduced. Dawn was greatly influenced by Méliès and his work, all the more so since the older man possessed much the same combination of photographic, theatrical, and artistic talents as his youthful admirer.

Dawn's interest in the then fledgling motion-picture industry was further heightened by his subsequent acquaintance with the pioneer film producers, Louis and Auguste Lumière; the French camera manufacturer, André Debrie; and the American businessman, Arthur Lee, who was at that time manager of the New York Office of the Gaumont Film Co.

Early in 1907, Dawn purchased a motion-picture camera from André Debrie at a cost of approximately $500. Basic instruction in its operation and in the fundamentals of motion-picture processing was given to Dawn by Joseph Dubray of the Lumière organization. The purchase of the camera was made at a time when the Motion Picture Patents Co. in America, through vigorous legal action, sought to prevent the manufacture of cameras within the United States or importation of equipment from abroad other than that licensed under its own patents. Following the advice of Arthur Lee, Dawn kept his Debrie camera and French raw stock carefully hidden during his return trip to the United States in the spring of 1907. Like many independent film-makers of the period, he was very soon in California after his return so there was as much distance as possible between him and the Motion Picture Patents Co.

Dawn's original intention had been to experiment with the Debrie camera more for his own amusement than for profit. Due to the efforts of the Motion Picture Patents Co., however, there were very few cameras in the United States available to independent producers, and still fewer cameramen who knew how to operate them. The demand for footage was considerable and Arthur Lee suggested that Norman put together a short film about the California missions. Accordingly, Dawn set out in the late

Fig. 2. Dawn (right) with 1-cylinder Reo packed with Debrie camera, film, tools and camping equipment used while filming his first production, *Missions of California* (Apr. 10, 1907).

Fig. 3. An early glass shot made by Dawn for the Selig studio. Entire picture area is painted except window insert where actors are seen (Oct. 8, 1911).

spring of 1907 in a newly-purchased, $750, one-cylinder Reo automobile; he was equipped with his Debrie camera, raw stock, an automobile tool kit and camping equipment (Fig. 2). Despite the rigors of auto transport over horse trails and muddy roads, and persistent mechanical breakdowns of camera and car, Dawn managed to film the missions at San Diego, San Luis Rey, San Juan Capistrano, San Gabriel, San Fernando and Ventura. The footage was assembled into a one-reel picture entitled *Missions of California*. In the course of the film's

production, Dawn applied, for the first time in his professional motion-picture career, some of the special-effects techniques he had invented for his own use. These will be described later in this paper.

Missions of California was purchased for release by Gaumont Studios for the sum of $150. During the next few years, from 1907 to 1910, Dawn traveled throughout the world as a newsreel and scenic cameraman contributing films to the Gaumont, Pathe, Keystone View and Universal companies, and as an

independent short subjects producer. Among the travel shorts which he filmed during this period were *Stage Coach to Taxco*, *Digging the Big Ditch* (Panama), *Gorges of the Yangtze*, *The Great Barrier Reef* and *Land of Padre Escalante*. He also shot railroad footage in Mexico for George C. Hale, owner and promoter of *Hale's Tours*, a pre-1910 novelty film attraction which presented audiences with a simulated railroad ride through internationally famous scenic locales, as recreated by motion pictures projected within an artificial railway-car theater.

During these years Dawn's skill as a cameraman increased considerably and he began to employ regularly the special-effects processes which he had developed. Early in 1911 while in Bolivia, he produced, directed and photographed what he considered to be his first genuinely professional production, a two-reel drama entitled *Story of the Andes*. The actors in the film were recruited from the land-

Fig. 4. Dawn (with foot on stairs) directing *Western Skies* (1914). Camera is a pre-market model of the Bell & Howell Standard which incorporated fixed registration pins to make quality effects work possible for the first time.

Fig. 5. An early matte shot (1915–1916) for Ince's *The Eye of the Night*. Matte line is just above first story of nearest house.

Fig. 6. Matte shot from Keystone's *Oriental Love* (1916). Trade papers acclaimed film's novelty for its many effects shots. This test shot was made between takes on the picture.

Fig. 7. Matte shot for Universal's *Girl in the Dark* (1917). Simulating a Tibetan landscape, the foreground was shot in Griffith Park in Los Angeles and the background painted and matted in by Dawn.

owning Bolivian aristocracy and the total cost of production was about $2,100. Dawn developed the negatives on location and shipped them off to France where the film was edited, titled, and released by Arthur Lee.

Returning to California in 1911, Dawn began attracting the attention of Los Angeles film producers by demonstrating his effects techniques, many of which were unknown in the industry at that time. In the latter part of 1911 he undertook his first Hollywood assignment as a special-effects cinematographer on the Selig lot. In the several decades of professional work which followed, he worked at nearly every major studio in the industry, as well as with many smaller organizations which have long since disappeared. These included Universal (where he worked for five years under eleven different managers), Keystone, F.B.O., Kalem, Selig, Ince (Triangle), M-G-M and Republic. Apart from his concurrent work as a producer and director, Dawn served as special-effects cinematographer on over thirty features and innumerable shorts and serials, in the course of which he made 860 different effects shots, all of them carefully recorded in his notebooks. Among these many films were Thomas Ince's *Civilization* and Eric Von Stroheim's *Blind Husbands*.

As a cameraman, however, Dawn had considerable difficulty in selling directors on the value of his effects work for their productions. Then, as even now, many directors understood little of the complicated techniques involved in special-effects cinematography and hesitated to spend money on sequences which were necessarily removed from the director's immediate control. Dawn decided that the only way in which he could exploit the technology which he had developed was to become a producer and director himself. In 1913, he acquired the half completed negative

of a western feature entitled *The Drifter*, the producers of which had gone bankrupt. Dawn, together with the actors and crew, took over the completion of the film, most of the remainder of which was shot on location in Utah. Dawn contributed several thousand dollars of his own money, the actors and crew worked on a deferred-money basis, and the Selig organization provided the laboratory work. The film was subsequently states-righted by the Lee-Bradford-Casey group.

Numerous other features followed, most of them filled with special-effects shots of an increasingly complex nature: combination shots for otherwise impossible scenic effects; artificially created architectural composites for increased production value; explosions, avalanches,

stampedes, fires, floods, earthquakes and other catastrophes for spectacle and dramatic emphasis.

Dawn's earliest demonstration of the wholesale use of cinematic effects was in the 1916 Keystone comedy, *Oriental Love*. The picture provoked wide comment in the trade papers of that day for its extensive trick work. Many years later, this two-reeler was used by the Motion Picture Producers and Distributors Association in court suits brought against it and its members. The film provided evidence of prior use of effects techniques claimed by various inventors.

Dawn directed pictures for Universal for over five years, besides working as effects cinematographer for the studio's other directors. Among the Universal Specials which he directed were: *Sin-*

Fig. 8. Birthday party for Carl Laemmle, founder and President of Universal, Jan. 1920. Left to right: (front row) Isidore Bernstein, Studio Head; Edith Roberts; Laemmle; Pricilla Dean; Eddie Polo; (back row) Lee Kohlmar; Hoot Gibson; Dawn; Frank Mayo; director John Ford, and Lee Moran.

143

Fig. 9. Matte shot for Universal's *The Right to Happiness* (1919). Matte line is just above first story of building on left.

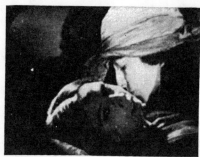

Fig. 10. One of Dawn's more intricate matte shots. Dorothy Phillips kisses her own cheek in a double role in *The Right to Happiness*. (Original nitrate test film clip has begun to decompose.)

Fig. 11. Three-element matte shot for Dawn's production of *The Adorable Savage* (1920). Foreground water was photographed at Santa Catalina, middle foreground set was built and photographed on the Universal back lot, background of trees is painted.

Fig. 12. Intricate matte shot of tarantula crawling over the face of a sleeping man from Dawn's *The Firecat* (1920) for Universal. Composite required usual two exposures. In first, the actor was photographed with upper part of cheek in shadow. In second, upper cheek of a plaster head was lit and tarantula was enticed into position by honey rubbed into model's make-up.

Fig. 13. Effective matte shot for *Five Days to Live* (1921), starring Sessue Hayakawa, for F.B.O. Simulated Chinese river, matted in above second row of glass panels, was shot at Venice, Calif.

bad the Sailor (1917), *Two Men of Tinted Butte* (1918–19), *The Line Runners* (1919), *Lasca* (1919), *A Tokio Siren* (1920), *White Youth* (1920), *The Adorable Savage* (1920), *The Firecat* (1920), *Wolves of the North* (1921) and *Thunder Island* (1921).

For F.B.O. he directed *Five Days to Live* (1921), *The Vermillion Pencil* (1921), *Son of the Wolf* (1922) and *After Marriage* (1923).

When Irving Thalberg left Universal to join Louis B. Mayer in the founding of what became M-G-M, Dawn went along as special-effects and special-unit producer to Thalberg. In 1923 Dawn traveled 800 miles by dog-team to Great Slave Lake and other northern regions to get special material for their production of *Master of Women*.

During the 1920's Dawn also produced a number of films in foreign or distant locales. These included *Lure of the Yukon* (1923–24), *The Eskimo* (1924), *Typhoon Love* (1924), *Black Hills* (1925), *Ranges of Doom* (1925) and *Girl of the Golden North* (1925).

In 1926 Dawn traveled to Australia where he produced and directed a film adaptation of the Marcus Clarke novel, *For the Term of his Natural Life*. Before production began, he found it necessary to construct a large studio and a complete laboratory facility in Sydney; by the time the picture was finished, it had cost over $650,000. Dawn subsequently described the film as the first major Australian production to compete successfully in the world market. The production was enthusiastically received, particularly in Australia and Asia, and was said by Dawn to have grossed more income than any previously released film in that part of the world.

Following this production, Dawn traveled to the Fiji Islands in 1927 where he made his last silent film, *The Adorable Outcast*. While finishing this production he learned of the imminent commercial introduction of "talking pictures." Hastily finishing the Fiji film, Dawn put it into immediate release and hurried back to the United States to learn more about

the new medium. Four years later, in 1931, he returned to Australia, this time with over $150,000 worth of sound equipment. He built a new studio on the fair grounds at Sydney and between June and September shot the first sound feature produced in that country — a musical entitled *Show Girl's Luck*. Running nine reels, the film was originally recorded with a sound-on-disc track and later released with sound-on-film.

Returning to Hollywood, Dawn directed several sound features for other producers between 1935 and 1938. These included *Tundra* (1935; re-released in 1949 as *Arctic Fury*), *Trail of the Yukon* (1937), and *Orphans of the North* (1938).

Early Special-Effects Techniques

Glass Shots. Long before he produced his first motion picture in 1907, Dawn had begun to experiment with special-effects techniques. In 1898, at the age of 12, he was given a portable "camera obscura" by his aunt. The camera obscura, a tent-like affair, was essentially

Figs. 14 A & B. Shots of a composite from *The Vermillion Pencil* (1921) for F.B.O., shows blending of matte elements: left, painted surround; right, complete scene with actors.

Fig. 15. Miniature "hanging ceiling" shot for *The Vermillion Pencil*. Ceiling is 4 or 5-ft wide miniature hung from above and interposed between camera and live action to provide proper matching of perspective lines with set. (Nitrate test film clip has begun to decompose.)

Fig. 16. Advertising poster for Dawn's *Show Girl's Luck* (1931) first soundfilm made in Australia.

a gigantic camera incorporating an optical system in a turret at its top which projected a large circular image within the tent downward onto a viewing screen. Dawn used the device in much the same fashion as 19th-century artists used the "camera lucida" — as an aid in the sketching of landscapes. He soon found that he could combine separate landscape components which had been viewed at entirely different locales. He would sketch in the foreground portion of a scene with the turret or tent in one position, then turn the turret or move the tent to a new locale, position his sketching pad on the projection screen with respect to the new scene, and then add the background component, thus creating a composite image which did not actually exist in nature.

The camera obscura was intended only as a toy, of course, but it revealed to Dawn the possibilities of artistic image manipulation. A few years later, in 1905, as a still photographer and commercial artist at the Thorpe Engraving Co., he had an opportunity for the first

time to apply some of his earlier special-effects experiments to the photographic art. Assigned to photograph architectural scenes in the Los Angeles area, Dawn discovered that the buildings which he was supposed to record were frequently rooted in unattractive settings or partially obscured by telegraph poles, wires, trees and other environmental bric-a-brac.

Dawn hit upon the idea of mounting a large sheet of plate glass in front of his 8 by 10-in. view camera and replacing the objectionable portions of the scene before him with painted images. The paints were laid directly onto the glass sheet and the images arranged in such a fashion that the perspective lines, image densities, contrast and tonal values of the painting matched that of the real scene. The painting was photographed with reflected sun or sky-light, and the real scene was photographed directly through the glass. Suitably small relative apertures, together with long exposures, were employed to secure sufficient depth-of-field to render both com-

ponents sharply focused. Dawn made his first still photograph with this process on February 11, 1905 (Fig. 17). For lack of a better name, he called these composite photographs "glass-shots." The term has survived to the present day, although whether derived from his own terminology or someone else's, Dawn is not able to say.

Dawn used his glass-shot process on numerous occasions in still photography, and upon his return from France in 1907, employed it for the first time as a motion-picture cameraman during the production of *Missions of California*. The technique was utilized there to reconstruct, with painted images, those early mission buildings which had partially disintegrated with time.

The glass-shot process which he developed during this period was virtually identical to that employed today. The camera and tripod were mounted on a sturdy parallel and focused upon the scene which was to be altered. A large sheet of glass was mounted in front of the camera. The artist-cameraman painted the new image components directly onto the glass, guided in his work by frequent sightings through the "through-the-lens" optical system of the camera. (In the case of the Debrie

145

Fig. 17. First glass shot was made by Dawn on Feb. 11, 1905 while employed as a still photographer for Thorpe Engraving Co. He replaced unattractive surroundings of building he was photographing with paintings laid onto a glass sheet mounted in front of his 8 x 10 view camera. He applied same technique two years later on his first motion picture, *California Missions*. (Sketched from memory by Dawn.)

camera, this was accomplished with great accuracy by focusing and composing directly on the film itself.) In most cases, a canvas cover was suspended over the entire work area to prevent reflections of the camera in the clear portion of the glass. Figure 18 shows a typical 1908 set-up. Oftentimes, additional light was provided for the illumination of the painting by means of reflectors or artificial light. Test footage was shot before each production take and developed in portable tanks. The wet negative was examined on the spot and further changes in painting or image alignment could be made, if necessary, before the final shot was made.

Dawn employed the glass-shot process in many of his own and other directors' films. The process achieved great popularity in the industry once its intricacies were known; it survives in practice to some extent today. The limitations of the process lie in the tedious and time-consuming painting which is required. In practice, all production on location must cease until the artist has completed his work. Once the painted element is finished, the shot must then be made within a reasonable length of time or the sun will move relative to the earth's surface and the position and direction of shadows in the painting will no longer match that of the real scene.

The Matte-Shot Process. Although Dawn's glass-shot survives today in professional circles, the previously described shortcomings have never rendered it very popular with either cameraman or producers. Far and away the most important contribution which Dawn made to the technique of effects cinematography was an entirely different process which was designed to overcome the limitations of the glass shot. Dawn called it a "matte-shot," although whether he was the first to use that term or not, it is not possible to say.

Certainly, other types of "matte-shots" had been employed by film makers long before Dawn had begun to experiment with the technique. In conventional earlier practice, part of the image recorded by the camera was obscured by a "matte" — an opaque card or plate inserted either into the external matte box or in the optics of the camera — during a first exposure to prevent the recording of certain portions of a set or scene. During a subsequent exposure, a "counter-matte" which conformed to the first exactly was similarly inserted, and a new scene was exposed and fitted into place with the rest of the already recorded image. Sometimes a portion of a set was matted out during first exposure by black velvet drapes or a black backdrop to achieve the same effect. Two of the earliest examples of this matting technique will be found in Edwin S. Porter's 1903 classic, *The Great Train Robbery*.

Although effective when properly executed, this type of matte-shot was completely unsuited for professional production. The process was time consuming, requiring that the same camera, matte box assembly and film be employed for both shots, the first scene being shot in one locale, the camera moved and the second exposure being made in the second locale. Moreover, the success of the shot was always uncertain; there was no provision for testing during the making of the composite. If the matte inserts were not precisely matched and aligned, or if the exposures of the two scenes were not properly balanced, the shot would be ruined; the whole process had to be repeated and both scenes had to be restaged.

In 1911, Dawn developed a more practical variation of the matte-shot technique which successfully overcame these limitations. It also provided for far more

complex and sophisticated manipulation of the image components. In the Dawn matte-shot process, a large sheet of glass was mounted in front of the camera, just as was formerly done with the glass shot. However, instead of painting the new, artificial image elements upon the glass, Dawn "matted out" the area of the new image by laying opaque black paint onto the surface of the glass sheet, the edges of the black paint conforming exactly to the "blend-line" or boundary between the real scene (photographed through the glass) and the new image components which would be added later. The painting of the black matte on glass could be accomplished fairly rapidly, following which the first exposure, with performing actors in the foreground, could be made.

Once this first shot had been made, a partially exposed negative resulted, on which only the live action portion of the scene had been recorded. Since the painted black matte in front of the camera neither reflected nor transmitted light, those portions of the negative which recorded the matte area were not exposed.

Immediately after the first exposure had been made, and while the camera and glass matte were still set up in the same position, an additional 50 to 100 feet of film were photographed on the same roll. This extra, nonproduction footage would be used later for test purposes at the time that the artificial image elements were added.

Back at the studio effects laboratory, Dawn removed the magazine of the first camera, containing the partially exposed but as yet undeveloped roll of film, and prepared to transfer it to a second camera. The second camera was mounted on a lathe bed which, in turn, was set on top of a concrete base, this massive support being designed to reduce camera vibration. The laboratory camera was aimed towards an art board easel which, in those early days, was illuminated by blue nitrogen bulbs (Fig. 19).

The laboratory camera which he employed had been modified to permit insertion of a right-angle prism and an optical system behind the intermittent movement, the pressure plate of which had been cut out. By means of such a viewfinding system, it was possible to view an image formed by the camera lens exactly as it was focused upon a strip of film in the camera aperture. (The camera described here is a Bell & Howell Standard. Prior to the introduction of this camera, Dawn employed a Debrie camera which provided a "straight-back" optical system for focusing directly on the film.)

In the darkroom a couple of feet of the extra test footage were cut out of the roll of production footage in the magazine and quickly developed, fixed and dried.

Fig. 18. Early glass shot set-up used by Dawn in 1908 to shoot scenic footage in Tasmania. The painted element, a rooftop, can be seen on sheet of glass. Canvas prevents reflection of the camera by the glass.

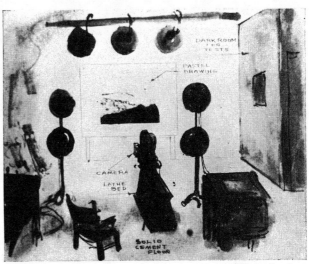

Fig. 19. Sketch of Dawn's laboratory at Universal during late teens and early twenties. Modified Bell & Howell camera is mounted on a lathe bed and focused on a matte board illuminated by blue nitrogen bulbs.

This negative was then inserted by Dawn into the modified intermittent movement of the camera.

The work area of the matte board in front of the camera was then illuminated with artificial light and its image focused through the lens system onto the processed test negative in the movement. It was now possible for Dawn to view any art work painted on the matte board, superimposed optically on the negative. The edge of the matted-out area produced during the original photography (which was clear on the negative) was now traced on the surface of the matte board with light pencil. The accuracy of the tracing could be checked by constant viewing through the special optical system installed behind the intermittent movement. Once the matte line had been traced, the lower portion of the matte board was painted in solid with black paint, thus creating a counter-matte which covered the same area of the picture as the original live action component.

With the black counter-matte completed, Dawn then began painting in the appropriate landscape or architectural details in the clear area of the matte board, developing proper perspective, density, and tone relationships between live action and painted components as he went along. As the painting on the matte board progressed, the accuracy with which the matte lines were aligned and the artistry with which the live action and painted elements were matched could be checked, step by step, by viewing the image of the matte board painting superimposed onto the developed, first-exposure negative in the camera aperture.

Having completed the painted element, Dawn removed the negative test strip from the intermittent movement and threaded the previously exposed

but still undeveloped production footage into the camera. Ten or fifteen feet of the remaining test footage at the end of this roll were then exposed in the camera, thus producing a composite image of the live action and painted elements. During this composite exposure test, several different exposure values were tried for density matching purposes. The short test strip was then cut out of the roll in a darkroom and quickly processed. By examining the developed composite test negative, Dawn could determine, first, which exposure value was appropriate for the matching of densities, and second, whether the matte line blend had been properly executed. Any necessary changes in matte line position or in the painting itself could be made at this point, and, if necessary, another ten or fifteen feet of composite test strip could be exposed, developed and examined.

Finally, once the proper matching of visual elements had been achieved in the test footage, the entire roll of production footage was run through the camera, producing the final composite of the live action, photographed on location or on stage, and the artificial elements, painted in the laboratory.

Dawn made his first matte shot with this process on January 14, 1911, using a black cardboard matte instead of glass, for his own production of *Story of the Andes*. As he perfected the technique over the years, both glass and cardboard mattes were used as the occasion demanded. By 1914 Dawn had supplemented the glass and cardboard mattes with small, frame-sized, hand-cut fiber mattes which he inserted into the internal, focal-plane matte slot within the camera's intermittent movement. Dawn cut the mattes by eye with a pen knife, an operation which required considerable skill and practice, not only because of the small size of the mattes but also because

they had to be cut upside-down and reversed right-to-left so as to match the inverted image formed by the lens system. After a few year's experience, Dawn got to the point where he could cut such miniature mattes in about one minute — a considerable saving in time over that previously required for the painting of an external matte.

Although Dawn used his matte-shot process frequently in professional productions of the day, the quality of his earliest work was oftentimes compromised by the registration inaccuracies of the intermittent movements then available to him. Such cameras as the Debrie and Pathe were perfectly good enough for conventional production work but lacked film movements sufficiently accurate to produce composites free of weave and jiggle. It became necessary for Dawn, when using such cameras, to expose the final composite a single frame at a time so as to minimize registration error. Even so, many a shot was ruined by the inadequate film movements and had to be completely re-taken. Finally, around 1914, the Bell & Howell Standard camera became available, featuring a fixed pilot-pin movement. Dawn secured a prototype model of the camera from Mr. Reynolds of the Bell & Howell organization and, for the first time, found himself with an intermittent movement sufficiently accurate for the kind of composite photography in which he was engaged. The same Bell & Howell shuttle-type movement remains in use today and can be found operating in such special-effects cameras as the Acme and Oxberry.

Dawn found that a number of precautions were necessary in the execution of such matte shots. As in the case of glass shots, a canvas cover was necessary to prevent reflections when a glass

147

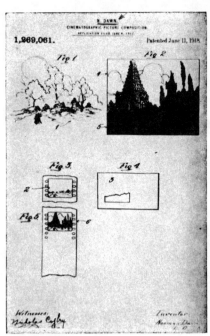

Fig. 20. Patent #1,269,061 granted Dawn in 1918 for his matte-shot process was subsequently sold to the Producers Association. Note, scene is that of Fig. 6.

Fig. 21. Early background projection set-up for *The Drifter* (July 1913). Dawn used two such shots in the picture but abandoned the process because of its poor quality. (Sketched from memory by Dawn.)

matte was used. A particularly rigid tripod support was necessary to minimize composite matte line weave due to movement of the production camera. In those cases in which the tripod was required to be mounted on the ground, Dawn found it necessary to sink hollowed stakes into the earth, into which the points of the tripod legs were set, thus minimizing slippage. He also mounted miniature automobile-type jacks under the corners of the camera between the camera body and the tripod head, so as to insure maximum rigidity in camera support.

Dawn used his matte-shot process extensively on all of his own and other producers' films throughout his long career. In many cases, two or more live action scenes were matted together instead of live action and painting. In some cases, the live action portions of the composite were combined with miniatures. For *Two Men of Tinted Butte* (1919), Dawn had a miniature of a complete desert canyon built, about twelve feet deep and sixty feet long. For a scene in which a desert cloudburst-flood inundated the valley, Dawn flooded the miniature with water released by sluice gates set in tanks out of camera range. The scene was photographed by two cameras, the first of which was a high-speed model (built for him by Fred Thalheimer) operating at between 64 and 90 frames per second. The lower portion of this shot was matted out. A second camera filmed the same action, the negative of which was used later as an "action cue track" in directing the actors who were to be matted into the lower section of the film. In the com-

posite, the actors are seen to barely escape from the flood of water which bears down upon them from the canyon valley in the matted-in miniature background.

Dawn's matte-shot process was obviously a valuable one, and, on June 8, 1917, he filed for a patent which was quickly granted a year later on June 11, 1918 (Fig. 20). Subsequently, Dawn was prevailed upon by his employer, Irving Thalberg, to sell the patent to the Motion Picture Producers and Distributors Association.

Several years later, with the introduction of quality duplicating stocks, Dawn's matte shot was further sophisticated by technicians in the film industry by means of "bipack printing." In this variation of the process, the original production scene is photographed "as is," with the actors performing in those areas of the scene which are to be retained in the final composite. No attempt is made at this time to matte out the unwanted portions of the image. A master positive is printed from the original negative and inserted into the intermittent movement of a bipack printer. A projection system in the printer produces an image of the master positive frame upon a matte board. The section of the image which is to be retained is matted out on the board and the painted image is added to the remaining clear portion. Following this, a second, counter-matte is prepared which is obscured with black paint in the area of the painting and left clear in the live action section. The composite of painting and live action occurs during the bipack printing operation, which requires two passes through the printer/camera. During these passes, the different mattes and the painting on the matte board are

imaged by a lens system on the printer which provides the light necessary to print the master positive through to a dupe negative, running in bipack with it, emulsion-to-emulsion. There are many variations of technique which are possible using this system, but the process is so well known that it does not require amplification here.

Background Projection. In today's production practice, few special-effects processes are so widely used as that of background projection, in which actors are posed in front of a translucent screen onto which a "stereo" diapositive or moving "plate" is projected from behind. Properly executed, the process offers a convincing composite of foreground action and background environment.

Most accounts of background projection development date its practical applications as beginning in the late 1920's and early 1930's, at which time the introduction of sound rendered interior stage photography of exterior scenes desirable. Long before 1930, however, many people in the industry had experimented with such a system and Norman Dawn was one of the earliest of these.

In July of 1913 he made his first background projection shots — two of them — for his own production of *The Drifter*. In these shots, his actor was posed in front of a ground-glass screen onto which a still-photo transparency was projected by means of a stereopticon projector (Fig. 21). The illumination employed for both projector and actor was limelight. Dawn used both shots in *The Drifter*. However, the quality of the composite was so poor that he abandoned the process.

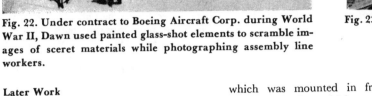

Fig. 22. Under contract to Boeing Aircraft Corp. during World War II, Dawn used painted glass-shot elements to scramble images of sceret materials while photographing assembly line workers.

Fig. 23. Dawn preparing rendering of Boeing bomber (1943).

Later Work

With the outbreak of World War II in 1941, Norman Dawn offered his services as an artist to the wartime defense industry. Working under contract to the Boeing Aircraft Corp., he employed an interesting application of his glass-shot process for the production of public information and training films. The need arose for the photography of airframe construction on the Boeing production line. At the same time, it became necessary to avoid revealing secret components and equipment mounted on the airframe and in full view of the camera. Dawn prepared a glass-shot painting which was mounted in front of the camera and which satisfactorily scrambled the appearance of these components so that their true nature would not be apparent (Fig. 22). He also produced many of the exquisitely rendered paintings of the Boeing bombers which were used for both instructional and public relations purposes.

Summary

In this article we have sketched, very superficially, the career and contributions of Norman O. Dawn in the field of special-effects cinematography. Although Dawn declines to claim historical prece-dence in his work, it seems apparent from the dates indicated here that he was among the very first workers to utilize the techniques described for professional film production.

Today, at the age of 77, Norman Dawn is still active in the graphic arts, at times illustrating children's books and other special assignments. He continues to experiment in photography.

Note. Material for this article was secured by the author from the notebooks of Norman Dawn and from interviews with him during 1962. Illustrations for the article were prepared by the author from still photographs, sketches, and original nitrate test film clips in Mr. Dawn's collection.

The Motion-Picture Laboratory

By J. I. CRABTREE

The evolution of the motion-picture processing laboratory is traced from the early days of reel-and-trough processing by Pathé and Gaumont up to the present day of highly efficient and complicated machine handling. During this half-century, many changes have been introduced in order to render the necessary services, to guarantee a uniformly high quality, and to meet economic requirements. In the early operations, processing was controlled largely by visual judgment. When photographic sound recording was introduced, sensitometric and other instrumental controls were adopted and a general refinement of laboratory methods soon followed. The complications of color photography required new techniques and new tools, especially as regards printing machinery. Laboratory work in the service of television is one in which the element of time is emphasized greatly.

During the latter half of the period, a system of motion-picture photography for the amateur involving the making of direct positives by reversal has resulted in the growth of a system of custom processing laboratories. At the same time the ramification of services to professional motion-picture production has been met by the development of new techniques and new functions while a high standard of quality and service has been maintained.

T HE BIRTHDAY of the motion-picture laboratory may be considered as coincident with the date of August 1889, when George Eastman sent a supply of motion-picture film to W. K. L. Dickson at the laboratory of Thomas A. Edison in Newark, N.J., for use in his Kinetoscope.[127]

Many previous workers had made pictures of moving objects consisting of a series of photographs on sheets or strips of film or bands of paper; but it would seem reasonable to apply the term "motion-picture" to a laboratory or workroom handling strips of film not less than 50 ft in length.

Dickson has described his method of processing this film as follows[127]: "Attached to this room, which was about 18 by 20 ft in size, were two darkrooms — one for punching, trimming, joining the films, and printing the positives; the other for developing, fixing, washing, and 'glycerining'* the films. These operations were done by using large, black, enameled drums adjustably suspended at each end when immersed in long, shallow troughs [Fig. 1].

"The films were spirally wound around these drums and the ends clamped to hold the film in place. When deemed to be thoroughly developed, the drum was carried to a similar trough to revolve in water coming from a spray over the length of the film or drum. The used water was carried away by an overflow from the trough. The film was then carried to the fixing trough and back to the

washing arrangement, thence to the glycerine trough, and dried before a fan while revolving on the motor-driven drum.

"As to our method of printing negatives, I had a large 8- or 10-inch sprocketed drum made, geared to run slowly, over which the films came in contact, the unexposed film being under the negative and the pins engaging both films. A small pea-lamp and reflector were placed above the negative. A square of ground glass was interposed between the light and the film, and the light was regulated by a small slide resistance to give the right exposure. Two spools on each side were used, geared to pick up the

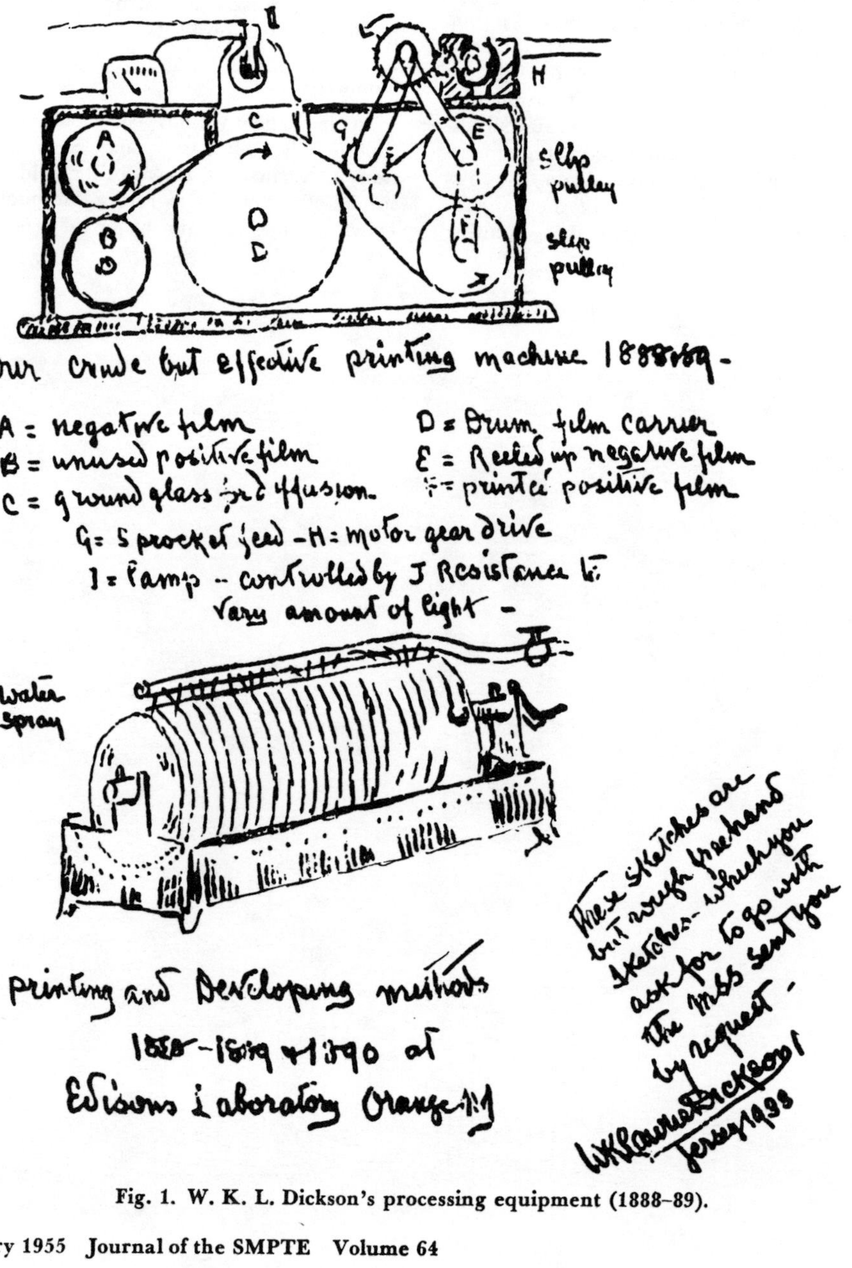

Communication No. 1668 from the Kodak Research Laboratories, presented on May 6, 1954, at the Society's Convention at Washington, D.C., by J. I. Crabtree, Research Laboratories, Eastman Kodak Co., Rochester 4, N.Y. (This paper was received on July 12, 1954.)

* A bath of glycerine and water, used to render the film more flexible.

Fig. 1. W. K. L. Dickson's processing equipment (1888–89).

Fig. 2. The Robert W. Paul Printer (1895).

Fig. 3. Paul's Laboratory Outfit (1895).

negative and positive films." Thus the principles of "spray impingement" and printing over the surface of a drum were born at an early age.

In the year 1895, L. Lumière gave a public showing of motion pictures with film prepared from "base" obtained from the New York Celluloid Company "which we coated with a sensitive emulsion in our machines and made into perforated rolls" and which, presumably, was processed in the same manner as by Dickson.[131]

In the same year (1895), Robert W. Paul in England had manufactured and distributed several duplicates of the Kinetoscope which was not patented in England and, being unable to obtain film subjects from Edison, built a studio and processing laboratory. To quote his own words: "In Birt Acres I found a photographer willing to take up the photography and processing, provided I could supply him with the necessary plant, which I did early in 1895.[130] For perforating the film I made, for use in an ordinary fly-press, a set of punches, 32 in number, made to the Edison gauge and fitted with pilot pins.

"Our printer [Fig. 2] was of the rotary type, consisting merely of a sprocket over which the positive and negative films passed together, behind a narrow slot illuminated by a gas jet. The sprocket was turned by hand at a speed judged by the operator, who inspected the negative as it travelled past a beam of red light. For development, a 40-ft. length of film was wound upon a birch frame with spacing pegs [Fig. 3]. Horizontal or vertical troughs held the solutions and washing water. At first drying was done in festoons, but a little later on light wooden drums. In 1899 a laboratory was erected adjacent to the studio having a capacity for processing up to 8000 feet of film per day." Thus was born the rack-and-tank system (Fig. 4).

Other film producers in England of this period included G. A. Smith, Charles Urban, J. Williamson, A. C. Bromhead and C. Hepworth. Hepworth has described some of his experiences before the British Kinematograph Society.[128] He writes: "My first effort was to photograph the boat race — it must have been the one of 1898, I think — and I took the negative to Wrench's place in Gray's Inn Road to develop on a pin-frame. With the arrogance of youth and the experience of one fifty-foot film behind me I then said that that was not the proper way to develop a continuous strip like a cinematograph film and that it ought to be developed continuously in a machine. So I set to work and made, and afterwards patented, an automatic machine [Fig. 5] in which the film was drawn through a succession of troughs in which it was developed, rinsed, fixed, and washed. Afterwards a printer and a perforator were added to the same machine so that

Fig. 4. Paul's Laboratory (1899). (Reproduced from *Moving Pictures* by F. A. Talbot, Lippincott, Philadelphia, 1923.)

we fed the unperforated film, just as it came from the maker, in at one end and it came out a finished print at the other. That was in 1898. In the tiny scullery we installed a vertical gas-engine, direct-coupled to a dynamo. It was just about as noisy as the average road-drill. We always had our meals in the same room. The automatic developing and printing machine was brought from Warwick Court and set up in the drawing-room. The best bedroom became the drying room, where the films were hung in festoons from wires stretched across it; the other bedroom served a similar purpose. The bathroom was the cutting-room and the front sitting-room was the office. My own patent ran out years before the rest of the trade began to feel the need of automatic developing, but it lasted me the whole of my film life, and I still have the consolation of knowing it was the first in the world."

In the same periodical, A. C. Bromhead[125] states: "At that time practically all film producers perforated their own films in their own laboratories. The types of perforator used were chiefly rotary. Laboratories recovered quite a sum by the sale of their punchings or perforations in the residue market. The perforators referred to were chiefly made by Wrench & Prestwich. In the result, perforations varied very widely, because the teeth wore smaller, the matrixes wore larger, and the perforation holes became ragged and irregular, causing unsteadiness of projection. It was really a great boon to the trade when Eastman and

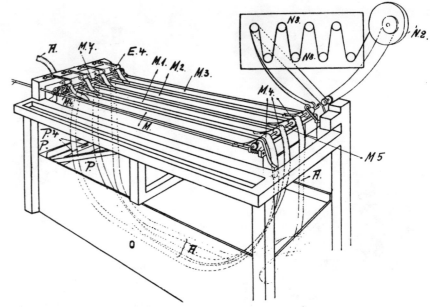

Fig. 5. The Hepworth Processing Machine, British Patent 13,315 (1898).

Pathé began to supply their stock perforated to an accurate gauge by an instrument of precision."

Simultaneously with technical developments in England, stimulated by the Kinetoscope, many firms in France entered the field of motion-picture production including Lumière, Pathé, Gaumont, George Meliès, Eclair, Lux, George Maurice, Debrie, etc., and during the next two decades they pioneered both in studio work and in the development of processing equipment. Likewise in Germany the motion-picture industry progressed under the leadership of Oskar Messter, Max and Emil Sladanowsky and the firms of Askania, Geyer and Agfa.

The Société des Etablissements Gaumont in 1907 was the first to put into service "batteries" of automatic developing machines.[133] In these, the processing solutions were held in tubes and later in tanks. A single-strip straight-line tank machine was employed by Lobel in 1912 (Fig. 6).

Fig. 6. The Lobel Single-Strip Straight-Line Machine (1912). (Reproduced from *La Technique Cinématographique* by L. Lobel, Dunod et Pinat, Paris, 1912.)

Fig. 7. The rack-and-tank system (1918).

In the United States, the drum-and-trough and rack-and-tank systems largely prevailed (Figs. 7 and 8), but in 1913 Leon Gaumont brought to Rochester, N.Y., a "tube" processing machine of the type illustrated in Fig. 9, in the operation of which I had the privilege of assisting. However, continuous processing machines were not universally adopted until several years later.

In France, the motion-picture laboratory by this time was organized broadly on present-day lines and those in England and the United States soon followed but, in the half-century since that time, many changes have been introduced in order to render the necessary services, to guarantee uniformly high photographic quality, and to meet economic requirements.

Owing to World Wars I and II, motion-picture development was greatly retarded in England, France, Germany and Italy, with the result that during these periods the major technical developments in laboratory processing occurred in the United States but these have been adopted in recent years by most laboratories throughout the world.

It is beyond the scope of this paper to consider the details of laboratory construction and organization which are adequately covered in the literature[137–149];

Fig. 8. Transferring film from developing rack to drying drum (1918).

however at this stage it is perhaps desirable to get a mental picture of the complexity of a modern processing laboratory so as to better evaluate the importance of the various milestones in the path of progress to be discussed later.

The nuclei of the laboratory are the developing and printing rooms containing complex machinery and, to insure their efficient operation, the basement may contain chemical mixing and circulating systems with flow meters (Fig. 10), refrigeration and air-conditioning apparatus, air compressors, electrical generators, water filters and softeners, silver recovery apparatus, a machine shop and a chemical laboratory.

Other departments provide for cleaning the negatives and positives, negative and positive assembly (Fig. 11), splicing, edge-numbering, negative timing, lubrication, editing, projection and storage. Although several types of machines have been devised for applying cleaning liquids and buffing the film[39] in order to avoid possible damage to negatives, many laboratories still clean their film by first winding it onto a plush-covered drum (Fig. 12).

We shall now consider the outstanding developments appertaining to processing laboratories which have occurred during the past half-century and which have been responsible for present high standards in photographic quality and efficiency. These developments may be tabulated as (a) functional milestones and (b) technical milestones.

(a) Functional Milestones

(1) Emergence of the laboratory as a separate organization to produce rush or daily prints and release prints. This occurred about 1900 when the laboratory work was no longer done by the cameraman and his helper.

(2) Additional functions beyond those of developing negatives and printing and developing positives were added in stages, namely, special printing, dissolves, dupes, tinting and toning, titles, reduction prints, "blow-ups," etc.

(3) Entry of the release print laboratory as separate from the studio laboratory.

(4) Establishment of special service laboratories such as for "process work."

(5) Specialist color laboratories: Technicolor, Cinecolor, and others.

(6) Specially equipped newsreel laboratories.

Fig. 10. Chemical mixing room with flow meters. Pathé Laboratories, Inc., New York, N.Y., 1953.

Fig. 11. 35mm and 16mm assembly. Pathé Laboratories, Inc., New York, N.Y., 1953.

Fig. 12. In order to avoid possible damage to negatives, many laboratories clean the base side by first winding on a plush-covered drum. Consolidated Film Industries, Hollywood, Calif., 1953.

(7) Sound production and printing as a laboratory function (1928).

(8) Refined chemical, mechanical and sensitometric control functions brought about largely by (7) (1930).

(9) Amateur service laboratories for reversal of originals and later for making duplicate positives. (This occurred about the same time as (4) and (5).)

(10) Color work in the nonspecialist laboratories (1950).

(11) Rapid and specialized work for the TV industry. This involved quicker service and prints with less than normal density and contrast.

(12) Miscellaneous work, including sound striping, electrical printing of sound and anamorphic printing.

(b) Technical Milestones

With regard to outstanding developments which have contributed to prog-ress in laboratory processing, the following milestones are merely the opinion of one person who has been intimately associated with processing laboratories for over forty years. However, there are un-doubtedly errors in precise chronology because, in many cases, several years elapsed before a new procedure made its impact on laboratories as a whole after its initiation.

1886 The old adage, "there is nothing new under the sun" would appear to apply also to processing machines since, in 1886, British Patent 16,327 was issued to John Urie, Sr., and John Urie, Jr., for a processing machine incorporating most of the elements which were adopted in one form or another in later types of processing machines. The machine employs (1) a constant but adjustable running speed, (2) a light-tight feed-on box, (3) feed-on rollers, (4) rollers which guide the film through the machine, (5) deep processing tanks, (6) agitation and uniform distribution of processing solutions, (7) regulation of treatment time by number and lengths of film loops, (8) auxiliary drive rollers, (9) replenisher system and constant liquid level of solutions, (10) storage tanks for collecting overflow, (11) recirculation of processing solutions, (12) means for relieving film tension and taking up of film slack and (13) portable racks which could be raised and lowered in the baths. However, no mention is made either of a drier or re-serve elevator.

1898 So far as is known, the first machine actually used for processing motion-picture film is that of C. Hep-

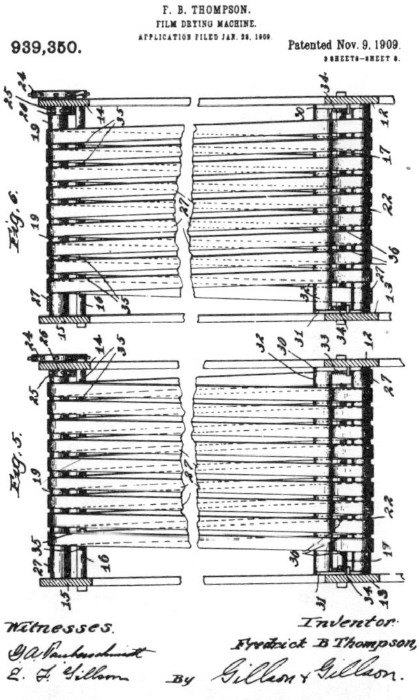

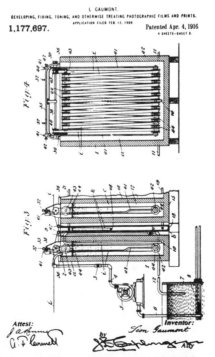

Fig. 14. The Gaumont Processing Machine, with spiral path of film travel (1916).

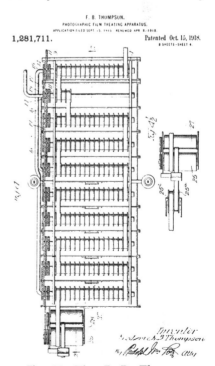

Fig. 13. The F. B. Thompson Film Drying Machine, with helical rack (1909).

Fig. 15. The F. B. Thompson Full Friction Lower Roller Driven Sprocketless Machine (1918).

worth described in British Patent 13,315 (1898) which consisted of a plurality of long shallow troughs, side by side, having feed sprockets at each end (Fig. 5).

The complete system included a perforator, and a printer from which the film was fed into the first trough over a movable rod which controlled the time of immersion. After passing through the various troughs in succession, the film was fed to a drier and rewind spool. Some years later, H. V. Lawley replaced this principle with a system of long vertical tubes which overcame the excessive aerial oxidation of the developer in the Hepworth troughs.

1907 Installation of "batteries" of tube processing machines by L. Gaumont, Paris.[133]

1909 In U.S. Patent 939,350, F. B. Thompson described a film-drying machine with helical rack, the top and bottom rollers being driven by a chain-and-sprocket combination (Fig. 13).

1913 Installation of a Gaumont tube machine for positive film at Kodak Park, Rochester, N.Y. In this year the first experimental lengths of panchromatic negative motion-picture film were made and processed by the reel-and-trough system at Kodak Park.

1916 United States Patent 1,177,697 (1916) was issued to Leon Gaumont for a motion-picture processor having a plurality of tanks in which upper and lower crowned rollers rotating on shafts afforded a helical path of travel for the film (Fig. 14). This fundamental idea has been adopted in many of the modern processing machines. An accompanying

patent (U.S. 1,209,096, 1916) by Gaumont described a drier with means for spiral travel of the film, a safety loop between the tanks and drier for protection against breakage, and an alarm system.

1918 United States Patent 1,260,595 was issued to F. B. Thompson for a processing system having a helical path of rollers of varying diameter to compensate for shrinkage during drying. United States Patent 1,281,711, also issued to F. B. Thompson (Fig. 15), described a full-friction, lower roller-driven sprocketless machine conveying the film in a spiral path in each tank.

In a later patent, U.S. 1,569,156 (1926), Thompson applied the same spiral path idea to the drier using graded diameter rollers to compensate for shrinkage (Fig. 16).

1920 The above-mentioned principles were incorporated in the "Spoor-Thompson" machine which contained the basic principles of most modern processors. Table I lists the various schemes for driving the film in processing machines in present-day laboratories. By eliminating sprockets, potential damage to the film, such as sprocket-hole tears, has been eliminated, unperforated film can be developed with equal facility, and a high speed of film travel in excess of 200 fpm has been made possible.

In the intervening years, many engineers have contributed to the perfecting of the modern processing machine in addition to Gaumont and Thompson, including DeMoos, Hubbard, Chanier, Tronolone, Sentou and Jacquet, Wescott, the Carleton Brothers, Hunter, Gage,

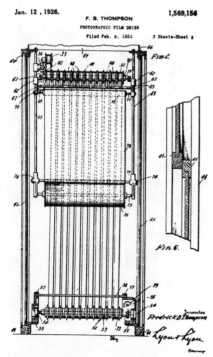

Jan. 12, 1926. 1,569,156
F. B. THOMPSON
PHOTOGRAPHIC FILM DRIER
Filed Feb. 9, 1924 3 Sheets-Sheet 3

Fig. 16. The F. B. Thompson Film Drier, using graded diameter rollers to compensate for shrinkage (1926).

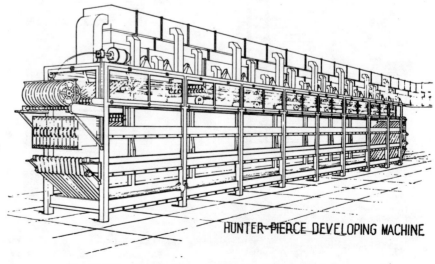

HUNTER-PIERCE DEVELOPING MACHINE

Fig. 17. The Hunter-Pierce Horizontal Tank Machine (1931).

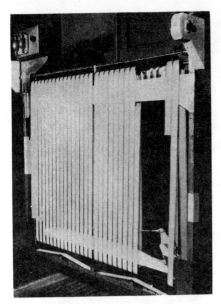

Fig. 18. Roller rack used in rack-and-tank process (1935).

Fig. 19. The Erbograph Machine (1920).

Griffith, Leshing, Nicholaus, Spray, Capstaff, Lootens, Duryea, Tondreau, Bertram, Solow, Miller, Gaski, Vinten, Debrie, Geyer and others.

The Hunter-Pierce machine (Fig. 17) which is typical of Type V (c), consists of three horizontal shallow troughs, one above the other, and accommodates 10 strands of film, each of which is pulled through the entire machine by a single sprocket, although several booster friction drives are desirable. Film enters in the top trough, passes to the second, and then to the lower trough, and up again to the drying box on top at a speed of about 12 fpm.[156]

A typical roller rack for use in the rack-and-tank system, which serves to keep a loop of film moving continuously so as to avoid rack marks, is shown in Fig. 18 and is capable of giving a development uniformity of the same order as that of continuous machines.[32]

Fig. 20. Spray-washing section of Erbograph Machine (1920).

Fig. 21. Scene tester (C. E. Ives and J. I. Crabtree, 1922).

Fig. 22. Double-reel equipment for processing 16mm film (1925).

1920 *Duplitized Film* was supplied by the Eastman Kodak Company for use in two-color subtractive color processes, and many schemes were devised for processing this film, such as floating the film on the surface of the treating liquid or protecting one side by varnishing before immersion and then removing the varnish for the second treatment.

A panchromatic negative film was by now in general use, necessitating a change in darkroom illumination from red to low-level dark green.[223]

1921 The SMPE Committee on Film and Emulsions[222] listed the following existing processing machines: Spoor-Thompson, Duplex, Lawley (England), Pathé, Jaeps (England), Erbograph, Gaumont (Flushing, L.I.), all being tube machines except the Erbograph and the Spoor-Thompson. Some machines used double-toothed sprockets and others sprockets with teeth alternating from one side to the other on successive sprockets.

In the Erbograph machine (Fig. 19), the processing solutions were in troughs superimposed one above the other,[150] the film traveled horizontally and the troughs could be lowered for threading. This machine was one of the first to employ "spray washing" (Fig. 20).

The Lawley machine employed vertical tubes 30 to 40 ft long even for drying, which extended into the third story, but the film tended to adhere to the sides of the tubes causing scratches and breakage.

1922 A simple method of scene testing[251] was devised by printing through a series of neutral densities calibrated in terms of printer steps (Fig. 21), although around 1920 Max Handschiegl in Hollywood manufactured a scene tester employing a stepwise shutter, which varied the time of exposure instead of the light intensity as in the printer. This was later improved by Crabtree, Ives and Tuttle (1930),[252] and the principle was applied, still later, in the Cinex, Reeves, Houston, and Herrnfeld[210] scene testers.

1923 The 16mm reversible Cine-Kodak Film employing a controlled light exposure for the redevelopment stage was born[121] and, in the initial stages, was processed on a reel and later on a double reel illustrated in Fig. 22, the film being transferred to the upper reel for drying.

1926 Cine-Kodak Film was processed commercially on a 7-fpm machine employing removable racks (Fig. 23), one of which is shown suspended from an upper beam. In later machines the speed was increased to 40 fpm.

1927 *Duplicating.* Up to this point, release printing was done from original negatives but, for foreign release, a print on positive stock or a duplicate negative on regular negative stock was supplied which, at best, was of inferior quality. The introduction of Eastman Duplicating Film,[101] which contained a

Fig. 23. The First Ciné-Kodak Continuous Processor (1926).

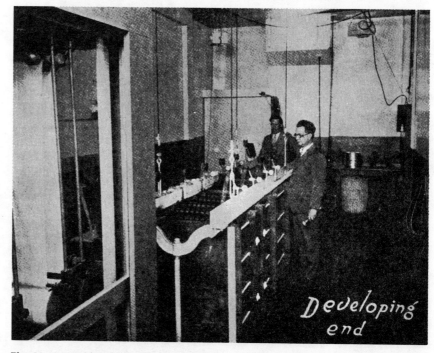

Fig. 24. A machine in which negative film was first developed commercially in the United States (1928).

158

Fig. 25. The Eastman Transmission Densitometer (1930).

yellow dye, permitted contrast control by printing with yellow or violet filters and was employed for making both the master positive and the duplicate negative. At a later date (1937),[105] individual films for making the master positive and the duplicate negative made greater control possible with improved quality and graininess.

In this year, the borax developer, Kodak D-76, was introduced.[100] Hitherto, the only trend in developer substitution had been the use of Metol and hydroquinone in place of pyrogallol or glycin, but the borax developer, with its high content of sulfite and its low pH value, gave finer-grained negatives, better H and D curves, and permitted conveniently longer developing times. Most

present-day sound and motion-picture negative developers are derivatives of this formula.

1928 *Machine Development of Negatives.*
Up to this time, very few laboratories had dared to develop negative film by machine for fear of damage, although the hope of doing this was expressed in a paper entitled "The Technical Status of the Film Laboratory"[138] in 1928 by L. M. Griffith, of the Paramount Hollywood Laboratory, who stated: "The progress of development technique may ultimately lead to chemically automatic developers capable of yielding the highest quality by simple time-temperature methods and machine processing of negatives will soon be the rule."

In discussing this paper, I stated: "...it is apparently up to the cameraman or whoever is responsible for the lighting to so light the set, that with a constant degree of development it will give the negative required. I think it is almost impossible for a man in a darkroom to develop a negative to the correct degree so that it will give a print of the type required. I don't see how he can know unless he knows exactly what each scene is all about. I think that better results will be obtained by standardizing the development. Then if the negative is not right, the lighting is wrong."

Machine development of negative was brought to fruition by C. R. Hunter[153,154] in 1928 who described a modified Spoor-Thompson machine in which he had been successfully developing negative film for over a year (Fig. 24). In discussing this paper, M. S. Leshing (Fox Laboratories) stated: "I was present when the first foot of film went through the negative machine at Universal City and as a 'Doubting Thomas' I sent in over

400 feet of negative. The Universal people didn't know what the subject was or which stock it was. I was agreeably surprised when I saw the results. As a matter of fact, we laboratory men are discouraged when we see this machine working. We 'expert' laboratory men have tried to 'photograph' for the cameramen. I do believe that this is a great step forward in producing uniformity of results."

In August, 1932,[227] the Report of the Progress Committee of the Society stated: "Three of the largest studios in Hollywood have established the practice of developing all negatives to a fixed gamma. The practice at first caused confusion among cameramen, but after becoming familiar with the laboratory technique, they adapted themselves readily to the situation."

Processing of Sound Records. This was an epoch-making year when sound on film became universal although both Fox-Case of Movietone and the General Electric Co. had given exhibitions in 1927 and DeForest in 1923.[132]

Very little was known about the processing of sound records until Engl studied the sensitometric aspects.[264] Sponable and Nicholson of Fox-Case made further sensitometric studies of the flashing-lamp technique[257] with collaboration of the Kodak Research Laboratories, but D. MacKenzie, of the Bell Telephone Laboratories, was largely responsible for working out initially the necessary conditions for processing variable-density sound records.[270]

Since that time a great amount of research has been applied to the determination of the optimum conditions for processing variable-density and variable-

Fig. 26. Film storage cabinets with individual drawers installed in a film vault at Kodak Park, Rochester, N.Y. (1929).

Fig. 27. Eastman Edge-Waxing Machine (1930).

width records by the research departments of the film and apparatus manufacturers and the film studios.

At an early stage it was recognized that sound records should be developed to a fixed degree or "gamma" which necessitated the establishment of sensitometric tests in all studios and laboratories, but the situation in the early days was chaotic until the introduction by Kodak of the Eastman Type IIb Sensitometer[234] and by ERPI of the Western Electric 1100 Densitometer,[73] which instruments greatly facilitated the testing methods. Photoelectric densitometers were later supplied by Eastman Kodak,[85] Ansco,[81] Herrnfeld[84] and others.

After sensitometry had proved its worth in the control of variable-density sound tracks, the next step was to apply it to the control processing of picture negatives and prints.

Previously, negative scenes were developed to different degrees and also the positives to some extent, but now that all positives were to be developed for a fixed time at a given temperature, this tended to compel the cameramen to employ light meters in order to obtain the necessary uniformity from scene to scene.

Provided with a sensitometer and densitometer (Fig. 25) and other refined instrumental aids, the laboratory was able to measure not only variations in the activity of the developer and variations in the degree of uniformity of processing resulting from changes in temperature and degree of agitation, but likewise variations in uniformity of the photographic characteristics of the film emulsions. This had the beneficial effect of compelling the film manufacturers to improve the uniformity of their product, the lack of which it was previously possible to blame on the laboratory.

In the beginning, sound quality of film records was quite inferior by modern standards owing to many causes, including lack of quality-control methods in processing, and it was not until 1935 that a planned system of replenishment of developers was found possible.[93,94] More thorough chemical control by analysis, pH measurement, and replenishment was not realized until 1940.[14−25]

At present (1954), control of laboratory processing of sound tracks is also accomplished by means of intermodulation distortion measurements for variable-density tracks and cross-modulation analyses for variable-area tracks.[276,277] Use of these two techniques has supplemented and, in some instances, replaced laboratory instrument control in the development of sound records.

1929 *Preservation and Storage.* A novel storage cabinet (Fig. 26) for insuring maximum protection to all films stored in a vault and minimum danger from spreading of fire consisted of a series of metal drawers of 1000-ft capacity

Fig. 28. Eastman Electrolytic Silver Recovery Unit (1931).

Fig. 29. The original printing machine: the Lumière Camera (1895).

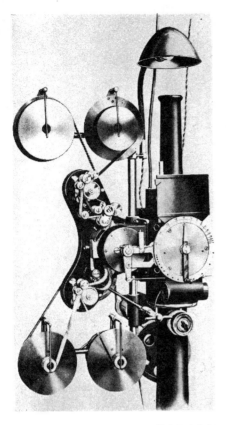

Fig. 30. The Bell & Howell Model D Printer (1912).

Fig. 31. Bell & Howell Model E Printer and Sound Printer (1932).

contained in fire-resisting wood cabinets.[180] The back end of each drawer was vented into a large flue pipe leading out of the building. Fire tests showed that one roll could be burned up completely without damaging any other rolls in the cabinet.

Most laboratories, however, employed the type of storage vault permitted by the National Board of Fire Underwriters for protection to surroundings, relying on duplicates for insurance of preservation. The universal use of safety film in 1950 tended to simplify the problem of storing future productions.

Apart from the fire hazard, increasing attention was given to the necessity for thorough washing of film[293] to insure its perpetuation, a sensitive method of determining hypo in film was devised[179] and limits of hypo content were established which have since become standard throughout the industry.[193]

1930 *Surface Treatment and Renovation.*
After processing and before projection, positive film requires lubrication to prevent offsetting of gelatin in the gate of the projector. In 1922 this was effected by edge-waxing with molten wax[284] and later (1930)[288] with a solution of wax in a readily volatile solvent (Fig. 27); and today many laboratories follow this procedure at the end of the drying cabinet before rewinding.

In order to minimize abrasion of the picture and sound record, a solution of wax was applied to the entire surface of the film, followed by buffing,[287] but this treatment was never universally adopted. Later, in 1941, Talbot[290] described a method of applying a varnish to the emulsion surface of processed film which could be removed and reapplied as the coating became scratched after a period of use.

Throughout the years numerous proprietary preparations have been applied to film with a view to increasing its life and preventing brittleness but none has been sufficiently effective to gain universal adoption.

A scratch-removing process which had some merit consisted in swelling the gelatin coating in a caustic solution and the base side with a suitable solvent, and then drying.[289]

Wide Film. During 1930 there was a great flurry of interest in wide film, various standards being proposed, namely, 70mm for Fox Grandeur, 63mm for "Natural Vision" by Spoor and Berggren, and 56mm for Magnafilm by Del Riccio and LaPorte of Paramount.[123] Special processing machines were devised for each of these dimensions but none has survived beyond the pseudo-commercial stage.

1931 *Electrolytic Silver Recovery.* As a result of the researches of Hickman, Sanford and Weyerts,[262] electrolytic recovery of silver from exhausted fixing baths was initiated in many laboratories. A typical electrolytic unit, shown in Fig. 28, provides for rapid agitation of the solution by paddles operating between the electrodes, thus permitting the use of high current density without sulfurization of the bath. A U.S. Patent (1,866,701) was issued to Garbutt and Ingman in 1932, but filed in 1929, for a method of silver recovery utilizing air agitation of the electrolyte, and this method was adopted in the Hollywood Paramount Laboratory.

For many years previously, laboratories had recovered silver by precipitating it as sulfide and then discarding the bath, although by this method it is possible to re-use the fixing solution after filtration provided an excess of silver ion is maintained during precipitation. Apart from the economy effected by electrolytic recovery, the necessary attendant analyses serve to insure uniform fixation and hardening properties of the fixing bath.

1932 *Automatic Printing.* At this stage, picture prints had been made on step printers such as the Lawley, Williamson, Duplex (flat and curved gate), Vinten, Debrie, Depue, Askania, Geyer, etc., machines and, in the earliest stages, the camera, such as the Lumière,[131] was employed also as a printer (Fig. 29).

By now, the Bell & Howell Model D continuous printer (Fig. 30) and the Duplex step printers were prevalent types throughout the industry. Negative timing was largely by eye and, surprisingly, for black-and-white work, this method is almost universally employed today. Ex-

Fig. 32. A modern multihead printer. The Calvin Co., Kansas City, Mo. (1952).

Fig. 33. The Peterson Optical Printer (1952).

posure sequence was effected with the aid of edge notches which activated mechanisms for varying the lamp voltage or the diaphragms in the New York laboratories, although in Hollywood most timing is accomplished by the light test method.

Sound negatives were printed by contact in a separate operation on the Model D printer with a mask in the gate to eliminate the picture area. Optical printers were in the development stage.

With the advent of the Bell & Howell Model E printer (Fig. 31) in 1932, the picture and sound were printed in one operation and by this time an infinite variety of printers were devised by laboratories and manufacturers, each laboratory usually modifying the Bell & Howell Model D or Duplex printer head and using these in tandem or in combination with a soundhead. Rewinding was avoided by making printers reversible or printing from the looped negatives. A multiple-head printer is shown in Fig. 32.[219]

Optical printing was being adopted about this time, making possible either a 1:1 ratio or 16mm:35mm or vice versa, both with picture and with sound. Several optical printers are in common use today, including the Depue, Acme-Dunn, Peterson (Fig. 33), Maurer, Arnold & Richter, Union Tonfilm (Germany), and the RCA and Eastman Model D sound printers.

1935 This was another epoch-making year, being the birthday of the three-color 16mm Kodachrome Process,[42] in which a multilayer film was utilized which could be processed by successive immersion in solutions without recourse to imbibition or other treatments.

In the earlier years, selective development of the emulsion layers was dependent on the differential penetration of the

processing solutions but later, in 1938, the film layers were so sensitized that development of each layer could be initiated by exposing the film in succession to cyan and yellow light. A typical processing machine is shown in Fig. 34.

1937 Agfacolor Reversible 35mm Film was made available and Eastman Kodak and Du Pont fine-grain sound-recording films in 1938, which made it feasible to develop variable-density sound negatives in the regular picture negative developers. Eastman Kodak also supplied 32mm film for slitting to 16mm after printing from a tandem negative and processing.

1939 Photoelectric densitometers were rapidly replacing the visual types.[71-85] It is interesting that as early as 1921 W. G. Story, Jr., measured the transmission of photographic images with a photocell and suggested this ap-

plication to the determination of printing exposure.[211]

1940 Integral printing was in use involving a hookup of printer, processor and projector. The printer and projector ran faster than the processor but elevators were interposed to accommodate the differential speeds. Such a hookup was in full operation in the Fort Lee laboratories of the Consolidated Film Industries in 1934. The current layout in the Consolidated Hollywood laboratories is shown in Fig. 35.

Turbulation. This term is often applied to the extent to which the solutions are removed at the surface of the film during processing and is usually proportional to the degree of agitation or "turbulence" of the liquid.

The importance of agitation in photographic processing has been frequently

Fig. 34. A Kodachrome Continuous Processing Machine (1953).

Fig. 35. Illustrating integral printing involving a hookup of printer, processor and projector. Consolidated Film Industries, Hollywood, Calif. (1953).

Fig. 36. 400-gpm capacity circulating system for jet agitation in color processing. Pathé Laboratories, Inc., New York, N. Y. (1953).

stressed in the literature but its significance in motion-picture laboratory processing was only fully revealed when attempts were made to improve the quality of sound records. Crabtree, of the Bell Telephone Laboratories,[1,2] was the first to study this subject in detail in relation to variable-density sound records but the first published account of attempts in a commercial laboratory using the Spoor-Thompson type of machine to increase the degree of turbulation in order to decrease "directional effects" or "sprocket-hole modulation" was by Leshing, Ingman and Pier in 1939–1940,[6] although in 1935 Ingman was granted U.S. Patent 1,991,251, which claimed the use of submerged jets for increasing turbulence in processing solutions. The normal degree of agitation resulting from the rapid motion of the film in this type of machine had been only partially effective in preventing the above defects but, by emptying about 75% of the developer in the tank and flowing the developer from the top down the vertical moving strands of film, the "directional effects" were largely eliminated, although this procedure was conducive to aerial oxidation of the solution. This method constitutes an application of the scheme used at the Warner Studios many years ago, the film being developed on a reel. The developer was poured over the reel, across the surface of the film, thus turning the reel in the manner of a water wheel.

In the same year, Capstaff patented a "spray rack" (U.S. 2,169,758) which provided immersed nozzles or spray pipes arranged adjacent to the film loops, and "backing rollers" were provided to maintain the position of the film. This method

is currently used in many laboratories, especially for color development. A typical arrangement of the pumps and piping for such a system is shown in Fig. 36.

Other methods of turbulation involve agitation with air or nitrogen.[3]

E. A. Bertram has advised that in 1936, under-surface turbulation and "waterfall" application of developer was employed for negative development in the DeLuxe Laboratories, New York, N.Y.

Likewise at the DeLuxe Laboratories, spray application of all processing solutions was in force for positive 16mm film in 1937 (Fig. 37) while in 1941 complete spray application of all solutions was in use for the development of 35mm negative films (Fig. 38).

An almost unique method for reducing directional effects was that of Davidge (1935),[31] which involved winding the film on a reel with an interleaving apron to separate the convolutions and rotating the reel in the developer solution, baffle plates in the tank serving to force the developer across the film surface. A 1000-ft unit is shown in Fig. 39.

1941 Coating of film with a removable lacquer to prevent abrasion and scratches was initiated.[290]

1942 Printing of sound records with ultraviolet light[271] served to prevent depth penetration of the latent image and image-spreading, giving better resolution.

In 1928 Sandvik and Silberstein[265] demonstrated the improvement in resolving power by the use of ultraviolet radiation but later Oswald and Foster in a series of patents claimed the use of ultra-

violet for the recording and reproduction of sound and the printing of motion-picture film (U.S. 1,928,392, 1933; 2,030,760, 1936; 2,055,261, 1936; 2,213,-531, 1940).

1945 Processing procedures for Ansco reversible[43] negative and color positive film were made available to laboratories.

1946 *Rapid Processing.* Although most laboratories employ the ASA standard development temperature of 68F, rapid processing of motion-picture film at temperatures up to 125 F was accomplished[243] by the use of (a) specially hardened emulsions or prehardening baths, (b) elevated temperatures for the developer, fixer and wash water, (c) optimum agitation by spray application of the solutions and wash water, and (d) drying by contact with a heated surface or by jets of air.

In the 35mm machine shown in Fig. 40, the film passes successively through spraying chambers which apply the processing solutions at 130 F, the film being finally air-squeegeed and dried by jets of hot air applied at numerous points as the film passes around the periphery of a "bicycle wheel."

Several adaptations of this machine have been made for television kinescope recording and microcopying (Fig. 41).

Commercially available rapid processors include the General Precision 16mm[167] and the Paramount.[246] The Debrie Aiglonne, while of relatively slow speed, is of novel design and is self-threading.[36]

Construction Materials. With the introduction of continuous processing machines, it was necessary to employ a variety of corrosion-resisting construction materials more amenable to fabrication to replace the wood, stone, brass, glass, etc., previously employed for rack-and-tank work. Molybdenum stainless steel A.I.S.I. Type 316 was available and since has been extensively employed in modern processors.[51-59] A large number of plastics were also introduced, many of which are suitable for tank linings, bearings, rollers, piping, etc.

1947 Another epoch-making year was 1947, when magnetic recording was tending to replace photographic recording in the studios, thus eliminating the laboratory processing, and by the fall of 1948 was almost generally adopted.[274] However, re-recordings continued to be made photographically.

Magnetic striping of processed and unprocessed film was proposed by Camras.[173]

1949 Du Pont color positive film for printing from three-color separation negatives was issued which employed synthetic binders for the silver halides which were, at the same time, color couplers.[45] Procedures for processing Kodachrome film were made available to laboratories.

Manufacture of nitrate film was discontinued by Kodak and soon after by other manufacturers and so only safety film was supplied. This had the effect of reducing fire hazards in the laboratory and making available construction sites for new laboratories in zoning areas previously forbidden. A fluorescent dye was incorporated in the safety film for identification with ultraviolet light.

1951 Eastman and Ansco color negative and positive films were introduced[47, 48] and rapidly adopted by many laboratories which, for many years, had been anxiously awaiting the availability of a color process which they could handle themselves with a minimum of alteration to their existing equipment.

Fig. 37. 16mm spray application machine for positive film. DeLuxe Laboratories, New York, N.Y. (1937).

Fig. 38. 35mm spray application machine for positive film. DeLuxe Laboratories, New York, N.Y. (1941).

Fig. 39. The Davidge 1000-Ft Developing Reel, which is rotated in the processing solutions (1935).

Fig. 40. A machine for rapid processing at 125 F (Ives and Kunz, 1950).

Fig. 41. The Recordak Rapid Processor (1953).

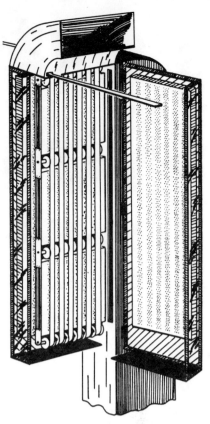

Fig. 42. Illustrating method of rapid drying by impingement of warm air from a large number of air jets (Miller, 1953).

1952 Supplementing color negative and color positive, a color internegative film[49] was introduced for duplication and for use in special-effects work.

With improvements in emulsions, processing solutions and machinery, it was now possible to increase the speed of processing color films from 20 to 40 fpm and later, in 1954, to 60 and as high as 150 fpm in some laboratories. The speed of processing black-and-white positive film in some cases exceeded 200 fpm.

Rapid drying of film[37] was being accomplished by impingement of warm air (125 to 210 F) through a large number of small orifices in a plenum placed in close proximity to the film, as illustrated diagrammatically in Fig. 42. In 1953 the general trend was toward this type of drier construction and the adoption of higher processing temperatures to insure more rapid production.

Figure 43 illustrates the complete drying section of the 150-fpm machine at the DeLuxe Laboratories, New York, N.Y. Eastman Color Positive Film (35mm) is dried in 1 min 45 sec with air at 155 F (October 1953).

1953 Magnetic striping of 16mm and 35mm films was in progress in many laboratories either by disk application of a slurry of magnetic material (Fig. 44)[178] or by laminating a strip of magnetic tape.

Electrolytic regeneration of a rapid developer containing vanadium salts was accomplished by means of electrolysis[99] but it is doubtful if this scheme will replace the existing developing solutions in the immediate future.

Current practice (1953) in the Precision Film Laboratories, New York, N.Y., for optimum quality in 16mm prints, is to print picture and sound separately, the picture on the (step) contact, or reduction printers, and the sound on 1:1 optical printers or electronically from

Fig. 43. The complete drying section of the 150-ft/min machine (35mm) at the De-Luxe Laboratories, New York, N.Y. (1954). It is only 5 ft in width.

Fig. 44. A magnetic striping machine (Dedell, 1953).

Fig. 45. Modern color processing machine (Eastman Kodak, 1953).

a magnetic track distributed to several optical printers.

The Impact of Color on the Laboratory. Until the advent of multilayer subtractive color films and their general availability, color photography had little effect on the majority of service laboratories since most processes such as Technicolor, Gaumont, Keller-Dorian, Prizma and Cinecolor were operated by individual laboratories, each system requiring specific treatment.

The Consolidated Film Industries operated the Magnacolor Process which was later superseded by the Trucolor Process. Magnacolor was similar to Cinecolor, being a toning process using Duplitized Positive. Trucolor was a color development process utilizing color couplers incorporated in both sides of a Duplitized Positive.

Multilayer films can be handled on processing machines essentially similar to those employed for black-and-white films but require more tanks, more complicated solutions, auxiliary tanks for processing the sound track and, in printing, it is necessary to control both the hue and intensity of the light source. A typical processing machine is shown in Fig. 45.

In view of the complexity of the chemical and optical reactions involved, rigid control methods must have even greater precision than is required for sound.

For color sensitometry, several intensity-scale instruments and photoelectric densitometers with color filter attachments have been made available, including the Eastman Processing Control, Ansco, Houston and Herrnfeld sensitometers, and the Ansco, Eastman Type 31A (Fig. 46) and Westrex color densitometers.[79-85]

In printing color film, variation of the hue as well as of the intensity of the printing light is accomplished either by

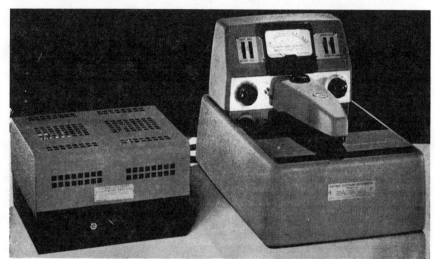

Fig. 46. The Eastman Electronic Densitometer, Model 31A (1954).

Fig. 47. The Streiffert Printer (1952).

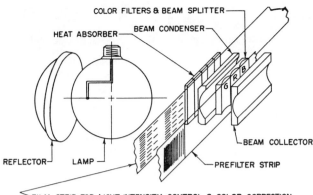

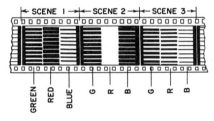

Fig. 48. Illustrating the optical principles of the Debrie Matipo Step Printer. Additive color mixture is effected by the use of a line-screen control matte in combination with prismatic lenses and three filter elements (1953).

Fig. 49. The Herrnfeld Scene Tester (1951).

means of individual filters, filter packs with or without neutral density filters, or by intermixing the three primary colors projected onto the printing aperture. For each scene, the filter or pack may be changed as is done in an automatic slide projector, or, more generally, a traveling matte or "cuing strip" is employed with varying apertures in combination with filters to modulate the intensity and hue of the printing light.

Additive printing with narrow band filters gives improved color saturation. In the Streiffert printer (Fig. 47), light from a single lamp is divided into three beams which are individually filtered, controlled in intensity by rotating vanes, and projected onto the printer aperture. Control is by means of punch holes in a control filmstrip which can also be adapted for scene testing.[220] The Debrie Matipo step color printer likewise employs the additive color-mixture principle effected by the use of a line screen control matte in combination with prismatic lenses and three filter elements (Fig. 48).[50]

It is customary to check the intensity and color quality at the printer aperture with a suitable photocell using standardized filters.[218] Notching of the film for scene changes is avoided by painting the edge of the film at intervals with a conducting paint which serves to actuate a solenoid.

For scene testing, the color positive may be exposed through the negative with a range of color-correcting filters under conditions which correspond to the printer exposure times, intensity and color balance. Typical scene testers include the Reeves, Houston-Fearless and the Herrnfeld instruments. The latter employs a curved platen with sixteen filter variants and the light, modulated by varying apertures, is directed to the film by a rotating mirror which scans the curved printing platen (Fig. 49).

The Future

The work of the motion-picture laboratory is becoming more and more technical, requiring the combined efforts of mechanical engineers, chemists and physicists to produce pictures having the maximum definition and photographic quality of which the film is capable, in the shortest possible time and at the least cost.

The significant growth of 16mm film in the professional field, and especially that of television, combined with the demands of color processing, will necessitate greater refinement of laboratory mechanisms and procedures in the future but I am sure that the facilities which our Society is providing for cooperative effort will contribute greatly to attainment of these goals.

The author wishes to acknowledge the assistance of his colleagues, C. E. Ives and A. R. Turner, in the preparation of this paper.

Discussion

John G. Frayne (Westrex Corp.): I saw no reference to the Western Electric 1100A Densitometer which was introduced around 1940, I believe, and which played a great part in standardizing sensitometry and the processing of variable-density films as well as black-and-white pictures. I believe this instrument should have some reference in the paper.

Mr. Crabtree: I gave a reference to that, although I didn't show an illustration.

E. W. Kellogg (Consulting Engineer, formerly of RCA): How large a part in the overall picture of sound printing was played by the nonslip printer, first brought to public attention through the work of C. N. Batsel about 1932?

Mr. Crabtree: The nonslip principle has not played a very important part in the evolution of the laboratory and, so far as I know, is not currently employed. Although the films do not tend to slip longitudinally, they may periodically slip laterally.

Mr. Kellogg: May I add an item to what you just said? A recent letter I had from Art Blaney was to the effect that although the nonslip printers were not very widely used, and displaced other types of printer only in a few laboratories, they did, by demonstrating what they could do with variable-area tracks in the way of improving definition, force refinements and better performance of sound printers throughout the industry.

Sidney P. Solow (Consolidated Film Industries): I think your paper helps point out that rather than being an adjunct, the laboratory is really the nucleus of a motion-picture enterprise and that if a country somewhere in the world would like to establish a native motion-picture industry they had better first consider establishing a laboratory.

BIBLIOGRAPHY

AGITATION, DEVELOPER

1. J. Crabtree, "Directional effects in continuous film processing," *Jour. SMPE, 18:* 207, Feb. 1932.
2. J. Crabtree, "Uniformity in photographic development," *Jour. SMPE, 25:* 512, Dec. 1935.
3. C. E. Ives and C. J. Kunz, "Solution agitation by means of compressed air," *Jour. SMPE, 34:* 364, Apr. 1940.
4. J. I. Crabtree and C. H. Schwingel, "Effect of aeration on the photographic properties of developers," *Jour. SMPE, 34:* 375, Apr. 1940.
5. B. C. Sewell, "The directional effect in machine development," *J. Brit. Kinemat. Soc., 3:* 84, Apr. 1940.
6. M. S. Leshing, T. M. Ingman and K. Pier, "Reduction of development sprocket-hole modulation," *Jour. SMPE, 36:* 475, May 1941.
7. C. E. Ives and E. W. Jensen, "The effect of developer agitation on density uniformity and rate of development," *Jour. SMPE, 40:* 107, Feb. 1943.
8. M. S. Leshing and T. M. Ingman, "Some turbulation characteristics of the new Twentieth Century-Fox Developing Machine," *Jour. SMPE, 44:* 97, Feb. 1945.
9. G. I. P. Levenson, "Chemical economics of spray processing," *Jour. SMPE, 53:* 665, Dec. 1949.
10. C. E. Ives, "The application of treating liquids and drying air in photographic processing," *Phot. Eng., 2:* No. 3, 116, 1951.

AIR CONDITIONING

11. D. C. Lindsay, "Air conditioning as applied in theaters and film laboratories," *Trans. SMPE,* No. 11, 334, Aug. 1927.
12. A. H. Simonds and L. H. Polderman, "Air conditioning in film laboratories," *Jour. SMPE, 17:* 604, Oct. 1931.
13. E. C. Holden, "Silica gel air-conditioning for film processing," *Jour. SMPE, 18:* 471, Apr. 1932.

ANALYSES (CHEMICAL), OF PROCESSING SOLUTIONS

14. R. M. Evans and W. T. Hanson, Jr., "Chemical analysis of an MQ developer," *Jour. SMPE, 32:* 307, Mar. 1939.
15. H. L. Baumbach, "Chemical analysis of hydroquinone, metol, and bromide in a photographic developer," *Jour. SMPE, 33:* 517, Nov. 1939.
16. R. B. Atkinson and V. C. Shaner, "Chemical analysis of photographic developers and fixing baths," *Jour. SMPE, 34:* 485, May 1940.
17. R. M. Evans, W. T. Hanson, Jr. and P. K. Glasoe, "Synthetic aged developers by analysis," *Jour. SMPE, 38:* 188, Feb. 1942.
18. J. G. Stott, "Application of potentiometric methods of developer analysis," *Jour. SMPE, 39:* 37, July 1942.
19. W. R. Crowell, W. W. Luke and H. L. Baumbach, "Potentiometric determination of bromide in the presence of chloride in photographic developer solutions," *Jour. SMPE, 44:* 472, June 1945.
20. V. C. Shaner and M. R. Sparks, "Application of the Polarograph to the analysis of photographic fixing baths," *Jour. SMPE, 45:* 20, July 1945.
21. H. L. Baumbach, "An improved method for the determination of hydroquinone and metol in photographic developers," *Jour. SMPE, 47:* 403, Nov. 1946.
22. V. C. Shaner and M. R. Sparks, "Application of methyl ethyl ketone to the analysis of developers for elon and hydroquinone," *Jour. SMPE, 47:* 409, Nov. 1946.
23. G. I. P. Levenson, "Controlling the elon-hydroquinone developer," *Brit. Kinemat., 12:* No. 2, 37, Feb. 1948.

24. A. H. Brunner, P. B. Means and R. H. Zappert, "Analysis of developers and bleach for Ansco Color Film," *Jour. SMPE, 53: 25,* July 1949.
25. H. L. Rees and D. H. Anderson, "Simultaneous determination of elon and hydroquinone in photographic developers," *Jour. SMPE, 53:* 268, Sept. 1949.

APPARATUS (PROCESSING)

26. J. I. Crabtree and C. E. Ives, "Improvements in motion picture laboratory apparatus," *Trans. SMPE,* No. 18, 161, May 1924.
27. J. I. Crabtree and C. E. Ives, "A pneumatic film squeegee," *Trans. SMPE,* No. 11, 270, Aug. 1927.
28. C. E. Ives, A. J. Miller and J. I. Crabtree, "Improvements in motion picture laboratory apparatus," *Jour. SMPE, 17:* 26, July 1931.
29. J. A. Dubray, "The evolution of motion picture film processing apparatuses," *Cinemat. Ann., vol. 2:* 271, 1931.
30. C. E. Ives, "A roller developing rack for continuously moving the film during processing by the rack-and-tank system," *Jour. SMPE, 24:* 261, Mar. 1935.
31. "The Davidge Developing Apparatus," *Jour. SMPE, 24:* 452, May 1935.
32. C. E. Ives, "An improved roller type developing rack with stationary drive," *Jour. SMPE, 31:* 393, Oct. 1938.
33. R. S. Leonard, "A reel and tray developing machine," *Jour. SMPE, 34:* 168, Feb. 1940.
34. B. Robinson and M. S. Leshing, "New gadgets for the film laboratory," *Jour. SMPE, 37:* 274, Sept. 1941.
35. C. E. Ives and C. J. Kunz, "The flat spiral reel for processing 50-foot lengths of film," *Jour. SMPE, 42:* 349, June 1944.
36. G. I. P. Levenson, "New Debrie processing machine," *Funct. Phot., vol. 2:* 13, Sept. 1951.
37. F. D. Miller, "Rapid drying of normally processed black-and-white motion picture film," *Jour. SMPTE, 60:* 85, Feb. 1953.

CLEANING

38. T. Faulkner, "Cleaning motion picture positive film," *Trans. SMPE,* No. 25, 117, Sept. 1926.
39. J. I. Crabtree and H. C. Carlton, "Cleaning liquids for motion picture film," *Trans. SMPE,* No. 11, 277, Aug. 1927.
40. A. S. Dworsky, "The Dworsky film-renovating machine, polishing machine, and film rewind," *Trans. SMPE,* No. 11, 774, Sept. 1927.

COLOR FILM, PROCESSING

41. W. V. D. Kelley, "The Handschiegl and Pathéchrome Color Processes," *Jour. SMPE, 17:* 230, Aug. 1931.
42. E. R. Davies, "The Kodachrome process of 16-mm colour kinematography," *Phot. J.* (Roy. Phot. Soc.), *76:* 248, Apr. 1936.
43. J. L. Forrest, "Machine processing of 16-mm Ansco Color Film," *Jour. SMPE, 45:* 313, Nov. 1945.
44. J. E. Bates and I. V. Runyan, "Processing color procedures for Ansco Color Film," *Jour. SMPE, 53:* 3, July 1949.
45. A. B. Jennings, W. A. Stanton and J. P. Weiss, "Synthetic color-forming binders for photographic emulsions," *Jour. SMPTE, 55:* 455, Nov. 1950.
46. W. Hedden, T. Weaver and L. Thompson, "Processing of 16-mm Kodachrome Prints," *Jour. SMPTE, 57:* 308, Oct. 1951.
47. W. T. Hanson, Jr., "Color negative and color positive film for motion picture use," *Jour. SMPTE, 58:* 223, Mar. 1952.
48. H. H. Duerr, "The Ansco color negative-positive process," *Jour. SMPTE, 58:* 465, June 1952.

49. C. R. Anderson, N. H. Groet, C. A. Horton and D. M. Zwick, "An intermediate positive-internegative system for color motion-picture photography," *Jour. SMPTE, 60:* 217, Mar. 1953.
50. R. H. Cricks, "New processing equipment for colour film," *Funct. Phot., 5:* 10, Oct. 1953.

CONSTRUCTION MATERIALS

51. J. I. Crabtree, G. E. Matthews and J. F. Ross, "Materials for the construction of motion picture processing apparatus," *Jour. SMPE, 26:* 330, Mar. 1931.
52. W. M. Mitchell, "Applications of stainless steels in the motion picture industry," *Jour. SMPE, 24:* 346, Apr. 1935.
53. R. L. Foote, "Laminated Bakelite in the motion picture industry," *Jour. SMPE, 24:* 354, Apr. 1935.
54. F. L. LaQue, "Inconel as a material for photographic film processing apparatus," *Jour. SMPE, 24:* 357, Apr. 1935.
55. F. L. LaQue, "Some general characteristics of chromium-nickel-iron alloys as corrosion-resisting materials," *Jour. SMPE, 32:* 505, May 1939.
56. B. H. Thompson, "Present and proposed uses of plastics in the motion picture industry," *Jour. SMPE, 43:* 106, Aug. 1944.
57. L. E. Muehler and J. I. Crabtree, "The relative corrosion effect on stainless steels of rapid fixing baths containing ammonium chloride and ammonium sulfate," *PSA Jour., 13:* 30, Jan. 1947.
58. A. B. Everest and F. Hudson, "Metals in kinema and related equipment," *Brit. Kinemat., 12:* 109, Apr. 1948.
59. L. E. Muehler and J. I. Crabtree, "Materials of construction for photographic processing equipment," *PSA Jour.* (*Phot. Sci. & Tech.*), *vol. 19B:* No. 2, 79, May 1953; *ibid., vol. 19B:* No. 3, 92, Aug. 1953.

DEFECTS

60. J. I. Crabtree and G. E. Matthews, "A study of the markings on motion picture film produced by drops of water, condensed water vapor and abnormal drying conditions," *Trans. SMPE,* No. 17, 29, Oct. 1923.
61. J. I. Crabtree and C. E. Ives, "Rack marks and airbell markings on motion picture film," *Trans. SMPE,* No. 24, 95, Oct. 1925.
62. J. I. Crabtree and G. E. Matthews, "Oil spots on motion picture film," *Trans. SMPE,* No. 11, 728, Sept. 1927.
63. J. I. Crabtree and G. E. Matthews, "Effect of the water supply in processing motion picture film," *Jour. SMPE, 16:* 437, Apr. 1931.
64. R. W. Henn and J. I. Crabtree, "Calcium scums and sludges in photography," *Jour. SMPE, 43:* 426, Dec. 1944.

DENSITOMETERS

65. J. G. Capstaff and N. B. Green, "A motion picture densitometer," *Trans. SMPE,* No. 17, 154, Oct. 1923.
66. J. G. Capstaff and R. A. Purdy, "A compact motion picture densitometer," *Trans. SMPE,* No. 11, 607, Sept. 1927.
67. F. L. Eich, "A physical densitometer for sound processing laboratories," *Jour. SMPE, 24:* 180, Feb. 1935.
68. C. M. Tuttle, "A recording physical densitometer," *J. Opt. Soc. Am., 26:* 282, July 1936.
69. C. M. Tuttle and M. E. Russell, "Note on the use of an automatic recording densitometer," *Jour. SMPE, 28:* 99, Jan. 1937.
70. W. W. Lindsay and W. V. Wolfe, "A wide range, linear-scale photoelectric cell densitometer," *Jour. SMPE, 28:* 622, June 1937.
71. R. M. Evans, "Color densitometer for subtractive processes," *Jour. SMPE, 31:* 194, Aug. 1938.

72. D. R. White, "A direct reading photoelectric densitometer," *Jour. SMPE, 33:* 403, Oct. 1939.
73. J. G. Frayne and G. R. Crane, "A precision integrating sphere densitometer," *Jour. SMPE, 35:* 184, Aug. 1940.
74. J. G. Frayne, "Measurement of photographic printing density," *Jour. SMPE, 36:* 622, June 1941.
75. M. H. Sweet, "Precision direct-reading densitometer," *Jour. SMPE, 38:* 148, Feb. 1942.
76. J. G. Frayne and G. R. Crane, "Automatic recording of photographic densities," *Jour. SMPE, 45:* 370, Nov. 1945.
77. A. F. Thiels, "A direct-reading equivalent densitometer," *Jour. SMPE, 56:* 13, Jan. 1951.
78. G. Barnes, "An automatic recording photographic densitometer," *J. Opt. Soc. Am., 43:* 1176, Dec. 1953.

DENSITOMETERS (COLOR)
79. R. M. Evans, "A color densitometer for subtractive processes," *Jour. SMPE, 31:* 194, Aug. 1938.
80. M. H. Sweet, "The densitometry of modern reversible color film," *Jour. SMPE, 44:* 419, June 1945.
81. M. H. Sweet, "An improved photomultiplier tube color densitometer," *Jour. SMPTE, 54:* 35, Jan. 1950.
82. A. C. Lapsley and J. P. Weiss, "A versatile densitometer for color films," *Jour. SMPTE, 56:* 23, Jan. 1951.
83. "Color densitometer," Photo Research Corp., *Jour. SMPTE, 57:* 400, Oct. 1951.
84. F. P. Herrnfeld, "Integrating-type color densitometer," *Jour. SMPTE, 59:* 184, Sept. 1952.
85. K. G. Macleish, "Transmission densitometer for color films," *Jour. SMPTE, 60:* 696, June 1953.

DEVELOPERS AND REPLENISHMENT
86. J. I. Crabtree and M. L. Dundon, "Investigations on photographic developers. Sulfide fog by bacteria in motion picture developers," *Trans. SMPE,* No. 19, 28, Sept. 1924.
87. J. I. Crabtree, "The handling of motion picture film at high temperatures," *Trans. SMPE,* No. 19, 39, Sept. 1924.
88. J. I. Crabtree and M. L. Dundon, "The staining properties of motion picture developers," *Trans. SMPE,* No. 25, 108, Sept. 1926.
89. J. I. Crabtree and M. L. Dundon, "Investigations on photographic developers. The effect of desensitizers in development," *Trans. SMPE,* No. 26, 111, Nov. 1926.
90. M. L. Dundon and J. I. Crabtree, "The fogging properties of developers," *Trans. SMPE,* No. 36, 1096, Sept. 1928.
91. H. C. Carlton and J. I. Crabtree, "Some properties of fine grain developers for motion picture film," *Trans. SMPE,* No. 13, 406, May 1929.
92. H. W. Moyse and D. R. White, "Borax developer characteristics," *Trans. SMPE,* No. 13, 445, May 1929.
93. J. I. Crabtree and C. E. Ives, "A replenishing solution for a motion picture positive film developer," *Jour. SMPE, 15:* 627, Nov. 1930.
94. R. M. Evans, "Maintenance of a developer by continuous replenishment," *Jour. SMPE, 31:* 273, Sept. 1938.
95. J. I. Crabtree and R. W. Henn, "An improved fine grain developer formula," *PSA Jour., 4:* 1, 1938.
96. J. I. Crabtree and G. E. Matthews, *Photographic Chemicals and Solutions,* American Photographic Publishing Co., Boston, Mass., 1939.
97. H. L. Baumbach, "Continuous replenishment and chemical control of motion picture developing solutions," *Jour. SMPE, 39:* 55, July 1942.

98. H. A. Miller, R. W. Henn, and J. I. Crabtree, "Methods of increasing film speed," *PSA Jour. 12:* 586, Nov. 1946.
99. A. A. Rasch and J. I. Crabtree, "Development of motion-picture positive film by vanadous ion," *Jour. SMPTE, 62:* 1, Jan. 1954.

DUPLICATION
100. Booklet: *Eastman Duplicating Film—Its Properties and Uses,* Eastman Kodak Co., Rochester, N.Y., Jan. 1927.
101. J. G. Capstaff and M. W. Seymour, "The duplication of motion picture negatives," *Trans. SMPE,* No. 28, 223, Feb. 1927.
102. C. E. Ives and E. Huse, "Notes on making duplicate negatives," *Trans. SMPE,* No. 34, 382, Apr. 1928.
103. O. B. Depue, "Machinery for making duplicate negatives," *Trans. SMPE,* No. 12, 1170, Sept. 1928.
104. J. I. Crabtree and C. H. Schwingel, "The duplication of motion picture negatives," *Jour. SMPE, 19:* 891, July 1932.
105. C. E. Ives and J. I. Crabtree, "Two new films for duplicating work," *Jour. SMPE, 29:* 317, Sept. 1937.
106. W. H. Offenhauser, Jr., "Some notes on the duplication of 16-mm integral tripack color films," *Jour. SMPE, 45:* 113, Aug. 1945.
107. N. L. Simmons and E. Huse, "Current black-and-white duplicating techniques used in Hollywood," *Jour. SMPE, 49:* 316, Oct. 1947.

EDITING
108. G. E. Hoglund, "Apparatus for preparing moving picture films," U.S. Pat. 971,889, Oct. 4, 1910.
109. F. D. Williams, "Methods of blooping," *Jour. SMPE, 30:* 105, Jan. 1938.
110. W. H. Offenhauser, Jr., "Current practices in blooping sound-film," *Jour. SMPE, 35:* 165, Aug. 1940.
111. I. J. Wilkinson and W. H. Hamilton "Motion picture editing," *Jour. SMPE, 36:* 101, Jan. 1941.
112. L. A. Elmer, "A non-cinching film rewind machine," *Jour. SMPE, 37:* 418, Oct. 1941.
113. H. A. Witt, "Practical aspect of edge-numbering 16-mm film," *Jour. SMPE, 39:* 67, July 1942.
114. F. Y. Smith, "Cutting and editing of motion pictures," *Jour. SMPE, 39:* 284, Nov. 1942.
115. L. Sherwood, "Editing and photographic embellishments as applied to 16-mm industrial and educational motion pictures," *Jour. SMPE, 41:* 476, Dec. 1943.
116. L. Thompson, "16-mm edge-numbering machine," *Jour. SMPE, 45:* 109, Aug. 1945.

FIXING
117. J. I. Crabtree and H. A. Hartt, "Some properties of fixing baths," *Trans. SMPE,* No. 38, 364, May, 1929.
118. J. I. Crabtree and H. D. Russell, "Some properties of chrome alum stop baths and fixing baths—Part I," *Jour. SMPE, 14:* 483, May 1930; Part II, *ibid., 14:* 667, June 1930.
119. J. I. Crabtree, L. E. Muehler and H. D. Russell, "New stop bath and fixing bath formulas and methods for their revival," *Jour. SMPE, 38:* 353, Apr. 1942.
120. D. B. Alnutt, "Some characteristics of ammonium thiosulfate fixing baths," *Jour. SMPE, 41:* 300, Oct. 1943.

HISTORY, EARLY
121. C. E. K. Mees, "A new substandard film for amateur cinematography," *Trans. SMPE,* No. 16, 252, May 1923.
122. G. Coissac, *Histoire du cinématographe,* Gauthier Villars, Paris, 1925, p. 309.
123. C. L. Gregory, "Early history of motion picture cameras for film wider than 35-mm," *Jour. SMPE, 14:* 27, Jan. 1930.
124. E. K. Scott, "Career of L. A. A. LePrince," *Jour. SMPE, 17:* 46, July 1931.

125. A. C. Bromhead, "Reminiscences of the British film trade," *Proc. Brit. Kinemat. Soc., 21:* 12, 1933.
126. E. R. Theisen, "The history of nitrocellulose as a film base," *Jour. SMPE, 20:* 259, Mar. 1933.
127. W. K. L. Dickson, "A brief history of the Kinetograph, the Kinetoscope and the Kineto-Phonograph," *Jour. SMPE, 21:* 435, Dec. 1933.
128. R. W. Paul, C. M. Hepworth and W. G. Barker, "Before 1910 kinematograph experiences," *Proc. Brit. Kinemat. Soc.,* No. 38, 9, 1936.
129. O. Messter, *Mein weg mit dem film,* Schoneberg, Paris, 1936.
130. R. W. Paul, "Kinematographic experiences," *Jour. SMPE, 27:* 495, Nov. 1936.
131. L. Lumière, "The Lumière cinematograph," *Jour. SMPE, 27:* 640, Dec. 1936.
132. W. E. Theisen, "Pioneering in the talking picture," *Jour. SMPE, 36:* 415, Apr. 1941.
133. Jean Vivié, *Traité général de technique du cinéma. Vol. I—Historique et développement de la technique cinématographique,* Editions B. P. I., Paris, 1946.
134. R. H. Cricks, "British influence in the technical development of kinematography," *Brit. Kinemat., 11:* 1, July, 1947.
135. G. Sadoul, *Les pionniers du cinéma,* Editions Denoel, Paris, 1949, p. 282.
136. A. Cornwell-Clyne, *Colour cinematography,* Chapman & Hall, London, 3rd edition, 1951.
137. J. I. Crabtree, "The development of motion picture film by the reel and tank systems," *Trans. SMPE,* No. 16, 163, May 1923.
138. L. M. Griffith, "The technical status of the film laboratory," *Trans. SMPE,* No. 33: 173, Apr. 1928.
139. T. E. Shea, "A modern laboratory for the study of sound picture problems," *Jour. SMPE, 16:* 277, Mar. 1931.
140. B. Burns, "The multicolor laboratory," *Jour. SMPE, 17:* 11, July 1931.
141. I. D. Wratten, "Motion picture film processing in Great Britain," *Jour. SMPE, 26:* 204, Feb. 1936.
142. Report of Committee on Laboratory Practice, D. E. Hyndman, Chairman, *Jour. SMPE, 26:* 345, Apr. 1936.
143. C. L. Lootens, "A modern motion picture laboratory," *Jour. SMPE, 30:* 363, Apr. 1938.
144. G. M. Best and F. R. Gage, "A modern studio laboratory," *Jour. SMPE, 35:* 294, Sept. 1940.
145. J. R. Wilkinson, "Motion picture laboratory practices," *Jour. SMPE, 39:* 166, Sept. 1942.
146. L. Thompson, "Practical side of direct 16-mm laboratory work," *Jour. SMPE, 41:* 101, July 1943.
147. W. H. Offenhauser, Jr., "A 16-mm commercial film laboratory," *Jour. SMPE, 41:* 157, Aug. 1943.
148. W. H. Offenhauser, Jr., *16-mm Sound Motion Pictures,* Interscience Publishers, New York, N.Y., 1949.
149. H. C. Harsh and K. Schadlich, "Laboratory for development work on color motion pictures," *Jour. SMPE, 53:* 50, July 1949.
149a. C. E. K. Mees, "History of professional black-and-white motion-picture film, *Jour. SMPTE, 63:* 134, Oct. 1954.

MACHINES, PROCESSING
150. R. C. Hubbard, "Erbograph machine. A friction feed developing machine for developing positive motion picture film," *Trans. SMPE,* No. 17, 163, Oct. 1923.
151. R. C. Hubbard, "The straight line developing machine," *Trans. SMPE,* No. 18, 73, May 1924.
152. A. B. Hitchins, "Machine development of negative and positive motion picture film," *Trans. SMPE,* No. 22, 46, May 1925.
153. C. R. Hunter, "Developer perfected," *Am. Cinemat., 8:* 17, Feb. 1928.

154. C. R. Hunter, "A negative developing machine," *Trans. SMPE*, No. 33, 195, Apr. 1928.

155. H. J. Jamieson, "A horizontal tray type of continuous processing machine," *Trans. SMPE*, No. 36, 1093, Sept. 1928.

156. C. R. Hunter and R. M. Pierce, "A method for quantity developing of motion picture films," *Jour. SMPE*, 17: 954, Dec. 1931.

157. H. D. Hineline, "Continuous photographic processing," *Jour. SMPE*, 26: 38, Jan. 1936.

158. W. Stull, "The Paramount transparency air-turbine developing machine," *Am. Cinemat.*, 17: 236, June 1936.

159. A. Reeves, "Laboratory equipment for the smaller laboratory," *Jour. SMPE*, 29: 446, Oct. 1937.

160. J. M. Blaney, "A new 16-mm film developing machine," *Jour. SMPE*, 32: 495, May 1939.

161. J. F. VanLeuven, "Simplifying and controlling film travel through a developing machine," *Jour. SMPE*, 33: 583, Nov. 1939.

162. W. G. C. Bosco, "An all-friction drive for developing machines," *Am. Cinemat.*, 26: 122, Apr. 1945.

163. R. P. Ireland, "A motion picture film developing machine," *Jour. SMPE*, 50: 50, Jan. 1948.

164. G. I. P. Levenson, "An experimental processing machine," *Kinemat. Weekly*, 392: No. 2217, 41, Oct. 27, 1949.

165. A. M. Gundelfinger, "Cinecolor three-color process," *Jour. SMPTE*, 54: 74, Jan. 1950.

166. R. H. Bomback, "Agfacolor process," *Funct. Phot.*, 1: No. 4, 15, Jan. 1950.

167. J. S. Hall, A. Mayer and G. Maslach, "A 16-mm rapid film processor," *Jour. SMPTE*, 55: 27, July 1950.

168. H. E. Hewston and C. H. Elmer, "Continuous processing machine for wide film," *Jour. SMPTE*, 56: 613, June 1951.

169. A. L. Holcomb, "Film-spool drive with torque motors," *Jour. SMPTE*, 58: 28, Jan. 1952.

170. J. W. Kaylor and A. V. Pesek, "Cinecolor multilayer color developing machine," *Jour. SMPTE*, 58: 53, Jan. 1952.

171. J. A. Tanney and E. B. Krause, "The Bridgamatic developing machine," *Jour. SMPTE*, 60: 260, Mar. 1953.

MAGNETIC STRIPING

172. S. J. Begun, "Recent developments in the field of magnetic recording," *Jour. SMPE*, 48: 1, Jan. 1947.

173. M. Camras, "Magnetic sound for motion pictures," *Jour. SMPE*, 48: 14, Jan. 1947.

174. M. Camras, "Recent developments in magnetic recording for motion picture film," *J. Acoust. Soc. Am.*, 19: 322, Mar. 1947.

175. E. Schmidt and E. W. Franck, "Manufacture of magnetic recording materials," *Jour. SMPTE*, 60: 453, Apr. 1953.

176. E. Schmidt, "Commercial experiences with Magnastripe," *Jour. SMPTE*, 60: 463, Apr. 1953.

177. B. L. Kaspin, A. Roberts, Jr., H. Robbins and R. L. Powers, "Magnetic striping techniques and characteristics," *Jour. SMPTE*, 60: 470, Apr. 1953.

178. T. R. Dedell, "Magnetic sound tracks for processed 16-mm motion picture film," *Jour. SMPTE*, 60: 491, Apr. 1953.

PRESERVATION AND STORAGE

179. J. I. Crabtree and J. F. Ross, "A method of testing for the presence of sodium thiosulfate in motion picture film," *Jour. SMPE*, 14: 419, Apr. 1930.

180. J. I. Crabtree and C. E. Ives, "The storage of valuable motion picture film," *Jour. SMPE*, 15: 298, Sept. 1930.

181. J. A. Norling and A. P. Rippenbein, "Treatment for rejuvenating and preserving motion picture film," *Jour. SMPE*, 16: 766, June 1931.

182. E. W. Fowler and L. B. Newell, "Storage and handling of motion picture film," *Jour. SMPE*, 16: 773, June 1931.

183. J. R. Hill and C. G. Weber, "Stability of motion picture films as determined by accelerated aging," *Jour. SMPE*, 27: 677, Dec. 1936.

184. J. G. Bradley, "Changing aspects of the film-storage problem," *Jour. SMPE*, 30: 303, Mar. 1938.

185. J. E. Gibson and C. G. Weber, "Evaluation of motion picture films by semimicro testing," *Jour. SMPE*, 32: 105, Jan. 1939.

186. Report of the Committee on Preservation of Film, *Jour. SMPE*, 35: 584, Dec. 1940.

187. R. H. Talbot, "New treatment for the prevention of film abrasion and oil mottle," *Jour. SMPE*, 36: 191, Feb. 1941.

188. J. I. Crabtree, G. T. Eaton and L. E. Muehler, "A review of hypo testing methods," *Jour. SMPE*, 42: 34, Jan. 1944.

189. W. H. Offenhauser, Jr., "A plan for preserving 16-mm originals of educational films," *Jour. SMPE*, 43: 418, Dec. 1944.

190. G. L. Sarchet, "Preservation and postwar utilization of U.S. Navy combat film," *Jour. SMPE*, 48: 476, May 1947.

191. J. G. Bradley, "Film vaults: construction and use," *Jour. SMPE*, 53: 193, Aug. 1949.

192. H. G. Brown, "Problems of storing film for archive purposes," *Brit. Kinemat.*, 20: 150, May 1952.

193. American Standard Method for Determining the Thiosulfate Content of Processed Photographic Film, PH4.8-1953, ASA, New York, N.Y.

PRINTERS

194. O. B. Depue, "A daylight optical reduction printer," *Trans. SMPE*, No. 28, 242, Feb. 1927.

195. A. B. Hitchins, "Duplex optical printers," *Trans. SMPE*, No. 32, 771, Sept. 1927.

196. C. L. Gregory, "An optical printer for trick work," *Trans. SMPE*, No. 34, 419, Apr. 1928.

197. O. B. Depue, "Machinery for making duplicate negatives," *Trans. SMPE*, No. 36, 1170, Sept. 1928.

198. O. B. Depue, "A printer for simultaneous printing of sound and picture negatives," *Trans. SMPE*, No. 37, 150, May 1929.

199. O. B. Depue, "A machine for printing picture and sound simultaneously and automatically," *Jour. SMPE*, 18: 643, May 1932.

200. R. V. Wood, "A shrinkage-compensating sound printer," *Jour. SMPE*, 18: 788, June 1932.

201. A. S. Howell, B. E. Stechbart and R. F. Mitchell, "The Bell & Howell fully automatic sound picture production printer," *Jour. SMPE*, 19: 305, Oct. 1932.

202. A. S. Howell and R. F. Mitchell, "Recent improvements in the Bell & Howell fully automatic printer," *Jour. SMPE*, 22: 115, Feb. 1934.

203. A. F. Victor, "Continuous optical reduction printing," *Jour. SMPE*, 23: 96, Aug. 1934.

204. C. N. Batsel, "A non-slip sound printer," *Jour. SMPE*, 23: 100, Aug. 1934.

205. O. Sandvik and J. G. Streiffert, "A continuous optical reduction sound printer," *Jour. SMPE*, 25: 117, Aug. 1935.

206. D. H. Geary, "The Vinten Dufaycolor printer," *J. Brit. Kinemat. Soc.*, 2: No. 3, 185, July 1939.

207. The Bell & Howell 35-mm non-slip sound printer," *Jour. SMPE*, 33: 125, Aug. 1939.

208. L. S. Dunn, "The new Acme-Dunn optical printer," *Jour. SMPE*, 42: 204, Apr. 1944.

209. C. W. Clutz, F. E. Altman and J. G. Streiffert, "35-mm to 16-mm sound reduction printer," *Jour. SMPE*, 52: 669, June 1949.

210. F. P. Herrnfeld, "Printing equipment for Ansco color film," *Jour. SMPTE*, 54: 454, Apr. 1950.

PRINTING METHODS

211. W. E. Story, Jr., "Actinic measurements in the exposing and printing of motion picture film," *Trans. SMPE*, No. 13, 106, Oct. 1921.

212. R. C. Hubbard, "Printing motion picture film," *Trans. SMPE*, No. 28, 252, Feb. 1927.

213. J. Crabtree, "Sound film printing," *Jour. SMPE*, 21: 294, Oct. 1933; *ibid.*, 22: 98, Feb. 1934.

214. G. L. Dimmick, C. N. Batsel and L. T. Sachtleben, "Optical reduction sound printing," *Jour. SMPE*, 23: 108, Aug. 1934.

215. G. L. Dimmick, "Improved resolution in sound recording and printing by the use of ultraviolet light," *Jour. SMPE*, 27: 168, Aug. 1936.

216. P. S. Aex, "A photoelectric method for determining color balance of 16-mm Kodachrome duplicating printers," *Jour. SMPE*, 49: 425, Nov. 1947.

217. F. LaGrande, C. R. Daily and B. H. Denney, "16-mm release printing using 35- and 32-mm film," *Jour. SMPE*, 52: 211, Feb. 1949.

218. C. A. Horton, "Printer control in color printing," *Jour. SMPTE*, 58: 239, Mar. 1952.

219. R. L. Sutton, K. B. Curtis and L. Thompson, "Prints from 16mm originals," *Jour. SMPTE*, 58: 145, Feb. 1952.

220. J. G. Streiffert, "A fast-acting exposure control system for color motion picture printing," *Jour. SMPTE*, 59: 410, Nov. 1952.

PROCESSING

221. J. Lachenbruch, "German efficiency in their laboratories," *M. P. News*, 26: No. 24, 2958, Dec. 9, 1922.

222. Report of Committee on Film and Emulsions, *Trans. SMPE*, No. 16, 274, May 1923.

223. L. A. Jones and J. I. Crabtree, "Panchromatic negative film for motion pictures," *Trans. SMPE*, No. 27, 131, Jan. 1927.

224. V. A. Stewart, "Improvements in laboratory practice," *Trans. SMPE*, No. 32, 651, Sept. 1927.

225. R. F. Nicholson, "The processing of variable-density sound records," *Jour. SMPE*, 15: 374, Sept. 1930.

226. J. Crabtree, "Directional effects in continuous film processing," *Jour. SMPE*, 18: 207, Feb. 1932.

227. Report of the Progress Committee, *Jour. SMPE*, 19: 134, Aug. 1932.

228. J. Crabtree and J. H. Waddell, "Directional effects in sound-film processing, Part II," *Jour. SMPE*, 21: 351, Nov. 1933.

229. J. Crabtree, "Uniformity in photographic development," *Jour. SMPE*, 25: 512, Dec. 1935.

230. *Motion Picture Laboratory Practice*, Eastman Kodak Co., Rochester, N.Y., 1936.

231. I. D. Wratten, "Motion picture film laboratory practice," *Proc. Brit. Kinemat. Soc.*, No. 41, 1936.

232. L. J. Wheeler, *Principles of Cinematography*, Fountain Press, London, 1953.

PROCESSING CONTROL

233. E. Huse, "Sensitometric control in the processing of motion picture film in Hollywood," *Jour. SMPE*, 21: 54, July 1933.

234. G. A. Chambers and I. D. Wratten, "The Eastman Type IIb Sensitometer as a control instrument in the processing of motion picture film," *Jour. SMPE*, 21: 218, Sept. 1933.

235. H. L. Baumbach, "Continuous replenishment and chemical control of motion picture developing solutions," *Jour. SMPE*, 39: 55, July 1942.

236. R. H. Bomback, "The chemical control of processing solutions," *Brit. Kinemat.*, 20: 119, Apr. 1952.

237. R. H. Bomback, "Technical control in the film processing laboratory," *Brit. Kinemat.*, 20: 142, May 1952.

RAPID PROCESSING

238. H. Parker, Jr. and J. I. Crabtree, "Rapid processing methods," *Jour. SMPE, 26:* 406, Apr. 1936.
239. F. E. Tuttle and C. H. Green, "Photographic race-timing equipment," *Jour. SMPE, 27:* 529, Nov. 1936.
240. H. A. Miller, J. I. Crabtree and H. D. Russell, "A prehardening bath for high-temperature processing," *PSA Jour. 10:* 397 and 453, Sept. and Oct. 1944.
241. J. I. Crabtree and H. D. Russell, "Rapid processing of photographic materials," *PSA Jour., 10:* No. 9, 541, Nov. 1944.
242. R. Hodgson, "Theatre television system," *Jour. SMPE, 52:* 540, May 1949.
243. C. E. Ives and C. J. Kunz, "Simplification of motion picture processing methods," *Jour. SMPTE, 55:* 3, July 1950.
244. J. S. Hall, A. Mayer and G. Maslach, "A 16-mm rapid film processor," *Jour. SMPTE, 55:* 27, July 1950.
245. R. L. Garman and B. Foulds, "Some commercial aspects of a new 16-mm intermediate film television system," *Jour. SMPTE, 56:* 219, Feb. 1951.
246. R. Hodgson and J. Hammer, "High-temperature film processing—its effect on quality," *Jour. SMPTE, 56:* 261, Mar. 1951.
247. L. Katz, "Ultrarapid drying of motion picture film by means of turbulent air," *Jour. SMPTE, 56:* 264, Mar. 1951.

REVERSAL PROCESSING

248. H. V. Verkinderen, "Reversal processing," *Brit. Kinemat., 13:* 37, Aug. 1948.
249. H. A. Miller, H. D. Russell and J. I. Crabtree, "Direct-positive processing of the new Kodak blue base reversal films," *PSA Jour., 15:* 382, June 1949.

SCENE TESTING

250. L. A. Jones and J. I. Crabtree, "A new sensitometer for the determination of exposure in positive printing," *Trans. SMPE,* No. 15, 89, Oct. 1922.
251. C. E. Ives and J. I. Crabtree, "A trial and error method of preparing a motion picture sensitometer tablet," *Trans. SMPE,* No. 32, 740, Sept. 1927.
252. J. I. Crabtree, C. E. Ives and F. E. Tuttle, "A semi-automatic timing device for motion picture negatives," *Jour. SMPE, 15:* 587, Nov. 1930.

SENSITOMETRY

253. L. A. Jones, "A motion picture laboratory sensitometer," *Jour. SMPE, 17:* 536, Oct. 1931.
254. L. A. Jones, "Photographic sensitometry, Part I," *Jour. SMPE, 17:* 491, Oct. 1931; Part II—*ibid., 17:* 695, Nov. 1931; Part III—*ibid., 18:* 54, Jan. 1932; Part IV—*ibid., 18:* 324, Mar. 1932.

255. A. Kuster and R. Schmidt, "The sensitometric control of sound records on film," *Jour. SMPE, 19:* 539, Dec. 1932.
256. H. Meyer, "Sensitometric studies of processing conditions for motion picture films," *Jour. SMPE, 25:* 239, Sept. 1935.
257. D. R. White, "Equipment for developing and reading sensitometric tests," *Jour. SMPE, 26:* 427, Apr. 1936.
258. M. H. Sweet, "A precision direct-reading densitometer," *Jour. SMPE, 38:* 148, Feb. 1942.
259. G. A. Johnson, "A processing control sensitometer," *Jour. SMPE, 47:* 474, Dec. 1946.
260. "Principles of Color Sensitometry, Report of the Color Sensitometry Subcommittee," *Jour. SMPTE, 54:* 653, June 1950.

SILVER RECOVERY

261. J. I. Crabtree and J. F. Ross, "Silver recovery from exhausted fixing baths," *Trans. SMPE,* No. 26, 70, Nov. 1926.
262. K. Hickman, C. Sanford and W. Weyerts, "The electrolytic regeneration of fixing baths," *Jour. SMPE, 17:* 568, Oct. 1931.
263. K. Hickman, W. Weyerts and O. E. Goehler, "Electrolysis of silver-bearing thiosulfate solutions," *Ind. Eng. Chem., 25:* 202, Feb. 1933.

SOUND RECORDS, PROCESSING

264. J. B. Engl, "A new process for developing and printing photographic sound records," *Trans. SMPE,* No. 30, 257, Aug. 1927.
265. O. Sandvik and G. Silberstein, "The dependence of the resolving power of a photographic material on the wavelength of light," *J. Opt. Soc. Am., 17:* 107, Aug. 1928.
266. D. MacKenzie, "Sound recording with the light valve," *Trans. SMPE,* No. 35, 730, Sept. 1928.
267. J. W. Coffman, "Sound film processing," *Trans. SMPE,* No. 35, 799, Sept. 1928.
268. J. A. Maurer, "The photographic treatment of variable-area sound-films," *Jour. SMPE, 14:* 636, June 1930.
269. R. F. Nicholson, "The processing of variable-density sound records," *Jour. SMPE, 15:* 374, Sept. 1930.
270. D. MacKenzie, "Straight-line and toe records with the light valve," *Jour. SMPE, 17:* 172, Aug. 1931.
271. G. L. Dimmick, "Improved resolution in sound recording and printing by the use of ultraviolet light," *Jour. SMPE, 27:* 168, Aug. 1936.
272. J. O. Baker and D. H. Robinson, "Modulated high-frequency recording as a means of determining conditions for optimal processing," *Jour. SMPE, 30:* 3, Jan. 1938.
273. J. G. Frayne and R. R. Scoville, "Analysis and measurement of distortion in variable-density recording," *Jour. SMPE, 32:* 648, June 1939.

274. R. V. McKie, "Commercial processing of 16-mm variable area," *Jour. SMPE, 43:* 414, Dec. 1944.
275. R. M. Corbin, N. L. Simmons and D. E. Hyndman, "Two new Eastman fine-grain sound recording films," *Jour. SMPE, 45:* 265, Oct. 1945.
276. H. W. Moyse, "Du Pont fine-grain sound films—Types 232 and 236," *Jour. SMPE, 45:* 285, Oct. 1945.
277. W. C. Miller, "Magnetic recording for motion picture studios," *Jour. SMPE, 48:* 57, Jan. 1947.

SPLICING

278. J. I. Crabtree and C. E. Ives, "A new method of blocking out splices in sound film," *Jour. SMPE, 14:* 349, Mar. 1930.
279. J. G. Capstaff and J. S. Beggs, "Film splicer for developing machines," *Jour. SMPE, 34:* 339, Mar. 1940.
280. A. Wallingsford, "A film-splicing and repair machine," *Jour. SMPE, 47:* 254, Sept. 1946.
281. E. Baumert and J. V. Noble, "The development of an invisible 16-mm film splice," *Jour. SMPE, 48:* 231, Mar. 1947.
282. I. I. Merkur, "A new motion picture film splicer," *Jour. SMPE, 48:* 238, Mar. 1947.
283. M. S. Leshing, "An improved film splicer," *Jour. SMPE, 50:* 68, Jan. 1948.

SURFACE TREATMENT OF FILM

284. J. G. Jones, "A film waxing machine," *Trans. SMPE,* No. 15, 35, Oct. 1922.
285. J. I. Crabtree and C. E. Ives, "The lubrication of motion picture film," *Trans. SMPE,* No. 31, 522, Sept. 1927.
286. A. S. Dworsky, "The Dworsky film-renovating machine, polishing machine, and film rewind," *Trans. SMPE,* No. 32, 774, Sept. 1927.
287. J. I. Crabtree, O. Sandvik and C. E. Ives, "The surface treatment of sound film," *Jour. SMPE, 14:* 275, Mar. 1930.
288. J. I. Crabtree and C. E. Ives, "A modified film-waxing machine," *Jour. SMPE, 15:* 370, Sept. 1930.
289. J. A. Norling and A. P. Rippenbein, "Treatment for rejuvenating and preserving motion picture film," *Jour. SMPE, 16:* 766, June 1931.
290. R. H. Talbot, "A new treatment for the prevention of film abrasion and oil mottle," *Jour. SMPE, 36:* 191, Feb. 1941.
291. R. H. Talbot, "Lubrication of 16-mm films," *Jour. SMPE, 53:* 285, Sept. 1949.

WASHING

292. G. T. Eaton and J. I. Crabtree, "Washing photographic films and prints in sea water," *Jour. SMPE, 40:* 380, June 1943.
293. J. I. Crabtree, G. T. Eaton and L. E. Muehler, "The removal of hypo and silver salts from photographic materials as affected by the composition of the processing solutions," *Jour. SMPE, 41:* 9, July 1943.

Some Accomplishments of Eugene Augustin Lauste— Pioneer Sound - Film Inventor

By MERRITT CRAWFORD

In any historical outline of the important inventions which have contributed to the technical development of motion pictures those of Eugene Augustin Lauste, pioneer experimenter in sound-film processes, ought properly to have a prominent place.

They are unique, in that they relate directly not only to one, but to two periods of the utmost importance in the evolution of the modern screen. Mr. Lauste contributed to the early mechanical inventions which made the silent motion picture possible and later developed the fundamental theories which made practical the addition of synchronized sound to the animated scene upon the same film. In both these fields this modest Frenchman played by no means a minor part. He was—and is—in the truest sense, a pioneer—a discoverer.

It is not possible, in this brief record, prepared on behalf of the Historical Committee, to do more than indicate the principal contributions which he made to the development of the silent and the sound-film art. Nor is it possible here to quote all the authorities consulted by the writer in support of the now generally accepted contention that Mr. Lauste is entitled to recognition as an experimenter and inventor of premier rank in film history.

This will be done, however, in a fully documented biography, which is now being prepared and in which Mr. Lauste's early researches and discoveries will be amply set forth.

It is sufficient to say here that published accounts of his experiments extended over a perior of years. The testimony of many members of our Society's London Section, who personally observed his work at various stages of its progress between the years 1908 and 1916—the records of the United States Courts—the existence of much of his early apparatus—the issuance of his British patent of 1906, covering basic means and methods for synchronously recording and reproducing sound and scene upon the same film—all serve to furnish a most complete picture of this remarkable man's researches and definite achievements in motion and sound picture history.

Mr. Lauste, who will be seventy-four his next birthday, is now living quietly in semi-retirement in Bloomfield, New Jersey. He has sold all his experimental

*A contribution of the Historical Committee.

apparatus to the Bell Telephone Laboratory, where it is expected it will eventually be placed on exhibition in the Bell Telephone Museum, at West and Bethune Streets, New York City, to take its place alongside of the epoch making inventions of Dr. Alexander Graham Bell and the long list of distinguished scientists and engineers who followed him to the development of sound and telephonic communication processes.

Mr. Lauste was born in the Montmarte district of Paris, January 17, 1857. It is said that he early displayed inventive and mechanical talents of a high order, and it is certain that before he was twenty-three he had filed with the French patent office no less than 53 models and designs on a variety of devices.

His connection with motion picture experimental and research work began in 1887, when he joined the technical staff of Thomas A. Edison at Orange, N. J. He was chief mechanical assistant to William Kennedy Laurie Dickson, for many years chief of Mr. Edison's technical and research staff, and shared with him in many of the early experiments in producing animated photography, which eventually resulted in the disclosure of the famous kinetoscope.

Mr. G. F. Atwood, now in charge of the Model Department at the Bell Telephone Laboratories, who occupied a similar post with Mr. Edison in that early day, tells me that Mr. Lauste was rated as one of the ablest mechanics in the Edison organization of that period and was highly regarded by all his superiors, including Mr. Edison himself. His assignments were seldom blueprinted, but were such as might be described as requiring much more than mere mechanical ability, as Mr. Lauste's ingenuity and inventive talents were fully recognized.

Mr. Lauste left the Edison organization in 1892 to develop a gasoline engine, which he had designed in association with another French engineer. His model worked, but he became discouraged and discarded it, when experts assured him that an engine of this type, with its noise and inflammable potentialities, could never be made commercial because it would not be permitted on the streets. But for this mischance he might well have figured as an inventor in the beginnings of the automobile as well as the motion picture.

In 1894 he became associated with Major Woodville Latham, a teacher, who had become interested in the possibilities of a step-photography as disclosed by Mr. Edison in his kinetoscope. Major Latham, himself, had little mechanical knowledge or experience, but had conceived the idea of devising a projector for the infant film and engaged Mr. Lauste to perform the actual experimental and mechanical work.

While associated with Major Latham, Mr. Lauste designed and constructed the first wide film projector—the Eidoloscope—which embodied the famous socalled "Latham Loop," which is a fundamental feature in all modern projection machines and which was an important matter in the patent litigation of a quarter of a century ago. Mr. Lauste also designed and built for Major Latham several wide film cameras and a complete printing equipment. With the Eidoloscope public exhibitions were given in May, 1895, at No. 153 Broadway, New York, and during the following summer at Coney Island in a tent on Surf Avenue. The pictures shown were views of the Griffo-Barnet prize-fight, which Mr. Lauste had photographed on the roof of the old Madison Square Garden.

In 1896 Mr. Lauste joined the American Biograph Company, with which he was associated for several years, much of the time being in charge of their laboratory and experimental plant near Paris, France.

Mr. Lauste's invention of the "Loop," in connection with the projection machine, as well as other features of the Eidoloscope, which have borne Major Latham's name, has been fully set forth in the testimony in the case of Edison vs. The American Mutoscope Company, brought in 1898 in the United States Circuit Court, Southern District of New York. Major Latham, Mr. Lauste, and Mr. Dickson, who had then left Mr. Edison's employ to become one of the founders of the Biograph Company, all testified in this action and their testimony leaves no question as to the authorship of the invention of the first wide film projector, the Eidoloscope.

Mr. Dickson, in a letter written as recently as March 28, 1927, in referring to the early inventors in the art, says: ". . . full credit must be given Mr. Lauste, who invented the indispensable 'Loop' and the second sprocket."

The foregoing will suffice to indicate the importance of Mr. Lauste's contributions to the early mechanical development of the art, but his chief fame will doubtless eventually rest upon his work in the field of the sound-film and its processes.

According to Mr. Lauste, himself, it was while he was employed at the Edison plant in 1888, that he first conceived the idea of photographing and reproducing sound and scene. In an old issue of the *Scientific American* dated May 21, 1881, which he found in the cellar of the Edison laboratory, he read a description by Dr. Alexander Graham Bell of his invention of the Photophone and the successful transmission of sound by means of radiant energy, using a microphone and selenium cell in conjunction.

The idea fascinated Mr. Lauste and it occurred to him that the sound waves might be recorded photographically and then reproduced by means of a light sensitive cell as Dr. Bell had done.

At first it was his idea to record the sound waves photographically upon a ribbon or strip of bromide paper and to reproduce them, using a mirror and reflected light. He had then not yet seen a sample of Mr. Eastman's film. Early in 1890, however, in the Edison laboratory he saw for the first time a specimen of this film in the *Blacksmith,* one of the earliest kinetoscope subjects, and at once realized that the commercial material was available which would solve this phase of his problem.

Until the year 1900, however, the pressure of other work and his limited resources prevented Mr. Lauste from making much progress with his idea. In that year he made his first "light gate" of the grate type and drafted some sketches. But it was not until 1904 that he was enabled to build his first complete apparatus for experimental purposes.

It was very crude, but it demonstrated to him that he was following the right lines and on August 11, 1906, he applied at the British Patent Office for an invention described in its preliminary specifications as: *"A new and im-proved method of and means for simultaneously recording and reproducing movements and sounds."*

His complete specification was accepted and a patent, No. 18,057, issued August 10, 1907, which has often since been described as the "master patent" in the field of synchronized sound and movement photography. There certainly has never been another patent in this field which has quite compared with this in general interest and attention, for it has long been the "best seller" of the British Patent Office.

It has already gone through seven editions and an eighth is presently in prospect, so unprecedented has been the demand for this paper with the tremendous increase in experimental and research work on the sound-film in recent years.

To sketch, even in the most cursory fashion, Mr. Lauste's later experiments is difficult within the limits of this article. Until 1910 he devoted most of his efforts to obtaining adequate results in sound recording and reproduction. He had, of course, no amplification.

He experimented with and devised various types of mechanical and optical slits and lighting means. The grate light valves he first made for recording were unsatisfactory because of the inertia of the mechanical slit used. His limited mechanical equipment made it impossible for him to make a slit of this type sufficiently narrow.

He used an oscillating mirror with good results, but eventually found this also impracticable because the vibrations of the camera interfered with the light waves and distorted them. His ultimate sound gate, which embodied a vibrating diamagnetic wire (silicon) acting between the poles of two strong magnets, was entirely successful. He devised this early in the year 1910.

In this year also, he paid his first visit to Ernst Ruhmer, the eminent German experimenter, in Berlin. It is generally recognized now that these two pioneers, a Frenchman and a German, laid down the fundamental theories for photographic sound recording and reproduction. They collaborated and exchanged notes on their experiments until 1913, the year in which Ruhmer died, and for a time considered combining their research activities.

In 1910 Mr. Lauste first photographed sound and scene on the same film at his Brixton, London, studio. Between that date and 1914 he photographed many thousand feet of sound pictures. He came to America for a short visit in 1911, with the idea of interesting capital, but was recalled to England too soon for him to make and definite arrangements.

In his short stay in America in the Spring of 1911 he demonstrated his sound camera-projector to a number of people and photographed at least one short length picture, recording sound and scene. This, doubtless, may properly be described as the first true sound picture to be taken in America.

In 1912 Mr. Lauste, having sufficiently perfected his recording and reproducing systems, began experiments to devise an amplifier for his sound films. But for the fact that his capital was limited and the later interruption of the war, it is quite possible that the sound picture might have made its public appearance at least a decade before its commercial possibilities were demonstrated by means of the sound amplifying system developed by the Bell Telephone engineers.

The fact that Mr. Lauste never succeeded in making his sound processes commercial or profiting from them, will have no bearing on the measure of fame which future film historians will accord him.

There can be no doubt but that he was the first to record sound and scene upon the same film and to reproduce it, and the importance of his researches and early experiments will become increasingly apparent with the passing of the years.

History of Sound Motion Pictures

By EDWARD W. KELLOGG

Excellent accounts of the history of the development of sound motion pictures have been published in this Journal by Theisen[5] in 1941 and by Sponable[6] in 1947. The present paper restates some of the information given in those papers, supplementing it with some hitherto unpublished material, and discusses some of the important advances after 1930.

One of the numerous omissions of topics which undeniably deserve discussion at length, is that, except for some early work, no attempt is made to cover developments abroad. The subject of 16mm developments is discussed with a brevity altogether out-of-keeping with its importance. This has been on the theory that basically the problems are similar to those of 35mm sound, and that whatever has brought improvement to one has been applied to both.

Edison invented the motion pictures as a supplement to his phonograph, in the belief that sound plus a moving picture would provide better entertainment than sound alone. But in a short time the movies proved to be good enough entertainment without sound. It has been said that although the motion picture and the phonograph were intended to be partners, they grew up separately. And it might be added that the motion picture held the phonograph in such low esteem that for years it would not speak. Throughout the long history of efforts to add sound, the success of the silent movie was the great obstacle to commercialization of talking pictures.

Early Sound Pictures Using the Phonograph

The idea of combining recorded sound with the motion pictures is as old as the motion picture itself[33] (if we exclude the early "zoetrope" invented in 1833 by W. G. Horner).[39] In a paper, "What Happened in the Beginning," F. H. Richardson[7] reproduced a letter in which Thomas A. Edison quoted from his early notes: "In the year 1887, the idea occurred to me that it would be possible to devise an instrument which should do for the eye what the phonograph does for the ear, and that by a combination of the two all motion and sound could be recorded and reproduced simultaneously." The letter proceeds to tell of the development of the motion picture (and is followed by letters from Thomas Armat, George Eastman, C. Francis Jenkins and others, related to motion-picture inventions). Edison in 1895 tried on the public the combination of a phonograph with his "peep show" moving picture.[5,11] He built at least 50 (and probably more) of the combination machines.

Gaumont. Leon Gaumont, in France,[5] began as early as 1901 to work on combining the phonograph and motion picture. He worked on the project during several widely separated intervals. Theisen[5] refers to a series of shows of the "Film Parlant" at the Gaumont Palace in Paris in 1913 and to demonstrations in the United States. After 1926 the "Eta-

Presented on May 5, 1954, at the Society's Convention at Washington, D.C., by Edward W. Kellogg, Consulting Engineer, 276 Merion Ave., Haddonfield, N.J.
(This paper was received on October 25, 1954.)

blissements Gaumont" used the system developed by Peterson and Poulsen.

Laemmle. An attempt by Carl Laemmle of Paramount in 1907 to exploit a combination of phonograph and motion picture is mentioned in Sponable's paper.[6] This was a German development called "Synchroscope." It was handicapped by the short time which the record would play, and after some apparently successful demonstrations, was dropped for want of a supply of pictures with sound to maintain programs in the theaters where it was tried.[13]

Pomerede, Amet, Bristol. Theisen's paper[5] mentions combinations of phonograph and motion pictures using flexible shafts or other mechanical connections, by Georges Pomerede[2] (1907 patent), and E. H. Amet[14] (1912 to 1918) who used electrical methods for the sound. Wm. H. Bristol[15] began his work on synchronous sound about 1917.

Siren Type of Amplifier. An ingenious attempt to obtain amplification in reproduction used the movements of the phonograph needle to vary the opening of an air-valve, connected to a source of air pressure. This device was employed for sound pictures by Oskar Messter[5,16] (Germany 1903–4). In England, where it was known as the "Auxetophone," it had some use for phonographs. Its invention is credited by the Encyclopedia Britannica to Short (1898), with improvements by the Hon. C. A. Parsons.

Edison. In 1913 Edison made a serious effort to provide synchronized phonograph sound. The equipment is on exhibit at the Edison Museum in West Orange, N.J. The phonograph is of

special construction, to provide maximum volume and long playing, the cylinder record was oversize, and the horn and diaphragm considerably larger than those of home phonographs. Between the reproducing stylus and the diaphragm was a mechanical power amplifier, apparently using the principle of capstans used on shipboard. There was a continuously rotating amber cylinder and a hard rubber brake-shoe subtending about 130° of arc. One end of the shoe was connected to the reproducing stylus in such a manner that an upward displacement of the stylus would increase the pressure between shoe and cylinder; and the other end of the shoe was connected through a slender rod to the diaphragm, in such a way that the shoe movement resulting from increased friction would give an upward push on the diaphragm.[17] One may well imagine that the adjustment of this device to give substantial gain without producing chattering must have tested the skill of the best of operators. Nevertheless, it must have worked, for the record indicates that the Edison talking-picture show ran for several months in Keith's Colonial Theatre in New York, with much acclaim, and was shown in other large cities of America and in other countries.

The arrangement for synchronizing was not in accordance with present practices. The phonograph behind the screen determined the speed, being connected through a string belt to a synchronizing device at the projector. The belt pulleys were about 3 in. in diameter. The belt passed from the phonograph up over idler pulleys and overhead, back to the booth. The synchronizing device applied a brake to the projector, and the brake-shoe pressure depended on the relative phase of phonograph and projector, increasing rapidly as the projector got ahead in phase. With an even force

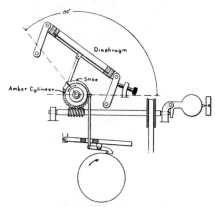

Fig. 1. Mechanical power amplifier of Thomas A. Edison and Daniel Higham.

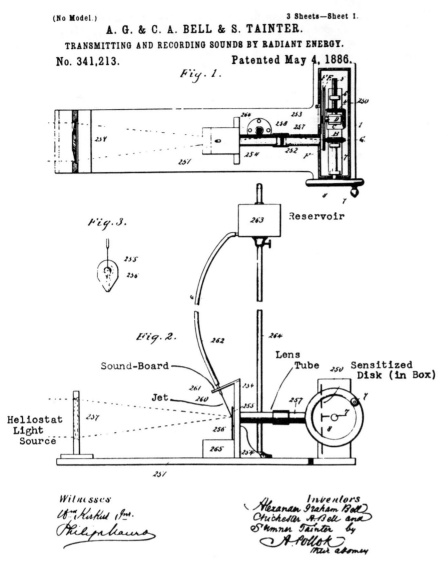

(No Model.)   3 Sheets—Sheet 1.

A. G. & C. A. BELL & S. TAINTER.
TRANSMITTING AND RECORDING SOUNDS BY RADIANT ENERGY.
No. 341,213.   Patented May 4, 1886.

Fig. 1.

Fig. 3.

Fig. 2.

Reservoir

Sound-Board

Lens
Tube   Sensitized
Disk (in Box)

Jet

Heliostat
Light
Source

Witnesses

Inventors
Alexander Graham Bell
Chichester A. Bell and
Sumner Tainter by
A. Pollok
their attorney

Fig. 2. Variable density recording system of A. G. Bell, C. A. Bell and Sumner Tainter, 1886.

on the projector crank, normal phase relation was maintained. The projectionist watched for synchronism and had a slight degree of control by turning the crank harder if the picture was behind or easing it off if it was ahead.

So far as I have learned, there were few further efforts (at least in the U.S.) to provide sound for pictures by means of phonograph (mechanical) recording until the Warner Brothers' Vitaphone system of 1926.

Photographic Sound Recording

A history of sound pictures necessarily includes the many efforts to record sound photographically, whether or not the experimenters made any attempt to combine the sound with pictures, or were even interested in that application. Despite the obvious advantages, from the synchronized-sound standpoint, of a photographic record of the sound on the same film with the picture, it does not appear that this consideration was necessarily an important factor in directing experimen-

tation toward photographic recording, nor even that ultimate application to synchronous sound for motion pictures was (in many cases) a main objective. It was rather that photographic recording represented a new medium, which seemed to offer promise of much superior results. A mechanical system seems inherently crude where such delicacy is needed as in reproducing sound; in contrast to which recording by a beam of light would seem ideal. The experimenters have all been conscious of the handicap imposed by the necessity of making ponderable mechanical parts vibrate at high frequency.

So we find that efforts to record sound photographically began before there were such things as motion pictures on strips of film. Before the invention of the telephone, Alexander Graham Bell, interested in aiding the deaf, had made photographic records of "manometric flames," showing voice waves. His patent, No. 235,199, filed in 1880, shows a system for transmitting speech over a

beam of modulated light, and uses a light-sensitive device (selenium cells) to detect the received fluctuations, thus anticipating the essential principle of the reproducing system which was used in many later experiments.

Blake. Prof. E. W. Blake of Brown University in 1878 made photographic records of speech sounds on a moving photographic plate, using a vibrating mirror.[6,18]

Fritts. U.S. Patent No. 1,203,190, filed in 1880 by Charles E. Fritts,[5,6] discloses photographic soundtracks and a great variety of devices for recording and reproducing, but there does not appear to be evidence of much significant experimental work.

Bell and Tainter. In the Smithsonian Museum in Washington, D.C., are a number of large glass disks carrying spiral sound tracks. These were made by a method described in U.S. Patent No. 341,213 (filed 1885) to Alexander Graham Bell, Chichester A. Bell and Sumner Tainter. Light from a steady source was transmitted in a relatively narrow beam through a piece of stationary glass, and then further restricted by a slit where it reached the circular photographic plate. Just above the place where the light entered the stationary glass, a tiny jet of ink (or other light-absorbing liquid) was directed against the surface. The nozzle was attached to a "sounding board" (small plate) which picked up the sound vibrations. The jiggles of the nozzle caused waves in the stream of ink which flowed down over the surface, and these modulated the transmitted light.

Some years ago it became desirable, in connection with a patent suit, to demonstrate that the spiral track was really a soundtrack. Contact prints (on celluloid films) were made of several of the most promising looking of the glass plates, and a reproducing system arranged, giving the record the benefit of modern equipment in this respect. The approximate best speed was found by trial. (The original recording machine was hand-cranked). The photographic image had suffered from age and was very noisy, and the total recording lasted only a few seconds. But it was with something of the thrill of an antiquarian that we listened to the voice from the past. "This is . . . . I am . . . in the . . . laboratory." The date was given too " . . . , eighteen eight- . . .?"

Others. Sponable's historical paper mentions numerous other workers and their patents. Several of these modulated the light by means of a small mirror connected to a diaphragm so that vibration caused rotation, thus anticipating features of equipment used by C. A. Hoxie in the work at General Electric Co. Of the developments which, although

175

not leading to any commercial system, deserve special mention, I shall speak of several inventions or discoveries which laid foundations for later developments, and of the direct contributions to photographic recording of Rühmer, Lauste, de Forest, Reis and Tykociner.

Basic Inventions and Discoveries

Selenium Cells. For many years, reproduction from photographic-sound records was made possible by the selenium cell. The photoconductive properties of selenium were discovered by Willoughby Smith in 1873, and a practical selenium cell was made by Werner Siemens in 1876.[19] The response of a selenium cell to changes in illumination is sluggish, making it a very imperfect tool for sound reproduction, whereas the photoemissive effect on which photocells depend is practically instantaneous, but the electrical output from a selenium cell is very much greater.

The Photocell. The first indication of photoemission was discovered by Hertz in 1887 and later studied by Hallwachs (1888), Stoletow (1890) and Elster and Geitel (1889 to 1913).[19,20] Although by 1900 much had been learned, practical photocells did not become generally available till some years later, nor were they of help toward sound reproduction without electronic amplifiers.[21,22]

Thermal Emission — The "Edison Effect." Edison discovered in 1883 that a small current could flow through evacuated space in a lamp bulb, between a hot filament and a separate electrode. The Fleming "Valve," invented in 1905, made use of this principle, played an important part in early wireless telegraphy and was the forerunner of thermionic amplifiers.[26]

The Audion. The invention of the "Audion" by Lee de Forest in 1907 marked the beginning of the electronic era. As has been emphasized by many writers, it was the electronic amplifier which unlocked the door to progress and improvement in almost every phase of sound transmission, recording and reproduction. However, amplifying tubes did not become generally available to experimenters for over a decade. The de Forest patent[23] (acquired by the Telephone Company) was basic and unchallenged, but the vacuum techniques of some of the foremost laboratories of the country[24] were needed to make of the audion a dependable and reasonably rugged tool.*

The Oscillograph. The oscillograph, consisting of a small mirror mounted on a pair of conductors, close together, in a

strong magnetic field, was invented by Blondel in 1891 and improved in 1893 by Duddell, who put it into practically the form still used. It has played a vital part in photographic sound recording.

Magnetic Recording. The invention by Poulsen of Copenhagen in 1900 of recording magnetically on a steel wire laid the foundation for modern tape recording, which has almost revolutionized methods of making original recordings.[27]

Auditorium Acoustics. The modern science of room acoustics and acoustic treatment dates from the work of Prof. Wallace C. Sabine of Harvard in the years 1895 to 1900.[28] With little other equipment than a whistle, a stop watch and brains, he worked out the acoustic principles on which successful sound recording and reproduction so largely depend.

Gas-Filled Incandescent Lamps. Beyond a certain point, optical-recording systems cannot give increased exposure by increasing the size of the source, but only by increasing the intensity (candles per square centimeter), which means higher temperature. Early incandescent lamps were well exhausted because all gas results in loss of heat by convection and hence lowered efficiency. In 1911–13 Irving Langmuir of General Electric Co. studied the effects of inert gas not only on heat loss, but also on the rate of evaporation of tungsten from the filament surface, which is the factor which determines permissible operating temperature. He showed that such gases as nitrogen, or better yet argon (the heavier the better), at pressures well up toward atmospheric or even higher, could with suitably formed filaments so retard the evaporation of tungsten that the higher permissible temperature much more than compensated for the added heat convection, thus giving several-fold increase in efficency as well as whiter light. With the gas, the evaporated tungsten is carried to the top of the bulb instead of blackening the sides, in the optical path.[29]

Magnetic Materials. The development of several alloys of iron, nickel and cobalt having extraordinary magnetic properties is reported by H. D. Arnold and G. W. Elmen in the *Bell System Technical Journal* of July 1923, and by Elmen in the January 1929 and July 1929 issues. The extremely high permeability and low hysteresis of Permalloy have made it possible to greatly reduce distortion in transformers and in many electromechanical devices, and to provide more successful magnetic shielding than would otherwise be possible. In another alloy which has been called Perminvar, constancy of permeability and low hysteresis (making for low distortion) have been carried still farther. Another alloy named Permendur can carry very high flux den-

sities before saturation, making it possible to produce intense fields which make for sensitivity and damping in devices of the moving conductor type.

Important for the reduction of cost and weight of magnetic devices was the discovery by the Japanese physicist T. Mishima of the properties of certain aluminum-nickel-cobalt alloys for permanent magnets,[30] and subsequent improvements.

Improvements in Vacuum Tubes and Phototubes. In any list of the advances which contributed in an important way to the technical attainments in modern sound reproduction, several improvements in amplifier tubes deserve an important place. Among these are:

(1) The Wehneldt (oxide coated) cathode and other low-temperature emitters, which in turn made indirectly heated unipotential cathodes possible.

(2) The screen-grid tube.

(3) The pentode.

(4) Remote cutoff or exponential tubes, and other variable gain tubes.

(5) The caesium phototube with its high sensitivity to infrared light.

(6) The gas-filled phototube with its increased output.

Early Work on Sound on Motion-Picture Film

Rühmer. Ernst Rühmer in Berlin[5,6,31] in 1901 began publication of the results of his work on photographic sound recording, which extended over a period of about twelve years. As sources of modulated light he superimposed voice currents on the continuous currents in electric arcs. He used considerably higher film speeds than those used for pictures. Sponable reported (ref. 6, p. 278) that some of Rühmer's Photographophon films were brought to this country by the Fox Film Corp., and that the articulation was clear; also, this reference shows a sample of Rühmer's soundtrack. A variable-area track by Rühmer is shown in the Theisen history (ref. 5, p. 421), the *Scientific American* of 1901[31] being cited as reference. Presumably Rühmer experimented with both systems.

Lauste. This Society has taken special note of the work of Eugene Augustine Lauste, in a 1931 report of the Historical Committee,[32] in a paper by Merritt Crawford[32] and in placing his name on the Society's Honor Roll. The young Frenchman joined the staff of Thomas A. Edison in 1887, where he did construction and experimental work till 1892. For two years he worked on another project and then, in association with Maj. Latham, developed a projector which was the first to incorporate the extra sprocket and free loops with the intermittent. Lauste's interest in photographic sound recording was first aroused when in 1888 he found in an old copy of the *Scientific American* (May 21,

---

* Much higher vacuum than de Forest had been able to obtain was necessary. This was independently accomplished by I. Langmuir of General Electric Co. and H. D. Arnold of Western Electric Co.[24]

1881) an account of Dr. Bell's experiment in transmitting sound over a modulated light-beam, and converting to electrical modulation by means of a selenium cell. This suggested the thought of recording the sound photographically on the same strip with the picture. It was not till about 1900 that he began to find opportunity to work on this project. He worked for several years in the United States and then went to England where he pursued his experiments. A British patent (No. 18,057, filed in 1906) shows a well thought-out system. Lauste received some financial backing in 1908 from the manager of the London Cinematograph Co.

To modulate the recording light, Lauste used rocking mirrors and what have been described as "grate-type light-valves." The mirror system was too sensitive to camera vibrations, and the grate-type valves which he was able to build had too much inertia. In 1910 he began working with modulators of the string galvanometer type, with excellent results. The historical account by Theisen,[5] shows photographs of some of Lauste's apparatus. He spent some time with Ernst Rühmer in Berlin, a stimulating and profitable association. He visited America in 1911 and as part of his demonstration made what was probably the first actual sound-on-film motion picture made in the U.S. A necessary return to England, shortage of capital, and the war, halted Lauste's sound-picture researches. In his paper on Lauste, Crawford expresses the thought that had it not been for this unfortunate interruption, plus very limited resources, and had electronic amplifiers been available to Lauste, commercialization of sound pictures might well have gotten started a decade before it actually did.

E. E. Ries filed application in 1913 for a patent (No. 1,473,976, issued in 1923) in which broad claims were allowed on the essentials of a single-film system. The patent became the basis of later litigation.[6]

Tykociner. In 1918 and following, Prof. J. T. Tykociner of the University of Illinois carried on experiments and developed a system. This work was described before the American Institute of Electrical Engineers and in the *SMPE Transactions*.[34] After pointing out that three new tools had in comparatively recent times become available for the solution of the sound-picture problem, (namely, high-frequency currents, photoelectricity, and thermionic amplifiers), Prof. Tykociner gives a broad discussion of requirements and possible arrangements. As a source of modulated light he used for the most part a mercury arc with either modulated continuous current or modulated high-frequency current, and for reproduction a Kunz (cathode of potassium on silver) photo-

cell. The light from the mercury arc is particularly potent photographically, but is sluggish in following the input modulation, which results in some loss of the higher audio frequencies.

Foreign Developments Which Led to Commercial Systems

Tri-Ergon (meaning "the work of three"). Josef Engl, Joseph Massole and Hans Vogt, in Germany, began in 1918 the development of a system of sound pictures which later was commercialized under the name Tonbild Syndicat AG (abbreviated to Tobis).[6,35] They used a modulated glow discharge for recording, and a photocell for reproducing. Of chief concern in this country were the Tri-Ergon patents,[35] in which numerous claims allowed by the U.S. Patent Office were so broad that had their validity been sustained they would have almost swamped the industry. In particular, one patent (1,713,726) which claimed the use of a flywheel on the shaft of a roller or sprocket which carries the film past the translation point, to take out speed variations, was the basis of prolonged litigation, being finally declared invalid by the U.S. Supreme Court (1935).[114] But in the meantime the efforts to avoid what were thought to be dangerous infringements of the Tri-Ergon flywheel claims, had for seven years steered the course of mechanical designs on the part of the major equipment manufacturers into inferior or more complicated constructions. (See section on Mechanical Systems.)

In Germany the Tri-Ergon patents controlled the situation. The large picture producing companies, U.F.A. and Klangfilm (a subsidiary of Siemens & Halske and A.E.G.), took licenses under the Tri-Ergon patents. A brief account of the patent negotiations and agreements in this company and in Germany will be found in the Sponable paper.[6]

Peterson and Poulsen in Denmark developed a system (1923) which was commercialized in Germany under the name Tonfilm.[6] They used an oscillograph as the recording light modulator (giving a variable-area soundtrack), and a selenium cell for reproduction. (One of the Tri-Ergon U.S. patents[35] claimed the use of a photocell for this purpose, and it is likely that a German patent accounts for the use of a selenium cell by Poulsen and Peterson.) This system was used by Gaumont in France and by British Acoustic Films, Ltd.

The de Forest Phonofilm

Dr. de Forest tells the story of this work in the 1923 *Transactions*.[36] The account is particularly interesting because he tells much of his viewpoint as he started, and then, after describing the system which he had evolved, gives his

reflections on the applications and future of sound motion pictures.

The man whose invention gave us amplifiers in which the heaviest object that had to be moved was an electron, surely had a right to wish to do away with moving mechanical parts in microphones, light-modulators and loudspeakers. For microphones he experimented with the conductivity of gas flames and of open arcs as affected by sound waves, and with fine platinum wires heated to a dull red by a direct current and subjected to the cooling effect of the air vibrations superimposed on a slight continuous air movement. The changes in resistance of the wires with variations of temperature gave rise to telephonic currents.

For light modulators he tried "the speaking flame" (probably the "manometric" flame of König) and a tiny incandescent lamp, carrying voice currents superimposed on direct current. The lamp was designed to have very rapid filament cooling (partly by using a short filament, so that heat conduction to the lead-in wires would be high). On listening to these sources by means of a photocell and amplifier, de Forest was convinced that they gave exceptional quality (even compared with the condenser microphone), but they proved entirely inadequate for making a useful soundtrack giving very small percentage of modulation and probably also underexposure. Finally a successful source of modulated light for recording was found in a gas-filled tube excited by modulated high-frequency currents from a 5- to 10-w radio telephone transmitter. This was named the "Photion." A slit, $1\frac{1}{2}$ to 2 mils wide and 3/32 in. long, adjacent to the film, was used to restrict the size of the exposing beam.

A similar slit was used in reproduction. Both potassium photocells and Case Thalofide[37,40] cells were used in reproducing equipment, the greater sensitivity obtainable with the Thalofide cell being a consideration offsetting the faster response of the photocell. The design and construction of amplifiers using his Audion were of course very familiar to de Forest.

Lament is expressed that loudspeakers depending on some principles other than diaphragms and horns were not to be had, but after some discouragements with "talking arcs" and sound radiators on the thermophone principle, the commercially available horn and diaphragm speakers were accepted as the only solution at the time.*

Practical models of recording and reproducing equipment were built, and re-

---

* It is of interest that in the early part of our investigation which led to the direct radiator dynamic speaker (*Trans. AIEE*, 1925, p. 461) Chester W. Rice and I tried talking arcs and thermophones, and also a corona discharge device — all of which avoid mechanical moving parts — but none of these appeared promising.[38]

cordings made, using principally a combined camera and recorder, and many demonstrations given.

The de Forest paper[36] reviewed earlier history of efforts to record sound photographically, and gave appreciative acknowledgment of the help that had been given by Theodore W. Case.[37]

To have guessed wrong on some subject is no reflection on the insight of an experimenter, but several instances are striking, in the light of later developments. Speaking of the efforts to provide sound by means of the phonograph, the author said: "The fundamental difficulties involved in this method were so basic that it should have been evident from their inception, that commercial success could hardly be achieved in that direction." (Consider the Warners' Vitaphone.) Speaking of loudspeakers, after saying that the loudspeaker has been developed "to a high state of perfection" but left much to be desired, he said: "I am convinced that final perfection will come not through any refinements of the telephone and diaphragm, but by application of entirely different principles." (Yet phenomenal improvements were made with the identical elements, through refinements.)

In speaking of the future of sound pictures, Dr. de Forest gave a definite "No" to the question whether the existing type of silent drama could be improved by the addition of voice. But he foresaw the evolution of an entirely new type of dramatic scheme and presentation, taking advantage of the freedom which had been such an asset to the silent moving picture (as contrasted with the stage) but using sound and voice where these could be effective. He also had visions of great utility for travel films, newsreels, records of notable persons, and educational films.

The work just described was done from 1918 to 1922. About a year and a half later[36] Dr. de Forest gave a brief account of progress, reporting improvements in many details, better articulation, thirty theaters equipped, much interest on the part of operators, films made of a number of celebrities and contracts with leading chain exhibitors. Again the opinion was expressed that the talking picture would not ever take the place of the silent drama.

The Phonofilm system was used in numerous theaters, with sound films made under Dr. de Forest's direction; but he did not succeed in interesting the established American picture producers. Perhaps the industry was prospering too well at the time, but judging from the initial coolness of film executives to the technically greatly improved systems a few years later, it is easy to imagine that numerous imperfections which undoubtedly existed (as, for example, defective film-motion, limited frequency range, and loudspeakers that gave unnatural voices, and perhaps too, demonstration films that were uninteresting) contributed to loss of the impressiveness needed for doing business.

Several years later the "de Forest Phonofilm Co." was bought by Schlesinger of London and South Africa.

Work at the Theodore W. Case Laboratory (Movietone)[6]

Theodore W. Case[37] became interested in modulating light and deriving telephonic currents from it in 1911, while a student at Yale. In 1914 he organized his laboratory at Auburn, N.Y., devoting special attention to the study of materials whose resistance is altered by light, of which selenium was the best known example. These studies resulted (1917) in the development of the Thalofide cell, in which the photosensitive material is thallium oxysulfide.[40] These cells, which are especially sensitive in the near infrared range, were widely used in Navy communication systems during World War I. Case was joined in 1916 by E. I. Sponable. Experiments were continued with the help of an Audion amplifier obtained from de Forest. One of Case's postwar developments was the barium photoelectric cell.

In 1922 attention was turned seriously to sound pictures. Manometric* flames (oxyacetylene) were tried as a possible source of modulated light. Soon afterward Case found that the light from an argon arc in one of the tubes that had been used for infrared signalling could be readily modulated and was photographically potent. These tubes had oxide-coated hot cathodes. A tube for recording, based on this principle, was developed and named the Aeo-light.[6,41] It operated at between 200 and 400 v. Helium was substituted for argon in 1922, with benefit to the actinic power and also to the speed with which the light followed the current variation. The commercial Aeo-lights were rated at 350 v.

From 1922 to 1925 Case cooperated with de Forest, furnishing numerous items of experimental equipment.

Several sound cameras were built under the direction of Sponable, in 1922, 1923 and 1924. The 1924 model was a modified Bell & Howell camera rebuilt to Sponable's specifications by the Bell & Howell Co. The film motion in this and other cameras was unacceptable until they had been reworked for greater mechanical precision. In the final designs of sound camera the sprocket was driven through a mechanical filter, consisting of damped springs and a flywheel on the sprocket shaft. The sound was recorded on the sprocket.

* A gas jet so arranged that sound vibrations produce changes in the gas supplied to the jet.

The Aeo-light was mounted in a tube which entered the camera at the back. Directly against the film was a light-restricting slit made by silvering a thin quartz plate, ruling a slit 0.0006 in. wide in the silver, and cementing over it a thin piece of glass which was then lapped to a thickness of about 0.001 in. The slit was thus protected from collecting dirt from the film. The end of the Aeo-light, where the glow was concentrated, was close behind the slit. A Bell & Howell contact printer was modified to make possible the independent printing of picture and sound.

Up to the fall of 1925, when the working arrangement with de Forest was terminated, the Case laboratory efforts were directed largely to recording principles and apparatus. It was decided then to work on a system independently of de Forest, and one of the next projects was to build reproducing equipment in the form of an attachment which could be used with existing picture projectors. It was in this design that the decision was reached to place the soundhead under the projector, and the offset of 20 frames or $14\frac{1}{2}$ in. between picture and sound was established. The speed of 90 ft/min was adopted for the Case system. In the first projector attachment a light-restricting slit was used similar to the one used in the camera, but later a straight tungsten filament was imaged on the film, and in a still later model, a concentrated straight-axis helical filament was imaged on a slit which was in turn imaged on the film.

With the essential elements of a sound-on-film system developed, Case and Sponable began study of the patent situation, with a view to obtaining licenses, if necessary, for the commercial use of their system. There appeared to be no very strong patents to interfere, except those on the use of thermionic amplifiers. A contract between General Electric, Westinghouse and Radio-Corporation on the one hand and Western Electric Co. on the other, was in effect, specifying the fields of activity in which each might use amplifiers, but, if I have not misinterpreted the account in Sponable's historical paper, sound-pictures had not been specifically mentioned, and there was some question as to the right to license use in the Case system, the eventual decision being that both groups had rights. The Bell Telephone Laboratories were interested themselves in developing sound pictures, and so were not immediately ready to license what would be a competing system. However their engineers were much interested in the performance attained, and there was some thought of combining efforts. There were demonstrations of both systems, but no plan to merge them was reached. The experience of Case and Sponable at

General Electric Co. was rather similar.

In 1926 demonstrations were made to representatives of the Fox Film Corp., who became greatly interested, and finally to William Fox. After thorough testing on their own premises, the Fox Film Corp. purchased rights to the Case developments (July 23, 1926), leaving the question of amplifier rights to be worked out later. The Fox-Case Corp. was organized to exploit the system, which was given the name Movietone. Courtland Smith, who had been with the Fox Film Corp. and had been instrumental in bringing about the purchase, was made president of the Fox-Case Corp. The Movietone News service was established.

Sponable left the Case organization to give his services to the new company, one of the first of his activities being the design of recording studios in New York and later in Hollywood. In 1927 he developed a screen which transmitted sound freely, permitting loudspeakers to be located directly behind the picture. The first public showing of Movietone recordings was in January 1927.

The Fox-Case Corp. obtained license to use amplifiers, first in 1926 through the Western Electric Co. and the Vitaphone Corp., and the next year revised contracts were made with Electrical Research Products, Inc. (ERPI), which was formed in January 1927 to handle the sound-picture business for the Western Electric and Telephone companies.

In the Movietone reproducing system, Western Electric amplifiers and loudspeakers were used. The years 1928 and 1929 were marked by rapid expansion in facilities and personnel, successful showings and stepped-up schedules of newsreel releases. In March 1929 the making of silent pictures by Fox was discontinued. Six months later the Fox and Hearst newsreel services were united.

The British Movietone News was organized in 1929. In 1930 William Fox sold his interests in Fox Film and Fox Theatres.

As the Fox Film Corp. was already an ERPI licensee, and therefore had rights to use other Western Electric developments, the Western Electric light valve was adopted for the Movietone service (as well as for Fox studio recording), displacing the Aeo-light.

Work at Western Electric Co. and Bell Telephone Laboratories

The Western Electric Co. brought to a commercial stage almost simultaneously a sound motion-picture system based on disk records, and one based on sound on film. Various developments which laid the foundations for these systems had been taking place through a number of years. The citation of the life and work of Edward B. Craft in this *Journal*[42] indicates that his interest and enthusiasm were in large measure responsible for the undertaking of a full-scale project for developing systems of sound for motion pictures. Craft was assistant chief engineer of the Western Electric Co. from 1918 to 1922, when he became chief engineer. With the transfer in 1924 of research activities to the newly organized Bell Telephone Laboratories, Craft was made executive vice-president, and continued to guide activities.[42]

Whether or not there was a definite policy of not putting all of the eggs in one basket, work on both systems was stepped up at about the same time (1922) and pushed with equal vigor.

The two systems had identical requirements with respect to many elements, but, in particular, microphones, amplifiers and loudspeakers. The Western Electric Co. had acquired rights to de Forest's Audion in 1913 and made great improvements in it during the next few years, building up wide experience in its applications and circuitry.

Second only to electronic amplifiers in importance for the development of high-quality recording and reproducing systems was a microphone of uniform response and with low distortion. With amplifiers available Dr. E. C. Wente[43] was able largely to ignore the question of output level, and to develop by 1916 a microphone of the condenser type, having extraordinarily high fidelity and freedom from distortion and noise.[44–47]

In the loudspeaker field, the company had had considerable experience and had developed units for public address work. The public address installations had afforded experience with auditoriums and requirements for intelligibility, while experience in acoustics for sound pickup had been gained in radio broadcasting.

With respect to the recording itself and reproduction, I shall separate the two stories of the disk and photographic systems.

The Disk System

In 1946 there was published a history of sound recording in the laboratories of the Western Electric Co.[48] Since the transmission of speech was the main business of the Telephone Co., a program of studying every aspect of speech waves was initiated about 1912, and as part of this project, efforts were directed to recording the sound. The interest soon spread to include music. In connection with work with disk records, Crandall and Kranz built an electromagnetic reproducer in 1913. In 1915 H. D. Arnold suggested that the improvement of disk recording be undertaken, using the then available electrical equipment (which included amplifiers). By this time the electrical reproducer had been improved.

The war interrupted these projects, but they were resumed soon after its close. A group under J. P. Maxfield undertook the improvement of wax recording and the phonograph. The story of this development was told in 1926 to the American Institute of Electrical Engineers.[49] The recording system made use of a magnetically driven cutter so designed that with constant current input, the vibratory velocity of the cutting stylus was substantially constant from about 200 to 5000 cycles, while from 50 to 200 cycles the amplitude was constant, a characteristic practically necessary to avoid overcutting by the low notes. Two features of the design were of special interest: (1) the separation of the total mass that must be driven into three parts (armature, stylus-bar and coupling disk), connected together through portions of shaft whose torsional flexibility was carefully calculated to make of the structure a mechanical low-pass filter of calculable mechanical impedance; and (2) a mechanical resistance consisting of a thick-walled rubber tube (which may be thought of as practically a rod of soft rubber) subjected at one end through the coupling disk to torsional vibrations. The propagation of torsional waves in such a soft rubber rod is so slow that in a length of about 6 in. there would be many wavelengths for all but the lowest frequencies.

Vibrations imparted to the rubber reach the far end very much attenuated, are reflected, and propagated back toward the start, but are of negligible magnitude when they reach it. Under such conditions the rubber line acts as a nearly pure mechanical resistance to load the filter, and, if properly matched to the filter impedance, results in practically complete (and therefore uniform) transmission through the filter structure, throughout the frequency band below the filter cutoff. The features just described are, I believe, the inventions of H. C. Harrison. The great improvement in records which electrical recording brought, is well known to all of us.

Without a better reproducing system than the phonographs of the types in use about 1920, the improvements in the records would have been largely lost, so there was developed a greatly improved (nonelectrical) phonograph called the Orthophonic (also largely the outcome of H. C. Harrison's approach to the problem). However this part of the program had no direct bearing on the talking-picture project. In early 1925 the Columbia and Victor Companies took licenses from Western Electric Co. to use the recording methods and apparatus, and to build phonographs of the Orthophonic type.

Sound-on-Disk Synchronized With Pictures. Little time was lost in trying and demonstrating synchronized sound and pictures using the new electrically recorded disks. Craft arranged for a demonstration at Yale University in 1922 and another in February 1924, the equipment and many details of the system having

179

been developed and improved in the interval.

To provide sound for pictures, using the disk-record system,[50] it was necessary to have records which would play continuously for at least the projection time of a 1000-ft reel (about 11 min), to plan a synchronous drive, and to use electrical reproduction in order that, with the help of amplifiers, adequate sound output could be had.

It was not desirable (in view of background noise) with record materials then available, materially to reduce amplitudes of cuts, and so groove pitch had to be kept nearly the same as then in current use (about 100 grooves per inch). To maintain quality the minimum linear groove velocity must not be reduced. With a given groove pitch and minimum velocity, the maximum playing time for a given record diameter is obtained by recording to half the maximum diameter, and the required playing time determines the needed size and corresponding rotation speed. While the engineers could take some leeway, the choice of 16 in. outside diameter and $33\frac{1}{3}$ rpm, approximately met the conditions indicated.

For synchronous recording, the camera and the recording turntable can be driven by selsyn motors, which driving system gives the equivalent of both being geared together and driven from one shaft. Starting marks on both film and disk are of course essential.

For reproducing, the turntable and projector were mechanically geared together. A simple magnetic pickup, if not damped, has a high-frequency resonance in which the armature whips, giving excessive output and high mechanical impedance at the needle tip.[51] The magnetic pickup used in the sound-picture system was designed for use with replaceable steel needles and damped by enclosing the moving elements (except the needle-holder and needle) in oil.[52]

The turntable driving systems[52-54] evolved for the sound pictures are discussed in the section on "Mechanical Systems" — the great problem being (as had been the case throughout the history of sound recording) to obtain sufficiently nearly constant speed.

The loudspeakers which had been developed for public address applications[55] were of the "balanced armature" type, had good power-handling capacity, and were regarded as fairly satisfactory from the standpoint of articulation. Designs of horns had been evolved which fairly successfully controlled the directivity for auditorium purposes. In 1923 Dr. Wente built a speaker of the moving-coil type which gave greatly improved quality[56] (especially the better bass response which is possible with the moving-coil drive), but in terms of efficiency and power-handling capacity it was not satisfactory. It was not until 1926 that a speaker of

the moving-coil type was developed by Wente and Thuras[57] which met the requirements for quality, efficiency and power-handling capabilities. Speakers of this design rapidly superseded those of earlier design, and continued in use for years.

According to the account of Lovette and Watkins[48] the sound-on-film system, on which another group of engineers had been engaged, was capable in 1924 of matching the quality of the disk system, but the latter represented an older art in which there were fewer uncertainties. The greater confidence with which the company could offer the disk system, and with which a potential customer would consider it, were responsible for choosing it as the first to be pushed. However, interest on the part of most of the picture producers was cool, nor did Craft, conscious of the numerous failures of previous efforts by others, think it desirable to hasten the commercialization of either system until its weaknesses were worked out.

Samuel Warner and Vitaphone.[58] With many details omitted, the foregoing is the description of the sound-on-disk system which became known as Vitaphone. Col. Nathan Levinson,[48] then serving the Western Electric Co. in the Pacific district where he had had close association with Samuel L. Warner, made a business trip to New York early in 1925 and saw a demonstration of the sound pictures. He felt sure that Mr. Warner would be interested, and arranged for a demonstration at the first opportunity. Samuel Warner was more than convinced, and his enthusiasm quickly spread to his brothers. More thorough tests were arranged, using cameramen, technicians and artists of the Warner staff, in cooperation with Western Electric engineers. The adoption of sound by a large picture-producing company would mean a huge outlay, and its success was a question not only of technical performance, but of the artistic, dramatic and psychological results which could be achieved through the addition of sound. The tests were convincing to the Warner Brothers, if not to the executives of some other picture companies who witnessed them. To develop and market sound motion pictures and equipment, the Vitaphone Corporation was organized in April 1926, with Samuel L. Warner as its president.

The first major Vitaphone sound picture to be released was *Don Juan*,[1,48] (August 1926) in which music by the New York Philharmonic Orchestra was featured. The new loudspeaker developed by Wente and Thuras was ready in time for this. Preparations were made for producing sound pictures in Hollywood, where sound stages were erected embodying the recommendations of the foremost experts in acoustics. The pro-

duction of *The Jazz Singer* with Al Jolson, was begun in the spring of 1927 and it was shown in New York on October 6. Its success was such that the industry was convinced "overnight" that the day of sound pictures had arrived.

Improvements in the Disk System. Under the title "Recent Advances in Wax Recording"[50] H. A. Frederick tells of a number of advances subsequent to the 1926 account by Maxfield and Harrison. By improvements in record material and wax processing techniques, it had been possible to reduce surface noise by 3 to 6 db. A new pickup (4A) is described with smoother response and good to about 4500 cycles, as compared with 4000 cycles for the previous model. A response curve for the commercial recorder shows practically uniform response to 5500 cycles. Laboratory models of recorder and reproducer are mentioned as carrying the response to 7500 cycles. The new recorder used a longer rubber damping line. Frederick gives the groove pitch as 10 mils and the minimum groove velocity as 70 ft/min. He also reported very satisfactory results with re-recording.

Western Electric Sound on Film

Mention has been made of fundamental studies of speech waves, begun in 1912 and carried on through several years until interrupted by the war. Amplifier tubes became available as laboratory tools in 1913. Photographic records of speech waveshapes were made, using at first a carbon transmitter, an amplifier and a Duddell oscillograph. The weakest link in this chain of equipment was the transmitter, whose response varied greatly with frequency and which had a high level of background noise, making it difficult to get reliable traces of consonants and other relatively weak speech sounds. The development of a better transmitter was one of the first undertakings of Edward C. Wente,[43] who came to the company in 1914.[44-47]

The Condenser Transmitter. If the charge on a pair of condenser plates is maintained through a sufficiently high resistance, the voltage is directly proportional to the separation of the plates, so that a transmitter based on this principle is an amplitude-sensitive device. If the diaphragm, which is one of the condenser plates, is so stiff in relation to its mass that resonance occurs above the required frequency range, the diaphragm deflection is proportional to the instantaneous air pressure. Wente met this mechanical requirement by using a stretched steel diaphragm 0.002 in. thick and spaced 0.001 in. from a relatively massive backplate. The very thin layer of air contributes greatly to the stiffness of the diaphragm, but the flow of air through the narrow space toward and from a relief space around the edges causes damping, so

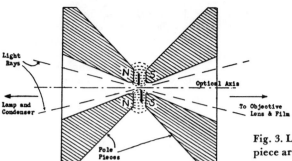

Fig. 3. Light-valve ribbon and pole piece arrangement; section at right angles to ribbons.

that a nearly flat (uniform) response was obtained up to about 15,000 cycles.

Wente left the company in 1916 for graduate study and returned in 1918. In the meantime Dr. I. B. Crandall had made a theoretical analysis of the air-film damping, and improved the instrument by means of grooves of appropriate size and shape in the backplate.[45] For measurement purposes it was essential to calibrate the condenser transmitter, and Wente accomplished this by working out the theory of the thermophone, which enabled him to make a reliable pressure calibration.[46] Free field calibrations were made later, using a Rayleigh disk as reference. In a later design,[47] which was used commercially for sound recording, the sensitivity was greatly increased, in part by use of aluminum alloy 0.001 in. thick instead of 0.002 in. steel for the diaphragm, and in part by not carrying the response as far into the high-frequency range. (In 1931 W. C. Jones published a pressure calibration curve for a #394 transmitter which showed a rapid drop above about 7000 cycles.[47]) The condenser tramsmitter is rated as a a very insensitive device, but it is of interest that a diaphragm deflection of a millionth of an inch will give a fifth of a volt, the gradient in the space between electrodes being 200 v per mil. It is the extreme stiffness of the diaphragm which makes the sensitivity low.

Photographic Recordings. The condenser transmitter with amplifier gave better waveshape traces, but the narrow mirror of the bifilar (or Duddell) oscillograph causes diffraction effects which make the light-spot at the film blurred or fuzzy. Prof. A. C. Hardy showed[59] that this trouble could be largely eliminated by radical changes in the optical system in which the oscillograph vibrator is used, but his analysis was not published until 1927 (in time to be of much help in the General Electric recording developments, but the Western Electric experiments with the oscillograph were before 1920).

An article in a British Journal (1920) came to Wente's attention, describing experiments of Prof. A. O. Rankine in transmission of sound over a beam of light. The light modulator, in which a rocking mirror caused an image of one

grating formed on another grating to move transversely to the bars, appeared well adapted to making photographic records of the variable-density type. While a variable-density record would not give as much information to the eye as a variable-area record, it could be analyzed by instruments of the microdensitometer type. The faithfulness of the recording could be checked by playing it back. (The previous oscillographic recordings had not been designed for playing back.)

Some of the recordings were played in May 1922 for Craft and others. A few months later apparatus-development engineers were requested to construct an electrically interlocking driving system for camera and recorder. Further demonstrations were given in December 1922. In these recordings the principle was recognized, that for linear relations between exposing light and print transmission, the product of positive and negative "gammas" should be unity.[61,62]

Light Valve. The grating type of modulator had several drawbacks, one of which was diffraction by the grating. Because of these difficulties, Wente in January 1923 proposed using a two-string light valve.[63—65,4] Such a valve was ready for test a month later. The tension on the ribbons was adjusted to bring their resonance to 6500 cycles. Condensing lenses imaged the light source on the slit between the ribbons, and an objective lens imaged the valve slit on the film.

Results with the light valve were definitely better than with the previous modulators, and arrangements were made for tests on a larger scale. A recording studio was set up in 1923 and sound pictures made for demonstration purposes.

In the latter part of 1922 and subsequently, much of the study of film emulsions, exposures and developments was carried on by Dr. Donald MacKenzie. He showed that by running the lamp at slightly over-voltage, it was possible adequately to expose positive film, which thereafter was the standard sound-recording stock. The relatively fine grain of the positive stock was of great benefit from the standpoint of resolution and low background noise.

In 1928 MacKenzie described the light-valve model in use at the time, and recording and processing practice (exposure ranges and developments) as worked out at the Bell Telephone Laboratories.[64] The valve is mounted with the slit between ribbons horizontal — so that its image on the film is transverse to the film. The ribbons are in a strong magnetic field and currents in the two are in opposite directions, so that they are deflected (edgewise) to increase or decrease their separation depending on the direction of the current. The width of the slit with no current in the ribbon was 0.002 in., and it was masked to a length of about 0.2 in. It was imaged on the film with a 2:1 reduction. With the slit width 0.002 in., the light could be modulated 100% by a vibration of each ribbon of 0.001 in. amplitude. Since the ribbon need be only slightly wider than its double amplitude, thick enough to be opaque, reasonably easy to handle and long enough between supports to make the deflection substantially uniform throughout the length of the slit, it can be extremely light and readily put under enough tension to place its mechanical resonance above the required audio range. Rather than attempting to control the resonance by damping beyond that obtainable electromagnetically, an electrical low-pass filter was used in the input, to prevent the passage of any impulses of high enough frequency to excite the resonance. However the cutoff was not too far below the frequency of resonance to permit a considerable rise in amplitude just before cutoff, the maximum being at about 7000 cycles. This rise was regarded as advantageous in that it compensated for loss of high-frequency response due to image spread in the film. For monitoring, a photocell behind the film picked up some of the light which went through the film.

The subject of sensitometry for sound-tracks of the variable-density type also received attention from many other writers for a number of years after the advent of photographic sound.

In the matter of the frequency range attained in the early light-valve recordings, MacKenzie shows an overall (light-valve input to photocell output) curve which was substantially flat to 5000 cycles, a figure not far from what could be obtained at the time with disks.

Recorder. The Western Electric recording machine employed a sound sprocket, having a filtered drive and protected by a feed sprocket from jerks from the magazines.[4] The film was exposed while on the sound sprocket. For synchronism the camera and recorder were driven by selsyn motors.

Soundhead. For reproduction from photographic soundtracks the Western Electric Co. built a "soundhead," to be mounted under the picture projector,[52-54] similar in many respects to that previously mentioned as used in the Fox-Case development. I shall come back to the subject of the mechanical features of the film-motion system, so shall mention here only some optical and electrical features. The scanning light on the film was an image of a mechanical slit, illuminated by a low-voltage incandescent lamp, with condensing lenses. The filament was a close-wound helix with straight horizontal axis. The photocell and preamplifier were cushion-mounted to prevent microphonic noises. Owing to the very high impedance of the photocell and its small output, a very short (low-capacity) connection to the first amplifier tube is important. The preamplifier brought the level up to about equal to that of the disk pickups.

Standard Speed. In the early theater installations most projectors were equipped for both disk and film reproduction. It was obvious that for sound pictures the recording and reproducing speeds must be closely held to a standard. The practice had become widespread of projecting silent pictures at considerably higher speeds than that of the camera, which had for years been nominally 16 pictures/sec or 60 ft/min. The higher projection speeds shortened the show so that more shows could be run in a day, and the public had become inured to the fast action. But there was a better justification in that flicker was much reduced.

For pictures with sound on film there was further benefit from increased speed in that it resulted in better high-frequency response and, in some degree, reduced percentage of speed fluctuation. A speed of 85 ft/min for silent pictures had been recommended for a standard, but practice varied widely. A speed of 90 ft/min or 24 frames/sec was chosen for both of the Western Electric sound-picture systems (sound on disk and sound on film) and this became the standard. On the theory that exhibitors would demand the option of running silent films at other speeds, the Western Electric engineers adopted a driving system with an accurate control which could be made inactive at the option of the projectionist.[54] Either a repulsion motor or a d-c motor might be used. For 90 ft/min a 720-cycle generator fed a bridge with one arm tuned to 720 cycles. At the correct speed the bridge was balanced, but if the speed was not correct the unbalance gave rise to a correcting current which increased or decreased the motor speed as required.

Commercialization. In January 1927 Electrical Research Products Inc. was formed as a subsidiary of Western Electric and the Telephone Co. to handle commercial relations with motion-picture producers and exhibitors.

The adoption of sound systems by the motion-picture industry (except for the case of Fox Movietone and Warner Vitaphone) is discussed in another section of this paper.

Developments at General Electric Co.

Interest in photographic sound recording at the General Electric Co. in Schenectady stems from the development prior to 1920 of a photographic telegraph recorder for radio reception,[66] by Charles A. Hoxie. Transoceanic radio service was by long waves, and static interference caused the loss of many letters. It was thought that a visual record of the incoming signals, even though mutilated by static, might be deciphered at leisure in many cases in which the signals were forever lost if the operator, depending on ear alone, failed to recognize a letter.

For the usual reception, by ear, the incoming continuous-wave code signals were heterodyned to give interrupted tones of audio frequency, short for dot and longer for dash. Hoxie's recorder made an oscillographic record of these code signal tones, on a moving strip of sensitized paper. Instead of actuating a receiver diaphragm the electrical signals vibrated a reed armature, which, through a delicate knife-edge arrangement, imparted rotary motion to a mirror, which caused a small spot of light to dance back and forth across the sensitive strip.

Since the code recorder vibrated at audio frequency, it was a short step to try it and modifications of it for recording voice, and this was one of the many experiments which Hoxie tried which started him on more systematic experimentation in the field of photographic sound recording. Negative film was used at first, in order to get adequate exposure, but Hoxie was among the first to appreciate the advantage of the finer-grain positive film.

As in the case of the telegraph recorder, the track ran down the middle of the film, and was nearly an inch in width. In Hoxie's recording and reproducing machine the film was drawn over a physical slit on which intense light was concentrated. The width of the slit was about 0.001 in. Since an open slit would quickly fill with dirt, a wedge of fused quartz was ground to a thin edge and cemented in place between the metal edges which formed the slit. The face against which the film was to run was then lapped and polished. A photocell close behind the film picked up the transmitted light, and an amplifier and loudspeaker completed the reproducing system. The results were highly gratifying. Theisen[5] says that Hoxie's first sound recorder was completed in 1921, and with it he recorded speeches by President Coolidge, the Secretary of War and others, and the recorded speeches were broadcast over Station WGY (Schenectady) in 1922.

Hoxie called his optical phonograph the Pallophotophone, meaning "shaking light sound." We do not know the identity of the Greek scholar. In another experimental development, Hoxie caused the vibration of a sound-pickup diaphragm to rock the mirror. This device, called the Pallotrope, was used with a photocell as a photoelectric microphone.

Narrow Sound Track Found Sufficient. Hoxie continued his experimenting for several years before any decision was reached to embark on an all-out program of developing a system of sound for motion pictures. One of Hoxie's experiments which undoubtedly played a part in interesting executives in such a program was that of reproducing with part of his track width masked. The development of the General Electric model of the Duddell oscillograph had centered in the General Engineering Laboratory (where Hoxie worked) and it was extensively used as a laboratory tool throughout the company. With such a background it would be natural to think of a photographic sound track as showing the outlines of the sound waves.

In any case the wide soundtracks made in the Hoxie equipment were of the variable-area type. A spot of light moved parallel with the slit, illuminating a larger or smaller fraction of its length. However, the active edge of the light spot was by no means sharp. While experimenting with reproduction from this sound track, Hoxie observed that masking off part of the track had little effect on the sound except some reduction in volume. He repeated the experiment with still more of the track masked off, until he was using only a sample, about $\frac{1}{16}$ in. wide. This experience was sufficient to demonstrate that a track wide enough to show the wave outlines was by no means necessary for sound reproduction. The narrow strip being scanned was obviously a variable-density record of the sound.

At that early stage of the experimenting we had not seen it demonstrated by actual accomplishment that a satisfactory variable-area recording could be confined within so limited a band, but at any rate this test proved that a photographic sound record could be placed along the side of the picture without stealing more picture width than could be tolerated.

Loudspeaker and Phonograph Developments. Another factor which undoubtedly influenced General Electric executives toward increased interest in sound was the success of the loudspeakers developed by C. W. Rice and myself for broadcast radio reception.[38] The coil-driven (or "dynamic") paper cone, freely suspended, surrounded by a baffle and driven by an amplifier with adequate undistorted power, so far surpassed its predecessors in quality of reproduction that within a few years its use for radio receivers and phonographs became practically universal.*

Following the loudspeaker development, the success of the electric phonograph helped to make the sound motion picture seem like a logical next project.

Chester W. Rice. I trust that I will be excused if I take this opportunity to pay a brief tribute to my colleague, whose vision and initiative were largely responsible for our undertaking the loudspeaker project. His thoroughness and tireless energy insured that no hopeful lead was left unexplored. He brought to bear on his work an extraordinary measure of ingenuity and mastery of engineering and physical principles, which he was constantly supplementing by study, and his standards of excellence would permit no compromise with an inferior result.

No one could have been more scrupulously fair and generous in giving credit to other workers. His death in 1951 was a great loss to his associates and to science.

C. W. Stone's Leadership. In addition to L. T. Robinson, head of the General Engineering Laboratory, the man who played the major role in initiating and promoting a large-scale project for developing talking pictures, was C. W. Stone, manager of the Central Station Dept., who had taken great interest in all of the sound developments. His enthusiasm, confidence and influence encouraged those who were engaged in development, helped to secure the financial backing and established fruitful contacts outside the company.

Practical designs; Assistance of Prof. A. C. Hardy and L. E. Clark. When, about 1925, a program of developing commercial sound-on-film equipment was undertaken, Robinson was made responsible for the general program, and, together with others in the Research Laboratory, I was asked to assist in problems where there seemed to be call for research. Engineers in the General Engineering and Research Laboratories had had experience in sound, first with loudspeakers[38] and then in cooperation with the Brunswick Balke Callender Co., electrical recording and reproduction for phonographs[51] (the work represented in the Brunswick Panatrope[51] and the

Brunswick electrically recorded disks). Our part in the phonograph project was tapering off, freeing some of the personnel to devote time to the newer development. Our group, however, had inadequate background in optics and photography. Professor A. C. Hardy was engaged as consultant and soon did us two invaluable services: he straightened us out on a number of optical and photographic questions, and he recommended that we engage the services of L. E. Clark, then completing some advanced work at Massachusetts Institute of Technology. "Pete's" presence was a guarantee that we would not again get off the beam on optical questions, but his associates at General Electric, then at Photophone headquarters in New York, and later in Hollywood, carry a memory of something far more cherished than his valuable technical help.

Variable-Area System Chosen. A fundamental question on which we took Prof. Hardy's advice was in regard to the advantages of the variable-area type of soundtrack.[61] At the time of Hoxie's tests with a masked track, the only tracks that had been made, sufficiently narrow and still fairly satisfactory, were of variable density. A better understanding and application of optical design was needed to make clear, sharp-edged variable-area tracks within permissible limits of width.[59,60]

With the right kind of lenses and optical design, an imaged slit soon displaced the contacting physical slit with which the first tracks had been made. Hoxie's special galvanometer was not adequately damped, but General Electric had long since been building oil-damped oscillographs of the Duddell type, whose response was good up to 5000 cycles. The optics of the recording system are similar in principle to those of the oscillograph, as explained in one of Hardy's papers.[59] Prof. Hardy had shown how important design improvements could be made, greatly increasing the light intensity at the film. An optical system was designed[60] using a regular oscillograph galvanometer, and following suggestions of Prof. Hardy and of L. E. Clark.

The general mechanical features of the first recording machines were due principally to Hoxie, while H. B. Marvin (of the General Engineering Laboratory) designed amplifiers, optical systems and other necessary equipment. High-quality microphones were available in the Western Electric Condenser Transmitter (developed by E. C. Wente of the Bell Laboratories)[44-47] which was used in broadcast studios and had been an essential tool in the loudspeaker[38] and phonograph developments.[51]

General Electric had a well established motion-picture laboratory under the direction of C. E. Bathcholtz, for general company and publicity service,

so that with the cooperation of that department, pictures with sound could be made. A number of demonstrations were given in 1926 and 1927, using this equipment. Motion-picture producers showed interest, but no contracts were made at that time.

An incident of much interest to those who were connected with the photographic recording project was a visit to Schenectady in December 1925 by E. I. Sponable from the Case Laboratories.[6] He showed and demonstrated the combined camera and sound-recording system which he and his associates had developed, giving us the benefit of his experience and participating in some demonstrations. However, no arrangements for combining the efforts resulted.

The Road-Show Wings. The first public entertainment picture to be shown, with the General Electric developed sound system, which by this time had been named the Kinegraphone, was a story of the Air Force activities in World War I, entitled *Wings* and produced by Paramount. The sound effects were added after the picture had been shot. The system and equipment were demonstrated and briefly described by H. B. Marvin.[67]

Wings was exhibited in 1927 as a "road show" (about a dozen sets of equipment having been supplied), for few motion-picture theaters at the time *Wings* was shown were equipped for optical sound reproduction. Multiple-unit cone-and-baffle type loudspeakers[38] were used, with a bank each side of the screen. The sound-reproducing device or "head" was mounted on the top of the projector, no standard sound offset having been established at the time the apparatus was designed. The picture width was reduced from 1 in. to $\frac{7}{8}$ in. to make room for a soundtrack. Ninety ft./min had by this time been agreed upon for film speed.

There were many, even of the most enthusiastic advocates of sound-picture development at General Electric, who did not think of the chief function of the synchronized sound as giving speech to actors in plays, but there was high confidence that there was a large potential market for sound systems for furnishing sound effects and background music and providing voice for lectures and speeches.

G.E.–Westinghouse–RCA Working Arrangements

At the time that the synchronized sound development was taking shape, the three-cornered arrangement between General Electric, Westinghouse and RCA was in effect. RCA was the sales outlet for all radio and kindred equipment. Manufacturing was divided between General Electric and Westinghouse. Research and development continued to be carried on at both manufacturing companies, and before production was

---

* Many of the elements of this type of loudspeaker, such as coil drive, cone diaphragms and the baffle had been proposed individually by early inventors, but not in the full combination. Nor, I believe, was the principle of placing the mechanical resonance of the diaphragm (with its suspension) at or below the lowest important frequency proposed, except that Adrian Sykes (U.S. Pats. 1,711,551 and 1,852,068) advocated it for a microphone. The Farrand loudspeaker (U. S. Pat. 1,847,935, filed 1921. See Radio Club of America, Oct. 1926) had a large cone, coil-drive and low resonance-frequency, but no baffle or associated power amplifier. It had considerable commercial success during the 1920's.

started, designs were coordinated between them and had also to be acceptable to RCA, which maintained a Technical and Test Dept. in New York, to pass on performance.

At Schenectady, in view of the prospects of manufacturing on a much larger scale than could be handled in the General Engineering Laboratory, the film project had been transferred (1927) to the Radio Dept. where it was under the direction of E. W. Engstrom. The change brought new personnel into the activity. The names of E. D. Cook and G. L. Dimmick deserve mention.

Developments at Westinghouse

Engineers at the Westinghouse Electric and Manufacturing Co. in East Pittsburgh did not turn their attention to photographic sound recording until about 1926 when the project at Schenectady had gained some momentum.

One of the first research projects undertaken was to adapt the Kerr cell to photographic recording. The development was described to this Society in 1928 by V. K. Zworykin, L. B. Lynn and C. R. Hanna.[68] Nitrobenzene has the property of rotating the plane of polarization of a light beam, when the liquid is subjected to an electrical field at right angles to the direction of the light. The amount of rotation depends on the square of the field gradient. Practically, several hundred volts per millimeter are required. Nicol polarizing prisms are used on each side of the cell and rotated to extinguish the light at minimum applied voltage. With increase of voltage, the transmitted light then varies as the sine of the increase in angle of rotation.

One of the design problems is to keep within satisfactory limits the distortion resulting from the nonlinear relation between voltage and transmitted light. Another difficulty is that commercial nitrobenzene is yellow, absorbing the photographically valuable blue light. The investigators were able by double distillation to reduce very largely the absorption of blue light. A third problem was avoidance of electrical arcs through the liquid, which quickly contaminate it. Proper choice of electrode material and surfaces, and purification of the liquid made it possible to produce cells which were regarded as practical.

The unique property of the Kerr cell light modulator which makes it of special interest is its extreme speed. The only limitation is in the ability of the modulation-voltage supply system to charge the extremely small capacity of the cell. As contrasted with this, other light-modulation systems either involve moving mechanical elements, or electrical discharges through gases, which have definite frequency limitations.

Zworykin, Lynn and Hanna were in the Westinghouse Research Laboratory, which was under the direction of Mr.

Kintner. A group under Max C. Batsel was responsible for development and design of commercial equipment. One of this group was J. D. Seabert, whose contribution to the theater loudspeaker problem will be described in the paragraph with that heading. Hanna's analysis of the damped flywheel problem[69] laid the foundation for the highly successful rotary stabilizer discussed under that heading in the section dealing with Mechanical Systems.

Organization of RCA Photophone, Inc.

RCA Photophone, Inc. was organized in 1928 as an RCA subsidiary to carry on commercial exploitation of the sound-on-film system. Carl Dreher (later with RKO) was its first chief engineer, followed in 1929 by Max C. Batsel from the Westinghouse Co. A laboratory was established in New York to which a number of engineers were transferred from the Technical and Test Dept. of RCA.

New Designs of Commercial Units. Between the launching of the *Wings* show and the offering by RCA Photophone, Inc., of a commercial sound system,* a number of design changes and advances had been made. C. L. Heisler had designed a new recording machine (R-3) and a combined picture and sound projector (P-2),[70] both of which embodied new principles in film motion. A sound attachment or "soundhead" was developed, by which existing silent projectors could be adapted for sound. The offset between picture and sound had meantime been standardized at $14\frac{1}{2}$ in., with the soundhead mounted under the projector. Because of the much more stringent requirement for accurate and constant speed for sound than for picture, the driving motor was made part of the soundhead, and the projector mechanism driven from the soundhead through gears. The first commercial soundhead to be offered by the RCA group (designated as PS-1) was of Westinghouse design, but the manufacturing was carried on by both companies.

Theater Loudspeakers. The flat baffle type of loudspeaker[38] used in the *Wings* equipment and in almost universal use for home receivers, while excellent for music and sound effects, had not proved satisfactory for *speech* reproduction in reverberant theaters. While a certain kind of directivity can be had by using arrays of direct-radiator loudspeakers, vibrating in phase, this did not confine the radiation in the direction of the

* H. B. Franklin in *Sound Motion Pictures*[2] gives May 14, 1928, as the date of an announcing advertisement in New York and Los Angeles papers; however the Progress Report, *Trans. SMPE*, No. 31, 438, May 1927, states that Photophone equipment is to be sold direct to theaters, and that recording efforts would be concentrated on music scores.

audience as successfully as the use of short horns. The first successful units of this type were developed by J. D. Seabert in 1929 (then of Westinghouse). The horns used at first expanded from about the cone area to an opening abut 3 ft by 4 ft. The name "directional baffle" was used to distinguish these horns, whose primary function was to confine the radiation within a limited angle, from the small-throat horns whose basic function was to load the diaphragm, in addition to confining the radiation. The directional baffle type of unit was the subject of later developments by Dr. H. F. Olson and his associates.[71-73]

In spite of the benefits of directive baffles, in many motion-picture theaters satisfactory speech reproduction was not achieved until absorption had been applied to reduce reverberation.

Location Equipment. The RCA equipment also included a truck for location and newsreel service.[75] With batteries for power supply, the truck carried a motor generator for driving apparatus designed for 60-cycle operation, and a studio-type film recorder, to be driven in synchronism with a cable-connected camera. For more remote or inaccessible locations, a single-film system was provided, with portable batteries and amplifier, governed direct-current camera motor, and a sound attachment, mounted on the top of the camera.[74] The first commercial uses of RCA Photophone recording equipment were for newsreel service. Two types of light modulator were employed in the earliest Photophone single-film location equipments, one of which used a galvanometer designed by W. O. Osborn and K. A. Oplinger, under the direction of C. R. Hanna, with optics generally similar to those of the studio system, and the other the Kerr cell (or Carolus cell) system developed by L. B. Lynn and V. K. Zworykin.[68]

Location equipment (sound trucks) of improved design followed within a short time. Of special interest was a new optical system requiring only 3 w for the lamp.[76]

Disk Equipment. Although the RCA group was convinced of the inherent advantages of sound on film for motion-picture sound, disk equipment was wanted in all of the earlier theater installations, and accordingly combined sound-on-film and synchronous disk equipment was designed and built by the G.E. and Westinghouse companies and supplied by RCA Photophone, Inc.

A number of developments and inventions took place at both of the manufacturing companies which did not come into commercial use for several years, and these will be described presently.

Commercialization. The establishment of commercial relations with picture producers is described in the latter part of the following section.

184

Bibliography and References

1. Lester Cowan, *Recording Sound for Motion Pictures*, McGraw-Hill Book Co., New York, 1931; H. G. Knox, "Ancestry of sound pictures," Chap. 1.
2. H. B. Franklin, *Sound Motion Pictures*, Doubleday, Doran and Co., 1929.
3. Academy of Motion Pictures Arts and Sciences, *Motion Picture Sound Engineering*, D. Van Nostrand & Co., New York, 1938.
4. J. G. Frayne and H. Wolfe, *Elements of Sound Recording*, J. Wiley & Sons, New York, 1949.
5. W. E. Theisen, "Pioneering in the talking picture," *Jour. SMPE*, 36: 415–444, Apr. 1941.
6. E. I. Sponable, "Historical development of sound films," Pt. 1–2, *Jour. SMPE*, 48: 275–303, Apr. 1947; Pt. 3–7, *ibid.*, 407–422, May 1947.
7. F. H. Richardson, "What happened in the beginning," *Trans. SMPE*, No. 22, 63–114, 1925.
8. T. A. Edison, U.S. Pat. 200,521, 227,679.
9. Terry Ramsaye, *History of the Motion Picture*, Simon & Schuster, New York, 1925.
10. Terry Ramsaye, "Early history of sound pictures," *Trans. SMPE*, No. 35, 597–602, 1928.
11. A. Dickson and W. K. L. Dickson, *History of the Kinetograph, Kinetoscope and Kineto-Phonograph*, Albert Bunn, N.Y., 1895.
12. W. K. L. Dickson, "A brief history of the Kinetograph, Kinetoscope and Kineto-Phonograph," *Jour. SMPE*, 21: 435–455, Dec. 1933.
13. Will H. Hays, *See and Hear*, p. 40, Motion Picture Producers and Distributors of America, New York, 1929.
14. E. H. Amet, U.S. Pat. 1,124,580 and 1,162,433, 1915.
15. W. H. Bristol, "An electrical synchronizing and resynchronizing system for sound motion picture apparatus," *Trans. SMPE*, No. 35, 778–789, 1928; and "New synchronizing apparatus for 16 mm films with disk records," *Jour. SMPE*, 14: 361–365, Mar. 1930; also U.S. Pat. 1,234,127, 1917.
16. Oskar Messter, *Mein Weg Mit dem Film*, Max Hesse Verlag, Berlin Schöneberg, 1936; Bk. Rev., *Jour. SMPE*, 332, Sept 1937; also Brit. Pat. 22,563, 22,564, 22,565.
17. T. A. Edison, U.S. Pat. 1,182,897, 1916; also Daniel Higham, U.S. Pat. 1,036,235, 1,054,203, 1,036,236 and 1,226,883.
18. E. W. Blake, *Am. J. of Science*, No. 16, 54, 1878.
19. A. C. Hardy and F. H. Perrin, *The Principles of Optics*, McGraw-Hill Book Co., New York, 1932.
20. V. K. Zworykin and E. G. Ramberg, *Photoelectricity and Its Application*, J. Wiley & Sons, New York, 1949.
21. L. R. Koller, "Characteristics of photoelectric cells," *Trans. SMPE*, No. 36, 921–939, 1928.
22. M. F. Jamieson, T. E. Shea and P. H. Pierce, "The photoelectric cell and its method of operation," *Jour. SMPE*, 27: 365–385, Oct. 1936.
23. L. de Forest, U.S. Pat. 841,386, 841,387, 879,532.
24. See refs. 392–399.
25. Frederick V. Hunt, *Electroacoustics*, J. Wiley & Sons, London and New York, 1954.
26. T. A. Edison, U.S. Pat. 307,031; and J. A. Fleming, U. S. Pat. 803,684.
27. V. Poulsen, U.S. Pat. 661,619, 789,336, 873,078, 873,083. "Der Telegraphon," *Annal. der Physik*, 1900.
28. Wallace C. Sabine, *Collected Papers on Acoustics*, Harvard University Press, 1922; and *Acoustics and Architecture*, McGraw-Hill Book Co., New York, 1932.
29. See refs. 400 et seq. — on lamp developments.
30. T. Mishima, "Nickel-aluminum steel for permanent magnets," *Stahl und Eisen*, 53: 79, 1933; and U.S. Pats. 2,027,994 to 2,028,000 incl; also W. E. Ruder, "New magnetic alloys," *Proc. IRE*, 30: 437, 1942.
31. Ref. 6, also gives the references *Annal. der Phys.*, 103, 1901, and *Phys. Zeit.*, No. 34, 498, 1901; Ref. 5, p. 421, and Crawford, ref. 32, refer to an article by Rühmer in the *Scientific American*, July 29, 1901.
32. Report of the Historical Committee, *Jour. SMPE*, 16: 105–109, Jan. 1931; Merritt Crawford, "Pioneer experiments of Eugene Lauste in recording sound," *Jour. SMPE*, 17: 632–644, Oct. 1931.
33. R. W. Paul, "Kinematographic experiences," *Jour. SMPE*, 27: 495–512, Nov. 1936; *also*, Thomas Armat, "My part in the development of the motion picture projector," *Jour. SMPE*, 24: 241–256, Mar. 1935. (These are of interest, though they do not deal with sound.)
34. J. T. Tykociner, "Photographic recording and photo-electric reproduction of sound," *Trans. SMPE*, No. 16, 90–119, 1923.
35. Hans Vogt, Joseph Massole and Josef Engl, U.S. *Tri-Ergon* Pats. 1,512,681; 1,534,148; 1,555,301; 1,557,678; 1,558,032; 1,566,413; 1,590,185; 1,597,323; 1,608,261; 1,628,377; 1,634,201; 1,756,681; 1,825,598; 1,713,726; Re. 20,621; 2,140,003 and others.
36. L. de Forest, "The Phonofilm," *Trans. SMPE*, No. 16, 61–75, May 1923; "Phonofilm progress," *Trans. SMPE*, No. 20, 17–19, 1924; "Recent developments in the Phonofilm," *Trans. SMPE*, No. 27, 64–76, 1927; "Pioneering in talking pictures," *Jour. SMPE*, 36: 41–49, Jan. 1941.
37. Theodore W. Case, Honor Roll Award, *Jour. SMPE*, 48: 437–440, May 1947.
38. Chester W. Rice and E. W. Kellogg, "Notes on the development of a new type of hornless loud speaker," *Trans. AIEE*, 44: 461, Apr. 1925.
39. Carl L. Gregory, "Resurrection of early motion pictures," *Jour. SMPE*, 42: 159–169, Mar. 1944.
40. Theodore W. Case, "Thalofide cell, a new photoelectric substance," *Phys. Rev.*, Apr. 1920, and *J. Opt. Soc. Am.*, No. 6, 398, 1922; U.S. Pats. 1,301,227 and 1,316,350.
41. Theodore W. Case, "Aeo-Light," U.S. Pat. 1,816,825.
42. Edward B. Craft, Honor Roll Award, *Jour. SMPE*, 48: 440–443, May 1947.
43. J. I. Crabtree, "The work of Edward Christopher Wente," (1935 Progress Medal Award), *Jour. SMPE*, 25: 478–482, Dec. 1935.
44. E. C. Wente, "A condenser as a uniformly sensitive instrument for the absolute measurement of sound intensity," *Phys. Rev.*, July 1917; U.S. Pat. 1,333,744.
45. I. B. Crandall, "The air damped vibratory system: theoretical calculation of the condenser transmitter," *Phys. Rev.*, 449, June 1918.
46. E. C. Wente, "Electrostatic transmitter," *Phys. Rev.*, 498, May 1922.
47. W. C. Jones, "Condenser and carbon microphones, their construction and use," *Jour. SMPE*, 16: 3–22, Jan. 1931.
48. Frank H. Lovette and Stanley Watkins, "Twenty years of talking movies, an Anniversary," *Bell Telephone Magazine*, Summer, 1946.
49. J. P. Maxfield and H. C. Harrison, "Methods of high quality recording and reproducing of music and speech based on telephone research," *Trans. AIEE*, 45: 334, 1926.
50. H. A. Frederick, "Recent advances in wax recording," *Trans. SMPE*, No. 35, 709–729, 1928.
51. E. W. Kellogg, "Electrical reproduction from phonograph records," *Trans. AIEE*, 46: 903, June 1927.
52. E. O. Scriven, "Western Electric sound projecting systems for use in motion picture theatres," *Trans. SMPE*, No. 35, 666–678, 1928.
53. H. Pfannenstiehl, "A reproducing machine for picture and sound," *Trans. SMPE*, No. 38, 253–267, 1929.
54. H. M. Stoller, "Synchronization and speed control of synchronized sound pictures," *Trans. SMPE*, No. 35, 696–708, 1928.
55. I. M. Green and J. P. Maxfield, "Public address systems," *Trans. AIEE*, 42: 64, 1923.
56. E. C. Wente, U.S. Pat. 1,812,389, "Acoustic device" (i.e. loudspeaker).
57. E. C. Wente and A. L. Thuras, "A high efficiency receiver of large power capacity for horn type loud speakers," *Bell Sys. Tech. J.*, Jan. 1928, p. 140.
58. Samuel L. Warner, Honor Roll Award, *Jour. SMPE*, 48: 443–446, May 1947.
59. A. C. Hardy, "Optical system of the oscillograph," *J. Opt. Soc. Am.* 14: 505, June 1927.
60. A. C. Hardy, "The optics of sound recording systems," *Trans. SMPE*, No. 35, 760–777, 1928.
61. A. C. Hardy, "The rendering of tone values in photographic recording of sound," *Trans. SMPE*, No. 31, 475–491, 1927.
62. L. A. Jones, "On the theory of tone reproduction with a graphic method for the solution of problems," *Jour. SMPE*, 16: 568–599, May 1931.
63. E. C. Wente, U.S. Pat. 1,638,555, "Translating devices" (light-valve).
64. Donald MacKenzie, "Sound recording with the light valve," *Trans. SMPE*, No. 35, 730–747, 1928.
65. T. E. Shea, W. Herriott and W. R. Goehner, "Principles of the light valve," *Jour. SMPE*, 18: 697–731, June 1932.
66. C. A. Hoxie, "A visual and photographic device for recording radio signals," *Proc. IRE*, 9: 506, Dec. 1921; and U.S. Pat. 1,758,794 (filed Aug. 1927).
67. H. B. Marvin, "A system of motion pictures with sound," *Trans. SMPE*, No. 33, 86–102, 1928.
68. V. K. Zworykin, L. B. Lynn and C. R. Hanna, "Kerr cell method of recording sound," *Trans. SMPE*, No. 35, 748–759, 1928.
69. C. R. Hanna, U.S. Pat. 2,003,048 (conditions for critical damping).
70. E. W. Kellogg, "A review of the quest for constant speed," *Jour. SMPE*, 28: 337–376, Apr. 1937.
71. H. F. Olson, "Recent developments in theater loudspeakers of the directional baffle type," *Jour. SMPE*, 18: 571–583, May 1932.
72. Louis Malter, "Loudspeakers and theater sound reproduction," *Jour. SMPE*, 14: 611–622, June 1930.
73. H. F. Olson and F. Massa, *Applied Acoustics*, P. Blakiston & Son, Philadelphia, 1934.
74. C. R. Hanna, "The Mitchell Recording Camera, equipped interchangeably for variable area and variable density sound recording," *Trans. SMPE*, No. 38, 312–317, 1929.
75. Harry W. Jones, "The modern newsreel," *Jour. SMPE*, 14: 204–208, Feb. 1930.
76. P. M. Robillard and E. B. Lyford, "Recent developments in RCA Photophone portable recording equipment," *Jour. SMPE*, 16: 269–276, Mar. 1931.

185

History of Sound Motion Pictures

By EDWARD W. KELLOGG

For the abstract of this paper which was presented on May 5, 1954, at the Society's Convention at Washington, D.C., see the first installment published in last month's Journal.

The Motion Picture Industry Adopts Sound

Many Commercially Unsuccessful Efforts. The historical outline with which our story began contains a very incomplete account of the many efforts to combine sound and picture, some of which attained a fair degree of technical success, elicited praise and held public interest for short periods. We mentioned the work of Edison, Lauste, Rümer, and de Forest, and might add Pathé Frères and Léon Gaumont* in France.[5] Many of these were ahead of their time, for without amplifiers, the production of adequate and natural sound was practically impossible. Even after amplifiers became available the experimenters had little better success in getting picture producers seriously interested. The article by Lovette and Watkins[48] states that by the end of 1924 practically every major producer in Hollywood had rejected Western Electric's sound-picture system.

Economic Hurdles. The same authors give such a convincing statement of the financial obstacles from the producer's standpoint that I cannot do better than quote them:

"The motion picture producers had large inventories of silent films, which had cost millions to produce. They had great numbers of actors and actresses under long term contracts, most of whom knew no dramatic technique except that of pantomime. The industry was universally equipped with stages and studios suited only to the silent film technique.

"Moreover, world-wide foreign markets had been established for silent films. To serve these markets, it was merely necessary to translate the words printed upon the film from English to any language desired. Finding stars and supporting casts who spoke the various languages of the world, or finding ways to give the illusion of their speaking them, appeared to be an insuperable task.

"The art of the silent film had attained superb quality and the public was satisfied. Why then, producers asked, should Hollywood scrap the bulk of its assets, undertake staggering conversion costs, and force upon the public a new and doubtful experimental art?

"Nor were the exhibitors equipped for sound. Many, it was argued, would not be able to meet the cost of sound picture equipment."

These obstacles would not have prevented the producers from introducing synchronized sound, had they been convinced that it would give their pictures greater appeal. A factor which many developers of sound equipment probably did not fully recognize, was that to contribute to the illusion, the sound must have a degree of naturalness far surpassing that which had sufficed for simply transmitting information, or making words understood.

How It Looked in 1926-7. To many, the silent motion picture, with its freedom of action, its settings for much of its action in natural backgrounds, was better entertainment than stage drama, and when one tried to imagine what a talking motion picture would be like, one's thoughts immediately turned to examples of theater drama. I have already quoted some of Dr. de Forest's reflections. The prevailing thought at the General Electric Co. as our system began to take shape is probably typical. Many, even of the most enthusiastic advocates of the sound-picture development were not convinced that the chief function of the synchronized sound would be to give speech to the actors in plays. The art of telling stories with pantomime only (with the help of occasional titles) had been so highly developed, that giving the actors voices seemed hardly necessary, although readily possible. Such a view was actually a very high tribute to the movie makers of the silent era. However, a very large business in synchronized sound seemed assured (even without any use of the system for dialogue) in furnishing sound effects, background music, and providing voice for lectures, speeches and travelogue commentary.

As one who shared in this misjudgment, I would like to suggest to readers that it is difficult today to divest oneself of the benefit of hindsight. At that time, the principal examples of sound pictures we had seen were demonstration films, very interesting to us sound engineers working on the project, but scarcely having entertainment value. None of us had seen a talking motion picture with a good story, and picture and script well designed for the purpose. When in 1927 such a picture was shown (*The Jazz Singer*) the story, the music and the dialogue were splendidly adapted to produce a fascinating picture with great emotional appeal, in which no element could have been spared without serious loss. In short, the excellence of showmanship played no small part in making it clear to everyone who saw it that the day of "Talkies" was here.

The Jazz Singer and its predecessor *Don Juan*, it might be noted, had the benefit of a newly designed loudspeaker,[57] very much superior to those used in the Western Electric 1924 demonstrations.

Warners and Fox Take the Step. Warner Brothers committed themselves to the adoption of sound pictures in 1926, license contract being concluded in April, followed by large investments in sound stages and equipment. In July of the same year the Fox Film Corp. became committed, forming the Fox Case Corp. which took license for the Case Laboratory developments in April, and in December from Western Electric Co. for rights to use amplifiers. Both Warners and Fox operated theater chains. With two major picture producing and exhibiting organizations definitely launched on a program of making and showing pictures, could the other great picture companies remain on the sidelines?

Large Producers Agree to Choose Same System.[6] Early in 1927 the first Fox Movietone Newsreel subjects were shown. The other picture companies must by this time have become convinced that sound pictures were inevitable, for a part, if not the whole of motion-picture entertainment. In February 1927, the "big five" — M-G-M, First National, Paramount, Universal and Producers' Distributing Corp. (or PDC), jointly asked the Hays organization to study and make recommendation as to what system should be adopted. The Movietone and Vitaphone (disk) had already

---

* Gaumont, in addition to many inventions and other activities, was a pioneer and successful leader in the motion-picture business, and probably came nearer to success with phonograph sound than others. See account, and references given in the Theisen history[5] from which ref. 77 is taken.

become commercial systems, Western Electric was offering a sound-on-film (light-valve) system, and General Electric had made a number of demonstrations of a variable-area system (later offered to the industry with some modifications through RCA Photophone). There had as yet been no formal standardization, and those participating in the conference probably felt some uncertainty about interchangeability of recordings. It is not strange that the picture companies thought it would be advantageous for all to adopt the same system.

By far the most ambitious demonstration of sound motion pictures that had as yet (February 1927) been witnessed was the Warner Vitaphone *Don Juan* (shown August 1926),[1, 43] with performances by noted artists and score and background music for the play by the New York Philharmonic Orchestra. And the sound quality was good. But it was a demonstration of synchronized sound, and not of sound motion-picture drama. The producers, still "on the fence," continued their "watchful waiting."

The presentation of *The Jazz Singer* in October 1927 dispelled all doubts. But whether the future lay with the disk or the film system was a question not completely settled for several years.

"Big Five" Sign Contracts with ERPI.[6] With such large producers as Warners making pictures with sound on disk and Fox with Movietone releases on film, it appeared that exhibitors might be saddled with a dual system. Perhaps it was the hope that one or the other would very soon forge ahead in the race that caused further hesitancy, but in April and May of 1928 (about six months after the showing of *The Jazz Singer*) Paramount, United Artists, M-G-M, First National, Universal and several others signed agreements with Electrical Research Products Inc. (the commercial outlet for the Western Electric systems) for licenses and recording equipment.

Getting Started.[1] There followed a period of feverish activity in erection of sound stages, and procurement and installation of recording channels and equipment. Deliveries of apparatus were far behind the desires of the customers, and there was great shortage of engineers and technicians with sound-picture background. The manufacturers and associated organizations lent or lost many of their personnel. Intensive training courses and much instructive literature alleviated the situation. The Transactions of the SMPE for the fall of 1928 are little short of an encyclopedia of sound recording and reproduction by both disk and film. To this body of literature, the engineers and processing laboratory experts from the producing companies soon began making their contributions.

Scarcely a step behind the building and equipping of recording studios was the installation of sound reproducing systems in theaters. Theater chains controlled by the picture-producing companies which had already signed contracts, used sound systems of the corresponding make, but the business of furnishing sound equipment to the great number of independent theaters was competitive between ERPI, RCA Photophone and many other suppliers. An idea of the rate of growth of the sound pictures, may be had from the following figures given in Sponable's paper.[6] At the end of 1927 there were some 157 theaters in the U.S. equipped for sound, of which 55 were for both disk and film and 102 for disk only. At the end of 1928, of the 1046 ERPI theater installations, 1032 were for disk *and* film. By the end of 1929 ERPI had equipped about 4000 theaters in the U.S. and 1200 abroad, and RCA Photophone had equipped some 1200 in the U.S. and 600 abroad, most of these being for both disk and film. The SMPE Progress Report of February 1930 states that at the time, Hollywood studios were producing only 5% silent pictures. Installations by other manufacturers brought the total number of theaters equipped for sound in the U.S. to over 8700. There were at the time 234 *different types* of theater sound equipment including the large number which were designed for disk only. At the end of 1930 there were about 13,500 theaters equipped for sound, and about 8200 not equipped, according to the SMPE Progress Report of August 1931.

Contracts for Photophone Variable-Area Recording. In 1928 RCA bought the theater chain interests of B. F. Keith and of Orpheum, and the film producing company Film Booking Office or F.B.O., and organized Radio Keith Orpheum or RKO. The new company (RKO), with Photophone equipment, and drawing heavily on the RCA group for much of its initial sound personnel, made many feature and shorter pictures, using the name Radio Pictures for its product. RCA Photophone made arrangements for license and equipment with Pathé Exchange Inc., Mack Sennett, Tiffany Stahl and with Educational Pictures Corp.

One of the first feature pictures made by Pathé was *King of Kings* directed by Cecil de Mille. The Pathé Newsreels were an important item, using a number of RCA mobile recording equipments or "sound trucks."

Disney switched to the RCA Photophone system in January 1933. Republic Pictures Inc. used the RCA system beginning October 1935 and Warner Brothers in June 1936. Columbia Pictures Inc. began May 1936 to use the RCA variable-area system for part of its operations, but continued for several years to release on variable-density.

Cinephone. The Powers Cinephone system was developed by R. R. Halpenny and William Garity for Patrick A. Powers, who financed the project. It was basically similar to the system of de Forest, with whom Powers had permissive contracts. Cinephone was put on the market in September 1929 and used for several years by Walt Disney and others.

Type of Contract. Most of the initial contracts between the equipment-manufacturing companies and the picture producers were on a lease (rather than outright sale) basis, for a stipulated term of years, with equipment servicing and engineering assistance as part of the suppliers' obligation, and royalties depending on the film footage recorded.

Evolution of a New Art,* Under Difficulties. The idea that the silent motion picture would continue to have its place in theater entertainment died hard. What *The Jazz Singer* had proved was that with a suitable story and presentation, a sound picture could have an appeal far beyond what was possible without sound. It had not proved that sound would help in *all* types of presentation. In March 1929, Fox discontinued making silent pictures. In speaking of this in his historical paper[5] of 1941, W. E. Theisen calls it a daring decision, "since a large number of the leaders of the industry still felt that sound films were only a passing fad." In "The Entertainment Value of the Sound Movie" (*Trans. SMPE*, No. 35, 1928), H. B. Franklin, President of West Coast Theatres, says: "The silent motion picture is too well established. . .to vanish because of this new development."

It took time, much work and some mistakes for the industry to learn to use sound to full advantage, and the great pressure under which writers and producers worked during the years of transition was not conducive to best results. Two quotations from 1928 papers are illuminating. In "The Public and Sound Pictures" (*Trans. SMPE*, No. 35) Wm. A. Johnson, Editor of *Motion Picture News*, speaks of the great demand for sound pictures, and says: "The present hastily turned out crop of talkies are for the most part crude and disappointing." In "Reaction of the Public to Motion Pictures with Sound" (*Trans. SMPE*, No. 35), Mordaunt Hall, motion-picture editor of the *New York Times*, describes the shortcomings of many efforts as due to stories not adapted to talkies, actors who didn't articulate, or had poor voices, and misjudgments in production.

---

* Many excellent discussions of the requirements for the new form of entertainment have been published. One such is Chapter IX "Comments on Production," of H. B. Franklin's *Sound Motion Pictures.*[2]

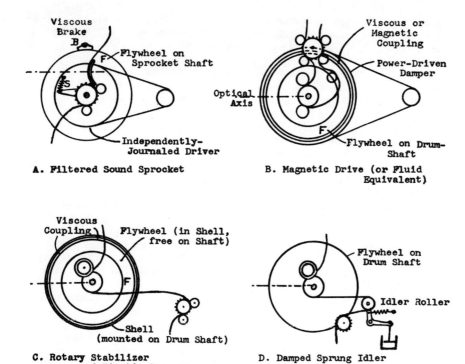

A. Filtered Sound Sprocket

B. Magnetic Drive (or Fluid Equivalent)

C. Rotary Stabilizer and Kinetic Scanner

D. Damped Sprung Idler

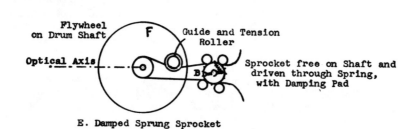

E. Damped Sprung Sprocket

Fig. 4. Mechanical filter systems for reducing irregularities in film motion.

We tend, fortunately, to forget the troubles that are past. Still more do we forget the troubles other people had. We who took part in the development of sound equipment may be tempted to think that we made the talking picture possible. But if we give the credit they deserve to the writers, directors, actors and their bosses, and to the patient guinea pigs who bought tickets, perhaps the only bouquet left to hand ourselves is to say that our stuff was not so bad as to make the talkies impossible.

Mechanical Systems

Of all the tell-tales that remind the listener that the sound he hears is from a record and not "live pickup," the most unmistakable is that due to speed variations — known as "wow" or "flutter," and it is probably the most painful and devastating to realism. The importance of correct and constant speed was recognized by Edison and all his successors in sound recording, but standards were not very high. Phonographs sold despite their shortcomings. But sound for pictures could succeed only by providing better entertainment than silent pictures. In those systems which gained eventual accept-

ance by the motion picture industry, the engineers spent much effort on providing constant speed. In his story of the development of the Fox-Case system, for example, Sponable[6] tells of having to rebuild cameras, and of mounting a flywheel on the sprocket shaft and driving the combination through damped springs.

The literature dealing with speed fluctuations has been devoted largely to discussions of measures for improving the performance of recorders and reproducers in this respect.[70] Until the recent important contribution by Frank A. Comerci,[84a] such information as has been published regarding subjective thresholds or tolerances has been limited largely to continuous tones. Further systematic quantitative studies with typical program material are very desirable. There is no question however that all the present and future improvements in equipment performance are well justified in terms of more satisfying sound reproduction. Some of the more general discussions of the subject will be found in the literature.[70,79—84a]

Wow Meters. Of prime importance toward improving recording and repro-

ducing machines is ability to measure the departures from uniform speed. One of the first such meters was built about 1928 by M. S. Mead[85] of the General Engineering Laboratory at Schenectady. It was improved by H. E. Roys and used extensively at Camden, N.J., being the basis of the flutter-measuring equipment described by Morgan and Kellogg.[86] This meter made an oscillographic recording of the fluctuations. An extremely simple and light-weight indicating flutter bridge used in RCA servicing is described in the *Journal.*[87] Flutter-measuring instruments are described by Scoville.[88] These are of the indicating type with band filters, by which flutter at different rates can be separated. Another design is described by Herrnfeld.[89] A widely used wow meter designed by U. R. Furst of Furst Electronics, Chicago, has been commercially available since 1947 or earlier.[90]

Disk System. In the disk system the change from 78 to $33\frac{1}{3}$ rpm increased the difficulties, for at the low speed even a very heavy turntable (although very helpful toward eliminating rapid flutter) was not a practical answer. A flywheel driven through springs, or what we call a "mechanical filter," was a well-known expedient, but such a system is oscillatory and will multiply rather than reduce the speed fluctuations if the disturbances are of a frequency anywhere near that of the resonance, unless the system is damped by adequate mechanical resistance.[69,70,81,91,94,100,102,104,105] The requirement that the transient disturbance of starting shall disappear in not more than one revolution is more difficult to meet with extremely large inertia. The acceptable $33\frac{1}{3}$-rpm reproducing turntables had much more inertia than had been customary for 78-rpm machines, and were driven through springs, with enough damping to reach equilibrium reasonably quickly, and dependence was not placed on making the natural frequency low in comparison with that of the slowest disturbance (once per revolution). Damping in some designs was provided by applying friction to the springs,[52,53] and in others by a viscous drag on the turntable. In either case it was essential to have high indexing accuracy in the low speed gear or worm-wheel.

For $33\frac{1}{3}$-rpm recording turntables, the Western Electric engineers went to extraordinary refinement.[70,91] On the theory that it would not be practically possible to produce gears with no eccentricity or indexing errors, they made their $33\frac{1}{3}$-rpm worm-wheel in four laminae, all cut together in one operation. Then they separated and reassembled them, each rotated 90° with respect to its neighbor. Each had its own spring connections to the turntable. Damping was by means of vanes in oil. Four vanes

188

were rigidly connected to the turntable, while the pot and four other vanes were driven from the gears through a system of equalizing levers (which might be compared to whiffletrees) which imparted to the pot and its vanes a rotation which was the average of that of the four gear laminae. The effect of this was to divide by four the magnitude of each disturbance due to imperfection in the cutting of the gear, but to make it occur four times per revolution instead of once, and both of these effects are helpful toward filtering out irregularities.

Filtering Systems for Film. In a very judicial appraisal of the relative advantages of film and disk, P. H. Evans[92] speaks of the disk system as giving better speed constancy. He was of course referring to the experience up to the time of writing. There can be no question that film presents a more difficult problem. Synchronous drive and the maintenance of free loops require that it be propelled by sprockets. In the earlier systems of driving the film, it seems to have been regarded as sufficient to provide constant rotational speed for the sprocket (often called the "sound sprocket") which carries the film through the point of recording or reproduction. To obtain such constant sprocket speed it was practically necessary to use mechanical filtering to take out irregularities originating in the gearing.[4,70] But the spring-driven sprocket was very sensitive to jerks from the film, so that it was necessary to employ extra sprockets with slack film between to isolate the filtered sound sprocket. It was also necessary to have an unusual degree of precision and concentricity in the sound sprocket. (Fig. 4A).

But there remained the question of what imperfections there might be in the film perforations, or how much it had shrunk since the holes were punched. Shrinkages up to 1% were not uncommon.

A sprocket can propel a film at uniform speed only when the pitch of the teeth and that of the holes match perfectly.* Otherwise there are continual readjustments of the film on the sprocket, producing in general 96-cycle flutter, plus random small variations. A paper by Herbert Belar and myself[82] shows graphically the startling breaking up of single tones into a multiplicity of side tones by a 96-cycle speed change such as might result from a shrinkage of about $\frac{1}{2}$%.

Recorders, since they are working with fresh film, may give very little 96-cycle flutter at the sprocket. The

* Sprocket propulsion of the film through the light beam has certain advantages for printers, as will be explained in the section on printer improvements. This mechanical section, however, seems the logical place for a brief review of studies by J. S. Chandler and J. G. Streiffert of the Eastman Co., directed to the reduction of sprocket-tooth flutter.

Dec. 27, 1932.   E. W. KELLOGG   1,892,554
FILM SUPPORTING AND DRIVING APPARATUS
Filed July 27, 1928

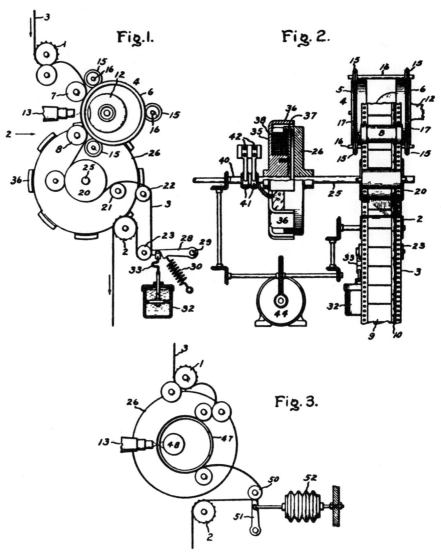

Film 5. Schematic representation of the magnetic drive for film motion, showing also provision for damping by use of a movable roller with dashpot.

Western Electric recorders of the earlier 1930's were designed on this basis.[4,93] The large sprocket was of precise construction and a nearly perfect fit for unshrunk film. It was on the shaft with a flywheel, and driven through damped springs. Another sprocket (unfiltered) drew the film from the magazine and resisted the pulls from the take-up magazine.

The engineers who designed the recorders supplied by RCA took no chances with sprocket teeth. In the first General Electric recording machines the film was carried past the recording light on a smooth drum (with a flywheel on its shaft) and a soft-tired pressure-roller prevented slipping.[67] Between the drum and the sprocket which fed the film through the machine at synchronous speed were flexible loops of film which

(so long as they remained under sufficiently low tension to retain their flexibility) would not transmit appreciable disturbances from the sprocket to the drum. Because of uncertain shrinkage the drum must be free to choose its own speed. The simplest expedient was to let the film pull the drum, like a belt. Machines built this way worked so well at times that they delayed the effort to design something on sounder principles. My own part in the development of a better machine lay originally in the recognition that the stretch of film which pulled the drum, in combination with the inertia of the flywheel, constituted an oscillatory system, although its period varied so greatly that the irregular action did not look like that of any oscillator we were accustomed to seeing. Another trouble was that the film loop

189

Fig. 6. Original model of magnetic-drive recorder.

was not free enough for isolating the drum. The cure for the bad effects of oscillatory action would be to provide damping. One way to provide this would be by bending the film around a flexibly supported idler roller,[105] connected to a dashpot. Another measure would be to use eddy-current damping at the flywheel by mounting a copper flange on the flywheel, spanned by a set of magnets. To use stationary magnets would provide damping but would also produce a steady drag, making a really flexible film loop impossible.[102,102a] By mounting the magnets so that they could be driven somewhat above flywheel speed, it became possible to provide a forward torque as well as damping, thereby relieving the film of all but a small part of its tension. (Figs. 4B, 5).[94-96]

The first magnetic-drive machine (an experimental model) (Fig. 6) employed both the damped idler roller and the rotating magnetic damper, but the latter was so effective that the first was superfluous. By adjusting the magnet current the film loop could be caused to run anywhere between a very slight deflection and a nearly semicircular bend. A production model (the R-4) recorder was designed in 1929 and was in production in 1930.[94] It was followed by other models (PR23 in 1933[98] and PR-31 in 1947[99]) employing the same principle.

The magnetic drive probably carried the idea of isolation of the film drum from disturbing forces farther than it has been carried in any other film-recording machine. Its extreme effectiveness as a filter system was demonstrated by Russell O. Drew and myself at the SMPE's 1940 spring convention.[96]

Although only a few were built, I should mention another recorder, the R-3,[70] designed by C. L. Heisler of the General Electric Co., which preceded the magnetic type. This had the smooth drum with flywheel to carry the film past the recording point, and the sprocket drive to hold synchronism. The drum was driven through a continuously adjustable-speed friction drive, which might be compared to a cone pulley, and the speed adjustment was automatically controlled by the length of the loop of film between the sprocket and drum, which loop was measured by the position of a movable deflecting roller.

Effect of the Tri-Ergon Patents.[35,114] Mention has been made of the development, beginning in 1918, of a sound system by Vogt, Massole and Engl, to which the name Tri-Ergon was given. They obtained very broad patents in Germany and were allowed some extremely broad claims in the United States. The patent which figured most seriously in litigation was No. 1,713,726 in which one claim covered the use of a flywheel on the shaft of the roller which carried film past the translation (recording or reproducing) point. Another claim covered carrying the film on a short roller and scanning it at the overhanging edge, and a third (based on a showing of flexibly mounted rollers pressing against and deflecting the stretches of film on either side of the drum) called for a spring-pressed roller engaging the film between

the sprocket and the roller (drum). Patent attorneys in the RCA group and Western Electric felt very confident that the broad flywheel claims could be safely disregarded because anticipated in many old sound-recording and reproducing devices, but the patent departments would not approve constructions using the overhung film for scanning until after about 1930, when W. L. Douden of the RCA patent department discovered an older disclosure of the same idea in a patent application of C. A. Cawley* (to which RCA obtained rights).

Film-Transport System of Soundheads. So the first reproducing machines to be marketed avoided the overhanging film feature, and instead pulled the film through a sound gate, where the scanning light passed through it and into the photocell. Friction in the gate made this arrangement much less favorable to constant speed than the use of the overhung principle. For constancy of film speed no further measures were used than to try to provide good sprockets to pull the film through the gate, and to filter the motion of the sprocket by use of a flywheel, and driving through springs. To damp this filter, the RCA PS-1 used grease-pads acting on the flywheel (Fig. 4A) and the Western Electric used a balanced pair of oil-filled sylphon bellows which acted as a dashpot supplementing the driving springs.[53] A practical improvement over filtering the sound sprocket was to drive a heavy flywheel on the sound-sprocket shaft by multipleV belts directly from the motor, and then by gearing take from this shaft whatever power is needed to drive the projector. The heavy flywheel and tight coupling to the motor gave the sound-sprocket drive such high mechanical impedance that its speed constancy was not materially disturbed by the irregularities of the projector load.

The Rotary Stabilizer. The discovery of the Cawley patent application by Douden made the RCA Patent Department consider it safe to build machines in which the reproducing light passed through the film where its edge overhung a short roller. With this privilege the way was open to make the film motion in reproducing machines comparable with that which had been attained in the magnet-drive recorder. However a less expensive construction was very desirable. The damping in the recorder was by eddy-current coupling between the flywheel and a coaxial magnet running at nearly the same

---

* The Cawley application had been filed Jan. 28, 1921, but had been held up on technicalities. It was put into suitable shape and issued Sept. 29, 1931 as a parent patent, No. 1,825,438, and three divisional patents, of which No. 1,825,441 contained the claims to the overhang feature.

speed. The functional equivalence of eddy-current coupling and viscous-fluid coupling was well recognized. I had tried some experiments with viscous coupling to a coaxial member which was not independently driven but was free to pick up the flywheel speed. The inertia of the viscously coupled member would tend to keep its speed constant so that a change in flywheel speed would cause relative movement and hence energy loss.[100] But I gave up in view of the feebleness of the damping I obtained.

It remained for C. R. Hanna of Westinghouse to make an analysis of the system. He showed that in order to get critical damping of the mass which is rigidly connected to the drum, the viscously coupled mass must have eight times as much moment of inertia, and the coupling coefficient must have the right value.[69] In 1932 and 1933 E. W. Reynolds and F. J. Loomis of the RCA Victor Co. in Camden did the job right.[101] The directly connected mass was an oil-tight shell of aluminum alloy inside which was a heavy cast-iron flywheel supported on a ball bearing whose friction was negligibly small in comparison with the oil coupling. Small clearance between concentric surfaces and a suitable oil gave the desired coupling. The inertia ratio was less than 8:1, but damping somewhat short of critical is satisfactory. By use of high-grade ball bearings the drum with attached stabilizer was caused to run with so little tension on the film which pulled it that the loop had plenty of flexibility for effective filtering.[102, 102a] (See Figs. 4C and 7.) The rotary stabilizer introduced in 1933 proved so satisfactory that it has been retained with little change for twenty years. A device on similar principles, called the "kinetic scanner" was used in Western Electric soundheads early in 1936[103] (Type 209).

In 1941 Alberscheim and MacKenzie[81] and Wente and Müller[104] described damped flywheels in which the entire viscously coupled mass was liquid. In order that there might be sufficient viscous resistance to movement of the liquid with respect to the container, partial obstructions were placed in the annular channel. This type of damped flywheel was used in the recorders and reproducers of the stereophonic system developed and demonstrated by the Bell Telephone Laboratories. Study has been given to the problem of finding suitable fluids. A low-temperature coefficient of viscosity is desirable, and if the entire coupled mass is liquid, high density is valuable.

Filters Using Movable Idler Rollers. The use of this type of filter was avoided in this country because of the danger of infringement suits on the basis of either the Tri-Ergon patent (No. 1,713,726)[35] or the Poulsen and Peterson patent (No.

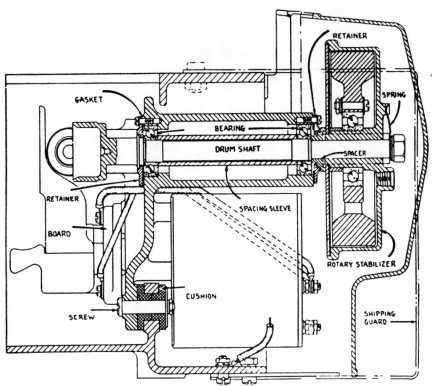

Rotary stabilizer construction of F. J. Loomis and E. W. Reynolds.

Fig. 7. Cross section, showing construction of the "rotary stabilizer."

1,597,819). Both of these show rollers elastically pressed against the film to deflect it from a straight path and thereby provide flexibility. Neither patent shows or mentions provision for damping, and yet the great merit of such an arrangement is in the simplicity with which damping can be obtained and not in the extra flexibility, for plenty of flexibility can be had by simply freeing the film of too much tension.[102, 102a] The flywheel may be solid and the arm on which the film-deflecting roller is mounted can be connected to a dashpot. (Even a cruder frictional device may give good results, but resistance of the viscous type is better.) A laboratory model of a soundhead using this type of filter was built about 1928 by the writer and performed very well, but did not receive patent approval (Fig. 4D).

After the patent obstacle to the use of the sprung-idler type of filter was ended, soundheads employing this principle were brought out by the Century Projector Corp. and the Western Electric Co.[105] and a recorder by Western Electric.[106] RCA adopted this film-motion system for 16mm machines and lightweight recorders R-32 and R-33,[107] but for 35mm soundheads continued to use the rotary stabilizer, the advantage of the movable-idler design being not so much a matter of performance as of lower manufacturing costs, an item which is contingent on schedules and tooling costs. Recently the flexibly mounted idler filter system has been utilized by RCA[108] and others[109, 110] in soundheads for use with multiple magnetic soundtracks.

Filter System With Drum and Sprung Sprocket. A film-motion system developed by engineers of M-G-M is described by Wesley C. Miller.[111] Recording or reproduction takes place on a drum with solid flywheel, and the drum is driven from a sprung sprocket isolated from other sprockets by loose loops. The film passes from the sprung sprocket, around the drum and back to engage the opposite side of the sprung sprocket, and this portion of the film is maintained under tension by a roller pressing against a free span of the film. The tight film affords the required traction between film and drum. Adjustable friction pads between the sprocket and its shaft cause frictional resistance whenever the deflection of the sprocket driving springs changes, thereby damping the system. Excellent film motion was obtained in these machines (Fig. 4E).

Minimizing Sprocket-Tooth Flutter. J. S. Chandler, in 1941[112] showed it to be possible to so shape sprocket teeth that the film speed would fluctuate between a maximum and minimum value which are the same at perfect fit and spread progressively with increasing misfit, but with a net flutter which can for a moderate range of shrinkage be quite small. However the realization of the calculated flutter values demands perfect perforation uniformity and freedom from any sticking on the teeth as the film is fed on or stripped off.

A further development in improving sprocket action is described by J. G. Streiffert.[113] The driving faces of the

191

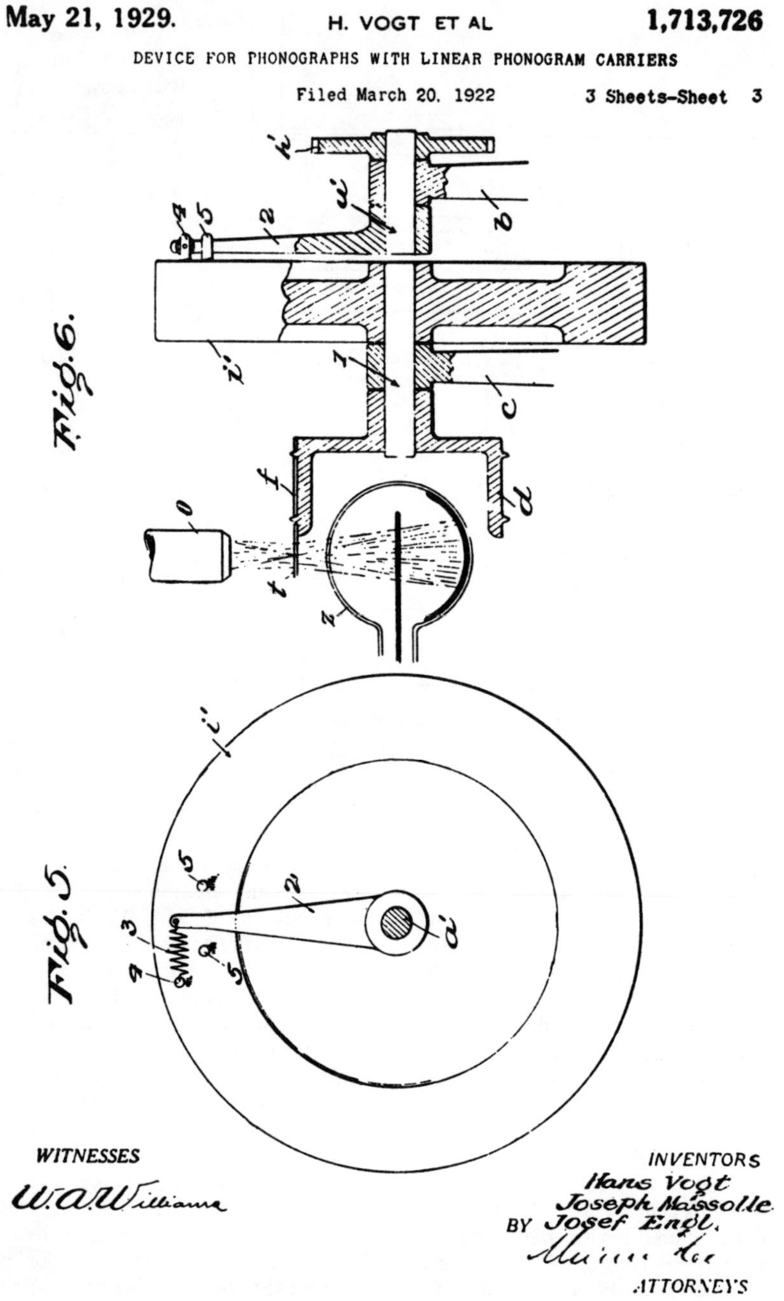

WITNESSES

W. A. Williams

INVENTORS
Hans Vogt
Joseph Massolle
BY *Josef Engl.*

Marcus Lee

ATTORNEYS

Fig. 8. Tri-Ergon showing of filtered sound-sprocket and overhanging sound-tract.

teeth are radial and the film is supported on a cylindrical surface which is slightly eccentric with respect to the sprocket. The film is fed on at a point where the teeth project only slightly above the film support, and as it travels around its arc of engagement the film gets closer to the roots of the teeth. The radius from the sprocket center to the film thus keeps decreasing, and therefore the velocity of the tooth face at the plane of the film decreases. The effect is essentially as though the tooth speed and the tooth pitch decreased correspondingly. The design is such that the tooth enters the hole with a margin of clearance and with the effective velocity (since the working radius is here near maximum)

slightly greater than that of the film. The tooth face therefore gains with respect to the film, closing up the clearance, and as soon as it touches the edge of the perforation begins propelling the film. While it is doing so the next tooth is catching up. Each tooth in turn propels the film from the moment that it reaches the perforation edge until the next tooth, which at the instant is moving slightly faster, touches the edge of its perforation. Thereafter, the effective speed of this tooth, which continues to decrease, is less than that of the film, so that a gap or clearance develops between the tooth and the leading edge of the perforation. The design is such that the film is not stripped from the teeth until, in all cases, sufficient clear-

ance has accumulated to avoid possible interference during the stripping.

Assuming that the film velocity is equal to that of the driving-tooth face at the radius where it touches the film, the film speed will fluctuate by the amount by which the effective tooth speed decreases as it travels one tooth pitch. This can be a very small change, especially if there is a large number of teeth and the eccentricity no more than needed to take care of a reasonable shrinkage range.

The region on the circumference of the sprocket where the propelling action takes place varies with the shrinkage of the film. Thus with unshrunk film the propulsion will be relatively near the place where the tooth enters the perforation, while with shrunk film it will be where the teeth are projecting farther, so that the point of contact is nearer the root of the teeth.

One way of describing the action of the system is to say that a film of any given shrinkage finds the appropriate radius where the pitch of the teeth equals the pitch of the perforations, and this is the region where propulsion takes place.

The Eastman Co. has used this system with excellent results in experimental printers. The Streiffert paper gives wowgrams of negative recordings made on such a sprocket, and also of contact prints, and for comparison wowgram (or flutter recordings) of prints made in a conventional sprocket-type printer, showing a major reduction in flutter with the new sprocket.

Litigation. Despite the efforts to avoid infringement of such claims of Tri-Ergon patent No. 1,713,726* as appeared to have any likelihood of being held valid, the American Tri-Ergon Corp. brought suit against Altoona Publix Theatres Inc., who were using an RCA Photophone (PS-1) projector attachment or soundhead. The case was tried at Scranton, Pa., in the U.S. District Court for the Middle District. The apparatus had been sold with a guarantee against patent liability, and the suit was defended by RCA, Electrical Research Products Inc. giving technical assistance in the defense. The court ruled (Feb. 10, 1933) that seven of the claims were valid and infringed. The case was appealed and reviewed by the U.S. Circuit Court of Appeals for the third circuit (in Philadelphia), which affirmed (June 13, 1934) the findings of the lower court. The defendents then appealed to the U.S. Supreme Court, which at first refused to review the case, but finally decided to do so, and on Mar. 4, 1935, ruled that the seven claims in the suit were all invalid (294 US 477).[114]

* This patent, issued May 21, 1929, was filed in the U.S. Mar. 20, 1922, and had a German filing date of Mar. 24, 1921.

This removed the threat to the equipment manufacturers of what might have been almost crippling damages, for had the findings of the lower courts been sustained the plaintiffs would have been in a position to bring suits for damages for infringement by most of the recording and reproducing equipment in this country, and covering a period of over five years.

The American Tri-Ergon Corp. applied on Feb. 18, 1937, for a reissue patent with modified claims, and this was granted Jan. 11, 1938, as Re. No. 20,621. On Oct. 25, 1946, RCA reached an agreement with American Tri-Ergon Corp. whereby it was granted rights under both the original and reissue patents.

Two other patents placed restrictions on the film-motion systems which American engineers could safely employ, namely Poulsen and Peterson No. 1,597,819 (filed July 9, 1924, and issued Aug. 31, 1926) and Poulsen No. 2,006,719 (filed Germany Sept. 1, 1930, and U. S. Aug. 19, 1931, and issued July 2, 1935). These patents to Danish inventors were owned by British Acoustic Films Ltd., which brought infringement suits against RCA Mfg. Co. and against Electrical Research Products Inc. The trial (in Wilmington, Del.) was before the U.S. District Court for the District of Delaware (43 USP–Q69). The arrangement shown in the patent comprised a drum propelled by the film, the film being passed around a flexibly mounted idler roller. Some of the claims in suit described the invention as "means contacting the film for increasing its flexibility." The apparatus in suit was the RCA PS-24 (rotary stabilizer type), which has no flexibly mounted roller, but was alleged to have the equivalent in that the film loop was so formed by the fixed rollers as to be very flexible. The court ruled Sept. 22, 1939, that the claims in suit were not infringed and not valid (the flexibly mounted idler having been disclosed in the earlier Tri-Ergon patent).

Plaintiffs appealed and the case was reviewed by the Circuit Court of Appeals of the Third Circuit which affirmed the findings of the lower court (46USP–Q107, June 27, 1940).

To forestall possible future trouble RCA obtained rights under these patents by agreement with British Acoustic Films Ltd., Dec. 21, 1944.

Immediate Requirements for Sound

Our historical story thus far has been confined almost entirely to the three fundamental elements, sound pickup (or microphone), a recording and reproducing system and loudspeakers. These represented the difficult phases of the problem, but before sound could become commercial certain items of equipment had to be made available and techniques established. Before discussing the advances in the art that followed commercialization, we shall mention some of these items.

Standard Track Position and Width.[115] Agreement between the makers of variable-width and variable-density systems was reached in 1928. The reproducing light spot must cover more than the extreme width of the clear area of a variable-area track, with both ends on black areas, but should fall entirely within the width of a variable-density track. This requirement is met with margins of safety, by recording density tracks 0.100 in. wide, while the scanning spot is 0.084 in. long. The modulated area of a variable-width track is limited to 0.071 in. with the black parts extending to the 0.100-in. width. The track center line is to be 0.243 in. ± 0.002 in. from the edge of the film.

Printers. Continuous contact printers previously used for pictures only could be adapted to sound by providing masks by which light could be confined to either the picture or the soundtrack area. Except for certain newsreel negatives, the sound and picture were on separate negatives, so that the print film had to be run through the printer twice. Even when the sound was on the same negative as the picture, the offset was not usually the required 14.5-in. and independent light controls were needed. Combination printers were soon developed which were essentially two printers in cascade, so that the print was complete with one passage through the machine.[116–120]

Bloops. The development engineer can overlook many defects so long as he knows their cause and that the apparatus he is testing is not at fault, but before sound pictures could be shown the public, these faults had to be corrected. The noise which a splice makes as it passes through the scanning beam can be made almost inaudible by cutting off the light gradually instead of suddenly. This was accomplished at first by painting a black spot with sloping edges over the splice. Later, black patches which could be quickly cemented in place where the splice crosses the sound track were made available. These are called "bloops." They are of trapezoid shape, masking off the entire sound track for a distance sufficient safely to cover the splice and with end slopes designed to change the light gradually enough to keep the noise just below noticeability at normal gain settings. The design of bloops is discussed in several papers.[121–123] To prevent a disturbance due to a printed-through negative splice, Sponable[124] described a punch which made a hole in the negative, resulting in a suitably-shaped black spot on the print.

Electrical blooping of splices in negatives has come into extensive use. When a negative splice goes through the printer an auxiliary light exposes (through the base) a suitable area of the print film, an edge notch or other means being employed to control the blooping light.

Lewin (Apr. 1947)[124a] describes a system of silencing splices in re-recording positives in which the output is momentarily suppressed in response to a punched hole.

Blimps.[125] Cameras which were entirely satisfactory for silent pictures were much too noisy for making sound pictures. Much quieter cameras were developed eventually,[126–128] but for immediate requirements it was necessary to reduce the noise radiated by existing cameras by building shells around them with thick layers of sound-absorbing material. These were called "blimps," or sometimes "bungalows." To smother the sound and still give access for the necessary operations was enough to tax the skill and ingenuity of the designer. Even with the quieter cameras it is still common to resort to partial or complete sound-insulating housing.

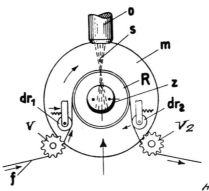

Fig. 9. Tri-Ergon showing (U.S. Pat. 1,713,726) of flexibly mounted rollers deflecting the film between sprockets and drum.

193

Sound Stages.[129,130] The requirement of freedom from noise necessitated the building of sound stages in which extreme measures were taken to exclude noise of outside origin. Many of these had double concrete walls and double floors, with sound absorbing material between, the inner walls and floor being supported on cushion mounts to prevent transmission of earth tremors. The roof and ceiling structures were designed on the same principle.

The high absorption (or short reverberation time) desirable for recording purposes helped control noises originating inside, but so far as possible all sources of noise were eliminated. Noisy arc lights gave way to incandescent or other quiet lamps, and all mechanisms were made to operate as noiselessly as possible. Ventilating systems required extreme measures.

In recording dialogue, the better the suppression of general room reverberation, the farther (within limits) from the action can the microphone be placed, thus affording more uniform coverage and making it easier to keep the microphone out of the field of the camera. If some echoes are wanted the "set" can frequently be designed to produce enough. Artificial reverberation using echo chambers in the recording channel or equivalent devices has many applications.

In contrast to the requirements for speech, the recording of music calls in general for rooms with considerable reverberation.[131-133]

Theater Acoustical Treatment.[134,135] The acoustical treatment of auditoriums has probably received more study than any other phase of architectural acoustics, perhaps because the desired characteristics are most difficult to attain. The reverberation must be sufficient to make music pleasing and to help equalize sound intensity in the various parts of the space, but must be short enough not appreciably to impair clarity of speech. A high order of directivity in the loudspeakers plus application of absorbent materials to any large surfaces toward which they are directed has helped with this part of the problem.

In general every theater or auditorium, many of which were built before the era of sound pictures, presents its own problems and calls for individual study. For new theaters there is optimum shape to consider as well as best distribution of absorption. The multiple loudspeaker systems (discussed later) besides making new effects possible have given the acoustical designer somewhat more freedom.

Booms and Dollies. In order that microphones might be suspended as near the action as might be wanted but just above the field of the camera, and in order

that their positions might be readily changed, microphone booms of various types came quickly into use. The more elaborate of these were much like derricks on platforms, with rubber-tired wheels on which they could be moved quickly and almost noiselessly.

Similarly, rubber-tired, battery-operated camera dollies enabled the cameraman rapidly and quietly to change the position or height of his camera.

Equipment of the kind just described underwent improvements through the years, but the main features were available from the start of commercial sound pictures.

Monitoring and Level Control.[136-139] Another line of equipment the essentials of which were made available as soon as recording machines, and which has been improved from time to time, was that providing for monitoring and level controls and (especially in re-recording operations) for adjusting the relative levels from several sources, or "mixing." Volume indicators[140,141] of several types were in use in broadcasting stations, and the design of mixing controls was well established.

The man responsible for recording judged the quality by means of a monitoring loudspeaker. He could check quality as represented by the current supplied to the light modulator, or by means of a photocell, in terms of the light reaching the film.[1,64,254] In the case of the RCA Photophone system there was a card on which the modulator projected a light-spot, the movements of which showed the amplitude being recorded on the sound track.[142]

It was for a time held by some that the monitoring speaker should be of the same type as a theater speaker, but high-quality monitoring speakers of the direct-radiator type were soon made available, and these were much better suited to the small rooms where the controls were located. In terms of frequency range covered, the cabinet-type monitoring speakers kept pace with the improvements in theater speakers (see section on loudspeakers). High-quality headphones have also found wide use in monitoring.[143,211] Whatever type of listening device is used, it should obviously be designed to give the recordist about the same range and tonal balance that a theater patron would get.

Screens. Our sense of the direction from which sounds come is too keen for us to be fooled by loudspeakers placed alongside or above the screen. Sound must come from directly behind the screen to give a good illusion. This is one of the lessons that was learned early. Screens of the types developed for silent pictures caused excessive loss and distortion if placed between the loudspeaker and the audience.

Mention has been made of a sound-transmitting screen developed by E. I. Sponable in 1927.[6] One of the first papers in the SMPE *Journal* dealing with screens for sound pictures was that in 1930 by H. F. Hopkins.[144] His curves of measured transmission indicate good results with screens having perforations whose total area is 4% or 5% of the screen area, and show definite advantage in a thin (0.013-in.) screen rather than a thicker (0.030-in.) material. With such screens the loss of brightness need be no greater than the proportion of the area taken out by the holes. Allotment of about 8% of the area to holes has been common, for example about 40 holes of 0.050-in. diameter per square inch.[145]

Processing, Variable-Density.[146] In the story of the work at Western Electric and Bell Laboratories I said that it was recognized by Wente and by MacKenzie that for the correct, or linear, relation between negative exposure and print transmission, the product of the negative and print gamma* should equal unity.† This is in accordance with principles set forth in early SMPE papers by L. A. Jones[62] and by A. C. Hardy.[61] Since practice in making pictures had been to develop the print to a gamma of approximately two, and both sound and picture would receive identical development, the sound negative should be developed to a gamma of about 0.5 or slightly higher. Picture-positive film was used for a number of years for sound negatives. Developers of the types used for picture negatives tend to give low contrast and fine grain, and the use of such developers helped to give the desired low value of gamma for the sound negatives.[147,148] MacKenzie[64] gives some information about the harmonic distortion which results from departures from the unity product, and thus gives an indication of tolerances with respect to development.

With the advent of sound, with its requirement for more strict control of development, control by use of sensitometric test strips, and by specified time, temperature and developer formulas[149-152] supplanted dependence on visual judgments of operators, where that practice had prevailed.[153,154] Maintenance of developer activity received much attention,[155-158] and stop baths assumed increased importance.[159,160] Rack-and-tank methods, where these had been followed,

---

* Gamma is the slope of the straight portion of a curve plotted with density $\left(\text{or log of } \dfrac{1}{\text{transmission}}\right)$ as ordinates and log exposure as abscissae. This is known as the Hürter and Driffield, or H & D curve. Gamma product is a measure of overall contrast as compared with that in the original exposure.

† In practice, because of some loss of contrast due to stray light in optical systems, best results with pictures had been found with somewhat higher gamma product.

194

gave way to continuous machine processing.[161-163]

How generally the distinctions between specular and diffuse density,[164] and between exposure modulation by varying time (light valve) and varying intensity (as by glow lamp)[165] were understood at first is a question, but these points were well covered in the literature. The Eastman Capstaff Densitometer,[166] which was developed primarily for measuring picture negatives for contact printing, reads diffuse densities. This would be appropriate for measuring the densities of sound negatives for use in contact printers, but not for densities of soundtrack prints, for it is the specularly transmitted light which reaches the photocell in a reproducer.

The widely used Eastman IIb Sensitometer, brought out about 1932,[167] which gives an accurately standardized series of test exposures in the form of a step tablet with exposure time increasing in the ratio $\sqrt{2}$ per step, and ranging from about 0.004 sec to 4 sec, has been of utmost value in maintaining controls. However, it does not simulate soundtrack recording conditions, where the intensity is extremely high and the time for average exposure was approximately 1/18000 sec (1/36000 sec with a later light-valve system and in present practice about 1/90000 sec) and still shorter for low exposures. The 1934 paper by Jones and Webb[165] gives an indication of the magnitude of the error. The Eastman Sensitometer on the other hand gives exposures which approximate sufficiently well those which a print receives, and are thus suitable for determining gamma of contact prints. For many purposes it has been satisfactory to draw conclusions by applying correction factors, if needed, to the readings of these instruments.

In the course of a few years densitometers employing photocells were developed which had the advantages of greater accuracy and much faster operation than the Capstaff visual-balance type.[168-172] For exposing sound negatives for sensitometry purposes, the light valve itself, with suitable calibration, can be used. The subject is again discussed under "Intermodulation Test."

While the conditions for low distortion were to keep both negative and positive exposures on the straight parts of the H & D characteristics, studies reported in 1931 by D. MacKenzie[172a] showed that low distortion was still possible while using the "toe" range of both films ("toe recording") or that of the positive only ("composite"). Toe recording using positive stock for the sound negative might, if the recording-system light was limited, be preferable to resorting to faster and coarser-grained recording stock. In the case of single-film systems (sound recorded on the picture negative) where the development of both the negative and positive soundtracks is fixed by picture requirements, MacKenzie found that the composite system offered best promise of low distortion. Both the toe and composite systems give higher output than a classical or straight-line system, but poorer signal-to-noise ratios.

It took a number of years to bring about the full transformation from the methods (depending much on visual judgments) which had been employed for making silent pictures, to the close controls and scientific precision needed for satisfactory and consistent sound. The constant and close checking of every element exerted a pressure for improvement along the whole front, including the manufacture of the film, in which departures from uniformity were quickly detected. The story is interestingly told by J. I. Crabtree.[146] An early account is given by J. W. Coffman.[153]

Processing, Variable-Area. Since the ideal variable-area track is part clear and part black with a sharp boundary between, there is no question of preserving correct shades of gray, but in general the higher the contrast (or gamma product) the better. As in the case of variable-density tracks it must be assumed that the print development will be that which is wanted for the picture, and that has been taken in general to give a gamma of about 2.0. Variable-area negatives as well as the prints are processed in high-contrast developers. The variable-area system is noncritical with respect to gamma product but, for a given positive emulsion and processing, there is for any given negative a best setting of printer light.

A comprehensive study of available sound-recording films and their processing was published by Jones and Sandvik.[173] Another study was made by J. A. Maurer.[174] From his curves it appeared that negative densities of 1.3 or higher were desirable, and the prints which gave maximum outputs were the ones having densities (in the dark areas) about equal to those of the negatives from which they were made. This held true for negative densities ranging from 0.6 to 1.3 and higher. The maxima however were very broad.

In November 1931, Dimmick[175] reported the results of a series of determinations of conditions for maximum output from a 6000-cycle recording, using Eastman positive 1301 for negatives and prints, and 4, 6, 8 and 10 min in D-16 developer. The study covered an adequate range of the four variables — negative (recording) exposure, negative development or gamma, printing exposure and print development. The results showed that wide ranges in each of the variables could be used with comparatively small loss of output, but for any negative there was a print density at which output was greatest. It made a comparatively small difference (except near the extremes) whether a given density of either negative or print was reached with small exposure and longer development or more exposure and less development, but in general the maxima were broader with the higher values of gamma, especially that of the print. The two highest gamma values in the series, 2 and 2.18 of both negative and print, in general gave best results, with negative densities (measured in the black areas) in the range 1.5 to 2, and print densities a little less in each case than that of the negative.

While maximum high-frequency output is of less consequence than avoidance of cross-modulation (which is discussed in the section on distortion) it is of interest that recommended practices based on the test just described come very close to those found to be best in later experience and after current testing methods had become established. The cross-modulation test did not come into general use until 1938.[176]

For a number of years a print density of 1.4 or slightly higher, with appropriate corresponding negative density, was taken as a practical objective. As galvanometers and optical systems were improved and finer grain films came into use, the tendency was toward higher densities for both negatives and prints, especially for the negatives.

Evolution in a Growing Industry

Greatly Expanded Developmental Activities. The development work prior to commercialization of sound was carried on largely in laboratories supported by manufacturers of supplies or equipment, or in independent laboratories, and it was done on the basis of hope for returns which might be realized either through patent royalties or through sales of equipment or both.

Once sound pictures began to be made and shown, developmental work was on a different basis. Research and investigations of numerous incompletely solved problems took on rather the character of plowing in profits, with greatly increased total expenditures for research and participation by all the major picture-producing organizations.

Of all of the problems, the most fundamental and greatest in magnitude was learning how to use sound pictures, or the evolution of a new art. This is discussed by J. E. Abbott.[177] The expression "growing pains" aptly describes the less successful phase of this evolution. Capacity for readjustment is one of the qualities of greatness in individuals and in organizations, and the motion-picture industry came through splendidly.

When any industry becomes large, and especially if its requirements are as diverse as those of sound pictures, it provides a market for numerous special-

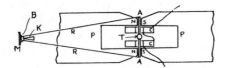

Fig. 10. Arrangement employed by G. L. Dimmick in 1929 galvanometer, for multiplying the rotation of the mirror.

ties and services. Many of these requirements are met by comparatively small organizations and others by branches of companies having many other activities and products. A few such items will serve to illustrate: special lamps, arc carbons, screens, cameras, acoustic treatment materials and service, chemicals, printers, testing equipment and studio apparatus. Many important improvements and contributions to technical advances are due to those who develop and supply such auxiliary equipment.

Mingled with the natural rivalry between picture producers has been a spirit of cooperation and sharing of experience and knowledge which has greatly accelerated progress. In 1930 this society began issuing the monthly *Journal* instead of the quarterly *Transactions*, an appropriate step to accommodate the rapidly expanding literature of sound-picture technology, covering almost every phase of the making and showing of motion pictures. The Academy of Motion Picture Arts and Sciences also played an important part in promoting interchange of information. Engineers and technicians from the sound-picture laboratories have reported experiences with various problems related to processing and controls and to sensitometry, while film and photographic suppliers have spared no efforts to enable those using their product to get the best possible results.

So many have been the contributions to the art and science along these lines, that I find it quite beyond my ability to do more than pay this general tribute and to mention a very few developments which have seemed to me to be of outstanding importance. I trust that I may be forgiven for showing partiality to the types of development with which I am most familiar, and also if I unjustly fail to mention many important advances.

Some of the Improvements After 1930

Galvanometers for Variable-Area Recording. The galvanometers used in the first variable-area recorders supplied by RCA Photophone were practically standard oscillograph vibrators, as these had been built at General Electric. They were oil-immersed and responded well up to 5000 cycles or above. An improved smaller model was brought out in 1930,[178] completely sealed instead of having an open oil well and with no external adjustments. This used molybdenum ribbon

(much stronger than the bronze) and was tuned to about 6000 cycles.

When recording was started at the RKO studios in Hollywood, one of the men from the General Engineering Laboratory who had had much experience with oscillographs, F. B. Card, joined the RKO staff. The RKO engineers soon decided that their sound would be better if the frequency range were extended. The ribbons of the oscillographs had been of phosphor-bronze. A small supply of duralumin ribbon was obtained, and with this Card succeeded in re-stringing the RKO galvanometers, with sufficient tension to tune them to nearly 9000 cycles. A thinner damping fluid was then appropriate, a change almost necessary to realize the benefits of the higher natural frequency.

G. L. Dimmick came to the General Electric Co. in 1929, and one of his first projects was the development of a new galvanometer which was promptly used in newsreel equipment.[178] He used a magnetic driving system of the balanced rocking armature type and by an ingenious mechanical arrangement, shown in Fig. 10, made his mirror rotate through about ten times the angle of the armature. The important advantage of this galvanometer was that the mirror was about ten times the area of that of the previous galvanometers. A few years later Dimmick designed a new galvanometer on the same principle (Fig. 11) but improved in numerous details.[142,179,180] This became the RCA Photophone standard for all photographic recording. These galvanometers were tuned to about 9000 cycles. Damping was by means of a block of rubber, the action of which was analogous to that of the rubber line of H. C. Harrison,[*,49] but since it

---

* See June *Journal*, p. 296, third col.

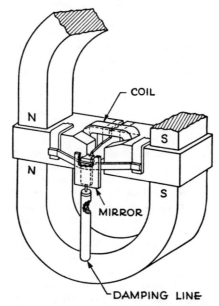

Fig. 12. Construction of RCA recording galvanometer (shown in section in Fig. 11).

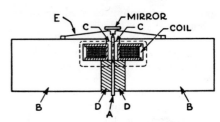

Fig. 11. Cross section of improved recording galvanometer, G. L. Dimmick. A—armature; B,B—pole pieces; C,C—working air gaps; D,D—nonmagnetic spacers; E—tensioned bronze ribbon.

had to work only at high frequency it could be of quite small dimensions. Dimmick found that he could increase the effectiveness of such damping blocks by incorporating tungsten powder in the rubber to increase its density (Fig. 12).

Further improvements in the galvanometer were reported by Dimmick in July 1947.[181] By the substitution of better magnetic materials he was able to reduce hysteresis almost to zero, to increase the sensitivity, and to avoid a slight saturation effect which had been present in the previous design.

A More Efficient and Versatile Optical System. In order that the galvanometer in one of our experimental optical systems might be closer to the slit, and thus send more light through it, I arranged a galvanometer to work on its side, so that it would move the light spot up and down across, instead of parallel to, the slit. I used a light spot with a sloping edge at an acute angle such that the change from zero to full-length slit illumination was accomplished with a movement equal to only one-fourth of the slit length.[*,182] Dimmick improved on this by making the light spot symmetrical with respect to middle of the slit, and having two sloping edges (see Fig. 13, and in Fig. 14 compare C with B). An advantage of the transverse-movement system was that it became very simple, by changing the masks which were imaged on the slit, to produce a variety of tracks which had their special applications.[142,180,183,184]

The combination of larger mirror and reduced distance between galvanometer and slit practically eliminated the diffraction trouble that had, with the small mirrors, impaired the formation of clean, sharp, high-contrast images at the plane of the slit.

Ground-Noise Reduction—GNR.[185] Scratches and dirt on film and graininess of emulsion cause a background noise

---

* All galvanometers have practical limits to the angle through which they can swing the light beam. And the required light spot movement sets a minimum to the distance between galvanometer and slit. The light which a galvanometer can send through the slit is proportional to the mirror area and the inverse square of its distance from the slit, up to the point at which the objective lens is "filled."

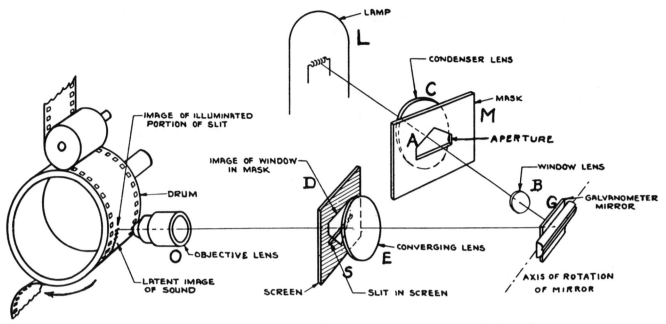

Fig. 13. Variable-area recording optical system. (Lens B images A on slit-plate D.)

which is particularly conspicuous when the modulation is low. The noise is reduced by reducing the transmitted light. At the same time, for a given modulation level there is no need for the average transmission to be more than about half the maximum. The noise may thus be reduced when the reduction is most needed, by decreasing the average light when the level of the recorded sound is low. This can be accomplished by biasing the light modulator toward zero, and then using a current derived by rectifying some of the modulation current to increase the mean light transmission when this is needed. The reduced transmission when the modulation is low means a darker track in a variable-density system, or a narrower clear area in a variable-area system, and in either case the noise is reduced. The early patent on this idea was to E. Gerlach.[186] This was assigned to Siemens & Halske, but to the best of my knowledge it occurred independently to L. T. Robinson in Schenectady and C. R. Hanna at Westinghouse,[187] and a system applicable to light valves was developed at Bell Laboratories.[188] The first trials at Schenectady with variable-area tracks did not indicate an impressively large reduction of noise, and there was an objection (in the case of the earlier, unilateral, variable-area tracks) in that the bias threw all of the low-level modulation over to one edge of the track, where many reproducing light beams were of reduced intensity. The project was revived by Hugh McDowell of RKO who got around the objection by screening off the surplus light by means of a shutter instead of biasing the galvanometer.[189] This method and the results obtained were reported to the Academy of Motion Picture Arts and Sciences by

Townsend, McDowell and Clark in 1930.[190] Thereafter a commercial form of shutter was designed[191] and ground-noise reduction became standard in the RCA system (Fig. 15).

With the introduction slightly later of the symmetrical track, the objection just mentioned to depending on galvanometer bias instead of a shutter no longer applied, but there was still some danger of saturating the galvanometer. Therefore a double-vane shutter was developed to mask down the light from both sides.[192]

The Bell Laboratories system is described by Silent and Frayne.[188] In the variable-density system there is no objection to accomplishing the result by biasing the valve.

In case of a sudden increase in modulation level the rectified current would change so rapidly as to cause an audible sound. The current for the shutter or for bias is therefore passed through a filter which reduces the rate of change. Limiting the speed with which the average light can increase means some clipping of the first few modulation peaks.

The light valve is a very low impedance device, and since the bias current may have to be sustained for consider-

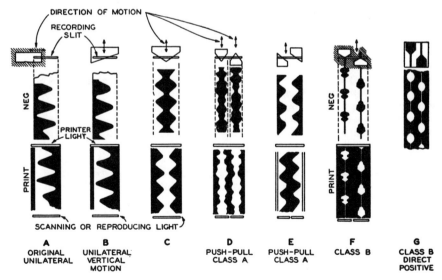

Fig. 14. Various types of area soundtracks, and light-spot shapes which produce them.

Fig. 15. Soundtrack produced by McDowell ground-noise reduction shutter.

able periods of time transformers cannot be used for impedance match coupling to the output tube of the ground-noise reduction amplifier. In the system most widely used with light valves the modulation current is rectified, passed through the timing filter, and used to modulate a 20,000-cycle oscillator, the output of which is amplified and rectified for supply to the valve. The design of the timing filter is much simpler when it can operate at interstage impedance.[193]

As compared with variable-area, the variable-density system is characterized by ground noise which is less in the nature of "ticks" and "pops" and more a continuous hiss. Another difference is that in the density system the noise falls more rapidly with reduced light transmission, so that a given amount of noise reduction is obtained with a smaller change in transmission. The continuous hiss type of noise is especially noticeable if it comes and goes, which changing bias causes it to do. This is often called the "hush-hush" effect, and becomes noticeable if the valve opening does not immediately fall when the modulation drops to a low level. At the same time the fact that smaller changes in transmission suffice to control the ground noise makes it possible to change transmission (or bias) more quickly without causing "thump." The filters for density systems are therefore designed for much faster timing than those of area systems, particularly in closing down when modulation falls.

While clipping of initial modulation peaks is a less serious problem in density than in area recording (because of faster opening and larger margin) engineers working with both systems have given much study to minimizing such clipping. Increased margin will decrease the frequency of occurrence of clipping, but this would be at the price of more noise. In all systems, opening (increasing light) is about as fast as it can be made without becoming audible, while the closing is much slower so that very brief reductions in level will not produce incessant closing and opening.[194]

A nonlinear characteristic has been given to RCA ground-noise reduction amplifiers, which causes the opening, as a function of modulation amplitude, to rise more steeply at first and then more slowly.[185] Relatively low-level modulation is then sufficient to cause an increase in margin and thus reduce subsequent clipping. It is when the modulation is nearly zero that close margin is urgent.

Certain characteristics of speech sounds have an important bearing on the design of ground-noise reduction systems. The positive pressure peaks are higher than the negative, and it is important to maintain correct polarity from microphone to valve, or to shutter and galvanometer.[192,195] R. O. Drew and I made an investigation to determine how often

speech sounds build up rapidly.[196] Instances in which maximum amplitude was reached in less than three or four waves (voice fundamental) were surprisingly rare.

The ideal solution to the problem of avoiding initial clipping would be to anticipate increases in sound level. This is discussed by J. G. Frayne.[197]

Anticipation by use of a second microphone was used experimentally in the stereophonic system described in the October 1941 *Journal* (p. 351) for operation of the compressor.[329a] A system employing a 14-msec electrical delay network is described (March 1950) by Whitney and Thatcher.[198]

When reported it had been in use for over a year by Sound Services Inc. with very favorable results. Besides reduced clipping, advantage was taken of the system to increase ground-noise reduction in density recordings by 5 db, and in area recordings to work with a bias line only 1 to 1½ mils wide. A low-distortion network good to 8000 cycles necessarily employs many sections (several hundred). Cost is probably the reason that this expedient has not been widely employed. A direct-positive variable-area recording system with the anticipation effect provided by means of an auxiliary exposure was designed and demonstrated by Dimmick and Blaney and has been used in the Warners' studios.[199]

In the re-recording operation anticipation should be a simple matter, involving only a double reproducing system (with scanning points a fraction of an inch apart) with separate amplifiers.* Mueller and Groves (June 1949)[200] mention use of this system at Warners. I understand however that little advantage has been taken of this possibility, presumably on account of costs. The explanation is probably that when initial clipping occurs in a well adjusted re-recording system, there was probably also some at the same spots in the original recording and the possible gain from anticipation in the re-recording operation is hard to detect. If clipping, in systems using ground-noise reduction, causes an appreciable impairment to sound quality, the ideal solution is to use for original recording a system whose ground noise is inherently so low that it needs no such expedient, and then introduce the ground-noise reduction when re-recording to the photographic tracks. Similar considerations apply to the use of compressors. Among the systems which in more or less measure meet this specification are Class B area recording, wide-track push-pull (with fine-grain film and fast-acting noise reduction) direct positives with the auxiliary exposing light,[199] and direct-playback disks. A real answer

to this problem seems to have come in the recent adoption of magnetic recording.†[200, 352—388]

Pre- and Post-Equalization. The practice of electrically exaggerating the high-frequency components in recording, as compared with the low-frequency components, in order to compensate for inevitable losses, began early in the recording of sound. Studies of the distribution of energy in program material had indicated that this could be done without resulting in overloads in the high-frequency end of the scale. A large amount of high-frequency pre-emphasis had been employed in cutting transcription disk records. In film records as well as disk records, ground noise can be made less noticeable by decreasing the gain at high frequency. Therefore, in addition to such relative attenuation of high-frequency sounds as was caused by the imperfections of reproducing systems and loudspeakers, the practice became prevalent of producing a drooping characteristic in the electrical circuits.

In order that all films might have good balance in all theaters, a committee of the Academy of Motion Picture Arts and Sciences made recommendations for a standard reproducing characteristic.[201] With such a standard adopted, the producers of sound pictures would have incentive to use recording characteristics which would give good balance when their films were played in a theater with the typical or standard reproducing characteristic.

The problem is discussed by J. K. Hilliard[202,203] and by Morgan and Loye.[204]

Better Lamps. Among the lamps used in the late 1920's for recording were some of the ribbon-filament type. These were ideal from the standpoint of uniformity, but required an inconveniently large current (18 amp) and did not have as long life at a given temperature as was obtainable with lamps of the helical-filament type. A series of lamps for sound recording and reproduction was made available by the lamp companies. The filaments were close-wound helices, of relatively heavy tungsten wire, and to permit operation at high temperatures with satisfactory life, the pressure of the inert gas (argon) with which the bulbs were filled was increased above that employed in lamps from which less intensity was required.

In the series of lamps described by F. E. Carlson of General Electric in 1939[205] the recording lamps were rated as operating at above 3100 K (color temperature) which is several hundred degrees higher than that of common

---

* In a set-up for mixing numerous sounds, it would for practical purposes be sufficient to equip only the dialogue film-phonograph with double scanner and amplifier.

† Some experimenting has been done with a double magnetic pickup for anticipation. Cross-talk between the two heads was a problem. The difficulties will undoubtedly soon be worked out.

incandescent lamps. Somewhat later, krypton-filled lamps were introduced, permitting still higher temperatures. The krypton, being heavier, more effectively retards evaporation of tungsten. (See the section on basic inventions.)

The light from a helical filament varies somewhat, depending on the angle from which the lamp is viewed. At the suggestion of L. T. Sachtleben of RCA, the helix of the lamp used in the variable-area recordings was curved, the convex side being presented toward the lenses. The helix with the curved axis gives definitely better uniformity.[183,205,205a]

Improvements in Light-Valves and Density Optical Systems. In June 1932 Shea, Herriott and Goehner[65] described the development of improved duralumin ribbon (stronger and with straighter edges) and better methods of adjusting and anchoring the ribbons at the ends of the free span. The new anchoring system practically eliminated the frictional hysteresis which had been found in the earlier design, thus reducing waveform distortion and making for greater stability. Stability became increasingly important as the mean spacing between the two ribbons in the valve was reduced. The ground-noise reduction system called for reducing the ribbon spacing when the modulation was low, and when it was found possible in view of required exposures to reduce the unbiased spacing from 0.002 in. to 0.001 in. this was done, while still keeping the optical reduction from valve to film at 2:1.

At high frequency and high modulation, the images of the ribbon edges move with velocities comparable with the speed of film travel. This results in a waveshape distortion which would convert a sine wave into a saw-tooth wave. Fortunately such a combination of high frequency and amplitude is not often encountered in program material, and the harmonics generated would probably not be reproduced, nor noticed if they were. However, it is desirable to minimize this "ribbon-velocity" distortion, and the reduced slit width helps in that respect and also in giving better resolution or high-frequency response.

In order that harmful effects (harm to sound quality if not to the ribbons themselves) might not result when the modulation current drives the ribbons to the point of touching or hitting each other (light-valve "clash") light valves have been built with the ribbons slightly offset, or in two planes.[207] There appears to have been difference of opinion about the necessity of this precaution. It should be remembered that in a density system the downward light modulation normally stops considerably short of zero, to avoid photographic nonlinearity. In other words touching of the ribbons would represent considerable overload.

The two-plane design of valve has become generally standard for variable-density recording.

The optics of light-valve recording systems[207] have been modified by the addition of a small horizontal cylindrical lens close to the film, which results in greater optical reduction between valve and film and therefore a narrower image (0.0002 in.). This makes for improved high-frequency recording and for further reduction of ribbon-velocity distortion. One of the factors which has made the narrower image possible without sacrificing exposure is that new lamps of higher intensity have become available.

Light-valve optics have been adapted to making variable-area tracks, for example as used in the stereophonic system described in 1941.[208] The valve is turned with the ribbons vertical, or parallel to direction of film travel. The lens system, which employs cylinders, magnifies the ribbon motion ten to one. This means that the lens must be close to the ribbons, hence with little depth of focus. Therefore in this application the ribbons are in the same plane, and an electrical current-limiting expedient prevents clash.[209]

A strong magnetic field is advantageous for the sake of sensitivity and damping. In the design described by Wente and Biddulph[208] an air gap flux density of 32,000 gauss is attained, an achievement which testifies to the excellence of the permanent magnet materials and the high flux capacity of the pole-piece material. There is some further discussion of light valves in the section on variable density vs. variable area.

Microphones. While condenser microphones had excellent characteristics they were more expensive and required more servicing than magnetic microphones, and it was practically necessary to provide a stage of amplification close to the microphone. On the other hand, the electrical impedance of a magnetic microphone is such that a transformer may be used if wanted, and the output transmitted at a convenient impedance. A magnetic microphone of the flexibly mounted rigid-diaphram, moving-coil type is described by Jones and Giles in December 1931.[210,211] It is a pressure-type (rather than velocity or pressure-gradient) microphone. Damping is obtained by flow of air when the diaphram vibrates, back and forth between two cavities, through passages which are of such small dimensions as to make air viscosity effective in dissipating energy.

In June 1931 H. F. Olson described the velocity microphone,[212] consisting of a ribbon of very thin aluminum (0.0001 in.) in a magnetic field between pole pieces which are adjacent to the edges of the ribbon, so that when the ribbon moves in a direction normal to its surface

a voltage is induced in the ribbon. A transformer is used to step up this voltage, which is then applied to the grid of an amplifier tube. Transverse corrugations are formed in the ribbon, which prevent it from curling and give it lengthwise flexibility. It is mounted under only such tension as is needed to keep it between the pole pieces. Olson shows that theoretically such a microphone should give uniform frequency response, and that it should have a polar directivity curve like a figure 8 (cosine law), the directivity being the same throughout the frequency range. Experimental results are also given confirming the theory. The velocity of movement of the ribbon is proportional to the velocity of air movement, so that it is often called a "velocity microphone."

Since a microphone of this type responds less and less as the direction of the sound departs from normal, it picks up much less reverberation (random in direction) than a nondirectional microphone having the same sensitivity for sound of normal incidence. The ratio of direct to reverberant sound in many cases sets the limit to how far from the source the microphone can be placed, and under such circumstances a ribbon microphone can get satisfactory pickup some 70% farther from the source than a nondirectional microphone, such as one of the pressure type.[213] Advantage has been taken of the directional characteristics of the ribbon microphone to exclude certain sounds or disturbances (for example camera noise), for it is deaf to sounds originating in the plane of the ribbon.

If the output of a pressure microphone is combined in correct phase and amount with that of a velocity microphone, the combination becomes unidirectional, having a cardioid-shaped directivity curve. It has a dead-spot 180° from the direction of maximum sensitivity. The forward directivity is much less sharp than that of a velocity microphone, and such a unidirectional microphone is better suited for picking up sound over a wide angle, as for example from a large orchestra. The cardioid directivity pattern has the same advantage as the figure 8 pattern in picking up less noise from random directions than a nondirectional microphone.

Before making a unidirectional microphone, Olson worked out an arrangement for converting a velocity microphone into a pressure microphone. He placed close behind the ribbon a combination shield and absorber consisting of an open-ended tube of the same cross-sectional area as the active area of ribbon. He distributed through the tube tufts of absorbent fiber. The length of the tube was made sufficient to dissipate wave energy. The impedance of the mouth of the tube then becomes equal to that of so much free air (to plane waves) but air in which there is no other sound to react on the ribbon. The ribbon is then actuated only by the pressure on the exposed side.[214]

Having successfully made this conversion, Olson applied the same treatment to only one half of the length of the ribbon, leaving the other half to act as a bidirectional velocity microphone, and the combination has the cardioid directional characteristics.[215]

Bell Laboratory engineers also developed bidirectional or velocity microphones, and unidirectional types, but differing from the Olson type in employing a second microphone more nearly like their standard pressure microphone. The unit and its applications were discussed by Marshall and Harry in September 1939.[216]

All studios use directional microphones for situations where the maximum ratio of direct to random sound is wanted.

Loudspeakers[4,25,73,222]

Single Range Loudspeakers. For several years after the industry had adopted sound the theater loudspeakers were of the kinds already mentioned, (1) the directional baffle-type, using a coil-driven cone, much like those used in direct radiator speakers, with a short, straight-axis exponential horn of large throat area, and (2) those using long exponential horns[217,218] with small throats, and coil-driven metal diaphragms. In view of their length the horns were coiled or otherwise bent to a form which took up less space.

Multi-Range Loudspeakers and Improved Single-Range Speakers. The idea of providing separate devices to radiate high and low frequencies is undoubtedly of early origin. When practically all radiators had strong fundamental resonances, the double or triple unit could spread the range of reasonably high response over a wider frequency band. With the advent of coil-driven, untuned diaphragms, resort to separate radiators was a measure for improving efficiency, in that the design did not have to be a compromise between what was best for low and for high frequencies. A triple-horn speaker designed with special consideration to efficiency and load capacity was advocated and demonstrated by C. R. Hanna of Westinghouse in 1927.[219]

However theater speakers of the single-unit type were so far improved (by the coil-driven unit of Wente and Thuras in 1926,[57] and by the adoption of directive baffles for the GE-RCA cone-type speakers in 1929) that they handled quite well the frequency range then obtainable from film or disk.

As recording improved, the benefits from extending the loudspeaker range became more noticeable. After various improvements in the recording system including the new galvanometer, the

symmetrical track, ground-noise reduction (by galvanometer bias), ribbon microphone for sound pickup, and a film-phonograph using the magnetic drive, Dimmick and Belar gave a demonstration of extended frequency range at the SMPE 1932 Spring Convention.[179] They did not resort to two-way (divided-range) speakers, for the straight-axis, directional baffle units, which had 6-in. cone diaphragms with aluminum voice-coils, had good response even at 10,000 cycles. The range was extended downward (to 60 cycles) by using slow expansion exponential horns (of the large-throat or directional-baffle type) 10 ft long, with mouth openings 75 in. square.

Multi-Range Speakers of Bell Telephone Laboratories. A divided-range speaker system was used by H. A. Frederick in the demonstrations of vertically cut disk records in the fall of 1931.[220] The high-frequency units were of the type described by Bostwick in the October 1930 *Journal of the Acoustical Society of America*, and in the May 1931 *SMPE Journal.*[221] These were equipped with small horns better to load the diaphragms. The low-frequency units were of the direct-radiator or flat-baffle type, using (as I recall it) approximately 12-in. diameter dynamic cone units,[38] a number of units being distributed over a large baffle. A curve indicates a response within ±5 db from 50 to 10,000 cycles.

A triple-range system is described by Flannagan, Wolf and Jones,[222] whose review of the development of theater loudspeakers is comprehensive and of much interest. The system is also discussed by Maxfield and Flannagan in the January 1936 *Journal.*[222a] The mid-range units were essentially like the previous single-range speakers, using the Western Electric No. 555 driver units. The radiators for the high-frequency range (3,000–13,000) were the same as used in the Frederick demonstrations. The authors state that for the range below 300 cycles large coil-driven conical diaphragms in a large flat baffle gave better results than designs using horns.

In April 1933 the Bell Telephone Laboratories gave a demonstration of reproduction of orchestra music in "*auditory perspective,*"[223,224] the orchestra being in Philadelphia and the reproduction in Constitution Hall in Washington, D.C. Three microphones picked up the music at three well-separated positions, and at the other end the independently transmitted and amplified currents were supplied to three correspondingly placed loudspeakers.

In this demonstration no recording and reproduction entered to affect frequency range, and it was essential for the purpose to provide abundant sound power and frequency range. A dual-range system was decided on.

The low-frequency unit was designed to work from 40 to 300 cycles, and consisted in a large-diaphragm, moving-coil unit, working into the 8-in. diameter throat of a horn which expanded exponentially to a mouth 60 in. square in a total length of approximately 10 ft.

The high-frequency driver unit, which covers the range 300 to 13,000 cycles is shown in cross section as Fig. 10 in the Flannagan, Wolf and Jones paper.[222] Particular attention is given in the design to the air space and passageways leading from the diaphragm surface into the horn or group of horns.

If a single straight-axis exponential horn is used, the tones of highest frequency are radiated in a direction close to the axis, while those of lower frequency are spread through much larger angles. This defect is avoided by dividing the total cross section of the passage into a number of smaller passages each of which is a small exponential horn. In this case there were sixteen horns for each driver. These are nested with their mouths adjacent and with their axes pointed in different directions to cover a total angle of about 30° vertically and horizontally. Since the horns are of equal length, the waves, whatever their frequency, unite at the ends of the horns to form a practically continuous spherical front, which is the condition for uniform distribution throughout the 30° angle. Two of these 16-horn nests were placed side by side to give the desired total of 60° horizontal coverage.

First Commercial RCA Two-Way Theater Speakers. In the RCA line of theater equipment a dual-range loudspeaker system was briefly described by J. Frank, Jr., at the 1935 fall meeting.[225] The speakers demonstrated by Dimmick and Belar, in 1932, using 6-in. cone diaphragms with aluminum voice coils, and 10-ft horns, were not seriously lacking in frequency range and were used in a number of deluxe installations, but they had two drawbacks. There were many theaters without sufficient room to install the long straight axis horns, and in addition, the high-frequency sound components were not well distributed. When a wave front reaches a point in an exponential horn at which the dimensions of the passageway are about a wavelength, its ultimate angle of spread will not greatly exceed the angle between the walls at that place. From this consideration it follows that a rapid flare horn would distribute the high-frequency sounds through considerably larger angles. Moreover with short rapid-flare horns, it is not impractical to multiply the number of units and thereby further control the sound distribution. In the theater speaker described by Frank, there were three high-frequency horns diverging in direction, the driver units being 6-in. cones with aluminum voice-coils.

These units were rated to operate effectively from 125 to 8,000 cycles, and a separate folded horn unit took care of sounds in the 40 to 125 cycle range.

One of the practical advantages of a direct-radiator (flat baffle) loudspeaker is the small space it requires. However a horn makes it possible to radiate more sound from a given-sized diaphragm without increasing the amplitude of motion, and is therefore desirable for increasing the sound output capacity. It also affords some control of the direction of radiation. But to radiate low frequencies the rate of expansion (ratio of increase in cross section per unit distance along axis) must be small, which for a given total ratio of expansion means length. One way to provide a long passageway without requiring excessive depth of space back of the screen is to coil up the horn. Drawings of coiled horns are shown in ref. 1, p. 298, and on p. 251 of the March 1937 *Journal*. The bending of large sound passageways is objectionable. Instead of expanding continuously as in the ideal horn, short waves suffer repeated reflections by the walls, causing some irregularities in the response and making the direction of radiation of high-frequency sounds rather unpredictable.* On the other hand if the horn is to handle only low-frequency sounds, the shapes of the bends are not at all critical, and the condition is easily fulfilled that the difference between the shortest and longest paths around a bend is a small fraction of a wavelength.

In a common form of low-frequency horn (in the sense of an approximately exponentially expanding passageway) the driver unit (or units) is at the middle of the back of a box-shaped space, and the passage is forward for a short distance, dividing and forming two passages which turn back and then forward and expand to form a pair of large adjacent rectangular openings, which together form the mouth of the horn. This roughly describes the low-frequency unit of the theater speaker system reported by Frank, the drivers in that case being a pair of 8-in. coil-driven cones.

Shearer System.[226] In 1936 Douglas Shearer, sound director for M-G-M, gave demonstrations of improved sound, using loudspeakers described by J. K. Hilliard in the July 1936 *Journal*. The high-frequency radiators in this system were similar in many respects to those used for the Auditory Perspective demonstrations (see figure in Hilliard paper). The frequency range to be covered was 50 to 8000 cycles, and the division or cross-over was at 250 cycles.

The low-frequency unit was a folded horn, with four 15-in. cones in a vertical column. For simplicity of construction the expansion was all in the horizontal

* This effect can be largely reduced by careful design of re-entrant (zig-zag passage) horns.

Fig. 16. Horizontal cross section showing sound passages of folded low-frequency horn.

plane, accomplished by suitably arranged vertical partitions. The horn cross section was divided into two expanding passageways, whose final openings together form a 68-in. square (Fig. 16). This was surrounded by a flat baffle 10 × 12 ft, to reduce end reflections and improve the loading of the units. The mean length of each passageway was 40 in. (very short as low-frequency horn designs go), nor was the expansion ratio large, the throat area being sufficient to accommodate the four 15-in. cones.

A nest of high-frequency horns, similar to that used for the Auditory Perspective demonstrations, three high by six horizontally, covered a horizontal angle of about 100°. With the lengths of the high- and low-frequency horns nearly the same, there would be little time difference in the arrival of the sounds at the plane of the mouths, thus simplifying the avoidance of a "phasing" error which has been found to have detrimental effects with transients. However, in all divided-range speaker systems the best relative positions of the high- and low-frequency units have been determined by careful trials. This problem of "phasing" is discussed by Maxfield and Flannagan,[222a] by Hilliard[226] and others. It appears to be not wholly a question of minimizing the mean time difference, although that is a part of it.

In all divided-range speaker systems, dividing networks[227] have been used to separate the high- and low-frequency portions of the amplifier output and direct each to the appropriate speaker units. The networks consist in general of simple filter sections, and their design has received much study.

Commercial Two-Way Systems. Commercial models of dual-range or "two-way" theater speakers were brought out in 1936, employing the multicell high-frequency horn system, and low-frequency units much like those described by Hilliard. The high-frequency driver units of the RCA system differed from the ERPI and Lansing designs in that the diaphragms were of molded phenolic instead of aluminum. This resulted in a more rugged, if less sensitive, device. The reduced sensitivity and greater "roll off," or falling off at high frequency, can be readily compensated electrically, and do not mean any serious increase in amplifier output power, because the high-frequency components of the sound represent only a small part of the total sound power.

The ERPI "Diphonic" speaker system

is described in the Flannagan, Wolf and Jones paper.[222]

The description by Hilliard of the Shearer low-frequency unit may be taken as in general typical of the commercial speakers of 1936–7.

Divided channel or "two-way" speakers came into wide use during the several years following 1936.

In some later designs of low-frequency units, the sound passageway was not folded, and consisted only of a short flaring connection between the driver units (which presented a large total radiating surface) and the large opening in the flat baffle.* It is of interest that the evolution of low-frequency sound sources has been toward a closer resemblance to the cone and baffle speakers of 1925, but greatly magnified in size, and with some "directive baffle" effect better to control sound distribution.

Higher crossover frequencies than the 250-cycle point of the Shearer system have prevailed, 400 cycles being the choice in many of the postwar units. In 1948 Hopkins and Keith[228] described the design of a two-way theater speaker in which the crossover had been raised to 800 cycles, observations having been made that the irregularities which are apt to occur at the crossover frequency are less prejudicial if the crossover is above the frequency range of maximum energy (250 to 500 cycles for orchestra music).

A photograph of a loudspeaker designed to use with "Cinerama" is shown in the May 1954 SMPTE Progress Report, p. 343. This is more or less typical of recent practice. The horn (or directive baffle expansion passage) of the low-frequency units as well as that of the high-frequency unit is designed to give exponential expansion of the total cross section by side walls which are radial, the floor and ceiling of each passage being curved to compensate. The reflex, phase-inversion principle (mentioned under "Monitoring Speakers") is employed to utilize radiation from the backs of the diaphragms, for the extreme bass. Note in the illustration the outlet slots on either side of the horn mouth.

Alternatives to Multicellular Horns. A somewhat simpler way of achieving the directive characteristic for which the multicellular high-frequency horns were designed has been developed in the postwar period by RCA and others. Horns are used with linear expansion in the horizontal plane (i.e. walls radial with respect to the throat), while in the vertical plane the rate of expansion

* This would raise the "cutoff" frequency of the horn, but where the total expansion ratio is comparatively small that is not necessarily very significant. Below its "cutoff" frequency, an exponential horn does not impede sound transmission. It merely fails to multiply the volume displacement as it does above cutoff.

is such as to bring the total expansion of the cross section to an exponential relation.

Another expedient for gaining the desired spread of high-frequency sounds was described by Frayne and Locanthi at the May 1954 convention of this Society.[229] If the waves issuing from a straight-axis exponential horn can be made to assume a spherical instead of nearly flat front, they will spread as desired. An acoustic equivalent of a concave optical lens is placed in the mouth of the horn, in order to retard the off-axis parts of the waves relative to the central part. The reduced velocity of propagation is achieved by means of a series of closely-spaced perforated sheet-metal baffles, the number of layers being progressively greater toward the edges. This system was reported to have given smoother distribution than the multicell horns.

Monitoring Loudspeakers.[4,230,231] Wider-range monitoring speakers kept pace with theater speakers. While a single conical diaphragm can be designed so that the center portion radiates high frequencies and the outer area radiates low frequencies, best results have been obtained by using separate diaphragms and separate voice coils, or in other words resorting to the dual-range system. The upper- and lower-range units may be adjacent or concentric. In the latter case the low-frequency diaphragm becomes a directive baffle for the high-frequency radiator.

Permissible cabinet size tends to set the lower limit of the frequency range, air reaction on the back of the diaphragm creating the problem if the back is enclosed, or inadequate baffling if an open-back cabinet is used. In order to utilize the radiation from the back of the low-frequency diaphragm, a second opening is often provided (for example below the diaphragm) and the space in the cabinet used to provide a folded horn between the diaphragm and the opening, or else to serve as a simple chamber which acts in conjunction with the inertia reactance of the air at the second opening as a phase inverter. This does not greatly augment the low-frequency output except near the resonance, set by the elastic reactance of the cavity and the inertia reactance of the combination of openings (one with the diaphram and one without). Sound-absorbing material is often used in the cabinet to reduce the magnitude of other resonances. If the horn-type back-wave system is used, its augmentation of output is limited at the lower end when the phase shift through the horn becomes less than about a quarter cycle, and at the upper end by the fact that it is deliberately designed to have a low-pass filter characteristic.

References (Continued)

1. Lester Cowan, *Recording Sound for Motion Pictures*, McGraw-Hill Book Co., New York, 1931; H. G. Knox, "Ancestry of sound pictures," Chap. 1.
4. J. G. Frayne and H. Wolfe, *Elements of Sound Recording*, J. Wiley & Sons, New York, 1949.
6. E. I. Sponable, "Historical development of sound films," Pt. 1–2, *Jour. SMPE, 48:* 275–303, Apr. 1947; Pt. 3–7, ibid., 407–422, May 1947.
57. E. C. Wente and A. L. Thuras, "A high efficiency receiver of large power capacity for horn type loud speakers," *Bell Sys. Tech. J.*, Jan. 1928, p. 140.
70. E. W. Kellogg, "A review of the quest for constant speed," *Jour. SMPE, 28:* 337–376, Apr. 1937.

The five references above, which are referred to in the current installment of this paper, are reprinted from the first installment for the convenience of readers.

77. *L'Industrie du Film Parlant*, Conservatoire des Arts et Métiers, Feb. 17, 1929. *Contains a resume covering the Gaumont and the Gaumont-Peterson-Poulsen sound systems. (The foregoing is from the Theisen historical paper—ref. 5.)*
78. H. E. Roys, "The measurement of transcription-turntable speed variation," *Proc. I.R.E., 31:* 52–56, Feb. 1943.
79. T. E. Shea, W. A. MacNair and V. Subrizi, "Flutter in sound records," *Jour. SMPE, 25:* 403–415, Nov. 1935.
80. E. G. Shower and R. Biddulph, "Differential pitch sensitivity of the ear," *J. Acoust. Soc. Am., 3:* 275–287, Oct. 1931.
81. W. J. Albersheim and D. MacKenzie, "Analysis of sound film drives," *Jour. SMPE, 37:* 452–479, Nov. 1941.
82. E. W. Kellogg and H. Belar, "Analysis of the distortion resulting from sprocket hole modulation," *Jour. SMPE, 25:* 492–502, Dec. 1935.
83. SMPE Committee on Sound, "Proposed standard specifications for flutter or wow as related to sound records," *Jour. SMPE, 49:* 147–159, Aug. 1947.
84. E. W. Kellogg, "Proposed standard for measurement of distortion in sound recording," *Jour. SMPE, 51:* 449–467, Nov. 1948. Further discussion of the Flutter Standard by the same author appears in an editorial in the *Trans. I.R.E.*, July–Aug., 1954.
84a. Frank A. Comerci, of the Material Laboratory, Bureau of Ships New York Naval Shipyard, Brooklyn, N. Y., "Perceptibility of flutter in speech and music," *Jour. SMPTE, 64:* 117–122, Mar. 1955. Discussion, 318, June 1955.
85. M. S. Mead, U.S. Pat. 1,854,949.
86. E. W. Kellogg and A. R. Morgan, "Measurement of speed fluctuations in sound recording and reproducing equipment," *J. Acoust. Soc. Am., 7:* 271–280, Apr. 1936.
87. A. Goodman, R. J. Kowalski, W. F. Hardman and W. F. Stanko, "Safeguarding theater sound equipment with modern test instruments," *Jour. SMPE, 34:* 409–423, Apr. 1940.
88. R. R. Scoville, "A portable flutter-measuring instrument," *Jour. SMPE, 25:* 416–422, Nov. 1935 Also: "Laboratory flutter-measuring instrument," *Jour. SMPE, 29:* 209–215, Aug. 1937.
89. F. P. Herrnfeld, "Flutter-measuring set," *Jour. SMPTE, 55:* 167–172, Aug. 1950.
90. U. R. Furst, "Periodic variations of pitch in sound reproduction by phonographs," *Proc. I.R.E., 34:* 887–895, Nov. 1946.
91. L. A. Elmer and D. G. Blattner, "Machine for cutting master disc records," *Trans. SMPE, 37:* 227–246, 1929.
92. P. H. Evans, "A comparative study of sound on disk and film," *Jour. SMPE, 15:* 185–192, Aug. 1930.

93. H. Pfannenstiehl, "High-precision sound-film recording machine," *Jour. SMPE, 29:* 202–208, Aug. 1937.
94. E. W. Kellogg, "A new recorder for variable area recording," *Jour. SMPE, 15:* 653–670, Nov. 1930. (*The title of this paper is misleading, in that the main features of the recorder were in no wise related to the type of sound track to be recorded.*)
95. E. W. Kellogg, U.S. Pat. 1,892,554, 1,899,571, and Re19,270.
96. R. O. Drew and E. W. Kellogg, "Filtering factors of the magnetic drive," *Jour. SMPE, 35:* 138–164, Aug. 1940.
97. See ref. 94.
98. A. G. Zimmerman, "Film recorders," *Jour. SMPE, 20:* 211–227, Mar. 1933.
99. M. E. Collins, "A deluxe film recording machine," *Jour. SMPE, 48:* 148–156, Feb. 1947. (*Model PR-31*)
100. H. A. Rowland, an early disclosure (1902) of the general principle of the damped flywheel is in U.S. Pat. 691,667, 1899, and 713,497. (See refs. 81 and 104.)
101. F. J. Loomis and E. W. Reynolds, "New Apparatus—A new high fidelity sound head," *Jour. SMPE, 25:* 449–460, Nov. 1935; and "New rotary stabilizer sound head," *Jour. SMPE, 27:* 575–581, Nov. 1936.
102. E. D. Cook, "The technical aspects of the high-fidelity reproducer," *Jour. SMPE, 25:* 289–313, Oct. 1935.
102a. Gerhard Schwesinger, "The compliance of film loops," *Jour. SMPTE, 57:* 320–327, Oct. 1951.
103. G. Puller, "Sound-picture reproducing system for small theaters," *Jour. SMPE, 27:* 582–589, Nov. 1936; Report of the Progress Committee, *Jour. SMPE, 27:* 29, July 1936.
104. E. C. Wente and A. H. Müller, "Internally damped rollers," *Jour. SMPE, 37:* 406–417, Oct. 1941.
105. C. C. Davis, "An improved film-drive filter mechanism," *Jour. SMPE, 46:* 454–464, June 1946.
106. G. R. Crane and H. A. Manley, "A simplified all-purpose film recording machine," *Jour. SMPE, 46:* 465–474, June 1946.
107. M. E. Collins, "Lightweight recorders for 35 and 16 mm films," *Jour. SMPE, 49:* 415–424, Nov. 1947. (*Models PR-32 and PR-33.*)
108. J. D. Phyfe and C. E. Hittle, "Film-pulled theater-type magnetic sound reproducer for use with multitrack films," *Jour. SMPTE, 62:* 215–220, Mar. 1954.
109. C. C. Davis and H. A. Manley, "Auxiliary multitrack magnetic sound reproducer," *Jour. SMPTE, 62:* 208–214, Mar. 1954.
110. S. W. Athey, W. Borberg, and R. A. White, "Four-track magnetic theater sound reproducer for composite films," *Jour. SMPTE, 62:* 221–227, Mar. 1954.
111. Wesley C. Miller, "M-G-M recorder and reproducer equipment units," *Jour. SMPE, 40:* 301, May 1943.
112. J. S. Chandler, "Some theoretical considerations in the design of sprockets for continuous film movement," *Jour. SMPE, 37:* 164–176, Aug. 1941.
113. J. G. Streiffert, "The radial-tooth, variable-pitch sprocket," *Jour. SMPTE, 57:* 529–550, Dec. 1951.
114. "Rulings of the U.S. Supreme Court in recent patent cases of the American Tri-Ergon Corp.," *Jour. SMPE, 24:* 529–550, June 1935.
115. Report of Standards and Nomenclature Committee, *Jour. SMPE, 14:* 126, 133, Jan. 1930.
116. Oscar B. Depue, "A machine for printing picture and sound simultaneously and automatically," *Jour. SMPE, 18:* 643–648, May 1932.

117. A. S. Howell, B. E. Steckbart and R. F. Mitchell, "The Bell & Howell fully automatic sound picture production printer," *Jour. SMPE, 19:* 305–328, Oct. 1932.

118. A. S. Howell and R. F. Mitchell, "Recent improvements in the Bell & Howell fully automatic printer," *Jour. SMPE, 22:* 115–126, Feb. 1934.

119. Roscoe C. Hubbard, "Printing motion picture film," *Trans. SMPE,* No. 28, 252, Feb. 1927.

120. J. Crabtree, "Sound film printing-I," *Jour. SMPE, 21:* 294–322, Oct. 1933; "Sound film printing-II," *Jour. SMPE, 22:* 98–114, Feb. 1934.

121. J. I. Crabtree and C. E. Ives, "A new method of blocking out splices in sound film," *Jour. SMPE, 14:* 349–356, Mar. 1930.

122. F. D. Williams, "Methods of blooping," *Jour. SMPE, 30:* 105–106, Jan. 1938.

123. W. H. Offenhauser, Jr., "Current practices in blooping sound-film," *Jour. SMPE, 35:* 165–171, Aug. 1940.

124. E. I. Sponable, "Elimination of splice noise in sound film," *Jour. SMPE, 26:* 136–144, Feb. 1936.

124a.George Lewin, "A new blooping device," *Jour. SMPE, 48:* 343–347, Apr. 1947.

125. L. E. Clark, "Some considerations in the design of sound-proof camera housings," *Jour. SMPE, 15:* 165–170, Aug. 1930.

126. Report of Progress Committee, *Jour. SMPE, 27:* 3–44, July 1936. Twentieth Century-Fox camera, p. 8.

127. H. R. Kossman, "A silent camera," *Jour. SMPE, 21:* 420–425, Nov. 1933.

128. D. B. Clark and G. Laube, "Twentieth century camera and accessories," *Jour. SMPE, 36:* 50–64, Jan. 1941.

129. J. P. Maxfield, "Acoustic control of recording for talking motion pictures," *Jour. SMPE, 14:* 85–95, Jan. 1930.

130. A. S. Ringel, "Sound-proofing and acoustic treatment of RKO stages," *Jour. SMPE, 15:* 352–369, Sept. 1930.

131. M. C. Batsel, "Recording music for motion pictures," *Jour. SMPE, 25:* 103–108, Aug. 1935.

132. R. H. Townsend, "Some technical aspects of recording music," *Jour. SMPE, 25:* 259–268, Sept. 1935.

133. M. Rettinger, "Scoring-stage design," *Jour. SMPE, 30:* 519–534, May 1938.

134. V. O. Knudsen, "Hearing of speech in auditoriums," *J. Acoust. Soc. Am., 56,* Oct. 1929.

135. W. A. MacNair, "Optimum reverberation time for auditoriums," *J. Acoust. Soc. Am., 242,* Jan. 1930.

136. S. S. A. Watkins and C. H. Fetter, "Some aspects of a Western Electric sound recording system," *Jour. SMPE, 14:* 520–530, May 1930.

137. B. Kreuzer, "Recent improvements in the variable-width recording system," *Jour. SMPE, 27:* 562–574, Nov. 1936.

138. W. P. Dutton and S. Read, Jr., "Some new RCA photophone studio recording equipment," *Jour. SMPE, 16:* 315–329, Mar. 1931.

139. S. Read, Jr., "RCA Victor high-fidelity film recording equipment," *Jour. SMPE, 20:* 396–436, May 1933.

140. S. Read, Jr., "Neon type volume indicator," *Jour. SMPE, 28:* 633–642, June 1937.

141. F. G. Albin, "Linear decibel-scale volume indicator," *Jour. SMPE, 29:* 489–492, Nov. 1937.

142. L. T. Sachtleben, "Characteristics of Photophone light-modulating system," *Jour. SMPE, 25:* 175–191, Aug. 1935.

143. L. J. Anderson, "High fidelity headphones," *Jour. SMPE, 37:* 319–323, Sept. 1941.

144. H. F. Hopkins, "Considerations in the design and testing of motion picture

screens for sound picture work," *Jour. SMPE, 15:* 320–331, Sept. 1930.

145. Charles R. Underhill, Jr., "Practical solution to the screen light distribution problem," *Jour. SMPTE, 56:* 680–683, June 1951; Report of Progress Committee, *Jour. SMPTE, 56:* 575, May 1951.

146. J. I. Crabtree, "The motion picture laboratory," *Jour. SMPTE, 64:* 13–34, Jan. 1955.

147. H. W. Moyse and D. R. White, "Borax developer characteristics," *Trans. SMPE,* No. 38, 445–452, 1929.

148. H. C. Carlton and J. I. Crabtree, "Some properties of fine grain developers for motion picture film," *Trans. SMPE,* No. 38, 406–444, 1929.

149. E. Huse, "Sensitometric control in the processing of motion picture film in Hollywood," *Jour. SMPE, 21:* 54–82, July 1933.

150. L. A. Jones, "Photographic sensitometry," *Jour. SMPE, 17:* 491–535, Oct. 1931; Part 2, 695–742, Nov. 1931; Part 3, *18:* 54–89, Jan. 1932; Part 4, 324–355, Mar. 1932.

151. A. Küster and R. Schmidt, "The sensitometric control of sound records on film," *Jour. SMPE, 19:* 539–545, Dec. 1932.

152. J. B. Engl, "A new process for developing and printing photographic sound records," *Trans. SMPE,* No. 30, 257–266, 1927.

153. Joe W. Coffman, "Sound film processing," *Trans. SMPE,* No. 35, 799–808, 1928. Also "Art and science in sound film production," *Jour. SMPE, 14:* 172–179, Feb. 1930.

154. W. Leahy, "Time-and-temperature vs. the test system for development of motion picture negatives," *Jour. SMPE, 18:* 649–651, May 1932.

155. J. I. Crabtree and C. E. Ives, "A replenishing solution for a motion picture positive film developer," *Jour. SMPE, 15:* 627–640, Nov. 1930.

156. R. M. Evans, "Maintenance of a developer by continuous replenishment," *Jour. SMPE, 31:* 273–286, Sept. 1938.

157. H. L. Baumbach, "Continuous replenishment and chemical control of motion picture developing solutions," *Jour. SMPE, 39:* 55–66, July 1942.

158. C. E. Ives and E. W. Jensen, "Effect of developer agitation on density uniformity and rate of development," *Jour. SMPE, 40:* 107–136, Feb. 1943.

159. J. I. Crabtree and H. D. Russell, "Some properties of chrome alum stop baths and fixing baths," *Jour. SMPE, 14:* Part 1, 483–512, May 1930; Part 2, 667–700, June 1930.

160. J. I. Crabtree, L. E. Muehler and H. D. Russell, "New stop bath and fixing bath formulas and methods for their revival," *Jour. SMPE, 38:* 353–372, Apr. 1942.

161. R. C. Hubbard, "The straight line developing machine, *Trans. SMPE,* No. 18, 73–85, May 1924.

162. Alfred B. Hitchins, "Machine development of negative and positive motion picture film," *Trans. SMPE,* No. 22, 46–53, 1925.

163. H. D. Hineline, "Continuous photographic processing," *Jour. SMPE, 26:* 38–53, Jan. 1936.

164. Clifton Tuttle and J. W. McFarlane, "The measurement of density in variable-density sound-film," *Jour. SMPE, 15:* 345–351, Sept. 1930.

165. L. A. Jones and J. H. Webb, "Reciprocity law failure in photograph exposures," *Jour. SMPE, 23:* 142–159, Sept. 1934.

166. J. G. Capstaff and R. A. Purdy, "A compact motion picture densitometer," *Trans. SMPE,* No. 31, 607–612, 1927.

167. G. A. Chambers and I. D. Wratten, "The Eastman type IIb densitometer as a control instrument in the processing of

motion picture film," *Jour. SMPE, 21:* 218–223, Sept. 1933.

168. F. L. Eich, "A physical densitometer for sound processing laboratories," *Jour. SMPE, 24:* 180–183, Feb. 1935.

169. W. W. Lindsey, Jr. and W. V. Wolfe, "Wide-range, linear-scale photoelectric cell densitometer," *Jour. SMPE, 28:* 622–632, June 1937.

170. D. R. White, "Direct-reading photoelectric densitometer," *Jour. SMPE, 33:* 403–409, Oct. 1939.

171. J. G. Frayne and G. R. Crane, "Precision integrating-sphere densitometer," *Jour. SMPE, 35:* 184–200, Aug. 1940.

172. C. M. Tuttle and M. E. Russell, "Note on the use of an automatic recording densitometer," *Jour. SMPE, 28:* 99–111, Jan. 1937.

172a.D. MacKenzie, "Straight-line and toe records with the light-valve," *Jour. SMPE, 17:* 172–202, Aug. 1931.

173. L. A. Jones and Otto Sandvik, "Photographic characteristics of sound recording film," *Jour. SMPE, 14:* 180–203, Feb. 1930.

174. J. A. Maurer, "The photographic treatment of variable-area sound-films," *Jour. SMPE, 14:* 636–649, June 1930.

175. G. L. Dimmick, "High-frequency response from variable-width records as affected by exposure and development," *Jour. SMPE, 17:* 766–777, Nov. 1931.

176. J. O. Baker and D. H. Robinson, "Modulated high-frequency recording as a means of determining conditions for optimal processing," *Jour. SMPE 30:* 3–17, Jan. 1938.

177. J. E. Abbott, "Development of the sound film," *Jour. SMPE, 38:* 541–545, June 1942.

178. G. L. Dimmick, "Galvanometers for variable-area recording," *Jour. SMPE, 15:* 428–438, Oct. 1930.

179. G. L. Dimmick and H. Belar, "Extension of the frequency range of film recording and reproduction," *Jour. SMPE, 19:* 401–406, Nov. 1932.

180. M. C. Batsel and E. W. Kellogg, "RCA sound recording system," *Jour. SMPE, 28:* 507–533, May 1937.

181. G. L. Dimmick, "A newly developed light modulator for sound recording," *Jour. SMPE, 49:* 48–56, July 1947.

182. E. W. Kellogg, U.S. Pat. 1,740,406.

182a.L. T. Sachtleben, "Characteristics of the Photophone light-modulating system," *Jour. SMPE, 25:* 175–191, Aug. 1935.

183. G. L. Dimmick, "RCA recording system and its adaptation to various types of sound-track," *Jour. SMPE, 29:* 258–273, Sept. 1937.

184. E. W. Kellogg, "ABC of photographic sound recording," *Jour. SMPE, 44:* 151–194, Mar. 1945.

185. E. W. Kellogg, "Ground-noise reduction systems," *Jour. SMPE, 36:* 137–171, Feb. 1941.

186. Siemens and Halske, British Pat. 288,225, Convention Apr. 9, 1927.

187. L. T. Robinson, U.S. Pat. 1,854,159 and 1,935,417; C. W. Hewlett, U.S. Pat. 1,853,812; and C. R. Hanna, U.S. Pat. 1,888,724.

188. H. C. Silent and J. G. Frayne, "Western Electric noiseless recording, *Jour. SMPE, 18:* 551–570, May 1932.

189. H. McDowell, Jr., U.S. Pat. 1,855,197.

190. R. H. Townsend, H. McDowell, Jr. and L. E. Clark, "Ground-noise reduction RCA Photophone system," Reprint 26, *Tech. Bul. Acad. Mot. Pict. Arts & Sci.,* Feb. 1931.

191. E. W. Kellogg and C. N. Batsel, "A shutter for use in reduction of ground-noise," *Jour. SMPE, 17:* 203–215, Aug. 1931.

192. H. J. Hasbrouck, J. O. Baker and C. N. Batsel, "Improved noise-reduction system

for high-fidelity recording," *Jour. SMPE, 29:* 310–316, Sept. 1937.

193. R. R. Scoville and W. L. Bell, "Design and use of noise-reduction bias systems," *Jour. SMPE, 38:* 125–147, Feb. 1942.

194. B. Kreuzer, "Noise reduction with variable-area recording," *Jour. SMPE, 16:* 671–683, June 1931.

195. J. L. Hathaway, "Microphone polarity and overmodulation," *Electronics,* Oct. 1939, p. 28.

196. R. O. Drew and E. W. Kellogg, "Starting characteristics of speech sounds," *Jour. SMPE, 34:* 43–58, Jan. 1940; and *J. Acoust. Soc. Am., 12:* 95–103, July 1940.

197. J. G. Frayne, "Noise-reduction anticipation circuits," *Jour. SMPE, 43:* 313–320, Nov. 1944.

198. J. R. Whitney and J. W. Thatcher, "Increased noise reduction by delay networks," *Jour. SMPTE, 54:* 295–302, Mar. 1950.

199. G. L. Dimmick and A. C. Blaney, "Direct positive system of sound recording," *Jour. SMPE, 33:* 479–487, Nov. 1939. See also Progress Committee Report, *Jour. SMPTE, 58:* 401, May 1952.

200. W. A. Mueller and G. R. Groves, "Magnetic recording in the motion picture studio," *Jour. SMPE, 52:* 605–612, June 1949.

201. Academy Research Council, "Report of basic sound committee on pre-and-post-equalization," *Jour. SMPE, 42:* 187–192, Mar. 1944.

202. J. K. Hilliard, "Projects of the committee on standardization of theater sound projection equipment characteristics," *Jour. SMPE, 30:* 81–95, Jan. 1938.

203. J. K. Hilliard, "Variable-density film-recording system used at MGM studios," *Jour. SMPE, 40:* 143–175, Mar. 1943.

204. K. F. Morgan and D. P. Loye, "Sound picture recording and reproduction characteristics," *Jour. SMPE, 32:* 631–647, June 1939; *33:* 107–108, July 1939.

205. F. E. Carlson, "Properties of lamps and optical systems for sound reproduction," *Jour. SMPE, 33:* 80–96, July 1939.

205a. L. T. Sachtleben, U.S. Pat. 2,158,308.

206. O. O. Ceccarini, "Recent contributions to light-valve Technic," *Jour. SMPE, 17:* 305–325, Sept. 1931.

207. W. Herriott and L. V. Foster, "Recent optical improvements in sound-film recording equipment," *Jour. SMPE, 23:* 167–174, Sept. 1934.

208. E. C. Wente and R. Biddulph, "Light-valve for the stereophonic sound-film system," *Jour. SMPE, 37:* 397–405, Oct. 1941.

209. R. R. Scoville, "Overload limiters for the protection of modulating devices," *Jour. SMPE, 31:* 93–98, July 1938.

210. W. C. Jones and L. W. Giles, "A moving-coil microphone for high-quality sound reproduction," *Jour. SMPE, 17:* 977–993, Dec. 1931.

211. E. C. Wente and A. L. Thuras, "Moving coil telephone receivers and microphones," *J. Acoust. Soc. Am., 3:* 44–55, Jan. 1931.

212. H. F. Olson, "The ribbon microphone," *Jour. SMPE, 16:* 695–708, June 1931; and *J. Acoust. Soc. Am., 3:* 56, July 1931.

213. H. F. Olson, "Collection of sound in reverberant rooms, with special reference to the application of the ribbon microphone," *Proc. IRE, 21:* 655, May 1933.

214. H. F. Olson and Frank Massa, *Applied Acoustics,* P. Blakiston's Sons & Co., Philadelphia, 1934.

215. H. F. Olson, "Unidirectional microphone," *Jour. SMPE, 27:* 284–301, Sept. 1936.

216. R. N. Marshall and W. R. Harry, "Cardioid directional microphone," *Jour. SMPE, 33:* 254–277, Sept. 1939.

217. A. G. Webster, "Acoustical impedance and theory of horns and phonograph," *Proc. Nat. Acad. of Sci., 6:* 275, 1919.

218. C. R. Hanna and J. Slepian, "The Function and design of horns for loud speakers," *Trans. AIEE, 43:* 393, Feb. 1924.

219. C. R. Hanna, "Loudspeakers of high efficiency and load capacity," *Trans. AIEE, 47:* 607, Apr. 1928.

220. H. A. Frederick, "Vertical sound records: recent fundamental advances in mechanical records on wax," *Jour. SMPE, 18:* 141–163, Feb. 1932.

221. L. G. Bostwick, "A loud speaker good to twelve thousand cycles," *Jour. SMPE, 16:* 529–534, May 1931.

222. C. Flannagan, R. Wolf and W. C. Jones, "Modern theater loud speakers and their development," *Jour. SMPE, 28:* 246–264, Mar. 1937.

222a. J. P. Maxfield and P. Flannagan, "Wide range reproduction in theaters," *Jour. SMPE, 26:* 67–78, Jan. 1936.

223. Symposium on Auditory Perspective, pub. in *Elec. Eng.,* (AIEE), *53:* 9, Jan. 1934; and *Bell Sys. Tech. J., 13:* 239, Apr. 1934. This equipment is again described in *Jour. SMPE, 37:* 331–417, Oct. 1941. See also refs. 329–332.

224. H. Fletcher, "Transmission and reproduction of speech and music in auditory perspective," *Jour. SMPE, 22:* 314–329, May 1934.

225. J. Frank, Jr., "RCA photophone high-fidelity sound reproducing equipment," *Jour. SMPE, 27:* 99–104, July 1936.

226. J. K. Hilliard, "Study of theater loud speakers and the resultant development of the Shearer two-way horn system," *Jour. SMPE, 27:* 45–60, July 1936.

227. J. K. Hilliard and H. R. Kimball, "Dividing networks for loud speaker systems," *Jour. SMPE, 27:* 61–73, July 1936.

228. H. F. Hopkins and C. R. Keith, "New theater loud speaker systems," *Jour. SMPE, 51:* 385–398, Oct. 1948.

229. J. G. Frayne and B. N. Locanthi, "Theater loudspeaker system incorporating an acoustic-lens radiator," *Jour. SMPTE, 63:* 82–85, Sept. 1954.

230. H. F. Olson and John Preston, "Wide-range loudspeaker developments," *Jour. SMPE, 47:* 327–352, Oct. 1946.

231. James B. Lansing, "New permanent magnet public address loudspeaker," *Jour. SMPE, 46:* 212–219, Mar. 1946.

FINAL INSTALLMENT

History of Sound Motion Pictures By EDWARD W. KELLOGG

For the abstract of this paper which was presented on May 5, 1954, at the Society's Convention at Washington, D.C., see the first installment published in the June Journal. The second installment appeared in the July Journal.

Developments Which Extended the Frequency Range

Better Light-Modulating System for Variable Area. Mention was made in the section on loudspeakers of a demonstration by Dimmick and Belar[179] of sound with extended frequency range. Aside from the improved loudspeakers and the ribbon microphone (whose response was practically uniform from 60 to 10,000 cycles) there were a number of advances that contributed to the result. The new galvanometer and optical system made so much more light available that it was feasible to reduce the width of the recording beam to $\frac{1}{4}$ mil, thus improving resolution. No small factor in giving clean high frequencies is avoidance of flutter, particularly rapid flutter such as 96 cycles. In the demonstrations, both recording and reproduction were on magnetic-drive machines.* (The rotary stabilizer was not yet available.)

Ground-noise reduction was by galvanometer bias with a single narrow line of transparent film when the modulation was zero, and it is my recollection that a measurement indicated a ratio better than 50 db between signal at full modulation and the ground noise when biased for zero modulation.

Nonslip Printer and Improved Sprocket-Type Printers. With the sprocket-type contact printers in almost universal use, a certain amount of slipping of the negative with respect to the print film is almost inevitable. The curvature at the sprocket compensates for a certain negative shrinkage at which the ratio of radii of the shrunk negative and unshrunk print stock is just equal to the ratio of their lengths. The sprocket diameter is designed to make this compensation correct for an average negative shrinkage, but it will be only approximate for negatives whose shrinkage

differs from this assumed average. By mechanically stretching whichever film is shorter, two films can be moved together through an appreciable distance in perfect nonslipping contact. A printing system in which this was done was developed by the Technicolor engineers for their color transfer, but it was not used for sound prints. An extended investigation of the losses and irregularities in high-frequency response which result from slippage and imperfect contact during printing is reported by J. Crabtree in the October 1933 and February 1934 *Journals.*[232]

In 1934 C. N. Batsel described a nonslip contact printer[233] employing a principle proposed and demonstrated earlier by A. V. Bedford for a different application.[70,234] Bending a film stretches one face and compresses the other, and it is only necessary that the contacting surfaces of the two films be made equal. In the nonslip printer, the negative is rolled through the machine at fixed curvature, and the print stock (held against the negative at the printing point, where it is propelled solely by friction) is made automatically to assume the curvature at which identical numbers

April 8, 1930.   A. V BEDFORD   1,754,187

BELT OR STRIP DRIVING ARRANGEMENT

Filed Nov 3, 1927

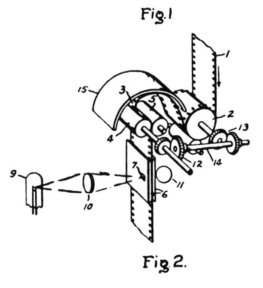

Fig. 1

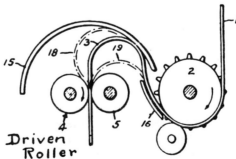

Fig 2.

Driven Roller

Fig. 17. Control of film speed by flexure (A. V. Bedford). Principle later used in nonslip printer.

---

* The special film-phonograph used in the demonstrations was a prototype of those used in the Disney *Fantasia* reproduction (see Fig. 7, p. 136, *Jour. SMPE*, Aug. 1941). The film was pulled by the magnetically driven drum over a curved supporting plate where the tracks were scanned, and was steadied at the other end of the plate by another drum with flywheel. This was an anticipation of the double flywheel system now used with magnetic tape and film.

of sprocket holes are fed through in a given time.

The nonslip printer was not built for sale by RCA, but free license and drawings were offered, and numerous laboratories built and used them, notably Consolidated Film Industries in Hollywood and Ace Film Laboratory in Brooklyn.[235]

A printer based on the identical principle was developed independently by R. V. Wood.[236]

Although nonslip printers were not made in large numbers, and did not to any great extent displace the conventional sprocket type of contact printer, they served to demonstrate how much improvement was possible through better printing, and in this way stimulated makers and users of sprocket printers to improve their machines and maintain them in the best possible condition. In a number of laboratories it appeared that better prints resulted if the teeth were removed from the side of the sprocket next to the soundtrack, leaving only a smooth supporting rim. The theory behind this is not clear unless it is that such disturbances of contact as are due to film sticking on the teeth are thus kept further from the soundtrack.

There were two reasons which limited the use of the nonslip printer. Since there is a very narrow region of close contact, the printing beam had to be narrow. Under such conditions any speed irregularities cause variation in print exposure, which sometimes becomes audible in density prints. While there is no valid excuse for such speed variations, this trouble contributed to the conclusion that the nonslip printer was unsatisfactory for density printing. Film laboratory operators were naturally averse to maintaining one type of printer for area and another for density. A more fundamental fault of the nonslip printer in making density prints is due to the fact that negative and positive perforations are not maintained in register. The more active developer circulation close to sprocket holes tends to darken these areas, resulting in a slight 96-cycle hum. The effects on the negative and print are compensatory provided the printing is done with the holes in registration, but cumulative if out of register. With a purely friction drive at the printing point the relative positions of positive and negative perforations are unpredictable and may drift slowly between one condition and the other. This results in a hum that comes and goes and is therefore more conspicuous than if steady. Area tracks are far less sensitive to such development variations.

Optical printers with independent filtering of negative and positive film motion would be subject to the same uncertainty with respect to relative perforation positions, but this problem comes up only with 35mm-to-35mm printing, for which optical printers are rarely used.

In spite of such improvements as have been made in developer turbulation in the processing machines, the sprocket type of printer does not appear to have any strong competitor for density prints. In such a situation the efforts of several Eastman engineers[112,113] to improve sprocket action are well justified. The shrinkage-compensating sprocket described above under "Mechanical Systems" should result in great improvements. The new film-base materials with their reduced shrinkage should also make for better results with printers of the sprocket type.[391]

Optical Printers. Cost and quick production have been dominating considerations in much 16mm production, and contact printing on the sprocket has prevailed, the printers being simpler than other types and available in large numbers to meet the heavy wartime demands. However, registration of negative and positive perforations is not a factor in the quality of 16mm prints of either density or area tracks. There is thus no obstacle on this score either to nonslip printers or to optical printers with independently filtered film motion, and both types have been used, the nonslip for printing from 16mm negatives, and the optical principally for printing on 16mm film from 35mm negatives,[237–239] but also with a 1 : 1 optical system for printing from 16mm negatives (Precision Film Laboratories, New York).[240]

The Eastman Co. has designed several models of optical reduction printers in which the 35mm and 16mm films are on sprockets on opposite ends of a single shaft and a U-shaped optical system is employed.[241] This system minimizes chances of slow "wows," but depends for good results on the degree of excellence attainable with sprocket action. The shrinkage-compensating, radial-tooth sprocket described in the section on "Mechanical Systems"[113] was developed with printer applications particularly in view.

Ultraviolet Light for Recording and Printing

For truly distortionless recording the ideal light spot would be of infinitesimal width. In practice, as various improvements made light of greater intensity available, the nominal width of the recording spot was reduced (to 0.00025 in.), but a limit is set by diffraction. With light of shorter wavelength lenses of the same dimensions can form a more nearly perfect image. This is one of the considerations that led to a study by Dimmick of the possibilities of recording with ultraviolet light. Even more important than the improved image definition was the fact that ultraviolet light is more rapidly absorbed in the emulsion than is visible light. The increased absorption must be compensated for by increased intensity, but the net effect is that the exposure is confined more nearly to the surface where the silver halide grains are more completely used, and the result is less graininess. Most important of all is that the light scattered by the emulsion does not spread as far sidewise, and thus enlarge the image, as does visible light.[242,243]

Dimmick reported the results of tests with ultraviolet in August 1936.[244] He had found it possible to obtain adequate exposure with the regular incandescent lamps and Corning No. 584 filters.

Conversion for ultraviolet recording involved provision for the filter, redesign of the objective lens, and substitution of glasses with less ultraviolet absorption for other lenses in the system. Many of the variable-area recording systems were converted. Single-film newsreel systems (with the sound recorded on panchromatic negatives) were especially benefited by use of ultraviolet.[245,246]

The results obtainable by the application of ultraviolet exposure to variable-density films were studied and reported by Frayne and Pagliarulo in June 1949.[247] They found major improvement in definition and reduced distortion, but only about 1 db reduction in ground noise. Further experiences with ultraviolet are reported by Daily and Chambers.[248]

Many printers were modified to print sound with ultraviolet. High-intensity mercury arc lamps were widely used for the printers.

Ultraviolet exposure gives lower gamma for the same development than does white light. Advantage has been taken of this in certain cases of density recording to reduce the gamma of the sound print without departing from optimum development for the picture.

Coated Lenses. Each time any optical or light-source improvement made an increase in image intensity possible, the benefit could be realized in terms of finer resolution and better high-frequency response.

When the results were published of some tests in which the reflection from glass surfaces had been materially reduced by applying quarter-wavelength coatings of certain low-index minerals,[249] Dimmick procured equipment, mastered the techniques of applying such coatings by evaporation in vacuum, and compared the merits of various materials and methods of hardening the deposited layer. Having found a satisfactory procedure, he treated all the glass-air surfaces in the RCA recording optical system. Although the loss at each glass-air surface is only about 5%, there are sixteen such surfaces (excluding the lamp bulb), and by reducing each to a magnitude of between 1 and 2%, a gain of more than 50% was possible in the brightness of the image on the film. Not only is the image thus brightened, but the stray light due to "lens flare" is reduced to a small fraction of its previous magnitude. A review of the subject, containing further references, has been published by W. P. Strickland.[250]

The first RCA coated-lens optical system to be field-tested was a "variable-intensity" system taken to Hollywood by Dimmick early in 1938 and used experimentally during some months at the Fox studios, C. N. Batsel being the RCA liaison engineer.[251] I believe that I am right in saying that the demonstrations of this system were partly responsible for arousing interest in the benefits to be had by such treatment of glass surfaces.

Within a short time the lenses in a number of the RCA recording systems were given low-reflection coatings, and the practice of coating lenses in both area and density recording systems spread rapidly.[252]

Dichroic Reflectors. As a by-product of the work on low-reflection coatings, Dimmick studied multilayer coatings of alternate high- and low-index materials.[253] With these he was able to produce plates having very high reflectivity in one part of the visible spectrum and very high transmission in another (65% reflection at 7500 A and better than 95% transmission between 4000 A and 5000 A).

The first motion-picture application of his "dichroic reflector" was for reflecting the red light of the recording light beam to a caesium phototube for monitoring, while losing practically none of the blue and violet light that produces the exposure.[254]

During the war there was heavy demand for dichroic reflectors, designed to various specifications, for the armed forces, and also great demand for low-reflection treatment of many optical devices. Selective reflectors of this type have also played an important part in color-television developments.[255]

Heat-Transmitting Reflectors. Another outcome of the development work on dichroic reflectors is a design in which the transition from high to low reflectivity occurs just beyond the end of the visible spectrum, so that as a mirror it would compete well in efficiency and whiteness with the best silver or aluminum mirrors, while the invisible heat rays are better than 75% transmitted.[255,256] No comparably effective means of separating the useful visible from the infrared radiation has been hitherto available, and we may look forward to extremely valuable applications.[257,258]

Measures for Reduction and Control of Distortion

There is hardly space here to mention the many refinements, including principles of good design, by which distortion has been kept low in microphones, amplifiers, recording devices, optical systems and reproducing systems. We shall confine ourselves to discussing the sources of distortion associated with photographic soundtracks. These may be listed as:

(1) background noise caused by graininess (especially in density tracks) or by scratches or dirt in the track area (most serious in area tracks);

(2) noise (hum) and amplitude modulation resulting from sprocket hole proximity;

(3) fluttter or "wows;"

(4) high-frequency loss;

(5) irregular high-frequency loss, and modulation of recorded sound, due to printer defects;

(6) waveform distortion due to misalignment of the aperture (slit) either in recording or reproducing, and to uneven reproducing-slit illumination;

(7) waveform distortion and production of spurious tones due to nonlinear input-output relations (more frequent in density recording than in area);

(8) waveform distortion and production of spurious sounds due to finite width of the recording slit and image spread in the film emulsion (a problem in the area system); and

(9) distortion due to overloading.

Measures for improving sound records with respect to background noise are discussed in part under "Ground-Noise Reduction," but also include extreme care as to cleanliness (especially in processing), to hardening and lubricating (waxing) the film,[259] to maintenance of projector condition, and to the several expedients by which the maximum reproduced volume can be increased.

Fine-grain film has made perhaps the greatest single contribution to improvement in ground-noise ratio, especially for density recordings, but its benefits have been in so many directions that only the present topic heading (Reduction and Control of Distortion) seems broad enough to include it.*

Various developments which improved high-frequency response have already been mentioned, and to these should of course be added the use of fine-grain film. The topic "Improved Printers" has also been included in the section on better high-frequency response. Reduction of flutter is dealt with in the section on "Mechanical Systems." Analytical studies of the distortion that results from misalignment (or azimuth

---

* It has been said that the entire evolution of sound reproduction can be divided into two parts: (1) the learning how to make a noise and (2) the reduction of distortion.

errors) of recording or reproducing slits in the case of area recordings, have been published by Cook[260] and by Foster.[261] In the case of density tracks the effect of misalignment is practically equivalent to widening the scanning slit, the results of which in terms of high-frequency loss are given in a paper by Stryker.[262] Both Cook and Foster have published analyses of the distortion in area recording due to slit width.[263,264]

Calculations of the distortion resulting from certain cases of uneven slit illumination and with several types of area track have been published by Cartwright and Batsel.[265] A test film has been made available for checking light uniformity.[266] It has a number of very narrow recordings of a tone in a series of positions across the track, and their relative outputs when played indicate light intensity at the corresponding positions in the scanning beam.

Sprocket Holes and Irregular Development. The proximity of sprocket holes to the soundtrack causes various difficulties. Mechanically the variations in stiffness of the film cause it to bend in a form resembling a polygon instead of a true circle.[232,267] This causes 96-cycle flutter, less perfect contact in printers, and 96-cycle modulation of high-frequency tones if optical systems have small depth of focus and are not exactly focused for the average emulsion plane. More serious from the sound standpoint is the effect of the holes on development.[268,269]

In film development there is always a tendency to nonuniform developer activity due to local exhaustion. For example, over and near a large dense area the developer is slightly weaker in its action than over the middle of a lightly exposed area, and this in turn is weaker than the average of the bath. If the partly exhausted developer as it diffuses out of the emulsion is not immediately carried away from the film by currents in the liquid, it may creep along the film surface and weaken the development in such areas. If there is little fluid movement except that caused by the travel of the film, the direction of travel is often evident from the appearance of pictures.[270,271] Circulation of the liquid is somewhat freer near the holes and edges of a film than elsewhere, and therefore the development and average density greater. This was discussed in connection with printers.

The irregular development troubles are reduced by very active stirring or turbulation of the developer while the film is passing through.[272] Improvements on this score are reported by Leshing, Ingman and Pier.[273]

Uniformity of development is further improved if the emulsion has such characteristics that its "gamma infinity" is only slightly higher than the desired gamma. Film manufacturers have been successful in producing fine-grain emulsions which come much closer to this desideratum than earlier types.

Waveform Distortions. The sensitometric studies and analyses about which we have already spoken are a part of the large body of literature bearing on the subject of distortion of the nonlinear type in density soundtracks. There have also been a number of experimental studies reported in this *Journal* giving distortion measurements with both density and area tracks. Two of the earliest of these were by Sandvik and Hall (October 1932)[274] and by Sandvik, Hall and Streiffert, October 1933.[275]

One of the most effective measures for reducing such distortions (second in importance only to avoiding overload) is by the use of push-pull soundtracks, and this applies about equally to density and area systems, although the causes of their distortions (Nos. 7 and 8 in the list) are quite different.

Two systems of testing for distortion (one for area and one for density systems) have assumed great importance since their introduction for ascertaining optimum ranges of exposure of negatives and positives. These are known as the "cross-modulation"[176] and the "intermodulation"[277] tests, and will be briefly described.

Overload. Overload in any element of the entire sound system other than in the soundtrack (either in the original recording or in the re-recording) means that the system has not been properly designed. It is easy to say that the way to avoid distortion due to overloads is not to overload, but that is asking too much. The price in terms of reduced average level is from a practical standpoint excessive. The levels set in recording are a compromise between too low an average level (with ground noise therefore more conspicuous) and too many and too bad-sounding overloads.*

In sections to follow, a number of expedients are mentioned for compassing a wider range between background noise and maximum reproduced level. These devices may be used either to make the background quieter or the loudest noises louder, and if properly applied can accomplish the latter with reduced instances of soundtrack overload.

Cross-Modulation Test to Determine Best Processing for Variable Area. While the variable-area system is not critical to gamma product it is subject to distortion, particularly at high frequency, due to the spread of the exposure outside the area of the actual image, caused by the scattering of light in the emulsion. This

image spread increases with exposure. The distortion is largely in the form of a change in average transmission when a high-frequency wave is present. It is often referred to as "zero shift." It was particularly troublesome in some of the earlier 16mm recordings. It is possible however, by selecting the proper printing exposure, to make the image spread in the print neutralize that in the negative.[276]

In January 1938, J. O. Baker and D. H. Robinson described tests and equipment which became the standard method for ascertaining the correct relative negative and print densities.[176] For 35mm tests a 9000-cycle tone is 100% modulated at 400 cycles, but there must be no 400-cycle component in current supplied to the galvanometer. For a given negative exposure and development, a series of prints having different black area densities are made. They are then reproduced and the magnitude of the 400-cycle output measured and plotted (in db below the 9000-cycle level, or other reference) as a function of print density. The curve goes through a sharp minimum at optimum print density. With a negative of greater (black area) density the optimum print density is found to be higher. One of the most frequent problems is to select a recording exposure which will give maximum (or at least satisfactory) cancellation of cross modulation, when printed for a certain desired print density (say 1.4 to 1.6).*

Experience shows that if the 400-cycle cross-modulation is 30 db or more below full modulation, the sound is satisfactory. In similar manner if the print exposure and development are specified, the optimum negative density can be determined. For 16mm processing control, a 4000-cycle tone is modulated at 400 cycles. In push-pull recording the cross-modulation in the two parts of the track largely cancel each other and tolerances are extremely broad.

At the 1954 spring convention Singer and McKie[278] reported good results with an electrical compensating circuit, so that cross-modulation can be practically neutralized when making direct positives. This involves determining what function of frequency, exposure and (possibly) amplitude comes nearest to expressing the magnitude of the cross-modulation products.

Intermodulation Test for Variable-Density Control.[277] In the June 1939 *Journal* Frayne and Scoville describe a test for control of variable-density processing.

In the earlier years of recording, the conditions for linear relation between negative exposure and print transmission were figured out by conventional sensitometric methods, with correction for the ratio of projection (or semispecular) density to diffuse density. But this is tedious, and a testing system which duplicated soundtrack recording and reproducing conditions was found preferable. In 1935 F. G. Albin[279] described a dynamic check on processing which consisted in making several recordings of a tone, all at the same fairly low amplitude, with a series of increasing mean valve-ribbon spacings. Comparison of the relative outputs from the print showed whether the slope of the curve of print transmission vs. negative exposure was constant or not. This was something of a forerunner of the intermodulation test. In the latter a tone of 1000 cycles or higher is superimposed on a low-frequency tone of, say, 60 cycles. Normally the level of the high-frequency tone is 12 db below that of the low tone, and the combined amplitude just short of overload. The print is run through a reproducing system, and the reproduced high-frequency tone separated out and measured for fluctuations in amplitude. Nonlinearity (distortion) becomes evident as fluctuations of the high-frequency tone, in general at rates equal to the frequency of the low tone or multiples of that frequency.

Fine-Grain Films.[280-282] While the many components of sound recording and reproducing systems were being improved, the great film companies were busy. In the period 1930–1940, the Eastman Co. offered at least seven new emulsions,[283] each of which offered some advantages for soundtrack application as compared with the currently used picture positive (Eastman No. 1301). In 1932 Eastman brought out No. 1359, intended for variable-density recording It was however similar to No. 1301 in contrast. In 1936 No. 1357 was brought out for variable-area recording, slightly faster than No. 1301 without sacrifice with respect to grain and resolution. With ultraviolet exposure it proved popular for variable-density recording. For release prints, however, the positive No. 1301 continued the almost universal choice except as similar films of other manufacture were used.

What was primarily wanted was finer grain, for this would mean cleaner, sharper images for variable-area tracks, less background noise in variable-density tracks, and better resolution and high-frequency response in all tracks. But fine grain in general means lower speed, or more exposure required, and too great sacrifice in this direction would make new films unacceptable. Another difficulty was that with many of the earlier fine-grain emulsions the image had a

---

*Most movie fans have probably forgotten what a gun sounds like.

*This test is made simpler than it might appear by the fact that when a high-contrast negative is used, the print black-area density is scarcely affected by differences in the black-area density of the negative, hence the printer light setting can generally be kept the same for the entire series of negatives.

brownish tone, which was objectionable in the picture, and so ruled these emulsions out for the release prints. Measures were found for correcting this fault in Eastman fine-grain positive No. 1302. The problem of exposure was less serious in the case of fine-grain films for release and for duplicating than for recording stock, although some changes in printers were required. Special films were introduced about 1937 for duplicating purposes.[284]

One of the chief problems in variable-area recording was due to image spread (beyond the exposed area), but it was found possible to make image spread in the print compensate for that in the negative. The criticism of one of the trial emulsions intended for variable-area negatives (No. 1360) was that it was *too* good in this respect for the currently used print stock.

Re-recording is the universal practice. Graininess and other imperfections in the original negative are transferred to the print, passed on to the second negative by the re-recording operation, and in the final printing are added to the graininess of the release print. The use of direct positives offered promise of eliminating at least one step which was contributing its share of noise. In 1937 Eastman introduced its No. 1360, and Du Pont its No. 216, both fine-grain films designed for making variable-area direct positives.

Changing to a new release stock represented a greater hurdle than the use of special films for negatives and for the re-recording print, so the general thought was to evolve the best possible films for these applications, and take what improvement could be gained in this way. As the story turned out, use of the fine-grain films did not become general until they were used also for the final release prints.

Film graininess contributes to background noise in much greater measure in the density system than in the area system, but the requirements seem to have been harder to meet. Many tests were run and studies made during the years 1938–1940, and a special committee representing those particularly interested in variable-density recording reported in the January 1940 *Journal*,[289] in which tentative specifications were given to guide in the development of the needed fine-grain films.

Du Pont No. 222 was one of the first fine-grain films to gain considerable acceptance, especially at the M-G-M and Paramount studios, where it was used for original negatives, re-recording prints, re-recorded negatives and for a limited number of release prints. High-pressure mercury lamps were substituted where needed to give the required printing exposure. Experience at the Paramount studios is reported by C. R. Daily in the same issue.[286] Figures published in

these reports indicate that while a re-recording print might be 8 to 12 db better in signal-to-noise ratio than one made on the previous types of film, only 4-to-6 db net gain was to be expected in the release print if this were on the usual stock. This indicates why the real gains from use of fine-grain film were not achieved until they were used for the release prints as well as in the earlier stages. (See also references 287–290.)

Some difficulty was encountered in processing the negatives to a suitably low gamma, but it was accomplished by use of special developers. (Uniformity of development is almost impossible if the time is cut so short that the gamma is far below the "gamma-infinity" for the given emulsion and developer.) In order to permit somewhat higher values of gammas in the fine-grain negatives the practice was adopted in some laboratories of holding down that of the fine-grain release prints by printing the sound with ultraviolet light, which gives lower gamma for a given development than does white light.

In 1938 the Eastman Co. brought out a high-resolution film (No. 1360) for variable-area recording and in 1939 a recording film (No. 1366) for variable density. In 1941 the No. 1302 fine-grain positive which has been widely used for release prints, became available. In 1945 the Eastman Co. brought out a high-contrast fine-grain film (No. 1372) for variable-area recording and a low-contrast fine-grain film (No. 1373) for variable-density recording, which could be processed in regular picture-negative developers instead of requiring special low-energy developers. The same year Du Pont brought out a new fine-grain recording negative (No. 236) for variable density, whose contrast could be more easily controlled than previous types because of low gamma infinity.

The fine-grain recording films are all much slower than the previous recording films, (No. 1302, for example, requiring about four times the exposure of No. 1301), and recording optical systems, although improved by coated lenses, could not with tungsten lamps provide sufficient exposures for the combination of fine-grain and ultraviolet light, but use of the fine-grain films with white-light exposure went so far in affording the benefits of high resolution and low noise that the combination seemed hardly needed. On the other hand, printing fine-grain positives with ultraviolet light from high-intensity mercury arcs has been widely employed.

It is of interest that the Callier coefficient (ratio of specular to diffuse density) is less with fine-grain than with coarser-grain films, and the result is that a higher control gamma (in which the measurements are of diffuse density) is needed to give the optimum picture on the screen—for example 2.5 for

No. 1302 as compared with 2.1 for No. 1301.[290]

Variable-Density vs. Variable-Area.[291,292] The rivalry between advocates of variable-density and variable-area recording is nearly as old as commercial talking pictures and has unquestionably promoted progress in both systems. The fact that the industry did not standardize on one or the other track does not seem to have been any handicap, for all theaters could play either type of track.

During the earlier years of commercial sound, the advantage seemed to be on the side of area for music but density for speech intelligibility. With both at their best there was little to choose in clarity of speech reproduction, but the density system seemed able to take more abuse without too serious loss of articulation. Before control of zero-shift was well in hand (see cross-modulation test[276]) this type of distortion seemed to do more damage to the quality of the high-frequency reproduction than the nonlinearity to which the density system is more subject. With improved techniques and equipment this difference disappeared.

Another factor which for a time was prejudicial to the area system was that, as compared with density recordings, low-level passages seemed to be excessively weak when the controls were set for satisfactory normal and high-level passages. One theory was that, due to some fault in equipment or system, there was "volume expansion," or actual exaggeration of level difference. To those most familiar with area recording such a theory appeared untenable. Measurements did not bear it out. Monaural or single-channel listening itself makes level differences seem greater than direct binaural listening. Could it not be that the density recordings by their nonlinearity produced a compression effect? I recall that one of the most confident exponents of this explanation was M. C. Batsel. One of the fundamental differences in the systems is that an area track overloads very abruptly, whereas in a density track the upper and lower limits of light transmission are approached more gradually. With such a characteristic, considerable overload (i.e. beyond the range of true linearity) can be tolerated without too objectionable effect, and it was thought that considerable advantage had been taken of what might be called permissible overloading in the density recordings as compared with those made on the area system.

A nearly equivalent effect in an area recording can be obtained by rounding the corners of the V-shaped opening in the aperture plate (whose image is the light spot on the slit as shown in Fig. 13). Transition curves are introduced at the outer (full-slit illumination) ends, while the vertex is drawn out to a finer point. Such curved apertures were tried and largely overcame the cause of criticism.

However, the use of electronic compressors (long employed in broadcasting studios) appeared preferable to sacrificing the range of low-distortion light modulation. Compressors were introduced in the recording channels with very satisfactory results. The first such compressors were tried at RKO and Warner studios and compression became the standard. If the original recording is on a wide-range (or low-background-noise) system, most of the compression is introduced in the re-recording to the release-print negative, but I am told that even with magnetic recording some compression is used (or at least available) in the initial recording.

Any simple and general statement of the relative signal-to-noise ratios of the two systems is impossible, since each has its own cause and type of ground noise: grain hiss in density, and ticks and pops due to dirt or scratches in the area system. Area starts with an initial advantage of about 6 db greater output, and if the film remains in good condition its signal-to-noise ratio is better. The variable-area system was chosen by the Bell Laboratories engineers for their stereophonic demonstrations.

As various improvements became available to the industry they worked to the benefit now chiefly of one system and now of the other. Fine-grain films helped both, but helped density more.

The higher output from variable-area tracks led to the proposal by Levinson[293] that intercutting of the two types of track be used as means for increasing reproduced volume range.

The RCA light-modulation system has been modified to record variable-density, by use of an out-of-focus image or "penumbra" on the slit in place of the usual sharply focused triangular spot.[183,294] This system modulated the light reaching the film by changing its *intensity*, whereas the light valve produced a spot on the film of constant intensity but varying height, and therefore varied the *time* of exposure.

The light valve also was modified to make variable-area records by turning it 90° so that the ribbons were vertical (parallel with the direction of film motion) and the motions of their edges imaged at 10 : 1 magnification on the film. This was the system employed for the stereophonic demonstrations.[208,295,296] Variable-area optical systems using light valves were shortly thereafter offered as optional equipment to licensees.

By using valves having one, two or three ribbons as needed, the light-valve system has been made to produce many of the various types of area track that are produced by the RCA galvanometer

optical system by changing apertures.[183,184,297]

The strict adherence to one system (area or density) on the part of the major picture companies has in considerable measure broken down, and several are employing both systems, depending on the type of operation required.[298] For example M-G-M, while continuing to use double-width push-pull density for initial recordings,* releases on variable area. One of the reasons for changing to area for release prints is that projectionists often neglected to change their gain settings when switching back and forth between area and density tracks, with a result to the disadvantage of the film with lower output (note also interest in Perspecta Sound.)

Mention is made, in the discussion of control tones, of a system in which the control tone is of subaudible frequency and superimposed on the recorded sound. Modulation of the sound by the control tone is much more easily avoided in area recording.

Compressors.[299] In the previous section comparing the area and density systems, the first urgent need of electronic compressors was described, but their use has proved so advantageous as to have become quite general, both in recording and re-recording channels.[300] Electronic compressors had long been in use in radio broadcasting.[304,304a] In their application to sound recording, if there is no provision for re-expansion, they do not actually increase the reproduced volume range although they may seem to. A common characteristic compresses 20 db into 10 db at a uniform rate. This would rob any passage of expression only to a slight degree. As the overload point is approached it is common to make the compression more drastic, for example 20 into 3 db. This is sometimes called a limiter type of compressor. If (for example by means of control tone) provision is made for re-expansion, the compression may be such as to keep the loud passages, whatever their original magnitude, at nearly full track amplitude. (See section on "Stereophonic.")

Since initial consonants usually carry little power compared with vowels, the compressor may wait to act for the vowel, with resulting relative exaggeration of consonants (especially sibilants). This has been corrected by a high-frequency pre-emphasis in the modulation which controls the compressor.[301–303]

Anticipation in compressor systems is desirable (see section on "Ground-Noise Reduction"). Fast action of compressors is essential and avoidance of "thump" is one of the problems.[305,306] Experiences in recording with compressors are reported by Aalberg and Stewart of RKO[300]. Experience with

_____
* Probably later adopted magnetic recording.

compressors at the Warner Bros. Studios is reported by B. F. Miller.[301]

Squeeze Track.[307] In view of the limited range of loudness which a soundtrack permits, and the very great range encountered in our ordinary experience, many expedients were tried for the purpose of increasing the range obtainable from the film. One of these was the "squeeze track" described by Wesley C. Miller of M-G-M.[307] If a variable-density track is reduced in width, both the noise and the modulation are reduced. The ground-noise reduction system described by Silent and Frayne in May 1932[188] may not have been as yet available, but the two devices are not equivalent and can be complementary. There is a practical limit set by film characteristics as to how far the ground-noise reduction, by reducing mean negative exposure, could be carried, and this was at about 10 db of reduction, but the noise can be still further reduced by narrowing the track. The controls in recording or in re-recording are used to avoid too low levels on the track, but some of the range can be restored by narrowing the track in the release print. There were several ways in which this could be done; one, for example, was by preparing a masking film and running the print through the printer a second time with the track width determined by the mask.

"Reversed Bias" System.[308] An expedient for obtaining greater output for bursts of high level sound was described by Hansen and Faulkner[308] of Twentieth Century-Fox. In effect the light-valve bias operates in the usual way for normal and low levels, but for passages of extra high level the mean ribbon spacing is increased to as much as twice normal while still being fully modulated. There is some resulting distortion, but substantial increase in print output. The loss of some relatively high-frequency output is probably not objectionable.

Wide Track and Push-Pull. By doubling the width of the track the noise would be expected to increase 3 db but the usefully modulated light would increase 6 db. While the improvement is not large, it is worth while, and has been widely employed for original recordings and for special purposes, when the sound print does not have to carry a picture.

Push-pull systems have also been developed for both density[309] and area[183] systems and for wide tracks[310,311] and standard-width tracks. Standard-width push-pull systems have been considered for general theater reproduction, but their actual use has been limited to places where the required special reproducing systems did not involve large investment. The push-pull system does not give any improvement in signal-to-noise ratio except for the few film

210

blemishes or other disturbances which affect the light through both sides alike. The principal advantage of the push-pull system is that it reduces distortion, and in the density system it may thereby somewhat increase the permissible ratio of light modulation. As applied to area recording it almost eliminates zero-shift distortion. With both systems, push-pull operation permits the use of faster-acting ground-noise reduction, since the "thump" caused by rapid change in transmitted light is largely cancelled. Milestones in the progress toward better sound are usually fixed in our minds by major demonstrations. Such a demonstration was given at the 1935 spring convention. Using wide-track push-pull density recordings, improved two-way (divided-frequency-range) loudspeakers and amplifiers with abundant reserve power, the engineers of the M-G-M Sound Department, under the direction of Douglas Shearer, gave impressive demonstrations.

Push-pull wide-track is regarded as the last word in photographic recording and has for years been used in many studios for original recording.

If the original recording is wide-track push-pull, the positive (which is edited and then used as the master for re-recording to the release-print negative) would be a print of the original. If the original is magnetic, the favored practice has been to re-record to a wide-track push-pull direct positive for the edited film. In eliminating the step of printing, the direct positive minimizes quality losses.

Control Tone.[312] The most effective way to reproduce the great range of sound volume encountered in natural sounds is to resort to compression for the recording and to expand in reproduction. It has always been the practice for the recordist to use his controls to maintain the recorded levels between the limits set by overload and a satisfactory margin above noise. Were a record made of each change in recording gain, and the projectionist given a cue sheet by which he could at the right times make the inverse changes in reproducing gain, the natural levels could be restored. Such a method of operation was at one time contemplated. However, manual controls in recording are too slow, and manual restoration of level too unreliable. Automatic control of gain on the other hand has been used very effectively. If space can be found on the film for an extra soundtrack, a continuous tone can be recorded with either its amplitude or its frequency automatically correlated with the gain of the recording amplifiers, so that it provides a complete record of the recording gain throughout the recording.

For example, a voltage derived from the modulation to be recorded (and thus a function of its initial level) can operate on the recording amplifier to change its gain as in any automatic compressor, and the same voltage can operate simultaneously on the control tone to make the appropriate change in either its amplitude or frequency. In reproduction the output of the control-tone track is then used to provide a voltage which is directly related to that which altered the recording gain, and can therefore be used to produce inverse, or compensating, changes in the reproducing gain.

The use of an extra soundtrack or recording to be used in the manner just described was, I believe, first proposed by C. F. Sacia of the Bell Laboratories, and described in U.S. Pat. No. 1,623,756. One of the first in the RCA group to become interested in control tones was Charles M. Burrill who experimented with tones superimposed on the modulation, but of either too high or too low frequency to be reproduced by the audio system, especially a subaudible tone such as 20 cycles. For film recording he proposed scanning the sprocket-hole area, and varying the magnitude of the resulting 96-cycle tone by blackening more or less of the film between perforations. Thus, if these areas are left clear, the 96-cycle tone is comparatively feeble, while the maximum is produced if they are black.

The sprocket-hole control track was developed for application by H. I. Reiskind and adopted by Warner Brothers for their "Vitasound" system, which will be described in the section on multiple-speaker systems.[326]

Control tones of the subaudible type have in recent years found use for producing spread-sound and stereophonic effects which are particularly appropriate for accompanying large-screen pictures. (See Perspecta Sound, under "Multiple-Speaker Systems" below.) The chief advantage of this method of recording the control tones is that it requires no changes in the recorders and scanning systems, the changes being confined to the electrical circuits. It meets the important practical requirement that reproduction must be acceptable on standard equipment (with no provision for control-tone use). Variable-area recording is better suited than variable-density for use with subaudible control tones, since with suitable processing more accurate linear relationship between input and output can be maintained throughout the range of modulation, thus avoiding modulation of the audio by the control tones. The maximum level which can be recorded must be reduced 2 or 3 db, to make room for the control tones, so that the sum of the two will not exceed the permissible maximum. Tones of 30, 35 and 40 cycles have been used for the controls.

A control-tone system used by adherents of the variable-density system was described by Frayne and Herrnfeld.[313] Between the normal soundtrack and picture areas, space was found for a soundtrack 0.005 in. wide. The authors give their reasons for believing that frequency modulation of the control tone would be more reliable than amplitude modulation. With a frequency range of one octave and using a bandpass filter, they found that in spite of the narrowness of the track it provided a 38-db signal-to-noise ratio. The system was designed to afford changes of gain for the sound up to 30 db, thus expanding the dynamic range by that amount. The soundtrack was of the standard-density type.

In certain systems in which three or more independently recorded soundtracks are used, the sound and picture are on separate films. This gives plenty of room for the control track, but the practice has been to allot only one track to the control and to superimpose the tones, separating them in reproduction by bandpass filters.

Class B Push-Pull. Of the possible systems of photographic recording, the Class B area track undoubtedly carries furthest the principle of low print transmission when the modulation is low. Such a system was described by Dimmick and Belar in 1934,[314] and favorable experience in its use was reported in 1939 by Bloomberg and Lootens of Republic Pictures,[315] where it had been adopted for original recordings and been used in the making of fourteen pictures at the time of the report. They have continued to the present time using the Class B push-pull system for all original recordings. They also reported the methods used for test and adjustment. In the Class B system one side of the track carries only the positive parts of the waves and the other only the negative. When there is no modulation there is no clear film, and no ground-noise-reduction system is needed; therefore the transient or initial clipping which ground-noise-reduction systems can produce are avoided. Two triangles of light (see Fig. 13) are formed at the plane of the slit (one for each half of the track) and their vertices just touch the slit with no current in the galvanometer. Exposure takes place only as one or the other triangle illuminates more or less of the slit. A feature not described in the papers just mentioned is shown in a September 1937 paper by Dimmick.[183] In the mask which is imaged at the plane of the slit to form the triangular light spots, a narrow slit extends from the vertex of each triangular opening, so that light is never completely cut off at this point. There is thus formed a continuous line at the middle of each half track, not wide enough to let an appreciable amount of light through the film, for it is so narrow that it is largely fogged in, but it prevents a slight wave-shape distortion which might otherwise be produced by image spread, just as the tip of the triangle crosses the slit.

Direct Positives. Recording direct positives, instead of recording negatives and then making prints from which to make re-recordings, would seem to offer important advantages in simplifying operations and reducing time loss. There would also be an advantage in reduced ground noise since one less film is used and thus one less source of graininess. The high-frequency losses due to the printer would also be avoided. In the section on "Ground-Noise Reduction," it was stated that a ground-noise reduction system applicable to variable-area direct positives had been developed with the feature of anticipation, so that initial clipping need never occur. It was further possible under these conditions to work with closer margins, and so reduce the width of clear film. This system and results of tests with it are described by Dimmick and Blaney in 1939,[199] with a further report by Blaney in 1944.[316]

The chief obstacle to making variable-area direct positives had been that an entirely satisfactory way of avoiding distortion due to image spread had not been found. In the negative-positive process image spread in the negative could be compensated by that in the print, but the direct-positive system left no place for that solution. There is, to be sure, a certain density for any film at which there is no image spread, and below which the blackened area is slightly less than the exposed area. With the recording films available for a number of years, the density which gave no spread, or zero shift, was so low that light passing through the darkened areas would result in considerable noise. In some of the later fine-grain recording films, however, the balance occurred at densities which were satisfactorily high, thus making direct positives feasible under conditions in which they had not been before. However, the direct-positive system described by Dimmick and Blaney was not limited to the use of special films. They used a push-pull system which goes so far toward neutralizing the effects of image spread that excellent results were obtained with the standard fine-grain recording stock for variable-area.[316,317]

In variable-density recording the same anticipation feature is not applicable, but the other advantages of direct positives for original recordings apply. The problem of recording a positive lies in the requirement that the film transmission shall not be a reciprocal of the exposure (hyperbola) which a non-reversing film tends to produce, but must have an inverse relationship expressible by a downward-sloping straight line, covering a large range of transmission. A method of correcting *in the reproduction* for the nonlinear transmission characteristic of a variable-density negative was described by Albersheim in 1937,[318] but this would limit the usefulness of the direct positives. Electrical compensation in the recording was described by O. L. Dupy of M-G-M in 1952.[319] An approximation to the desired relation is possible by recording on the toe of the H&D curve, but high-level output is not possible from such direct positives without serious distortion.

A radically different solution of the problem was described by Keith and Pagliarulo in 1949.[320] Superimposed on the audio current supplied to the valve was a 24-kc bias current of twice the magnitude required to modulate fully the light-valve opening at normal unmodulated spacing. The ribbons are in different planes so that they can overlap without clashing. The authors reported 8-db higher output from the direct-positive than from a standard-density print, and 6-db higher signal-to-noise ratio than a standard print without ground-noise reduction. Direct positives, generally push-pull, have come into wide use for editing and re-recording service.[321,322]

Electrical Printing. Successful recording of direct positives opens the way to "electrical printing," or putting sound-tracks on release prints by a re-recording operation instead of by contact printing. This is discussed by Frayne.[323] While such a method would necessarily be more expensive, the elimination of the flutter and irregularities resulting from the action of most contact printers is a strong argument in its favor. Frayne finds possibilities of greatly improved sound by this method, particularly for 16mm color prints of the reversible type such as Kodachrome or Ansco-color.

Engineers have long been attracted by the possibility of improved resolution and reduced distortion in 16mm positives by direct recording,[324] but until the more recent developments, direct positives (except on reversal films) were not a success.

Limits of Volume Range. While ideal sound reproduction would seem to call for duplication of original sound levels it is questionable whether illusion or seeming naturalness is improved by going as far as this in the direction of loudness. In the applications of control-tone systems, where very high levels are attainable, the extremes have been scaled down by 10 db or more. With respect to the desirability of carrying reproduction to extreme low levels, W. A. Mueller[325] has shown that there is a definite practical limit set by general theater noise.*

Multiple-Speaker Systems

It has often been observed that musical reproduction gives greater satisfaction if it comes from several sources. The Music Hall at Radio City in New York has been equipped to make this possible, and thus has afforded numerous opportunities to verify the advantages of multiple sources. With reference to the effort to obtain "dynamic range," Garity and Hawkins[333] state that: "Three channels sound louder than one channel of three times the power-handling capacity. In addition, three channels allow more loudness to be used before the sound becomes offensive, because the multiple source, and multiple standing-wave pattern, prevents sharp peaks of loudness of long duration."

That dialog should be reproduced on a speaker as near as possible to where the actors are seen is never questioned, but music and many sound effects such as thunder, battle noise and the clamor of crowds are far more impressive and natural if coming from sources all around the listener. The effects obtainable are discussed by H. I. Reiskind[326] who also describes the equipment used in the sprocket-hole control-track system.

Vitasound. This system, used by Warner Brothers, is described by Levinson and Goldsmith.[327] It is the simplest of the systems employing spread-sound sources and control tone. It uses three similar loudspeakers, the usual screen-centered dialog speaker and two side speakers outside the screen area. The design of the system is based on the theory that the volume range which the film (with the usual ground-noise reduction) affords is adequate for dialog and such other sounds as come from the center speaker only, and that higher sound levels will be wanted only for music and sound effects for which the spread-sound source will also be wanted. The control-tone output is therefore used, first to switch in the side speakers, with no change in total sound power. Further increase in control-tone output raises the gain on all three speakers, up to a total of 10-db increase.

Stereophonic Sound. Mention has been made in the section on loudspeakers of the transmission of music and other sounds "in auditory perspective" from Philadelphia to Washington in 1933. Three microphones were spaced across the stage and their outputs separately transmitted to three similarly located loudspeakers at the auditorium where the sound was reproduced. The various

---

* Background noise makes the useful sound seem fainter than sound at the same level in a quiet place. This holds even though the background noise is not loud enough to interfere nor even to make the listener conscious of its presence.

orchestral sounds seemed to come from the appropriate places, and a moving source such as a man walking across the stage and talking seemed at the receiving end to move about. In 1941 and earlier,[328,329] similar demonstrations were given, with the difference that this time the sound was recorded and reproduced. As in the previous case, every effort was made by the engineers of the Bell Telephone Laboratories and Electrical Research Products Inc. to minimize all forms of distortion and to reproduce the sound in the full dynamic range of the original.

Since it appeared that for the immediate purposes of the project the films could be maintained in good condition with respect to abrasions and dirt, and that under such conditions the advantage in terms of signal-to-noise ratio is with the variable-area system, the recordings were of the variable-area type, made with an adaptation of light-valve optics. The recorder and reproducing machine carried the film through the translation points on smooth (toothless) drums, on whose shafts were damped flywheels of the liquid-filled type described by Wente and Müller.[81,104]

On the basis that the film track was capable of giving a signal 50 db above noise, while the orchestral music to be reproduced had a range of 80 db, compressors were used in recording, and expandors in the reproducing system designed to compensate exactly* for the compression in recording. The compressors made no change of gain until the signal neared full track level and above this made the gain the inverse of the sound level, thus keeping the recorded level just below track overload. The level of the amplified microphone output controlled the magnitude of an oscillator tone, which tone was simultaneously recorded in a fourth track and applied to the recording-circuit compressor. In reproduction the same tone controlled the expandor gain. Because the levels at the three microphones did not necessarily rise and fall together, the compressors in the three channels were independently controlled by their own modulation levels. This necessitated use of three control tones, but these were recorded superimposed in one track and separated in reproduction by filters.

In order to give the compressor time to operate when a sudden increase of sound level occurred, an "anticipation" system was employed, using two microphones. The compressor operation was determined by the output of the microphone closer to the source, while the second microphone furnished the sound to be recorded.

As further insurance against audible background noise, the system of "pre-

* Exactly, in terms of timing, but not necessarily fully restoring the 30 db of compression range.

emphasis and post-equalization" of high-frequency components of the sound was employed. The usual ground-noise-reduction system by light-valve bias was not used, being made less necessary by the compressor-expandor (or "Compandor") system.

The October 1941 issue of the *Journal* carries discussions by Fletcher,[329] Steinberg,[330] Snow and Soffel,[331] Wente and Müller,[104] and by Wente, Biddulph, Elmer and Anderson,[332] of various aspects and elements of the stereophonic system.

Despite the unquestionable success of the stereophonic system in reproducing the subjective effects of sounds coming from the sources located as seen on the screen, and the impressiveness of the musical and sound effects which it was capable of handling, the motion-picture industry made no immediate move to adopt or apply it. A factor which undoubtedly militated against interest in utilizing the stereophonic system was that only for the patrons near the front of a theater did the screen subtend a large enough angle to make the difference between stereophonic and single-channel reproduction impressive. It appears to be another case of a development ahead of its time. With the recent advent (commercially) of the wide-film systems CinemaScope and Cinerama, stereophonic sound, supplemented by "spread sound," plays an essential role in providing the desired overall effects.

Fantasound: Fantasia. Walt Disney and his engineers had a somewhat different idea of what might be accomplished by means of multiple-track recordings with control tones. It might be appropriate to say that they proposed to make their spread-sound effects an art rather than a science. Duplication of an original distribution of sound sources was a secondary consideration, and the choice of directions from which sounds were to come was to be entirely at the discretion of the directors, musicians and technicians.

The story of the development of Fantasound and its evolution through numerous experimental forms beginning in 1937, was told by Garity and Hawkins,[333] with further reports by Garity and Jones,[334] and by E. H. Plumb.[335] Garity and Hawkins reported from tests that if a sound source (from loudspeakers) was to seem to move smoothly from one position to another, the output power from the two speakers should be held constant. This condition is not necessarily met by having the actual source move from near one microphone to near the other, but it can be met when the gain is reduced to one speaker and increased to the other by means of a knob or control tone.

The animated picture was designed specifically for the music, which was

taken from great classics. In the initial orchestral recordings many microphones and separate recording channels were used. Recordings were selected or mixed in the re-recording to obtain desired effects such as predominance in turn of various orchestral groups (strings, brass etc.). Sound and picture were on separate films. The final sound film carried three 200-mil push-pull variable-area soundtracks, and three superimposed variable-amplitude control tones on a fourth track. The amplitude of the several control tones was determined by manual adjustments.

The theater equipment consisted of three loudspeakers at the center and to the sides of the screen and additional speakers at the sides and back of the auditorium. The latter could be brought into operation by relays responsive to notches in the edge of the film. They were used effectively for various sound effects and for the music of a large chorus. Abundant sound power and volume range were employed, the volume range being readily obtained by use of the control tracks.

The final Fantasound equipment was designed by RCA engineers. A special optical printer was used to print sound from separate negatives onto the multi-track positive, and special film phonographs in which a single system illuminated all four tracks, the transmitted light being received by four independent double-cathode photocells.

Fantasia was enthusiastically received but was not a financial success because of the heavy expense not only of its production but of "road-showing" with such elaborate equipment. The advent of World War II hastened its withdrawal, but Disney had performed a great service to the industry and art by pioneering in a sound-effects field which is now finding important applications.

Recent Multiple-Channel Systems.[336–342] During 1952 and 1953 three new systems of presenting pictures were introduced, known as "3-D" (Three-Dimensional), "Cinerama" and "CinemaScope." All of these represent more elaborate and expensive picture-projection systems, and with them would logically go whatever could be offered in the way of more impressive sound. The principles of stereophonic sound, plus the surround speakers distributed around the auditorium (as used in Fantasound), have been applied.

In the 3-D system two projectors are required, and a third synchronized machine, a film phonograph, is added for the sound. The sound system is stereophonic and uses three 200-mil magnetic tracks.[370,371]

The CinemaScope system[339] (developed by Twentieth Century-Fox) presents a much wider screen picture than does the standard system, and therefore presents an excellent opportunity for the use of stereophonic sound since the screen speakers are distributed over a large enough distance to make the shifts in the position of the sound source noticeable and needed for realism. The sound system developed to go with Cinema-Scope uses four magnetic stripes or tracks, two just inside the sprocket holes and two outside. To make more room for the tracks and leave as much as possible for the picture, sprocket holes of new shape have been designed. In the new perforation no valuable feature is believed to have been sacrificed, and the film will still run on standard sprockets. Three of the tracks provide the regular stereophonic sound (three speakers behind the screen) and the fourth carries sound effects for transmission by the surround speakers. For multitrack magnetic reproducing equipment see references 108–110.

Cinerama[340] (developed by Fred Waller and Hazard E. Reeves, and commercialized by Cinerama Productions Corp.) carries the wide-screen principle much further, employing three projectors to project adjacent edge-blended pictures on a curved screen. For the sound six magnetic tracks are used, and five speakers behind the screen, while the sixth track feeds a set of surround speakers.

The surround speakers, wherever these are used, are of the direct-radiator type, much less bulky than the screen speakers and with more limited frequency range.

Recent Multiple-Speaker Systems With Photographic Track.[339] A simpler multispeaker (or sound-placement) system has been developed by Robert Fine[342] and named "Perspecta Sound." Mention was made under the heading "Control Tones," of the use of control tones of subaudible frequency. In the Fine system there is only one soundtrack (variable-area, photographic) in the standard position, but three loudspeakers behind the screen, fed through separate variable-gain amplifiers. Three control tones, superimposed on the sound recording and separated in reproduction by filters, control the gains of the three amplifiers so that the apparent source can be made to shift across the screen, and the total sound level may be varied as desired to increase the dynamic range. The Perspecta-Sound recording if reproduced on a standard system (not equipped to make any use of the control tones) would, except for a slight reduction in level, be indistinguishable from a standard recording. M-G-M and Paramount have been particularly interested in Perspecta Sound and have equipped numerous theaters with it.[342]

Another sound-placement system was developed by the Dorsett Laboratories of Norman, Okla., and has been installed in a number of theaters in Texas and Oklahoma. It is described in the May 1954 Progress Report[339] as using a standard optical track, but with provision for shifting the sound from the center speaker to either of two screen speakers to right or left, or to peripheral (surround) speakers. This is accomplished by "switching cues in the form of a binary code marked into both sprocket-hole areas," and optically scanned. "Standard single-track optical release prints are cued for use with this system by the Dorsett representatives." (Quotations are from the Progress Report.)

Sound and Color. Since in color pictures the silver is removed from the emulsion, special handling of the soundtrack is required. In the Technicolor imbibition process the soundtrack is printed in the usual way, the remainder of the film is then cleared of all silver, and the pictures produced by dye transfer from relief masters.

With the multilayer color films such as Kodachrome, Kodacolor, Anscocolor and a number of more recent types it would be possible to expose the track with white light so that all three dyes contributed to the density, or with colored light so that the sound image would be principally in the top layer, and reproduce with a filter of the complementary color. The principal problem with this procedure is that existing projectors are nearly all equipped with caesium photocells whose sensitivity extends well into the infrared, in which range all of the dyes in use are transparent.[343] Substitution of phototubes of other types would mean an objectionable loss of sensitivity. In May 1946, A. M. Glover of RCA reported the development of a blue-sensitive phototube which could replace the caesium tubes in projectors without loss of output.[344,345] However, by this time the makers of color film had begun the use of edge-development processes that form a track of silver or of a metallic salt (opaque to infrared) not removed by the bleach which was part of the picture processing.[346] In one system the silver is in the top layer only, and the dyes in the other two layers contribute to the opacity. The metallic track became general in the handling of sound on color films.[347–350]

Sound on 16mm Film. I have confined my story to developments in the 35mm field in the belief that the general principles and practices which solved problems or led to improvements in one case were applicable in the other. It is probably a gross injustice to pass over the valuable work of engineers whose efforts were devoted to 16mm sound, but it seems to be a necessity.

From the start, the recording of sound at 36 instead of 90 ft/min. pre-sented great difficulties. Only the fact that standards were much less exacting made the project practicable. But with each advance in the resolution of high frequencies in 35mm recording, the corresponding principles were applied to 16mm. One factor at least was in the favor of the low film speed, namely the providing of adequate exposure. By the time of the outbreak of World War II sound on 16mm film had improved to the point which made it acceptable for a great number of military applications.[351]

Recording sound on black-and-white reversal film was not too satisfactory, but years later when color films came into wide use, it again became necessary to put the sound on what was essentially a reversal type of film. Particularly successful for this purpose is recording on the individual prints or electrical printing. (See the section with that heading, and the December 1950 paper by J. G. Frayne.[323])

Black-and-white prints, with original sound recorded either on 16 or 35mm films, formed the great bulk of the product before and during the war. Fortunately, fine-grained emulsions could be used. Cost considerations dictated for the most part the use of 16mm negatives and contact prints, and unhappily nearly all of the printers were of the sprocket type. One laboratory adopted 1 : 1 optical printing as its standard.* Much study was given to the possibilities of recording direct positives. Still more development work was devoted to direct optical reduction from 35mm negatives, and this certainly helped resolution and high-frequency response,[239] but in the case of area tracks, neutralization of image spread in the positive by spread in the negative was not easily achieved.[276] The same factor made difficulty in the recording of direct positives, which had advocates since early in the era of sound pictures. Since 35mm negatives for optical reduction, or 35mm re-recording positives to be used for making 16mm negatives give best results if recorded with different degrees and kinds of high-frequency pre-equalization, the organizations producing these masters have worked together to establish standards of recommended characteristics.[352]

Adding sound to 16mm films by use of a stripe of magnetic material promises to become of great popular and commercial importance.[353]

Drive-in Theaters.[354] The drive-in theater was first proposed and advocated by R. M. Hollingshead, a businessman of Camden, N.J., not affiliated with motion-picture or electronic interests. The first such theater was built near Camden in 1933. In the earlier experiments with the system effort was made

---

* Precision Film Laboratories, New York, operated by J. A. Maurer.[240]

to put out enough sound power from a screen speaker to enable patrons to hear satisfactorily in their cars. This presented great technical difficulties, and also would have restricted theaters to locations where the noise would not be too objectionable. Several arrangements were tried, one with loudspeakers distributed over the field so that each speaker provided sound for two cars side by side. This was a great improvement from the noise standpoint, and the theaters previously equipped with screen speakers were converted. However, these "outcar" speaker arrangements still left something to be desired on the score of general noise. The "in-car" speaker, introduced by RCA in 1941, provided sound which was much more satisfactory to patrons and practically eliminated the neighborhood-noise problem. In the design of "in-car" speakers, the qualities of ruggedness, conveniently small size without too much sacrifice of sound quality, and immunity to damage by weather were design objectives.[355] The amplifier and audio-power distribution system had to be such that the individual levels would not be too much affected by the number of speakers in use. During the 1930's a number of drive-in theaters were built in New England, in the South, and (through the efforts of Philip Smith) in Indianapolis, Cleveland, Detroit, Milwaukee, St. Louis, Kansas City and Pittsburgh. Building activities were practically at a standstill during the war, but after its close the number increased rapidly. Underhill[356] gives the number of drive-in theaters at the end of the war as about 60 and four years later as 1000. He attributed the rapid growth just after the war in part to the greatly increased number of cars on the road, especially after the end of gasoline rationing, and in part to the shortage of building materials which made the construction of indoor theaters relatively difficult and expensive. The May 1954 Progress Report puts the number of drive-in theaters at the end of 1953 at 4000, and estimated that six months later there would be 4500.

The most serious problem of the drive-in theater is the provision of sufficient light for the large screen, a consideration, however, which lies outside the scope of this paper.

Magnetic Recording

The principle of magnetic recording was demonstrated in 1900 by Valdemar Poulsen, who called his device the "Telegraphone."[27,357] About 1917 the American Telegraphone Co. marketed a dictation machine under that name which performed well by existing standards but was complicated and could not compete commercially with cylinder machines. Recording was on 0.010-in. "piano" wire, contacted from opposite sides by a pair of offset steel pole-pieces.

Erasure was by a saturating d-c field, and a d-c bias was combined with the recording-voice current in sufficient magnitude to maintain all the recorded magnetization of the reversed polarity.

An alternating magnetic field has for years been the accepted means of demagnetizing magnetic materials, and it seemed a paradox that a superimposed alternating current would assist in, rather than obliterate, recording. However, it was found in 1921 by W. L. Carlson and G. W. Carpenter, then working on a government project of recording telegraph signals, that a bias current of supersonic frequency could be very advantageous in magnetic recording of audio-frequency signals.[358]

The development of magnetic recording was carried on by the Bell Telephone Laboratories during the 1930's. A thin steel ribbon about $\frac{1}{8}$ in. wide was found better than wire, and alloys of superior magnetic properties were developed. Direct current erase and bias were used in the equipment.

The developments and publications of Marvin Camras[359,360] of Armour Research Foundation aroused widespread interest in magnetic recording and the results obtainable with high-frequency bias. The essential difference between a recording made with d-c bias, and one made with high-frequency bias is that with the latter (1) modulation is through zero, with resultant increase in maximum recordable amplitude, and (2) there is no remanent magnetism when the modulation falls to zero. The second feature is the condition for low background noise. The comparison is analogous to that between a Class B push-pull photographic record, and a unilateral recording without ground-noise reduction.

There was much developmental activity in wire recording just before and during the war, with numerous applications for the armed services. The extreme compactness of recordings stored as magnetized wire plus the ruggedness of the system with respect to mechanical injury made it of especial value for military uses. Better wires were developed, 4- to 5-mil diameter sizes being widely used. The Brush Development Co. developed a compound wire in which an alloy of superior permanent magnetic properties was plated on a brass core.[357] The National Standard Co. of Niles, Mich., developed a successful stainless-steel recording wire.

S. J. Begun[357] quotes an article in *Machinery* of January 1917 about the Telegraphone in which mention is made of a stripe of powdered iron to be painted on a motion-picture film to provide synchronous sound. It was more than 30 years later before use was made of this principle — one of the many examples of development in which the basic concept is only a small part of the invention, and the real contribution to

progress the result of laborious experimentation and wise application of refinements and better techniques. Not until a sound quality was attained in magnetic recording surpassing that of any other known system did it become of great concern to motion pictures.

Development of magnetic coatings on paper or other base materials was undertaken by the AEG in Germany about 1928, but up to the outbreak of war nothing of outstanding quality had appeared. At the close of the war the American occupying forces brought back samples of a new German magnetic tape and equipment. The magnetic material was a finely divided iron oxide, mixed with a binder and coated on a thin cellulose base (total thickness about 0.002 in.). In the recording magnet a supersonic bias current was superimposed on the audio current. Magnetization was longitudinal, produced by C-shaped magnets of high-permeability alloy, with very short gaps where they contact the tape. Reproducing magnets were similar. In cleanness of reproduction, low ground noise and volume range the German system set a new high standard.

A period of intensive development followed the demonstrations. Some time was required before American firms could match the quality of the German tape, especially with respect to freedom from noise. Numerous papers were published describing basic properties of magnetic materials,[361,362] analysing the action of the supersonic bias,[363,364] and reporting tests on various tapes to determine optimum bias, relation of distortion to recorded amplitude, and amount of residual noise.[365] Among the first in this country to produce acceptable tapes was the Minnesota Mining & Mfg. Co.[361] Experimenters tried the magnetic black oxide (Fe_3O_4) in powder form and found it capable of producing higher output levels but noisier than the red oxide used in the German tapes. The red oxide (Fe_2O_3) in a certain crystal form ("gamma phase") is magnetic. Grinding to a particle size of about 1 μ or less was found essential, and prolonged mixing. Many tape-recorder-reproducer equipments were developed, both for amateur and professional use, the latter principally for broadcast stations.

Advantages of the Magnetic System. The compactness and portability of the magnetic-tape equipment, its freedom from dependence on laboratories, the immediate playback, the small storage space required, the relatively small cost of recording stock, plus the ability to reuse tape when the recorded sound on it is no longer wanted, the ability to work in daylight, and finally the excellent sound quality and dynamic range, combined to make the magnetic system a great advance from both the economic and performance standpoints.

Uses in the Motion-Picture Industry of Nonsynchronous Recording. The prompt interest of motion-picture producers in magnetic recording was shown in two lines of activity. The Basic Sound Committee of the Motion Picture Research Council held meetings in *1946* to which prospective suppliers of magnetic-recording equipment and record materials were invited.[366] The purpose was to formulate the requirements of the motion-picture industry in order that developments might be better directed toward meeting these requirements. The other activity was making experimental use of the nonsynchronous thin-tape recording equipment which was the first to be developed.[200] While the most important use which might be made of the magnetic system would be for the original synchronous recordings, there are numerous operations for which the lack of exact synchronism of magnetic tape would not be too serious an obstacle, such as for immediate playback after rehearsals, for training singers and actors, and for recording of music and sound effects which do not have to synchronize exactly with the picture. In musical numbers the picture is often secondary to the sound, and in many cases the practice had been followed of recording the sound first, without picture, and subsequently fitting the picture to the music. For this, initial recording on tape was applicable, the sound being re-recorded to film while musicians or vocalists performed synchronously for the camera.

Papers on Progress in Magnetic Sound. At the October 1946 convention of this Society Marvin Camras described and demonstrated synchronous magnetic sound, using 35mm film coated at Armour Research Foundation. However, the coated film was not offered commercially. At the same meeting H. A. Howell[362] of Indiana Steel Products Co. gave data on several magnetic materials and described a coated-paper tape which could be perforated if desired. While paper offered certain advantages which commended its use at the time, it has not been possible with coatings on paper to attain the quality and low noise that are realized with bases of clear plastic.

In February 1947 the Du Pont Co. furnished RCA with samples of coated 35mm film base. A conversion kit was developed so that a standard RCA photographic recorder (PR-23) could record and reproduce magnetically. The November 1948 issue of the *Journal* contains a description of the kit by Masterson,[367] measurements of the properties of the Du Pont film reported by O'Dea[368] and bias studies by Dimmick

and Johnson[365] of $\frac{1}{4}$-in. thin tapes made by Du Pont and by Minnesota Mining & Mfg. Co. as compared with one of the German tapes. The commercial version of the conversion kit was described by Gunby[369] at the October 1948 convention. In the June 1949 *Journal* Mueller and Groves[200] describe experiences at Warner Bros. Studios with various uses of nonsynchronous magnetic recording, and such experience as had been had up to that time with synchronous magnetic recording. The practice of re-recording from magnetic to direct-positive photographic tracks is mentioned. This has sometimes been called "electrical printing," and soon became the prevalent method of providing a sound film to be edited and then re-recorded to the final release negative. The January 1952 paper by Carey and Moran[322] states that the practice of re-recording from a magnetic original to a 200-mil push-pull variable-area direct positive for editing had been followed by Universal International Pictures since January 1951.

The Progress Report of May 1951 shows RCA synchronous magnetic recording equipment, designed to make one, two, or three tracks on the film.* This was being used by Columbia, the sound being re-recorded to direct positives for editing. The same report tells of Westrex portable synchronous magnetic-recording equipment, suited (optionally) to 35mm, $17\frac{1}{2}$mm or 16mm film, describing this equipment as in wide use in this country and abroad. Triple-track Westrex equipment is described by Davis, Frayne and Templin[371] in the February 1952 *Journal*.

Portable magnetic-recording equipment (the complete channel weighing less than 100 lb) using $17\frac{1}{2}$mm film was described by Ryder[372] at the April 1950 convention. The May 1951 Progress Report states that since April 1, 1950, all Paramount production recording had been done on this equipment.

The Progress Report[373] of May 1952 states that by the end of 1951 approximately 75% of the original production recording, music scoring and dubbing in Hollywood was being done on magnetic-recording equipment.

Editing. While it is entirely possible to edit magnetic recordings with the help of quick-stop reproducers, sound-film editors have come to depend in part on the visibility of modulation in a photographic track. This is probably one of the chief reasons for the retention of

---

* The use of three tracks on a 35mm film was begun by Columbia in November 1950. In single-channel recording the three tracks could be used in succession, or in recordings calling for combined voice, orchestra and sound-effects these could be independently and simultaneously recorded and later mixed for desired balance.

photographic-sound records for this intermediate function. Push-pull recording is usual, and in order to add as little ground noise as possible, preferably wide-track. The use of direct positives saves time as well as printing losses. When the editing is completed, the negative for release printing is made by another re-recording operation.

To provide the visual advantages of the photographic track for purposes of editing while retaining the quality advantages of the magnetic system, an arrangement has been tried which registered by an ink line on the magnetic film the amplitude of the modulation being recorded.[372] Another expedient, described by Frayne and Livadary,[374] is to make simultaneous tracks on the film to be edited, one magnetic and the other photographic variable-area, the magnetic to be used for the re-recording.

A system in which both pictures and sound can be backed up at any time without loss of synchronism is described by George Lewin[377] of the Signal Corps Pictorial Center. This makes it possible for a narrator to correct or change his speech, erasing portions of the previous record as he substitutes the new.

Synchronous Thin Tape. While use of perforated film afforded the necessary synchronism, the thin tape has the important advantages of reduced size and weight of equipment, smaller space required for storage, lower cost, and better contact between magnet and record surface because of its greater flexibility. A number of systems have, therefore, been developed to drive tape in strict synchronism. These have for the most part used the principle of recording a tone on the tape in addition to the audio modulation and of controlling the speed of the driving system so as to hold within limits the phase relation between the reproduced tone and a reference frequency, usually the 60-cycle power which drives the camera. The recorded tone may be 60 cycles[375] (excluded from the audio by a high pass filter) or a tone slightly above the audio range for example 14,[376] 15[377] or 18[378] kc, and modulated at the 60-cycle rate.

An optical tone on the tape, as by stripes on the back of the tape would have certain advantages (one of which is that full voltage can be developed from standstill), but this has to the best of my information not been made commercial.

Experiments have indicated that with a suitably designed mechanical system, perforations and sprockets are not out of the question, even with tape as small as 0.002 in. thick by $\frac{1}{4}$ in. wide.[379]

Striping. While magnetic sound has been thus far used mainly in the preliminary operations of making sound pictures, and release prints are still optical, there are some exceptions, for example the films for the CinemaScope system, on which the sound is all-magnetic. This calls for applying stripes of magnetic coating on the photographic film which carries the picture. There are also numerous applications, especially with 16mm films, for which it is desirable to add sound to an existing picture film, and other uses for which the stripe is applied to the unexposed film.

The application of the magnetic material in stripes of closely controlled width, position and thickness is no simple problem. The April 1953 *Journal*, Part II, carries a series of papers dealing with problems of magnetic recording. Striping is discussed by representatives of Reeves Soundcraft Corp.,[380] Minnesota Mining and Mfg. Co.,[381] Eastman Kodak Co.[382] and Bell and Howell.[383] The Minnesota Mining and Mfg. Co. developed a method of application of a stripe by transfer from a temporary supporting tape. Only heat (no solvent or wet cement) is required for the transfer. The Reeves engineers also have papers on the preparation of the magnetic material,[384] and the study of the minute surface irregularities which tend to lift the tape from the magnet causing sound "drop-outs."[385] In spite of the utmost effort to prevent the formation of such high spots they are not entirely eliminated, and polishing operations are helpful. Other papers in the group deal with wear on magnets,[386] measurements of magnetic induction,[387] and standardization.[388]

The May 1954 Progress Report mentions new high-output magnetic-oxide coatings introduced in 1953 and 1954 by Minnesota Mining and Mfg. Co., greatly increased use of striping, new machines for applying the stripes, and several designs of theater soundheads (to be mounted above the projector head) for reproducing multiple-track magnetic sound.

A Sound Committee Report by J. K. Hilliard in the June 1953 *Journal* tells of arrival at agreement for a standard of track positions for triple 200-mil magnetic tracks on 35mm film, of projects for standardizing theater magnetic-reproducing characteristics, and plans for making available various magnetic test films, corresponding to the long-used photographic test films.

Theater reproducing systems for magnetic tracks are designed to be mounted on the tops of projectors, and do not interfere with the optical reproduction.

New Safety-Film Base.[280,389] For years the motion-picture industry struggled to minimize the fire hazard of nitrate film. Safety-film base had early been developed and used for certain purposes for 35mm film, and was mandatory for amateur equipment (16mm), but the stability and mechanical properties of

the safety base were so inferior to the nitrate base that it was not a satisfactory substitute.

The film companies worked long and diligently on the problem of improving film-base stock. In 1937 the Eastman Co. adopted an improved safety base,[390] and in 1948 announced a new safety base which combined the needed properties to replace the long-used nitrate base, being superior to the nitrate in heat resistance and low shrinkage. It is described by Fordyce[391]. With these virtues the new film has rapidly supplanted nitrate.

The improvement in sound quality due to reduced shrinkage may not be noticeable to the average listener, but it must inevitably mean better performance especially in the action of contact printers. The importance of this new base can hardly be exaggerated.

Acknowledgments

I wish to express my appreciation and indebtedness to the many who have supplied information, and reviewed portions or the entire text, submitting comments and indicating corrections. Special acknowledgment must be made to E. C. Wente who supplied me with much of the story at Western Electric, and to J. G. Frayne who reviewed a large part of the text, indicating corrections and answering many questions. A. C. Blaney gave particularly generously of time and thought in answering questions and filling in gaps of information. My thanks also go to E. M. Honan, and W. V. Wolfe, O. B. Gunby, E. W. Templin, Kurt Singer, Barton Kreuzer, and Walter L. Tesch for reviews and comments.

APPENDIX

Development of High Vacuum Amplifier Tubes from the Audion

A brief account of the improvement of the audion by Dr. Arnold of the Western Electric Co., and of the subsequent patent interference and litigation, appeared in *Jour. SMPE, 17:* 658–663, Oct. 1931. In view of the vital part played by the electronic triode, it seems appropriate to tell something more about the parallel developments at the General Electric Co. The results, in terms of practical, high-vacuum amplifier tubes, were attained independently and at very nearly the same time at the two laboratories. The Telephone Co. had immediate use for audio amplifiers and promptly put them to use on a large scale, whereas, at the General Electric Co., the work was much more nearly a pure research.

Study at the Research Laboratory of the General Electric Co. of the relation of "Edison Effect" current to residual gas was an outgrowth of incandescent lamp development. Because of serious effects in some cases of the minutest traces of impurities or of certain gases or vapors, the techniques of producing high vacua had been developed to a high degree.

In the early days of the Fleming valve and the de Forest audion the opinion was widely held that these depended for their conducting properties on the presence of some gas. Experiments in 1907 by Prof. Soddy[395] of the University of Glasgow lent support to the belief that the space current would become zero if a true vacuum were obtained. On the other hand, the English scientists J. J. Thompson (who first proved that there was such a thing as an electron) and O. W. Richardson believed that high temperature would cause a conducting body to throw off electrons into the adjacent space, without dependence on the potent effects (in releasing electrons) of impacts on the cathode surface by positive gas ions. It was the question which of these theories was right that enlisted the interest of Dr. Irving Langmuir. By using the known techniques for driving occluded gases from glass and metal surfaces, the Gaede diffusion pump, and adding a liquid-air cooled trap in the exhaust line, Dr. Langmuir exhausted his experimental tubes to about the highest possible vacuum. He showed that (with adequate temperature of the tungsten cathode) a pure electron space current flowed, and that this current followed the theoretically predicted 1.5 power relationship to the anode potential.[397]

With high enough anode voltage to carry over all the electrons emitted by the cathode ("saturation current") Langmuir was able to verify O. W. Richardson's prediction ("The electrical conductivity imparted to a vacuum by hot conductors," *Phil. Trans. 201:* 497, 1903) that the rate at which electrons are "boiled" out of the cathode bears a similar relation to temperature that vapor pressure does in the case of an evaporating substance. The presence of small quantities of ordinary gases (other than the "noble" gases) was found to "poison" the tungsten surface and greatly reduce emission, but this effect disappeared at high enough temperatures.[397]

These studies were begun in August 1912, and continued through that year and the following. Three electrode tubes exhausted to high vacuum were found to be free from the voltage limitations and erratic behavior of the previous audions.[398] Another important outcome of the development of the pure electron discharge was the Coolidge X-ray tube (hot-cathode, high-vacuum type) in which the electron velocities at the anode (and thereby the frequency or penetrating power of the X-rays) could be accurately and reliably controlled, and carried to much higher values than had been possible in the previous tubes where gas ionization had limited the effective anode voltage. The use of chemical "getters" for improving the vacuum in sealed-off tubes was also much advanced by work at this time at General Electric. In October 1913, a patent application was filed for Langmuir on "Electrical Discharge Apparatus" (triode) in which conduction is entirely by electrons, the effects of gas ions being negligible.

The audions which de Forest supplied for radio reception broke into a glow discharge if anode potentials of more than 20 to 40 were applied, and all control by the grid then vanished. The very limited output with low-voltage operation was not serious for radio detectors, but made the tubes of little or no use as amplifiers. During the years 1909–1912 de Forest was employed by the Federal Telegraph Co. of California. The company wanted amplifier tubes and de Forest ordered some made with better vacuum, calling in some cases for re-exhaust, so that by August 1912, a tube was being used at 54 v and by November, one at 67½ v. This was held in some of the later court actions to be a clear indication of the direction from which improvement in the audion could be expected and thus, so far as invention or discovery goes, an anticipation of possible patent claims by others, directed to improving the audion by employing higher vacuum.

At the time that the work just described was going on, the Telephone Co. was making plans to establish transcontinental telephone communications in time for the opening of the San Francisco Panama-Pacific Exposition in 1915. There had been a long-felt need for a voice-current amplifier, much effort had been expended on the project, and devices based on various principles tried.

For the 3000-mile transmission the possession of amplifiers would be imperative and they must have low distortion to permit cascading. According to the accounts by Lovette and Watkins,[48] and by Wm. R. Ballard,[393] a visit by de Forest in October 1930 served to direct attention to the possibilities of the audion, other devices of promise having till then claimed the research efforts. De Forest gave demonstrations and left a sample for tests and study. The demonstrations were repeated next day for the benefit of research engineer Dr. H. D. Arnold, who was quick to recognize the potentialities of the audion, the requirement for high vacuum and the role of space charge in limiting and controlling electron current. He expressed entire confidence that an amplifying tube which would meet the requirements could be developed from the audion, and he was assigned the task. Progress was rapid, and tubes with much higher vacuum were quickly available, but vacuum of the desired value was not achieved until a Gaede molecular pump, which was ordered from Germany, arrived. Long-lived cathodes were of great importance for telephone applications, and cathodes of the Wehneldt oxide-coated type were developed to replace de Forest's tungsten cathodes.

More details about the developments at the Western Electric Co. will be found in the references already cited.[48,293] Doubting the patentability of the improvement brought about by higher vacuum, Arnold and his attorneys did not file any application until they learned that an application based on a similar development had been filed by the General Electric Co. The prolonged interference which followed is summarized in the footnote on page 657 of the October 1931 *Journal*, "After various conflicting opinions by successive tribunals, U.S. Pat. No. 1,558,436 was issued to Langmuir in 1925."

In 1926 the General Electric Co. brought suit for infringement against the de Forest Radio Corp. Again there were decisions, appeals, and reversals, ending with the ruling of the Supreme Court, May 25, 1931, that the patent did not involve invention.

Some light on the questions at issue may be found in opinions written by the successive courts.

Court of Appeals of the District of Columbia (339 *Official Gazette* 56). Patent issued pursuant to finding of this court.

Federal District Court for Delaware before which the General Electric vs. de Forest suit was tried (*Federal Reporter, Vol. 23, 2nd Series*, p. 698).

U.S. Circuit Court of Appeals for the Third District (44 *Federal Reporter 2nd Series*, p. 931, and *U. S. Pat. Quarterly*, Oct.–Dec. 1930, p. 67). Majority opinion for plaintiffs and dissenting minority opinion.

U.S. Supreme Court (283 U.S. 664, *Baldwin Vol. XI* 664).

References (Continued)

232. J. Crabtree, "Sound film printing," *Jour. SMPE, 21:* 294–322, Oct. 1933, and "Sound film printing—II," *Jour. SMPE, 22:* 98–114, Feb. 1934. (Repetition of ref. 120.)
233. C. N. Batsel, "A non-slip sound printer," *Jour. SMPE, 23:* 100–107, Aug. 1934.
234. A. V. Bedford, U.S. Pat. 1,754,187.
235. F. W. Roberts and E. Taenzer, "Photographic duping of variable-area sound," *Jour. SMPE, 34:* 26–37, Jan. 1940.
236. R. V. Wood, "A shrinkage-compensating sound printer," *Jour. SMPE, 18:* 788–791, June 1932.
237. G. L. Dimmick, C. N. Batsel and L. T. Sachtleben, "Optical reduction sound printing," *Jour. SMPE, 23:* 108–116, Aug. 1934.
238. M. E. Collins, "Optical reduction sound printer," *Jour. SMPE, 27:* 105–106, July 1936.
239. R. O. Drew and L. T. Sachtleben, "Recent laboratory studies of optical reduction printing," *Jour. SMPE, 41:* 505–513, Dec. 1943.
240. John A. Maurer, "Optical sound-track printing," *Jour. SMPE, 50:* 458–473, May 1948.
241. O. Sandvik and J. G. Streiffert, "A continuous optical reduction sound printer," *Jour. SMPE, 25:* 117–126, Aug. 1935.
242. O. Sandvik and G. Silberstein, "The dependence of the resolving power of a photographic material on the wavelength of light," *J. Opt. Soc. Am., 17:* 107, Aug. 1928.
243. Carl L. Oswald and Warren D. Foster, U.S. Pat. 1,928,392, 2,030,760, 2,055,261, 2,213,531.
244. G. L. Dimmick, "Improved resolution in sound recording and printing by the use of ultraviolet light," *Jour. SMPE, 27:* 168–178, Aug. 1936.
245. G. L. Dimmick and L. T. Sachtleben, "Ultraviolet push-pull recording optical system for newsreel cameras," *Jour. SMPE, 31:* 87–92, July 1938.
246. J. O. Baker, "Processing of ultraviolet recordings on panchromatic films," *Jour. SMPE, 31:* 28–35, July 1938.
247. J. G. Frayne and V. Pagliarulo, "Effects of ultraviolet light on variable-density recording and printing," *Jour. SMPE, 34:* 614–631, June 1940.
248. C. R. Daily and I. M. Chambers, "Production and release applications of fine-grain films for variable-density sound recording," *Jour. SMPE, 38:* 45–55, Jan. 1942.
249. J. Strong, "On a method of decreasing reflections from non-metallic substances," *J. Opt. Soc. Am.,* vol. 26, 73, Jan. 1936.
250. W. P. Strickland, "An analysis of low-reflection coatings as applied to glass," *Jour. SMPE, 49:* 27–36, July 1947.

251. C. W. Faulkner and C. N. Batsel, "Operation of the variable-intensity recording system," *Jour. SMPE, 36:* 125–136, Feb. 1941.
252. W. C. Miller, "Speed up your lens systems," *Jour. SMPE, 35:* 3–16, July 1940; and "Recent improvements in nonreflective lens coating," *Jour. SMPE, 37:* 265–273, Sept. 1941.
253. C. H. Cartwright and A. F. Turner, "Multiple films of high reflecting power," *Phys. Rev., 55:* 595, June 1939.
254. G. L. Dimmick, "A new dichroic reflector and its application to photocell monitoring systems," *Jour. SMPE, 38:* 36–44, Jan. 1942.
255. Mary Ellen Widdop, "Review of work on dichroic mirrors and their light-dividing characteristics," *Jour. SMPTE, 60:* 357–366, Apr. 1953.
256. G. L. Dimmick and Mary Ellen Widdop, "Heat-transmitting mirror," *Jour. SMPTE, 58:* 36–42, Jan. 1952.
257. Progress Reports, *Jour. SMPTE, 56:* 575 May 1951; and *Jour. SMPTE, 62:* 336, May 1954.
258. G. J. Koch, "Interference mirrors for arc projectors," *Jour. SMPTE, 55:* 439–442, Oct. 1950.
259. See reference 146 and accompanying classified bibliography. (J. I. Crabtree, "The motion-picture laboratory," *Jour. SMPTE, 64:* 13–34, Jan. 1955.)
260. E. D. Cook, "The aperture alignment effect," *Jour. SMPE, 21:* 390–402, Nov. 1933.
261. D. Foster, "Effect of orientation of the scanning image on the quality of sound reproduced from variable-width records," *Jour. SMPE, 33:* 502–516, Nov. 1939.
262. N. R. Stryker, "Scanning losses in reproduction," *Jour. SMPE, 15:* 610–623, Nov. 1930.
263. E. D. Cook, "The aperture effect," *Jour. SMPE, 14:* 650–662, June 1930.
264. D. Foster, "The effect of exposure and development on the quality of variable-width photographic sound recording," *Jour. SMPE, 17:* 749–765, Nov. 1931.
265. C. N. Batsel and C. H. Cartwright, "Effect of uneven slit illumination upon distortion in several types of variable-width records," *Jour. SMPE, 29:* 476–483, Nov. 1937.
266. American Standard, Scanning Beam Uniformity Test Film for 35mm, *Jour. SMPE, 51:* 542–544, Nov. 1948; and American Standard, *Jour. SMPTE, 59:* 427–431, Nov. 1952.
267. J. O. Baker and R. O. Drew, "New and old aspects of the origins of 96-cycle distortion," *Jour. SMPE, 37:* 227–255, Sept. 1941.
268. J. G. Frayne and V. Pagliarulo, "Influence of sprocket holes upon the development of adjacent sound track areas," *Jour. SMPE, 28:* 235–245, Mar. 1937.
269. J. Crabtree and W. Herriott, "Film perforation and 96-cycle frequency modulation in sound-film records," *Jour. SMPE, 30:* 25–29, Jan. 1938.
270. J. Crabtree, "Directional effects in continuous film processing," *Jour. SMPE, 18:* 207–231, Feb. 1932.
271. J. Crabtree and J. H. Waddell, "Directional effects in sound-film processing-II," *Jour. SMPE, 21:* 351–373, Nov. 1933.
272. C. E. Ives and E. W. Jensen, "Effect of developer agitation on density uniformity and rate of development," *Jour. SMPE, 40:* 107–136, Feb. 1943. (Repetition of ref. 158.)
273. M. S. Leshing, T. M. Ingman and K. Pier, "Reduction of development sprocket-hole modulation" *Jour. SMPE, 36:* 475–487, May 1941.
274. O. Sandvik and V. C. Hall, "Wave form analysis of variable-density sound recording," *Jour. SMPE, 19:* 346–360, Oct. 1932.
275. O. Sandvik, V. C. Hall and J. G. Streiffert, "Wave-form analysis of variable-width sound records," *Jour. SMPE, 21:* 323–336, Oct. 1933.

276. C. E. K. Mees, "Some photographic aspects of sound recording," *Jour. SMPE, 24:* 285–326, Apr. 1935. See page 324.

277. J. G. Frayne and R. R. Scoville, "Analysis and measurement of distortion in variable-density recording," *Jour. SMPE, 32:* 648–673, June 1939.

278. Kurt Singer and Robert V. McKie, "Cross-modulation compensator," *Jour. SMPTE, 63:* 77–81, Sept. 1954.

279. F. G. Albin, "A dynamic check on the processing of film for sound records," *Jour. SMPE, 25:* 161–170, Aug. 1935.

280. C. E. Kenneth Mees, "The history of professional black and white motion picture films," *Jour. SMPTE, 63:* 134–137, Oct. 1954.

281. R. M. Corbin, N. L. Simmons and D. E. Hyndman, "Two new Eastman fine-grain sound recording films," *Jour. SMPE, 45:* 265–285, Oct. 1945.

282. Hollis W. Moyse, "DuPont fine-grain sound films—Types *232* and *236*," *Jour. SMPE, 45:* 285–293, Oct. 1945.

283. L. A. Jones and Otto Sandvik, "Photographic Characteristics of sound recording film," *Jour. SMPE, 14:* 180–203, Feb. 1930. (Repetition of ref. 173.)

284. C. E. Ives and J. I. Crabtree, "Two new films for duplicating work," *Jour. SMPE, 29:* 317–325, Sept. 1937.

285. Progress Report, *Jour. SMPE, 48:* 305, Apr. 1947.

286. C. R. Daily, "Improvement in sound and picture release through the use of fine-grain film," *Jour. SMPE, 34:* 12–25, Jan. 1940.

287. W. H. Offenhauser, Jr., "Notes on the application of fine grain film to 16mm motion pictures," *Jour. SMPE, 41:* 374–388, Nov. 1943.

288. J. R. Wilkinson and F. L. Eich, "Laboratory modification and procedure in connection with fine-grain release printing," *Jour. SMPE, 38:* 56–65, Jan. 1942.

289. Report on the adaptation of fine-grain films to variable-density sound technics, *Jour. SMPE, 34:* 3–11, Jan. 1940.

290. V. C. Shaner, "Note on the processing of Eastman 1302 fine-grain release positive in Hollywood," *Jour. SMPE, 38:* 66–73, Jan. 1942.

291. E. W. Kellogg, "A comparison of variable-density and variable-width systems," *Jour. SMPE, 25:* 203–226, Sept. 1935.

292. John G. Frayne, "Comparison of recording processes," (reprint) *Jour. SMPTE, 59:* 313–318, Oct. 1952.

293. N. Levinson, "New method of increasing the volume range of talking motion pictures," *Jour. SMPE, 26:* 111–116, Feb. 1936.

294. G. L. Dimmick, "Optical control of waveshape and amplitude characteristics in variable-density recording," *Jour. SMPE, 33:* 650–663, Dec. 1939.

295. John G. Frayne, "Variable-area recording with the light valve," *Jour. SMPE, 51:* 501–520, Nov. 1948.

296. Lewis B. Browder, "Variable-area light-valve modulator," *Jour. SMPE, 51:* 521–533, Nov. 1948.

297. E. M. Honan and C. R. Keith, "Recent developments in sound tracks," *Jour. SMPE, 41:* 127–135, Aug. 1943.

298. J. P. Livadary and S. J. Twining, "Variable-area release from variable-density original sound tracks," *Jour. SMPE, 45:* 380–388, Nov. 1945.

299. W. K. Grimwood, "Volume compressors for sound recording," *Jour. SMPE, 52:* 49–76, Jan. 1949.

300. J. O. Aalberg and J. G. Stewart, "Application of non-linear volume characteristics to dialog recording," *Jour. SMPE, 31:* 248–255, Sept. 1938.

301. B. F. Miller, "Elimination of relative spectral energy distortion in electronic compressors," *Jour. SMPE, 39:* 317–323, Nov. 1942.

302. M. Rettinger and K. Singer, "Factors governing the frequency response of a variable-area film recording channel," *Jour. SMPE, 47:* 299–326, Oct. 1946.

303. Kurt Singer, "High-quality recording electronic mixer," *Jour. SMPE, 52:* 676–683, June 1949.

304. A. C. Norwine, "Devices for controlling amplitude characteristics of telephonic signals," *Bell Sys. Tech. Jour., 17:* 539–554, Oct. 1938.

304a. D. E. Maxwell, "Dynamic performance of peak-limiting amplifiers," *Proc. I.R.E., 35:* 1349–1356, Nov. 1947.

305. Kurt Singer, "Preselection of variable-gain tubes for compressors," *Jour. SMPE, 52:* 684–689, June 1949.

306. Harold E. Haynes, "New principle for electronic volume compression," *Jour. SMPTE, 58:* 137–144, Feb. 1952.

307. W. C. Miller, "Volume control by the squeeze track," *Jour. SMPE, 15:* 53–59, July 1930.

308. E. H. Hansen and C. W. Faulkner, "Mechanical reversed-bias light-valve recording," *Jour. SMPE, 26:* 117–127, Feb. 1936.

309. J. G. Frayne and H. C. Silent, "Push-pull recording with the light-valve," *Jour. SMPE, 31:* 46–64, July 1938.

310. John G. Frayne, T. B. Cunningham and V. Pagliarulo, "An improved 200-mil push-pull density modulator," *Jour. SMPE, 47:* 494–518, Dec. 1946.

311. Lawrence T. Sachtleben, "Wide-track optics for variable-area recorders," *Jour. SMPE, 52:* 89–96, Jan. 1949.

312. J. E. Jenkins and S. E. Adair, "The control-frequency principle," *Jour. SMPE, 22:* 193, Mar. 1934.

313. J. G. Frayne and F. P. Herrnfeld, "Frequency-modulated control-track for movietone prints," *Jour. SMPE, 38:* 111–124, Feb. 1942.

314. G. L. Dimmick and H. Belar, "An improved system for noiseless recording," *Jour. SMPE, 23:* 48–54, July 1934.

315. D. J. Bloomberg and C. L. Lootens, "Class B push-pull recording for original negatives," *Jour. SMPE, 33:* 664–669, Dec. 1939.

316. A. C. Blaney, "Notes on operating experience using the direct positive push-pull method of recording," *Jour. SMPE, 42:* 279–282, May 1944.

317. A. C. Blaney and G. M. Best, "Latest developments in variable-area processing," *Jour. SMPE, 32:* 237–245, Mar. 1939.

318. W. J. Albersheim, "Device for direct reproduction from variable-density sound negatives," *Jour. SMPE, 29:* 274–280, Sept. 1937.

319. O. L. Dupy, "A method of direct-positive variable-density recording with the light valve," *Jour. SMPTE, 59:* 101–106, Aug. 1952.

320. C. R. Keith and V. Pagliarulo, "Direct-positive variable-density recording with the light valve," *Jour. SMPE, 52:* 690–698, June 1949.

321. Lewis B. Browder, "Direct-positive variable-area recording with the light valve," *Jour. SMPE, 53:* 149–158, Aug. 1949.

322. L. I. Carey and Frank Moran, "Push-pull direct-positive recording, an auxiliary to magnetic recording," *Jour. SMPTE, 58:* 67–70, Jan. 1952.

323. John G. Frayne, "Electrical printing," *Jour. SMPTE, 55:* 590–604, Dec. 1950.

324. C. N. Batsel and L. T. Sachtleben, "Some characteristics of 16mm sound by optical reduction and re-recording," *Jour. SMPE, 24:* 95–101, Feb. 1935.

325. W. A. Mueller, "Audience noise as a limitation to the permissible volume range of dialog in sound motion pictures," *Jour. SMPE, 35:* 48–58, July 1940.

326. H. I. Reiskind, "Multiple-speaker reproducing systems for motion pictures," *Jour. SMPE, 37:* 154–163, Aug. 1941.

327. N. Levinson and L. T. Goldsmith, "Vitasound," *Jour. SMPE, 37:* 147–153, Aug. 1941.

328. J. P. Maxfield, "Demonstration of stereophonic recording with motion pictures," *Jour. SMPE, 30:* 131–135, Feb. 1938.

329. H. Fletcher, "Stereophonic reproduction from film," *Jour. SMPE, 34:* 606–613, June 1940; ibid., "Stereophonic sound-film system—general theory," *Jour. SMPE, 37:* 339–352, Oct. 1941. (*See p. 352.*)

330. J. C. Steinberg, "The stereophonic sound-film system—pre- and post-equalization of compandor systems," *Jour. SMPE, 37:* 366–379, Oct. 1941.

331. W. B. Snow and A. R. Soffel, "Electrical equipment for the stereophonic sound-film system," *Jour. SMPE, 37:* 380–396, Oct. 1941.

332. E. C. Wente, R. Biddulph, L. A. Elmer and A. B. Anderson, "Mechanical and optical equipment for the stereophonic sound-film system," *Jour. SMPE, 37:* 353–365, Oct. 1941.

333. W. E. Garity and J. N. A. Hawkins, "Fantasound," *Jour. SMPE, 37:* 127–146, Aug. 1941.

334. W. E. Garity and W. Jones, "Experiences in road-showing Walt Disney's Fantasia," *Jour. SMPE, 39:* 6–15, July 1942.

335. E. H. Plumb, "Future of Fantasound," *Jour. SMPE, 39:* 16–21, July 1942.

336. See group of papers on stereophonic sound, *Jour. SMPTE, 61:* No. 3, Sept. 1953, Pt. II.

337. Panel Discussion, J. K. Hilliard, moderator "Equipment for stereophonic sound reproduction," *Jour. SMPTE, 62:* 228–237, Mar. 1954.

338. L. D. Grignon, "Experiment in stereophonic sound," *Jour. SMPTE, 62:* 64–70, Sept. 1953, Pt. II.

339. Progress Committee Report, *Jour. SMPTE, 62:* 338, May 1954.

340. Progress Committee Report, *Jour. SMPTE, 60:* 535, May 1953. See also Progress Committee Report, *Jour. SMPTE, 64:* 226–228, May 1955.

341. Russell J. Tinkham, "Stereophonic tape recording equipment," *Jour. SMPTE, 62:* 71–74, Jan. 1954.

342. C. Robert Fine, "Perspecta Stereophonic Sound," paper presented at 75th SMPTE Convention, Washington, D. C., May 1954.

343. R. Görisch and P. Görlich, "Reproduction of color film sound records," *Jour. SMPE, 43:* 206–213, Sept. 1944.

344. Alan M. Glover and Arnold R. Moore, "Phototube for dye image sound track," *Jour. SMPE, 46:* 379–386, May 1946.

345. Lloyd T. Goldsmith, "Preliminary report of research council photocell subcommittee," *Jour. SMPE, 48:* 145–147, Feb. 1947.

346. J. L. Forrest, "Metallic-salt track on Ansco 16-mm color film," *Jour. SMPE, 53:* 40–49, July 1949.

347. Report of the SMPTE Color Committee, L. T. Goldsmith, chairman, "Characteristics of color film sound tracks," *Jour. SMPTE, 54:* 377, Mar. 1950.

348. Robert C. Lovick, "Optimum exposure of sound tracks on Kodachrome films," *Jour. SMPTE, 59:* 81–88, Aug. 1952.

349. Robert C. Lovick, "Densitometry of silver sulfide sound tracks," *Jour. SMPTE, 59:* 89–93, Aug. 1952.

350. C. H. Evans and J. F. Finkle. "Sound track on Eastman color print film," *Jour. SMPTE, 57:* 131–139, Aug. 1951.

351. J. A. Maurer, "Present technical status of 16-mm sound-film," *Jour. SMPE, 33:* 315–325, Sept. 1939.

352. W. C. Miller, "Preliminary report of Academy Research Council Committee on rerecording methods for 16-mm release of 35-mm features," *Jour. SMPE, 45:* 135–142, Aug. 1945.

353. E. E. Masterson, F. L. Putzrath and H E. Roys, "Magnetic sound on 16-mm edge-coated film," *Jour. SMPTE, 57:* 559–566, Dec. 1951.

354. Geo. M. Peterson, *The Drive-In Theater,* Associated Publ. Kansas City, Mo. Book Rev., *Jour. SMPTE, 62:* 401, May 1954.

355. R. H. Heacock, "Improved equipment for drive-in theaters," *Jour. SMPTE, 60:* 716–720, June 1953.

356. C. R. Underhill, Jr., "The trend in drive-in theaters," *Jour. SMPTE, 54:* 161–170, Feb. 1950.

357. S. J. Begun, "Recent developments in the field of magnetic recording," *Jour. SMPE, 48:* 1–13, Jan. 1947.

358. G. W. Carpenter and W. L. Carlson, U.S. Pat. 1,640,881, filed Mar. 26, 1921; issued Aug. 30, 1927.

359. M. Camras, "Theoretical response from a magnetic wire record," *Proc. IRE and Waves and Electrons, 34:* No. 8, 597, Aug. 1946.

360. M. Camras, "Magnetic sound for motion pictures," *Jour. SMPE, 48:* 14–28, Jan. 1947.

361. R. Herr, B. F. Murphy and W. W. Wetzel, "Some distinctive properties of magnetic-recording media," *Jour. SMPE, 52:* 77–88, Jan. 1949.

362. H. A. Howell, "Magnetic sound recording on coated paper tape," *Jour. SMPE, 48:* 36–49, Jan. 1947.

363. Hershel Toomin and David Wildfeuer, "The mechanism of supersonic frequencies as applied to magnetic recording," *Proc. IRE, 32:* 664–668, Nov. 1944.

364. Lynn C. Holmes and Donald L. Clark, "Supersonic bias for magnetic recording," *Electronics, 18:* 126, July 1945.

365. G. L. Dimmick and S. W. Johnson, "Optimum high-frequency bias in magnetic recording," *Jour. SMPE, 51:* 489–500, Nov. 1948.

366. Research Council Basic Sound Committee, (Acad. Mot. Pict. Arts and Sciences), Discussion of Magnetic Recording, *Jour. SMPE, 48:* 50–56, Jan. 1947.

367. Earl Masterson, "35-mm magnetic recording system," *Jour. SMPE, 51:* 481–488, Nov. 1948.

368. Dorothy O'Dea, "Magnetic recording for the technician," *Jour. SMPE, 51:* 468–480, Nov. 1948.

369. O. B. Gunby, "Portable magnetic recording system," *Jour. SMPE, 52:* 613–618, June 1949.

370. Progress Committee Report, *Jour. SMPTE, 56:* 572–573, May 1951.

371. C. C. Davis, J. G. Frayne and E. W. Templin, "Multichannel magnetic film recording and reproducing unit," *Jour. SMPTE, 58:* 105–118, Feb. 1952.

372. Loren L. Ryder, "Motion picture studio use of magnetic recording," *Jour. SMPTE, 55:* 605–612, Dec. 1950.

373. Progress Report, *Jour. SMPTE, 58:* 400–401, May 1952.

374. John G. Frayne and John P. Livadary, "Dual photomagnetic intermediate studio recording," *Jour. SMPTE, 59:* 388–397, Nov. 1952.

375. R. H. Ranger, "Sprocketless synchronous magnetic tape," *Jour. SMPTE, 54:* 328–336, Mar. 1950.

376. D. G. C. Hare and W. D. Fling, "Picture-synchronous magnetic tape recording," *Jour. SMPTE, 54:* 554–566, May 1950.

377. George Lewin, "Synchronous 1/4-in. magnetic tape for motion picture production," *Jour. SMPTE, 56:* 664–671, June 1951.

378. Walter T. Selsted, "Synchronous recording on 1/4- in. magnetic tape," *Jour. SMPTE, 55:* 279–284, Sept. 1950.

379. Warren R. Isom, "Synchronized recordings on perforated tape," *Jour. SMPTE, 63:* 26–28, July 1954.

380. Edward Schmidt, "Commercial experiences with magnastripe," *Jour. SMPTE, 60:* 463–469, Apr. 1953. Part II.

381. Andrew H. Persoon, "Magnetic striping of photographic film by laminating process," *Jour. SMPTE, 60:* 485–490, Apr. 1953, Pt. II.

382. Thomas R. Dedell, "Magnetic sound tracks for processed 16-mm motion picture film," *Jour. SMPTE, 60:* 491–500, Apr. 1953, Pt. II.

383. B. L. Kaspin, A. Roberts, Jr., Harry Robbins, and R. L. Powers, "Magnetic striping techniques and characteristics," *Jour. SMPTE, 60:* 470–484, Apr. 1953, Pt. II.

384. Edward Schmidt and Ernest W. Franck, "Manufacture of magnetic recording materials," *Jour. SMPTE, 60:* 453–462, Apr. 1953, Pt. II.

385. Ernest W. Franck, "A study of dropouts in magnetic film," *Jour. SMPTE, 60:* 507–515, Apr. 1953, Pt. II.

386. G. A. del Valle and L. W. Ferber, "Notes on wear of magnetic heads," *Jour. SMPTE, 60:* 501–506, Apr. 1953, Pt. II.

387. J. D. Bick, "Methods of measuring surface induction of magnetic tape," *Jour. SMPTE, 60:* 516–525, Apr. 1953, Pt. II.

388. Ellis W. D'Arcy, "Standardization needs for 16 mm magnetic sound," *Jour. SMPTE, 60:* 526–534, Apr. 1953, Pt. II.

389. W. E. Theisen, "The history of nitrocellulose as a film base," *Jour. SMPE, 20:* 259–262, Mar. 1933.

390. J. M. Calhoun, "The physical properties and dimensional behavior of motion picture film," *Jour. SMPE, 43:* 227–267, Oct. 1944.

391. Charles R. Fordyce, "Improved safety motion picture film support," *Jour. SMPE, 51:* 331–350, Oct. 1948.

392. See Appendix.

393. Report of Historical Committee. *Jour, SMPE, 17:* 655–663, Oct. 1931. Address by Robert A. Millikan and communication by Wm. R. Ballard.

394. Paul Schubert, *The Electric Word, The Rise of Radio;* The MacMillan Co., New York. 1928, pp. 108 to 129.

395. W. Rupert Maclaurin, *Invention and Innovation in the Radio Industry,* The Macmillan Co., New York, 1949, pp. 95–98, 129.

396. Gleason L. Archer, *History of Radio,* publ. by the Am. Hist. Soc. Inc., New York, 1938, pp. 106–108, 114.

397. Irving Langmuir, "The effect of space charge and residual gases on thermionic currents in high vacuum," *Phys. Rev., N.S.* Vol. II: Nol 6, Dec. 1913.

398. Irving Langmuir, "The pure electron discharge and its applications in radio telegraphy and telephony," *Proc. IRE, 3:* 261, 1915.

400. Just and Hanaman, U.S. Pat. 1,108,502, "Incandescent bodies for electric lamps," filed 1905—issued 1912.

401. W. D. Coolidge, "Ductile tungsten," *Trans. AIEE, 29:* Pt. 2, 961–965.

402. C. G. Fink, "Ductile tungsten and molybdenum," *Trans. Electrochem. Soc., 17:* 229, 1910.

403. Irving Langmuir, "Thermal conduction and convection in gases at extremely high temperatures," *Trans. Electrochem. Soc., 20:* 225, 1911.

404. Irving Langmuir, "Convection and conduction of heat in gases," *Phys. Rev., 34:* 401, 1912.

405. Irving Langmuir, "Nitrogen filled lamps," *Gen. Elec. Rev., 16:* 688, 1913.

406. Irving Langmuir and J. A. Orange, "Tungsten lamps of high efficiency," *Trans. AIEE, Pt. II, 32:* p. 1935, 1913.

Joseph T. Tykociner:
Pioneer in Sound Recording

By JOHN B. McCULLOUGH

Professor Joseph T. Tykociner, now 90 years old, demonstrated his system of recording sound optically by means of a variable-density soundtrack in 1922. During that year he held one of the earliest public showings of talking motion pictures. His early background and later achievements are described.

On June 9, 1922, Prof. Joseph T. Tykociner of the University of Illinois presented one of the first public exhibitions of sound on motion-picture film. This did not, of course, represent the materialization of an entirely new idea. Such scientists as Edison, Lauste, Case, Sponable and De Forest had been interested in research leading to the goal of talking pictures before that date. The 1922 sound-on-film demonstration followed approximately one year of developmental work at the University (with a reported budget of less than $1000.00) but the idea of sound-on-film seems to have been in Tykociner's mind for nearly a quarter of a century. During those years the development of the electronic equipment that made it possible to put his ideas into effect was gradually taking place.

Joseph Tykocinski-Tykociner is a quiet, thorough scientist of great warmth and humanity. He is now retired, but despite his 90 years, he is still interested in scientific problems. At present he is studying phenomena associated with high voltage discharges through rarefied gases and their resemblance to the colors in the Aurora Borealis.

He was born in Poland in 1867. His father was a grain broker whose fervent hope it was that his son would follow in the family business. This hope was doomed when young Joseph, according to a later account, chanced upon a French magazine describing in words and pictures the telephone. The boy's older sister translated the article and the whole pattern of his future life was set. The impressions formed from this literary encounter were reinforced when Tykociner traveled to Warsaw and there had the opportunity of examining an actual telephone in operation. He was also impressed by the lights of that city which, as a junior engineer and later served with Telefunken in Berlin. A few years later he was asked to organize the wireless department of Siemens & Halske in Russia, and shortly thereafter became

for the first time, was electrically illuminated by means of arc lamps.

His father strongly opposed his desires for scientific training, and at the age of 18 the son abandoned home ties and emigrated to America. His scientific mind was ready for absorbing further technical advances of the time. The crude Edison phonograph aroused his keenest interest and he recognized a challenge to develop more accurate sound reproduction.

In 1897, while he was living in New York, he saw his first motion picture and the possibility of combining sound in synchronism with its visual images may then have occurred to his agile mind. During his years of service in the electrical industry this possibility continued to be a challenge.

He first experimented with a manometric flame with the thought of photographing on a moving film strip the fluctuations caused by the impingement of sound waves on a diaphragm. His plan was to run this film record, after processing, through a mechanism incorporating a light source which would pass through the variable density of its photographed sound image to the then crude selenium cell. Problems arose from the lack of inherent sensitiveness in the selenium cell and the nonexistence of the amplifying and electronic devices for proper reproduction.

In 1900 Tykociner's father relented and he returned to Poland where he finally began formal scientific training. Early in the century he became associated with the British Marconi Company its Chief Engineer and Manager of Research. He pioneered in short wave radio and was successful in equipping the Russian Navy with wireless equipment prior to the 1904 Russo-Japanese War.

During World War I, he headed the group supplying wireless equipment to the Russian Government, and it was at this time that he made the acquaintance of his good friend Dr. Vladimir Zworykin,

who was then in charge of the Imperial Russian Government's Department responsible for the procurement of communications equipment.

With the advent of the Bolshevik regime, he escaped to his native Poland and was successful in organizing its first wireless communication system.

In 1920 he returned permanently to the United States where he once again met Dr. Zworykin. In 1921 he became the first research professor of Electrical Engineering for the University of Illinois. Professor Ellery B. Paine, then head of the University's Department of Electrical Engineering, one day chanced to question Professor Tykociner regarding a possible project study of his personal choice, and it was only natural that he described his interest in photographing sound on a motion-picture film, stressing his belief that if perfected it would provide an entirely new educational and entertainment medium. Factors which aided this experimentation were the availability of the stable and sensitive photoelectric cell invented in 1913 by Professor Jakob Kunz, of the Department of Physics of the Univ. of Illinois, and a mercury vapor lamp that could be modulated for recording. These developments plus the availability of recently perfected vacuum tube amplifiers and oscillators were all needed to make his dream come true.

Development work proceeded rapidly, and he was able to give his first public demonstration by projecting and reproducing a composite print of both motion-picture and variable-density soundtrack before the Urbana Section of the American Institute of Electrical Engineers on June 9, 1922. It should be noted that Professor Tykociner never patented his devices nor was there any profit to either himself or the University of Illinois from this development. The sound reproduced was far from perfect, but it proved that the system would work provided there was additional electronic improvement. This demonstration, based on his studies,[*] heralded the advent of sound on film processes later brought to a higher stage of development.

[*] J. Tykocinski-Tykociner, "Photographic recording and photoelectric reproduction of sound," *Trans. SMPE, 16:* 90–119, May 1923.

Editorial Note: *Following the presentation of this paper at the 1957 Fall Convention at Philadelphia, the Tykociner film was shown. It is the Society's good fortune that the only existing 35mm print of this experimental film had been secured by Mr. McCullough before it had decomposed beyond reclamation. Crude by present standards, talking and projection speeds vary so widely that it is impossible to reproduce its feeble sound recording in a modern projector. The task of reproducing the sound on this historic film was assigned to Joseph E. Aiken, who also was personally acquainted with Prof. Tykociner. In the following paper, Mr. Aiken describes the technical problems involved in carrying out this assignment.*

Technical Notes and Reminiscences on the Presentation of Tykociner's Sound Picture Contributions

By JOSEPH E. AIKEN

The task of reproducing the sound on the historic film of Prof. J. T. Tykociner presented certain technical problems. These problems are described. The author's recollections of the sound on film demonstration in 1922 and his recollections of a personal association with Tykociner are recounted.

THE TASK of reproducing the sound on the historic film of Prof. J. T. Tykociner was a very welcome assignment, since the author had a brief personal association with him at the University of Illinois in 1921 and 1922 while he was conducting his experiments. At that time the author was a candidate for the degree of Bachelor of Science and for a thesis had built and was operating the University's first broadcasting station which employed the only two 50-w vacuum tubes on the campus. Professor Tykociner was permitted to borrow these tubes during the day with the agreement that he would return them before any evening broadcasts. This was a satisfactory arrangement except on one occasion when it was necessary to burglarize the Professor's laboratory in order for the station to go on the air.

The basic features of the recording system developed by Tykociner are described in his paper published in the *Transactions* of this Society in 1923 (referred to in the preceding paper). It is shown that exposure on the film was made by a modulated mercury vapor lamp, and reproduction of sound was by means of the photoelectric cell which had been developed by Prof. Jacob Kunz at the University. It is recalled that he used a carbon-grain telephone transmitter for a microphone, and an early Magnavox speaker with upright "morning glory" horn for reproduction. His penthouse sound recorder, mounted on a Bell & Howell "Professional" camera constituted an early "single system" equipment. He used a Simplex projector with the sound system mounted above the picture mechanism rather than below as in present practice.

Reproduction of the sound from the Tykociner film is handicapped by the location of the soundtracks which prevents their being played on a modern projector. His first recording, made in October 1921, placed the soundtrack down the center of the film (Fig. 1). In this recording, the Professor's voice announced that this was "an experiment in the reproduction of sound" and he counted numbers up to ten, concluding the test with a loud, "Hello!" Undoubtedly this is one of the oldest intelligible sound-on-film records which has been preserved. Figure 2 illustrates the track placement in all subsequent recordings. Here, the track is on the side of the film opposite from modern practice. It is approximately 0.155 in. in width and its outer edge is placed 0.125 in. from the edges of the sprocket holes. Thus, even with the film threaded in a reversed, or "turned over" position in a modern projector, the track is not scanned. Tykociner used several different film speeds and those examined were made at some higher rate than the present 90 ft/min.

Tape recordings to play at normal speed were made from some of the Tykociner film for the Historical Committee and were demonstrated at the 82d Convention in Philadelphia. To reproduce the track in the middle of the film (Fig. 1) the optical system of a Moviola reader was modified for center scanning and was clamped in a horizontal position on the side of a Westrex RA-1570 Re-recorder which served only as a film transport. With the re-recorder operating at 90 ft/min, the sound was transferred to a $\frac{1}{4}$-in. tape with Rangertone synchronizing pulses. In reproducing the sound of the violin scene (Fig. 2) it was found that the lateral adjustment of the optical system of the RA-1570 Re-recorder was sufficiently flexible to move the scanning into the soundtrack region when the film was threaded in a reversed position. To reduce noise caused by double exposure with picture on the inboard edge of the track, only the outboard 0.100 in. of the track was scanned. This sound was also transferred to $\frac{1}{4}$-in. tape with Rangertone synchronization.

It was necessary to devise means by which these tape recordings could be played back at continuously variable speeds. The Rangertone synchronizing system driving an Ampex Model 350 recorder was modified so that the inverter was fed from a variable-frequency oscillator instead of the usual corrected 60-cycle signal from the synchronizer. Thus, the speed of the tape could be made to vary over a wide range.

The reproduction speed of the tape recording of Tykociner's voice was established solely by ear, choosing a speed that seemed to provide the most natural voice pitch. The tape speed of the violin scene was established with more accuracy. The picture was shown to a violinist in repeated screenings who observed the fingering until he was able to write down the notes which were played by the original violinist. A recording of the modern violinist playing these same notes was made on 35mm magnetic film at standard speed. Then by listening to the Tykociner tape from one speaker, and comparing it with the new recording heard from another speaker, there was no difficulty in varying the frequency of the oscillator until the two recordings were brought into exact pitch. Finally the Tykociner sound on the tape was transferred at the newly established speed to a tape recorder operating at the standard speed of $7\frac{1}{2}$ in./sec.

By multiplying the ratio of the oscillator frequency to 60 cycles by 90 ft min, an approximation of the original film speed used by Tykociner was made. This proved to be 102 ft min for the first voice recording, and 162 ft min for the violin scene. Credit is due Jack C. Greenfield for the details of these procedures.

These tape recordings are not an accurate representation of the original quality and intelligibility of Tykociner's sound on film. By 1954 the only surviving Tykociner film was a print on nitrate base film which was in an advanced stage of decomposition. A dupe negative was made at that time and the print was destroyed. These tape recordings were made from a print from this dupe negative. Without question, some of the original quality of the variable-density soundtracks has been lost and the signal-to-noise ratio has suffered. The author witnessed the demonstration given at Urbana on June 9, 1922, and another demonstration on Municipal Pier, Chicago, in July 1922. Some scenes are recalled which are not included in the surviving film. There is a distinct recollection that the speech was intelligible throughout.

Presented on October 8, 1957, at the Society's Convention at Philadelphia by Joseph E. Aiken, Naval Photographic Center, Anacostia, D.C., in the form of a commentary accompanying the film presentation.
(This paper was received on February 15, 1958.)

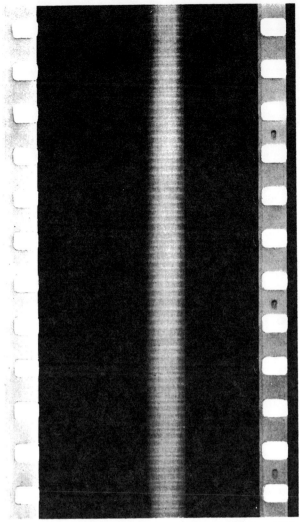

Fig. 1. Soundtrack recorded by Tykociner in October 1921.   Fig. 2. Typical Tykociner soundtrack and picture.

Part III
Historical Papers -- Television

Historical Sketch of Television's Progress

By L. R. LANKES*

Summary.—*This is a brief review of published material and, in its original form, was an introductory part of a symposium on the various aspects of television which will affect the photographic industry. It is not an attempt to answer directly the question, "Who invented television?" for, as Waldemar Kaempffert, Science Editor of the New York Times, has already pointed out, Professor William F. Ogburn in his "Social Change" has listed 148 major discoveries and inventions which were made simultaneously and independently by at least two workers in the particular field concerned in each case; and if the list were to include developments of secondary importance, it would undoubtedly have grown into a volume at least as large as an unabridged dictionary. Rather, then, it should be construed as an attempt to convey a general understanding of the subject by considering how it was pieced together.*

Of all the pursuits to which one can turn his attention, perhaps none has aroused a higher degree of curiosity, enthusiasm, and hope than the development of television. It has been said that television holds the promise of being the medium that can bring the peoples of far places emotionally face to face with one another's manners, customs, and problems, and thereby make them understand that they are all essentially human. It could be said that the motion picture also holds this promise since television is essentially motion pictures with radio as the means of conveyance. However, there may be advantages in television's claim to immediacy: namely, that what is being viewed at the receiver is occurring *now* at the transmitter.

Contrary to general opinion, the concept of television is not a twentieth-century product. Even in Biblical times abstract thinkers predicted that it would be possible to develop the ability to see events occurring beyond the horizon. However, the crystallization of specific inventions which led to television as we know it today, began with the transition of the eighteenth to the nineteenth century. The first items are Alexander Volta's electric battery, the voltaic pile; Professor Berzelius' isolation of the element selenium; Oersted's discovery of the principle of electromagnetic induction; and the efforts of Ampere, Ohm, and Faraday.

The middle of the nineteenth century might be said to have borne the infant, television, for in 1842 Alexander Bain,[1] an English physicist, first proposed a device to send pictures from one place to another by electric wires. Bain's plan was so correct basically that it embraced the fundamentals of all picture transmission, having recognized the particular problems posed by the need for synchronization between transmitter and receiver. In 1847, Bakewell[2] devised a "copying telegraph" employing an elementary scanning device. Specifically, this was an instrument for transmitting writing or drawings in the form of nonconducting shellac ink on tin foil. The foil was then wrapped around a cylinder which rose as it rotated, thereby tracing out a spiral with a fixed metal needle pressing against the foil. At the receiver, a similar cylinder was covered with chemically treated paper. In 1862, Abbe Caselli[2] transmitted the first electric picture from Amiens to Paris.

The latter part of the nineteenth century saw the groundwork for the construction of the present video industry. The light-sensitive properties of selenium were discovered in 1873 by a telegraph operator named May.[3] In a terminal station for the Atlantic cable on the coast of Ireland, May observed the effect of sunlight falling on selenium resistors in some of his circuits. This indicated that light values can be converted into equivalent electrical values. In 1875, G. R. Carey, in Boston, and Ayrton and Perry, in England, proposed to build a large mechanical eye using a plate of tiny selenium cells as the retina.[3] Each cell would be connected by wire to a corresponding spot on the receiver. Electromagnets connected to each of the small sections of the receiver plate were to regulate the amount of light on each section. Many other suggestions, all very similar in principle, were advanced through this period. These were followed by Sir William Crookes' discovery of cathode rays in his famous vacuum tube. In 1880, Leblanc[2] developed the complete principle of scanning wherein a picture is divided into lines and each line into tiny segments. Hertz,[4] in 1886, confirmed Maxwell's theories of electricity and discovered the photoelectric effect in 1887, when he noticed that a spark could be made to jump over a gap more readily if one of the electrodes were illuminated than if the event occurred in darkness. The German Hallwachs[4] later studied the photoelectric effect systematically and concluded that light set free electrical particles from the electrode surface. Sir J. J. Thompson identified them as electrons and Einstein announced the theory of the photoelectric effect. The practical side was advanced by Elster[4] and Geitel[4] who, as early as 1890, built practical photoelectric cells. Thus the method was defined by which a television camera would turn a picture into electricity.

As a noteworthy aside, Thomas Edison[5] filmed his first motion picture in 1889; and Marconi,[6] in 1895, sent and received his first wireless signals across his father's estate.

Coincidental with these latter developments came the invention, in 1884, by the German Nipkow[4] of the rotating scanning disk. This disk made use of the very significant technique, previously suggested, of dissecting the scene to be transmitted into points of light which would then be measured on a time scale in orderly fashion. Nipkow's work ranks high in the history of the medium because he realized so early a system which was not improved upon, basically, for nearly fifty years.

In 1890, the Englishman Sutton[4] proposed a system for a television receiver which ranks in importance with Nipkow's system for the transmitter. Sutton's apparatus used a scanning disk and a light source controlled by a Kerr cell. This method of reassembling the image was likewise remarkable in that it was used widely in practical television systems for nearly forty years.

At the turn of the century, Sir J. J. Thompson,[7] in his work to determine the charge-to-mass ratio of the electron, showed that the cathode ray was in reality a beam of high-speed electrons. His methods involved the application of both electric and magnetic deflecting forces. At about the same time, Professor Braun[8] built a cold-cathode-ray tube. With it he could show the effect of magnetism on electron beams in tracing their paths on a fluorescent screen. From the viewpoint of television, this was to be the means of scanning control for Crookes' cathode rays. Amplitude control, on the other hand, was to come later.

By the end of the first decade of the twentieth century, Professor Boris Rosing[2] had patented a television system, using a receiver resembling the modern set, based on the Braun cathode-ray tube. In 1911, A. A. Campbell Swinton,[3] a man of great imagination and foresight, saw the possibility of tele-

*Eastman Kodak Company, Rochester 4, New York.

vision communication with variations of Rosing's cathode-ray tubes at both transmitter and receiver. Recent years have shown that Swinton actually predicted television apparatus used today, having developed the theory of a cathode-ray-tube camera. Meanwhile, Knudson[2] had sent the first drawing by radio.

Only a few of the early discoveries and inventions are directly employed in modern television. However, the original work and inventions gave impetus to experiments in demonstrating that light could be converted into electrical impulses which, in turn, could be transmitted and later reconverted. Fortunately for television, the development of the radio and electrical arts coincided with the advanced phases of research in the fields of optics and vision.

World War I delayed progress universally, for the next important date is 1923 when Zworykin filed patent application on the first electronic television camera tube, the iconoscope, wherein the means for scanning control, as well as for picture signal-amplitude control, were all self-contained on a completely electronic basis. While the idea had been proposed early in the art, this was the first practical means of achieving it.

At this time J. L. Baird[4] in England, and C. F. Jenkins[4] in the United States, working independently, produced and demonstrated systems of television based on mechanical scanning through the use of the Nipkow disk or something similar to it. The disk carried holes along a spiral in such a way that a scene, when viewed through a portion of it, would be broken into parallel lines or arcs, thereby providing the means of measuring light values along the short time-base which represented the frame interval. The pictures were mere shadowgraphs at first, but Baird soon demonstrated television transmission of half-tone pictures as well as infrared television.

This method of scanning, having serious limitations in definition, is not in use today, nor is the receiving system that reconstructed the picture by reversing the process. While the low-definition (less than 60-line) images of those days may seem to have little bearing on techniques which produce present-day, continuous-tone pictures in a 525-line system, much of the theory which makes present equipment possible was proved during this mechanical era.

In 1927 the Bell System demonstrated the transmission of television over substantial distances; between Washington and New York over wire line, and between Whippany, New Jersey; and New York over radio link. With this was published an analysis, thorough for the time, of the transmission problems facing television, particularly the frequency bandwidth requirements which have become so characteristic of the art.[9]

The decade 1925 to 1935 produced many developments in steady succession. These began with the National Broadcasting Company's first radio network and Warner Brothers' "Vitaphone" sound-on-disk system synchronized with motion pictures. Concurrently Congress established the Federal Radio Commission; progress continued with Bairds' first trans-Atlantic television picture and his first crude systems of color and stereoscopic television; Farnsworth's system and Zworykin's system of all-electric television were introduced employing special cathode-ray receiver tubes called kinescopes; Bell Laboratories demonstrated television in color, delivering a picture of postage-stamp size; theater television was shown on screens as wide as 10 feet; two-way-wire television-telephone demonstrations were made by Bell; improved photoelectric cells and electronic tubes were introduced; an extensive program of field tests by the Radio Corporation of America was initiated starting with 240-line all-electronic television employing radio relay, to continue right through the period of commercial operation; and, finally, the 1935 announcement of the principle of frequency modulation by Edwin Armstrong.

Through the efforts of men like Zworykin, Engstrom, and Goldsmith of RCA; Farnsworth; Ives and others at the American Telephone and Telegraph Company; Alexanderson of General Electric; Dumont, and Goldmark of the Columbia Broadcasting System, well-planned and well-executed programs made public participation in the United States possible in 1934.

The Philips Company of Holland built the first iconoscope in Europe in 1935. Television transmitters appeared in places such as the Eiffel Tower and Stockholm. As the advance continued, A. T. and T. successfully demonstrated the capabilities of coaxial cables in 1936. Such cables were laid from New York to Philadelphia, from Paris to Bordeaux, and from Berlin to Nuremberg. The first patent on coaxial cable was granted in England at this time and cables were laid from the British Broadcasting Corporation transmitter to Buckingham Palace and Victoria Station for the first direct televising of coronation-procession street scenes.[10–12]

In 1938 television signals from London, on ultra-short waves, were picked up on Long Island, although badly distorted.

The point was reached wherein one saw the telecasting of plays from thea-ter stages, the New York World's Fair, major-league baseball, and professional football. Meanwhile RCA introduced an improved television camera tube, the orthicon. It is beyond the scope of this paper to enumerate the many developments from that point to date.

The lack of uniformity in choice of number of lines for the picture structure was never satisfactory to the non-technical observer who was quick to compare television with motion pictures. Because of this, and in keeping with the steady advances, "definition" was standardized at 343 lines in 1935. Later this was raised to 441. In 1940 it was increased to 525 where it remains as today's standard.

Although World War II brought an apparent period of inactivity, an abundance of knowledge and technical personnel grew out of government-sponsored radar and guided-missile programs. Accelerated research and development produced items such as the high-sensitivity image-orthicon and phosphors to withstand the bombardment of highly accelerated electron beams, for brighter pictures.

The highly controversial issue of color versus black-and-white television brought the industry to a virtual standstill. After this was settled early in 1947 in favor of black-and-white, the prospective broadcaster, the equipment manufacturer, and the receiving-set purchaser appeared ready to invest in the fast-growing business. By December 31, 1947, the score totaled 12 cities with television service; 18 stations operating and 55 licensees; 287 sponsors; 142,400 receivers in private homes; 27,600 receivers in public places; 195,000 total receiver production; and an estimated audience of 1,200,000 with assurance of nationwide networks in the reasonably near future.

BIBLIOGRAPHY

(1) RCA Institutes, Inc.. "Radio Facsimile," vol. 1, 1938.

(2) American Television Society Inc., "American Television Directory," 1st Ann. Ed., 1946.

(3) Lee de Forest, "Television To-day and Tomorrow," Dial Press, Inc., New York, N. Y., 1942.

(4) J. Porterfield and K. Reynolds, "We Present Television," W. W. Norton and Co., New York, N. Y., 1940.

(5) Deems Taylor, "A Pictorial History of the Movies," Simon and Schuster, New York, N. Y., 1943.

(6) New York World Telegram, "Chronology of radio and television," Source: The National Broadcasting Company, The World Almanac, 1945, p. 650.

(7) J. J. Thompson, "Cathode rays," Phil. Mag. vol. 44, p. 293; 1897.

(8) F. Braun, "Ueber ein Verfahren zur Demonstration und zum Studium des zeitlichen Verlaufs variabler Strome." Ann.

Phys. und Chemie (Wied. Ann), New Series, vol. 60, p. 552; 1897.

(9) H. E. Ives, F. Gray, J. W. Horton, R. C. Mathes, H. M. Stoller, E. R. Morton, D. K. Gannett, E. I. Green, and E. L. Nelson, "Television Symposium," *Trans Amer. Inst. Elec. Eng.,* vol. 46, pp. 913-962; June, 1927.

(10) British Patent No. 284,005.

(11) K. Lake, "The coaxial cable," *Telev. and Short Wave World,* (known as *Television* (London), prior to 1939), vol. 10, p. 202; April, 1937.

(12) "Special television cable," *Elec. Rev.* (London), vol. 120, p. 889; June 11, 1937.

(13) O. E. Dunlap, "The Future of Television," Harper Brothers, New York, N. Y., 1942.

(14) William C. Eddy, "Television—The Eyes of Tomorrow," Prentice-Hall, New York, N. Y., 1945.

(15) D. G. Fink, "Principles of Television Engineering," McGraw-Hill Publishing Company, New York, N. Y., 1940.

(16) P. C. Goldmark, J. N. Dyer, E. R. Piore, and J. M. Hollywood, "Color television," *J. Soc. Mot. Pict. Eng.,* vol. 38, pp. 311-353; April, 1942.

(17) R. W. Hubbell, "4000 Years of Television," G. P. Putnam Sons, New York, N. Y., 1942.

(18) M. S. Kiver, "Television Simplified," D. Van Nostrand and Company, New York, N. Y., 1946.

(19) E. J. G. Lewis, "Television" (Dictionary), Pitman Publishing Company, New York, N. Y., 1936.

(20) National Television System Committee, "Television Standards and Practices," McGraw-Hill Publishing Company, New York, N. Y., 1943.

(21) Radio Corporation of America, "Collected Addresses and Papers on the Future of the New Art and Its Recent Technical Developments," vol. 1, 1936; vol. 2, 1937; vol. 3, 1946; vol. 4, 1947.

(22) "Televiser," *J. Telev.,* vol. 4, November-December, 1937.

The Early Days of Television

By JOHN V. L. HOGAN

This paper describes the beginnings of television, both in the U.S.A. and abroad. Once there had been formulated the desire to transmit pictorial intelligence, including motion, from one point to another, many ingenious attempts to solve the technical problems were proposed. The paper describes a number of the more significant early steps and points out that although they were broadly successful in obtaining the primary objective of "seeing at a distance," they were limited as to the amount of pictorial matter that could be transmitted.

HUMAN BEINGS, as well as the so-called lower animals, have long had the desire to see what is going on at places beyond their normal range of vision. It takes no Sherlock Holmes to deduce that when a dog stops running after something and sits up on his haunches, peering ahead attentively, he is impelled by some urge to see more than he could have seen if he had kept his forefeet on the ground. This same urge for expanded vision had certainly been felt by others than our canine friends. Maybe it explains why the giraffe and the ostrich grew long necks. However, except perhaps for the development of an erect posture, the human species seems to have attempted to extend its range of vision without falling back on biology or physical evolution. In order "to get a better view" of something or other, we first climbed trees. I have not been able to fix the earliest date when humans decided that they would prefer themselves to see what was going on beyond their normal limits of visual observation, rather than to be told about it by someone else. I suspect that our species made that decision a long time ago. Perhaps it has come down to us from Adam and Eve.

The first suggestions that machinery could be built to accomplish the miracle of seeing what was happening somewhere else were made many years later. Probably the first contribution to the solution was purely optical, coming into being with the invention of the equivalent of field glasses, about 1600 A.D. It had long been known that if a man stood on a mountain and looked into a valley or to another nearby mountain, he could see more of what was going on there than if he had stayed home. He could see large objects or mass movements, but he could not see much detail. So the optical experts came up with the ancient telescope, which supplemented the lenses of the observer's own eyes. With such an optical aid, he could see more detail, but only in a restricted field. Still he was unable to look around

a corner, unless he could persuade somebody to set up a mirror at the strategic time and place.

This human desire to see what was going on somewhere beyond the range of normal vision, and even around corners, led to our modern science of television. The first machines that carried us forward to television were probably those described by Bain in 1842 and by Bakewell in 1847. These inventors proposed schemes for the electrical transmission of still pictures from one point to another. Their systems provided for "seeing at a distance" or "seeing by electricity" in a limited sense, for they transmitted visual information over a telegraph line which could extend for a considerable distance and could go around almost any number of corners. However, the machines could handle only one view at a time and very slowly at that. Therefore, they could not reproduce motion, which is an essential part of complete vision. Bain and Bakewell laid the foundation for the modern facsimile transmission of text and pictures, and they introduced the process of synchronous sequential scanning which is now used in both facsimile and television, but their mechanical light-sensing devices were too crude to stimulate much thinking directed toward electrical transmission of scenes involving motion.

It was in 1873 that a British telegraph operator named May discovered that the chemical element selenium had the curious property of responding to light

by changing its electrical resistance. This discovery was put before the engineering public by Willoughby Smith. Almost immediately thereafter, suggestions as to how it might be possible to "see by electricity" began to crop up thick and fast.

The first electric television system was proposed only two years later, in 1875, by George R. Carey of Boston, Mass. This system was in many ways analogous to the human eye. Carey planned to build a transmitter comprising a mosaic of light-sensitive selenium cells and a receiver consisting of a similar bank or mosaic of electric lights. It is worth while to examine the principle of such a system, for, so far as I have been able to find, it offers the earliest plan that would transmit to a distant point not merely the form of a visible object, but also its motion.

One way in which such a system might operate is illustrated in Figs. 1 and 2. Figure 1 shows an elementary circuit that would meet Carey's requirements. The transmitter is shown at the left and the receiver at the right. If the selenium cell at the transmitter is in darkness, its electrical resistance is very high and the current from battery B_1 flowing through the line wire and returning through the ground connections E_2 and E_1 is insufficient to operate the relay at the receiver. Consequently the conditions are as illustrated in Fig. 1, and the lamp at the receiver is not turned on. Thus we have both transmitter and receiver in the dark or "black" situation. But if the selenium cell at the transmitter is illuminated by a bright light, its resistance falls, the current from B_1 increases and the relay at the receiver operates to close its contacts and to light the receiver lamp with current from battery B_2. This represents the lighted or "white" situation. It is a very elementary type of television, but an observer at the re-

Presented on May 7, 1954, at the Society's Convention at Washington, D.C., by John V. L. Hogan, President, Hogan Laboratories, Inc., 155 Perry St., New York 14.
(This paper was received on May 21, 1954.)

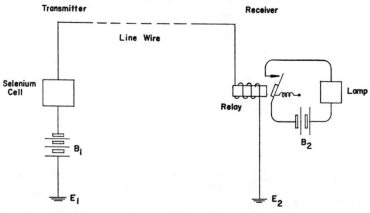

Figure 1

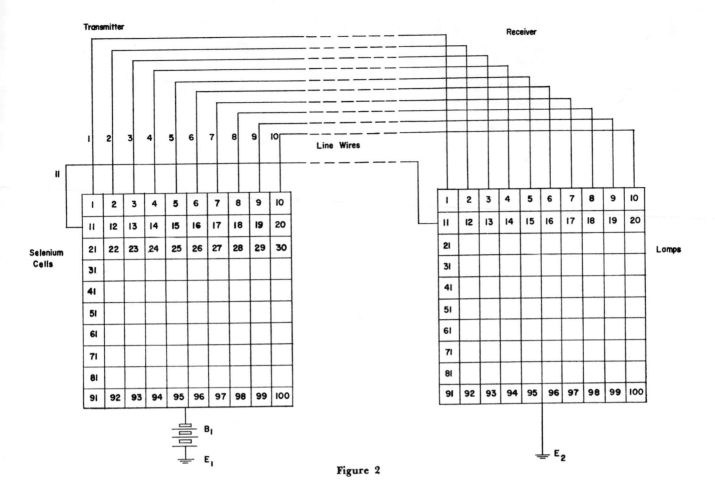

Figure 2

ceiver would know whether or not the selenium cell at the distant transmitter was illuminated. That information he could not have without the help of a system such as is shown in Fig. 1.

Carey proposed to send, from a transmitter to a distant point, much more information than the equipment shown in Fig. 1 could deliver. Figure 2 shows how he planned to accomplish that result.

Imagine the sending mechanism to consist of 100 light-sensitive cells, arranged in 10 rows of 10 cells each. The receiver comprises 100 small electric lights, also arranged in a square with 10 lights on a side. Cell 1, at the upper left corner of the sending mosaic will be connected by wire 1 with light 1, at the corresponding upper-left corner of the receiving mosaic. Cell 2 of the sender will be similarly connected by wire 2 to control light 2 at the receiver. Each of the remaining 98 cells will be connected by a separate wire to that one of the remaining 98 receiver lights which corresponds with its position in the bank. Thus 100 wires must be run from sender to receiver, plus a wire or ground common return circuit, such as from E_2 to E_1, and there must be connected into the system an on-off relay for each lamp together with the required sources of electrical power. In Fig. 2, I have omitted the relays and the battery B_2 for lighting the receiver lamps. Except

for the 100-wire cable and the 100 relays, the system is not very complicated.

But how does it work? Well, if the sending mosaic is in darkness, all the lamps at the receiver will be turned off, and the screen will be dark. If the sending mosaic is completely illuminated, all the receiver lamps will be turned on and the whole screen area will be brightly lighted. In either of these simple cases the receiver gives a true picture of what the sending mosaic sees, that is, either no light or full light. It will also give a true picture of any object inserted between the light source and the pickup mosaic at the sender, within the limits of definition imposed by our assumption that the entire picture contains only 100 elements. Suppose that at the transmitting station we hold a rod horizontally across the middle of the mosaic, and that the thickness of that rod is such that it will shadow the two middle rows of light-sensitive cells. Light will thus be cut off from cells 51–60 and 61–70, and the corresponding lights at the receiver will go out. Thus any one looking at the receiver mosaic will see a horizontal black bar in the middle of the screen, which is a true picture of what we have shown to the transmitter. If the rod is held vertically in midscreen, cells 5–6, 15–16, 25–26 . . . 95–96 will be shadowed and the corresponding lights at the receiver will be extinguished. Thus an

observer would see a centrally located vertical black bar, which again is a true picture of what was presented to the transmitter. It is not hard to appreciate that this crude system has the capacity of presenting at a distance, by electrical means, a visual image of the form of any object shown to the transmitter. If one desires to transmit pictures of more complicated subjects than rods, rectangles, alphabetical characters and so forth, it is only necessary to increase the resolving power of the system by adding light-sensitive cells at the pickup, together with corresponding wire-lines, relays and receiver-lights.

Perhaps I should insert here a word of warning as to this apparently simple way of increasing resolution by adding elements. We have been considering a 10×10 system, having 100 picture elements. The human eye uses a mosaic having millions of elements, so that a Carey television system which would convey as much visual information as the eye delivers to the brain would be many thousand times as complex as that shown in Fig. 2.

This multichannel television system is also capable of transmitting moving images, within the technical limitations of resolution and speed which are inherent in the equipment available at any particular date. It is not hard to see how motion can be reproduced at a distant point. Let us again imagine the fully illuminated transmitting mosaic and, therefore, the fully lighted receiving screen. Let us take the same rod, held horizontally above the transmitter cell-bank. Let us move the rod downward, so that first its shadow blacks out cells 1–10 and (at the receiver) lamps 1–10. Moving the rod a little further downward blacks out cells and lamps 11–20 also, and the receiving observer sees the full-width image of the rod at the top of his screen. As we continue to move the horizontal rod downward, the shadow leaves cells 1–10 and covers cells 21–30. So, at the receiver, the black band has moved down one step. This continues row by row until the rod has moved so far down that it no longer shadows the lowest row of cells (91–100). If the speed of downward movement of the rod does not overtax the frequency response of the light-sensitive cells at the transmitter, and of the relays and the lights available for the receiver, a distant picture showing the form and movement of the original scene will be created. That is television.

But of course it is television of a very crude type, and of little practical value. We may doubt the possibility of finding selenium cells that would turn lamps off or on, and we may point out that the selenium cell is so sluggish in operation that only very slow motion could be picked up and transmitted to the receiver. The basic defect of the system, however, is that a separate communication channel is required for each picture element to be transmitted. In the example that we have considered, the picture was divided into 100 elements, which would suffice to handle only the simplest images. Yet 100 wire circuits were required. To pick up and reproduce scenes having sufficient detail to tell even a simple story would call for a mosaic having at least 50 cells on a side, or a total of 2500. Such a system would require at least 2500 individual circuits from sender to receiver, and yet would convey very little pictorial information as judged by today's standards. When Shefford Bidwell much later considered Carey's simultaneous system, about 1908, he assumed that 90,000 circuits would be necessary to handle an adequate picture. I do not need to emphasize the impracticability of providing so many individual circuits from the transmitter to each receiver.

The scientists of the 1880 decade appear to have recognized the necessity of finding some way to obviate the need for using a separate channel to represent each picture element. Bain and Bakewell, nearly forty years earlier, had introduced the scanning idea of looking at a picture point by point and printing a copy of it, point by point, at a distant receiver. Faraday, even earlier, had indicated that if a series of time-spaced progressive still pictures could be rapidly

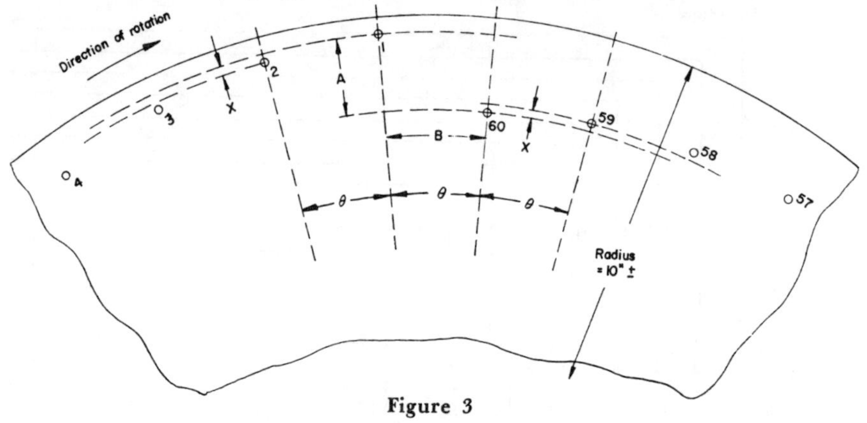

Figure 3

presented to the eye of a human observer the series of still pictures would be blended together because of the eye's "persistence of vision," and a realistic illusion of motion would result. If these two principles could be combined, so that ten or more completely scanned pictures could be transmitted per second, over a single channel, and could be displayed by a receiver, the multichannels of the simultaneous system would no longer be required. Carey later proposed the idea of moving the transmitting selenium cell in a spiral path, so examining the original image from point to point, but apparently he had in mind only a receiver that would print a simple picture on paper. Thus his concept seems to have been more nearly related to what we now call facsimile than to television. The same is true of the linear-scanning system constructed by Bidwell in 1881.

Looking back from today, it appears that Paul Nipkow was the first man to realize that television could be accomplished over a single channel by optically scanning the original scene, point by point, and fast enough to take advantage of human persistence of vision. About 1884 Nipkow explained that an image could be progressively scanned, point by point and line by line, if it were projected upon or viewed through the outer area of a large rotating disk having a number of small holes in spiral arrangement. Because the principles suggested by Nipkow were found useful in the first practical television operations and because his idea of progressive linear optical scanning is the basis of today's television, we should examine his 1884 proposal in some detail.

Figure 3 shows a portion of a scanning disk such as Nipkow described. The area to be scanned has the vertical dimension A and the horizontal dimension B. If we assume the conventional motion-picture aspect ratio of 4:3, A may be $\frac{3}{4}$ in. and B 1 in. Figure 3 shows the first and the last five holes in the disk, the holes being marked 1 to 5 on the left and 56 to 60 on the right. Since there are 60 of these holes equally spaced about the 360° comprising the

circumference of the disk, the angle θ must be 1/60 of 360°, or 6°. The radial center-to-center spacing of successive holes, indicated as X, must be 1/60 of $\frac{3}{4}$ in. (dimension A), or 0.0125 in. The diameter of each hole may be something over this figure, perhaps 1/50 of an inch. To get 60 holes one inch apart around the outer portion of the disk, it must have been a circumference of something over 60 in. or a diameter of about 20 in. Finally, the disk must be rotated at a speed that will scan the picture area at the rate desired. If the image is to be completely scanned in 1/20 sec, the disk must revolve at 1200 rpm.

Now let us see how such a scanning disk may be used in a television transmitter. Nipkow planned to project the scene upon the area A by B shown in Fig. 3. On the other side of the disk there was to be a selenium cell, the electrical output of that cell being delivered to the receiver over a single circuit. That cell had to look at each element of the picture to be transmitted and to translate its light value into a proportional current. As hole number one swept across the top line of the scene, the amount of light passing through the hole and, therefore, the electrical output of the selenium cell varied in accordance with the picture density, from element to element. When the scanning of the first line was completed, the second hole of the disk began to pass across the image and to scan the second line, a little below the first. Thus successive lines from the first (at the top) to the last (at the bottom) were scanned, and the selenium cell passed a series of current values corresponding to the density of all of the elements in the picture area, one after another.

This process of scanning successive points of the picture, one at a time and one after another, is quite different from the operation of the simultaneous mosaic system that I first described. The simultaneous system required a separate communication channel or wire, from sender to receiver, for each picture element. The scanning system requires only a single connecting channel, because the signals representing elemental picture brilliance are transmitted over that channel in a time series, one after another. But its use puts a heavy burden on the equipment in terms of frequency response to light variations, because, if motion is to be shown by relying upon persistence of vision, varying current corresponding to all of the picture elements of the image must be transmitted in less than 1/10 of a second.

How did Nipkow propose to make visible his single-channel transmission of a changing scene, at a distant receiving location? He showed that all one needed was a light source whose brilliance could be controlled by the arriving signals, plus a viewing disk which was substantially a duplicate of the scanning disk used at the transmitter, plus some way of keeping the sending disk and the receiving disk revolving at exactly the same speed and in the same phase. The light source at the receiver was to illuminate the picture area A X B on one side of the receiving disk, and the viewer was to look at the light source through the holes in the disk. Thus he would see only one element of the scene at a time. If the sending and receiving disks were rotated at the same speed and in the same phase, the particular picture element seen by the receiving observer at any particular instant would have the same position in the picture field as the element being projected upon the transmitter's selenium cell at the same instant. If a picture element being scanned at the transmitter was bright or brilliantly lighted, the selenium cell would let through enough current to light the lamp at the receiver, and the observer would see a pinpoint of light through the hole in the receiving disk at the appropriate position in the picture field. Similarly, if the element being scanned was dark, the selenium cell would not pass enough current to light the receiving lamp, and that particular spot of the area being viewed at the receiver would appear black to the observer. Thus the entire picture was to be analyzed point by point and line by line at the transmitter and to be simultaneously synthesized, point by point and line by line at the receiver. All of the picture elements in the picture were to be successively scanned so rapidly that the human eye would retain its impression of the brilliance of the first element, in the upper lefthand corner of the scene, until the brightness of the last element, in the lower righthand corner, had been transmitted. Thus the observer would appear to see a complete picture although he was actually viewing only one element at a time.

Carey and Nipkow were not the only inventors to propose electrical television systems in what we may call the speculative period from say 1875 to 1890. Senlecq, in France, Ayrton, Perry and Bidwell in England, and Bell in the United States were among those who suggested various types of equipment that might have been used for television. Senlecq's 1880 scheme was of particular interest, for his transmitter comprised a bank of small selenium cells, like Carey's, and his receiver a similar bank of incandescing platinum wires. However, he did not plan to connect each cell to its corresponding lamp by means of a separate line wire. Instead, he advanced the idea of using synchronous distributors at sender and receiver to connect a single line wire successively to each selenium cell and to the corresponding lamp. Here we have a scanning system of an electrical, rather than an optical, nature.

None of these workers in the "speculative period" produced and demonstrated a working television system. So far as I know, nobody developed hardware that could effectively meet the practical requirements of these early television systems until the twentieth century was well on its way. But all of us should remember that many, if not most, of the basic principles of today's television had been thought of some sixty to eighty years ago. That early thinking was highly creditable and constructive, and vastly more important than mere intellectual exercise.

Why did not these inventors produce working television systems? Well, what would we do in television today if we were limited to the slow and weak response of the selenium cell, as compared to the rapid action and high sensitiveness of the modern photocell? What would we do if we had no vacuum-tube amplifier? What would we do if we had no light source whose brilliance could be easily and rapidly controlled by varying the applied voltage? Before 1900 not even one of those essential elements was available. But soon thereafter they began to appear, at first in undeveloped and unsatisfactory but nevertheless promising forms, and in the first two decades of the twentieth century all of them became practical. By 1913 Elster and Geitel had produced the fast and sensitive potassium hydride photoelectric cell, and de Forest had succeeded in making the grid audion work as an audio-frequency amplifier. Thus two essential tools for practical television came on the horizon. The third need was a light source which could be rapidly controlled in brilliance by a varying electric current. A number of magnetic shutter or light-valve schemes were available, at least in theory, but the most practical solution seems to have been provided by D. McFarlan Moore, then of the General Electric Co. About 1917 he produced a negative-glow neon lamp which could be electrically modulated in brilliance. Working with Jenkins in the following years, and using the de Forest amplifier, he developed this glow lamp into an operative light source for a television receiver.

It was not until 1925, however, that these new tools were well enough understood and sufficiently available to end the hiatus of some thirty years that separated the speculative period ending about 1890 from what might be called the experimental period beginning about 1920.

1925 seems to have been the "magic year" for the first electrical transmissions of moving images from one place to another. Jenkins in the United States and Baird in the United Kingdom are both credited with accomplishing such image transmission within the first half of that year. Historians do not agree as to which of these experimenters should be recognized as having been in the lead. The available records suggest that the credit should be more or less equally divided between them, for they seem to have been running a neck-and-neck race for a number of years. Sometimes one was ahead and sometimes the other but together they did a great deal to bring television before the public. Each of them showed considerable ingenuity in applying the newly available scientific tools to the practical application of the principles that had long before been suggested by Nipkow and his contemporaries. Both Baird and Jenkins adopted the Nipkow single-channel time sequential or scanning system rather than the Carey multiple-channel simultaneous or mosaic system. The validity of their choice has been demonstrated by the fact that all television from 1925 to the present day has followed their lead in that respect. Many of the things that Baird and Jenkins accomplished should be recognized as new and useful, and, therefore, as "inventions." In any event, 1925 saw television as a fact and not merely as a dream. The experimental period was about five years old.

Once it had been proved that the early proposals for electrically seeing at a distance could really be implemented (or physically "reduced to practice") by using the newly available electronic tools, television entered an unbroken phase of application and improvement. From 1925 to the present time there has been no hiatus comparable to that which occurred between 1890 and 1920.

That is undoubtedly because after 1920 the experimenters and scientists had enough tools available to assure them that acceptable television could be developed. But what is acceptable television?

Perhaps the best way to answer that question is to review what actually happened.

In 1927, two years after the first showings by Baird and Jenkins, the Bell System demonstrated the results of a television research that must have been begun long before. Bell System engineers then showed how the Nipkow disk, the Elster and Geitel photocell, the de Forest amplifier and the Moore glow lamp could be used to transmit scenes electrically, either by wire or by radio, over distances of many miles. To attain this result they added new products of their own ingenuity and "know how" to what had been suggested by the pioneer thinkers and doers. The Bell accomplishments, for which Dr. Ives was largely responsible, marked a milestone in the progress of television and probably did more to show its practical utility than had any of the prior experiments. The picture was scanned in 50 horizontal lines at the rate of 18 frames/sec, which was adequate for the reproduction of easily recognizable full-face portraits or of relatively simple views. The halftone or photographic-transmission was good, so that the system was not limited to black-and-white silhouettes, and provision was made for the delivery of sound along with the picture. Thus an observer in New York could talk by telephone with another person in Washington and, during the entire conversation, could see a televised image of the distant speaker. For such "person to person" television communication the received image on the Nipkow disk was viewed through a lens, so that the picture appeared to be about $2 \times 2\frac{1}{2}$ in. in size.

To enable a number of viewers to see the same received picture, the Bell engineers devised a special neon glow lamp made up of a gas-filled tube bent back and forth to cover an area of some five square feet. The arriving picture currents were fed to external electrodes on this tube by way of a rotary distributor which was driven in synchronism with the distant scanning disk. Thus elemental areas of the display system were successively lighted to an intensity corresponding to the brightness of the similarly placed element in the original

scene. A complete field was scanned in about 1/18 sec, and so the observers could see the outlines, shading and motion of the televised view.

The next year, 1928, the General Electric Co., from Station WGY in Schenectady, began the regular radio broadcasting of televised pictures accompanied by sound. This work, under the guidance of Dr. Alexanderson, led to the showing of large-screen projected television pictures. The first broadcasts were put on the air three times a week, and used 24-line scanning which limited the pictorial content to about one-quarter of that which characterized the Bell System demonstrations. In July of the same year, 1928, Jenkins began television broadcasting from his experimental radio station W3XK near Washington, D.C. His pictures were scanned at 48 lines/frame and 15 frames/sec. Most of his subjects were on film, so that he was able to replace the Nipkow disk having spirally arranged holes by a scanning disk in which the holes or lenses were placed circumferentially at a single radial distance from the driving shaft. Fast or horizontal line scanning was accomplished by the sweeping of these apertures across the film, but the line-by-line advance or slow scanning in the vertical dimension was had by continuously moving the film lengthwise.

The increasing interest in television was shown by the establishment of additional picture-broadcasting stations in the next few years. In 1929 Baird, cooperating with the British Broadcasting Company, began to send out pictures scanned at 30 lines per frame and $12\frac{1}{2}$ frames/sec. That same year several new stations went on the air in the United States, including W2XBS of the National Broadcasting Company and my own W2XR. We both used a somewhat higher scanning standard, namely 60 lines/frame and 20 frames/sec.

If one must choose a date for the end of the "the early days of television" it might as well be 1930. By then the possibilities of mechanically driven optical

scanning systems had been quite thoroughly explored, and it had become evident that the apparently insatiable demand for the electrical transmission of more and more picture content could be appeased, if not satisfied, only by making use of the cathode-ray tube for fast scanning. The change to today's all-electronic television did not come at a single date. There was a large overlapping period in which the possibilities of cathode-ray tubes were being explored and the limits of mechano-optical television systems were being determined. In fact, the two concepts were proposed for use together in various ways. Rosing in 1907, suggested a mirror-drum transmitter to be used with a cathode-ray tube receiver. The Radio Corporation of America in 1932 used a refined mechanical scanner to feed television signals to a cathode-ray tube display. My own Laboratory worked out a television receiver in which a cathode-ray tube was used for the required fast scanning but the area or slow-scanning presentation was provided by rotating concave mirrors.

In closing, let me apologize for having omitted discussion of the early progress in connection with the difficulties involved in providing synchronization between sender and receiver. Briefly, the synchronizing problem was attacked by every means from clock work to electronic frequency standards, but was solved as a practical matter by using the same 60-cycle power source to drive the motors at the sender and at the receiver. The Bell Telephone Laboratories, in their 1927 work, used a much more elegant but equally practical system.

I have now carried you, at least in thought, from 1875 to 1930. In 1875 there was suggested a television system that could be made to work. In 1930 there were television pictures on the air, available to any one who had a suitable receiver. In another paper Mr. Jensen will tell you how these broadcast pictures have been improved in content and in quality over the past 25 years.

The Evolution of Modern Television

By A. G. JENSEN

This paper first describes the gradual transition from mechanical television to the present all-electronic television. It gives a brief account of the major developments leading to the present types of pickup and reproducing equipment, and describes the growth of network facilities which has made possible the present wide distribution of television programming in the United States.

In THIS PAPER modern television implies the type of television now used for commercial broadcasting in the United States and elsewhere. This is an all-electronic type of television which utilizes electronic pickup tubes of one form or another at the transmitting end and cathode-ray tubes for displaying the picture at the receiving end. Such a system is in contrast to earlier experimental television systems using mechanical-optical scanning means both at the transmitting end and at the receiving end. These earlier types of systems have been described by J. V. L. Hogan in a companion paper.[1]

It is obvious that the transition from the earlier mechanical systems to our present electronic systems was a very gradual one. Roughly speaking, we may say that the period before 1930 was that of the all-mechanical television system, the period from 1930 to 1940 was the period of the partially electronic system, and the period from 1940 on was that of the all-electronic television system. It was natural that the comparatively simple cathode-ray tube at the receiving end should be perfected sooner than the more complicated pickup tubes at the transmitting end, and, up to the middle thirties, the systems experimented with were mostly of a type that utilized mechanical-optical scanning means at the transmitting end but used a cathode-ray tube as the display device at the receiving end. From 1935 to 1940 the mechanical scanning means at the transmitting end were gradually superseded by steadily improved electronic camera tubes, but it is interesting to note that even as late as 1939 and 1940 some of the best television pictures were produced with transmitting equipment using Nipkow discs. This was the case here in the United States and also in England, Germany and Holland.[2] In an art which has developed as rapidly and in as revolutionary a way as television, it is rather extraordinary that this should be the case, considering that the Nipkow disc was invented sixty years earlier.

Presented on May 7, 1954, at the Society's Convention at Washington, D.C., by A. G. Jensen, Bell Telephone Laboratories, Inc., Murray Hill, N.J.
(This paper was received on September 15, 1954.)

Early Inventions

While the experimental development of electronic pickup and reproducing equipment did not really get started until around 1930, it is interesting to note that the conception of such devices is quite a bit older.

The earliest experiments with the use of a cathode-ray tube as a television receiver were probably those of Prof. Max Dieckmann in Germany. One is described in a German patent application dated September 12, 1906, called "A Method for the Transmission of Written Material and Line Drawings by Means of Cathode Ray Tubes."[3] A description of these early experiments and several pictures of the equipment can be found in a recent article in a German magazine giving the history of television in Germany up to 1945.[4] Figure 1 is reproduced from this magazine and shows Dieckmann's experimental setup, consisting of a cathode-ray tube receiver adjacent to a Nipkow-type scanner used as a transmitter. The cathode-ray tube used deflection modulation and magnetic deflection for both directions of scanning.

Due to a particular design of the Nipkow disc, the signals obtained from the transmitter were of a facsimile nature, indicating either black or white, but no halftones. For this reason it has been argued that Dieckmann's experiments were not true television, but rather facsimile transmission. The fact remains, however, that the cathode-ray tube receiver by itself did not have this limitation and would have been able to reproduce half-tones as well as any other cathode-ray tube of those early days. The equipment shown in Fig. 1 is still in existence and is housed in the Deutsches Museum.

Another early description of a cathode-ray tube used as a television receiver is due to Prof. Boris Rosing, who was a lecturer at the Technological Institute at St. Petersburg in Russia. Rosing called his invention the "electric eye," and it is described in two British patents of 1907 and 1911[5] and also in a couple of articles in the *Scientific American* of 1911.[6] Figure 2 is a reproduction of a drawing in Rosing's 1907 patent. The transmitter images the object (3) in the plane of the photosensitive cell (5), and by means of two rotating mirror drums this image is moved vertically and horizontally across the photosensitive element, which in this manner scans the entire picture. The receiver is a cathode-ray tube with a fluorescent screen (12), a pair of magnetic deflecting coils (14 and 15), and a

Fig. 1. Earliest experimental model of German cathode-ray tube television receiver (Dieckmann, 1906).

November 1954 Journal of the SMPTE Volume 63

pair of modulating plates (16). The saw-tooth deflecting current for the coils is obtained from rheostats mounted on the mirror drums and with contacts so arranged that the current from the rheostat varies linearly with the rotation o the drums. As the signal from the photosensitive element (5) on the transmitter is impressed on the modulating plates (16), it causes the electron beam to be deflected away from a hole in a diaphragm (13), thereby changing the strength of the beam impinging on the fluorescent screen. It must be remembered that cathode-ray tubes, or Braun tubes as they were called in those days, did not then have very well focused beams, and it is doubtful whether a very satisfactory picture could be obtained with tubes of that sort. But it is interesting to note that Rosing employed the principle of deflection modulation of the electron beam, a principle which was later utilized very successfully by Dr. C. J. Davisson in a cathode-ray tube built in the late 1930's. The patent descriptions of this system indicate that Rosing did some experimental work, but there is no record of any successful demonstrations.

A still more startling invention was made by A. A. Campbell Swinton in 1911. Swinton was an outstanding British consulting engineer, who was born in 1863 and died in 1930. He was mainly connected with the design and development of electric lighting and electric traction in England, and was also associated with Sir Charles Parsons in the development of the steam turbine. However, apart from his business, he was also keenly interested in the newer developments in physics and electronics, particularly in the fields of x-rays and television. He was a Fellow of the Royal Society, and made many experiments both in the field of x-rays and in the field of radio. Swinton's invention was triggered by a letter written by Shelford Bidwell to *Nature* in 1908.[7] Bidwell had been interested in experiments in television since 1880, and he wrote his letter to comment on an earlier letter by Armengaud of Paris, in which the author stated that he "firmly believes that within a year, as a consequence of the advance already made by his apparatus, we shall be watching one another across distances hundreds of miles apart."

Armengaud's television system was purely mechanical, and Bidwell takes issue with him with respect to the accuracy of synchronization obtainable by such a system. Bidwell assumes a picture 2 in. square and estimates that, to equal the definition of a good photograph, such a picture would require 160,000 elements. With 10 pictures per second this would mean 1.6 million synchronizing operations per second which, according to Bidwell, is "wildly impracticable."

Instead of such a system, Bidwell sug-

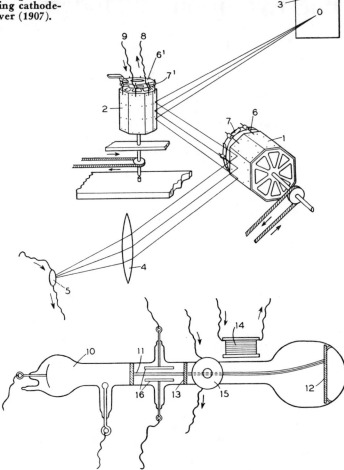

Fig. 2. Boris Rosing's television system using cathode-ray tube receiver (1907).

gests that one should consider a system based on the operation of the human eye, that is, a system with a large number of individual cells connected by separate wires. He estimates that for 90,000 picture elements one would require at the transmitting end a screen consisting of selenium cells and occupying a space 8 ft square. This screen would be illuminated by the object by means of a projection lens with a 3-ft aperture. He further estimates that the receiver would occupy a space of 4000 cu ft, although he does not specify what the actual receiving element would be. The 90,000-conductor cable is estimated to have a diameter of 8 to 10 in. and to cost about $1\frac{1}{4}$ million pounds for 100 mi. (It is interesting to note that this cost is at least an order of magnitude greater than the cost of present-day coaxial cables, and this is in spite of the fact that Bidwell's system would require less than one megacycle for its transmission, and that the pound of 1908 was worth a good deal more than it is today.)

In reply to Bidwell's letter, Swinton wrote as follows[8]:

"Distant Electric Vision

"Referring to Mr. Shelford Bidwell's illuminating communication on this subject published in NATURE of June 4, may I point out that though, as stated by Mr. Bidwell, it is wildly impracticable to effect even 160,000 synchronized operations per second* by ordinary mechanical means, this part of the problem of obtaining distant electric vision can probably be solved by the employment of two beams of kathode rays (one at the transmitting and one at the receiving station) synchronously deflected by the varying fields of two electromagnets placed at right angles to one another and energised by two alternating electric currents of widely different frequencies, so that the moving extremities of the two beams are caused to sweep synchronously over the whole of the required surfaces within the one-tenth of a second necessary to take advantage of visual persistence.

"Indeed, so far as the receiving apparatus is concerned, the moving kathode beam has only to be arranged to impinge on a sufficiently sensitive fluorescent screen, and given suitable variations in its intensity, to obtain the desired result.

"The real difficulties lie in devising an efficient transmitter which, under the influence of light and shade, shall sufficiently vary the transmitted electric current so as to produce the necessary alterations in the intensity of the kathode beam of the receiver, and further in making this transmitter sufficiently rapid in its action to respond to the 160,000 variations per second that are necessary as a minimum.

"Possibly no electric phenomenon at present known will provide what is required in this respect, but should something

* Apparently Swinton lost track of the fact that Bidwell suggested 10 pictures per second, each with 160,000 elements. The figure therefore should be 1,600,000 operations per second.

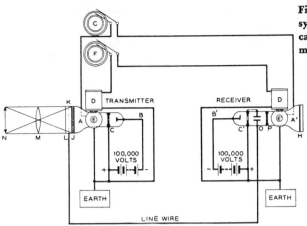

Fig. 3. Campbell Swinton's system of television using cathode-ray tubes as transmitter and receiver (1911).

witness the practical development of his ideas.

Cathode-Ray Tube Receiver

The experiments described above all dealt with the earlier types of Braun tubes which were only partially evacuated. They were generally filled with argon or some other rare gas with a pressure of 10^{-2} to 10^{-4}mm of mercury, and it was not possible in these tubes to obtain a very sharp focus. As the art progressed, however, the tubes were gradually improved, and by the middle 1920's several experimenters were working with such tubes, both here in the United States and abroad. One of the first experimenters in this field in the United States was Vladimir K. Zworykin, who came to this country in 1918 and did his early work with the Westinghouse Research Laboratories. In the years around 1910 he had been a student under Rosing at St. Petersburg and had worked with him in the early experiments with Braun tubes as television receivers. He continued this work here in America, and his first patent application describing a complete electronic television system was issued in 1923.[11] Figure 4 shows a picture of the cathode-ray receiving tube in the above-mentioned patent application. It will be noticed that the tube has a cathode (56), a modulating grid (54), an anode (57), and a fluorescent screen (60). No mention is made about the vacuum in the tube, but in a 1925 patent application a somewhat similar tube is described using low-pressure argon and it may be assumed, therefore, that this first tube also was argon-filled and depended on the argon for focusing the beam. The condenser plates (58 and 59) are used for producing electrostatic horizontal deflection, while the coils (69 and 70) produce magnetic vertical deflection.

According to Zworykin, the first demonstration of an all-electronic system using such a cathode-ray tube at the receiver and an early form of camera pickup tube at the transmitter took place in 1924. However, the pictures were scarcely more than shadow pictures with rather poor definition. It was apparent to Zworykin that the biggest problem was to produce a satisfactory pickup tube

suitable be discovered, distant electric vision will, I think, come within the region of possibility."

The foresight expressed in this letter is truly remarkable when one realizes that it was written in the early infancy of radio transmission, and at a time when the electron tube amplifier had not yet been invented and when photoelectric equipment was still very inefficient and primitive.

Three years later, Swinton elaborated on his suggestion in a presidential address to the members of the Röntgen Society in November 1911.[9] In this address he gave a detailed description of his proposal and illustrated it with a diagram which is reproduced in Fig. 3. The figure shows his conception of a camera tube involving the use of a mosaic screen of photoelectric elements which was scanned by an electron beam. The signal from the camera tube is impressed upon a pair of deflection plates in a cathode-ray tube receiver. Just as in Rosing's suggestion, Swinton makes use of deflection modulation in the receiving tube. Magnetic coils are used both at the transmitter and at the receiver for deflecting the electron beams, and synchronism is insured by using a common alternating-current supply for the two ends.

Swinton apparently never built a complete model of his system but he remained interested in it and, up to the time of his death, talks by him indicated that he had made several experiments to construct a satisfactory mosaic for the

transmitter tube. Thus in 1924 he gave a lecture before the Radio Society of Great Britain entitled "The Possibilities of Television."[10] In this lecture he dealt in detail with his earlier suggestion in 1911 and discussed his latest thoughts on the best design of the mosaic plate in the transmitting tube. He also pointed out that the advent of the electronic amplifier and of radio communication had greatly enhanced the possibilities of successful transmission of television signals. The lecture was followed by a lively discussion and, in his answer to a questioner, Swinton concluded as follows:

"...I wish to say that I agree entirely with Mr. Atkinson that the real difficulty in regard to this subject is that it is probably scarcely worth anybody's while to pursue it. That is what I have felt all along myself. I think you would have to spend some years in hard work, and then would the result be worth anything financially? If we could only get one of the big research laboratories, like that of the G.E.C. or of the Western Electric Company—one of those people who have large skilled staffs and any amount of money to engage on the business—I believe they would solve a thing like this in six months and make a reasonable job of it."

Here again Swinton shows an uncanny ability to foresee the future of television. It was indeed by the efforts of the large companies that modern-day high-definition television was finally developed, although it took a good deal longer than the six months estimated by him. It is to be regretted that he died too soon to

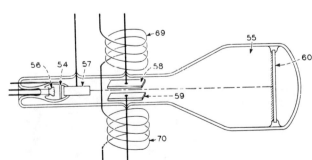

Fig. 4. Zworykin's earliest form of cathode-ray receiving tube (1923).

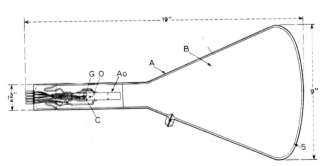

Fig. 5. Early Zworykin cathode-ray receiving tube (1933).

and, in order to achieve better results as soon as possible, he reverted for the next few years to the use of mechanical scanning means at the transmitter and concentrated on the design of better cathode-ray tubes for the receiver. The first published account of these early experiments will be found in an article in *Radio Engineering* for December 1929.[12] The article describes experiments which used a tube with a 7-in. diameter screen. It employed a simple form of electrostatic focusing, grid modulation, and both magnetic and electrostatic deflection. In this article Zworykin first coined the word "kinescope" for the receiving tube.

Around 1930 Zworykin joined the RCA Laboratories, and in the years 1931 and 1932, he and other RCA engineers constructed a complete television system utilizing a cathode-ray tube at the receiver. The transmitter still was mechanical, making use of a Nipkow disc for the scanning process, but the receiving tube had undergone a great deal of development and began to look more like present-day cathode-ray tubes.

This work was described in an article in the *Proceedings of the I.R.E.* for December 1933,[13] and Fig. 5 shows a cross-sectional picture of the cathode ray receiving tube taken from this article. Figure 6 is a diagrammatic view of the cathode and the two anodes of this tube, and it is obvious from the figure that the application of electron optics to proper focusing of the electron beam by means of electrostatic lenses was by that time quite well understood. In order to obtain such focusing the tube must have been of the same high-vacuum type as those employed in today's television receivers. The tube face was 9 in. in

Fig. 6. Constructional details of early Zworykin cathode-ray receiving tube (1933).

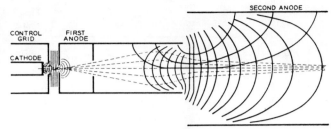

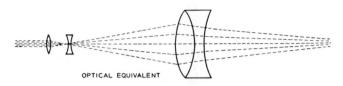

OPTICAL EQUIVALENT

diameter and the tube was 19 in. long. Magnetic deflection was used in both directions, and the pictures produced had 120 lines/frame and 24 frames/sec. Several photographs of such pictures are shown in the article mentioned above.

Another early experimenter with cathode-ray receiving tubes in this country was Philo T. Farnsworth, who did his early experimental work in San Francisco in the late 1920's and early 1930's. He too was working with an all-electronic system using cathode-ray tube devices both at the receiving and at the transmitting ends. The transmitting tube was of a different type than that conceived by Zworykin, and will be described later on. The receiving tube, however, was quite similar to the early types of receiving tubes used by Zworykin. The early experimental work by Farnsworth is described in articles appearing in *Wireless World* and *Television News* in 1931.[14] Figure 7 from the article in *Wireless World* shows a picture of the cathode-ray receiving tube which

Farnsworth called an "oscillite." A complete receiver using such a tube is shown in Fig. 8. The pictures had 200 lines/frame and 15 frames/sec, and Farnsworth stated that the bandwidth necessary for transmitting such a signal should be about 300 kc. Even in these earliest tubes, Farnsworth used magnetic deflection for both directions.

Another early experimenter with cathode-ray tubes for television was Manfred von Ardenne in Germany. His work is described in several articles in the German magazine *Fernsehen* during 1930 and 1931.[15] As will be discussed later, von Ardenne was probably the first to experiment with a cathode-ray tube as a flying-spot scanner at the transmitting end, and the experiments described in the above-mentioned article utilized this arrangement at the transmitter. Figure 9 shows a photograph of a table model receiver as taken from one of these articles, while Fig. 10 shows a photograph of a picture obtained on such a receiver. The pictures had 60 lines/frame and about 9000

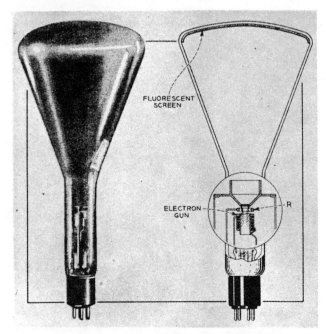

Fig. 7. Early model of Farnsworth cathode-ray receiving tube (1931).

Fig. 8. Early model of American cathode-ray tube television receiver (Farnsworth, 1931).

Fig. 9. Early model of German cathode-ray tube television receiver (von Ardenne, 1930).

Fig. 10. Photograph of early German cathode-ray tube television picture (von Ardenne, 1931).

picture points, which would correspond to a bandwidth of about 75 kc. According to von Ardenne, this limitation in detail was entirely due to the sending arrangement and the receiving tube by itself was capable of producing pictures with about 20,000 to 30,000 picture elements/frame.

During the next twenty years, the early forms of cathode-ray receiving tubes described above were steadily being developed and improved in a number of laboratories and by a number of different organizations. Increased knowledge and application of electron optical principles made it possible to design tubes with higher and higher definition. By the middle 1930's pictures were being shown with as many as 300 lines/frame. During the 1940's pictures were shown with 500 or more lines and, at present, tubes can be made which are capable of resolving 1000 or more lines. At the same time manufacturing methods were developed and steadily improved to permit the production of larger diameter tubes. Up to 1940 very few tubes with diameters over 10 or 12 in. were used, while nowadays television receiver tubes are made with diameters as large as 30 in.

As a somewhat unusual phase of this development, it might be of interest to mention a cathode-ray receiving tube designed by C. J. Davisson of the Bell Telephone Laboratories for use in the first transmission of television signals over the coaxial cable from New York to Philadelphia in 1937.[16] Davisson designed this tube on the basis of his knowledge of electron optics, and at no stage would he depart from a design which would allow him accurately to predict the performance. This accounts for the "thin" lenses used in the different focusing systems, for the small deflection angles employed to insure sharp focus all over the screen, and for the extreme care with which the deflection-plate system was made to avoid either "pin

cushion" or "barrel" distortion. It resulted in a very long tube (about 5 ft), as shown in Fig. 11, and an unusually complex assembly of precision mechanical parts, as shown by the diagrammatic representation of the tube in Fig. 12. It also resulted in an actual performance very close to the predicted performance and markedly superior to that of other television receiving tubes of the same period. It is interesting to note that Davisson in this tube reverted to the old method of deflection modulation in order to insure more complete control over the size and shape of the spot on the screen.

Cathode-Ray Tube Flying-Spot Scanner

The use of the light spot of a cathode-ray tube raster as a scanning means for scanning lantern slides or motion-picture film was first proposed by Zworykin in the 1923 patent application mentioned above.[11] Figure 13 shows the proposed arrangement in this patent application. The light from the scanning raster is made to fall on a lantern slide (78), and the light passing through the slide is focused by the lens (77) onto the photocell (76). While the optical arrangement proposed here is not altogether clear, the fundamental idea of obtaining a television signal in this manner is quite obvious.

The first experimenter to put this suggestion into practice was von Ardenne, and his experiments are described in the articles already mentioned above.[15] The general arrangement of the transmitter and receiver is shown in Fig. 14, taken from the article, and here the optical arrangement at the transmitting end is quite proper except that an additional condensing lens between the lantern slide and the photocell amplifier might have been advantageous. The frame frequency of 25 and the line frequency of 1500 would indicate that each picture consisted of 60 lines. Figure 15, also from the same article, shows an experimental setup of the cathode-ray tube

used for scanning motion-picture film, and a sample of the pictures obtained was shown above in Fig. 10.

The use of such a cathode-ray tube flying-spot scanner even for live pickup was proposed by von Ardenne, as indicated by Fig. 16 from the same article. Here the scanning raster of the tube is

Fig. 11. C. J. Davisson cathode-ray receiving tube (Bell Telephone Laboratories, 1937).

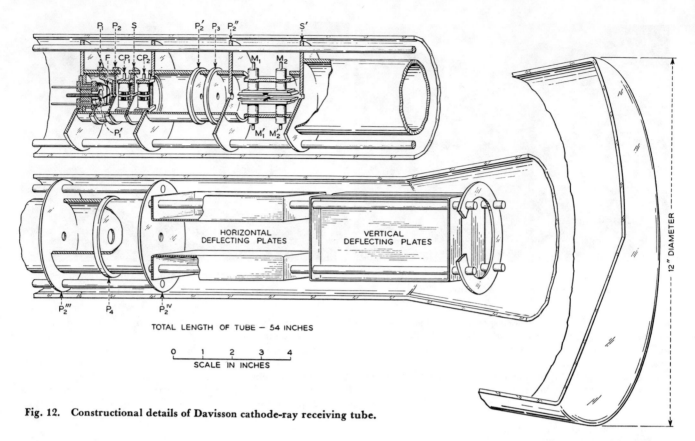

Fig. 12. Constructional details of Davisson cathode-ray receiving tube.

TOTAL LENGTH OF TUBE — 54 INCHES

SCALE IN INCHES

imaged by means of a lens in the plane of the object, in this case the head of a person. The light reflected from the object is then picked up by photocells arranged around the object, and the signals from the photocells are amplified and sent to the transmitter.

It appears that for many years following von Ardenne's experiments no further work was done with cathode-ray tubes as spot scanners. This probably was due to the fact that, as the art progressed toward pictures with higher and higher definition, the cathode-ray tube became inadequate as a spot scanner because of the comparatively slow decay in the phosphors. For receiving tubes it is necessary only that the light decay appreciably in the time between successive field scans, i.e., in 1/60th of a second, and phosphors with this order of decay time were well known even in the 1930's. For spot-scanning tubes, on the other hand, it is necessary that the light decay

appreciably in the time corresponding to one picture element. Otherwise the afterglow would result in an intolerable smearing or blurring of the image. For modern high-definition television this means that the phosphor decay can be only a very small fraction of a microsecond, and phosphors of this type were not known until around 1940. One of the earliest discussions of the requirement for spot-scanning phosphors can be found in an article in a German magazine in 1939.[17] A description of one of the first high-definition lantern slide spot scanners used in this country will be found in an article in the *Proceedings of the I.R.E.* in 1946.[18] This particular spot scanner was used for scanning motion-picture film, a purpose for which a cathode-ray tube scanner is particularly well

adapted. This problem will be discussed in more detail later on under Film Scanners. Since that time many types of cathode-ray tube spot scanners have been developed and are now available commercially.

Camera Tubes

Electronic camera pickup tubes may be divided into two types. One type is the instantaneous or nonstorage type tube, as exemplified by the Farnsworth dissector tube, while the other is the storage type of camera tube, as exemplified by Zworykin's iconoscope and practically all of the later types of camera tube types used today. In the following we shall discuss the development of both of these types of camera tubes.

Fig. 13. Earliest picture of Zworykin's cathode-ray tube spot scanner (1923).

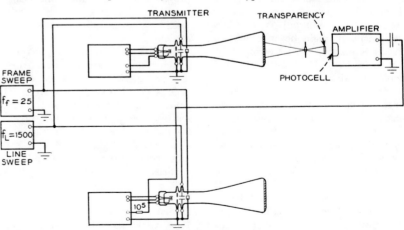

Fig. 14. Diagram of German proposal for cathode-ray tube spot-scanning transmitter (von Ardenne, 1930).

Fig. 15. Early German cathode-ray tube film scanner (von Ardenne, 1931).

A. Dissector Tube

The dissector tube was developed by Farnsworth and was first described by him in a patent application dated January 7, 1927.[19] While the fundamental principles of the tube are described in this patent application, there were still several essential improvements to be added before the tube would operate satisfactorily. These additions were incorporated in several subsequent applications, and a complete description of the method of operation of the tube was first given by Farnsworth in an article in the *Journal of the Franklin Institute* in 1934.[20]

One interesting feature of Farnsworth's earliest patent application is the fact that he does not use at the receiver a cathode-ray tube as in his later applications and as discussed above. Instead he uses a Kerr cell for controlling the intensity of a polarized light source in accordance with the received signal strength, and the light beam after leaving the Kerr cell is then deflected onto a screen by use of two galvanometer mirrors controlled by the scanning signals. This is probably one of the very few proposals, if not the only one, for a television system using electronic means at the transmitting end and mechanical scanning means at the receiving end.

Figure 17 shows a cross-sectional view of the dissector tube as described in the 1934 article. It consists of a cylindrical glass envelope with a plain circular cathode at the left and an anode enclosed in a pencil-shaped shell, called "target," at the right. The end face of the tube consists of plane glass of optical quality, and through this end plate an optical image of the object to be televised is formed on the face of the cathode. Since the surface of the cathode is photosensitive, electrons will leave each point of this surface in an amount corresponding to the illumination in the image at that point. These photoelectrons are pulled toward the anode by means of a high potential applied between the anode and the cathode. If no other arrangements were made, the electrons leaving any one point in the cathode would not all travel toward the anode in an axial direction, but would fan out in a narrow cone. However, by enclosing the entire tube in a solenoid and passing a direct current of the proper amplitude through this sole-

noid, it is possible to pull this cone of electrons together again in such a fashion that all electrons leaving any one point on the cathode will again come together in one point of a plane parallel to the cathode and located in the plane of the target. This focusing action is indicated by the curved electron patterns shown in Fig. 17. In other words, it is thus possible to insure that a complete electron image of the scene is reproduced in the plane of the target. The target has a small aperture facing the cathode and, by sweeping the entire electron image back and forth and up and down past this aperture, the electrons of each element of the image are made to pass successively through this aperture and reach the anode inside. That is, by the scanning of the electron image past the aperture, the image is "dissected" into its elemental areas, and a signal is produced which at each instant is proportional to the number of electrons entering the aperture at that instant, and therefore again proportional to the light falling on the corresponding point of the cathode at that same instant. The tube therefore is instantaneous in nature and no storage is involved. The sweeping of the electron image is effected by means of two sets of sweep coils placed at right angles around the cylindrical sides of the tube and energized by saw-tooth currents of the proper frequencies.

The earliest forms of dissectors built by Farnsworth were quite insensitive as compared with modern type tubes. In order to obtain television signals with any reasonable signal-to-noise ratio, it was necessary that the illumination in the optical images formed on the cathode be extremely high. This, in turn, meant that live pickup from studio scenes was out of the question since the required image illumination could be obtained only from lantern slides with high-intensity light sources. In order to remedy this situation, Farnsworth therefore replaced the original photocell with an electron multiplier capable of multiplying the original photocurrent by many orders of magnitude. The development of electron multipliers for this and other purposes will be discussed later.

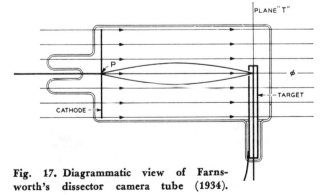

Fig. 16. Early German proposal for live pickup using cathode-ray tube spot scanner (von Ardenne, 1930).

Fig. 17. Diagrammatic view of Farnsworth's dissector camera tube (1934).

Fig. 18. Special Farnsworth dissector camera tube (Bell Telephone Laboratories, 1945).

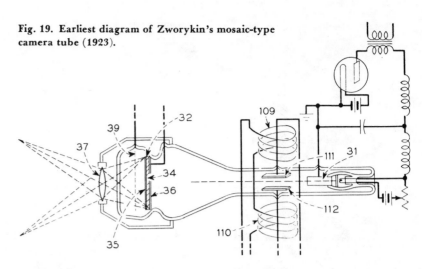

Fig. 19. Earliest diagram of Zworykin's mosaic-type camera tube (1923).

In the late 1930's dissector tubes with electron multipliers were used in television cameras for live pickup and demonstrated by Farnsworth, but even these later type tubes required studio lighting which was uncomfortably intense and the tubes were never used in any commercial television cameras. The tube, however, has been used very successfully in many types of motion-picture film scanners, although present types of commercial film scanners all use storage-type tubes. It also has been used and still is being used for several applications of industrial television, such as the reading of instruments in inaccessible or dangerous locations. It should be mentioned that the great advantage of the dissector tube over storage-type tubes is that it is completely linear in operation so that the output signal is strictly proportional to the light falling on the cathode. This is of particular advantage when scanning motion-picture film and was the principal reason for the use of the dissector tube for this purpose until the advent of the short-decay, cathode-ray tube flying-spot scanner.

Figure 18 shows a photograph of a special type of dissector tube designed for use in an experimental motion-picture scanner which was used in the Bell Telephone Laboratories until quite recently.[21]

B. The Iconoscope

The storage-type camera tube was invented by Zworykin and was first described in a patent application dated December 29, 1923.[11] Figure 19 shows a cross-sectional view of the tube as taken from this application. The right end of the tube shows the cathode and a cylindrical anode (31), and through this a beam of electrons is directed toward the target (32). This target has the characteristic mosaic structure consisting of a wire mesh screen (36) facing the cathode, a thin insulating layer (34) behind the wire screen, and a layer of insulated globules of photoelectric material (35) deposited on the insulating layer. This photoelectric mosaic thus faces the camera lens (37). By means of this lens the scene to be televised is imaged on the mosaic. It will be noticed that both electrostatic and electromagnetic deflection are used in this type. The tube was argon-filled and used gas focusing of the beam and, according to the description in the patent, this gas also played a part in the collection of signal current from the mosaic onto the signal grid (39). However, the exact nature of this collection is not very clear. Tubes of this sort were constructed by Zworykin in 1924, and Fig. 20 is a photograph of one of these early tubes. It was mentioned earlier that Zworykin demonstrated the use of such a camera tube in an all-electronic system using a cathode-ray tube at the receiver sometime during 1924, but that the pictures were scarcely more than shadow pictures with rather poor definition.

After spending the next few years in improving the cathode-ray tube at the receiver, Zworykin again took up the construction of camera tubes when he joined RCA around 1930. A description of an early form of iconoscope is given in an article by Zworykin in the *Proceedings of the I.R.E.* in 1934,[22] and Fig. 21 shows a cross-section of a tube used in these experiments. By this time it had been realized that proper focusing of the electron beam could be obtained only in a high-vacuum tube with proper design of focusing electrodes, as described earlier in the section on Cathode-Ray Tube Receivers. The tube has a signal plate consisting of a thin metal plate on which is deposited a thin layer of insulating material (in modern iconoscopes this insulating layer consists of a thin sheet of mica), and on top of the insulating sheet is deposited a mosaic consisting of a large number of minute globules of photosensitive material. The globules are insulated from each other and are small enough so that the cross-section of the beam covers a large number of globules at any one time.

The method of operation of the iconoscope may be described in a somewhat simplified form as follows. An object is imaged on the mosaic by means of a camera lens and, as the globules are illuminated by this image, they give off photoelectrons which leave the mosaic and are collected by a collector electrode marked "Pa" in the figure. As the photoelectrons leave the mosaic, the globules are thus charged positive with respect to the signal plate, and the greater the illumination the more the globules are charged and, therefore, the higher the potential between the globules and the signal plate. This goes on as

Fig. 20. Earliest experimental model of Zworykin camera tube (1923).

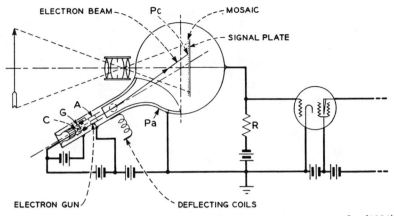

Fig. 21. Diagram of earlier model of Zworykin's iconoscope camera tube (1934).

long as the target is illuminated and the action, therefore, is cumulative. An electron beam from the cathode of the tube is made to scan over the mosaic in the usual manner by means of two sets of magnetic coils placed around the neck of the tube. As the scanning beam strikes the globules on any one point of the mosaic, these globules are thereby discharged and the discharge causes a corresponding pulse of current to flow from the signal plate to ground through the resistance, R. The varying potential across this resistance therefore constitutes the television signal. As soon as the beam has left a particular spot on the mosaic, this spot will again start to charge up in accordance with the light falling on it and will continue to do so until the beam strikes it again during the succeeding scan. In other words, energy is stored up in the mosaic by the action of light on the photoelectric globules, and this storage continues during the entire period between scans. This storage principle makes the iconoscope much more sensitive than the dissector tube, which depended for its action on the photoelectric emission from the cathode at any one instant.

The actual mode of operation of the iconoscope is somewhat more complicated than described above, due to the

fact that secondary emission takes place as the beam scans over the mosaic. The potential between the cathode and the anode is quite high, of the order of a thousand volts or so, and therefore results in a high velocity electron beam. As this beam strikes the mosaic it releases secondary electrons from the mosaic, and these secondary electrons are partly collected by the collector electrode but also partly pulled back onto the mosaic in a more or less random manner. Even if the mosaic were not illuminated by any image, such secondary emission would still take place and some of these secondary electrons would be pulled back to the mosaic and redistributed over the surface, thus giving rise to a false signal current. These spurious signals are called "shading" signals and are common to all iconoscope and other high velocity beam tubes. Since the secondary electrons are redistributed over the mosaic in a rather broad fashion, the resulting shading signals are low-frequency signals of rather simple waveforms, and they may therefore be compensated for by introducing a corresponding correcting signal from special shading signal generators incorporated as part of the camera equipment. A photograph of an early iconoscope of the type described above is shown in Fig. 22.

Due to the storage action of the iconoscope, this tube theoretically should be some 50 to 100 times more sensitive than an instantaneous-type tube like the dissector (assuming that the dissector does not incorporate the use of an electron multiplier). Actually, the iconoscope is only some 5 to 10% efficient due to the secondary emission. In the first place, the secondary electrons released from the mosaic reduce the electric field in front of the mosaic and therefore make the photoemission of the globules less efficient; also, the fact that the secondary electrons are only partly collected by the collector electrode results in lower charging potentials of the globules and, therefore, in lower signal current. Even so, the inconoscope proved to be a much more sensitive tube than any tube hitherto produced and made it possible for the first time to build live pickup cameras for studio use with studio illuminations that were not too uncomfortable for the actors.

The number of secondary electrons emitted from any part of the mosaic depends on the potential of the mosaic at the time the electron beam strikes it, and this again depends on the amount of light falling on the mosaic at that point. The result is that the overall action of the iconoscope is not linear, that is, the output current is not proportional to the amount of light falling on the mosaic. The relation between illumination on the mosaic and signal output current is more nearly a square root relation for small values of illumination, and for large values it soon reaches a saturation point, so that increased illumination results in only very little increase in corresponding signal output.

For studio use the iconoscope has long since been superseded by more modern forms of camera tubes, but it is still extensively used in motion-picture film scanners. The tube shown to the right in Fig. 27 is a photograph of a modern-type iconoscope for this use.

C. Image Iconoscope

The first step towards further improving the iconoscope was the so-called image iconoscope, which was first described in an article by Iams, Morton and Zworykin in the *Proceedings of the I.R.E.* in 1939.[23] Figure 23 shows a cross-sectional diagram of such a tube, as

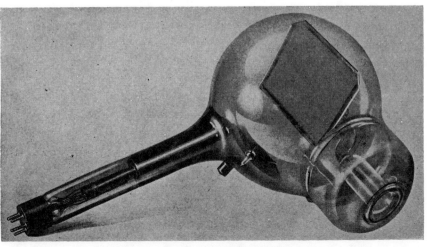

Fig. 22. Early iconoscope camera tube.

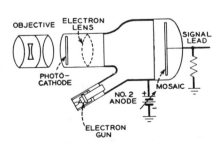

OBJECTIVE   ELECTRON LENS

SIGNAL LEAD

PHOTO-CATHODE

NO. 2 ANODE

MOSAIC

ELECTRON GUN

Fig. 23. Diagram of image iconoscope camera tube (1939).

taken from that article. The tube has a semitransparent photocathode on which an optical image is formed of the scene to be televised. As light falls on the photocathode, photoelectrons are emitted from this cathode and are pulled towards the mosaic at the right by means of a high electric potential. Close to the photocathode there is, in other words, an electron image corresponding to the optical image falling on the cathode, and by means of an electron lens system this electron image is focused in the mosaic in the same manner as described earlier for the dissector tube. The electron lens system may be either magnetic and consist of a coil, as in the case of the dissector, or it may be electrostatic and consist of a series of metal rings of proper potential.

Since the potential between the photocathode and the mosaic is high, the photoelectrons reach the mosaic and therefore give rise to the emission of secondary electrons from the mosaic. Since each incoming electron releases on the order of 4 or 5 secondary electrons, this in effect results in a charge image on the mosaic which is 4 or 5 times higher than if no secondary emission took place. On top of that, the high field between the photocathode and the mosaic results in a more efficient collection of current from the photocathode than in the case of the iconoscope, where the field near the photosensitive mosaic was reduced due to secondary emission. All in all, this arrangement results in a tube which is about ten times more sensitive than the ordinary iconoscope. Figure 24 shows a photograph of an image iconoscope for use in a studio camera. Tubes of this type were used here in the United States during the 1940's but were later replaced by the image orthicon. However, in England tubes of this type are used extensively for studio cameras. The English name for this type of camera tube is Super Emitron.

D. The Orthicon

It was mentioned above that the iconoscope was only 5 to 10% efficient. Due to secondary emission, only a small part of the photoelectrons emitted by the mosaic are drawn away and only a small part of the stored charge is effective in

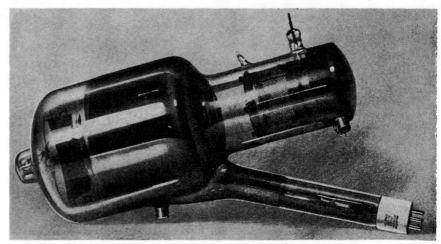
Fig. 24. Image-iconoscope camera tube (1939).

producing a signal. The image iconoscope is one attempt to improve this efficiency, but another and rather different approach consists in using a low-velocity electron beam for scanning. In this case it is possible to provide at the mosaic a field strong enough to draw away all the photoelectrons and, furthermore, no secondary electrons are emitted when the beam reaches the mosaic.

A tube of this type, called the orthicon, was developed at the RCA Laboratories, and is described by Rose and Iams in an article in *RCA Review* in 1939.[24] Figure 25 shows a cross-sectional diagram of this tube. The tube has a storage-type mosaic plate similar to that used in an iconoscope, and when light falls on this plate all the photoelectrons are drawn to the collector by means of a sufficiently high potential between the collector and the mosaic plate. In this case, however, the mosaic plate is kept at a potential equal to that of the cathode, and when the electron beam reaches the signal plate it therefore has zero velocity and does not release any secondary electrons. If the mosaic has been charged up due to light falling on it, the electron beam just resupplies the electrons that have left the mosaic due to photoemission and thus brings that part of the mosaic back to cathode potential. The remaining electrons in the beam thereafter return to the collector. The signal thus consists of the current pulses flowing in the output lead as each successive point of the mosaic is being discharged.

Since the electron beam in this tube has very low velocity, it would not stay sharply focused as it traverses the tube unless special precautions were taken. These consist in focusing coils arranged around the tube in such a manner as to produce a strong longitudinal magnetic field. This field has the effect of keeping the beam concentrated as it traverses the tube so that the cross-section of the beam at the mosaic is about the same as that leaving the gun. In order to avoid blurring near the edges of the mosaic it is further necessary to introduce correcting fields which insure that the beam is perpendicular to the mosaic over the entire surface. One of the great advantages of this type of tube is that no secondary emission takes place. For this reason the tube is nearly linear in operation and, furthermore, this also results in a complete absence of spurious shading signals. Tubes of this sort were built and used experimentally in pickup cameras. However, the tube was soon to be superseded by a still more efficient and sensitive tube and therefore never came into wide use.

E. Image Orthicon

In the description of the orthicon it was mentioned that the electron beam supplies to each part of the mosaic the electrons that have been lost by the electron image, and the remaining part of the electrons then return to the collector. This return beam, therefore, is in effect modulated by the signal current and,

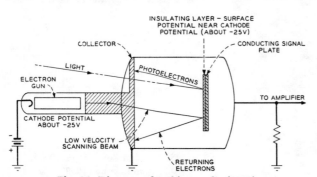
Fig. 25. Diagram of orthicon tube (1939).

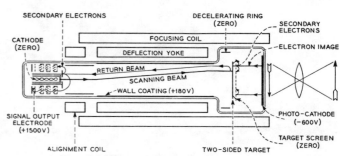
Fig. 26. Diagram of image-orthicon tube (1946).

Fig. 27. Modern vidicon, image-orthicon and iconoscope tube.

if properly collected, could indeed be used as the signal. This is one of the principles employed in the image-orthicon tube which was developed by RCA and first described in an article by Rose, Weimer and Law in the *Proceedings of the I.R.E.* in 1946.[25] Figure 26 shows a cross-sectional diagram of this tube which makes use of electron image amplification, as in the image iconoscope, of the efficient low-velocity beam, as in the orthicon, and of an electron multiplier, as in the later types of dissectors. The optical image is formed on a transparent photocathode placed on the inside of the end glass wall of the tube. The electron image emitted from this cathode is focused as a second electron image in the plane of a thin two-sided insulating target. Since a high electric field exists between the photocathode and the target, the photoelectrons strike the target with high velocity and give rise to the emission of secondary electrons, with the result that the charge image on the target is some 4 or 5 times stronger than the electron image leaving the photocathode. The other side of the target is scanned by a low velocity electron beam which discharges points of the target as it scans across it, thus resulting

in a return beam which is modulated with this discharge current. As in the orthicon, the electron beam is kept focused during its traverse from electron gun to target, and the same focusing field will therefore keep the return beam focused along the same path so that the return beam strikes the plate surrounding the gun aperture very close to this aperture. It strikes these plates with a velocity high enough to release secondary electrons and, by proper electrostatic focusing, these secondary electrons are in turn guided to the first dynode of a multistage electron multiplier located behind the gun. By thus making use of all the known methods of electron magnification it has been possible to construct a camera tube which is of the order of 100 times more sensitive than any previous type of camera tube. With tubes of this sort, it is possible to make television pictures at very low light levels and, in fact, when using television cameras with this type of tube it has been possible to televise outdoor scenes at light levels so low that no satisfactory motion picture could be obtained. When used in the studio this tube produces excellent television pictures at medium light levels and is now the tube

most commonly used for all studio cameras in the United States. A photograph of a modern image orthicon is shown as the center tube in Fig. 27.

F. The Vidicon

One of the earliest discoveries in the field of photoelectricity was that of the photoconductive properties of selenium. Selenium was discovered in the early part of the 19th century and was found to have a very high electrical resistance. In 1873 Willoughby Smith in England was making experiments with submarine cables and, in connection with those tests, he had use for some very high resistances. He therefore had made up some long wires of selenium enclosed in glass tubes, with the idea of using these as resistance elements. He found, however, that he could not obtain constant results in his measurements. The results varied from day to day for no apparent reason and, in an attempt to discover the cause of the discrepancies, Smith accidentally covered one of the selenium wires, excluding the light falling on the wire, and he found that it suddenly changed its resistance materially. Smith published his discovery, which caused great excitement and gave rise to many of the early proposals for "seeing by electricity." When Swinton tried to build a mosaic for his camera tube, it was selenium he thought about as a photoelectric material, and most of the other early experimenters thought in terms of selenium when translating light energy to electrical energy. It is interesting to note that, in spite of this early discovery of the photoconductive property of selenium, it was not until 1950 that a satisfactory photoconductive camera tube was built, a tube capable of producing the high-definition television signal required for modern television. It took the technique over half a century to catch up with the ideas and visions of the early inventors.

During the late 1940's the engineers at RCA experimented with an RCA photoconductive pickup tube, and in 1950 such a tube was described in an article by Weimer, Forgue and Goodrich appearing in *Electronics*.[26] They called the tube the vidicon, and Fig. 28 shows a cross-sectional diagram of such a tube

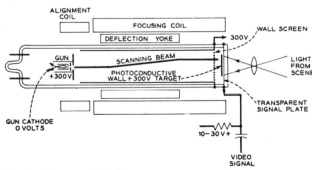

Fig. 28. Diagram of vidicon camera tube (1950).

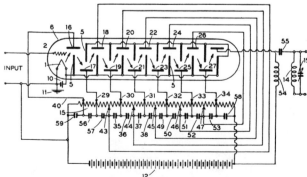

Fig. 29. Diagram of early electron multiplier amplifier tube (1926.)

as taken from the article mentioned. The tube uses a low-velocity scanning beam similar to that used in the orthicon, but instead of the photoemissive surface in the orthicon the vidicon uses a photoconductive target deposited on a transparent conductive signal plate. An optical image of the scene to be transmitted is focused onto the photoconductive surface through the transparent signal plate. This signal plate is kept at a potential of about 20 v positive with respect to the cathode, and when no light falls on the photoconductive surface this surface is kept at cathode potential by means of the scanning beam. When light falls on the photoconductive surface it increases the conductivity, and a charge current flows from the signal plate to the individual elements of the photoconductive surface, the charging current being proportional to the amount of light falling on the surface. When the scanning beam strikes the charged surface it deposits sufficient electrons to neutralize this charge and thereby generates the video signal in the signal plate lead. In other words, the operation is very similar to that of the orthicon except that the positive charging effect is achieved by photoconduction through the target itself rather than by photoemission from the scanned surface.

The advantage of using a photoconducting tube rather than a photoemissive tube is that the sensitivity of photoconductive materials is such that currents of several thousand microamperes per lumen may be obtained as compared to 30 to 50 μa/lm for the most efficient photoemissive materials. Thus a highly sensitive camera tube may be built without the additional complication of an electron image amplifier and an electron multiplier as incorporated in the image orthicon. This results in a simpler tube which is cheaper to build and can be made much smaller and more compact than any other camera tube. The photograph to the left in Fig. 27 is of a vidicon tube capable of producing satisfactory television pictures of more than 600 lines. It is about 6 in. long and 1 in. in diameter, and with tubes of this sort it has been possible to build portable field cameras that are not much bigger than an ordinary 16mm motion-picture camera.

Multiplier Phototubes

A multiplier phototube or photomultiplier is a photocell in which the photoelectrons emitted by the photosensitive surface are amplified inside the tube by making use of the phenomenon of secondary emission. The photoelectric effect itself was first discovered by Hertz in 1887, and photoelectric cells of the type we now know were first experimented with around 1900. The use of secondary emission as a means of amplification was first made use of by A. W.

Hull in a patent application dated 1915.[27] This application deals with the use of a dynatron as a device having negative electrical resistance characteristics. A second patent application by Hull, dated December 28, 1921,[28] deals with a vacuum tube amplifier which makes use of secondary emission to obtain increased amplification. Another electron multiplier amplifier is described in a patent application by Jarvis and Blair dated September 15, 1926.[29] Figure 29 shows a cross-sectional diagram of the amplifier taken from this application. In this amplifier tube, electrons from the cathode (1) are controlled by the grid (2) in the usual manner, and from there they flow to the first anode (16) which corresponds to the plate in an ordinary vacuum tube. If this anode is of the proper potential, the electrons striking it will have sufficiently high velocity so that each electron releases several secondary electrons. By means of electrostatic shields (5) of proper potential, these secondary electrons are guided to the next anode (17) which they strike, and release still more secondary electrons, and so on, through the entire tube until finally the multiplied electrons reach the collector plate at the end of the tube. With the proper potential gradient from anode to anode, and with the anodes made of the proper material, it is possible to insure that each primary electron striking an anode will release as many as 4 or 5 secondary electrons, and with enough stages of multiplication it is thus possible to obtain an electron multiplication of many thousand times.

If, in the tube shown in Fig. 29, the cathode and the grid are replaced by a photosensitive surface on which light can be projected, we have, in effect, a photomultiplier very similar to the type used nowadays. During the early development of photomultipliers some of the forms utilized external magnetic focusing or guiding of the electrons through the tube, but all of the photomultipliers used today employ electrostatic focusing similar to that described above. It is multipliers of this type that were used by Farnsworth in his later developments of the dissector tube, and it is also this type of multiplier which is employed in the image orthicon.

Motion-Picture Film Scanners

During the late 1930's it was established that future commercial television in the United States would use 30 frames/sec, that is, 60 fields interlaced. With regard to the scanning of motion-picture film, this created a problem, due to the fact that motion pictures are presented at 24 frames/sec, and some form of translation from 24 to 30 frames/sec was therefore necessary.

The problem was solved by using a storage type of camera tube as a pickup device in the scanner. The motion-

picture film was run in the usual intermittent fashion at 24 frames/sec, and the mosaic of the camera tube was illuminated by the image using very short flashes of intense light at the rate of 60/sec. These flashes were made to occur during the field blanking intervals of the television signal, and the mosaic was then scanned in the usual manner while the film was being pulled down to the next frame. Thus every other picture frame is scanned twice and the intervening frames three times in order to produce the 60/sec field scan.

The tube most commonly used for film scanners was the iconoscope and, in fact, many film scanners using the iconoscope are still in use in the broadcasting studios. As mentioned above, under the Iconoscope Section, this tube produces a spurious shading signal, the nature of which depends to some extent on the distribution of light in the image. This therefore creates an additional problem since sudden changes of scene in the film give rise to sudden changes in the shading signal. Satisfactory operation of such a film scanner calls for highly skilled personnel and, in general, requires rehearsals in order to insure prompt and accurate modifications of compensating signals when the scene changes. On top of this, the iconoscope is not capable of producing a range of tone gradations that is anywhere near that obtainable in high-grade motion-picture film.

For these reasons, television pictures from motion pictures have generally been quite inferior to those obtained with live pickup, and many attempts have been made to design a motion-picture film scanner capable of using a cathode-ray tube spot scanner as the light source, since this would result in a much better tone gradation and the absence of shading signals.

In order to accomplish this it is necessary to use a continuous or nonintermittent film drive and to incorporate in the machine a system of rotating mirrors or prisms so arranged that the scanning raster imaged onto the film via these mirrors is made to follow the motion of the film, and thus is capable of scanning the film as if the frames were stationary.

Continuous projectors with this type of optical arrangement have been known for a long time, and in one particular form were used quite extensively for commercial film projection in Germany in the 1930's. This projector was designed by Mechau, and a detailed description of its design and operation was given in 1928.[30] The optical arrangement of the projector is such that, as the film is pulled through the gate in a continuous motion, the light projected through the film passes via a series of mirrors moving in such a fashion as to keep the image of the film frame stationary on the screen. As one film frame leaves the gate, the image of this frame fades out and the image of the succeeding frame fades in. In other words, the picture on the screen consists of a continual lap-dissolve from one frame into the next.

If a machine of this sort is used backwards, that is, with a cathode-ray tube scanning raster in place of the screen and with a photomultiplier in place of the light source, then it fills all the requirements for a continuous motion-picture television scanner. In fact, quite a number of these Mechau machines were brought to England before and after the last war and are still being used by the British Broadcasting Corp. for film scanning and kinerecording.

In the United States a continuous film scanner made on a principle somewhat similar to Mechau's was designed and constructed in the Bell Telephone Laboratories around 1948.[31] It uses a system of moving mirrors like the Mechau, but the mechanical arrangement for controlling these mirrors is greatly simplified over that used in the Mechau machine. This machine is still used as a main source of television signals in the Laboratories and is capable of producing pictures with a detail corresponding to some 7 or 8 mc and with contrast ranges corresponding to theater release prints.

Lately several firms have brought on the market commercial film scanners using continuous film motion and a rotating prism as the moving optical element. Film scanners of this type are particularly significant since they greatly simplify the problem of scanning motion-picture film in color.[32]

It should be mentioned that in the last few years the advent of the image orthicon and the vidicon has made it possible to build intermittent-type film scanners with performance capabilities much higher than those of the original iconoscope film scanner, and such scanners are now being used to an increasing extent in the broadcating studios.

In England television pictures are scanned at the rate of 25 frames/sec or 50 fields interlaced. By simply running the motion-picture film continuously at the rate of 25/sec instead of 24/sec, it has therefore been possible for the British to construct and use very high-grade cathode-ray tube spot scanning machines with very much simpler optical arrangements than are required here in the United States. A description of two different types of such film scanners was given at the Television Convention in London in 1951.[33]

Development of Television Standards in the United States

It was long ago realized that in order to insure adequate synchronization between television transmitters and television receivers it is essential to establish a "lock-and-key" relationship between the two. It was therefore also realized that a widespread commercial television service would require a set of nationally adopted systems standards insuring such a lock-and-key relationship.

As early as 1929 the Radio Manufacturers Association set up a committee on television for the purpose of coordinating and guiding the experimental television work going on at that time. By 1935 this committee was requested to investigate the possibility of setting up a set of television standards for nationwide use, and by 1936 such a set of standards had been proposed and a report submitted to the Federal Communications Commission.

In this report it was recommended that seven television channels be allocated in the region from 42 to 90 mc and that each channel should be 6 mc wide. It was proposed that the system should consist of a 441-line picture and the transmission recommended was a double sideband AM transmission of the picture signal with 3.25-mc separation between the sound and the picture carriers. By August 1936 the Federal Communications Commission permitted experimental transmission of such signals in part of the frequency band proposed but took no further action on the standards since the transmissions were still experimental only.

During the next couple of years further developments resulted in a modified set of standards which was submitted by the Radio Manufacturers Association to the Federal Communications Commission in 1938 with the proposal that they be adopted as national standards. Furthermore, the National Broadcasting Company announced that, coinciding with the opening of the New York World's Fair in 1939, they would start a limited series of programs in accordance with these standards. By this time the standards recommended made use of vestigial sideband transmission, which enabled the frequency range occupied by the picture signal to be increased from about $2\frac{1}{2}$ mc to 4 mc.

NBC maintained such a program all through 1939 without any formal approval of the standards by the FCC, but in the latter part of 1939 the FCC issued a ruling which permitted limited commercial sponsorship of such transmission and announced their intention of holding a hearing in January 1940 for the purpose of arriving at a set of standards having general industry support.

During the hearing it developed that serious objections to the RMA proposed standards were raised by several sectors of the industry, and in the report of the hearing the FCC stated that commercialization would not be permitted until the industry agreed on one common system of broadcasting.

In order to establish such a system, the National Television System Committee was set up under the sponsorship of RMA. This Committee consisted of a group of technical experts from all interested parts of industry, and during the next year and a half this Committee concentrated on the formulation of a complete set of television standards supported by the industry as a whole. The final report of the Committee was delivered to the Commission in March 1940, and in May of that year the FCC announced that the NTSC standards had been adopted officially and that commercial television broadcasting based on these standards would be permitted as of July 1941.

By this time the standards called for a picture having 525 lines and, except for minor modifications, the standards were identical to those now in force. During the war years commercial television was temporarily discontinued except for a few special transmissions, and in 1945 the prewar standards were reaffirmed by the Commission with a few minor modifications. These reaffirmed standards are the present commercial standards for black-and-white television transmission in the United States.

A very complete report on this standardization work inside RMA and NTSC was assembled by D. G. Fink and published by McGraw-Hill in book form in 1943.[34]

The Development of Television Network Facilities

The first transmission of television signals over Bell System wire facilities took place in April 1927 when signals produced by Dr. H. E. Ives' mechanical-scanning arrangements were transmitted from Washington to New York.[35] At the same time, signals were also transmitted by radio from Whippany, N.J., to New York.[36] These signals were of the low-definition type produced at that time and required a band-width of only about 20,000 cycles.

Television signals approaching the present-day wide-band variety were first transmitted over the coaxial cable from New York to Philadelphia in 1937.[2] The pictures were produced from motion-picture films by means of a 6-ft scanning disc. Two hundred and forty lines per frame were used and the band-width required to transmit the signals was 800,000 cycles. In 1940 television signals were transmitted over the coaxial cable from New York to Philadelphia and return, but now the signals corresponded to 441-line television pictures and required a frequency band of about 2.7mc.[37] Later that year scenes from the Republican National Convention in Philadelphia were transmitted over the coaxial cable to the National Broadcasting Co. studio in New York for television broadcasts. During 1941 similar television signals were transmitted over coaxial cables for a total distance of 800 mi. by looping the coaxial units in the cable between Stevens Point, Wis., and Minneapolis.

During the war years very little television transmission took place, but after the war, in 1945, television service was furnished to the broadcasters on an experimental basis between New York and Philadelphia and New York and Washington, with dropping points at Baltimore. These signals were of the 525-line variety now used for commercial broadcasting.

In 1947 the first microwave relay system was inaugurated between New York and Boston, and a round-trip television signal from New York was sent to Boston and back again and was received both in New York and, in addition, in Washington over the coaxial cable from New York.[38]

In 1948 commercial service over Bell System networks was started and since that time the number of channel miles available for transmission has grown steadily, both over the coaxial system and over the microwave relay system. The Chicago-New York radio relay link was started in 1950, and the first commercial program transmission from coast to coast over the radio relay took place in September 1951 when President Truman spoke in San Francisco, and signals were broadcast from stations in New York City.[39]

At the end of February 1954, the total number of channel miles available for television transmission in the United States was about 52,000, of which 17,000 were coaxial and the remaining 35,000 microwave relays.

The establishment of satisfactory long-distance television transmission facilities has imposed some extremely severe requirements on the reliability and stability of the individual components of such systems. The reception of a satisfactory broadcast television picture, especially for color television, requires that the studio equipment, the transmitting equipment and the receiving equipment together provide a channel which has a gain characteristic flat within a fraction of a decibel over the entire band and for which the departure from phase linearity over the band is only a few degrees. When such a television signal is transmitted over a coaxial cable from New York to Chicago, it passes through over a hundred repeaters, each with a gain of about 40 db, or a total gain of over 4000 db. In order to insure that the television signal still meets the above-mentioned requirement after transmission over such a system, it will be realized that the design of the individual components requires extreme accuracy and care in order to insure the necessary precision and stability of both the repeaters themselves and their associated passive equipment, such as amplitude and phase equalizers. Similar stringent requirements exist for the components in microwave relay systems since the signal transmitted over such a system from New York to Los Angeles again has to pass through over a hundred repeaters on the way.

Conclusion

The purpose of this paper has been to sketch the development of modern television from the early days of mechanical scanning through the transition period of partly mechanical and partly electronic scanning up to the present-day all-electronic systems of high-definition television. This paper deals only with black-and-white television; the development of color television has not been included, partly because color television has only just been made commercial and a historical paper on this subject may therefore be somewhat premature, but partly also because this entire subject by itself has a long and interesting history and therefore merits a separate paper of its own.

Apart from some of the early historical developments, the author has limited himself largely to the development here in the United States, but for those readers interested in the development of television in England and in Germany, the author would refer them to two very excellent papers published during the last couple of years, one in the *Proceedings of the Institution of Electrical Engineers* in 1952[40] and the other in a German magazine article mentioned previously.[4] Both these papers are very extensive and both have excellent bibliographies, which will prove valuable and time-saving to any reader interested in source material.

References

1. J. V. L. Hogan, "The early days of television," *Jour. SMPTE*, 63: 169–172, Nov. 1954.
2. M. E. Strieby, "Coaxial cable system for television transmission," *Bell Sys. Tech. J.*, 17: 438–457, July 1938.
   D. C. Espley and D. O. Walter, "Television film transmitters using aperture scanning discs," *J. Inst. Elec. Engrs.*, 88: 145–171, June 1941.
   Kurt Thöm, "Mechanischer Universal Abtaster für Personen-, Film-, und Diapositivübertragungen," *Fernseh Ag.*, 1: 42–48, Dec. 1938.
   H. Rinia and L. Leblans, "The Nipkow disc," *Philips Tech. Rev.*, 4: 42–47, Feb. 1939.
3. M. Dieckmann and G. Glage, German Patent No. 190102, Sept. 12, 1906.
4. Gerhart Goebel, "Television in Germany up to the year 1945," *Arch. Post- u. Fernmeldewesen*, 5: 259–393, Aug. 1953.
5. Boris Rosing, British Patent No. 27570, June 25, 1908, application filed Dec. 13, 1907; British Patent No. 5486, 1911.
6. *Sci. Amer.*, p. 384, June 17, 1911; p. 574, Dec. 23, 1911.
7. Shelford Bidwell, letter to *Nature*, 78: 105, 1908.
8. A. A. Campbell Swinton, letter to *Nature*, 78: 151, 1908.
9. A. A. Campbell Swinton, Presidential Address, *J. Röntgen Soc.*, 8: 1–15, Jan. 1912.
10. *Wireless World*, 14: 51–56, 82–84, 114–118, 1924.
11. V. K. Zworykin, U.S. Patent No. 2,141,059 Dec. 20, 1938, applic. filed Dec. 29, 1923.
12. V. K. Zworykin, "Television with cathode ray tube for receiver," *Radio Eng.*, 9: 38–41, Dec. 1929.
13. V. K. Zworykin, "Description of an experimental television system and the kinescope," *Proc. I.R.E.*, 21: 1655–1673, Dec. 1933.
14. A. Dinsdale, "Television by cathode ray. The new Farnsworth system," *Wireless World*, 28: 286–288, Mar. 1931.
15. Manfred von Ardenne, "Die Braunsche Röhre als Fernsehempfänger," *Fernsehen*, 1: 193–202, May 1930; 2: 65–68, Apr. 1931, and 173–178, July 1931.
16. A. G. Jensen, "The Davisson Cathode Ray Television Tube using deflection modulation," *Bell Sys. Tech. J.*, 30: 855–866, Oct. 1951.
17. Kurt Brückersteinkuhl, "Über das Nachleuchten von Phosphoren und seine Bedeutung für den Lichtstrahlabtaster mit Braunscher Rohre," *Fernseh Ag.*, 1: 179–186, Aug. 1939.
18. "Simultaneous all-electronic color television," *RCA Review*, 7: 459–468, Dec. 1946.
19. Philo T. Farnsworth, U.S. Patent No. 1,773,980, Aug. 26, 1930, applic. filed Jan. 7, 1927.
20. Philo T. Farnsworth, "Television by electron image scanning," *J. Franklin Inst.*, 218: 411–444, Oct. 1934.
21. A. G. Jensen, "Film scanner for use in television transmission tests," *Proc. I.R.E.*, 29: 243–249, May 1941.
22. V. K. Zworykin, "The Iconoscope—a modern version of the electric eye," *Proc. I.R.E.*, 22: 16–32, Jan. 1934.
23. Harley Iams, G. A. Morton and V. K. Zworykin, "The Image Iconoscope," *Proc. I.R.E.*, 27: 541–547, Sept. 1939.
24. Albert Rose and Harley Iams, "The Orthicon, a television pickup tube," *RCA Rev.*, 4: 186–199, Oct. 1939.
25. Albert Rose, Paul K. Weimer and Harold B. Law, "The Image Orthicon—a sensitive television pickup tube," *Proc. I.R.E.*, 34: 424–432, July 1946.
26. Paul K. Weimer, Stanley V. Forgue and Robert R. Goodrich, "The Vidicon Photoconductive Camera Tube," *Electronics*, 23: 70–73, May 1950.
27. A. W. Hull, U.S. Patent No. 1,387,984, Aug. 16, 1921, applic. filed Aug. 30, 1915.
28. A. W. Hull, U.S. Patent No. 1,683,134, Sept. 4, 1928, applic. filed Dec. 28, 1921.
29. K. W. Jarvis and R. M. Blair, U.S. Patent No. 1,903,569, Apr. 11, 1933, applic. filed Sept. 15, 1926.
30. L. Burmester and E. Mechau, "Untersuchung der mechanischen und optischen Grundlagen des Mechau-Projektors," *Kinotechnik*, 10: 395–401, 423–426 and 447–451, Aug. 5, Aug. 20 and Sept. 5, 1928.
31. A. G. Jensen, R. E. Graham and C. F. Mattke, "Continuous motion picture projector for use in television film scanning," *J. SMPTE*, 58: 1–21, Jan. 1952.
32. E. H. Traub, "New 35mm television film scanner," *J. SMPTE*, 62: 45–54, Jan. 1954.
   Victor Graziano and Kurt Schlesinger, "Continuous all-electronic scanner for 16mm color motion-picture film," *J. SMPTE*, 62: 294–305, Apr. 1954, Part I.
   Jesse H. Haines, "Color characteristics of a television film scanner," 1954 I.R.E. Convention Record, Part 7, Broadcasting and Television, pp. 100–104.
33. T. C. Nuttall, "The development of a high-quality 35mm film scanner," *Proc. Inst. Elec. Engrs.*, 99: 136–144, Apr.-May 1952.
   H. E. Holman and W. P. Lucas, "A continuous-motion system for televising motion-picture films," *Proc. Inst. Elec. Engrs.*, 99: 95–108, Apr.-May 1952.
34. Donald G. Fink, *Television Standards and Practice*, McGraw-Hill Book Co., New York and London, 1943.

35. D. K. Gannett and E. I. Green, "Wire transmission system for television," *Bell Sys. Tech. J.*, *6:* 616–632, Oct. 1927.
36. Edward L. Nelson, "Radio transmission system for television," *Bell Sys. Tech. J.*, *6:* 633–652, Oct. 1927.
37. M. E. Strieby and J. F. Wentz, "Television transmission over wire lines," *Bell Sys. Tech. J.*, *20:* 62–81, Jan. 1941.

M. E. Strieby and C. L. Weis, "Television transmission," *Proc. I.R.E.*, *29:* 371–381, July 1941.
38. G. N. Thayer, A. A. Roetken, R. W. Friis and A. L. Durkee, "The New York-Boston microwave radio relay system," *Proc. I.R.E.*, *37:* 183–188, Feb. 1949.
39. A. A. Roetken, K. D. Smith and R. W. Friis, "The TD-2 microwave radio relay system,"

Bell Sys. Tech. J., *30:* 1041–1077, Oct. 1951, Part II.
T. J. Grieser and A. C. Peterson, "A broadband transcontinental radio relay system," *Elec. Eng.*, *70:* 810–815, Sept. 1951.
40. G. R. M. Garratt and A. H. Mumford, "The history of television," *Proc. Inst. Elec. Engrs.*, *99:* 25–42, Apr.-May 1952.

A Short History
of Television Recording

By ALBERT ABRAMSON

This paper describes the development of the three basic television recording processes since 1927. It also describes the film-recording processes used in both the United States and Great Britain. The introduction of television recordings made on magnetic material in both monochrome and color is noted. The paper concludes with a short résumé on the new art of electronic motion pictures produced with television cameras and recording facilities.

TELEVISION recording is an important part of the television industry today. Film recordings are made for a variety of useful purposes, some of which are: to compensate for time differentials, to delay presentation of a program to a more convenient time, and to provide network service to stations not connected by radio-relay or coaxial cable. In addition, programs may be recorded in advance to allow personnel to be elsewhere when the program is telecast, or even to provide a reserve program in case of emergency. As a result, the amount of film used to record programs by the major networks in the United States far surpasses that used by conventional film making means.

This recording of the television signal has been complicated lately with the adoption of a compatible color-television system. Since more and more network programs will be presented in color, a satisfactory commercial system of color recording must be developed that will have the same flexibility and speed as the monochrome recording. One of the answers to recording in color seems to have been solved with the introduction of magnetic television recording. This has been presented in both black-and-white and in full color, although only in a developmental stage. Magnetic television recording has many advantages such as: immediate playback of the picture, no development or chemical processing needed, and the saving if the magnetic material is used over and over.

Finally the possibilities of actually making high-quality motion pictures by means of television recording and electronic (television) cameras opens up a whole new field of endeavor. The advantages of this method have long been recognized but it has been only lately that equipment capable of the definition required has become available. It is to be expected that this process will eventually replace the more conventional film making methods.

Presented on October 19, 1954, at the Society's Convention at Los Angeles, by Albert Abramson, CBS Television, 1313 N. Vine St., Hollywood, Calif.
(This paper was received on December 22, 1954.)

Historical Development

Phonovision by Baird. Television recording is almost as old as television itself. To find the first efforts at recording the television image we must go back to the work of John L. Baird in England in 1927. Baird was a restless experimenter who covered the whole field of television. He tried long distance television, night-time television, stereoscopic television and color television.[1] It is little wonder that he even tried recording television. This he did on a machine called the Phonoscope.[2] Baird was experimenting with a process of "Phonovision" which was the recording of the television signal on phonograph records. At this time, Baird was transmitting a 30-line picture at a rate of $12\frac{1}{2}$ frames/sec. Thus the signal was actually of a very low frequency, so low, that it was easily carried on a regular telephone line or impressed on a wax record. The amplified signal was carried to an ordinary stylus head where the "picture" was converted into vibrations on the surface of the record. If desired, a synchronized record could be made of both the picture and the sound with either a double track being made, on one record, or else recording the sound on an accompanying record. To reproduce this record all that was necessary was a turntable synchronized with a scanning disc. The vibrations were converted back into electrical impulses which were fed to a neon light which illuminated the apertures in the scanning disc. Undoubtedly they were of poor quality for they were subject to the limitations of the crude mechanical system that produced them and there were other losses in the recording and reproduction processes. Baird soon tired of this facet of television and went on to more promising aspects of the field. However, we must credit him with making the first television recordings.

Rtcheouloff's Magnetic Recorder. While Baird was experimenting with his stylus recordings of the television signal another man filed a patent in England on January 4, 1927, for a process of recording the television signal on magnetic material. This was B. Rtcheouloff who indicated apparatus "...adapted for the production of a magnetic record of the Poulsen telegraphone type." Poulsen was the Danish physicist who invented magnetic recording in 1898. Rtcheouloff's patent indicated that the accompanying sound was to be recorded on the opposite side of the magnetic material. At the receiving end the record was to feed several television receivers and the telegraphone receivers.[3] There is no indication that this apparatus was ever built.

Hartley and Ives. On September 14, 1927, Hartley and Ives of Electrical Research Products proposed a new method of "interposed" film at both the transmitting and receiving ends. The reasons given were as follows: "Television of background details is improved and increased illumination is obtained by taking a kinematographic film of the scene to be transmitted." Thus they proposed a method of television in which the scene to be transmitted would first be filmed by conventional methods and then the resultant film would be scanned for transmission. They also stated that "...preferably a photographic process is also interposed at the television receiving station."[4] This, of course, is the basis of the "intermediate film" process which later came into being as one means of producing large screen television.

Thus the period of 1926—27 saw the birth of the three basic television recording processes; however, of the three, only one, the film recording process or "intermediate film" method, was to be of any consequence for the next twenty-five years.

During the early 1930's there were many attempts to project a large-screen television image. Most of these used large scanning disks with powerful arc lights modulated by a Kerr cell. But many experimenters tried to take advantage of the regular motion-picture film projector and its greater light-throwing capacity.

Lee De Forest's Large-Screen Projector. De Forest and his associates filed a patent on April 24, 1931, for a method of recording pictures, film or events, "at the receiver by the etching action of an electrical discharge upon a suitable coating applied to a moving picture film or strip."[5] Their apparatus consisted of a revolving wheel with a series of needle-points. These needle-points were connected to the receiving apparatus which impressed the video signal upon them. These points passed over a strip of moving 35mm film which was coated with pure metallic silver. As the impulses varied, so did the etching action of the needle-points as they passed over the film. Thus the dark and light portions of the picture were to be reproduced as modulated lines on the film. This etched film was to be projected on a standard motion-picture machine.[6] However, due to many difficulties, this method was soon abandoned as impracticable.

The Intermediate-Film Process

The Intermediate-Film Transmitter. Another attempt at large-screen television was made by Fernseh A.G. in Germany. In 1932 they introduced their "intermediate film" transmitter at the Berlin Radio Exhibition. This was a television apparatus that first photographed the image to be transmitted by means of an ordinary motion-picture camera.[7] The scene was photographed on film prepared with a rapid and sensitive surface. This film was then passed through tanks where it was developed, fixed and washed, and while still wet (or in some cases after it had been partially dried) fed through a film gate in the last tank. Here it was fed to a scanning disk where it was dissected for transmission. After transmission, the film was either resensitized for immediate re-use or else saved for future transmission.

The Intermediate-Film Receiver. At the 1933 Berlin Radio Exhibition Fernseh again demonstrated this intermediate-film transmitter. Also in this year they demonstrated for the first time their "intermediate film" receiver for large-screen television.[8] Here the received signal was "recorded" on motion-picture film and then rapidly processed and projected by a standard motion-picture machine onto a full-size screen.

At the receiving end, the television signals were made to modulate a powerful beam of light by means of a Kerr cell. Between the cell and the film was a scanning disk with 90 hexagonal holes. This was rotated at a speed of 3000 rpm. Thus with 25 frames/sec a 180-line picture was obtained. The resultant light was focused on the film by a special optical system.

An image of the aperture in the disk was focused onto the sensitized film that was passing down a recording window. In this manner a series of adjacent lines of varying amounts of light and shade along each line, were imprinted on the film, so building up a picture. The film was rapidly developed and fixed. It was then fed into a theater projector of the usual intermittent type. The picture was 10 ft by 13 ft in size.

Thus the first television film recordings were made in 1933. This system was again demonstrated in 1934 using the same apparatus. The film was either saved

or resensitized as in the intermediate-film transmitting process. The results were often marred by blotches on the film. There was a delay of some 20 sec between the time the image was received and the time it was projected on the screen.

In 1935 the intermediate-film receiving system dispensed with the mechanical scanning disk and the Kerr cell in favor of a cathode-ray picture tube. A patent was taken out by Rolf Möller of Fernseh A.G. in Germany on December 12, 1934, for recording television images on film from a cathode-ray tube using continuously moving film. This apparatus was shown at the 1935 Berlin Radio Exhibition.[9] Thus the first cathode-ray film recordings were made during the period of late 1934 and shown publicly in 1935. However, this new intermediate-film receiving system was not successful and was not shown at the annual radio exhibition in 1936.

The Visiogram. In England there also were interesting attempts made to record television images. A novel machine called the "Visiogram" was developed by Edison Bell Ltd. in 1934. Motion-picture film was used, with the television signals being recorded thereon by the variable-density method familiar in sound techniques. The video signal was not converted into the usual light values of the scene itself but into a modulated "sound" track of the image. By means of a simple attachment the film signals were to be translated back into a visual image in an ordinary television receiver. In a demonstration given to the press the results were extremely poor.[10] Both intermediate-film transmitters and receivers were studied in the laboratories of Fernseh A.G. in 1937; the intermediate-film receiver method disappeared in Europe after 1937. It was revived after World War II when one of the major American motion-picture companies turned to it as one solution to the large-screen television problem. It was to be many years before it would be possible to project an image as large or as bright with a cathode-ray projector as with the intermediate-film receiving process.

Early Film Recording in the United States

In 1938 the first attempts were made in the United States to record on film the screen of a cathode-ray picture tube. These early efforts used standard silent, 16mm, spring-wound cameras operating at 16 frames/sec. With the low light intensity of the monitor screen, it was necessary to use the fastest film emulsion then available.

Since the cameras were nonsynchronous with the 30-frame rate of the television screen, the film recordings were marred by the appearance of

banding or horizontal lines (shutter bar) of over and under exposure caused by the uneven matching of the odd and even fields recorded on each frame of film.

The film was then recorded at 15 frames/sec which succeeded in eliminating banding but was successful in recording only every other frame of the television 30-frame picture.

It became obvious that if commercial use was to be made of television film recordings in the United States, the 30-frame television picture would have to be recorded on film at 24 frames/sec to conform with the speed of standard 16mm sound film, thereby permitting projection of the film either in a conventional sound projector for direct viewing, or by a standard projector for rebroadcasting by television. Development of a suitable commercial television recording camera was to continue for the next ten years before a practical system was perfected.

Recording of Airborne Television Transmissions. Although commercial television started in the United States in 1939 there was no further development in television film recording until the middle of World War II. Experiments with airborne television equipment such as "Project Ring" and the "Block" system were carried out. With the development of "Block" and "Ring" equipment, it became necessary to make permanent records of the transmissions of this apparatus. Motion-picture film cameras were used to record the television images sent by these developments from aircraft and guided missiles. Film cameras were installed on television receivers on the ground and in other aircraft. One of these early motion-picture cameras was a standard Air Force camera with a speed control to adjust the shutter to about 8 frames/sec. Speeds as low as 4 frames/sec were available. The recorded pictures were very poor due to the different standards of the transmissions, the low light intensities of the recording monitors, and to the many steps involved in the photographic processes. Shutter banding was noticeable in the film but did not destroy its value as a record. Further work was done with a Cine Special camera at 15 frames/sec with a 170° open shutter.[11]

During the immediate postwar period there was created a new interest in the recording of television images. The U.S. Navy started a series of experiments with its airborne television equipment. The first postwar black-and-white television film recordings were made on March 21, 1946, at the Naval Air Station at Anacostia, D.C. These were secured during a public demonstration of the Navy "Block" and "Ring" airborne television equipment.

251

Need for Commercial Film Recording. The rapid growth of the television industry also necessitated the use of commercial film recordings. Television stations in the United States were opening faster than the telephone company could lay coaxial cable or erect radio-relay stations. With many new stations commencing operation it became necessary to serve them with program material from the two great centers of production, New York and Hollywood. Therefore the television film recording or transcription filled this need for program material.

Paramount's Large Screen Method. The film recording became one of the prime methods for large-screen television also. Paramount Pictures chose the "intermediate-film" method of recording for their large-screen television system. Paramount selected this system over the other immediate cathode-ray methods for a variety of reasons. Some of these were: the opportunity for cutting and editing the program before presentation; flexibility of programming around the regular film showing; and the use of regular projection equipment at the usual high light values.

With these advantages in mind, Paramount developed an intermediate-film system which used 35mm film exclusively. It used a special 35mm single-system (both sound and picture recorded on the same film), recording camera built by the Akeley Camera Co. This camera was unique at the time in that it used an electronic shutter. It could be loaded with 12,000 ft of film which permitted recording of over two hours. A Cooke $f/1.3$ coated lens was used at normal aperture, $f/2.3$. Du Pont Type 228, fine-grain, master positive film or Eastman 5302 film was used for recording either positive or negative pictures.

The film was processed by high-speed developing machines, in approximately 66 sec and was fed by a chute directly to a standard motion-picture projector.[12]

The Eastman Television Recorder. In January 1948 Eastman Kodak announced their new 16mm motion-picture camera for rerecording television programs on film. It had been developed in cooperation with NBC and the Allen B. Du Mont studios. It featured a 1200-ft magazine for continuous recording of a half-hour program, separate synchronous-motor drives for the shutter and film-transport mechanism an $f/1.6$ 2-in. lens, and a 72° closed shutter. The pulldown time was 57 degrees. Other features included a "bloop" light to provide registration with a sound-film recorder, a film loop-loss indicator, and appropriate footage indicators.[13]

First Color-Television Recordings. The first color film recording was made on August 18, 1949, in Washington, D.C. The film camera used was the Navy's Berndt-Maurer with a 25mm $f/1.4$ Cine Ektar lens. Daylight Type Kodachrome was used. Exposures were made at 15 frames/sec synchronous, and at approximately 8 and 4 frames using the hand crank. The results were quite promising, in that the exposures at 8 and 4 frames were both adequate.

Other cameras were used and it was claimed that the "...first completely successful color recordings were made from a CBS Color Television receiver at the speed of 25 frames per second." On February 6, 7, and 8, 1950, sound was recorded with the picture to make the first sound and picture color film recordings.

The first color recording of the RCA "dot sequential" color television system was made at the RCA Silver Spring Laboratory on March 10, 1950. The initial recording was made at 15 frames/sec with a 180° open shutter, the exposure time being one-thirtieth of a second. It was claimed that all exposures were good and, "...strangely enough, it was the consensus of opinion that the film record was superior in quality to the image on the color television receiver as viewed with the naked eye. This phenomenon may be partially explained by the fact that the recording camera lens was located on the axis of, and normal to, the color television image, whereas the observers were forced to view the image from an 'off center' position."

The last of the three experimental systems, the "line sequential" system of Color Television, Inc., San Francisco, was recorded from an RCA Receiver on March 16, 1950, for the first time. This was made at 15 frames/sec.[14]

Early Film Recording in Great Britain

Similar progress in television film recording took place in England immediately after World War II. However, the need for recordings was different since there was only one television station in operation right after the war. The English realized that many topical events occurred when the majority of viewers were unable to see the direct transmission. Also they considered it a waste of time when recording topical or news events to have both newsreel cameramen and television cameras cover the same event. This is especially true when the televised event can be recorded and readied for broadcasting in such a short time compared with the regular filmed version. In addition the British had developed the habit of repeating dramatic programs a few days after the original performance. The use of television film recording allowed them to repeat a performance without added expense of cast and crew.

$188\frac{1}{2}$-Line Recorder. The 1947 efforts of the British to record television programs on film were done along the same pattern as the Americans. They tried to use intermittent recording cameras with quick pulldown times. Here they faced a tremendous problem. They had to record a 25-frame television picture at 24 frames/sec and the amount of pulldown time was about 12°, so they compromised by recording only 50% of the television picture using the other 50% for pulldown time. These recordings were made on 35mm film but recorded only $188\frac{1}{2}$ lines of the British 405-line picture.[15]

$16\frac{2}{3}$-Frame Recorder. Later in 1947 they used another method of intermittent recording. A special shutter was designed which recorded for 240° and was closed for 120°. This produced a film recording that was nonstandard, being recorded at $16\frac{2}{3}$ frames/sec.[16] This recorder was also abandoned for a new one that used no intermittent mechanism at all.

The Mechau 35mm Recorder. Early in 1948 a 35mm continuous motion picture projector, the Mechau made by A.E.G. in Germany, was converted to a camera for continuous recording. It had a rotating mirror drum which for all practical purposes produced a stationary film frame. It used a form of optical compensation where as the drum rotated in sync with the film, the varying tilt of the mirrors made the reflected images of the television picture follow the film on its downward course. Thus the image was stationary in relation to the film. In this way a succession of images was formed on the film as it passed through the gate, the brilliance of each image rising from zero at the top of the gate, then increasing to a constant intensity over the central part of the gate and finally falling to zero at the bottom of the gate. This method eliminated any frame rate difference. This machine also eliminated the high rate of pulldown and the problem of the "picture splice" in the center of the frame common to the United States. There were no lines of the television picture lost in the recording process. It was claimed that this method could be used in the United States by blacking out a portion of the mirrors to avoid more than two fields being recorded on a single frame.[17]

Experiments with this equipment showed that the mirror drum was fully capable of providing correct optical compensation; however, the film transport mechanism did not attain the same high standard. Therefore the equipment was redesigned completely and three machines of this new type were to be installed in 1953 at the Lime Grove television studios.[18]

Application of "Spot Wobble." In addition, there was added an ingenious system of spot position modulation to eliminate the line structure that forms the television image. This was the application of a 10- to 15-mc modulation to the scanning beam. This caused the electron beam to oscillate vertically as it swept across a line and thus spread out. This increased the effective height of the scanning spot without increasing its width. It was claimed that a gain in light output in the order of two to one was made possible by the application of the "spot wobble."[19]

Double Gate 16mm Recorder. While this continuous recorder was more than satisfactory with 35mm film, more economical methods of recording became desirable by 1950 and development was concentrated on 16mm film. Due mainly to the fact that no continuous motion mechanism had been developed for 16mm film it was decided to develop a new recorder using an intermittent movement. This new 16mm film recorder had a double gate, that is, one gate above another, with an optical system capable of producing two images, identical in size, shape, and brightness at the normal 16mm frame spacing. A special pulldown mechanism was designed to work at 90°.

A full frame with two fields was recorded in the bottom aperture and then the second field of the first frame and the first field of the second frame recorded in the top aperture. The second field was lost and the film advanced two frames in this period. This cycle was then repeated. This gave an average film speed of 25 frames/sec. This recording camera gave good general definition with excellent interlacing. Movement was satisfactory although some jerkiness could be detected, especially on pan shots.[20]

Continuous Recording. In addition to the continuous mirror drum system and intermittent methods using either one or two gates there is a third method for recording television images on film. This was actually the oldest system of all as it was the basis of Fernseh's "intermediate-film receiver of the early 1930's. With the use of short decay and buildup phosphors, it was possible to make continuous recordings of television images from a cathode-ray picture tube, for example, merely by using the film motion as the vertical sweep and allowing it to spread a complete record of each frame of the television picture along the length of the film. There were no complications due to the difference in frame frequency and shutter frequency since there was no shutter used on the camera. This method is used in the present day "Ultrafax" facsimile recording apparatus.[21]

Magnetic Television Recording

Another advance in television recording was made on November 11, 1951, when the Electronic Division of Bing Crosby Enterprises gave its first demonstration of a video tape recorder in black-and-white.[22] The advantages of recording video signals on magnetic tape are many.

1. There is no lens system necessary, as there is in the film-recording camera. Thus all optical losses are eliminated.

2. The signals are recorded as electrical waveforms and not as visible images from the face of a cathode-ray monitor tube with its possible distortions and limitations.

3. There are no problems of pulldown time or frame-rate conversion.

4. There are no developing processes, and so losses due to chemical action and image transfer are avoided.

5. The video tape recording can be played back immediately.

6. Magnetic tape is cheaper than processed motion-picture film and can be used over many times if necessary.

7. It will eventually allow full color, stereoscopic pictures with stereophonic sound to be recorded on one strip of magnetic tape.

However, the recording of a video signal on magnetic tape presents many unique problems. Since the signal cannot be spread horizontally as it can in film recording, it must be spread along the length of the tape. It is possible to record the signal by use of special recording heads capable of responding to a 3- or 4-mc signal. Or the signal may be divided among a series of heads for recording. In either case the tape must be run many times faster than sound recording speed. The problem is also complicated by the fact that the tape must run at an absolute constant rate of speed. In addition, it must be remembered that the television signal consists of other necessary information such as synchronizing pulses. Finally, the tape must be played back on the same standard of definition (number of lines and frames/sec, etc.) as it was recorded.

A multiple-track method was chosen by the Electronics Division of Bing Crosby Enterprises for their first video tape recorder.[23] This apparatus used twelve recording heads. Ten were used to record the video signal, the eleventh was for a synchronizing track, and the twelfth was for recording audio. By combining an ingenious method of sampling each head in a stroboscopic manner with a unique switching device, an alternating signal was recorded on each track, with both positive and negative halves representing bits of picture information up to 1.69 mc for the whole group of ten heads. Early models of this apparatus used 1-in. brown oxide tape although later models use either one $\frac{1}{2}$- or $\frac{3}{8}$-in. tape. The tape ran at a speed of 100 ips. The recorder accommodated reels for 16 min of recording.

The October 2, 1952, demonstration of this video tape recorder proved that this process merited attention. The picture had the following good features:

1. The gray scale was outstandingly good.

2. The picture was sharp and clear. However, the following faults were apparent:

1. A diagonal pattern was always prominent.

2. Considerable flicker was noticeable.

3. Under certain conditions a series of ghosts was noticeable.[24]

Later developments by the Crosby Organization have resulted in highly improved definition of the picture and elimination of most of the previous deficiencies. The number of tracks required has been greatly reduced for black-and-white recording, thereby making the system more easily adaptable to color recording.

The RCA Video Tape Recorder. The Radio Corporation of America on December 1, 1953, demonstrated at the David Sarnoff Research Center a video tape recorder on both monochrome and color. It proved that the recording of images in color was as easily accomplished as in black-and-white. The recorder used paper thin plastic tape running at 30 fps. The reels were 17 in. in diameter and would record some four minutes of a program. RCA had achieved the recording of a 3-mc signal through the use of specially designed recording and reproducing heads which responded to frequencies much higher than the cutoff point for heads used in sound recording.[25]

The black-and-white programs were recorded on $\frac{1}{4}$-in. tape, using two tracks, one for the picture and synchronizing signal, and the other for the sound portion. The color program was recorded on $\frac{1}{2}$-in. tape, using five tracks. Three tracks were for the colors, red, blue and green, one was for the synchronizing signals and the last was for the audio portion. The playback of the color recording showed only a slight loss in definition, mostly in excess light values. There was a slight smearing, streaking and halo effect, as well as a high-frequency noise level hiss. Occasionally there was some jitter due to nonuniform speed control. However, the demonstration was considered to be an overwhelming success.

It is expected that these problems will be overcome and that video tape recording will emerge from the laboratory capable of reproducing pictures indistinguishable from the original "live" pickup. It is expected that this process will supplement if not supplant the film or visual recording.

The Electronic Motion Picture

A whole new field of television film recording is being introduced by the development of a completely new electronic picture recording system by High Definition Films Ltd., in London, which has a new concept of producing high-quality motion pictures, utilizing electronic (television) cameras and advanced film recording techniques.

High Definition Films Ltd. Norman Collins and T. C. Macnamara have carefully pointed out the limitations of ordinary film-making procedures while indicating the advantages of using the electronic camera.[26] Avoiding ordinary television broadcasting requirements, they are not bothered by such items as a restricted bandwidth, limited contrast range and tonal gradation, and the necessity for mixing in synchronizing signals. The whole apparatus is operated on closed-circuit under virtually laboratory conditions.

In the development of this equipment, it was decided to equal the standards of present 35mm motion-picture filming. This was accepted as some 30 to 40 lines/mm resolution. To equal this definition a 24-frame picture would have to have 992 lines with a bandwidth of 15.75 mc/sec. This may be increased to 1300 lines if necessary. However, it was felt that it would not be necessary to go much above a thousand lines to equal today's 35mm film standards.

The line scanning is sequential. It is known that interlacing is not needed for pure film recording purposes. Interlacing's main advantage of eliminating flicker while conserving available bandwidth does not overcome some of its more serious faults. These include "line-pairing," "line-crawl," and movement blur. Since in this system, the picture signals are kept separate from the synchronizing signal, the line frequency does not have to be related to the frame frequency. This simplifies the pulse generating apparatus and also enables the number of lines to be varied to suit the resolving power of the type of pickup tube selected.

When recording television images on film, any apparent flicker will be eliminated by the film projector due to its interruption of the light source two or three times during a frame. However, it was expected that monitoring would be difficult, but that the 24-frame flicker could be reduced by using cathode-ray screens having long delay times.

The recording unit is of the intermittent type. While it was felt that continuous motion was exceedingly attractive from many points of view the accuracy of registration which could be realized at the present state of development was insufficient for recording picture of the high definition required. In 1952 a standard film camera with a 70° pulldown was being used. The lens was also a standard motion-picture

75mm type operated at full aperture of $f/2$. Recording was on a slow, fine-grain sound recording stock.

Refinements of the High-Definition system were made and it was presented with the following features in 1954.[27]

1. The cameras in England were the Pye Radio type using the Pye Photicon image iconoscope pickup tube. Cameras for use in the United States and Canada were the General Precision Laboratory type using the 5826 image orthicon pickup tube.

2. The cameras used sequential scanning of either 625 or 834 lines per frame at 24 frames/sec.

3. The chain is essentially closed circuit with a bandwidth of 12 mc.

4. The picture and synchronizing signals are never mixed and a new method of signal control has been devised.

5. A special "staircase" signal is present on all picture monitors in the form of a step wedge. Its presence allows accurate adjustment of the signal amplitude and lift.

6. On the recording monitor two photocells are used for measuring brightness of the first and tenth suppression steps on the kinescope tube face. The monitor tube is a special HDF/Cintel tube with a 9-in. diameter flat screen, free from granularity, and aluminum backed. It presents a 3 × 4 in. picture.

7. The High Definition system employs a spot wobble oscillator to eliminate line structure.

8. There are two recording channels using HDF/Moy 35mm film cameras. These cameras have a specially designed 20° pulldown mechanism with a special film accelerator.

9. This system is designed to use any kind of sound recording method.

High Definition Films has acquired studios in London and was producing demonstration films by this process early in 1954.

Television recording has come a long way from Baird's crude grammophone recordings to today's high-definition film recordings. The television recording has an important place in the commercial television industry. It promises to play an even more important role in the motion-picture industry of tomorrow. The electronic motion picture using neither film cameras nor motion-picture film is an actuality. The television camera and the magnetic video recorder will allow the motion picture a perfection and flexibility that has never before been attained.

References

1. Sydney A. Moseley and H. J. Barton Chapple, *Television Today and Tomorrow,* Sir Isaac Pitman & Sons, Ltd., London, 4th ed., 1934.
2. A. Dinsdale, "Television sees in darkness and records its impressions," *Radio News,* 8: 1422–1423, June 1927.
3. B. Rtcheouloff: Brit. Pat. 288,680, June 7, 1928.
4. R. V. L. Hartley and H. E. Ives: Brit. Pat. 297,078, Mar. 19, 1928.
5. American Television Laboratories: Brit. Pat. 386,183, Apr. 14, 1932.
6. Lee de Forest, *Father of Radio,* Wilcox & Follett, Chicago, 1950, pp. 418–422.
7. A. T. Stoyanowsky, "A new process of television out of doors," *Jour. SMPE,* 20: 437, May 1933.
8. J. L. Baird, "The Kerr Cell and its use in television," *Jour. TV Soc.,* 11: 110–124, Jan. 1935 – Dec. 1938.
9. E. H. Traub, "Television at the Berlin Radio Exhibition," *Jour. TV Soc.,* 11: 56, Jan. 1935 – Dec. 1938, p. 56.
10. London Times, Nov. 29, 1934.
11. Robert M. Fraser, "Motion picture photography of television images," *RCA Review,* 9: 202–217, June 1948.
12. Richard Hodgson, "Theater television system," *Jour. SMPE,* 52: 540–548, May 1949.
13. J. L. Boon, W. Feldman and J. Stoiber, "Television recording camera," *Jour. SMPE,* 51: 117–126, Aug. 1948.
14. W. R. Fraser and G. J. Badgley, "Motion picture color photography of color television images," *Jour. SMPE,* 54: 736, June 1950.
15. H. W. Baker and W. D. Kemp, "The recording of television programmes," *B.B.C. Quarterly,* 6: 1, pp. 236–248, Winter, 1949–50.
16. D. A. Smith, "Television recording," *Wireless World,* 55: 305, 1949.
17. W. D. Kemp, "Video recordings improved by the use of continuously moving film," *Tele-Tech,* 9: 32–35, 62–63, Nov. 1949.
18. W. D. Kemp, "Television recording," an abstract (75% of the original paper, presented at the Convention on the British Contribution to Television, Apr. 28–May 3, 1952), *Jour. SMPTE,* 60: 367–384, Apr. 1953.
19. P. J. Herbst, R. O. Drew and J. M. Brunbaugh, "Factors affecting the quality of kinerecording," *Jour. SMPTE,* 58: 85–104, Feb. 1952.
20. W. D. Kemp, "A new television recording camera," *J. Brit. Kinemat. Soc.,* 21: 39–56, Aug. 1952.
21. D. S. Bond and V. J. Duke, "Ultrafax," *RCA Review,* 9: 99–115, Mar. 1948.
22. Frederick Foster, "Motion Pictures on Tape," *Am. Cinemat.,* 32: 500, Dec. 1951.
23. "Video magnetic tape recorder," *Tele-Tech,* 13: May 1954, 77, 127–129, May 1954.
24. John T. Mullen, "Video tape recording," Speech delivered at 7th Annual NARTB Conference, Thursday, Apr. 30, 1953. (A brief illustrated description appears in the New Products column, *Jour. SMPTE,* 62: 323–324, Apr. 1954.
25. H. F. Olson, W. D. Houghton, A. R. Morgan, J. Zenel, M. Artzt, J. G. Woodward, and J. T. Fischer, "A system for recording and reproducing television signals," *RCA Review,* 15: 3–17, Mar. 1954.
26. Norman Collins and T. C. Macnamara, "The electronic camera in film-making," *J. Inst. Elec. Engrs.* (London), 99: Part 111A, No. 20: 673–679, 1952. (Reprinted, *Jour. SMPTE,* 59: 445–461, Dec. 1952.
   Norman Collins and T. C. Macnamara, "High definition films," *J. Brit. Kinemat. Soc.,* 21: 32–38, Aug. 1952.
27. Information obtained from a brochure sent by High Definition Films, London, England, entitled *High Definition Electronic Picture Recording System,* Technical Description, May 1954.

Bibliography

Additional Historical Papers
from *The Journal of the Society of Motion Picture and
Television Engineers*

Abbott, J. E., "Development of the Sound-Film," June, 1942, p. 541.

———, "Organization and Work of the Film Library of the Museum of Modern Art," March, 1937, p. 294.

Bitting, Robert C., Jr., "Creating an Industry," November, 1965, p. 1015.

Crawford, M., "Some Accomplishments of Eugene Augustin Lauste—Pioneer Sound-Film Inventor," January, 1931, p. 105.

Davee, Lawrence W., "Remarks on the Beginnings of 'Talking' Pictures, December, 1966, p. 1184.

de Forest, L., "Pioneering in Talking Pictures," January, 1941, p. 41.

Didiee, Louis J. J., "Memories of the Early History of 9.5mm Film," December, 1966, p. 1181.

Epstean, E., "Centenary of Photography and the Motion Picture," March, 1939, p. 253.

Fleischer, Max, "Historical Note on Composite Production of Motion Pictures," April, 1960, p. 263.

Gillett, A., H. Chretien and J. Tedesco, "Panoramic Screen Projection Equipment Used at the Palace of Light at the International Exposition (Paris, 1937)," May, 1939, p. 530.

Gregory, C. L., "Early History of Motion Picture Cameras for Film Wider than 35-mm," January, 1930, p. 27.

Hineline, H. D., "Composite Photographic Processes," April, 1933, p. 283.

Hoorn, F. W., "Military Training and Historical Films," October, 1933, p. 337.

Ives, F. E., "Pioneering Inventions by an Amateur," September, 1934, p. 175.

Jenkins, C. Francis, "Society's History," November, 1918, p. 6.

Jones, L. A., "A Historical Summary of Standardization in the Society of Motion Picture Engineers," October, 1933, p. 280.

Kalmus, Herbert, "The Adventure of Technicolor," December, 1958, p. 829.

Kellogg, E. W., "The Development of 16-mm Sound Motion Pictures," January, 1935, p. 63.

Krainock, Mildred B., "An Annotated List of Articles Pertaining to the History of Motion Pictures: 1950-1956 (Including Some Historical References on Television)," November, 1958, p. 771.

Kruse, William F., "Willard Beach Cook—Pioneer Distributor of Narrow-Gage Safety Films and Equipment," July, 1964, p. 576.

Limbacher, James L., "Wide Screen Technology," (reprint), February, 1956, p. 116.

Matthews, Glenn E., "Historical Aspects of the SMPTE," September, 1966, p. 666.

Mees, C. E. K., "Development of the Art and Science of Photography in the Twentieth Century," January, 1937, p. 3.

Mole, P., "Evolution of Arc Broadside Lighting Equipment," April, 1939, p. 398.

Mueller, W. A. and M. Rettinger, "Anecdotal History of Sound Recording Technique," July, 1945, p. 48.

Nelson, Otto, "Early History and Growth of the Motion Picture Industry," November, 1926, p. 28.

Newman, Arthur S., "Camera Mechanism, Ancient and Modern," May, 1930, p. 534.

Niver, Kemp R., "Paper Prints of Early Motion Pictures" (Reprint), December, 1966, p. 1186.

Norath, Albert, "The Work of Film Pioneer Max Skladanowsky," December, 1966, p. 1168.

Norling, John A., "The Stereoscopic Art—A Reprint," March, 1953, p. 268.

Olmstead, A. J., "Motion Picture Collection at the National Museum," March, 1936, p. 265.

Peters, T. K., "A Museum of Motion Picture History," May, 1925, p. 54.

Rackett, Gerald F., "The Production of Motion Pictures in Color, 1930-1954," October, 1954, p. 138.

Ramsaye, Terry, "Early History of Sound Pictures," September, 1928, p. 597.

Rayton, W. B., "Status of Lens Making in America," October, 1939, p. 426.

Rhoads, James B., "Preserving Our National Heritage on Film: The Role of the National Archives," December, 1966, p. 1188.

Rose, Samuel G., "Alexander F. Victor—Motion Picture Pioneer," August, 1963, p. 614.

Sponable, E. I., "Historical Development of Sound Films," April, 1947, p. 275; May, 1947, p. 407.

Sulzer, A. F., "Epoch of Progress in Film Fire Prevention," April, 1940, p. 398.

Theisen, W. E., "Pioneering in the Talking Picture," April, 1941, p. 415.

———, "Work of Lee de Forest," December, 1940, p. 542.

Tuttle, Harris B., Sr., "Some Notes on the Early Reversal Processing of 16mm Film," December, 1966, p. 1174.

Waddell, John H., "The Rotating-Prism Camera: An Historical Survey," July, 1966, p. 666.

Walls, H. L., "Film-Collection Program," January, 1949, p. 5.

———, "Motion Picture Incunabula in The Library of Congress," March, 1944, p. 155.

Westhaver, J. L., "The Autochrome Plate of 50 years Ago," December, 1966, p. 1185.

Williford, E. A., "Twenty-Four Years of Service in the Cause of Better Projection," March, 1941, p. 294.

Withington, C. M., "Golden Jubilee Anniversary of the Motion Picture Industry, May, 1938, p. 570.